NATIONAL ACADEMIES *Sciences Engineering Medicine*

NATIONAL ACADEMIES PRESS
Washington, DC

Closing the Opportunity Gap for Young Children

LaRue Allen and Rebekah Hutton,
Editors

Committee on Exploring the Opportunity Gap for Young Children from Birth to Age Eight

Board on Children, Youth, and Families

Division of Behavioral and Social Sciences and Education

Consensus Study Report

NATIONAL ACADEMIES PRESS 500 Fifth Street, NW Washington, DC 20001

This activity was supported by contracts between the National Academy of Sciences and Administration for Children and Families (HHSP23320140002 0B/75P00120F37106), Bainum Family Foundation (6186), Bill and Melinda Gates Foundation (INV-001632), Brady Education Foundation (unnumbered), Foundation for Child Development (NAS 06-2020), Heising-Simons Foundation (2020-1415), and W.K. Kellogg Foundation (P0132304). Any opinions, findings, conclusions, or recommendations expressed in this publication do not necessarily reflect the views of any organization or agency that provided support for the project.

International Standard Book Number-13: 978-0-309-69461-2
International Standard Book Number-10: 0-309-69461-2
Digital Object Identifier: https://doi.org/10.17226/26743
Library of Congress Control Number: 2023942496

This publication is available from the National Academies Press, 500 Fifth Street, NW, Keck 360, Washington, DC 20001; (800) 624-6242 or (202) 334-3313; http://www.nap.edu.

Copyright 2023 by the National Academy of Sciences. National Academies of Sciences, Engineering, and Medicine and National Academies Press and the graphical logos for each are all trademarks of the National Academy of Sciences. All rights reserved.

Printed in the United States of America.

Suggested citation: National Academies of Sciences, Engineering, and Medicine. 2023. *Closing the Opportunity Gap for Young Children*. Washington, DC: The National Academies Press. https://doi.org/10.17226/26743.

The **National Academy of Sciences** was established in 1863 by an Act of Congress, signed by President Lincoln, as a private, nongovernmental institution to advise the nation on issues related to science and technology. Members are elected by their peers for outstanding contributions to research. Dr. Marcia McNutt is president.

The **National Academy of Engineering** was established in 1964 under the charter of the National Academy of Sciences to bring the practices of engineering to advising the nation. Members are elected by their peers for extraordinary contributions to engineering. Dr. John L. Anderson is president.

The **National Academy of Medicine** (formerly the Institute of Medicine) was established in 1970 under the charter of the National Academy of Sciences to advise the nation on medical and health issues. Members are elected by their peers for distinguished contributions to medicine and health. Dr. Victor J. Dzau is president.

The three Academies work together as the **National Academies of Sciences, Engineering, and Medicine** to provide independent, objective analysis and advice to the nation and conduct other activities to solve complex problems and inform public policy decisions. The National Academies also encourage education and research, recognize outstanding contributions to knowledge, and increase public understanding in matters of science, engineering, and medicine.

Learn more about the National Academies of Sciences, Engineering, and Medicine at **www.nationalacademies.org**.

Consensus Study Reports published by the National Academies of Sciences, Engineering, and Medicine document the evidence-based consensus on the study's statement of task by an authoring committee of experts. Reports typically include findings, conclusions, and recommendations based on information gathered by the committee and the committee's deliberations. Each report has been subjected to a rigorous and independent peer-review process and it represents the position of the National Academies on the statement of task.

Proceedings published by the National Academies of Sciences, Engineering, and Medicine chronicle the presentations and discussions at a workshop, symposium, or other event convened by the National Academies. The statements and opinions contained in proceedings are those of the participants and are not endorsed by other participants, the planning committee, or the National Academies.

Rapid Expert Consultations published by the National Academies of Sciences, Engineering, and Medicine are authored by subject-matter experts on narrowly focused topics that can be supported by a body of evidence. The discussions contained in rapid expert consultations are considered those of the authors and do not contain policy recommendations. Rapid expert consultations are reviewed by the institution before release.

For information about other products and activities of the National Academies, please visit www.nationalacademies.org/about/whatwedo.

COMMITTEE ON EXPLORING THE OPPORTUNITY GAP FOR YOUNG CHILDREN FROM BIRTH TO AGE EIGHT

LARUE ALLEN (*Chair*), Vice Dean for Faculty Affairs, New York University, Steinhardt School of Culture, Education and Human Development
RANDALL AKEE, Associate Professor, University of California, Los Angeles
ALFREDO J. ARTILES, Lee L. Jacks Professor of Education, Stanford University
RENÉE BOYNTON-JARRETT, Associate Professor of Pediatrics, Boston Medical Center Vital Village Networks, Boston University School of Medicine
KENNETH A. DODGE, William McDougall Professor of Public Policy, Sanford School of Public Policy, Duke University
BRENDA JONES HARDEN, Ruth Ottman Professor of Child and Family Welfare, Columbia School of Social Work
PAMELA K. JOSHI, Senior Scientist and Associate Director, Institute for Children, Youth and Family Policy, The Heller School for Social Policy and Management, Brandeis University
SHANTEL E. MEEK, Professor of Practice and Founding Director, The Children's Equity Project, Arizona State University
BELA MOTÉ, President and CEO, Carole Robertson Center for Learning
MILAGROS NORES, Codirector for Research, Associate Research Professor National Institute for Early Education Research, Rutgers The State University of New Jersey
CYNTHIA OSBORNE, Professor of Early Childhood Education and Policy, Executive Director, Prenatal-to-3 Policy Impact Center, Peabody College of Education and Human Development, Vanderbilt University
ALBERT WAT, Senior Policy Director, Alliance for Early Success

Study Staff

REBEKAH HUTTON, Study Director
PAMELLA ATAYI, Program Coordinator
IVORY DEAN, Program Officer (*until October 2021*)
SARAH PERUMATTAM, Research Assistant (*from October 2021 until May 2022*)
MEREDITH YOUNG, Associate Program Officer (*from May 2022*)

2020–2022 James C. Puffer, MD/American Board of Family Medicine Fellow
RITA HAMAD, Associate Professor in Residence, Director, Social Policies for Health Equity Research (SPHERE) Program, Department of Family & Community Medicine, Philip R. Lee Institute for Health Policy Studies, University of California, San Francisco

2020–2021 National Academy of Medicine Distinguished Nurse Scholar-in-Residence and Consultant to the Committee
ASHLEY DARCY-MAHONEY, Professor and Chair, George Washington University School of Nursing

BOARD ON CHILDREN, YOUTH, AND FAMILIES

JONATHAN TODRES (*Chair*), Georgia State University College of Law
RICHARD F. CATALANO, JR., University of Washington School of Social Work
TAMMY CHANG, University of Michigan
DIMITRI A. CHRISTAKIS, Seattle Children's Research Institute, University of Washington
ANDREA GONZALEZ, McMaster University
NANCY E. HILL, Harvard University
CHARLES HOMER, Economic Mobility Pathways
MARGARET KUKLINSKI, University of Washington
MICHAEL C. LU, UC Berkeley School of Public Health
STEPHANIE J. MONROE, Wrenwood Group
STEPHEN RUSSELL, The University of Texas at Austin
NISHA SACHDEV, Premnas Partners, Washington, DC
JANE WALDFOGEL, Columbia University School of Social Work
JOANNA L. WILLIAMS, Rutgers University

Staff

NATACHA BLAIN, Senior Board Director
EMILY P. BACKES, Deputy Board Director

Acknowledgments

This report would not have been possible without the contributions of many people. First, we thank the sponsors of this study without whom this work would not have been possible: the Administration for Children and Families at the Department of Health and Human Services, the Bainum Family Foundation, the Brady Education Foundation, the Foundation for Child Development, the Bill and Melinda Gates Foundation, the Heising-Simons Foundation, and the W.K. Kellogg Foundation.

The committee and project staff would also like to express their gratitude to the numerous experts and consultants who contributed to the development report. We would like to extend our deep gratitude to Ashley Darcy-Mahoney and Rita Hamad for their valuable insights, research and writing support, and contributions to the committee's work. We thank Marianne Bitler and Seojung "Cate" Oh for their work on a commissioned paper for the committee on the economic costs of the opportunity gap. Thanks are also due to the numerous experts who volunteered significant time and effort to address the committee during our public information-gathering and listening sessions: Carolyn Barnes, Ajay Chaudry, Janet Currie, Lisa Gennetian, Pamela Herd, Rucker Johnson, Ariel Kalil, Kimberly Noble, Sean Reardon, and Hirokazu Yoshikawa. The insights and perspectives shared with the committee played an essential role in informing the committees discussions, deliberations, and recommendations. We thank Nancy McArdle of diversitydatakids.org for preparing the summary tables of the population of children ages 0–8. Finally, we thank Rona Briere for her editing of the report.

We would also like to thank the many staff members of the National Academies of Sciences, Engineering, and Medicine who provided invaluable support throughout this process: Natacha Blain for her oversight as director of the Board on Children, Youth, and Families; Anne Marie Houppert, Christopher Lao-Scott, and Rebecca Morgan for their research support and fact checking; Faye Hillman, Javed Khan, and Micah Winograd for their financial management assistance; Christopher King and Sandra McDermin for their insights and guidance; Doug Sprunger and Meredith Fender for their assistance with communications and dissemination of the report; Natalie Nielsen, Patricia Morison, Maryjo Oster, Bea Porter, Kirsten Sampson Snyder, and Amy Stephens for their guidance throughout the report review process; and Clair Woolley for her assistance with the final production of the report. We would like to extend gratitude to the members of the project staff who worked directly with the committee over the course of the project—Rebekah Hutton, Pamella Atayi, Ivory Dean, Sarah Perumattam, and Meredith Young—for their significant contributions to supporting the committee's work.

Finally, the committee wishes to thank our chair, LaRue Allen, for her dedication to this work and the exceptional leadership and guidance that she has provided throughout this process.

This Consensus Study Report was reviewed in draft form by individuals chosen for their diverse perspectives and technical expertise. The purpose of this independent review is to provide candid and critical comments that will assist the National Academies of Sciences, Engineering, and Medicine in making each published report as sound as possible and to ensure that it meets the institutional standards for quality, objectivity, evidence, and responsiveness to the study charge. The review comments and draft manuscript remain confidential to protect the integrity of the deliberative process.

We thank the following individuals for their review of this report:

DOLORES ACEVEDO-GARCIA, Institute for Child, Youth and Family Policy, The Heller School for Social Policy and Management, Brandeis University
ERICA FRANKENBERG, Education Policy Studies, The Pennsylvania State University
VIVIAN L. GADSDEN, National Center on Fathers and Families, Graduate School of Education, University of Pennsylvania
BETH GRAUE, Center for Research on Early Childhood Education, University of Wisconsin–Madison
SANDRA G. HASSINK, Nemours Pediatric Obesity Initiative, Nemours Children's Health System

IHEOMA U. IRUKA, Department of Public Policy and Equity Research Action Coalition, University of North Carolina at Chapel Hill
DANIELLE LARAQUE-ARENA, New York Academy of Medicine
STEPHEN W. RAUDENBUSH, Department of Sociology, The University of Chicago
ARTHUR J. REYNOLDS, Institute of Child Development, University of Minnesota

Although the reviewers listed above provided many constructive comments and suggestions, they were not asked to endorse the conclusions or recommendations of this report, nor did they see the final draft before its release. The review of this report was overseen by **CLAIRE D. BRINDIS,** University of California, San Francisco, and **ELAINE L. LARSON,** Columbia University. They were responsible for making certain that an independent examination of this report was carried out in accordance with the standards of the National Academies and that all review comments were carefully considered. Responsibility for the final content rests entirely with the authoring committee and the National Academies.

Contents

Acronyms	xxiii
Preface	xxvii
Summary	1
1 Introduction	17

    ABOUT THIS STUDY, 18
    STUDY APPROACH, 18
    THE REPORT CONCEPTUAL FRAMEWORK, 22
    UNDERSTANDING THE HISTORICAL AND STRUCTURAL
        DRIVERS OF THE OPPORTUNITY GAP, 23
        Historical Precedents in Education, 25
        Segregation as a Structural Driver of the Opportunity Gap, 29
    DEMOGRAPHIC AND STRUCTURAL CHANGES
        AFFECTING CHILDREN AND FAMILIES, 36
        The Changing Demography of Children from Birth to Age 8:
            Implications for the Opportunity Gap, 36
        Structural Changes in the Economy and Labor Markets, 41
        Poverty, 42
        Geography, 44
    ACCESS TO RESOURCES, SUPPORTS, AND OPPORTUNITIES, 48
        Administrative Burden, 48
        Implementation of Programs, 50
    OVERVIEW OF THE REPORT, 51
    REFERENCES, 52

2   Opportunity Gaps in Early Care and Education
    Experienced by Children from Birth to Pre-K   63
    WHY EARLY CARE AND EDUCATION MATTERS, 64
    CURRENT POLICY, FUNDING, AND SYSTEMS, 70
    ACCESS TO EARLY CARE AND EDUCATION SYSTEMS, 76
        Disparities in Access, 79
        Gaps in ECE Capacity, 85
        Cost as a Barrier to Access, 85
        Access to Early Intervention and Early Special Education
            for Children with Disabilities, 86
        Administrative Barriers to Access, 92
    DIFFERENTIAL EXPERIENCES IN LEARNING SETTINGS, 93
    THE IMPORTANCE OF STRUCTURAL QUALITY
        STANDARDS, 97
        Physical Infrastructure, 98
        Ratios and Class Sizes, 99
        Language of Instruction, 101
        Harsh and Exclusionary Discipline Policies, 103
    THE EARLY CARE AND EDUCATION WORKFORCE, 105
        Education and Professional Preparation, 107
        Compensation, 110
        Access to Professional Development and Supportive
            Working Conditions, 111
        Professional Beliefs and Practices, 113
    PROCESS AND INTERACTIONAL QUALITY, 113
        Pedagogy, Instruction, and Access to Enrichment, 114
        Strong Family Engagement, 117
    THE IMPACT OF COVID-19 ON CHILDREN'S
        OPPORTUNITY GAPS, 120
    CONCLUSIONS, 121
    REFERENCES, 123

3   Opportunity Gaps in the Education Experienced by Children
    in Grades K–3   147
    CURRENT POLICY, FUNDING, AND SYSTEMS FOR
        EARLY ELEMENTARY EDUCATION, 149
        Access to and Funding for Out-of-School Time, 152
        Special Education, 154
        Absenteeism, 165
    DIFFERENTIAL EXPERIENCES IN EARLY ELEMENTARY
        LEARNING SETTINGS, 166
        Physical Infrastructure, 167
        Ratios and Class Sizes, 168
        Language of Instruction, 169
        Harsh and Exclusionary Discipline Policies, 169

THE EDUCATION WORKFORCE IN GRADES K–3, 175
    Supportive, Enriching, and Warm Teacher–Child Relationships
        and Interactions, 175
    Teacher Expectations and Perceptions of Behavior, 178
    Pedagogy, Instruction, and Access to Enrichment, 180
THE IMPACT OF COVID-19, 183
CONCLUSIONS, 184
REFERENCES, 186

4 Opportunity Gaps in the Physical Health and Health Care Experienced by Young Children and Their Parents   205
DRIVERS OF OPPORTUNITY GAPS IN HEALTH AND
    HEALTH OUTCOMES, 207
    Conditions Prior to Birth and Pregnancy, 207
    Maternal Access to Health Insurance, 208
    Maternal Access to Adequate Prenatal Care, 210
    The Medical Home and Developmental Screening, 213
    Poverty and Health Care, 215
    Racism and Culturally Responsive Care, 216
    Relational Health, 218
    Adultification, 218
    Antiracism and Dismantling Race-based Medicine, 220
    Nutrition, 224
    Food Insecurity for Households with Children, 226
    Safe and Healthy Environments, 226
ADDRESSING OPPORTUNITY GAPS IN PHYSICAL
    HEALTH AND HEALTH CARE, 237
    Poverty Reduction, 237
    Access to Pediatric and Family Health Care, 238
    Antiracism and Dismantling of Race-based Medicine, 239
    Screening for Social Influences of Health, 239
    Alternative Models for Delivering Health Care, 240
    Safe and Violence-free Environments, 240
CONCLUSIONS, 241
REFERENCES, 243

5 Opportunity Gaps in the Social-Emotional Development, Well-being, and Mental Health Experienced by Young Children   263
CONTEMPORARY CHILD DEVELOPMENT SCIENCE, 264
HOW DISPARITIES IN CHILD OUTCOMES DEVELOP, 266
    Historical and Current Inequities in Families' Access to
        Community Resources, 267

Disparities and Opportunity Gaps in Mental Health in
  Early Childhood, 267
Positive Socialization and Identify Formation, 274
REDUCING OPPORTUNITY GAPS IN MENTAL HEALTH
  IN EARLY CHILDHOOD, 275
  Screening and Assessment Strategies to Reduce Opportunity
    Gaps, 277
  Parent Beliefs about Child Development, Behavior, and Use
    of Mental Health Services, 280
  Strengthening Families Work Supports to Reduce Opportunity
    Gaps, 281
  Home Visiting Strategies to Reduce Opportunity Gaps, 283
  Program Strategies to Reduce Opportunity Gaps in Early
    Childhood Mental Health, 286
  School Nursing to Reduce Opportunity Gaps in School, 288
CONCLUSIONS, 290
REFERENCES, 291

6   The Economic Costs of the Opportunity Gap   309
    THE OPPORTUNITY GAP: COST ESTIMATES, 310
    SHARE OF OPPORTUNITY GAPS AND THEIR COSTS
      THAT CAN BE AFFECTED BY POLICY, 312
    APPROACHES TO EVALUATING THE NET BENEFITS OF
      INVESTMENT IN MITIGATING THE OPPORTUNITY
      GAP, 313
    EVIDENCE FOR WHETHER IMPLEMENTATION MAKES
      SENSE: REPRESENTATIVE EXAMPLES OF EFFECTIVE
      POLICIES IN THREE ARENAS, 315
      Reducing the Opportunity Gap Due to Income Differences
        through Cash and Near-Cash Means-Tested Assistance, 316
      Reducing the Opportunity Gap Due to Inequitable Access to
        Health Care and Health Insurance through Medicaid, 317
      Reducing the Opportunity Gap Due to Unequal Access to
        Early Education through the Head Start Program, 318
    CONCLUSIONS, 319
    REFERENCES, 320

7   Research, Policy, and Practice: Contexts and Efforts to
    Address Opportunity Gaps   323
    INCOME AUGMENTATION PROGRAMS AND
      POLICIES, 323
      Minimum Wage, 324
      Earned Income Tax Credit, 325
      Paid Family and Medical Leave, 326

PARENTS' POOR JOB QUALITY AND OPPORTUNITY GAPS
  FOR CHILDREN, 330
POLICY INTERVENTIONS AND PROGRAMS THAT ADDRESS
  PARENTS' JOB QUALITY, 335
  Federal Labor Standards and Social Protection Policies, 336
  Social Protection Policies, 339
  State and Local Paid Family and Medical Leave and
    Scheduling Laws, 340
  Programs Designed to Supplement Low Wages and Limited
    Benefits and Promote Career Advancement, 342
  Employer Policies and Practices, 345
ADDRESSING OPPORTUNITY GAPS AND OUTCOMES
  IN EDUCATION, 346
  Full Funding, 346
  Inclusive, Quality Standards, 347
  A Supported, Fairly Compensated, Competent Workforce, 348
  Data, Monitoring, and Accountability, 348
ADDRESSING OPPORTUNITY GAPS AND OUTCOMES
  IN PHYSICAL HEALTH, 349
  Improving Maternal Health and Birth Outcomes, 349
  Medicaid, 350
  Nutrition Assistance Programs, 351
  Reduction of Environmental Contaminants, 354
HUMAN-CENTERED DESIGN AND POLICY
  DEVELOPMENT, 357
PUBLIC–PRIVATE PARTNERSHIPS, 359
CONCLUSIONS, 360
REFERENCES, 362

8 **Key Conclusions and Recommendations** 379
  KEY CONCLUSIONS, 379
  RECOMMENDATIONS, 383
  FINAL THOUGHTS, 399
  REFERENCES, 399

Appendix A A Total Population of Children Ages 0–8 by
            Race/Ethnicity and Nativity, 2020   407
Appendix B Percentage of Children from Birth through Age 5
            and Not Yet in Kindergarten Participating in Various
            Weekly Nonparental Care Arrangements, by Child
            and Family Characteristics, 2019   409
Appendix C Committee Member and Staff Biosketches   415

Boxes, Figures, and Tables

BOXES

1-1 Statement of Task: Committee on Exploring the Opportunity Gap for Young Children from Birth to Age Eight, 19
1-2 Relevant Reports of the National Academies of Sciences, Engineering, and Medicine, 21

4-1 The Effect of Preterm Birth on Opportunity Gaps, 211
4-2 Policy Lessons: Lead Exposure and Academic Performance, 230

5-1 How the COVID-19 Pandemic Exacerbated the Opportunity Gap, 290

FIGURES

1-1 A conceptual framework for understanding the opportunity gap, 24
1-2 Changing racial/ethnic composition of the U.S. child population aged 0–18 (percent), 37
1-3 Racial/ethnic composition of children aged 0–8 in the United States, 2020 (thousands), 38
1-4 Racial/ethnic composition of children aged 0–8 by family immigration status, 2020 (thousands), 39

1-5   Racial/ethnic composition of children aged 0–8 by family immigrant status, 2020 (percent), 40
1-6   The Child Opportunity Index, 47

2-1   Percent of children aged 3-4 enrolled in early care and education, 2020, 82
2-2   Percentage of low-income children served by Head Start, by state, 83
2-3   Percentage of U.S. 3- and 4-year-olds enrolled in state-funded preschool, 84
2-4   Current enrollment in Head Start and state-funded preschool and the number of additional slots needed for universal pre-K, 85
2-5   Weekly child care costs as a percentage of household (HH) income for low-income households that pay out of pocket, by race/ethnicity and nativity status, 87
2-6   Percentage of states' populations of 3- and 4-year-olds enrolled in state preschool programs by number of National Institute for Early Education Research (NIEER) quality benchmarks, 95

3-1   Percentage of students aged 5–21 served under the Individuals with Disabilities Education Act (IDEA) Part B within racial/ethnic groups, by educational environment, fall 2019, 158

4-1   Leading causes of death among children and adolescents in the United States, 1999–2020, 236

7-1   Hypothesized pathways between parents' job quality and children's health and development, 331
7-2   Share of full-time working families with jobs without adequate family-supporting wages or benefits by race/ethnicity and foreign-born status, 334

TABLES

1-1   Historical Precents in Education in the United States across Systems and Settings for Children from Birth through Age 8, 26

2-1   Comparison of Child Care, Head Start, and State Pre-K Programs and Programs Covered by the Individuals with Disabilities Education Act (IDEA) Part C and Part B Section 619, 73
2-2   Median Hourly Wages (in dollars) of Center-Based Teachers and Caregivers by Age of Children Served and Sponsorship and Funding of Center-Based Program or Employment, 111

3-1 Risk Ratios for Students with Disabilities Ages 5–21 (served by Individuals with Disabilities Education Act [IDEA], Part B) by Racial/Ethnic Group and Disability Category, Fall 2019, 155
3-2 Odds Ratios for Special Education Identification by Grade Level and Student Group, 162
3-3 Behaviors Associated with Learning Disabilities and Second Language Acquisition, 163
3-4 Racial Disparities for Students with Disabilities (SWD) in Days of Lost Instruction per 100 Students Due to Disciplinary Removal: Top 10 States (including the District of Columbia), 171

4-1 Misrepresentation of Race in Preclinical Curricula, 223
4-2 Food Insecurity by Selected Household Characteristics, 226

5-1 Racial and Ethnic Differences in Diagnosis Rates for Attention Deficit/Hyperactivity Disorder (ADHD) and Autism Spectrum Disorder (ASD), 278
5-2 Outcomes of Interest for Home Visiting Programs at the Primary Prevention Level, 284
5-3 Outcomes of Interest for Secondary-Level Home Visiting Programs, 285

A-A Total Population of Children Ages 0–8, by Race/Ethnicity and Nativity, 2020, 408

A-B Percentage of Children from Birth through Age 5 and Not Yet in Kindergarten Participating in Various Weekly Nonparental Care Arrangements, by Child and Family Characteristics, 2019, 410

Acronyms

AAP	American Academy of Pediatrics
ABC	Attachment and Biobehavioral Catch-up
ACE	adverse childhood experience
ACOG	American College of Obstetricians and Gynecologists
ADHD	attention-deficit/hyperactivity disorder
AFDC	Aid to Families with Dependent Children
AI/AN	American Indian/Alaska Native
AIM	Alliance for Innovation on Maternal Health
AMA	American Medical Association
APHA	American Public Health Association
ASD	autism spectrum disorder
BIE	Bureau of Indian Education
BLL	blood lead level
BPA	bisphenol A
CCAP	Child Care Assistance Program
CCDBG	Child Care and Development Block Grant
CCDF	Child Care and Development Fund
CDA	child development associate
CDC	Centers for Disease Control and Prevention
CEP	Community Eligibility Provision
CHIP	Children's Health Insurance Program
CLASS	Classroom Assessment Scoring System
CMS	Centers for Medicare & Medicaid Services

COI	Child Opportunity Index
CPC	Chicago Child–Parent Center
CPP	Child Parent Psychotherapy
CPS	Current Population Survey
CPSC	Consumer Product Safety Commission
CRC	United Nations Convention on the Rights of the Child
CRDC	Civil Rights Data Collection
CTC	child tax credit
DB	Developmental and Behavioral
DOL	Department of Labor
EBT	electronic benefit transfer
ECE	early care and education
ECERS-R	Early Childhood Environmental Rating Scale-Revised
ECPP-NHES	Early Childhood Program Participation Survey of the National Household Education Surveys Program
EITC	earned income tax credit
ELA	English Language Arts
EPA	Environmental Protection Agency
ESSA	Elementary and Secondary Education Act
ESSA	Every Student Succeeds Act
FLSA	Fair Labor Standards Act
FMLA	Family and Medical Leave Act
FPL	federal poverty level
FWO	Fair Workweek Ordinance
GAO	Government Accountability Office
GDP	gross domestic product
HCD	human-centered design
HHS	Department of Health and Human Services
HMD	Health and Medicine Division
HomVEE	Home Visiting Evaluation and Effectiveness
HSIS	Head Start Impact Study
HSPPS	Head Start Program Performance Standards
IDEA	Individuals with Disabilities Education Act
IECMHC	Infant and Early Childhood Mental Health Consultation
IES	Institute of Education Sciences
IOM	Institute of Medicine
IRS	Internal Revenue Service

L1	first language
L2	second language
LAUNCH	Linking Actions for Unmet Needs in Children's Health
MIECHV	Maternal, Infant, and Early Childhood Home Visiting
MIHOPE	Maternal Infant Home Visiting Program Evaluation
MMRC	Maternal Mortality Review Committee
MMWR	Morbidity and Mortality Weekly Report
MVPF	marginal value of public funds
NAEP	National Assessment of Educational Progress
NAEYC	National Association for the Education of Young Children
NASEM	National Academies of Sciences, Engineering, and Medicine
NCHS	National Center for Health Statistics
NCSER	National Center for Special Education Research
NFP	Nurse-Family Partnership
NHANES	National Health and Nutrition Examination Survey
NHVY	National Home Visiting Yearbook
NICHD	Eunice Kennedy Shriver National Institute of Child Health and Human Development
NIEER	National Institute for Early Education Research
NIH	National Institutes of Health
NRC	National Research Council
NSECE	National Survey of Early Care and Education
NSF	National Science Foundation
NSLP	National School Lunch Program
OECD	Organisation for Economic Co-operation and Development
OMB	Office of Management and Budget
OST	out-of-school time
PCE	positive child experience
PEELS	Pre-Elementary Education Longitudinal Study
PPP	public–private partnership
pre-K	prekindergarten
PQC	Perinatal Quality Collaborative
PTFCEH	President's Task Force on Children's Environmental Health
QALY	quality-adjusted life year
QRIS	quality rating and improvement systems

RCT	randomized controlled trial
SAMHSA	Substance Abuse and Mental Health Services Administration
SBP	School Breakfast Program
SES	socioeconomic status
SNAP	Supplemental Nutrition Assistance Program
SSI	Supplemental Security Income
STEM	science, technology, engineering, and mathematics
SWD	students with disabilities
TANF	Temporary Assistance for Needy Families
TN-VPK	Tennessee Voluntary Pre-Kindergarten
UI	unemployment insurance
UNICEF	United Nations International Children's Emergency Fund
USDA	U.S. Department of Agriculture
VBAC	vaginal birth after cesarean
VSL	value of a statistical life
VSLY	value of a statistical life year
WIC	Special Supplemental Nutrition Program for Women, Infants, and Children
WONDER	Wide-ranging Online Data for Epidemiologic Research

Preface

The committee that produced this report was tasked with authoring a consensus report focused on identifying and describing causes, costs, and effects of the opportunity gap in children. We define the opportunity gap as **the unequal and inequitable distribution of resources and experiences on the basis of race, ethnicity, socioeconomic status, English proficiency, disability, immigration status, community wealth, familial situations, geography, or other factors that contribute to or perpetuate inequities in well-being across groups of young children in outcomes including health, social and emotional development, and education.**

Our statement of task specifies that the committee focus on children from birth to age 8 and make recommendations on how to improve conditions and promote success for children—at home, in communities, and in schools. Our work began with addressing the relationship between the opportunity gap and the persistent achievement gaps that disadvantage children from marginalized groups. In our view, opportunity gaps fuel achievement gaps as a result of various missed opportunities. Thus we reviewed evidence and consulted experts on family, school, economic, and community factors that promote, mitigate, or diminish opportunities for achievement. Reviewing and synthesizing this literature also made it clear that it would be naïve to approach fulfilling our task of recommending ways to improve outcomes and promote child success without focusing beyond academic achievement to encompass two other important developmental outcomes that greatly influence a child's ability to profit from available opportunities—physical health, and social and emotional well-being.

Complementing our scientific review of the opportunity gaps in these three major areas of development, we were tasked with summarizing the economic justification for addressing the opportunity gap—both the costs of the existing failures and the potential economic benefits of addressing them. Our review of evidence on promising federal and state policy interventions and practices that have addressed the opportunity gap is intended to move us forward in closing the gap through interventions based on practices and policies that have already shown some promise. Finally, while every sector of our society has a role to play in addressing the opportunity gap, the committee was also asked to pay particular attention to identifying the potential roles and actions appropriate for our sponsors from philanthropy in supporting federal, state, and local governments in working to address the opportunity gap.

In taking on the commitment to address a complex statement of task, the committee was aware of the many existing bodies of evidence documenting the ways in which disparities in early life opportunities have an impact on children's development. In fact, the National Academies of Sciences, Engineering, and Medicine have played a significant role in providing expert analysis of the need for better distribution of existing resources for young children in areas as diverse as health, access to quality early education, and the opportunity to participate in summertime programs that help children maintain and build on the gains of the prior school year. What was needed, in our opinion, was a broader lens on the problems with the persistent achievement gap among children. In addition to examining opportunity gaps that children face in unequally resourced academic settings (from preschool to second grade), we showed the gaps in resources that make children less able to benefit from their academic setting. Thus, as suggested above, our approach to addressing the committee's statement of task includes documenting the interconnection of education, physical health, and social and emotional development to a child's readiness to benefit from available educational opportunities.

Any chance of creating equity for all young children depends on understanding how activities in support of children's development, whether at the family and community levels, or at the levels of local, state, and federal government, are often misaligned and sometimes even in conflict. Though entities at each level may be committed to promoting positive outcomes for children, we perceived the need to document how historical practices of less favorable treatment of children with differing social class, immigration, racial, ethnic, linguistic, and ability backgrounds reinforce the existing opportunity gaps and undermine efforts to eliminate them.

Our task, then, was to (1) summarize the evidence that has shown the many negative effects on children of being on the wrong side of the opportunity gap; (2) highlight actions for change that have been recommended by several expert groups, including more than a half dozen National Academies panels; and (3) develop a coherent picture of the many conflicting, underimplemented, or inequitably implemented policies at the federal and state levels. All of this was intended to make the case that, more than creating new tools to close this pernicious gap, we as a nation need to mobilize what we already have and know, or what we could know if we compared notes and collaborated across policy and practice silos. We recognize that creating momentum for a shared national commitment to closing the opportunity gap will not happen overnight, so our recommendations include actions that can be addressed in the shorter term along with recommendations that will require changes at the state and federal levels—changes that may take longer to put in place.

On behalf of the committee, I would like to thank our sponsors from the world of philanthropy and government for requesting the creation of this important synthesis of research, practices, and policies aimed at creating a forceful and systematic attack on the gaps in access to resources that leave so many children behind. We could not have done this work without the incredible skill and diligence of the National Academies staff, led by Rebekah Hutton. I am deeply grateful to them all for their support—past, present, and future. My fellow committee members and I formed what I know, from chairing two earlier National Academies committees, to be an unusually strong bond and unwavering commitment to fully addressing our statement of task. Colleagues were unstinting in sharing their talents, resources, views, and time to achieve our shared goals on this very important project. My warmest regards and thanks to each and every one of you. As large as is the accomplishment we feel upon completing this report, we know that we have much work ahead of us to disseminate our recommendations to a wide range of audiences, including our sponsors who, in their wisdom, tasked the committee with identifying roles they could play in closing the gap.

LaRue Allen, *Chair*
Committee on Exploring the Opportunity Gap
for Young Children from Birth to Age Eight

Summary

While many young children are thriving and have access to the conditions and resources they need for healthy development, a substantial number of young children face challenging conditions. These conditions—rooted in the inequitable distribution of resources in the United States based on factors such as race/ethnicity, geographic disadvantage, socioeconomic status, and community wealth—have compounded over time, and today manifest as disparities that include inadequate access to health care and well-funded quality schools, poverty, food insecurity, lack of mental health care, and exposure to violence. In addition to their effects on future academic outcomes, these challenges can lead to disparities in healthy development across multiple domains. Children's academic outcomes and overall well-being might be improved by efforts to reduce disparities in opportunity in order to prevent them from becoming achievement gaps. For example, such efforts might include reducing barriers to social supports, improving community safety, increasing access to quality health care, addressing factors such as institutional racism, making parents' jobs higher quality and more family friendly, implementing culturally relevant pedagogy and learning, and reducing child poverty.

The Every Student Succeeds Act calls for schools to implement "whole child" strategies that promote physical health and healthy social-emotional development as a means of reducing disparities in academic achievement. Similarly, the Head Start Act promotes overall well-being and school readiness through a focus on addressing children's comprehensive developmental and health needs and the needs of their families. Because a wide variety of factors begin to influence the trajectories of children before they are even born, closing the opportunity gap requires a deeper and integrated examination of family and community factors, such as family and community engagement, parent/caregiver academic attainment, health of parents and/or child(ren), and cultural norms, as well as structural factors, such as social inequality, racism and discrimination, laws and policies, and other social determinants of health and well-being.

The Committee on Exploring the Opportunity Gap for Young Children from Birth to Age Eight was formed to identify and describe causes, costs, and effects of the opportunity gap in young children. In order to make recommendations on how to improve conditions and promote success for children at home, in communities, and in schools, the committee was asked to (1) identify and describe the opportunity gap and its relationship (if any) to the achievement gap; (2) review available research and evidence on the effects of the opportunity gap, as well as family, school, and community factors that promote or diminish opportunities for achievement; (3) discuss the economic costs of the opportunity gap and potential economic benefits of addressing it; (4) review evidence on promising federal and state policy interventions that have addressed the opportunity gap; and (5) identify the potential roles, actions, and supports appropriate for philanthropy to assist in addressing the opportunity gap (see Chapter 1 for the committee's full statement of task). The committee's statement of task specifies that the committee should focus on children from birth to age 8; however, we recognize that the causes of these gaps may begin before birth and that the effects of these gaps may persist well beyond third grade into adulthood. The statement of task asked the committee to identify and describe societal conditions with potential to preclude equal access to high-quality educational opportunities. Accordingly, the expertise represented on the committee (including early childhood and primary education, child development, public health, mental health, sociology, demography, neuroscience, economics, and public policy) reflects the complexity of this task.

For many young children in the United States, unequal opportunity exists across a number of contexts from the time they are born, which can have a long-lasting impact on future academic, health, and economic outcomes. Although achievement and opportunity are related, it is important to distinguish between the two. The potential causes of the achievement gap are individual opportunity gaps across numerous domains that we refer to *collectively* as the opportunity gap. We define the opportunity gap as **the unequal and inequitable distribution of resources and experiences on the basis of race, ethnicity, socioeconomic status, English proficiency, disability, immigration status, community wealth, familial situations, geography, or other factors that contribute to or perpetuate inequities in well-being across groups of young children in health, social-emotional development, and education.** The achievement gap refers to the effect of the opportunity gap—disparities in academic outcomes and well-being among different groups of children. To understand the nature of the opportunity gap, the committee examined the historical contexts that underpin the structures and barriers that allow disparities to persist and the ways in which these drivers continue to affect access to resources, supports, quality educational experiences, quality health care, and positive developmental experiences.

The committee examined opportunity gaps among children by identifying differences in experiences and outcomes by race/ethnicity, gender, socioeconomic status, disability, nativity/immigrant status, language learner status, child's age, and geographic location. With a focus on equity, the committee used its review of peer-reviewed publications and relevant grey literature—including policy briefs, reports, and evaluations, as well as expert presentations and a commissioned research synthesis—to better understand how certain subgroups of children may be differentially affected by the absence of specific opportunities and whether this has a negative impact on young children across a number of demographic designations.

KEY CONCLUSIONS ACROSS THE COMMITTEE'S DOMAINS OF FOCUS

The committee's key conclusions identify issues that cut across the domains discussed in this report—education, physical health, and social-emotional health and well-being. These conclusions highlight contexts that drive opportunity gaps and areas in which there are opportunities to change policies, programs, and interventions to close the opportunity gap for young children. Supporting evidence for the committee's key conclusions can be found in Chapter 8.

> *Conclusion 1: Differential experiences and access to resources in early childhood result in opportunity gaps, which can lead to long-term gaps in outcomes in education, physical health, and social-emotional development that are harmful to individuals, communities, and society.*

> *Conclusion 2: There is substantial evidence describing effective policies and practices that can increase opportunity across multiple domains. These domains range from health, such as increasing maternal access to prenatal care, access to health care, and insurance coverage to access to antipoverty programs and to early care and education. However, differential access as a matter of policy or practice, as well as inconsistent—and in some cases, uncoordinated—implementation and inadequate funding, has allowed barriers to accessing opportunities to persist, leaving the most vulnerable populations underserved. These*

barriers must be addressed for these promising policies and practices to be implemented equitably and effectively.

Conclusion 3: Restrictive eligibility criteria set at the federal and state levels and differences in state and local implementation of policies lead to vastly different experiences for children and families depending on who they are and where they live. Access to resources and services has been impeded by some state and federal policies, as well as service systems that create administrative barriers to access, barriers that disproportionately affect communities of color, immigrant families, and families with low income. These differences occur across all domains examined by the committee, from school funding and access, to quality schools and teachers, to access to health care and health insurance, to the neighborhood-level resources that shape the ability of parents to support and care for their children and provide the supports needed for healthy development.

Conclusion 4: Research shows that income from full-time employment does not cover the cost of basic needs for many working families. In addition, many employers do not provide benefits such as paid leave or child care. Limited access to paid family leave creates an opportunity gap for young children by limiting parents' and infants' bonding time, decreasing the time available to take care of serious health issues, elevating family stress, and exposing children to financial uncertainty. Limited access to high-quality child care can create opportunity gaps by limiting parents' employment, earnings, and job stability, ultimately leading to family economic insecurity.

Conclusion 5: Differential experiences and access to resources are associated with factors such as race/ethnicity, income, social class, gender, national origin, language background, and disability; however, the intersections of these factors with social determinants can result in interdependent systems of disadvantage that multiply negative effects. Thus, opportunity gaps for one age group can persist and compound, becoming the cause of future opportunity gaps.

Conclusion 6: Structural racism and discrimination perpetuate opportunity gaps and the achievement gap. Systematic exclusion, structural racism, racial and ethnic discrimination, poverty, unequal allocation of resources and services, labor market inequalities, biases in access to and experiences in services, and policies that create administrative burden for families all affect the ways in which families experience opportunity. While many of these structures have their origins in the past, they persist, and their effects—now compounded—continue to affect outcomes and the well-being of children and families.

RECOMMENDATIONS

The committee's recommendations draw on evidence-based conclusions presented throughout the report to identify actions that can be taken by policy makers, practitioners, community organizations, philanthropic organizations, and other stakeholders. Additional supporting text for each recommendation can be found in Chapter 8 of this volume.

Recommendation 1: Federal entities and agencies and private philanthropic organizations that collect data and fund research related to child health and development should create and adequately support an effective equity-focused policy- and services-monitoring data infrastructure (collection of both quantitative and qualitative data, data analysis, and program evaluation) to guide federal, state, and local policy decisions aimed at closing the opportunity gap across income, race/ethnicity, disability, gender, language background, and immigrant status. This data infrastructure should also be made available for research and learning.

To further a research agenda addressing the opportunity gap, actions such as the following could be taken by federal entities and private philanthropic organizations:

- All federal data (and data reported to the federal government by states and local communities) could be disaggregated for groups listed in Executive Order 13985, Advancing Racial Equity and Support for Underserved Communities through the Federal Government.
- Data could be shared across agencies that are responsible for individual safety net and social insurance programs (e.g., the Department of Health and Human Services/Centers for Medicare & Medicaid Services for Medicaid, the Internal Revenue Service for the earned income tax credit/child tax credit, the Department of Labor for unemployment insurance) and linked when possible to create merged data sets. These data could be used by each agency to monitor program access, quality, and outcomes across groups known to experience gaps in opportunity through internal and external research studies.
- The Office of Management and Budget (OMB), with input from the Office of Science and Technology Policy, could direct all federal

agencies to conduct audits and examine disparate treatment and administrative burden in state and local service systems responsible for serving families and children.
- OMB could direct each federal agency with significant federal expenditures on young children to create an equity research, evaluation, and technical assistance center.
- OMB could direct federal statistical agencies to assess current data collection on families and young children and make recommendations on improvements aimed at addressing opportunity and outcome gaps that can be evaluated and prioritized for investment.
- The Department of Labor could use its existing data to monitor differential trends in job quality, including wages, employer-provided benefits, schedules, and health and safety standards for all workers and working families with young children. With input from the relevant offices of the Executive Office of the President (e.g., the Council of Economic Advisers), the data could be used to formulate policy recommendations and set goals for improving job quality.
- The National Institutes of Health, National Science Foundation, and Institute of Education Sciences could prioritize studies that fill gaps in knowledge about policies, programs, and practices that reduce opportunity gaps for subgroups of young children that are underrepresented in the existing evidence base.
- The Internal Revenue Service and the Census Bureau could create a linked data system for use in analyzing all families' access to and take-up of tax credits—the most robust antipoverty programs, including the earned income tax credit and the child tax credit—in support of the development of a systematic outreach approach to reduce the burden associated with and increase take-up.
- The Department of Education could require the What Works Clearinghouse to report the evidence for subgroups of children and results from rigorous quasi-experimental studies.
- The Interagency Forum on Child and Family Statistics could evaluate each agency's existing systems for collecting data on young children and whether and how these systems could be linked. This assessment would lead to recommendations for improving these data systems so they could be used to evaluate and monitor developmental outcomes of young children, including disparities among groups in access, take-up, and outcomes across multiple programs.
- The philanthropic community could prioritize investments in further developing state and local data systems that include linked data on children's health and education outcomes, as well as measures of opportunity gaps by race/ethnicity, income, nativity, language, and disability, at a minimum. To monitor child opportunity

across communities and target funding to communities with lower resources, a consistent set of state/local measures from these systems could be added to the Child Opportunity Index. Investments are also needed to bolster the evaluation efforts of community-based organizations aimed at identifying, piloting, and expanding evidence-based practices that make families' access to systems more equitable and user-friendly and their experiences within systems positive and promotive.

Monitoring and accountability are key for the successful implementation of all of the committee's recommendations. Given the complexities surrounding the opportunity gap for young children, a system of metrics is needed to track disparities in opportunities and resources, such as access to qualified educators, rigorous and inclusive curricula, school funding, school ecologies that support learning, quality health care, and resources that promote healthy social and emotional well-being and development. In addition to tracking of these metrics, systematic cataloging of evidence-based, effective, and equitable policies and program interventions across domains in a centralized database/registry would provide a significant resource to communities, policy makers, researchers, and philanthropic organizations working to reduce disparities in opportunity for children.

Recommendation 2: The federal government and states should establish early learning opportunities—accompanied by both legal accountability guaranteeing access and inclusive, intentional quality standards that are aligned with scientific evidence—as a right afforded to all children and families who need and want services.

This recommendation is supported by a wealth of evidence demonstrating that high-quality early care and education (ECE) is a public good with social and economic returns that benefit all, one that is recognized as a fundamental right in many countries around the world. Despite this fact, ECE is available only to some and exists as a patchwork system of varying quality. As a result, many families, disproportionately those from marginalized backgrounds, are left in difficult positions, balancing the safety, care, and education of their children and their employment. To implement this recommendation, federal and state actors should consider codifying ECE as both a civil and a human right of all young children. This could be achieved at the federal level by ratifying the United Nations Convention on the Rights of the Child, which would build on existing precedent established at the federal level through, for example, the right to preschool services for young children with disabilities in the Individuals with Disabilities Education Act.

Recommendation 3: The federal government—in partnership with states—should fully implement a voluntary universal high-quality public early care and education system using a targeted universal approach (i.e., setting universal goals that are pursued using processes and strategies targeted to the needs of different groups). Such programs should be responsive to community needs, reflect the true cost of quality, and have strong monitoring and accountability systems that specifically address gaps in opportunity.

Such a unified system would:

- ensure that children and families from communities listed in Executive Order 13985, Advancing Racial Equity and Support for Underserved Communities through the Federal Government, are prioritized;
- allocate greater resources to historically marginalized communities to compensate for historical and current inequities in resources, experiences, and opportunities;
- allocate greater resources for parts of the early care and education system that have traditionally received fewer resources;
- require evidence-based program standards that improve population outcomes and explicitly remedy opportunity gaps;
- build a corps of diverse, competent, well-trained, well-supported, and appropriately compensated early childhood educators and program leaders, across all age groups and program settings; and
- require disaggregated data collection that can be linked with other relevant data sources, as well as continuous quality improvement aimed at bridging opportunity and outcome gaps.

Underinvestment in high-quality ECE disproportionately affects children from low-income families, children of color, children who speak languages other than English at home, and children with disabilities. This underinvestment, the result of a complex array of factors, persists despite the well-documented benefits—individual and societal—of high-quality ECE.

Quality frameworks adopted by the field may not, in many instances, include indicators that have a particularly salient effect on opportunity gaps and the experiences of children from historically marginalized communities, such as issues related to bias, language of instruction, and inclusion of children with disabilities. Underfunded and fragmented programs, underpaid workers, inconsistent access to high-quality programming, and inadequate quality frameworks contribute to opportunity gaps. Wide-scale implementation of such a system should take into account the challenges that can occur during scale-up, such as insufficient capacity to implement programs, lack of sustained funding, a mismatch between demand for and supply of programs, and barriers to access for targeted populations. A systematic approach to scaling up should be used to ensure that goals are clear and measurable, that progress is assessed regularly, and that challenges and opportunities are identified as they occur to inform iterative improvements in implementation.

Recommendation 4: The federal government, states, local communities, and districts should adequately and equitably support elementary school education and out-of-school programs. Elementary school education should operate under a common quality framework, with quality benchmarks aligned with those in the early care and education (ECE) system and based on evidence-based policies and practices.

Such a system would:

- address structural drivers of education opportunity, including segregation in learning settings by language, disability, race, and income; and
- be adequately funded to support the implementation of high-quality benchmarks aligned with those in the ECE system, including
  - high-quality instruction and asset-driven pedagogies, assessments, and curricula;
  - social-emotional and mental health supports and policies to explicitly reduce exclusionary and harsh discipline and eliminate disparities in such practices;
  - full inclusion of children with disabilities in general education settings, with high-quality and individualized services and supports;
  - bilingual learning opportunities for children who are English learners and dual language learners;
  - structurally sound, safe, healthy, and engaging learning environments;
  - a well-qualified, fairly compensated, and supported workforce;
  - data-driven continuous quality improvement efforts targeted at identifying and addressing opportunity and outcome gaps;
  - authentic and meaningful family engagement and partnerships;
  - strong partnerships with ECE systems that promote seamless transitions from ECE to the early grades; and
  - community partnerships and engagement to promote holistic family wellness.

Increasing funding for education, particularly for low-income students, has significant effects (e.g., improving achievement and graduation rates, employment, and wages, and reducing poverty rates). Thus, resource allocation would need to prioritize underserved populations, including high-poverty and minoritized communities and children with unique needs, such as English learners and students with disabilities. Increased resources could be used in a targeted way to meet quality benchmarks, close opportunity gaps, and meet the holistic and academic needs of students. ECE and the early grades would also need to be aligned so that what was attained in the early years would be built upon and expanded in the later grades rather than repeated or dropped altogether. Families and communities must be a part of these systems to ensure that children are immersed in the environments and conditions they need to thrive across settings.

Recommendation 5: The Department of Education should fully integrate Individuals with Disabilities Education Act programming with general early childhood and K–12 education. As part of achieving this goal, the Department of Education, states, and districts should undertake specific reforms explicitly addressing opportunity gaps identified in this report, including:

- uneven access to early intervention and preschool special education;
- uneven quality and dosage of early intervention and preschool special education;
- inclusion of children with disabilities across age groups, especially preschoolers, who are the most likely to be served in separate settings;
- nonbiased, accurate identification, specifically addressing over- and underidentification of specific groups of children, such as children of color, English learners, and others; and
- prohibition of harsh forms of discipline, including suspensions, expulsions, all forms of corporal punishment, seclusion, and inappropriate restraint for all students with disabilities, with special attention to students of color, who are disproportionately subject to these practices.

The maximum federal share of funding for the Individuals with Disabilities Education Act (IDEA) determined by Congress is 40% of the national average per pupil expenditure. Today, Congress funds about 18% of what it costs to educate children with disabilities. Indeed, the inadequate funding of these services has resulted in states restricting eligibility criteria, lowering the dosage of services, or stretching wait times for the evaluation and service delivery process to the upper limits of what is allowable by law.

IDEA policy reforms, through reauthorization, regulation, technical assistance, and monitoring and accountability systems, must intentionally address gaps in access, particularly for children of color; accuracy in identification; inclusion in general ECE settings; and the harsh discipline to which children with disabilities are disproportionately subject.

> **Recommendation 6:** The Department of Health and Human Services (HHS) should create, lead, and be accountable for coordinating an interagency group focused on children's mental health and social-emotional well-being that includes the several HHS operating divisions, including the Administration for Children and Families, the Health Resources and Services Administration, the Substance Abuse and Mental Health Services Administration, the Centers for Disease Control and Prevention, and the Centers for Medicare & Medicaid Services, among others, as well as the Department of Education, the Department of Justice, the Department of Housing and Urban Development, and other relevant agencies, for the purpose of designing, implementing, and evaluating a comprehensive system of primary psychosocial care for young children and their families.

Such a comprehensive system of primary psychosocial care for young children and their families would include:

- universal support across the lifespan from the prenatal period through third grade, consisting of regular screening and identification of needs in mental health and social-emotional development for both families and children, followed by facilitated access to community resources that address those needs;
- sufficient community capacity to address young children's needs through a comprehensive array of well-funded, evidence-based intervention programs and resources;
- an integrated data system, much like a child's electronic medical record, that charts a child's needs and interventions across the life course, to facilitate cross-agency communication and program and policy evaluation, and serve as a resource for future providers; and
- an evaluation plan and support for research to understand systemic and structural drivers (e.g., racism) that create or worsen physical and mental health challenges among young children from historically marginalized communities.

For families with children, no universal system provides care to support the social and emotional development, mental health, and well-being of their child from birth until age 5 when they enter the K–12 system with continuity of supports and services through the early school-age years. Families from minoritized groups (both parents and children) are disproportionately exposed to hardships and stress across the life course, including stress related to racism and discrimination; are less likely to have their mental health needs met; and are more likely to have treatment prematurely terminated. In addition, children from minoritized groups are less likely to have access to mental health services in schools and in the child welfare system. For many families, especially those experiencing poverty, health issues, and precarious jobs, uncoordinated public systems that provide support for the well-being of children create barriers to access and burden these families as they attempt to access services and supports. A centralized system for identifying and cataloging effective, evidence-based intervention programs, policies, and resources should be part of the development of this system of primary psychosocial care to assist communities in selecting appropriate evidence-based interventions that can then be evaluated and used to understand drivers of challenges that affect specific communities.

Recommendation 7: The Department of Labor and the Department of Health and Human Services, in partnership with other relevant federal agencies, should review, update, and enforce existing labor standards and employment policies to address disparities that disproportionately affect working families with young children.

To implement this recommendation, the federal government could:

- build on the current job protections offered under the unpaid Family Medical Leave Act to create a paid social insurance program, administered by the Social Security Administration, to support parents needing time away from work to care for infants and newly adopted children and attend to their own and their family members' serious health issues;
- address documented issues in access to paid family and medical leave for low-income families and families from marginalized communities by implementing progressive wage replacement rates, making coverage more inclusive by eliminating firm-size requirements, and using existing hours and duration criteria for Social Security Disability Insurance or Medicare Hospital Insurance;
- develop recommendations on the definition of good-quality jobs for families with children, an effort that should include setting standards for family-sustaining wages and family-friendly employer practices;
- update existing labor standards and policies, raise the minimum wage floor, make work schedules more predictable, budget more

resources for enforcement, and incentivize employers to provide training and career ladders; and
- partner with philanthropic organizations to conduct research on job quality standards and metrics to guide policy and employer-based interventions.

Research shows that many working families do not earn enough from full-time employment to cover basic needs, and that many employers do not provide benefits such as paid sick or medical leave, parental leave, or child care. Lack of access to paid leave creates an opportunity gap for young children by limiting bonding time for parents and infants, decreasing the time available to attend to serious health issues, elevating family stress, and exposing children to financial uncertainty. Overall, this body of research suggests that paid family and medical leave is an effective policy that improves the social-emotional well-being of parents and the health of their young children. Moreover, making the program nearly universal would lower per-worker costs. The policy could be further improved by reducing racial/ethnic and income disparities in take-up of leave through less restrictive eligibility criteria, higher wage replacement rates, targeted outreach, and improved administrative systems.

Recommendation 8: The federal government, in partnership with state and local governments, philanthropy, and relevant public and private organizations, should support policies and interventions targeting social determinants of health that create and perpetuate opportunity gaps at the community level.

To further the development of targeted policies and interventions for addressing the opportunity gap at the community level, the following actions should be taken by federal, state, and local entities and private philanthropic organizations:

- Federal and state governments should expand existing safety net programs that have been shown to address poverty and food insecurity as social determinants of health, including the Special Supplemental Nutrition Program for Women, Infants, and Children, the Supplemental Nutrition Assistance Program, and the earned income tax credit, as well as the 2021 expanded child tax credit. Eligibility applications for these programs could be unified and streamlined to reduce administrative hurdles to take-up.
- As with other programs such as child care subsidies, to reduce disruptions in insurance and health care access, the federal government should ensure continuous coverage with Medicaid for a

minimum 12-month period even if families experience temporary changes in income during the year that make them ineligible, and Medicaid should be provided to women for at least 12 months postpartum.
- Federal, state, and local governments should increase the supply of affordable high-quality housing, which would include access to green spaces, playgrounds, and parks.
- Local governments should engage in urban planning improvements to enhance traffic safety and eliminate road hazards (e.g., legislate speed limits), especially in marginalized communities.
- Governments at the federal, state, and local levels and philanthropy should prioritize support for communities with a level of high need and low resources, as measured by the Child Opportunity Index, program administrative data, and historical budget data.
- Early learning, education, and health care systems should act as anchor institutions and be coordinated through shared data systems and integrated service delivery to promote family wellness and community development by offering onsite or providing connections to health, mental health, after-school, nutritional support, and economic wellness services. The federal government should build on and expand existing programming that can facilitate this anchor organization approach, such as full-service community schools, Head Start, and federally qualified health centers.
- Community organizations, philanthropy, and local governments should support evidence-based programs for young people, such as those that include tutoring or mentoring; sports; and early childhood mental health programs, including parent–child interaction and cognitive-behavioral therapeutic approaches.

For children living in poverty and those from other marginalized populations, inequities in experiences and access to resources that support healthy developmental outcomes can vary greatly, leading to persisting opportunity gaps for young children. State and local governments have opportunities to examine existing policies that have demonstrated promising outcomes for young children and to leverage resources and partnerships with the private sector to invest in interventions with the potential to promote healthy development and close opportunity gaps for young children.

Recommendation 9: Early learning and K–12 education systems, health care systems, and employers should test and institute policies and protocols for identifying and addressing manifestations of institutional racism to reduce inequities in access to resources and quality services in education, health care, and public health.

To identify and address manifestations of institutional racism that create and perpetuate the opportunity gap, the following specific actions should be taken to reduce inequities in access to resources and quality services in education, health care, and public health:

- Systems leaders and administrators across all levels of government (federal, state, local) should work to address institutional racism and increase culturally and linguistically appropriate health care, public health, ECE, and early grade education.
- Policy makers should take into account historical inequities in resource distribution and current manifestations of racism and marginalization in developing policy and making budgetary decisions.
- Federal research agencies (e.g., the National Institutes of Health, the National Science Foundation) and philanthropic organizations should support and prioritize historically marginalized communities and groups to improve their access to professional development programs, apprenticeships, and scholarships, and to diversify the pipeline of health care professionals, public health practitioners, teachers, early educators, and early childhood researchers.
- National professional organizations and accreditors should improve curriculum training and require minimum competencies in antiracist approaches; social determinants of health inequities; and culturally competent, trauma-informed, and resilience-building health care, ECE, and early grade education.

A consistent finding across issue areas (e.g., early education, health, social-emotional development) is that opportunity is associated with race, and that race intersects with multiple other identities to result in compounded gaps in opportunity and outcomes. These gaps are the products of centuries of systemic racism across a number of domains of life. Any attempt to bridge unequal opportunity must be addressed by understanding and remedying historical inequities and their manifestations today.

1

Introduction

While many young children are thriving and have access to the conditions and resources they need to grow up healthy, a substantial number of young children face more challenging conditions. These conditions—rooted in an unequal and often racialized[1] distribution of resources in the United States—have compounded over time, and today manifest as inadequate access to health care and well-funded, quality early care and education (ECE) programs and schools; poverty; food insecurity; lack of mental health care; and exposure to violence. The opportunity gap represented by these challenges can easily translate to an achievement gap that can not only affect future academic outcomes but also lead to disparities in physical and mental health and well-being.

A central emphasis of this report is that, although the opportunity gap is usually defined in terms of its effects on future academic performance, one must understand the interconnectedness of gaps in other domains, such as physical health, mental health, and social-emotional development, in order to develop strategies for closing this gap that address the healthy development of the whole child. In recognition of this essential interconnectedness, the opportunity gap is defined in this report as **the unequal and inequitable distribution of resources and experiences on the basis of race, ethnicity, socioeconomic status, English proficiency, disability, immigration status, community wealth, familial situations, geography, or other factors**

---

[1] Racialization is defined as the act of giving a racial character to someone or something or the process of categorizing, marginalizing, or regarding according to race (Merriam-Webster, 2022).

that contribute to or perpetuate inequities in well-being across groups of young children in health, social-emotional development, and education. The purpose of this study was to identify and describe causes, costs, and effects of the opportunity gap among young children and to make recommendations on how to improve these conditions and promote success for children—at home, in communities, and in schools.

ABOUT THIS STUDY

To better understand the nature of the opportunity gap and the factors driving disparities in outcomes among young children, the sponsors of this study[2] asked the National Academies of Sciences, Engineering, and Medicine to convene an ad hoc committee of experts to respond to the statement of task presented in Box 1-1. The committee's membership represents the diverse areas of expertise—early childhood and primary education, child development, public health, mental health, sociology, demography, neuroscience, economics, and public policy—that must be brought to bear to fully understand the interconnectedness mentioned previously and the complexity of the statement of task.

In responding to its statement of task, the committee focused on opportunity gaps in three domains—education, physical health and health care, and social-emotional development and well-being. In each of these domains, the committee examined the numerous gaps that prevent young children from having equitable access to resources and experiences. It should be noted that, although the committee's statement of task specifies a focus on children from birth to age 8, we recognize that the causes of the opportunity gap may begin before birth, and its effects may persist well beyond third grade into adulthood.

STUDY APPROACH

Evidence presented in this report was gathered from a range of sources. The committee met in closed sessions six times over the course of the study to discuss its findings and develop conclusions and recommendations based on the evidence gathered. The committee's first (virtual) meeting in February 2021 provided an opportunity to hear presentations from representatives of the study sponsors during a session that was open to the public. This meeting allowed the committee members to ask clarifying questions related to

---

[2]This study was sponsored by the Administration for Children and Families (Department of Health and Human Services), Bainum Family Foundation, Bill and Melinda Gates Foundation, Brady Education Foundation, Foundation for Child Development, Heising-Simons Foundation, and W.K. Kellogg Foundation.

BOX 1-1
Statement of Task: Committee on Exploring the Opportunity Gap for Young Children from Birth to Age Eight

An ad hoc committee will conduct a consensus study on the causes and consequences of the opportunity gap for young children from birth to age 8. The committee will:

- Identify and describe the opportunity gap (the potential causes—societal conditions that preclude equal access to high-quality educational opportunities) and its relationship, if any, with the achievement gap (the effect—subgroups of children who demonstrate lower performance than others and subgroups of children who do not achieve at a recognized level of performance).
- Review available research on the effects of the opportunity gap on children from birth to age 8 and its relationship to demographic characteristics and institutional racism and discrimination.
- Review available evidence on family and community factors, and pre-K to grade 3 school factors, that promote, mitigate, or diminish opportunities and achievement for children.
- Discuss the economic costs posed by the opportunity gap and the potential economic benefits of investing in strategies, interventions, and policies to address opportunity gap concerns for children from birth to age 8.
- Review evidence on promising federal and state government policy and program interventions that have addressed opportunity gap concerns for children from birth to age 8.
- Develop recommendations for education policy, practice, and research to better understand the opportunity gap and promote success for all students pre-K to grade 3.
- Identify the potential roles, actions, and supports appropriate for philanthropy to assist in addressing the opportunity gap for young children from birth to age 8.

The committee will produce a consensus report that synthesizes the information gathered on the relationship between the opportunity and achievement gaps for young children from birth to age eight, and make recommendations on how to improve conditions and promote success for children—at home, in communities, and in schools.

the statement of task. Another virtual public information-gathering session, webcast live, was held in May 2021. This session was focused on measuring the opportunity gap and understanding barriers to accessing benefit programs.[3] The committee also held four public listening sessions at which invited speakers presented research on measuring the opportunity gap, on inequality and children's brain development, on child poverty and the opportunity gap, on behavioral insights and parental decision making, and on addressing inequality in the United States from "cradle to kindergarten." In addition to these meetings, the committee commissioned a paper on the economic costs of the opportunity gap to inform its recommendations and conducted extensive searches of the literature related to the domains outlined in the statement of task.

While a comprehensive systematic review of all primary literature related to all of the domains relevant to the committee's charge was not within the scope of this study, the committee developed a three-pronged approach to reviewing such a large research base. First, the committee reviewed several National Academies reports related to the scope of this work (Box 1-2), as well as additional up-to-date peer-reviewed analyses and reviews of the literature. The findings gleaned from these sources provided a base summary of the state of the evidence on child opportunity and outcome gaps and policies and practices that can improve or exacerbate access to opportunities. Relevant findings are briefly summarized throughout each chapter of this report. Second, to document inequities in access to opportunities and the sources of these inequities, the committee reviewed comprehensive historical analyses of inclusion and exclusion and policy analyses of state/local variations in program design, implementation, and funding; current program participation; unmet need; and take-up barriers, such as administrative burden. When data were available, the committee summarized access issues by race/ethnicity, immigrant status, income, and disability/health status, and examined qualitative research describing whether children's culture, racialized history, and language needs have been addressed in programs serving young children. Finally, the committee examined reviews of evaluation evidence for policies and programs, and recent studies if no such reviews were available. Causal and quasi-experimental evidence, broken down by subgroups, is summarized when available, as are research and data gaps. Given the limited number of national studies estimating the impact of opportunity gaps with large-enough sample sizes to enable subgroup analyses, the committee also considered high-quality correlational research studies making clear whether intervention effects are associations or causal and for which groups.

---

[3]The Proceedings of a Workshop—in Brief for this meeting is available at https://www.nap.edu/read/26416

> **BOX 1-2**
> **Relevant Reports of the National Academies of Sciences, Engineering, and Medicine**
>
> - *From Neurons to Neighborhoods: The Science of Early Childhood Development* (2000)
> - *The Integration of Immigrants into American Society* (2015)
> - *Transforming the Workforce for Children Birth Through Age 8: A Unifying Foundation* (2015)
> - *Parenting Matters: Supporting Parents of Children Ages 0-8* (2016)
> - *Communities in Action: Pathways to Health Equity* (2017)
> - *Promoting the Educational Success of Children and Youth Learning English: Promising Futures* (2017)
> - *Transforming the Financing of Early Care and Education* (2018)
> - *English Learners in STEM Subjects: Transforming Classrooms, Schools, and Lives* (2018)
> - *Fostering Healthy Mental, Emotional, and Behavioral Development in Children and Youth: A National Agenda* (2019)
> - *Monitoring Educational Equity* (2019)
> - *A Roadmap to Reducing Child Poverty* (2019)
> - *Vibrant and Healthy Kids: Aligning Science, Practice, and Policy to Advance Health Equity* (2019)
> - *Science and Engineering in Preschool Through Elementary Grades: The Brilliance of Children and the Strengths of Educators* (2022)

The statement of task asked that the committee examine the connection between the opportunity gap and potential resulting achievement gaps for young children. The approach to addressing this question was guided by a recognition that children and their families interact with numerous systems and environments in ways that can either mitigate or exacerbate disparities that affect both short- and long-term outcomes.

While the statement of task is oriented toward future educational achievement, it asked that the committee make recommendations not only for education policy, practice, and research, but also for how to improve conditions and promote success for young children more broadly. To understand how varying conditions can affect young children, the committee examined both historical and current drivers of inequities in education, health, and social and emotional well-being. The committee also reviewed evidence related to promising policies and practices with the potential to close the opportunity gap for young children.

THE REPORT CONCEPTUAL FRAMEWORK

The committee drew on a number of sources to inform its development of a framework that could describe the complexity of how various structural drivers and individual, family, and community factors interact across a wide variety of domains, not only during the period from birth to age 8, but also prior to birth and into later life, to create the opportunity gap (Start Early, n.d.; Bronfenbrenner, 1992; Kuh et al., 2003; Institute of Medicine & National Research Council [IOM & NRC], 2015; National Academies, 2016, 2019a,b; World Health Organization, United Nations Children's Fund, & World Bank Group, 2018). First, to identify areas for examination within the study scope, the committee looked to the United Nations Convention on the Rights of the Child (CRC). While it is important to note that the United States is one of two countries in the world that has not ratified the CRC (UNICEF, 1990), its provisions for what nations should do to ensure that children's rights are protected helped shape the committee's thinking on areas of research for discussion in this volume. Among other provisions, for example, the CRC asks that nations—to the extent possible—ensure the survival and development of the child (Art. 6); ensure the development of institutions, facilities, and services for the care of children and the right of children of working parents to benefit from child care services and facilities for which they are eligible (Art. 18); ensure that assistance to disabled children is provided free of charge, taking into account the financial resources of the parents or others caring for the child (Art. 23); and recognize the right of the child to the enjoyment of the highest attainable standard of health (Art. 24; UNICEF, 1990).

The committee also examined the frameworks and approaches presented in recent relevant National Academies reports and in literature related to the statement of task. The science of early development; the mechanisms of early adversity, stress, and resilience that affect sensitive periods of brain and biological development; and the implications for young children and their trajectories into adulthood is well established (National Academies, 2000, 2019c). Based on this scientific evidence, a strong case has been made for early intervention and investments and a strengths-based approach to support young children (García Coll et al., 1996; Walker et al., 2011). Ecological models have long acknowledged that disparities in children's access to opportunities are driven by structural factors, such as the macroeconomy, policy choices, and structural racism, that are beyond the direct control of families. There is growing recognition across disciplines that racial, ethnic, and immigrant stratification manifested by structural racism and the illegality associated with immigrant status should be incorporated as key components in traditional models focused on early adversity, brain development, and healthy child development (Acevedo-Garcia et al., 2021a; Shonkoff, Slopen, & Williams, 2021). Building on these frameworks and the body of scientific evidence, the committee developed a conceptual model of the opportunity gap experienced by many young children (Figure 1-1). This model recognizes that children and their families interact with numerous institutions and programs within their communities. These interactions are influenced not only by policy and economic contexts (e.g., drivers) but also by structural racism,[4] which often affects access to—and the quality of—opportunities. The model shown in Figure 1-1 depicts how family and social factors (e.g., culture, home language, parent education), environmental and community factors (e.g., access to safe spaces for play, lack of environmental contaminants, violence-free neighborhoods), structural inequities (e.g., structural racism, residential segregation, disparities in school funding), economic drivers (e.g., unemployment, prices of goods needed to raise children), and policy drivers (e.g., federal social safety net and social protection and support policies, local school funding formulas) interact with one another to influence—and have the potential to create inequities in—access to high-quality opportunities. As in other models, these opportunities include educational experiences and high-quality health, economic, and psychosocial supports from the prenatal period through the early years and across the life course. This report differs from others in presenting a comprehensive review of the evidence on structural factors that shape differences in children's opportunities based on race/ethnicity, immigration, and disability/health status and their intersection.

UNDERSTANDING THE HISTORICAL AND STRUCTURAL DRIVERS OF THE OPPORTUNITY GAP

As background for the detailed discussion in the following chapters, the remainder of this introduction provides historical contexts and examines structural factors that have created and continue to perpetuate the opportunity gap. Also provided is an overview of the changing demographics of children from ages 0 to 8 and evidence showing that the effectiveness of public policies designed to provide opportunities for these young children will increasingly be evaluated on how they affect the well-being of children of color and children of immigrants. Reviewed as well is research outlining barriers that impede access to sources of resources and supports for young children and their families.

---

[4]Structural racism is defined in this report as "a system in which historical and (or) contemporary public policies, institutional practices, cultural representations, and other norms work in different, often reinforcing, ways to maintain or compound racial inequalities" (Aspen Institute Roundtable on Community Change, 2004, p. 11; National Academies, 2022a, p. 1).

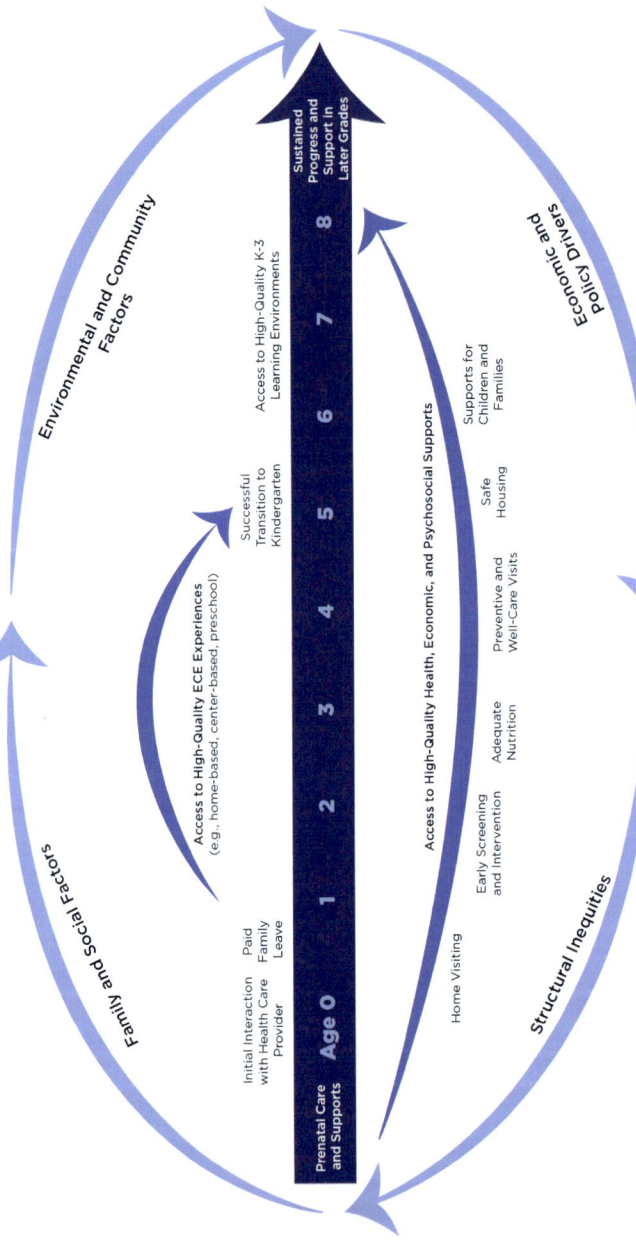

FIGURE 1-1 A conceptual framework for understanding the opportunity gap. Numerous drivers and factors interact and influence access to equitable high-quality experiences and supports for young children aged 0–8 and their families. These drivers and factors continue to interact and shape experiences in later stages of the life course.
NOTE: ECE = early care and education.

To understand the nature of the opportunity gaps experienced by young children, one must first understand the historical contexts that are their origins and that underpin the structures and barriers that often cause disparities in outcomes to persist. While rooted in history, many of these institutional and economic drivers continue to affect access to resources, supports, and high-quality experiences in ECE, health and health care, and social-emotional development and well-being. The resulting opportunity gaps disproportionately affect children from households with low income and from marginalized populations, not just in the early years from birth to age 8 but across the life course. The increasing racial/ethnic diversity of U.S. children is resulting in greater numbers of young children who are disproportionately low income; therefore, these opportunity gaps, if left unaddressed, will be experienced by more children over time.

Historical Precedents in Education

An analysis of opportunity gaps in the early years and the early grades requires a historical understanding of the evolution of the systems in which these gaps are experienced and of how, from these origins, structural and interpersonal inequities have interacted to create the opportunity gaps and outcome disparities of today. To provide context for issues covered in this report, Table 1-1 provides a brief review of historical precedents in education across systems and settings.

Preprimary and elementary education systems and settings have developed over time with relative independence from one another, in part because of the differences in origins and goals summarized in Table 1-1. This disconnect can affect factors such as teacher qualifications, program quality standards, and program oversight, which in turn affect the quality of children's learning experiences (IOM & NRC, 2015). Even with the growth in access to and investment in ECE over the last five to six decades as a mechanism for bridging early opportunity gaps—accomplished through the growth of Head Start, state pre-K, and the Child Care and Development Block Grant (CCDBG)—program funding, access, and quality remain inadequate (IOM & NRC, 2015; Lombardi et al., 2016; Malik et al., 2018; National Academies, 2018; Ullrich & Schmit, 2019; Keating et al., 2020; Meek et al., 2020; Friedman-Krauss et al., 2022).

It is important to note that the historical inequalities affecting children from marginalized populations may be compounded when one accounts for identity intersections. The concept of intersectionality describes the way in which inequality associated with multiple social categories of identity (e.g., class, race, ethnicity, nativity, gender) can overlap and compound inequities in outcomes for individuals and communities (Crenshaw, 1991). Indeed, such characteristics as race, social class, gender, national origin, language

TABLE 1-1 Historical Precedents in Education in the United States across Systems and Settings for Children from Birth through Age 8

Child Care in the Home during the Late 19th and Early 20th Centuries	Following the abolition of slavery, many Black women (and other women of color) entered the workforce as domestic workers for low pay (Lloyd et al., 2021). Workforce participation for White women was rare and largely viewed as socially unacceptable (Amott & Matthaei, 1996). Throughout the following decades, the composition of the workforce evolved on the basis of geography, with Black women, Latinas, and Japanese women making up a majority of domestic child care providers in the South, Southwest, and West, respectively. Indigenous girls and young women also were often placed in the homes of White families as part of federal assimilation policies (Jacobs, 2007). In the early 1900s, building on the model of "widows' pensions" that were created following the Civil War, many Northern states implemented "mothers' pension" or "mothers' aid" programs to enable mothers to stay home and care for their children (Minoff, 2020). In 1931, the only study examining the racial makeup of recipients of these benefits found that more than 96% were White, 3% were Black, and 1% were of another race (Bell, 1965; Minoff, 2020). These laws were later bolstered and ultimately replaced by the Aid to Dependent Children provision of the Social Security Act of 1935 (renamed Aid to Families with Dependent Children in 1962) (Floyd et al., 2021). This federally funded program was run by the states, many of which created eligibility restrictions that made it difficult for Black women and other women of color to access this income support for the first several decades (Gordon & Batlan, 2011; Banks, 2019).
Child Care Centers	Child care centers were established in the United States primarily to provide safe and secure settings for young children while their parents were at work, or in the case of philanthropy-funded "day nurseries," which emerged during the early 20th century, as a way to assimilate immigrant children into American society (Johnson-Staub, 2017) and provide child care for women who were not eligible for widows' pensions (National Academies, 2018). Child care practices are historically grounded more in employment and child protection traditions than in education traditions. Many federal funding streams and state licensing for child care programs still reflect this historical aim of subsidizing safe child care to enable adult workforce participation instead of being oriented primarily to providing an early learning environment for children (Kostelnik & Grady, 2009).

TABLE 1-1 Continued

Nursery Schools	Historically, nursery schools in the United States were established to provide supplemental early learning experiences for children below school age. Children attending nursery schools were primarily from middle- and upper-class families. The aim was to nurture children's social, emotional, physical, and intellectual development, and nursery school teachers were responsible for engaging children in activities that aligned with their interests and provided opportunities for creative expression, project work, and the use of natural materials (Kostelnik & Grady, 2009).
Kindergarten	In its early history in the United States, kindergarten, funded through philanthropy, was intended primarily to provide classroom learning, health services, home visits, and other assistance to children living in poverty and their families. Although kindergarten has moved over time into elementary schools, it originally functioned as a transition between home-based care and formal schooling and focused on play, self-expression, social cooperation, and independence. While the original emphasis was on development in the social and emotional domains, over time kindergarten also began to incorporate content-based learning, as well as the development of mathematics and literacy skills (Kostelnik & Grady, 2009).
Compensatory Education	Compensatory education programs provide services to children and their families who experience developmental, socioeconomic, or environmental circumstances that can negatively affect child development, such as poverty or disability. Examples in the United States include federally mandated programs under the Individuals with Disabilities Education Act, as well as Head Start, which provides early learning opportunities for young children from low-income families. The learning environments in these programs are influenced by other care and education traditions, and as they have become well established, these programs have also influenced other settings and services (Kostelnik & Grady, 2009).

(continued)

TABLE 1-1 Continued

Compulsory Education	Originally, schooling in the United States varied greatly, and included private institutions, church-sponsored schools, charity schools for low-income families, local schools created by parents, private tutors, and boarding schools for children from wealthy families, among others. This disjointed and uncoordinated approach led to schooling that was inconsistent and inequitable, with some children having limited access to opportunities to learn. A publicly funded, locally governed, universal system was subsequently established as a result of education reform movements. As described by Kostelnik and Grady (2009, pp. 48–49), the purpose of this compulsory education was to prepare children for citizenship in a democratic society; help students acquire the knowledge and skills to become economically self-sufficient; unify a diverse population; and help the nation address social problems related to poverty, violence, class conflict, and ethnic differences. At present, about half of states require children to attend school by age 6, while for some the minimum age is 5 and for others is as old as 8 (Francies & Perez, 2020).

SOURCE: Adapted from IOM & NRC, 2015.

background, and disability have been intricately interlaced throughout history and have been associated with reductions in opportunity (Valencia, 2010). In the late 1800s, for instance, the so-called ugly laws—also known as the "unsightly beggar ordinances"—prevented people with visible disabilities and deformities from accessing public spaces, including public transportation (Schweik, 2009). Of significance, ugly laws were enforced in various states as late as the 1970s. These legal barriers disproportionately impacted the lives of people of color, especially those with disabilities, in terms of community participation, civic engagement, and access to and use of services in multiple sectors (Walker, 1996; Lee, 2009).

Intersectional historical analyses of educational opportunity in ECE and in the early elementary grades are necessary to understand and reduce opportunity gaps among young children. Disability, for instance, has historically been a category subjected to exclusion and discrimination. However, an intersectional lens can provide insights into how the intersection of disability with other categories, such as race and language, increases barriers to opportunity. Herein lies a daunting challenge: understanding the dual nature of disability and its intersections in order to provide supports and protections to those who need them while avoiding the use of these intersections to produce opportunity gaps and perpetuate the stratification of certain groups (Artiles, Dorn, & Bal, 2016).

Segregation as a Structural Driver of the Opportunity Gap

Segregation is a major structural driver of inequalities in resource allocation, opportunity, and family and child outcomes related to health, education, and economic advancement. Over the course of U.S. history, segregation has been used as a tool for exclusion, separating children by race, income, language, and disability. Residential segregation, both racial/ethnic and income/wealth-based, separates families and children into neighborhoods with vastly different resources. The research reviewed in this section demonstrates that children from historically marginalized communities consistently and disproportionately experience resource gaps that can affect their developmental health (Acevedo-Garcia et al., 2010, 2020; Orfield & Frankenberg, 2014; Chetty et al., 2020). Residential segregation is the main driver of school segregation, which in turn is associated with inequitable exposure to qualified teachers, class size, curriculum, and pedagogy. Children may also be segregated within schools by language, disability, or other characteristics, further increasing their isolation.

Residential Segregation

Residential segregation—the physical separation of groups into different neighborhoods—is a result of discriminatory policies and practices, both historical (e.g., racial covenants, redlining, displacement through urban renewal; Rothstein, 2017) and ongoing (e.g., discriminatory lending and real estate practices, exclusionary zoning, "opportunity hoarding"[5]). Because most school assignments are residence based, residential segregation is also at the root of school segregation. In fact, residential and school segregation can be mutually reinforcing as a result of the local property taxes in funding public schools (Rothwell, 2012).

Residential Racial/Ethnic Segregation

Levels of residential segregation are higher for children than for adults for every major racial/ethnic group (Iceland et al., 2010; Jargowsky, 2014; Owens, 2017). This segregation is not benign, but leads to neighborhoods that are both separate and greatly unequal in terms of resources and opportunities (Acevedo-Garcia et al., 2010; McArdle & Acevedo-Garcia, 2018; Owens, 2020). In addition to its impacts on education, discussed in a

---

[5] Opportunity hoarding—"a behavior that reserves for one's own children the best possible educational opportunities, the inevitable flip side of which is excluding others from those same good opportunities" (Walters, 2007, p. 17)—contributes to and compounds the effects of segregation. It is related to individual behaviors, but these behaviors are facilitated by policies and structures (Hanselman & Fiel, 2017; Sattin-Bajaj & Roda, 2020; Cashin, 2021).

later section, residential segregation negatively impacts health outcomes by exposing residents to lower housing quality (Williams & Collins, 2001; Kramer & Hogue, 2009), concentrated poverty, and reduced access to economic opportunities (Williams & Collins, 2001; Schulz et al., 2002; Mays, Cochran, & Barnes, 2007; Kramer & Hogue, 2009; Kotecki et al., 2019). Research has found that high levels of residential segregation appear to be related to worse outcomes for Black infants (Polednak, 1991; Bird, 1995; Collins, 1999; Kotecki et al., 2019) and Black adults (Polednak, 1993; Hart et al., 1998; Collins, 1999; Jackson et al., 2000; Kotecki et al., 2019). Research has found further that it is not "racial isolation" in itself that drives gaps in opportunity but the associated conditions, including discrimination, disenfranchisement, and historical and current inequitable access to resources (Faber, 2020).

While racial/ethnic and economic integration are intertwined, high levels of racial/ethnic segregation cannot be explained by income alone. Children are more economically segregated than are adults, but after accounting for family income, racial/ethnic segregation among children remains high. Segregation of poor children of all major non-White racial/ethnic groups from poor White children is very high, even higher than that of children of all incomes combined (McArdle & Acevedo-Garcia, 2018). Further, while segregation by income has been increasing, racial/ethnic segregation of children is still higher than is income segregation.

The negative effects of residential segregation may persist throughout childhood into adulthood, providing opportunities for interventions aimed at mitigating those effects, as well as improving children's access to neighborhoods and schools with resources to support healthy development. Given that segregation is a structural problem with roots and manifestations in many sectors, interventions to mitigate it span housing, education, and health. Indeed, many in the public health field see segregation as a social determinant of health and health equity, and, accordingly, view as public health initiatives such nonhealth policies and programs as fair housing; programs to improve neighborhood choice, such as those targeting housing mobility; increased enforcement of laws focused on housing discrimination; and projects designed to improve neighborhood conditions (Acevedo-Garcia et al., 2008; Kotecki et al., 2019).

Residential Socioeconomic Segregation

Increases in income segregation have overwhelmingly been led by families with children. Indeed, segregation levels for such families are roughly double those for families without children, in large part because of rising income inequality and unequal school options along school district boundaries that incentivize families with children who can afford it to find housing in school districts with more resources. Upper-income families have thus been able to access neighborhoods with a larger property tax base and better schools, thereby separating their children from their lower-income counterparts (Owens, 2016). This economic segregation is further enabled by zoning codes that limit or entirely prohibit types of homes that are affordable to lower-income families, which tend to be disproportionately Black and Hispanic. Strict zoning codes are one example of the opportunity hoarding by which privileged families can sequester themselves in exclusive areas with neighbors and school populations that reflect local demographics.

School Segregation

School segregation is perhaps the most critical pathway by which residential segregation impacts child well-being, given that 84% of public school students attend assigned schools, usually based on place of residence (Noel, Stark, & Redford, 2016).

As a result of court rulings eliminating numerous desegregation orders and plans, especially throughout the 1990s and 2000s, prior gains in desegregation have gradually been reversed (Reardon et al., 2012; Frankenberg et al., 2019). Thus although diversity within student populations has increased over time, schools throughout the United States continue to be segregated along racial and ethnic lines; Latinos in the Western United States are particularly affected (GAO, 2022). This resegregation has also been shaped by the lasting effects of discriminatory housing and other local policies, such as school boundary gerrymandering (Richards, 2014), defined as the drawing of irregularly shaped borders (as opposed to borders around cohesive communities) that determine school attendance zones. School leaders make decisions about school attendance zone boundaries and school assignments within those zones, taking into account an array of community factors, including race, income, and parental education (Monarrez & Chien, 2021). Some research has explored the role of school boundary gerrymandering in preventing students from lower-income families from attending high-resourced schools, a practice generally associated with increases in segregation, particularly in communities undergoing rapid demographic shifts (Richards, 2014, 2017). School boundary gerrymandering has been used to reduce segregation in some communities, but it is also used to consolidate resources in more affluent communities and decrease school diversity (Saporito & Van Riper, 2016; Richards, 2017).

Similarly, research on the effects of school choice[6] policies has highlighted how these policies have the potential to exacerbate racial segregation of schools. For example, some families choose schools that have fewer students from marginalized populations and are better resourced, while other families choose schools where they can self-isolate within their own racial/ethnic community. Other parents may choose a school other than their local traditional public school, such as a charter, based on proximity to home, and these schools may reflect racially segregated demographics within the community (Bifulco & Ladd, 2007; García, 2008; Jacobs, 2011; Kotok et al., 2017). Private school vouchers have also been found to have the net effect of exacerbating segregation (Potter, 2017).

Racial/ethnic segregation is associated with concentrated school poverty, disproportionately inflicting the harms of concentrated poverty on Black and Hispanic students. While public schools have increasing shares of low-income students, Black and Hispanic students disproportionately attend high-poverty schools. In 2013, low-income students made up 52% of enrollment in public schools overall. The average White or Asian student attended a school that was 40% or 42% low income, respectively, but the corresponding percentage for the average Black or Hispanic student was 68% (Orfield et al., 2016). Segregated schools provide reduced access to resources, supports, and services for students of color, particularly Black, Latino, and Indigenous children and youth (Frankenberg et al., 2019). A National Academies report documents a $23 billion funding gap between schools serving predominantly non-White versus mainly White learners, "despite serving the same number of children" (National Academies, 2019a, p. 192). Segregation patterns are also negatively associated with achievement, college completion, income, and long-term employment (Condron et al., 2013; Frankenberg et al., 2019; Reardon et al., 2019).

The educational achievement gap between middle-income and low-income students has widened, in part as a result of income segregation (Owens, Reardon, & Jencks, 2016). Evidence suggests that when classrooms are more socioeconomically diverse, learning in both preschool and elementary school settings, specifically in language, math, and reading, is greater (Cascio, 2021). Some of these studies have found this association with greater learning gains regardless of children's own socioeconomic status (Schwartz, 2010; Reid et al., 2015). Schools with lower levels of concentrated poverty lead to improved achievement through a number of mechanisms, including "more equitable access to important resources such as structural facilities, highly qualified teachers, challenging courses, private and public funding,

---

[6]School choice allows public funds to follow students to the schools they attend and permits families to select alternatives to public schools, such as charter schools, private schools, or home school.

social and cultural capital," lower levels of social disorder and violence, and higher educational expectations compared with segregated schools (Wells, Fox, & Cordova-Cobo, 2016, p. 12). As with other structural drivers of opportunity, it is not the composition of children's socioeconomic status in itself that predicts learning gains; rather, the conditions resulting from underinvestment that affect nearly every other domain of life—health, education, and economic stability—are associated with deficits in learning. That is, concentrated poverty and community underinvestment suppress opportunity, including in learning (Coley et al., 2019; Wodtke et al., 2022).

Segregation in Early Childhood Education

Unfortunately, children are most segregated at the very young ages, a critical time in their development when their racial attitudes are still developing and when cross-racial friendships are most common. Segregation at the preschool level occurs both across and within programs. Head Start programs disproportionately enroll low-income and Black students (Joshi, Geronimo, & Acevedo-Garcia, 2016). Hispanic children are disproportionately less likely to attend center-based preschools, while children from families of higher socioeconomic status are more likely to do so (Frankenberg, 2016). And a study of 28,000 public preschools found that more than half of Hispanic and Black students attended preschools with at least 90% children of color, a level of isolation even greater than that of K–12 students (Frankenberg, 2016).

Data indicate that ECE classrooms with greater racial segregation of Latino and Black children are associated with lower-quality instruction, emotional support, and global quality scores (Reid et al., 2015). Similar patterns have been identified in the early grades, with greater racial isolation predicting lower math and literacy learning (Aikens & Barbarin, 2008; Benson & Borman, 2010; Ready & Silander, 2011). Other studies have replicated this finding in the early grades and throughout the K–12 continuum, indicating that residential segregation is a strong predictor of opportunity and outcome gaps in education and income (e.g., Johnson, 2011; Bischoff & Reardon, 2014; Reardon, 2015).

Disability Segregation

Research indicates that inclusion in high-quality general ECE programs is associated with a host of positive social and academic outcomes for children with and without disabilities, and that early inclusion is associated with inclusion later in children's school trajectories (Rafferty, Piscitelli, & Boettcher, 2003; Green, Terry, & Gallagher, 2014; Lawrence, Smith, & Banerjee, 2016). Yet, segregation by disability status is also a reality of the ECE system that extends into the early grades and across the K–12 education system. The Individuals with Disabilities Education Act (IDEA) is clear about the requirement to educate children with disabilities in the least restrictive environment possible and to secure placements for them in settings that they would attend if they did not have a disability (20 U.S.C. § 1400 [2004]). For children with disabilities, segregation can be a violation of this requirement, affecting their ability to learn alongside their peers without disabilities. Today, more than half of preschoolers with disabilities who receive IDEA services receive those services outside of general ECE programs (U.S. Department of Education, 2021). There are some disparities by age in this regard; for example, 3-year-olds are the least likely to receive services in inclusive settings, while 5-year-olds are the most likely. There are also substantial differences across and within states, with Colorado serving the highest percentage of preschoolers with disabilities in inclusive settings and Louisiana serving the lowest (Meek et al., 2020).

In many instances, preschool special education systems were required to be established long before robust public preschool systems were put in place. Over time, even as the number of public preschool slots expanded, the percentage of children with disabilities receiving services in those settings barely changed (Smith et al., 2020). Today, data indicate no association between the amount of public pre-K available for 4-year-olds in a state and the percentage of preschoolers with disabilities receiving services in those programs (Meek et al., 2020), pointing to underutilization of public pre-K in expanding inclusive learning for children with disabilities. In particular, the lack of coordination of IDEA service delivery in ECE settings outside of public schools and Head Start programs may be an important factor in these low inclusion numbers.

Many of these inequities are undergirded by chronic underfunding of identification and service systems, together with policies that affect children with disabilities inequitably, especially those from racialized backgrounds and those who speak languages other than English at home (Gillispie, 2021; Hinds, Newby, & Korman, 2022). At the current level of funding, IDEA cannot ensure sufficient quantity and dosage of high-quality services for children who need them. In addition, the system does not always ensure appropriate and accurate identification (specifically with respect to under- and overidentification); access to services, particularly early intervention and preschool special education services for children of color; high-quality supports and accommodations in sufficient dosage to promote learning and growth across learning and education goals; and discipline policies that address disproportionately high rates of harsh discipline for children with disabilities (National Center for Learning Disabilities, 2020; Gillispie, 2021). Each of these deficits contributes to the existing opportunity gaps for these children.

Language Segregation

The default use of English in the U.S. education system is long-standing; however, the contexts through which language policies are implemented have the potential to reinforce disparities and devalue the cultures and languages of marginalized populations. For example, language has been used as a tool for exclusion, segregation, and assimilation (described in Douglas & the Supreme Court's decision in *Lau v. Nichols*; Gándara & Orfield, 2010; Department of the Interior, 2021), as exemplified by the creation of Indigenous boarding schools and the establishment of Mexican schools in the Southwest and California (Gonzales, 2011; Glenn, 2015; Surface-Evans, 2016). In fact, as recently as 2016, California was an "English-only" state, mandating exclusively English instruction in public education. Arizona remains the sole English-only state in the nation today, and its policies require segregating English learners. Across the country, English learner policies vary greatly, but in practice, many of these children remain segregated in schools (Gándara, 2020). For children who speak a non-English language at home, segregated learning may deprive them of equal education opportunities (Castro & Meek, 2022), and is associated with poorer outcomes (Artiles et al., 2010; Rumberger & Tran, 2010; Estrada, Wang, & Farkas, 2020).

Today, language segregation significantly overlaps with racial and income segregation (Gándara & Aldana, 2014). Research shows that dual language learners and English learners are more likely than their non–dual language and non–English learner peers to attend schools that are racially, economically, and linguistically segregated (Orfield & Frankenberg, 2014). This finding points to the importance of considering the interconnectedness of race, income, and language as they relate to opportunity, and how the effects of systems and policies are compounded to inhibit opportunity for children. Many dual language learners and English learners are segregated at the classroom level for at least part of the school day to focus on English acquisition. Often these blocks of segregated English learning time are long, reducing the time students have to engage in learning other subjects, such as math and science. That deficit in turn creates an opportunity gap and contributes to disparities in longer-term outcomes, such as high school graduation (National Academies, 2018). Research has found that the level of segregation of English learners in a school is a significant predictor of the gap in academic outcomes between those children and their peers (Rumberger & Tran, 2010). Yet these segregation practices and policies persist in schools, despite research showing negative impacts on educational opportunity for English learners who are excluded from rigorous or advanced coursework (National Academies, 2018), and positive academic and social benefits of dual language immersion or bilingual learning models for both dual language and English learners and their native English-speaking peers (Serafini, Rozell, & Winsler, 2020).

DEMOGRAPHIC AND STRUCTURAL CHANGES AFFECTING CHILDREN AND FAMILIES

This section reviews a number of shifts affecting the opportunities available to young children, including changes in demographic characteristics, the economy and labor markets, poverty, and geography.

The Changing Demography of Children from Birth to Age 8: Implications for the Opportunity Gap

Understanding the overall size, needs, and demographic characteristics of the child population is critical to designing effective policies and programs that provide equitable opportunities for all children to reach their full potential. The size of the child population and children's specific needs determine the demand for institutions and services such as ECE, schools, pediatric health care practices, and family social services. In the United States, most national child-focused policies are not universal, nor do they provide funding to fully meet demand (Currie, 2006). A consequence of these national-level gaps is state variations in allocation of benefits that meet children's basic needs, resulting in deficits that can create opportunity gaps and lead to underserved groups of children (Bruch, Gornick, & Van Der Naald, 2022).

The size and demographics of the child population are changing rapidly. Children are the most racially/ethnically diverse age group in the United States, and children of color, multiracial children, and immigrant children are driving growth in the child population (Frey, 2018). The Census Bureau projects that the child population under age 18 will grow from 74 to 80 million from 2020 to 2060, by which time 60% of children are projected to be Black, Hispanic, Asian, American Indian, or multiracial (Vespa, Medina, & Armstrong, 2020). Figure 1-2 shows that the share of White children under 18 declined from 74% in 1980 to 50% in 2020, and is projected to decrease even further to 39% by 2050. The share of Hispanic children almost tripled between 1980 and 2020, rising from 9% to 26%, and is projected to grow further to 31% by 2050. The share of Asian and multiracial children is projected to grow to 7% and 8%, respectively, by 2050, while the share of Black and American Indian children is projected to remain constant at 14% and 1%, respectively. Other research indicates that the share of children in immigrant families will increase from 23% in 2009 to 34% by 2050 (Passel, 2011). These demographic shifts mean that the success of public policies will increasingly be evaluated according to their effects on the well-being of children of color and children in immigrant families.

INTRODUCTION 37

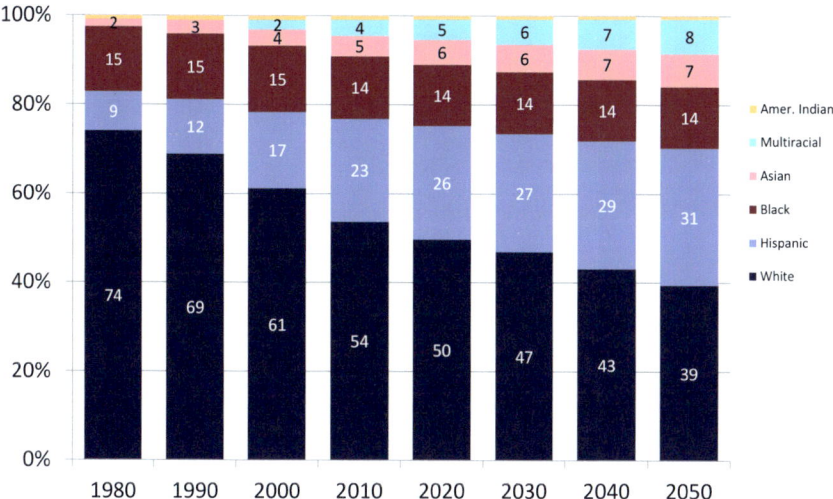

FIGURE 1-2 Changing racial/ethnic composition of the U.S. child population aged 0–18 (percent).
NOTES: Racial groups include only non-Hispanic members; Hispanics may be of any race. American Indian includes Alaska Native. Asian includes Pacific Islander. Data on multiracial children are not available before 2000. Data from 2000 onward are not directly comparable with data from earlier years.
SOURCE: Data from U.S. Census Bureau, Population Division. These data are available on the U.S. Census Bureau website on the Population Estimates and Population Projections pages. The data for 1980 to 2009 are intercensal estimates and incorporate the 1980, 1990, 2000, and 2010 Censuses as benchmarks. The data for 2010 to 2019 are based on the population estimates released for July 1, 2020. The data for 2020 to 2021 are based on the population estimates released for July 1, 2021. Data beyond 2021 are derived from the national population projections released in September 2018. Obtained from America's Children in Brief: 2022, Federal Interagency Forum on Child and Family Statistics, 2022.

Of the 74 million U.S. children under 18 in 2020, fewer than half, 35.4 million, were aged 0–8—the focus of this committee's work. There were 17.3 million White children aged 0–8, more than 9 million Hispanic children, 4.7 million Black children, 1.8 million Asian children, 2.3 million multiracial children, and fewer than 250,000 American Indian children (Figure 1-3). The demographic composition of the population of young children aged 0–8 in 2020 was similar to that of the total child population. Fewer than half of children under 8 were White (49%), more than a quarter were Hispanic (26%), 13% were Black, 5% were Asian, and 7% were other/multiracial; fewer than 1% were American Indian.

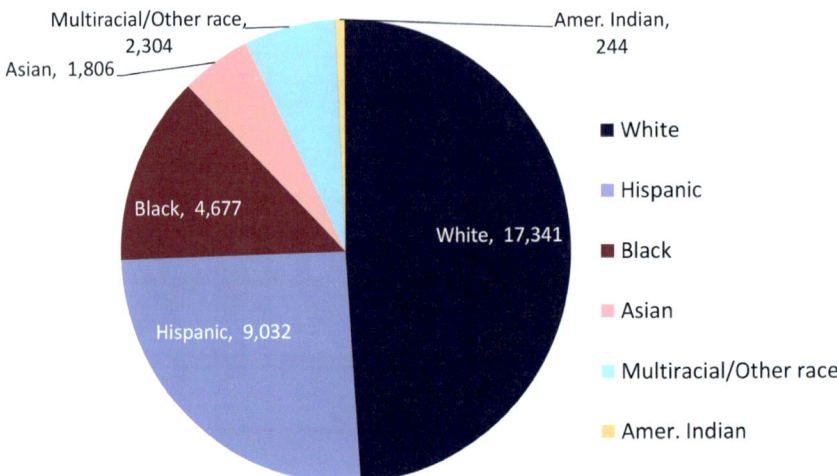

FIGURE 1-3 Racial/ethnic composition of children aged 0–8 in the United States, 2020 (thousands).
NOTES: Racial groups include only non-Hispanic members; Hispanics may be of any race. American Indian includes Alaska Native. Asian includes Pacific Islander.
SOURCE: Data from diversitydatakids.org calculations of data from the Integrated Public Use Microdata Series data sets drawn from the 2020 American Community Survey, 5-year data set.

The surge in the diversity of the child population is being driven by changing fertility patterns, the aging of the baby boom generation, and the most recent wave of immigration starting in the 1960s (Frey, 2018). Immigrants are fundamental to the U.S. economy and social fabric, fueling labor markets and contributing to the diversity of cultures and languages. The Immigration Act of 1965 opened up legal immigration to people from all over the world but restricted immigration from North America, setting the stage for the rise in the undocumented population (National Academies, 2015). In 2020, a significant share of the U.S. child population, about 18 million children under 18, lived in immigrant families, defined as having at least one foreign-born parent (Urban Institute, 2022). More than 8.7 million children aged 0–8 lived in immigrant families, representing 25% of young children (Figure 1-4). The majority of young children in immigrant families (92%) are born in the United States, and thus are U.S. citizens (see Appendix A). Compared with children under 8 who are second-generation immigrants born in the United States (8 million), a much smaller number (700,000) are first-generation immigrants born abroad. Since the second generation is younger than the first generation, there may be generational differences in

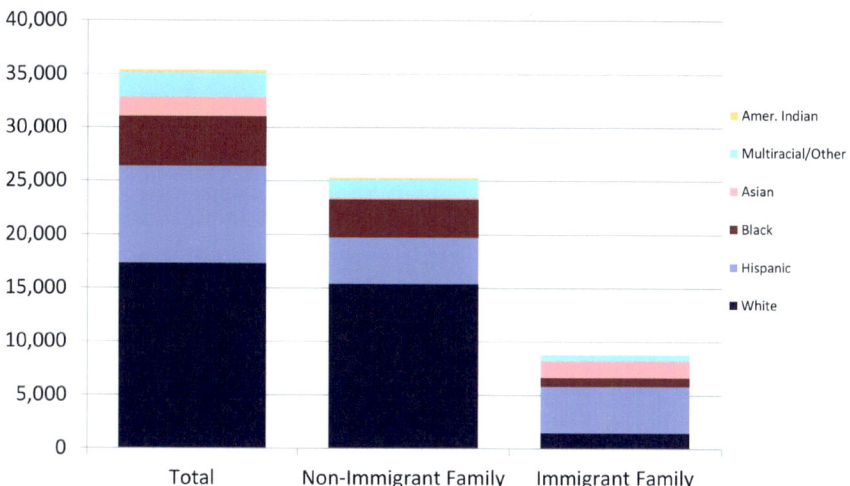

FIGURE 1-4 Racial/ethnic composition of children aged 0–8 by family immigration status, 2020 (thousands).
NOTES: Immigrant families are defined as those with at least one parent who is foreign born but not born abroad of American parents. Nonimmigrant families are defined as those with all parents either U.S. born or born abroad of American parents. Racial groups include only non-Hispanic members; Hispanics may be of any race. American Indian includes Alaska Native. Asian includes Pacific Islander. Data by immigrant status exclude approximately 1.26 million children who do not live with parents, so parent nativity is unknown.
SOURCE: Data from diversitydatakids.org calculations of data from the Integrated Public Use Microdata Series data sets drawn from the 2020 American Community Survey, 5-year data set.

educational needs (Passel, 2011); for example, a much higher share of the second generation of children in immigrant families will need ECE.

By design, children in immigrant families face opportunity gaps due to their exclusion from eligibility for antipoverty programs and other family policies based on their own and their parents' or other family members' immigration status (Acevedo-Garcia et al., 2021b). Even if children in immigrant families are eligible, they underutilize programs (Capps et al., 2020). Children who are immigrants and children in immigrant families who are U.S. citizens face severely high poverty rates—much higher than those of children in nonimmigrant families—due, in part, to their receiving less or no income from public supports (National Academies, 2019a; Acevedo-Garcia et al., 2022). Thus children in low-income immigrant families, the majority of whom are U.S. citizens, experience opportunity gaps resulting from their exclusion from antipoverty programs that have positive impacts on child health and development (National Academies, 2019a). A growing research base shows that state-level restrictions on immigrants can be harmful to children's health (Perreira & Pedoza, 2019); conversely, states that have less criminalizing immigrant policies have less health care inequity between citizens and noncitizens (Young, Beltrán-Sánchez, & Wallace, 2020).

Policies restricting immigrants' ability to access antipoverty programs also have implications for racial/ethnic inequities in child opportunities and outcomes. Although on their face, restrictions based on immigration status are race neutral, they have disproportionately negative impacts on Hispanic children. Recent waves of immigration, primarily from Asia and Latin America, are driving changes in the racial/ethnic composition of the child population as a whole and the portion of that population in immigrant families. While young children in immigrant families are more racially/ethnically diverse than those in nonimmigrant families, Figure 1-5 shows

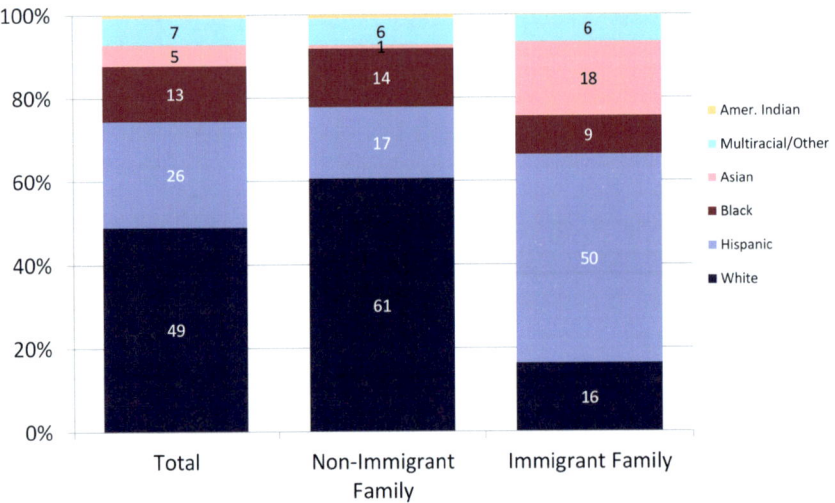

FIGURE 1-5 Racial/ethnic composition of children aged 0–8 by family immigrant status, 2020 (percent).
NOTES: Immigrant families are defined as those with at least one parent who is foreign born but not born abroad of American parents. Nonimmigrant families are defined as those with all parents either U.S. born or born abroad of American parents. Racial groups include only non-Hispanic members; Hispanics may be of any race. American Indian includes Alaska Native. Asian includes Pacific Islander. Data by immigrant status exclude approximately 1.26 million children who do not live with parents, so parent nativity is unknown.
SOURCE: Data from diversitydatakids.org calculations of data from the Integrated Public Use Microdata Series data sets drawn from the 2020 American Community Survey, 5-year data set.

that fully half of children in immigrant families are Hispanic, while 18% are Asian and 16% are White, whereas in nonimmigrant families, a larger share of children are White (61%), compared with 17% Hispanic and 1% Asian. Hispanic children represent the greatest share of immigrant children and also experience higher rates of poverty than Black and non-Hispanic White children (National Academies, 2019a). A disproportionate share of Hispanic children may be exposed to opportunity gaps due to restrictive eligibility criteria for immigrants that prevent them from accessing anti-poverty programs.

Structural Changes in the Economy and Labor Markets

Inflation, unemployment, and economic recessions decrease families' economic security, exposing their children to volatile and decreasing family income. Labor markets affect employment, hours worked, and wages earned by parents to cover the basic costs of raising their families (e.g., food, housing, child care). Economic opportunity gaps for families with children arise as a result of stagnant wages, growing wage inequality, greater job instability, and precarious work hours and schedules. Economic opportunity gaps also are driven by uneven economic growth and structural changes in the labor market, including the rise of skills-based technological jobs, domestic outsourcing, franchising, platform-based gig work, and monopsony (e.g., mergers); bias in hiring and promotion practices; declining unionization; and stagnant minimum wage levels (Weil, 2014; Bahn, 2019; National Academies, 2019a). The result is that the wages of many families in the bottom half of the labor market have not kept pace with inflation, and employers now offer fewer core benefits, including health insurance and support for workers' caregiving needs, such as paid family and medical leave and child care.

Stagnant wages and rising prices of basic goods mean that despite working full time and full year, many families do not earn enough to cover the minimum cost of raising their children. Prior to the COVID-19 pandemic, about one-third of families raising children did not earn enough income to cover minimum expenses, a situation that disproportionately affects low-income and Black, Hispanic, and immigrant families (Joshi et al., 2022). Conversely, those at the top of the wage distribution see wage growth and more employer benefits. The result is a growing divide between high-paying jobs with good benefits and low-wage jobs with no employer supports. Black, Hispanic, and immigrant workers are disproportionately concentrated in these latter, often essential frontline jobs. To reduce economic opportunity gaps driven by structural changes in the labor market, an ecosystem of supports is needed for parents to supplement low wages and provide health insurance, paid family and medical leave, and high-quality child care.

Labor regulations help protect workers from some of these structural changes by reducing mandatory overtime and increasing wages. However, racial exclusion from labor regulations designed to protect workers and raise wages contributes to economic opportunity gaps. When the Fair Labor Standards Act (FLSA) was passed in 1938 to protect the rights of employees across the country by establishing requirements for a minimum wage, bargaining rights, and overtime, domestic workers were exempted from these rights. At that time, more than 60% of gainfully employed Black women worked as domestic workers (Thernstrom & Thernstrom, 1998). Thus, this policy created an opportunity gap by disproportionately decreasing economic stability and wealth building for Black women and their families. Policy changes in 1967 that extended FLSA coverage to the retail, services, and agriculture sectors had substantial positive effects on wages for low-wage and Black workers, helping explain the reduction in the racial earnings gap during the civil rights era of the 1950s and 1960s (Derenoncourt & Montialoux, 2021). Research in this area provides insight into how policies can be changed to reduce the large racial disparities in economic opportunities that persist today.

Poverty

During the civil rights era, many social service programs that had been implemented in ways that explicitly discriminated against marginalized populations were dismantled, and equality in the ability to participate in public aid programs increased. Indeed, nearly 200 pieces of legislation were passed during the Great Society era under President Lyndon Johnson. Legislation and substantial investment during this time period ushered in new protections in civil rights (e.g., passage of the Civil Rights Act of 1964 and the Economic Opportunity Act of 1964), the creation of Medicare and Medicaid, projects for urban beautification and renewal, nutrition assistance, new consumer safety and environmental regulations, supports for social action, the beginning of the war on poverty, increased investment in K–12 education, and the creation of Head Start (Aaron, 2010; Meyer & Sullivan, 2013; Hinitz, 2014).

Although views on how Head Start should be structured initially varied, ultimately the program was innovative in its design as both a provider of comprehensive services (e.g., education, nutrition, health, early screening services) and a means of building social and emotional competencies in young children. In addition, Head Start implemented performance standards for family engagement as a way to involve families in the program's planning and administration to ensure that they had a voice in decision making around such issues as curriculum, finance, staffing, and other policies—a practice that set Head Start apart from many other social service programs (Hinitz, 2014).

The growth of research on educational interventions for children living in poverty, such as the HighScope Perry Preschool Project, and later, research pointing to the sensitive nature of brain development in the earliest years, made a strong case for public investment in ECE programs. The passage of the Elementary and Secondary Education Act in 1965 also increased support for promoting full educational opportunity in the K–12 system through grants for districts with higher populations of students from families with low incomes, grants for textbooks and library books, and funding for special education as a poverty-reduction strategy (Nelson, 2016).

Despite the many substantial advances in increasing equality achieved during the civil rights era, these efforts also coincided with an important paradigm shift in the early 1960s: instead of providing public funds to support mothers in caring for their own children, policies shifted to requiring work for public benefits and subsidizing child care as part of these work requirements (Vogtman, 2017; Minoff, 2020). In 1971, Congress passed the Comprehensive Child Development Act, which would have created public funding for a national ECE system. However, President Nixon vetoed the legislation, citing "family-weakening implications" and concerns about "communal approaches to childrearing over against the family-centered approach" and diminishing "both parental authority and parental involvement with children" (Nixon, 1971). As Kamerman and Gatenio-Gabel (2007) conclude in their review of ECE policy in the 21st century, the government's role in ECE "is still viewed by some as trespassing into the private lives of its citizens" (p. 27), and as such, not an area for public investment. In the 1990s, the CCDBG, representing a major step in child care programming and investment, became the major federal funding source for child care. States were responsible for setting standards beyond the minimal federal standards and operating the program. The result was wide variability in family access and eligibility, and in children's experiences in child care (Bipartisan Policy Center, 2021).

Also in the 1990s, as part of efforts to reform welfare programs, Aid to Families with Dependent Children was replaced by Temporary Assistance for Needy Families (TANF), which imposed more stringent work requirements and time limits on the receipt of benefits. TANF continues to demonstrate racial inequities in states' administration and resource allocation that contribute to higher poverty rates among Black children (Hahn et al., 2017; Parolin et al., 2021). Indeed, a 2019 study on the effects of TANF on the Black–White child poverty gap found that states with higher percentages of Black residents were less likely to prioritize investment in cash assistance programs and that eliminating the inequities in spending priorities among the states could reduce the Black–White child poverty gap by up to 15% (Parolin et al., 2021).

The National Academies report *A Roadmap to Reducing Child Poverty* (2019a) presents overwhelming evidence that, compared with children not living in poverty, those living in poverty generally experience worse outcomes that affect their development and well-being not just in the early years, but into adulthood. The effects of poverty and the ways in which it creates and perpetuates opportunity gaps are numerous. For example, parents living in poverty have fewer material resources and less access to services that promote healthy development relative to their wealthier peers. Young children living in families experiencing this kind of material hardship have less access to stable housing, adequate nutrition, medical care, and many other essential needs (National Academies, 2019a; Kalil & Ryan, 2020).

The effects of poverty on parents also have implications for child outcomes. Parents living in poverty are more likely to experience decreased emotional well-being, stress, and conflict, which can impact their ability to parent in ways that promote healthy cognitive and social-emotional development in their children (National Academies, 2019a). For children, the stressors associated with poverty within the home and neighborhood environment have been correlated with differences in brain development; lower achievement in education; and in the long term, reduced opportunities and income disparities in adults (National Academies, 2019a; Troller-Renfree et al., 2022). Gaps in outcomes in early skills begin early—some measures indicate as early as 9 months. Despite evidence that more than half of children—in particular, children from lower-income families and Black and Hispanic children—are entering kindergarten with lower literacy and math skills compared with their peers, it is in these early years that investments in children are the smallest (Chaudry, 2021). Although some children living in poverty may be resilient in the face of these negative effects, evidence shows that poverty is significantly linked to multiple negative effects that create opportunity gaps. Policies, programs, and practices with the potential to mitigate these effects are discussed in detail in Chapter 7.

Geography

The contexts in which families live vary greatly from state to state, among communities, and within neighborhoods. Across all of these contexts, however, environments in which families have access to safe and healthy neighborhoods and high-quality education and health care have been found to support healthy development. Conversely, as stressed throughout this report, young children living in neighborhoods with high poverty where families often have less access to high-quality care, educational opportunity, and supports are more likely to experience worse outcomes in education, development, health, and social-emotional well-being (e.g., lower school quality, lower health care quality, diminished health, increased crime, reduced economic mobility; National Academies, 2019a,b).

Children living in rural communities may have less regular parental supervision and often have less access to regular care and to community resources that can support healthy development (e.g., quality out-of-school programming) compared with their nonrural peers. For parents of young children living in rural communities, limited access to public transportation and fewer child care options can make it difficult to find stable employment. Children in these communities also are likely to have less access to high-quality educational opportunities. Poverty rates are higher in rural than in urban communities, and rural children are more likely to live in extreme poverty (O'Hare, 2009). The effects of poverty in rural communities, as well as in suburban and urban areas of concentrated poverty, are compounded by the fact that families living in these areas are less likely to live close to community social service organizations that can provide important supports (National Academies, 2019b).

Geography can also influence equity in educational experiences. The Elementary and Secondary Education Act of 1965, which was subsequently reauthorized in 2001 via No Child Left Behind and, in 2015, via the Every Student Succeeds Act, established state and local accountability for monitoring academic performance across a number of demographic characteristics (e.g., race, socioeconomic status, home language) as a way to ensure that all children would have equal access to rigorous academic content (National Academies, 2022b). At the state level, school education agencies play a major role in determining state academic standards, accountability measures, policies and priorities, and curriculum. Individual school districts also have a substantial amount of control over how schools and classroom teachers function. These policies—and the ways in which they may vary both among and within states—can affect a wide variety of factors, such as instructional time policies, teacher credentialing, access to public pre-K, and school funding, that impact children's access to high-quality educational opportunities (National Academies, 2022b).

Policies related to housing, segregation, urban planning, and school funding, among others, have resulted in systemic geographic disparities in outcomes for children and families. As discussed previously, segregation can be a strong predictor of opportunity gaps, especially when it leads to differential concentrations of groups in high- and low-poverty schools. In general, high-poverty schools cannot provide the types of opportunities provided by low-poverty schools, a differential that creates, maintains, and perpetuates opportunity gaps (Reardon, 2021).

The neighborhoods where children live, grow, and learn have substantial impacts on their current health and well-being (Acevedo-Garcia, Noelke, & McArdle, 2020), expectations (Galster, 2012), and future success (Chetty, Hendren, & Katz, 2016). Neighborhoods are characterized by both assets (e.g., high-quality schools, availability of healthy food, green spaces) and stressors (e.g., toxic environments, concentrated-poverty schools), which can either reinforce or mitigate the supports or deficits of the child's family environment and the child's own individual characteristics.

The connections between neighborhood socioeconomic status and a host of child and adolescent outcomes—including links to health, life expectancy, behavior problems, juvenile delinquency, and academic achievement—have been well documented (Kawachi & Berkman, 2003; Leventhal, Dupéré, & Brooks-Gunn, 2009; Aris et al., 2022; Shanahan et al., 2022; Slopen et al., 2023). Other neighborhood factors—such as public safety; levels of trust among neighbors; availability of safe recreational spaces; access to affordable, healthy food; and exposure to violence—also influence children (Newburger, Birch, & Wachter, 2011; Sharkey et al., 2012; Sharkey, 2013; Ellen & Glied, 2015). Although most of these studies do not establish causality between neighborhood conditions and child outcomes, they strongly suggest that a wide range of neighborhood characteristics affect child well-being across a number of dimensions.

Several rigorous studies have distinguished family from neighborhood influences and revealed independent neighborhood effects. For example, research on the Moving to Opportunity program showed that children who moved from a high-poverty to a low-poverty neighborhood before the age of 13 had greater earnings and higher-quality college education as adults compared with children remaining in high-poverty areas (Chetty, Hendren, & Katz, 2016). Other research found that neighborhood characteristics predicted outcomes for low-income Latino and African American children in such areas as exposure to violence, risky behaviors, physical and behavioral health, education, marriage and childbearing, and youth labor market outcomes, even after controlling for many household, child, and caregiver traits (Santiago et al., 2014).

Research on neighborhoods has advanced beyond the use of single indicators, such as poverty, to more complex aggregate indices that capture a range of neighborhood stressors and assets. These measures incorporate an understanding that the effects of neighborhood stressors on child well-being can be cumulative, as when high-poverty neighborhoods also have high levels of violent crime, but also can potentially be offset by positive neighborhood factors (Theall, Drury, & Shirtcliff, 2012; Wei et al., 2021).

One such aggregate measure of neighborhood characteristics is the Child Opportunity Index (COI) 2.0 (Figure 1-6). The COI combines 29 separate component indicators in three overall domains—education, health and environment, and social and economic—into a composite opportunity index score, which positions/ranks each neighborhood relative to all other neighborhoods in its metropolitan area, its state, and the nation. Each of the individual indicators was vetted for relevance to child development based on empirical literature on neighborhood effects and/or conceptual

Education

Early childhood education (ECE)
ECE centers within five miles
High quality ECE centers within five miles
ECE enrollment

Primary school
Third grade reading proficiency
Third grade math proficiency

Secondary and post-secondary
High school graduation rates
AP enrollment
College access/enrollment

Resources
School poverty
Teacher experience
Adult educational attainment

Health and Environment

Healthy environments
Access to healthy food
Access to green space
Walkability
Housing vacancy rates

Toxic exposures
Superfund sites
Industrial pollutants
Microparticles
Ozone
Heat

Health care access
Health insurance coverage

Social and Economic

Economic opportunities
Employment rate
Commute duration

Economic resource index
Poverty rate, public assistance rate, high skill employment, median household income, home ownership

Family structure
Single parenthood

FIGURE 1-6 The Child Opportunity Index.
SOURCE: http://new.diversitydatakids.org/sites/default/files/file/ddk_the-geography-of-child-opportunity_2020v2.pdf

frameworks of neighborhood influences on children (Acevedo-Garcia et al., 2020). While there now exist several publicly available, aggregate indices of neighborhood characteristics, the COI is specifically focused on characteristics important for children and includes child-relevant indicators, such as the presence of early childhood education centers, the availability of healthy food, and walkability. Furthermore, a recent evaluation comparing commonly used neighborhood indices recommended the COI's use in policy and decision making, finding that it performed consistently overall in terms of its relationship to 24 diverse life outcomes related to mortality, physical health, mental health, subjective well-being, and social capital (Lou et al., 2023).

Several recent studies using the COI have found significant associations between neighborhood opportunity and a range of child health outcomes. Growing up in a neighborhood with higher opportunity is associated with lower child and caregiver mortality (Slopen et al., 2023), longer life expectancy at birth (Shanahan et al., 2022), and better cardiometabolic health (Aris et al., 2022), and may protect children from poor families from the physiological impacts of stress (Roubinov et al., 2018). Conversely, lower neighborhood opportunity has been linked to increased emergency department visits and hospitalizations, longer hospital stays, and hospital readmissions (Kersten et al., 2018; Bettenhausen et al., 2022; Fritz et al., 2022), especially for conditions that could have been treated in or prevented through a primary care setting (Beck et al., 2017; Krager et al., 2021; Kaiser et al., 2022; Ramgopal et al., 2022). Others have shown that children from lower-opportunity areas have delayed access to care in the case of an acute emergency, such as appendicitis, which can increase the risk of complications (Bouchard et al., 2022).

The COI has also been used to demonstrate high levels of racial/ethnic inequity in children's neighborhood opportunity. For instance, in the 100 largest metropolitan areas, non-Hispanic White (39%) and Asian and Pacific Islander (40%) children are concentrated in very high-opportunity neighborhoods—those neighborhoods containing the 20% of the total U.S. child population living in the highest-opportunity neighborhoods across the United States. In contrast, Hispanic (33%) and Black (46%) children are disproportionately concentrated in very low-opportunity neighborhoods—those containing the 20% of the total U.S. child population living in the lowest-opportunity neighborhoods across the United States. Inequities persist even after controlling for poverty status: 66% of all poor U.S. Black children and 50% of all poor U.S. Hispanic children live in very low-opportunity neighborhoods, compared with 20% of all poor U.S. White children (Acevedo-Garcia et al., 2020). These stark inequities in the neighborhood opportunity levels of children by race/ethnicity reflect the high levels of child residential segregation discussed earlier (Acevedo-Garcia et al., 2008).

ACCESS TO RESOURCES, SUPPORTS, AND OPPORTUNITIES

Although a number of social programs exist to support families with young children, access to these programs and the opportunities they offer can be low as a result of administrative burden and barriers created by the ways in which the programs are implemented. This section summarizes program characteristics that can impede access to and uptake of these programs, contributing to the persistence of opportunity gaps. Further detail can be found throughout this report.

Administrative Burden

Administrative burden encompasses challenges related to the time and energy required to access—and maintain access to—public programs and the benefits they provide. While the intent of these programs is to provide assistance to those in need, many of these burdens result from deliberate policy choices that limit access and perpetuate disparities (Herd & Moynihan, 2018). A National Academies report on reducing child poverty highlights the importance of equitable and ready access to benefit programs and describes how bureaucratic processes, which may differ from state to state, can vary across and within programs. These variations in implementation create barriers to access for eligible families (National Academies, 2019a) and cause the benefits of these programs to reach some groups more than others and some states more than others. Likewise, administrative burdens may affect some groups more than others and can result in participation rates that differ substantially by race, ethnicity, neighborhood, or other individual characteristics (National Academies, 2019a).

Pamela Herd (Georgetown University) presented to the committee on barriers to accessing benefit programs and described two of the major social and behavioral costs related to administrative burden—learning costs and compliance costs (Herd, 2021; National Academies, 2021).

Herd defined learning costs as the way in which individuals or families gather information about how to access the services available to help meet their needs. Her presentation highlighted a project of the California Policy Lab that found that 20% of families in California's social welfare system were not accessing student stimulus benefits. In another example highlighted in the National Academies report referenced above (National Academies, 2019a), variations in enrollment requirements for the Supplemental Nutrition Assistance Program (SNAP) contributed to participation rates that varied from 59% to 100% of eligible families, depending on the state.

Compliance costs—those costs associated with following administrative rules and meeting program requirements—can also affect take-up of programs and benefits. Individuals and families attempting to access multiple programs and benefits face particular administrative hurdles because of a lack of program linkages. Compliance costs can include, for example, the time spent on administrative processes, the frequency of recertification, and the difficulties associated with gathering and submitting necessary documentation, among others. A barrier for people living in rural areas, for example, can be a lack of transportation to travel to in-person appointments required to maintain benefits, which can result in reduced participation (National Academies, 2021). Similarly, while nearly all infants eligible for the Special Supplemental Nutrition Program for Women, Infants, and Children participate in the program, only 25% of eligible 4-year-olds do so, in part because of the challenges of recertification (U.S. Department of Agriculture, 2022). Understanding and keeping track of policy changes can also create challenges that affect access to programs and benefits. In Tennessee, for example, 10% of children enrolled in Medicaid were dropped from the program in 2018 as the result of a recertification process, which included a 47-page form that could be completed only by mail. Families that failed to complete the form or submitted it late were dropped from the program (Herd & Moynihan, 2020).

In addition to learning and compliance costs, it is important to recognize the psychological costs associated with administrative burden. The difficulty of navigating these systems and the stigma associated with accessing these benefits can lead to chronic stress, frustration, and anger, with negative impacts on mental health (Herd & Moynihan, 2018, 2020; Herd, 2021).

Some states are working to decrease the administrative burden of benefit programs by automating the application process, allowing individuals and families to submit applications and renew eligibility online, connecting families to other support programs, and implementing presumptive eligibility policies that can allow individuals and families to access services before their applications are fully processed. Yet while these efforts to simplify processes at the state and local levels have been demonstrated to save both states and applicants money, inconsistent implementation across states and the associated administrative burdens present a significant challenge to families (National Academies, 2019a). Similarly, while some states enable families that participate in one safety net program to be enrolled automatically in others for which they are eligible, the vast majority require families to complete multiple burdensome application processes.

Policy interventions that recognize the diversity of needs of families and the challenges they encounter in accessing supports have the potential to improve health and education outcomes for young children and help close the opportunity gap. Reducing administrative burdens could help eliminate barriers to accessing and participating in programs designed to achieve this goal.

Implementation of Programs

As noted earlier, the implementation of benefit programs can vary substantially from state to state, leading to differing participation rates among those who qualify and vastly different levels of support. The previously cited National Academies report, for example (National Academies, 2019a), highlights variations in monthly payments to families through TANF that could not be accounted for by differences in the cost of living—from a low of $170 in Mississippi to a high of $1,021 in New Hampshire. State-to-state variations in supplements to federal programs and additional tax credits also influence the amounts families may receive and can create disparities resulting simply from where families live. For some programs, even when access is not the primary barrier, participation may be limited because of insufficient funding. For example, the Child Care and Development Fund is funded at a level that allows it to support only 17% of eligible children (National Academies, 2019a).

In certain cases, eligibility requirements may exclude certain groups (e.g., both documented and undocumented immigrants or individuals who have been convicted of felonies). Although these groups might otherwise be eligible for certain benefits based on their household income, they may be excluded from such programs as SNAP, Medicaid, and Supplemental Security Income. Children in immigrant families are much less likely to qualify for and benefit from such programs, even if they themselves are U.S. citizens. And even for groups that are eligible, the stigma associated with accessing these programs can reduce participation. In addition, fear of jeopardizing their opportunity to gain permanent resident status or U.S. citizenship—most prevalent among Latino families—may prevent some immigrant families from accessing these benefits (National Academies, 2019a; Herd, 2021). Policies that perpetuate disparate outcomes harm both citizen and noncitizen families and children and reduce the benefits and resources that would otherwise be available to them, creating opportunity gaps. This is especially the case for children and families who are racial and ethnic minorities.

OVERVIEW OF THE REPORT

As demonstrated by the broad range of background information presented in this chapter, the committee's review of evidence in this report is extensive and covers multiple domains in order to capture the complexity of the opportunity gap. Chapters 2 and 3 review gaps in access to and quality experiences in learning systems, gaps that have been shaped by history and persist as a result of policy; these chapters also describe promising policies for bridging these gaps, as well as an inclusive framework for narrowing or eliminating disparities in outcomes. Chapter 2 focuses on young children from birth through pre-K, and Chapter 3 on children in grades K–3.

Chapter 4 examines the effects of social determinants of health on physical health and how disparities in physical health and access to health care can be drivers of opportunity gaps from the prenatal period through the early years of life. Chapter 5 focuses on how gaps in opportunities to foster positive social-emotional development and well-being and mental health in parents and children create persistent opportunity gaps across the life course, and how community resources and targeted policies and practices that improve family functioning and mental health and well-being can help close these gaps. Chapter 6 looks at the economic costs of the opportunity gap and the associated gaps in research. Chapter 7 provides an overview of policies, promising practices, and potential opportunities that governments, community organizations, philanthropic organizations, and other stakeholders can consider to reduce, mitigate, and eliminate disparities among young children. Finally, Chapter 8 provides the committee's key conclusions and recommendations for addressing the opportunity gap among young children from birth to age 8.

REFERENCES

Aaron, H. (2010). *Politics and the professors: The great society in perspective.* Washington, DC: Brookings Institution.

Acevedo-Garcia, D., Osypuk, T.L., McArdle, N., & Williams, D.R. (2008). Toward a policy-relevant analysis of geographic and racial/ethnic disparities in child health. *Health Affairs (Project Hope), 27*(2), 321–33. https://doi.org/10.1377/hlthaff.27.2.321

Acevedo-Garcia, D., Rosenfeld, L.E., McArdle, N., & Osypuk, T.L. (2010). The geography of opportunity: A framework for child development. *Changing places: How communities will improve the health of boys of color,* 358–406. Berkeley, CA: University of California Press.

Acevedo-Garcia, D., Noelke, C., & McArdle, N. (2020). *The geography of child opportunity: Why neighborhoods mattter for equity: First findings from the Child Opportunity Index 2.0.* Heller School for Social Policy and Management, Brandeis Univeristy.

Acevedo-Garcia, D., Noelke, C., McArdle, N., Sofer, N., Hardy, E.F., Weiner, M., Baek, M., Huntington, N., Huber, R., & Reece, J., (2020). Racial and ethnic inequities in children's neighborhoods: Evidence from the New Child Opportunity Index 2.0. *Health Affairs, 39*(10), 1693–701. https://doi.org/10.1377/hlthaff.2020.00735

Acevedo-Garcia, D., Joshi, P.K., Ruskin, E., Walters, A.N., & Sofer, N. (2021a). Restoring an inclusionary safety net for children in immigrant families: A review of three social policies. *Health Affairs, 40*(7), 1099–107. https://doi.org/10.1377/hlthaff.2021.00206

Acevedo-Garcia, D., Joshi, P.K., Ruskin, E., Walters, A.N., Sofer, N., & Guevara, C.A. (2021b). Including children in immigrant families in policy approaches to reduce child poverty. *Academic Pediatrics, 21*(8S), S117–25. https://doi.org/10.1016/j.acap.2021.06.016

Acevedo-Garcia, D., Walters, A.N., Shafer, L., Wong, E., & Joshi, P. (2022). *A policy equity analysis of the earned income tax credit: Fully including children in immigrant families and Hispanic children in this key anti-poverty program. Data-for-equity research report.* Brandeis University and diversitydatakids.org. Available: https://www.diversitydatakids.org/research-library/research-report/policy-equity-analysis-eitc

Aikens, N.L., & Barbarin, O. (2008). Socioeconomic differences in reading trajectories: The contribution of family, neighborhood, and school contexts. *Journal of Educational Psychology, 100*(2), 235–51. https://doi.org/10.1037/0022-0663.100.2.235

Amott, T., & Matthaei, J. (1996). *Race, gender & work: A multicultural economic history of women in the United States.* Boston, MA: South End Press.

Aris, I.M., Perng, W., Dabelea, D., Padula, A.M., Alshawabkeh, A., Vélez-Vega, C.M., Aschner, J.L., Camargo, C.A., Sussman, T.J., Dunlop, A.L., Elliott, A.J., Ferrara, A., Zhu, Y., Joseph, C.L.M., Singh, A.M., Hartert, T.V., Cacho, F., Karagas, M.R., North-Reid, T., ... & Oken, E. (2022). Associations of neighborhood opportunity and social vulnerability with trajectories of childhood body mass index and obesity among US children. *JAMA Network Open, 5*(12), e2247957. https://doi.org/10.1001/jamanetworkopen.2022.47957

Artiles, A.J., Klingner, J., Sullivan, A.L., & Fierros, E. (2010). Shifting landscapes of professional practices: ELL special education placement in English-only states: English learners and restrictive language policies. *Forbidden language: English learners and restrictive language policies,* 102–17. Los Angeles, CA: Civil Rights Project.

Artiles, A.J., Dorn, S., & Bal, A. (2016). Objects of protection, enduring nodes of difference: Disability intersections with "other" differences, 1916 to 2016. *Review of Research in Education, 40*(1), 777–820. https://doi.org/10.3102/0091732x16680606

Aspen Institute Roundtable on Community Change. (2004). *Structural racism and community building.* Available: https://www.aspeninstitute.org/publications/structural-racism-community-building/

Bahn, K. (2019). *Research finds the domestic outsourcing of jobs leads to declining U.S. job quality and lower wages*. Washington Center for Equitable Growth. Available: https://equitablegrowth.org/research-finds-the-domestic-outsourcing-of-jobs-leads-to-declining-u-s-job-quality-and-lower-wages

Banks, N. (2019). *Black women's labor market history reveals deep-seated race and gender discrimination*. Economic Policy Institute. Available: https://www.epi.org/blog/black-womens-labor-market-history-reveals-deep-seated-race-and-gender-discrimination

Beck, A.F., Sandel, M.T., Ryan, P.H., & Kahn, R.S. (2017). Mapping neighborhood health geo-markers to clinical care decisions to promote equity in child health. *Health Affairs*, 36(6), 999–1005. https://doi.org/10.1377/hlthaff.2016.1425

Bell, W. (1965). *Aid to dependent children*. New York, NY: Columbia University Press.

Benson, J., & Borman, G.D. (2010). Family, neighborhood, and school settings across seasons: When do socioeconomic context and racial composition matter for the reading achievement growth of young children? *Teachers College Record*, 112(5), 1338–90. https://doi.org/10.1177/016146811011200505

Bettenhausen, J.L., Noelke, C., Ressler, R.W., Hall, M., Harris, M., Peltz, A., Auger, K.A., Teufel, R.J., Lutmer, J.E., Krager, M.K., Simon, H.K., Neuman, M.I., Pavuluri, P., Morse, R.B., Eghtesady, P., Macy, M.L., Shah, S.S., Synhorst, D.C., & Gay, J.C. (2022). The association of the Childhood Opportunity Index on pediatric readmissions and emergency department revisits. *Academic Pediatrics*, 22(4), 614–21. https://doi.org/10.1016/j.acap.2021.12.015

Bifulco, R., & Ladd, H.F. (2007). School choice, racial segregation, and test-score gaps: Evidence from North Carolina's charter school program. *Journal of Policy Analysis and Management*, 26(1), 31–56. Available: http://www.jstor.org/stable/30164083

Bipartisan Policy Center. (2021). *Building bipartisan support for child care toolkit: 2021 update*. Bipartisan Policy Center. Available: https://bipartisanpolicy.org/report/building-bipartisan-support-for-child-care-toolkit-2021-update/

Bird, S.T. (1995). Separate black and white infant mortality models: Differences in the importance of structural variables. *Social Science & Medicine*, 41(11), 1507–12. https://doi.org/10.1016/0277-9536(95)00029-7

Bischoff, K., & Reardon, S.F. (2014). Residential segregation by income, 1970–2009. *Diversity and disparities: America enters a new century*, 208–34. New York, NY: Russell Sage Foundation.

Bouchard, M.E., Kan, K., Tian, Y., Casale, M., Smith, T., De Boer, C., Linton, S., Abdullah, F., & Ghomrawi, H.M.K. (2022). Association between neighborhood-level social determinants of health and access to pediatric appendicitis care. *JAMA Network Open*, 5(2), e2148865. https://doi.org/10.1001/jamanetworkopen.2021.48865

Bronfenbrenner, U. (1992). Ecological systems theory. *Six theories of child development: Revised formulations and current issues*, 187–249. London, UK: Jessica Kingsley Publishers.

Bruch, S.K., Gornick, J.C., & van der Naald, J. (2022). Geographic inequality in social provision: Variation across the U.S. states. *Measuring distribution and mobility of income and wealth*. Chicago, IL: University of Chicago Press.

Capps, R., Fix, M., & Batalova, J. (2020). *Anticipated "chilling effects" of the public-charge rule are real: Census data reflect steep decline in benefits use by immigrant families*. Migration Policy Institute. Available: https://www.migrationpolicy.org/news/anticipated-chilling-effects-public-charge-rule-are-real

Cascio, E. (2021). *Early childhood education in the United States: What, when, where, who, how, and why*. (Working Paper No. 28722). National Bureau of Economic Research. https://doi.org/10.3386/w28722

Cashin, S. (2021). *White space, Black hood: Opportunity hoarding and segregation in the age of inequality*. Boston, MA: Beacon Press.

Castro, D.C., & Meek, S. (2022). Beyond Castañeda and the "language barrier" ideology: Young children and their right to bilingualism. *Language Policy*, 21(3), 407–25. https://doi.org/10.1007/s10993-021-09608-x

Chaudry, A. (2021). Addressing inequality in the United States from cradle to kindergarten. Presentation to the Committee on Exploring the Opportunity Gap for Young Children from Birth to Age Eight.

Chetty, R., Hendren, N., & Katz, L.F. (2016). The effects of exposure to better neighborhoods on children: New evidence from the Moving to Opportunity experiment. *American Economic Review*, 106(4), 855–902. https://doi.org/10.1257/aer.20150572

Chetty, R., Hendren, N., Jones, M.R., & Porter, S.R. (2020). Race and economic opportunity in the United States: An intergenerational perspective. *The Quarterly Journal of Economics*, 135(2), 711–83. https://doi.org/10.1093/qje/qjz042

Coley, R.L., Spielvogel, B., & Kull, M. (2019). Concentrated poverty in preschools and children's cognitive skills: The mediational role of peers and teachers. *Journal of School Psychology*, 76, 1–16. https://doi.org/10.1016/j.jsp.2019.05.008

Collins, C.A. (1999). Racism and health: Segregation and causes of death amenable to medical intervention in major U.S. cities. *Annals of the New York Academy of Sciences*, 896, 396–8. https://doi.org/10.1111/j.1749-6632.1999.tb08152.x

Condron, D.J., Tope, D., Steidl, C.R., & Freeman, K.J. (2013). Racial segregation and the black/white achievement gap, 1992 to 2009. *The Sociological Quarterly*, 54(1), 130–57. https://doi.org/10.1111/tsq.12010

Crenshaw, K. (1991). Mapping the margins: Intersectionality, identity politics, and violence against women of color. *Stanford Law Review*, 43(6), 1241–99. https://doi.org/10.2307/1229039

Currie, J.M. (2006). *The invisible safety net: Protecting the nation's poor children and families*. Princeton, NJ: Princeton University Press.

Department of Education. (2021). *43rd annual report to Congress on the implementation of the Individuals with Disabilities Education Act, 2021*. Available: https://sites.ed.gov/idea/files/43rd-arc-for-idea.pdf

Department of the Interior. (2021). *Federal Indian boarding school initiative*. Available: https://www.bia.gov/service/federal-indian-boarding-school-initiative

Derenoncourt, E., & Montialoux, C. (2021). Minimum wages and racial inequality. *The Quarterly Journal of Economics*, 136(1), 169–228. https://doi.org/10.1093/qje/qjaa031

Douglas, W.O., & the Supreme Court of the United States. (1973). U.S. Reports: Lau v. Nichols, 414 U.S. 563. [Periodical]. Library of Congress. Available: https://www.loc.gov/item/usrep414563/

Ellen, I., & Glied, S. (2015). Housing, neighborhoods, and children's health. *The Future of Children*, 25(1), 135–54. https://doi.org/10.1353/foc.2015.0006

Estrada, P., Wang, H., & Farkas, T. (2020). Elementary English learner classroom composition and academic achievement: The role of classroom-level segregation, number of English proficiency levels, and opportunity to learn. *American Educational Research Journal*, 57(4), 1791–836. https://doi.org/10.3102/0002831219887137

Faber, J.W. (2020). We built this: Consequences of New Deal era intervention in America's racial geography. *American Sociological Review*, 85(5), 739–75. https://doi.org/10.1177/0003122420948464

Federal Interagency Forum on Child and Family Statistics. (2022). *America's children in brief: Key national indicators of well-being, 2022*. Washington, DC: U.S. Government Printing Office.

Floyd, I., Pavetti, L., Meyer, L., Safawi, A., Schott, L., Bellew, E., & Magnus, A. (2021). *TANF policies reflect racist legacy of cash assistance: Reimagined program should center Black mothers*. Washington, DC: Center on Budget and Policy Priorities. Available: https://www.cbpp.org/research/income-security/tanf-policies-reflect-racist-legacy-of-cash-assistance

Francies, C., & Perez, Z. Jr. (2020). *50-state comparison: Free and compulsory school age requirements*. Education Commission of the States. Available: https://www.ecs.org/50-state-comparison-free-and-compulsory-school-age-requirements/

Frankenberg, E. (2016). *Segregation at an early age*. State College, PA: Center for Education and Civil Rights, Pennsylvania State University College of Education.

Frankenberg, E., Ee, J., Ayscue, J.B., & Orfield, G. (2019). *Harming our common future: America's segregated schools 65 years after Brown*. The Civil Rights Project. Available: https://www.civilrightsproject.ucla.edu/research/k-12-education/integration-and-diversity/harming-our-common-future-americas-segregated-schools-65-years-after-brown

Frey, W.H. (2018). *Diversity explosion. How new racial demographics are remaking America*. Washington, DC: Brookings Institution.

Friedman-Krauss, A.H., Barnett, W.S., Garver, K.A., Hodges, K.S., Weisenfeld, G., Gardiner, B.A., & Jost, T.M. (2022). *The state of preschool 2021: State preschool yearbook*. New Brunswick, NJ: National Institute for Early Education Research.

Fritz, B.A., Ramsey, B., Taylor, D., Shoup, J.P., Schmidt, J.M., Guinn, M., & Maddox, T.M. (2022). Association of race and neighborhood disadvantage with patient engagement in a home-based COVID-19 remote monitoring program. *Journal of General Internal Medicine*, 37(4), 838–46. https://doi.org/10.1007/s11606-021-07207-4

Galster, G.C. (2012). The mechanism(s) of neighbourhood effects: Theory, evidence, and policy implications. *Neighbourhood effects research: New perspectives*, 23–56. Springer. Available: https://link.springer.com/book/10.1007/978-94-007-2309-2

Gándara, P. (2020). Equity considerations in addressing English learner segregation. *Leadership and Policy in Schools*, 19(1), 141–3. https://doi.org/10.1080/15700763.2019.1711134

Gándara, P.C., & Aldana, U.S. (2014). Who's segregated now? Latinos, language, and the future of integrated schools. *Educational Administration Quarterly*, 50(5), 735–48. https://doi.org/10.1177/0013161x14549957

Gándara, P., & Orfield, G. (2010). *A return to the "Mexican room": The segregation of Arizona's English learners*. The Civil Rights Project. Available: https://civilrightsproject.ucla.edu/research/k-12-education/language-minority-students/a-return-to-the-mexican-room-the-segregation-of-arizonas-english-learners-1

García, D.R. (2008). Academic and racial segregation in charter schools: Do parents sort students into specialized charter schools? *Education and Urban Society*, 40(5), 590–612. https://doi.org/10.1177/0013124508316044

García Coll, C., Lamberty, G., Jenkins, R., McAdoo, H.P., Crnic, K., Wasik, B.H., & García, H.V. (1996). An integrative model for the study of developmental competencies in minority children. *Child Development*, 67(5), 1891–914. https://doi.org/10.2307/1131600

Gillispie, C. (2021). *Our youngest learners: Increasing equity in early intervention*. The Education Trust. Available: https://edtrust.org/increasing-equity-in-early-intervention/

Glenn, E.N. (2015). Settler colonialism as structure: A framework for comparative studies of U.S. race and gender formation. *Sociology of Race and Ethnicity*, 1(1), 52–72. https://doi.org/10.1177/2332649214560440

Gonzales, R.G. (2011). Learning to be illegal: Undocumented youth and shifting legal contexts in the transition to adulthood. *American Sociological Review*, 76(4), 602–19. https://doi.org/10.1177/0003122411411901

Gordon, L., & Batlan, F. (2011). The legal history of the aid to dependent children program. Social Welfare History Project, Virginia Commonwealth University. Available: https://socialwelfare.library.vcu.edu/public-welfare/aid-to-dependent-children-the-legal-history

Government Accountability Office (GAO). (2022). *K-12 education: Student population has significantly diversified, but many schools remain divided along racial, ethnic, and economic lines*. (GAO-22-104737). Available: https://www.gao.gov/products/gao-22-104737

Green, K.B., Terry, N.P., & Gallagher, P.A. (2014). Progress in language and literacy skills among children with disabilities in inclusive early reading first classrooms. *Topics in Early Childhood Special Education*, 33(4), 249–59. https://doi.org/10.1177/0271121413477498

Hahn, H., Aron, L.Y., Lou, C., Pratt, E., & Okoli, A. (2017). *Why does cash welfare depend on where you live? How and why state TANF programs vary*. The Urban Institute. Available: https://www.urban.org/sites/default/files/publication/90761/tanf_cash_welfare_final2_1.pdf

Hanselman, P., & Fiel, J.E. (2017). School opportunity hoarding? Racial segregation and access to high growth schools. *Social Forces*, 95(3), 1077–104. https://doi.org/10.1093/sf/sow088

Hart, K.D., Kunitz, S.J., Sell, R.R., & Mukamel, D.B. (1998). Metropolitan governance, residential segregation, and mortality among African Americans. *American Journal of Public Health*, 88(3), 434–8. https://doi.org/10.2105/ajph.88.3.434

Herd, P. (2021). Barriers to accessing benefit programs: Administrative burden. Presentation to the Committee on Exploring the Opportunity Gap for Young Children from Birth to Age Eight. May 25, 2021. Washington, DC: National Academies of Sciences, Engineering, and Medicine.

Herd, P., & Moynihan, D.P. (2018). *Administrative burden policymaking by other means*. New York, NY: Russell Sage Foundation.

———. (2020). How administrative burdens can harm health: Health policy brief. *Health Affairs*. Available: https://www.healthaffairs.org/do/10.1377/hpb20200904.405159/full

Hinds, H., Newby, L., & Korman, H. (2022). *Ignored, punished, and underserved: Understanding and addressing disparities in education experiences and outcomes for Black children with disabilities*. Bellwether. Available: https://bellwether.org/publications/ignored-punished-and-underserved

Hinitz, B.S. (2014). Head Start: A bridge from past to future. *Young Children*, 69(2), 94–7. Available: http://www.jstor.org/stable/ycyoungchildren.69.2.94

Iceland, J., Kimberly, A., Goyette, K., Nelson, A., & Chan, C. (2010). Racial and ethnic residential segregation and household structure: A research note. *Social Science Research*, 39(1), 39–47. https://doi.org/10.1016/j.ssresearch.2009.06.006

Institute of Medicine (IOM) & National Research Council (NRC). (2015). *Transforming the workforce for children birth through age 8: A unifying foundation*. Washington, DC: The National Academies Press. https://doi.org/10.17226/19401

Jackson, S.A., Anderson, R.T., Johnson, N.J., & Sorlie, P.D. (2000). The relation of residential segregation to all-cause mortality: A study in black and white. *American Journal of Public Health*, 90(4), 615–7. https://doi.org/10.2105/ajph.90.4.615

Jacobs, M.D. (2007). Working on the domestic frontier: American Indian domestic servants in white women's households in the San Francisco Bay Area, 1920-1940. *Frontiers: A Journal of Women Studies*, 28(1 and 2), 165–99. https://doi.org/10.1353/fro.2007.0028

Jacobs, N. (2011). Understanding school choice: Location as a determinant of charter school racial, economic, and linguistic segregation. *Education and Urban Society*, 45, 459–82. https://doi.org/10.1177/0013124511413388

Jargowsky, P.A. (2014). Segregation, neighborhoods, and schools. *Choosing homes, choosing schools: Residential segregation and the search for a good school*. New York, NY: Russell Sage Foundation.

Johnson, R.C. (2011). *Long-run impacts of school desegregation and school quality on adult attainments*. (Working Paper No. 16664). National Bureau of Economic Research. https://doi.org/10.3386/w16664

Johnson-Staub, C. (2017). *Equity starts early: Addressing racial inequities in child care and early education policy*. Center for Law and Social Policy, Inc. Available: https://www.clasp.org/publications/fact-sheet/equity-starts-early-addressing-racial-inequities-child-care-and-early

Joshi, P., Geronimo, K., & Acevedo-Garcia, D. (2016). Head Start since the war on poverty: Taking on new challenges to address persistent school readiness gaps. *Journal of Applied Research on Children: Informing Policy for Children at Risk*, 7(1). Available: http://digitalcommons.library.tmc.edu/childrenatrisk/vol7/iss1/11

Joshi, P., Walters, A.N., Noelke, C., & Acevedo-Garcia, D. (2022). Families' job characteristics and economic self-sufficiency: Differences by income, race/ethnicity, and nativity. *The Russell Sage Foundation Journal of the Social Sciences*, 8, 67–95. https://doi.org/10.7758/RSF.2022.8.5.04

Kaiser, S.V., Hall, M., Bettenhausen, J.L., Sills, M.R., Hoffmann, J.A., Noelke, C., Morse, R.B., Lopez, M.A., & Parikh, K. (2022). Neighborhood child opportunity and emergency department utilization. *Pediatrics*, 150(4), e2021056098. https://doi.org/10.1542/peds.2021-056098

Kalil, A., & Ryan, R. (2020). Parenting practices and socioeconomic gaps in childhood outcomes. *Future of Children*, 30(1), 29–54. https://doi.org/10.1353/foc.2020.0004

Kamerman, S.B., & Gatenio-Gabel, S. (2007). Early childhood education and care in the United States: An overview of the current policy picture. *International Journal of Child Care and Education Policy*, 1(1), 23–34. https://doi.org/10.1007/2288-6729-1-1-23

Kawachi, I., & Berkman, L.F. (2003). *Neighborhoods and health*. Oxford University Press. http://dx.doi.org/10.1093/acprof:oso/9780195138382.001.0001

Keating, K., Cole, P., & Schaffner, M. (2020). *State of babies yearbook: 2020*. Zero to Three: National Center for Infants, Toddlers, and Families. Available: https://stateofbabies.org/wp-content/uploads/2020/06/State-of-Babies-2020-Full-Yearbook-061820.pdf

Kersten, E.E., Adler, N.E., Gottlieb, L., Jutte, D.P., Robinson, S., Roundfield, K., & LeWinn, K.Z. (2018). Neighborhood child opportunity and individual-level pediatric acute care use and diagnoses. *Pediatrics*, 141(5), e20172309. https://doi.org/10.1542/peds.2017-2309

Kostelnik, M.J., & Grady, M.L. (2009). *Getting it right from the start: The principal's guide to early childhood education*. Thousand Oaks, CA: Corwin.

Kotecki, J.A., Gennuso, K.P., Givens, M.L., & Kindig, D.A. (2019). Separate and sick: Residential segregation and the health of children and youth in metropolitan statistical areas. *Journal of Urban Health: Bulletin of the New York Academy of Medicine*, 96(2), 149–58. https://doi.org/10.1007/s11524-018-00330-4

Kotok, S., Frankenberg, E., Schafft, K.A., Mann, B.A., & Fuller, E.J. (2017). School choice, racial segregation, and poverty concentration: Evidence from Pennsylvania charter school transfers. *Educational Policy*, 31(4), 415–47. https://doi.org/10.1177/0895904815604112

Krager, M.K., Puls, H.T., Bettenhausen, J.L., Hall, M., Thurm, C., Plencner, L.M., Markham, J.L., Noelke, C., & Beck, A.F. (2021). The Child Opportunity Index 2.0 and hospitalizations for ambulatory care sensitive conditions. *Pediatrics*, 148(2), e2020032755. https://doi.org/10.1542/peds.2020-032755

Kramer, M.R., & Hogue, C.R. (2009). Is segregation bad for your health? *Epidemiologic Reviews*, 31, 178–94. https://doi.org/10.1093/epirev/mxp001

Kuh, D., Ben-Shlomo, Y., Lynch, J., Hallqvist, J., & Power, C. (2003). Life course epidemiology. *Journal of Epidemiology and Community Health*, 57(10), 778. https://doi.org/10.1136/jech.57.10.778

Lawrence, S.M., Smith, S., & Banerjee, R. (2016). *Preschool inclusion: Key findings from research and implications for policy*. Child Care and Early Education Research Connections, National Center for Children in Poverty. Available: https://eric.ed.gov/?id=ED579178

Lee, C.D. (2009). Historical evolution of risk and equity: Interdisciplinary issues and critiques. *Review of Research in Education*, 33(1). https://doi.org/10.3102/0091732X08328244

Leventhal, T., Dupéré, V., & Brooks-Gunn, J. (2009). Neighborhood influences on adolescent development. *Handbook of adolescent psychology: Contextual influences on adolescent development*, 411–43. John Wiley & Sons, Inc. https://doi.org/10.1002/9780470479193.adlpsy002013

Lloyd, C.M., Carlson, J., & Alvira-Hammond, M. (2021). *Federal policies can address the impact of structural racism on Black families' access to early care and education*. Child Trends. Available: https://www.childtrends.org/publications/federal-policies-can-address-the-impact-of-structural-racism-on-black-families-access-to-early-care-and-education

Lombardi, J., Harding, J.F., Connors, M.C., & Friedman-Krauss, A. (2016). Executive summary. *Coming of age: A review of federal early childhood policy 2000-2015*. Build Initiative. Available: https://www.researchgate.net/publication/323400908_Coming_of_Age_A_Review_of_Federal_Early_Childhood_Policy_2000_-_2015

Lou, S., Giorgi, S., Liu, T., Eichstaedt, J.C., & Curtis, B. (2023). Measuring disadvantage: A systematic comparison of United States small-area disadvantage indices. *Health Place*, 80, 102997. https://doi.org/10.1016/j.healthplace.2023.102997

Malik, R., Hamm, K., Schochet, L., Novoa, C., Workman, S., & Jessen-Howard, S. (2018). *America's child care deserts in 2018*. Center for American Progress. Available: https://www.americanprogress.org/article/americas-child-care-deserts-2018

Mays, V.M., Cochran, S.D., & Barnes, N.W. (2007). Race, race-based discrimination, and health outcomes among African Americans. *Annual Review of Psychology*, 58, 201–25. https://doi.org/10.1146/annurev.psych.57.102904.190212

McArdle, N., & Acevedo-Garcia, D. (2018). Consequences of segregation for children's opportunity and wellbeing. *A shared future: Fostering communities of inclusion in an era of inequality*. Cambridge, MA: Harvard Joint Center for Housing Studies.

Meek, S., Smith, L., Allen, R., Catherine, E., Edyburn, K., Williams, C., Fabes, R., McIntosh, K., Garcia, E., Takanishi, R., Gordon, L., Jimenez-Castellanos, O., Hemmeter, M.L., Gilliam, W., & Pontier, R. (2020). *Start with equity: From the early years to the early grades: Data, research, and an actionable child equity policy agenda*. Children's Equity Project and The Bipartisan Policy Center. Available: https://childandfamilysuccess.asu.edu/cep/start-with-equity

Merriam Webster (n.d.). *Racialization*. Merriam Webster Dictionary. Retrieved August 20, 2023, from https://www.merriam-webster.com/dictionary/racialization

Meyer, B.D., & Sullivan, J.X. (2013). *Winning the war: Poverty from the Great Society to the Great Recession*. (Working Paper No. W18718). National Bureau of Economic Research.

Minoff, E. (2020). *The racist roots of work requirements*. Center for the Study of Social Policy. Available: https://cssp.org/resource/racist-roots-of-work-requirements

Monarrez, T., & Chien, C. (2021). *Dividing lines: Racially unequal school boundaries in US public school systems*. Urban Institute.

National Academies of Sciences, Engineering, and Medicine (National Academies). (2000). *From neurons to neighborhoods: The science of early childhood development*. Washington, DC: The National Academies Press.

———. (2015). *The integration of immigrants into American society*. The National Academies Press. https://doi.org/10.17226/21746

———. (2016). *Parenting matters: Supporting parents of children ages 0-8*. The National Academies Press. https://doi.org/10.17226/21868

———. (2018). *Transforming the financing of early care and education*. The National Academies Press. https://doi.org/10.17226/24984

———. (2019a). *A roadmap to reducing child poverty*. The National Academies Press. https://doi.org/10.17226/25246

———. (2019b). *Shaping summertime experiences: Opportunities to promote healthy development and well-being for children and youth*. The National Academies Press. https://doi.org/10.17226/25546

———. (2019c). *Vibrant and healthy kids: Aligning science, practice, and policy to advance health equity*. The National Academies Press. https://doi.org/10.17226/25466

———. (2021). *Measuring the opportunity gap for children from birth to age eight and understanding barriers to access: Proceedings of a workshop–in brief*. National Academies Press. https://doi.org/10.17226/26416

———. (2022a). *Structural racism and rigorous models of social inequity: Proceedings of a workshop*. The National Academies Press. https://doi.org/10.17226/26690.

———. (2022b). *The future of education research at IES: Advancing an equity-oriented science*. The National Academies Press. https://doi.org/10.17226/26428.

National Center for Learning Disabilities. (2020). *Significant disproportionality in special education: Current trends and actions for impact*. National Center for Learning Disabilities. Available: https://www.ncld.org/wp-content/uploads/2020/10/2020-NCLD-Disproportionality_Trends-and-Actions-for-Impact_FINAL-1.pdf

Nelson, A.R. (2016). The Elementary and Secondary Education Act at fifty: A changing federal role in American education. *History of Education Quarterly*, 56(2), 358–61. https://doi.org/10.1111/hoeq.12186

Newburger, H.B., Birch, E.L., & Wachter, S.M. (Eds.). (2011). *Neighborhood and life chances: How place matters in modern America*. University of Pennsylvania Press. http://www.jstor.org/stable/j.ctt3fhhvw

Nixon, R. (1971). *Veto of the economic opportunity amendments of 1971*. The American Presidency Project. Available: https://www.presidency.ucsb.edu/documents/veto-the-economic-opportunity-amendments-1971

Noel, A., Stark, P., & Redford, J. (2016). *Parent and family involvement in education, from the National Household Education Surveys Program of 2012: First look*. Washington, DC: Institute of Education Sciences, National Center for Education Statistics, Department of Education.

O'Hare, W. (2009). *The forgotten fifth: Child poverty in rural America*. (National Report No. 10). Durham, NH: Carsey Institute, University of New Hampshire.

Orfield, G., & Frankenberg, E. (2014). Increasingly segregated and unequal schools as courts reverse policy. *Educational Administration Quarterly*, 50(5), 718–34. https://doi.org/10.1177/0013161x14548942

Orfield, G., Ee, J., Frankenberg, E., & Siegel-Hawley, G. (2016). *Brown at 62: School segregation by race, poverty and state*. Los Angeles, CA: Civil Rights Project/Proyecto Derechos Civiles, University of California, Los Angeles.

Owens, A. (2016). Inequality in children's contexts: Income segregation of households with and without children. *American Sociological Review*, 81(3), 549–74. https://doi.org/10.1177/0003122416642430

———. (2017). Racial residential segregation of school-age children and adults: The role of schooling as a segregating force. *The Russell Sage Foundation Journal of the Social Sciences*, 3(2), 63–80. https://doi.org/10.7758/RSF.2017.3.2.03

———. (2020). Unequal opportunity: School and neighborhood segregation in the USA. *Race and Social Problems*, 12, 29–41. https://doi.org/10.1007/s12552-019-09274-z

Owens, A., Reardon, S.F., & Jencks, C. (2016). Income segregation between schools and school districts. *American Educational Research Journal*, 53(4), 1159–97. https://doi.org/10.3102/0002831216652722

Parolin, Z., Collyer, S., Curran, M., & Wimer, C. (2021). *The potential poverty reduction effect of the American Rescue Plan: Fact sheet*. Center on Poverty and Social Policy at Columbia University. Available: https://www.povertycenter.columbia.edu/publication/2021/poverty-reduction-analysis-american-rescue-plan

Passel, J.S. (2011). Demography of immigrant youth: Past, present, and future. *Future Child*, 21(1), 19–41. https://doi.org/10.1353/foc.2011.0001

Perreira, K.M., & Pedroza, J.M. (2019). Policies of exclusion: Implications for the health of immigrants and their children. *Annual Review of Public Health*, 40, 147–66. https://doi.org/10.1146/annurev-publhealth-040218-044115

Polednak, A.P. (1991). Black-white differences in infant mortality in 38 standard metropolitan statistical areas. *American Journal of Public Health*, 81(11), 1480–2. https://doi.org/10.2105/ajph.81.11.1480

———. (1993). Poverty, residential segregation, and black/white mortality ratios in urban areas. *Journal of Health Care for the Poor and Underserved*, 4(4), 363–73. https://doi.org/10.1353/hpu.2010.0094

Potter, H. (2017). *Do private school vouchers pose a threat to integration?* The Century Foundation. Available: https://tcf.org/content/report/private-school-vouchers-pose-threat-integration/

Rafferty, Y., Piscitelli, V., & Boettcher, C. (2003). The impact of inclusion on language development and social competence among preschools with disabilities. *Exceptional Children*, 69(4), 467–79. https://doi.org/10.1177/001440290306900405

Ramgopal, S., Attridge, M., Akande, M., Goodman, D.M., Heneghan, J.A., & Macy, M.L. (2022). Distribution of emergency department encounters and subsequent hospital admissions for children by Child Opportunity Index. *Academic Pediatrics*, 22(8), 1468–76. https://doi.org/10.1016/j.acap.2022.06.003

Ready, D.D., & Silander, M.R. (2011). Isolating family, neighborhood, and school influences. *Integrating schools in a changing society: New policies and legal options for a multiracial generation*. Chapel Hill, NC: University of North Carolina Press.

Reardon, S.F. (2015). School segregation and racial academic achievement gaps. (Working Paper No. 15–12). Stanford Center for Education Policy Analysis. Available: https://cepa.stanford.edu/sites/default/files/wp15-12v201510.pdf

———. (2021). Measuring the opportunity gap. Presentation to the Committee on Exploring the Opportunity Gap for Young Children from Birth to Age Eight: Speaker Series #1. Washington, DC: National Academies of Sciences, Engineering, and Medicine.

Reardon, S.F., Grewal, E.T., Kalogrides, D., & Greenberg, E. (2012). Brown fades: The end of court-ordered school desegregation and the resegregation of American public schools. *Journal of Policy Analysis and Management*, 31(4), 876–904. https://doi.org/10.1002/pam.21649

Reardon, S.F., Weathers, E.S., Fahle, E.M., Jang, H., & Kalogrides, D. (2019). Is separate still unequal? New evidence on school segregation and racial academic achievement gaps. (Working Paper No. 19–06). Stanford Center for Education Policy Analysis. Available: http://cepa.stanford.edu/wp19-06

Reid, J.L., Kagan, S.L., Hilton, M., & Potter, H. (2015). *A better start: Why classroom diversity matters in early education*. National Center for Children and Families, Teachers College, Columbia University. Available: http://www.prrac.org/pdf/A_Better_Start.pdf

Richards, M.P. (2014). The gerrymandering of school attendance zones and the segregation of public schools: A geospatial analysis. *American Educational Research Journal*, 51(6), 1119–57. https://doi.org/10.3102/0002831214553652

———. (2017). Gerrymandering educational opportunity. *Phi Delta Kappan*, 99(3), 65–70. https://doi.org/10.1177/0031721717739597

Rothstein, R. (2017). *The color of law: A forgotten history of how our government segregated America*. New York, NY: Liveright Publishing Corporation.

Rothwell, J.T. (2012). *Housing costs, zoning, and access to high-scoring schools*. Washington, DC: Brookings Institution, Metropolitan Policy Program.

Roubinov, D.S., Hagan, M.J., Boyce, W.T., Adler, N.E., & Bush, N.R. (2018). Family socioeconomic status, cortisol, and physical health in early childhood: The role of advantageous neighborhood characteristics. *Psychosomatic Medicine*, 80(5), 492–501. https://doi.org/10.1097/PSY.0000000000000585

Rumberger, R.W., & Tran, L. (2010). State language policies, school language practices and the English learner achievement gap. *Forbidden language: English learners and restrictive language policies*. New York, NY: Teachers College Press.

Santiago, A.M., Galster, G., Lucero, J., Ishler, K., Lee, E.L., Kypriotakis, G., & Stack, L. (2014). *Opportunity neighborhoods for Latino and African American children*. Department of Housing and Urban Development. http://dx.doi.org/10.2139/ssrn.2563141

Saporito, S., & Van Riper, D. (2016). Do irregularly shaped school attendance zones contribute to racial segregation or integration? *Social Currents*, 3(1), 64–83. https://doi.org10.1177/2329496515604637

Sattin-Bajaj, C., & Roda, A. (2020). Opportunity hoarding in school choice contexts: The role of policy design in promoting middle-class parents' exclusionary behaviors. *Educational Policy*, 34(7), 992–1035. https://doi.org/10.1177/0895904818802106

Schulz, A.J., Williams, D.R., Israel, B.A., & Lempert, L.B. (2002). Racial and spatial relations as fundamental determinants of health in Detroit. *The Milbank Quarterly*, 80(4), 677–707. https://doi.org/10.1111/1468-0009.00028

Schwartz, H. (2010). *Housing policy is school policy: Economically integrative housing promotes academic success in Montgomery County, Maryland*. New York, NY: The Century Foundation.

Schweik, S.M. (2009). *The ugly laws: Disability in public*. New York, NY: New York University Press.

Serafini, E.J., Rozell, N., & Winsler, A. (2020). Academic and English language outcomes for DLLS as a function of school bilingual education model: The role of two-way immersion and home language support. *International Journal of Bilingual Education and Bilingualism*, 25(2), 552–70. https://doi.org/10.1080/13670050.2019.1707477

Shanahan, K.H., Subramanian, S.V., Burdick, K.J., Monuteaux, M.C., Lee, L.K., & Fleegler, E.W. (2022). Association of neighborhood conditions and resources for children with life expectancy at birth in the U.S. *JAMA Network Open*, 5(10), e2235912. https://doi.org/10.1001/jamanetworkopen.2022.35912

Sharkey, P.T. (2013). *Stuck in place: Urban neighborhoods and the end of progress toward racial equality*. Chicago, IL: The University of Chicago Press.

Sharkey, P.T., Tirado-Strayer, N., Papachristos, A.V., & Raver, C.C. (2012). The effect of local violence on children's attention and impulse control. *American Journal of Public Health*, 102(12), 2287–93. https://doi.org/10.2105/AJPH.2012.300789

Shonkoff, J.P., Slopen, N., & Williams, D.R. (2021). Early childhood adversity, toxic stress, and the impacts of racism on the foundations of health. *Annual Review of Public Health*, 1(42), 115–34. https://doi.org/10.1146/annurev-publhealth-090419-101940

Slopen, N., Cosgrove, C., Acevedo-Garcia, D., Hatzenbuehler, M.L., Shonkoff, J.P., & Noelke, C. (2023). Neighborhood opportunity and mortality among children and adults in their households. *Pediatrics*, 151(4), e2022058316. https://doi.org/10.1542/peds.2022-058316

Smith, S., Ferguson, D., Burak, E.W., Granja, M.R., & Ortuzar, C. (2020). *Supporting social-emotional and mental health needs of young children through Part C early intervention: Results of a 50-state survey*. National Center for Children in Poverty, Bank Street Graduate School of Education. Available: www.nccp.org/wp-content/uploads/2020/11/Part-C-Report-Final.pdf

Start Early. (n.d.) *Start early and close the opportunity gap*. Available: https://www.startearly.org/campaign/start-early-and-close-the-opportunity-gap/

Surface-Evans, S.L. (2016). A landscape of assimilation and resistance: The Mount Pleasant Indian Industrial Boarding School. *International Journal of Historical Archaeology*, 20(3), 574–88. https://doi.org/10.1007/s10761-016-0362-5

Theall, K.P., Drury, S.S., & Shirtcliff, E.A. (2012). Cumulative neighborhood risk of psychosocial stress and allostatic load in adolescents. *American Journal of Epidemiology*, 176(7 Suppl), S164–74. https://doi.org/10.1093/aje/kws185

Thernstrom, A., & Thernstrom, S. (1998). Black progress: How far we've come, and how far we have to go. Brookings Institution. Available: https://www.brookings.edu/articles/black-progress-how-far-weve-come-and-how-far-we-have-to-go

Troller-Renfree, S.V., Costanzo, M.A., Duncan, G.J., Magnuson, K., Gennetian, L.A., Yoshikawa, H., Halpern-Meekin, S., Fox, N.A., & Noble, K.G. (2022). The impact of a poverty reduction intervention on infant brain activity. *Proceedings of the National Academy of Sciences of the United States of America*, 119(5), e2115649119. https://doi.org/10.1073/pnas.2115649119

Ullrich, R., & Schmit, S. (2019). *Inequitable access to child care subsidies.* Center for Law and Social Policy. Available: https://www.clasp.org/publications/report/brief/inequitable-access-child-care-subsidies

UNICEF. (1990). *Convention on the rights of the child.* Available: https://www.unicef.org/child-rights-convention/convention-text#

Urban Institute. (2022). Data from the Integrated Public Use Microdata Series datasets drawn from the 2005–2020 American Community Survey. Available: https://children-of-immigrants-explorer.urban.org/pages.cfm?p=technicalappendix

U.S. Department of Agriculture. (2022). *WIC eligibility and coverage rates.* Available: https://www.fns.usda.gov/wic/wic-eligibility-and-coverage-rates

Valencia, R.R. (2010). *Chicano school failure and success: Past, present, and future.* (3rd ed.). New York, NY: Routledge.

Vespa, J., Medina, L., & Armstrong, D.M. (2020). *Demographic turning points for the United States: Population projections for 2020 to 2060.* Available: https://www.census.gov/library/publications/2020/demo/p25-1144.html

Vogtman, J. (2017). *Undervalued: A brief history of women's care work and child care policy in the United States.* National Women's Law Center.

Walker, S.P., Wachs, T.D., Grantham-McGregor, S., Black, M.M., Nelson, C.A., Huffman, S.L., Baker-Henningham, H., Chang, S.M., Hamadani, J.D., Lozoff, B., & Gardner, J.M.M. (2011). Inequality in early childhood: Risk and protective factors for early child development. *The Lancet,* 378(9799), 1325–38. https://doi.org/10.1016/S0140-6736(11)60555-2

Walker, V.S. (1996). *Their highest potential: An African American school community in the segregated south.* University of North Carolina Press. Available: http://www.jstor.org/stable/10.5149/9780807866191_walker

Walters, P.B. (2007). Explaining the durable racial divide in American education: Policy development and opportunity hoarding from Brown to vouchers. Paper Presented at Conference on the Social Dimensions of Inequality. Los Angeles, CA: The Russell Sage Foundation and Carnegie Corporation.

Wei, W.S., McCoy, D.C., Busby, A.K., Hanno, E.C., & Sabol, T.J. (2021). Beyond neighborhood socioeconomic status: Exploring the role of neighborhood resources for preschool classroom quality and early childhood development. *American Journal of Community Psychology,* 67(3–4), 470–85. https://doi.org/10.1002/ajcp.12507

Weil, D. (2014). *The fissured workplace: Why work became so bad for so many and what can be done to improve it.* Cambridge, MA: Harvard University Press.

Wells, A.S., Fox, L., & Cordova-Cobo, D. (2016). *How racially diverse schools and classrooms can benefit all students.* The Century Foundation. Available: https://tcf.org/content/report/how-racially-diverse-schools-and-classrooms-can-benefit-all-students/

Williams, D.R., & Collins, C. (2001). Racial residential segregation: A fundamental cause of racial disparities in health. *Public Health Reports,* 116(5), 404–416. https://doi.org/10.1093/phr/116.5.404

Wodtke, G.T., Ard, K., Bullock, C., White, K., & Priem, B. (2022). Concentrated poverty, ambient air pollution, and child cognitive development. *Science Advances,* 8(48), eadd0285. Available: https://www.science.org/doi/10.1126/sciadv.add0285

World Health Organization, United Nations Children's Fund, & World Bank Group. (2018). *Nurturing care for early childhood development: A framework for helping children survive and thrive to transform health and human potential.* Geneva, CH: World Health Organization.

Young, M.E.D.T., Beltrán-Sánchez, H., & Wallace, S.P. (2020). States with fewer criminalizing immigrant policies have smaller health care inequities between citizens and noncitizens. *BMC Public Health,* 20, 1460. https://doi.org/10.1186/s12889-020-09525-4

2

Opportunity Gaps in Early Care and Education Experienced by Children from Birth to Pre-K

Historically, a major focus of education research and policy has been on achievement gaps, with much debate centered around remediation at the child level. Here, the committee takes a markedly different approach to transcend an exclusive focus on outcomes. We argue that a narrow focus on outcomes (e.g., gaps in health or achievement) ignores the critical role of the historical and structural precursors and processes that have preserved or increased such gaps in outcomes over time and across a child's early years. Instead, as discussed in detail in Chapter 1, the committee focused its attention on the opportunity gaps that have resulted in these outcome gaps, and on the historical and structural drivers of these opportunity gaps. In this chapter and Chapter 3, respectively, we review the evidence on those drivers and their effects on the outcomes experienced by young children with respect to early care and education (ECE) and early elementary education. We also examine gaps in access to services designed to benefit young children and their families in general, but further interrogate how even access to such programs is insufficient if the *experiences* children and families have in these programs are unfair, inadequate in quality, or even harmful.

The organizing focus of this chapter is an understanding of gaps in (1) access and (2) quality experiences as they relate to gaps in child outcomes in ECE systems and as shaped by history and perpetuated by policy. We examine the literature on policies that show promise in bridging gaps across these two areas. The evidence reviewed in this chapter serves as the basis for recommendations, presented in Chapter 8, on a targeted universal[1] approach to high-quality ECE systems, aligned with a well-funded, equitable, quality early education system, as well as recommendations on a more inclusive framework for quality programming in ECE and throughout the early grades that is essential to narrow or eliminate disparities in outcomes.

WHY EARLY CARE AND EDUCATION MATTERS

It has been more than 20 years since the publication of *From Neurons to Neighborhoods*, a National Academies study that solidified understanding of the critical role of the early years in brain development and later life outcomes and, equally important, the role of the child's environment in shaping early brain development (Institute of Medicine & National Research Council [IOM & NRC], 2000). This early work helped underscore the need to invest in supporting children during these malleable and influential early years. Decades of research on high-quality preschool and early education programs have shown that children reap from these programs both short-term benefits and long-term benefits that persist through adolescence and into adulthood (IOM & NRC, 2000, 2015).

A number of longitudinal studies initiated in the 1960s and 1970s have demonstrated the long-term promise of high-quality ECE. The Abecedarian program, for example, followed 111 children (98% of whom were Black) through age 21 (Barnett & Masse, 2007; Campbell et al., 2012). The children were randomized shortly after birth, with the intervention group accessing a center-based ECE program 8 hours a day until age 5 years (Ramey, 2018). The Perry Preschool Program followed a sample of 123 Black children from low-income households through age 40 (Schweinhart et al., 2005). This program provided the intervention group with 2 years of half-day high-quality preschool and weekly home visitation. And the Chicago Child–Parent Center study matched intervention children with peers of the same age and similar socioeconomic background, providing center-based half-day preschool for 3- and 4-year-olds in the intervention group, along with health and social services and free meals (Reynolds et al., 2011, 2017; Reynolds, Ou, & Temple, 2018). The study includes approximately 1,400 children, is federally funded, and is routinely implemented in the Chicago Public Schools. The evidence across these three longitudinal studies shows long-term positive outcomes in the areas of school experiences and trajectory, schooling outcomes, adult earnings, health, welfare dependency,

---

[1]Targeted universalism entails setting universal goals for all groups concerned while using processes and strategies that are targeted to the needs of different groups—based on how those groups are situated within various societal contexts (e.g., geography, culture, socioeconomic status)—in order to achieve those goals (powell, Menendian, & Ake, 2019).

risky behaviors, and crime (Campbell et al., 2002, 2012; Schweinhart et al., 2005; Barnett, 2011).

While acknowledging that these rigorously studied programs produce positive child outcomes over the long term, some scholars critique the original program approach (e.g., the terminology used and a deficit approach), the definitions of quality, and the lack of direct attention in program design to the racial experiences of young children (Derman-Sparks & Moore, 2016; Allen et al., 2021; Bruno & Iruka, 2022). Citing programs' goals of increasing the IQ and cognitive development of children from "disadvantaged homes" so they could succeed in general education, for example, Bruno and Iruka (2022) point out that Abecedarian focused on reducing perceived deficits such as "preventing mild mental retardation" rather than building on children's strengths. A strengths-based approach incorporates children's sociocultural context into the program design, such as in staffing, everyday activities, approaches to discipline, and the transition to elementary school. Another critique of the traditional ECE intervention framework is the primary emphasis on changing individual child outcomes without addressing structural barriers that create opportunity and outcome gaps, an emphasis that assumes the structural barriers as a given and forges a compensatory response. Although these compensatory efforts may be admirable, transformation of the structural system to promote equitable opportunity for all children may be much more powerful.

In part because of these epistemological limitations and consistent with recent efforts to address structural racism in such fields as biomedical research (Collins et al., 2021), contemporary scholars point to the need to reexamine these foundational early childhood models with a strengths-based approach using an antiracist lens. This approach entails examining whether measures of ECE outcomes, processes, and practices are relevant to the population participating in the program and addressing such factors as sociocultural history, language, culture, and positive racial identity, while advancing a mixed-methods research design (e.g., particularly in-depth qualitative data collection to understand the nuances of interactions; Bruno & Iruka, 2022). This evaluation approach can better inform policy and practices that support the development of Black children and other children of color (Allen et al., 2021; Bruno & Iruka, 2022).

More recently, research has found long-term benefits with respect to schooling or labor market outcomes for a mix of universal and targeted preschool programs, such as the Abbott preschool program in New Jersey (Jung & Barnett, 2021), the Boston preschool program (Gray-Lobe, Pathak, & Walters, 2021), North Carolina's Smart Start and More at Four (Muschkin, Ladd, & Dodge, 2015; Bai et al., 2020), the Chicago Child–Parent Centers (Reynolds, 2019); Georgia's Preschool Program (Han & Neuharth-Pritchett, 2021), the Tulsa pre-K program (Gormley, 2017; Gormley et al.,

2023), and Head Start (Joshi, Geronimo, & Acevedo-Garcia, 2016; Bailey, Sun, & Timpe, 2021). Positive outcomes have been found for targeted pre-K programs serving mainly children in low-income households, as well as for universal pre-K programs (Bartik, Gormley, & Adelstein, 2012; Cascio & Schanzenbach, 2013; Phillips et al., 2017; Jung & Barnett, 2021; Villareal & Lee, 2022), although the benefits appear to be greater for children from low-income households (Gormley et al., 2005; Barnett, 2011; Weiland & Yoshikawa, 2013; Yoshikawa et al., 2013). The benefits of improvements in child development and subsequent positive outcomes in the labor market are strongly associated with school-related experiences and are the source of most of the economic returns on quality preschool programs (Barnett, 2011; Reynolds, Ou, & Temple, 2018; Cannon et al., 2017; Gormley et al., 2023; Varshney, Temple, & Reynolds, 2022).

Findings from individual studies such as those described here are further supported by meta-analyses. For example, McCoy et al. (2017) reviewed medium- and long-term outcomes of ECE programs between 1960 and 2016 and found participation to be associated on average with significant reductions in grade retention and special education placement, and with increases in high school graduations. Other meta-analyses of preschool programs (Camilli et al., 2010; Duncan & Magnuson, 2013; Kay & Pennucci, 2014; Schindler et al., 2015; Joo et al., 2020) have similarly concluded that they have on average substantial positive effects on child learning and development across a range of developmental domains. In high-quality programs, the magnitude of the impacts appears to decrease as children progress through formal education, but on average, effects persist even at moderate levels, and impacts on children's school experience (e.g., with respect to special education, grade retention, school progress, and behavior) clearly emerge.

A combination of experimental and nonexperimental longitudinal studies of Head Start have found that it has significant impacts on children's school readiness in the short term and is associated with a host of positive benefits in the long term (Joshi, Geronimo, & Acevedo-Garcia, 2016; Meek et al., 2021).

Black and Latino children appear to demonstrate the greatest short-term gains in math and language by the end of their first year in the program; Black children demonstrate the greatest gains in writing, and Latino children demonstrate the greatest gains in applied problem solving (Aikens et al., 2013). Other scholars have found that the program narrows school readiness gaps (Pianta et al., 2009; Bitler, Hoynes, & Domina, 2014). Research has also identified associations between Head Start enrollment and health outcomes, including better overall health, less obesity, increased dental care, and higher likelihood of having health insurance, compared with non–Head Start ECE programs (Alford, 2009; Puma et al., 2010; Lumeng et al., 2015). In addition, positive family and parenting outcomes have been noted in Head Start families, including associations with more positive parenting practices, such as reading to children; decreases in spanking (Zill et al., 2001; Puma et al., 2010); and parental educational attainment and maternal well-being (Parker, Piotrkowski, & Peay, 1987; Sabol & Chase-Lansdale, 2015; Schanzenbach & Bauer, 2016).

In the long term, nonexperimental studies have found that Head Start enrollment is associated with a decreased likelihood of grade retention and a higher likelihood of high school and college graduation and skill certification (Ludwig & Miller, 2007; Schanzenbach & Bauer, 2016). Most recently, using large-scale administrative data from the program's first 15 years of operation, researchers found that Head Start was associated with increases in schooling, high school graduation, and college enrollment and completion (Bailey, Sun, & Timpe, 2021). Finally, a recently published study examining the intergenerational effects of Head Start on child and family outcomes identified several long-term benefits, including decreases in teen parenting and criminal engagement by 8 and 13 percentage points, respectively, and increases in high school graduation and college enrollment by 11 and 18 percentage points, respectively. In the second generation, researchers found reductions in grade repetition and criminal engagement. The researchers quantified these outcomes in terms of increased wages (Barr & Gibbs, 2022). Despite these findings, Head Start has never been fully funded to enroll all eligible children. Moreover, inadequate funding of existing slots, paired with wide-scale implementation, has contributed to varying quality (Joshi, Geronimo, & Acevedo-Garcia, 2016).

Despite the extensive evidence of the benefits of ECE reviewed by the committee, some research has shown that ECE does not always translate to long-term outcomes. Multiple reviews of pre-K evaluations have concluded that when children enroll in high-quality programs, they consistently outperform their peers without such experience in early language, math, and social-emotional skills at the end of the pre-K year and during the kindergarten year. However, the evidence that this advantage is sustained in the long term is mixed (Yoshikawa et al., 2013; Phillips et al., 2017; Meloy, Gardner, & Darling-Hammond, 2019). Specifically, longitudinal studies of Head Start (Puma et al., 2010, 2012) and the Tennessee Voluntary Pre-Kindergarten (TN-VPK) program (Lipsey et al., 2018; Durkin et al., 2022), which used random assignment to create treatment and control groups, found that children in these programs made significant gains initially, but by as early as first grade, their peers in the control group had caught up in their cognitive and social-emotional development. In the Head Start study, however, certain subgroups, such as dual language learners, children with disabilities, and children from "high-risk households," sustained gains made during the preschool year through first and third grade (Puma et al., 2010, 2012).

Evaluators of these programs and studies point to a few explanations that can guide the implementation of ECE in the future. First, the quality of the curriculum, teaching and learning training and supports, and the ability of teachers to engage in high-quality interactions and developmentally appropriate activities are key (Yoshikawa et al., 2013; Phillips et al., 2017; Meloy, Gardner, & Darling-Hammond, 2019). In a study in Tennessee in 2009–2011, for example, 85% of classrooms scored below "good" on a classroom observation measure (Farran et al., 2014). And evaluators of the TN-VPK study (Durkin et al., 2022) point out that findings stem partly from focusing strongly on "constrained" skills (e.g., names or sounds of letters) and less so on "unconstrained" skills (e.g., vocabulary, comprehension). In particular, they propose that greater focus on executive function skills could yield larger gains during the pre-K year and make those gains last longer. The focus on measuring such "constrained" skills in the Head Start Impact Study might also explain why even though the early gains in such measures appear to dissipate, other studies, such as those discussed earlier, have found significant impacts into adulthood and intergenerationally (Durkin et al., 2022).

Some research has sought to understand the mechanisms that contribute to long-term adult outcomes (Ramey & Ramey, 2019). Categorizing the evidence in relation to pathways that contribute to adult effects, various authors (Reynolds et al., 2011, 2017; Reynolds & Temple, 2019) have found that stimulating educational experiences in ECE direct children into positive scholastic development and attitudes toward school (and related transitions through school) that continue into adolescence and adulthood. This finding takes into account all outcomes—not just cognitive measures but also other markers, such as progression, attention, engagement, and motivation. Also included in this work is a family support hypothesis whereby ECE programs enhance family functioning and parenting practices, which in turn increases children's learning time, content learning, and access to learning materials, and has the indirect effect of enhancing motivation and attitudes toward learning (Reynolds et al., 2017; McCormick et al., 2020). Both of these pathways have featured prominently in the previously discussed landmark studies, and it is important to note that, particularly in Head Start, family engagement and wellness are a core part of the model.

This same research on pathways also includes a school quality hypothesis according to which sustained effects are related to whether subsequent schooling experiences are of sufficient quality, explaining why in some cases, children who did not attend pre-K programs appear to converge with their pre-K peers (Yoshikawa et al., 2013; Meloy, Gardner, & Darling-Hammond, 2019; Reynolds & Temple, 2019). Some evidence appears to align with this hypothesis, with several studies showing that children's pre-K gains persist only when they attend higher-quality elementary programs

(Bailey et al., 2017; Phillips et al., 2017; Carr et al., 2021). Some of the same researchers that conducted the TN-VPK study performed a subsequent analysis and found that pre-K students who later enrolled in high-quality elementary schools, as indicated by teacher and school ratings, maintained their advantage over non-VPK participants through third grade (Pearman et al., 2020). Similarly, Reynolds et al. (2017) show that enrollment in higher-quality schools for children in the Chicago Child–Parent Center program mediates the association between preschool participation and school achievement and attainment. And research on Head Start found that children who attended Head Start followed by a well-funded elementary school outperformed both their peers who attended a less well-resourced elementary school and those who did not attend Head Start at all (Johnson & Jackson, 2019).

Collectively, this research base—including longitudinal randomized controlled trials; program evaluations; meta-analyses; and nonexperimental longitudinal studies—sheds light on the potential effects of ECE on children's long-term trajectories. It also underlines, however, how differences in children's access to high-quality ECE programs and disparate experiences within programs can be major contributors to the opportunity gaps that lead to deficits in later development and achievement. Indeed, despite the well-documented and robust benefits of high-quality ECE, access to these programs has consistently been less attainable for children from such communities. Many children who do have access, particularly those from historically marginalized communities, have markedly different and lower-quality experiences compared with their White, higher-income, native English-speaking peers. Herein lies a paradox in the history of the United States: a commitment to the value of opportunity and mobility through education while systems that reproduce educational inequalities on the basis of race, gender, socioeconomic status, and language background are perpetuated. Eliminating inequities in basic access to and experiences in ECE programs, then, is one critical and basic step toward addressing the opportunity and outcome gaps experienced by some groups of young children (IOM & NRC, 2000; National Academies, 2018, 2019a,b,c).

While opportunity gaps exist in both the ECE system and the early elementary grades, the ways in which these gaps manifest in each of these two systems differ in important ways. In the United States, compulsory public education—beginning between ages 5 and 8, depending on the state—is a right to which all children are entitled and a public good whose cost is borne by federal, state, and local governments. Because it is a right embedded in state constitutions and in federal law, the public has legal recourse if faced with inequitable access to a quality education. By contrast, such rights for children and families in the pre-K years are established in neither state constitutions (with very limited exceptions) nor federal law, with the exception of children with disabilities, who have a right to preschool services under the Individuals with Disabilities Education Act (IDEA) Part B 619, although those services often fall short of the need in both quality and quantity (Rebell et al., 2017; Friedman-Krauss et al., 2021). The absence of a legal obligation for the states or the federal government to provide ECE means that unequal access to *any* early learning experiences is the de facto policy in the United States—an inequity that is felt most by children from marginalized populations.

This situation may be changing. The federal government has enacted relevant precedents that could pave a path forward toward a right to access ECE services. The Elementary and Secondary Education Act permits the use of funds for early childhood programs in those schools in which 40% or more of children come from low-income families or are dual language learners above age 3; IDEA Part B explicitly defines its age target as 3 through 21; and federal law also requires access to locally or state-administered preschool for children experiencing homelessness (Rebell et al., 2017). And in some states, courts have considered access to preschool for low-income children through litigation (Rebell et al., 2017).

CURRENT POLICY, FUNDING, AND SYSTEMS

The disparate histories of ECE programs in the United States—such as Head Start and state-funded pre-K, and child care—and the policy goals they were designed to address, as described in Chapter 1, have resulted in the lack of a coherent, intentional approach to ECE. The potential for ECE to address opportunity gaps head on is limited by the fact that its history does not "reflect a consistent philosophy or aim to achieve a unified set of objectives" for young children and families (Vogtman, 2017, p. 11). It is as if Head Start, pre-K, and child care were ill-fitting pieces from different jigsaw puzzles placed on the same board. As a result, children and families are falling through the cracks. Not only do ECE policies lack coherence, but their connection to child development has been tenuous. As stated in a recent National Academies report, "the various goals of ECE policy... were not always based on, nor consistent with, the developmental needs of all children as we understand them today" (National Academies, 2018, p. 45). Finally, because state and federal policy makers have failed to make such programs broadly available—even for eligible children and families—children from families with low incomes or from historically marginalized communities experience significant gaps in ECE opportunities compared with their peers from families not constrained by financial resources, racial discrimination, linguistic barriers, and/or barriers related to their immigrant status (National Women's Law Center, 2016; Phillips et al., 2017; Corcoran

& Steinley, 2019; Babbs Hollett & Frankenberg, 2022). In short, children from historically marginalized communities have less access to high-quality ECE programs and have lower-quality experiences in these programs, deficits that result in disparities in both opportunities and outcomes that have compounded over time. These disparities have been shaped in part by societal attitudes toward safety net spending and aid for people living in poverty, attitudes that in turn are entangled with racial and class bias, as well as the belief that hard work, talent, and effort allow all individuals to have an equal opportunity to succeed (DeParle, 2021). This belief is countered, however, by the previously summarized research evidence showing that strengthening of safety net supports (e.g., income supplements) is associated with later average higher earnings, better health, and reduced criminal arrests (National Academies, 2019c).

Head Start and state pre-K programs are designed to advance specific early learning and development goals, as reflected in the Head Start Early Learning Outcomes Framework and states' early learning standards, respectively. Child care programs funded by the Child Care and Development Block Grant (CCDBG) were originally developed to support parents' participation in the workforce and had little focus on child development and school readiness. These programs are required to adhere to minimal federal standards embedded in the law and relevant state rules and policies. And although CCDBG's program standards related to early learning remain significantly less rigorous than those of Head Start and public pre-K programs, the program's most recent reauthorization, in 2014, made some progress toward supporting child development, including the requirement to "develop, maintain, or implement early learning and developmental guidelines for statewide use by child care providers.... In addition, they must be incorporated into other parts of the child care system and align vertically and horizontally with the standards for other sectors (such as prekindergarten, Head Start, and Early Head Start)" (Administration for Children and Families, 2022, paras. 1–2).

The differences in intent among these three types of ECE programs lead to differences in policy, and ultimately in quality and children's experiences. Compared with child care programs, Head Start and state pre-K programs tend to have higher standards and compensation for lead teachers, more rigorous education program standards, and more access to public funding, although it is important to note that because state pre-K standards and investment amounts vary across states, quality and access vary accordingly, with some states having very poorly funded systems. Head Start also provides services—such as health screenings, mental health and dental health supports, and family engagement and leadership programs—that target the comprehensive needs of children and families from low-income households. The Head Start Program Performance Standards include provisions on such topics as teaching and the learning environment, curricula, screening and assessment, oral health practices, nutrition, mental health and social-emotional well-being, and family engagement. In addition, the standards address practice for specific populations, including tribal communities, dual language learners, children with disabilities, and pregnant women (Head Start Early Childhood Learning and Knowledge Center, 2022). Table 2-1 presents a comparison of the three major types of ECE programs discussed above, along with programs covered by IDEA Part C and IDEA Part B Section 619, along key dimensions.

In addition, Head Start and state pre-K programs receive funding from the federal or state government in the form of grants. They typically receive the funds in advance of implementing the programs and retain the funds as long as they adhere to standards mentioned previously and serve the number of children supported by the grant. It is important to note, however, that funding for pre-K and in some cases for Head Start often is based not on a systematic analysis of the cost of implementing a high-quality program, especially one that provides compensation and benefits commensurate with the staff's experience, training, and education and with those provided at the K–12 levels (Belfield & Schwartz, 2007; Barnett & Kasmin, 2018; Friedman-Krauss et al., 2021; Karoly et al., 2021; Kilander, Garver, & Barnett, 2022).

Programs funded by the Child Care and Development Fund (CCDF) receive funds as reimbursements (after services have been rendered) on a per child basis—and typically only if the child attends the program. Absences result in less funding. The federal government recommends that states set subsidy rates at the 75th percentile of the market rate, which is based on what the community is able to pay, not what it actually costs to provide quality care. This policy inherently creates an inequitable situation in which programs that serve communities with greater poverty receive lower subsidy payments. Even in this inequitable context, very few states actually meet this minimal standard (National Women's Law Center, 2016). Under this funding model, child care programs that are not part of the Head Start or state pre-K system rely on revenue streams that are much less stable and robust, which impacts the extent to which these programs can support and sustain quality services, including professional development and retention strategies for their staff. Moreover, this funding model ignores structural factors that can mediate program participation (e.g., access to transportation infrastructure, cost of transportation, flexibility of parents' work schedules), and funding is not based on assessment of the cost of delivering quality services. It should be noted that direct contracts to providers are allowable under CCDBG, but states rarely make use of this mechanism and operate largely with the subsidy and reimbursement system (Office of Child Care, 2022). In states that do make use of contracts, there is some

TABLE 2-1 Comparison of Child Care, Head Start, and State Pre-K Programs and Programs Covered by the Individuals with Disabilities Education Act (IDEA) Part C and Part B Section 619

Dimension	Child Care	Head Start and Early Head Start	State Pre-K	IDEA Part C	IDEA Part B Section 619
Goals for Children	State-defined early learning standards	Head Start Early Learning Outcomes Framework	State-defined early learning standards	Individual Family Service Plans	Individual Education Plans
Program Standards	Licensing standards, mainly for health and safety	Head Start Program Performance Standards	Varies by state (see National Institute for Early Education Research Yearbook)	Early intervention services for children with identified or suspected disabilities under age 3; standards in line with IDEA law and regulations	Preschool services for children with identified or suspected disabilities; standards in line with IDEA law and regulations, including access to a free and appropriate public education in the least restrictive environment possible
Funding per Child	Federal guidance suggests states provide subsidies at the 75th percentile of the current market rate, although only one state meets that standard[a]	$8,800 for preschool-aged children, $12,800 for infants and toddlers	Varies by state; per child spending ranges from $527 in North Dakota to $18,421 in Washington, DC[b]	Federal funds are allocated to states to support early intervention services for infants and toddlers; grants to states range from about $3 million in states with smaller populations to nearly $80 million in California	Federal funds are allocated to states to support special education and related services for preschoolers with disabilities; state grants range from less than $500,000 in Washington, DC, to more than $60 million in California

(continued)

Dimension	Child Care	Head Start and Early Head Start	State Pre-K	IDEA Part C	IDEA Part B Section 619
Copayment Requirements	Yes	No	No, although some state pre-K programs allow for tuition based on a sliding-fee scale, mainly for families above the income eligibility level		
Teacher Qualifications	Varies by state, but generally minimal education requirements beyond high school	BA in early childhood education for at least half of lead educators; currently, about 73% of Head Start teachers meet this standard	Varies by state; most programs require BA with specialization in early childhood education	Varies by type of service provided	Varies by type of service provided
Teacher Compensation[c]	$10.60 (median wage of all center-based ECE teachers)	$14.80 (median wage for Head Start teachers with BA or higher)	$15.00 (median wage for publicly funded pre-K teachers with BA or higher)	Varies by type of service provider	Varies by type of service provider

| Eligibility | Parents who are employed, in school, or in job training programs whose family income falls under 85% of state median income can be eligible for Child Care Development Block Grant Act subsidies; however, states have broad discretion to set more restrictive income eligibility levels[d] | 3- and 4-year-olds who live under the federal poverty level are eligible for Head Start, although programs are allowed to reserve 10% of their enrollment for children above that income level; the program also has categorical eligibility for children experiencing homelessness, children involved in the child welfare system, and children with disabilities | Varies by state; restricted mainly to children in low-income households, although many states take other family or child factors into consideration, such as disabilities, abuse and neglect, homelessness, linguistic background, military duty, low birthweight, substance abuse, or teen parent | State-determined, including infants and toddlers with developmental delays or diagnosed with disabilities that are likely to result in developmental delays | Children aged 3–5 with developmental disabilities or delays |

SOURCE: [a]Schulman, 2021; [b]Friedman-Krauss et al., 2021; [c]National Survey of Early Care and Education Project Team, 2013; [d]Ullrich, Schmit, & Cosse, 2019.

evidence that providers are more likely to be located in lower-income areas, which can increase ECE access in underserved communities and decrease opportunity gaps (Giapponi Schneider, Joshi, & Ha, 2021). Greater use of direct contracts has the potential to give the system more stability and, depending on the assumptions included in the calculation of those contract amounts, to increase quality. However, in order for child care providers to participate, they need to have the administrative capacity, through family child care systems or affiliation with larger social service organizations, to handle the contracting process (Giapponi Schneider et al., 2017).

One promising program that has bridged the differences between child care and Early Head Start, in particular, is the Early Head Start–Child Care Partnerships model. First launched in 2014, this model provides funding through the Head Start system to forge partnerships with licensed child care providers who agree to meet rigorous Head Start standards for infants and toddlers. The model relies on layering child care subsidy funding with Early Head Start funding to enable programs to meet the Head Start Program Performance Standards. Beyond direct effects on eligible children served, the model has spillover effects that benefit all the children in a program (e.g., through more highly trained teachers, safer playground equipment, or a new curriculum). Although some programs have reported that the model poses implementation challenges, it has ultimately resulted in a greater number of infants and toddlers being served in high-quality care (Bipartisan Policy Center, 2019; Bucher et al., 2022; Cardona et al., 2022).

As concluded in a National Academies report on financing in ECE (National Academies, 2018, p. 195):

> *Only a small share of children currently have access to such high-quality programs because the cost of providing access to affordable, high-quality early care and education for all children far exceeds current funding amounts. The majority of children in families choosing to use early care and education (ECE) services are in low- or mediocre-quality programs that do not have the resources necessary to support the emergence of the developmental and economic benefits that are possible [and]...a substantial number of children...are unable to use any early care and education because of a lack of either available ECE services or family resources to pay for placement in the available settings.*

ACCESS TO EARLY CARE AND EDUCATION SYSTEMS

Although the numerous short- and long-term benefits of participation in high-quality ECE (e.g., increased kindergarten readiness, lower referral rates to special education, higher rates of achievement in later grades) have been demonstrated in existing research, children of color are less likely than their White peers to attend or have access to high-quality ECE programs across a wide range of settings (Phillips et al., 2017; Babbs Hollett & Frankenberg, 2022; see Appendix B for detailed data on participation in nonparental care arrangements by child and family characteristics). To understand opportunity gaps in the context of ECE systems, it is critical to assess two key dimensions of systemic and programmatic functioning: (1) equitable access to services and resources (considered in this section), which is especially relevant in nonuniversal systems such as ECE; and (2) the quality of the experiences of children and families in the early childhood years. Currently, research suggests that gaps across these dimensions are associated with income, race, language background, geography, funding streams, and other factors, leading to significant differences in children's lifelong development and their success in the education system (Babbs, Hollett, & Frankenberg, 2022). Here, we review the literature on opportunity gaps in access to ECE programs that contribute to disparities in outcomes among groups of children.

In the absence of large-scale and systematic public investment in ECE in the United States, most families that need or wish to enroll their children in some kind of program must find and pay for the program on their own. In 2016, about 51% of families reported having difficulty finding programs or not finding a program at all (Corcoran & Steinley, 2019). These rates were higher for Black (53%), Hispanic (54%), and Asian American (57%) families and for families earning 100–200% of the federal poverty threshold (54%). Among White families, 47% reported difficulty finding programs or not finding a program at all. The rates were highest for non-English-speaking families (61%). In fact, in 2019, among parents reporting any difficulty in finding an ECE program, a lack of open slots and cost were cited as the main reasons by 27% and 37%, respectively, indicating that these two issues are central to access barriers faced by children and families (National Center for Education Statistics [NCES], 2017; Cui & Natzke, 2020).

Families' decisions about whether and where to enroll their children in ECE programs are based on individual preferences, demographic characteristics, family economic resources and employment schedules, and the supply of available local providers. While existing research on these decisions reveals differences both within and among different types of families, it also suggests that these decisions are associated with children's characteristics, parents' work arrangements, parents' income and education levels, race and ethnicity, place of residence, immigration background, and number of child care centers available within communities (Chaudry et al., 2011; Forry et al., 2013; Miller, Votruba-Drzal, & Coley, 2013; Coley et al., 2014; Crosnoe et al., 2016; Ackert et al., 2018; National Academies, 2018; Shuey & Leventhal, 2018). And since different types of ECE programs are shaped by different goals, standards, and funding levels, understanding these decision patterns can shed light on the opportunity gaps experienced by children from different demographic backgrounds.

At the same time, it is important to note that while this research, summarized in the section that follows, reviews how families answered a survey on child care decisions, it does not necessarily capture the range of choices families actually had or their true preferences if they had had more choices. Families in low-resourced communities or with low incomes likely have fewer choices than their wealthier peers in affluent communities. Thus their choices may be reflective of care they can afford that is available to them when they need it in order to work, as opposed to the choices they would make if these contextual variables were not a factor. Recent qualitative research suggests that parents, particularly in families with low incomes, make a range of trade-offs in child care arrangements as a result of affordability and availability constraints that can lead to compromising (accepting suboptimal choices) or sacrificing (accepting choices that conflict with needs or preferences) on child care (Savage & Robeson, 2020). With this caveat in mind, the research on family child care decisions based on survey data can be summarized as follows:

- While most families believe in the importance of quality, those with higher incomes and more education and those in which parents do not work full-time are better able to prioritize quality over such considerations as cost and location in their decision-making process (Forry et al., 2013).
- Families with more income and education, including immigrant families, are also more likely to choose center-based programs (Greenberg, 2011; Miller, Votruba-Drzal, & Coley, 2013; Coley et al., 2014).
- Parents who work outside the home tend to choose home-based over center-based care (Miller, Votruba-Drzal, & Coley, 2013; Coley et al., 2014; Ackert et al., 2018).
- Coley and colleagues (2014) found that families who prioritize providers with more training and greater English proficiency tend to enroll their children in center-based programs, while those who prioritize accessibility tend to choose home-based programs. Among immigrant families, a preference for "cultural similarity" was found to be most predictive of choosing a home-based program over other settings (Coley et al., 2014, p. 1351).
- Parents of infants and toddlers and those with unpredictable or nonstandard work hours are more likely to choose a home-based ECE arrangement, while parents of preschool-aged children are

more likely to choose a center-based program (Miller, Votruba-Drzal, & Coley, 2013; Coley et al., 2014).
- Parents of children with disabilities are more likely to choose home-based ECE settings (Forry et al., 2013).
- African American families are more likely to choose center- or home-based ECE programs (i.e., nonparental care) for their children compared with families of other races and ethnicities (Coley et al., 2014).
- Hispanic and Asian American families—both native and immigrant—tend to choose either home-based or parental care over center-based programs (Coley et al., 2014).
- Rural families tend to choose home-based programs over center-based or parental care (Coley et al., 2014).

As these findings indicate, parents have valid reasons for choosing certain types of ECE programs that may not possess the traditional markers of "quality." Some do so because these settings are more culturally and linguistically responsive or can provide more individualized attention to infants or children with disabilities, or can provide care when parents need it most. The findings also show why it is important to understand the differences and disparities in funding, standards, and policies among the major ECE program types discussed in this chapter. If certain types of families tend to choose certain types of ECE arrangements that enjoy more or less support for quality, the disparate policies across ECE funding streams and settings could exacerbate opportunity gaps during the early years. Importantly, instead of steering families toward one type of ECE arrangement, one example of an effective policy response would be to ensure that all publicly funded ECE programs receive the necessary and equitable support needed to provide high-quality programming.

Disparities in Access

Disparities in access to quality ECE programs relate to income, race/ethnicity, age group, and geographic region.

Disparities by Income

In 2019, about 62% of children under the age of 6 were enrolled in center-based care, with differences in enrollment by income (Cui & Natzke, 2021). For children in types of care other than parental, those in families whose income was classified at or above 200% of the federal poverty threshold[2] were more likely to be enrolled in center-based care (62.8%) than were children from families with incomes classified as either near poor or poor (51.7% and 58.7%, respectively; NCES, 2021). The lower enrollment for children under 200% of the poverty threshold is explained by public financing policies that make ECE programs inaccessible for families that fall just above eligibility thresholds for public subsidies or publicly funded programs (National Academies, 2018). Indeed, families at 100–200% of the poverty threshold report cost to be a central concern (NCES, 2018). While those with incomes below the federal poverty level generally participate without having to pay, expenses for those that do pay may amount to about 20% of their income, a greater proportion than what is paid by higher-income households (National Academies, 2018, Table 2-1). In addition, a 2017 study found that the cost of child care pushes about one-third of low-income families that pay for child care and have at least one child under age 6 into poverty. This was more likely to occur in families with three or more children, those with a head of household with less than a high school diploma, those with a head of household who did not work full-time, those with a single-parent head of household, and those with a Black or Hispanic head of household (Mattingly & Wimer, 2017).

Enrollment rates are less than desirable even for children in families living under 100% of the poverty threshold because while they qualify for subsidized programs, such programs are largely underfunded. In fact, as noted previously in this report, none of the major publicly funded ECE programs have enough funding to serve all eligible children. Only about 17% of families that meet states' eligibility criteria receive a child care subsidy funded by CCDF (Chien, 2022), while Head Start serves fewer than half of all eligible children, and an even smaller percentage of eligible children in more ethnically/racially diverse states (Schmit & Walker, 2016; Friedman-Krauss et al., 2022). Specific communities are even more underserved. For example, only 6% of low-income children with immigrant mothers receive subsidies (Johnson et al., 2014). Analyses of longitudinal cohorts in relation to participation show that, despite increases in total enrollment, socioeconomic gaps in access to ECE actually grew between 1998 and 2010 (Bassok et al., 2016a): in 2010, families with low incomes were less likely to enroll

---

[2]"Poor" is defined in these data as having family income below the Census Bureau's poverty threshold in the year prior to data collection; near-poor children are those whose family incomes ranged from the poverty threshold to 199% of the poverty threshold; and nonpoor children are those whose family incomes were at or above 200% of the poverty threshold. The poverty threshold is a dollar amount that varies depending on a family's size and composition and is updated annually to account for inflation. In 2015, for example, the poverty threshold for a family of four with two children was $24,257. Survey respondents are asked to select the range within which their income falls, rather than giving the exact amount of their income; therefore, the measure of poverty status is an approximation.

their children in publicly funded ECE (child care, pre-K, Head Start) in the year prior to kindergarten than they were in 1998.

Disparities by Race and Ethnicity

ECE enrollment rates also differ by race and ethnicity. Estimates of access to high-quality preschool for 4-year-olds show that access is lower for Hispanic children and starkly lower for Hispanic dual language learners relative to their White peers (Nores, Krauss, & Frede, 2018). One-third of low-income Hispanic children are enrolled in ECE settings, compared with half of low-income White children and two-thirds of low-income Black children (Mendez, Crosby, & Siskind, 2018; Nores, Krauss, & Frede, 2018). Research also shows that Hispanic and Asian children are less likely than Black children to have access to Head Start programs in their immediate neighborhood or to receive state-level child care subsidies (Schmit & Walker, 2016; Ullrich, Schmit, & Cosse, 2019; Hardy & Huber, 2020). As a consequence, Black and Hispanic children (together with children with a single parent or no mother in the household and children in households with incomes at 100–200% of the federal poverty threshold) are heavily dependent on care provided by relatives (NCES, 2017). High prices for full-time center-based care, coupled with lower earnings and family incomes, make center-based care more unaffordable for low-income Black and Hispanic parents working full-time year-round (Baldiga et al., 2018; Joshi et al., 2022). Thus, affordability will continue to be a barrier to enrolling children in ECE centers if the high price of child care is not addressed, leading to inequities in ECE access for low-income Black and Hispanic families.

Disparities by Age Group

Enrollment in ECE among children aged 3–5 has increased since the 1970s, although this growth has slowed in the last couple of decades (Cascio, 2017). In 2016, seven in 10 children aged 3–5 were enrolled in center-based care or received care from relatives or nonrelatives (NCES, 2018), with about eight million of these children, or close to 60%, being enrolled in center-based care (NCES, 2017). In 2021, a large portion of the latter children (36% of 4-year-olds and 12% of 3-year-olds) were enrolled in state preschool programs or Head Start, down from 44% and 17%, respectively, in 2020 (Friedman-Krauss et al., 2021, 2022; Figure 2-1).

For children under age 3, enrollment rates are lower than is the case for children aged 3–5. Lack of slots for this age group is reported as a significant issue by families, especially those with children under age 1 year (NCES, 2019). In 2016, only 13% of children under age 1 year and 25% of children under age 2 years were enrolled in center-based care (NCES, 2017),

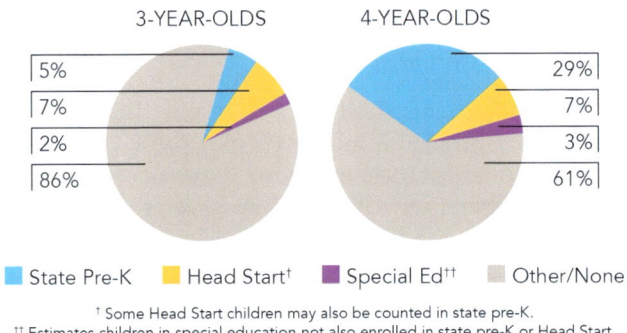

FIGURE 2-1 Percent of children aged 3–4 enrolled in early care and education, 2020.
SOURCE: Friedman-Krauss et al., 2022.

although children in this age group are more likely than older children to be enrolled in home-based programs. Fewer than one in four children in this age group were enrolled in publicly funded programs (Datta & Borton, 2020). Early Head Start and early intervention programs (discussed below) are arguably the only publicly funded programs designed to advance the early development of the youngest children (National Academies, 2018), and Early Head Start serves only 3% of eligible children (National Academies, 2018). The four states serving the highest percentage of children in Early Head Start—only 6–7% in families under 200% of the federal poverty threshold—are Arkansas, Mississippi, New Mexico, and Vermont (Friedman-Krauss et al., 2021).

Disparities by Geographic Region

Stark differences in ECE enrollment exist by state. In the 2020–2021 school year, the number of children served by Head Start represented 30% of 3- to 5-year-olds living in poverty, and this percentage varies greatly across states, most of which serve fewer than 25% of these children (Figure 2-2). On the high end, North Dakota served about 56% of these children, and on the low end, Nevada served fewer than 10% (Figure 2-2; Friedman-Krauss et al., 2022). Similar variation exists for state pre-K programs, with the District of Columbia serving 84% of its 4-year-olds and 73% of its 3-year-olds, while the respective percentages for Arizona are 3% and 2% (Friedman-Krauss et al., 2021).

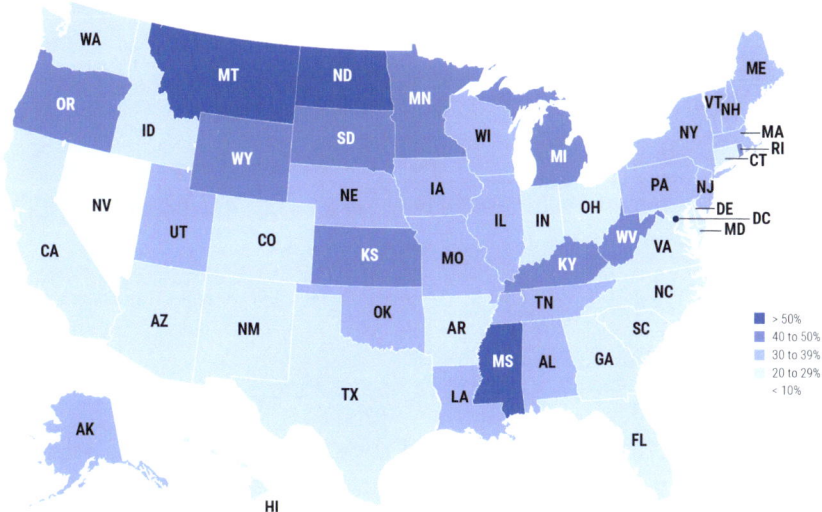

FIGURE 2-2 Percentage of low-income children served by Head Start, by state.
SOURCE: Friedman-Krauss et al., 2022.

The COVID-19 pandemic negatively impacted Head Start and Early Head Start enrollment in all 50 states, the District of Columbia, and the U.S. territories. During the 2020–2021 program year, 287,000 fewer children were enrolled in Head Start, Early Head Start, American Indian/Alaska Native Head Start programs, and Migrant and Seasonal Head Start programs. These enrollment rates represent a 33% decline in Head Start enrollment and a 10% decline for Early Head Start between 2018–2019 and 2020–2021. Enrollments began to increase again during the 2021–2022 program year but have not returned to prepandemic levels (Friedman-Krauss et al., 2022).

In 2020–2021, state preschool programs enrolled a total of 1.36 million children, including about 1.15 million 4-year-olds. These figures represented a decline to enrollment rates similar to those last seen in 2011 and a decline in coverage for the first time in 20 years (Figure 2-3). In 2021, all state pre-K programs collectively served 29% of all 4-year-olds and 5% of all 3-year-olds (Friedman-Krauss et al., 2022). As of this writing, six states still provide no preschool program at all, and 18 states serve no 3-year-olds. Only seven states serve more than 50% of their 4-year-olds, and only six serve more than 70%. In a few states, access is nearly universal; however, adequate duration and quality are not always present in these programs (Friedman-Krauss et al., 2022).

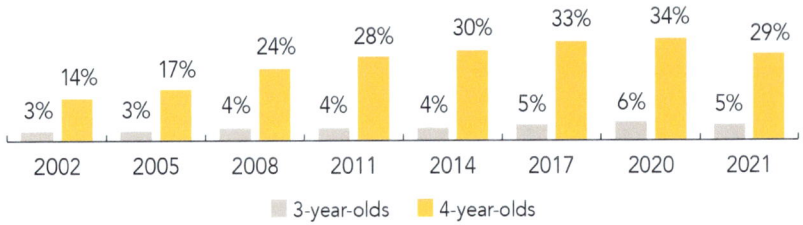

FIGURE 2-3 Percentage of U.S. 3- and 4-year-olds enrolled in state-funded preschool.
SOURCE: Friedman-Krauss et al., 2022.

The lack of available preschool slots, while predominant across the country, also varies by community and region (National Academies, 2018, p. 120). Analyses of the locations of licensed center- and home-based care across geographic U.S. regions have shown that more than half of families live in communities where the number of children exceeds the supply of preschool slots, and this gap is more pronounced for low-income families and those who live in rural communities (Malik et al., 2018). In fact, 60% of rural communities lack an adequate supply of child care. The prevalence of so-called child care deserts varies significantly across states, from fewer than 23% of neighborhoods in Maine to more than 75% in Utah. In addition, nearly 60% of Hispanic and Latino children reside in communities with an inadequate (or no) supply of licensed child care providers.

Growing evidence reveals the existence not only of child care deserts but also of subsidized child care deserts—there is shortage of subsidized child care slots in neighborhoods where eligible children live. In some cases, extreme deserts (e.g., shortages of subsidized child care slots in children's immediate and surrounding neighborhoods) affect large numbers of subsidy-eligible children (Hardy et al., 2018). One study found that, as a result of high levels of racial/ethnic segregation of children within and across contiguous neighborhoods (see Chapter 1), Black and Hispanic children were four to five times more likely to live in extreme subsidy deserts (Hardy et al., 2018). Targeting CCDBG funds to these extreme subsidized deserts that have high unmet need for subsidized care and a large gap in access to subsidies due to racial residential segregation represents a targeted universalism approach that can reduce racial/ethnic inequities in ECE access.

Gaps in ECE Capacity

Recent analyses suggest that more than 5 million more preschool seats are currently needed to attain universal pre-K (Friedman-Krauss et al., 2022; Figure 2-4). A recent national survey found that 81% of parents would likely use a free, universal pre-K program if it became available. Black and Hispanic parents reported a greater likelihood of participating, as did parents with annual incomes below $25,000 (Jung & Barnett, 2021).

Cost as a Barrier to Access

Cost is a central barrier to access to ECE. As of 2019, the estimated average cost of full-time, full-year ECE was $16,500 per child (Cascio, 2021). In 30 states plus the District of Columbia, the average yearly cost for an infant in full-time center-based care is more than the average cost of 1 year (tuition and fees) at a 4-year public university (National Academies, 2018). Families pay about 52% of the total cost of ECE in the United States, making it the only education level for which parents shoulder most of the

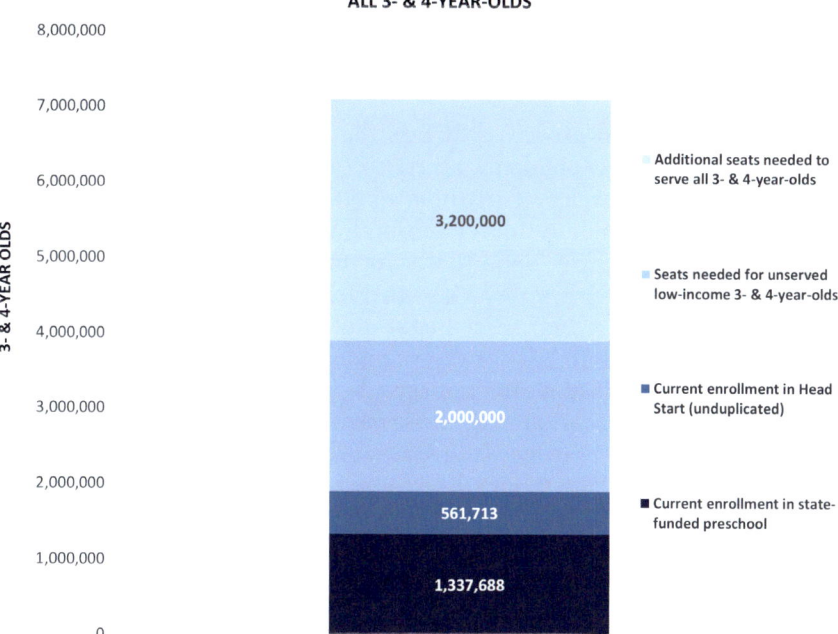

FIGURE 2-4 Current enrollment in Head Start and state-funded preschool and the number of additional slots needed for universal pre-K.
SOURCE: Friedman-Krauss et al., 2022.

financial burden. Moreover, the burden is not proportionally distributed: families with incomes at or below the federal poverty threshold spend about 20% of their income on ECE services, while those earning five times that amount spend about 6% (National Academies, 2018). (The Department of Health and Human Services [HHS] sets 7% of income as the threshold for affordable child care.)

The cost burden is even steeper for low-income Hispanic (immigrant and nonimmigrant households) and Black non-Hispanic families (Figure 2-5). Among Hispanic families that incur child care costs, 25% pay 7% or less of their household income for child care, while the rest spend on average nearly one-third of their income (Crosby, Mendez, & Barnes, 2019). If working parents had to pay out of pocket for full-time center-based care, based on market prices in their state, 63% would have to spend more than 7% of their household income, and this percentage is higher for Black (69%) and Hispanic (72%) parents (Baldiga et al., 2018). Hispanic families rely heavily on unpaid care from a home-based provider, which may stem from the high price of center-based care. In sum, enrollment rates, cost rates, and difficulties reported by families suggest that many low- and middle-income families are unable to afford center-based child care services without public supports.

Access to Early Intervention and Early Special Education for Children with Disabilities

Another critical aspect of ECE is the identification of children with disabilities and these children's access to early intervention and preschool special education services. Early intervention has been shown to have positive impacts on children's developmental and school trajectories (Snyder, 2021), making it a key opportunity for children with disabilities. IDEA established and governs states' early intervention (<3 years old; Part C) and preschool (3–5 years old) special education (Part B, Section 619) systems for children with disabilities or delays under age 5. The act establishes that children with identified disabilities aged 3–5 have the right to a free and appropriate public education in the least restrictive environment possible and to specialized services as needed (Assistance for Education of All Children with Disabilities). Part C mandates a system for identifying and serving infants and toddlers with disabilities (20 U.S.C. § 1400 [2004]).

Variability in access to early intervention and special education services is shaped by a host of structural factors, such as chronic underinvestment and differential availability of services across regions and locales, particularly in rural areas and in underserved communities of color. The lack of culturally and linguistically diverse evaluators, interventionists, and other service providers also presents a barrier to access to timely evaluation and

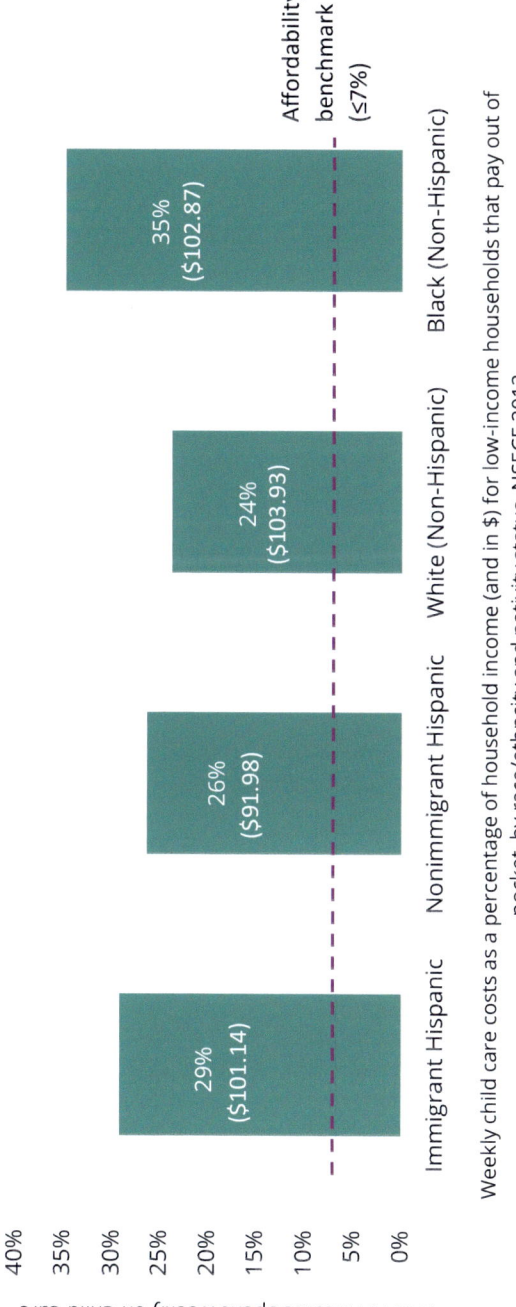

FIGURE 2-5 Weekly child care costs as a percentage of household (HH) income for low-income households that pay out of pocket, by race/ethnicity and nativity status.
SOURCE: Crosby, Mendez, & Barnes, 2019.

quality services for children of color and those from linguistically diverse communities. In addition, policy and technical factors mediate access to services; for instance, eligibility, screening, and early detection criteria and procedures vary across states (National Research Council [NRC], 2002; Macy, Marks, & Towle, 2014; Hirai et al., 2018; National Academies, 2019d). Access to health care is another key factor in attaining access to services (NRC, 2002; Artiles, Dorn, & Bal, 2016; National Academies, 2017).

The most recent report to Congress on IDEA data indicates that 424,318 children aged 0–2 were served under IDEA Part C in 2019 in the 50 states and the District of Columbia, representing 3.7% of that age group. Compared with their White peers, Latino, Native Hawaiian, and other Pacific Islander children were more likely to be served, while Black and American Indian/Alaska Native children were less likely to be served. Nearly 97% of these infants and toddlers received their services in a "natural" environment, defined as the home or a community-based setting.

Studies of children younger than age 3 show that large numbers of these children who may be eligible are not enrolled in Part C (Simpson, Colpe, & Greenspan, 2003; Peterson et al., 2004; Robinson & Rosenberg, 2004). For example, research on a U.S. longitudinal birth cohort showed prevalence rates of about 13% of this cohort at age 9 and 24 months based on existing eligibility criteria, compared with the provision of services to about 10% of this cohort at age 24 months (Rosenberg, Zhang, & Robinson, 2008). More generally, it is estimated that while about 10.55% of children aged 3–5 have a developmental delay, only approximately 2% to 3% of U.S. infants and toddlers with developmental and social emotional disabilities receive early intervention under IDEA Part C (Zablotsky et al., 2019; Office of Special Education Programs [OSEP], 2021).

Another study (Markowitz et al., 2006), on the characteristics of preschool children with disabilities, raises several questions regarding access to high-quality services. The authors found, for instance, that developmental or health concerns were first raised at a young age (<3 years) for a relatively small proportion of children (ranging from 10% to 30%), pointing to the need for more developmental screening across child-serving systems at younger ages and more frequent intervals, including in pediatric care, child care, and home visiting programs. Of note, children in higher-income households are 26% more likely to receive a developmental screening relative to their peers in lower-income households (Keating et al., 2022). Black and Latino infants and toddlers are much less likely (78%) to have their needs identified (Gillispie, 2021). These children are less likely to be screened, and, even when they are screened, are less likely to have a follow-up evaluation, a required step in determining eligibility before services are received (Gillispie, 2021). Indeed, one nationally representative study found that families of color had more negative experiences compared with their

White counterparts throughout the screening, evaluation, and identification process (Bailey et al., 2004; Evans, Feit, & Trent, 2016).

For Part B Section 619, 793,542 children aged 3–5 were served in 49 states, the District of Columbia, and Bureau of Indian Education schools, representing 6.7% of the resident population in this age group. The most common disability category was developmental delay[3] (40.1%), followed by speech or language impairment (39.9%) and autism (11.8%). The category "other disabilities combined" accounted for the remaining children (8.2%). American Indian/Alaska Native, Hawaiian and other Pacific Islander, and White children were more likely to be served, while Latino and Asian children were less likely to be served. Fewer than 40% of children receiving services in this age group received the majority of those services in a regular early childhood program. A substantial proportion of children received services in a separate classroom, but that number fluctuated by race/ethnicity: 20% of White children, 26.5% of Black children, 28.4% of Latino children, and 34.4% of Asian American children (OSEP, 2021).

Eligibility criteria for preschool special education systems are a significant concern that influences access. States have authority to define "developmental delay," the most common category for eligibility in this age group. State thresholds for eligibility in this category vary widely, with differences in the extent of delay and the number of domains of delay that meet the eligibility criteria. As a result, children may be eligible in one state and ineligible in another (OSEP, 2021).

The most recent data available through IDEA indicate that nearly 95% of preschoolers with disabilities were served by certified and qualified special educators and paraprofessionals in 2018 (OSEP, 2021), although researchers have previously found racial and income-based disparities in access to certified educators. Markowitz and colleagues (2006), for example, found that a larger proportion of White children (20%) and higher-income children (24%) were served by teachers with a speech and language pathology license compared with Black (8%) and lower-income (11%) children. Furthermore, proportionally more children in the emotional/behavioral disturbance (51%) and intellectual disability (50%) categories were taught by credentialed teachers in early childhood special education compared with those learners with low-incidence disabilities (29%) and specific language impairment (21%). Proportionally more children with developmental delays (54%), emotional/behavioral disability (52%), intellectual disability

---

[3]IDEA states that children with developmental delays include those aged 3–9 who (1) are experiencing developmental delays, as defined by the state and as measured by appropriate diagnostic instruments and procedures, in one or more of the following areas: physical development, cognitive development, communication development, social or emotional development, or adaptive development; and (2) by reason thereof, need special education and related services (20 U.S.C. § 1400 [2004]).

(51%), and autism (51%) had teachers with special education credentials. In contrast, children with specific language impairment (25%) or low-incidence disabilities (23%) were less likely to have credentialed teachers.

Research has found that receiving special education services in inclusive settings is associated with a host of positive social and academic outcomes for children with disabilities, with notable social benefits for children without disabilities as well (Wiener & Tardif, 2004; Odom, Buysse, & Soukakou, 2011). Unfortunately, progress toward greater inclusion of children with disabilities has moved extremely slowly and regressed during the pandemic (Steed et al., 2021). Importantly, research has found that families of children with disabilities have greater difficulty finding high-quality child care, or child care at all, for their children, with one study reporting that about a third of preschoolers with disabilities experienced gaps in accessing preschool (Markowitz et al., 2006). And despite the increase in access to state-funded pre-K over the last several years, there has not been a commensurate increase in children with disabilities receiving services alongside their peers without disabilities (Meek et al., 2020). Notably, the Head Start program requires that 10% of a program's funded enrollment be for children with disabilities, and the program has a long history of supporting high-quality inclusion and accommodations for these children that even predates IDEA. These data warrant more research to identify more precisely the barriers to accessing services and the quality of services for children with disabilities, particularly for children of color and those from low-income households.

For young children, all of these data vary across state lines as a result of state-determined eligibility thresholds, particularly in the domain of developmental delay. This variation across states represents another opportunity gap, such that in some states, children need to exhibit much more severe delays than they do in other states to be eligible for services. Issues associated with differential screening rates, state and local funding, and transitions between Parts C and B Section 619 also impact this dynamic for families. In all, the disparities in access to early supports, which research finds are critical to growth and development, combined with the uneven access to general education settings and the inadequate dosage and quality of the services many children receive, create substantial opportunity gaps for children with disabilities, particularly those of color.

In general, patterns of underidentification of students of color have been reported in ECE and in the early primary years (National Academies, 2017; Cruz & Firestone, 2022). However, this general finding must be qualified by noting that varying levels of over- and underidentification have been reported in early primary grades by gender, language status, race, grade, and disability category (Cruz & Firestone, 2022). Researchers have also pointed to the difference between the incidence of disability and its documentation, observing that children of color are most represented in disability categories that require subjective identification (e.g., emotional disturbance). And a group of researchers has been documenting that students of color are underidentified in special education (Morgan et al., 2015, 2017; Skiba et al., 2016; Artiles, 2019). While these differences in identification are not necessarily present for infants, they emerge as children become toddlers (Feinberg et al., 2011).

To summarize, access to high-quality early intervention and early childhood special education programs can have positive effects, although equity considerations need to be explicitly addressed throughout the identification and intervention processes because these factors can shape patterns of under- or overidentification of certain groups and the quality of services received. Recent attention to the contextual influences on disability identification for various racial groups, the consequences of identification and their links to educational opportunity, and recent legal cases offer important opportunities to advance a new generation of research on racial disparities in special education. For instance, promising research directions could stem from the recent *Endrew F. v. Douglas County School District RE-1* (2017) case, which interpreted the requirement of "appropriate education" included in IDEA. In that case, the Court stated (as cited in Turnbull, Turnbull, & Cooper, 2018, p. 126):

> *When all is said and done, a student offered an educational program providing "merely more than de minimis" progress from year to year can hardly be said to have been offered an education at all. For children with disabilities receiving instruction that aims so low would be tantamount to "sitting idly…awaiting the time when they were old enough to drop out" [interior quotes omitted]. The IDEA demands more. It requires an educational program reasonably calculated to enable a child to make progress appropriate in light of the child's circumstances.*

The *Endrew* decision added a requirement for "progress," called attention to students' "potential for growth," challenged educators to maintain high expectations for students, and has critical implications for parents' roles and professional development. Above all, *Endrew* "is a narrative about ethics" (Turnbull, Turnbull, & Cooper, 2018) and a timely reminder of the importance of dignity in education. Although *Endrew* has not been used in research or reforms surrounding disproportionality, it has great potential to add an ethical dimension to scholarship on this complex subject.

Administrative Barriers to Access

Even when ECE programs are available, they may not be *accessible*, especially to children of color and families with low incomes. Because the provision of publicly funded ECE is largely contingent on perceptions of which children or families "need" or "deserve" such programs instead of being viewed as a public good that confers benefits for individuals and society alike, an array of processes have been established to ensure that these programs are serving the intended beneficiaries. While restrictive program eligibility criteria and administrative systems help ensure that those children and families that most need ECE services receive them, they can also hinder access for eligible individuals. In other words, even when ECE programs exist in the community, administrative processes can create access barriers for eligible families, leading to disparities.

For immigrant families, accessing ECE programs and benefits is more challenging when the eligibility and enrollment processes (e.g., public information, paperwork, staff) fail to take into account that some eligible families may not be proficient in English. Also, immigrant parents with children who are legal residents or citizens and are therefore eligible for ECE programs may be hesitant to apply for assistance or enrollment because they do not think their child is eligible, the applications require social security numbers, or the families have fears—perceived or real—that they may risk deportation or be considered "public charges" for receiving ECE benefits (Gelatt, Adams, & Heurta, 2014; Ullrich, Schmit, & Cosse, 2019; Acevedo-Garcia et al., 2021; Adams & Pratt, 2021). Agency practices, such as requiring social security numbers on eligibility applications even though they are optional in ECE programs, can deter immigrant families' enrollment. Of the 13 states that contain 80% of the U.S. Hispanic population, 12 requested social security numbers in child care subsidy applications, and five did not indicate that providing the numbers was optional (Hill, Gennetian, & Mendez, 2019). Knowledge and information gaps also create barriers to program participation. Hispanic and immigrant families are less aware of the subsidy program relative to other groups (Pacheco-Applegate et al., 2020). One study found that more than one-third of foreign-born Hispanic parents who were noncitizen legal permanent residents and were eligible for public assistance believed that they were not eligible because of their immigrant status (Alvira-Hammond & Gennetian, 2015). Notably, while studies document information barriers experienced by Hispanic and immigrant families, the effects of these barriers on low-income White, Black, and Asian families have not been studied in depth

Child care subsidies are particularly difficult for families to access within publicly provided ECE programs because these programs have strict work requirements and can be housed in human service systems with other safety net programs that are administratively burdensome, with extensive application and documentation requirements, interim reporting, and benefit reassessments (Adams & Pratt, 2021). In addition to paperwork and compliance costs, subsidies can be difficult to access because of additional redemption costs (Barnes, 2021). Parents must find providers that will accept their subsidies (e.g., are willing to accept an amount lower than the market price) and that offer care that matches the parents' work schedules. These types of administrative burdens are linked to higher subsidy instability and low duration of benefit receipt (Henly et al., 2017), which in turn decrease the continuity of child care arrangements and can have negative consequences for children (Pilarz & Hill, 2014). On the other hand, when states ease administrative burden, there is growing evidence of positive effects on subsidy stability and duration of benefits (Ha et al., 2020; Jenkins & Nguyen, 2022).

These barriers are particularly salient for some families, depending on their race/ethnicity. As detailed in Chapter 7, working parents of color are more likely than their White counterparts to have low-wage jobs, often with unpredictable hours or offered as part-time employment, with no or limited paid time off or flexibility during the workday. They also are more likely to live in underresourced communities with less access to public transportation or with limited internet connection (Johnson-Staub, 2017; Ullrich, Schmit, & Cosse, 2019; Adams & Pratt, 2021). Immigrant families have similar working and living conditions (Acevedo-Garcia et al., 2021; Joshi et al., 2022). Taken together, these factors make it difficult for these families to document and prove (and maintain) their income- and work-related eligibility for subsidies, submit paperwork (online or otherwise), meet with agency staff, and afford copayments (Adams & Pratt, 2021). Thus, funding more ECE programs or slots will not be sufficient to increase access if agency staff and policy makers fail to understand and mitigate the barriers experienced by eligible families when they attempt to access services and benefits.

DIFFERENTIAL EXPERIENCES IN LEARNING SETTINGS

Previous discussion in this chapter has focused on various demographic characteristics that are associated with children's access, or lack thereof, to quality ECE opportunities. These characteristics, such as race, income, language, and disability, are also associated with children's differential experiences within ECE settings. It is important to note that it is not the demographic characteristics of children that cause these differences in experiences, but the structural drivers of opportunity, such as inequitable access to resources, segregation, discriminatory policies, and biased practices and interactions.

One driving factor that shapes children's experiences in ECE settings is program quality. Gaps in access to quality are pervasive and disproportionately affect children from historically marginalized groups. More than a fifth of parents cite quality as the primary driver of their difficulty in finding ECE for their children (NCES, 2017). A recent report by the Education Trust found that only 1% and 4% of Latino and Black children, respectively, were enrolled in public pre-K deemed "high-quality" according to the National Institute for Early Education Research's (NIEER's) quality benchmarks (Gillispie, 2019; Figure 2-6).

An evaluation of the implementation of New York City's rapid scale-up of universal public preschool found racial disparities in the quality experienced by White and Black children, with researchers attributing the gap to differential proximity to high-quality providers (Latham et al., 2021). Earlier studies examining pre-K systems yielded similar findings, such that children of color were more likely to attend programs rated as lower quality (Chien et al., 2010; Barnet, Carolan, & Johns, 2013; Hillemeier et al., 2013; Office for Civil Rights Data Collection [OCRDC], 2016; Bassok & Galdo, 2016; Bassok et al., 2016a; Valentino, 2018). Most recently, a review of tiered quality rating and improvement systems in Pennsylvania found that White children were the most likely and Black children the least likely to be enrolled in programs rated higher quality, with the largest racial gaps seen in the youngest children—infants (Babbs Hollett & Frankenberg, 2022). The study also found that Black and Latino children were the most likely to attend programs that served more children whose families received child care subsidies, that were rated lower in quality, and that received less funding through tiered quality rating and improvement systems, findings that could produce a cycle of perpetual inequity. It is important to note, however, that definitions of "quality" vary and often omit dimensions that are particularly important to the experiences of children from historically marginalized communities, particularly those who speak languages other than English at home, racialized[4] children, and children with disabilities, among others (Phillips, Johnson, & Iruka, 2022).

The only longitudinal birth cohort study of children in the United States examining childhood transition to early education programs and nonparental care (dating back to 2001) showed that Black and Hispanic children experienced lower average quality in home- and center-based care relative to their White peers as measured by the Early Childhood Environmental Rating Scale-Revised (Barnett, Carolan, & Johns, 2013). Using these same data, researchers found that only 18% of low-income children (as measured

---

[4]Racialization is defined as the act of giving a racial character to someone or something or the process of categorizing, marginalizing, or regarding according to race (Merriam-Webster, 2022).

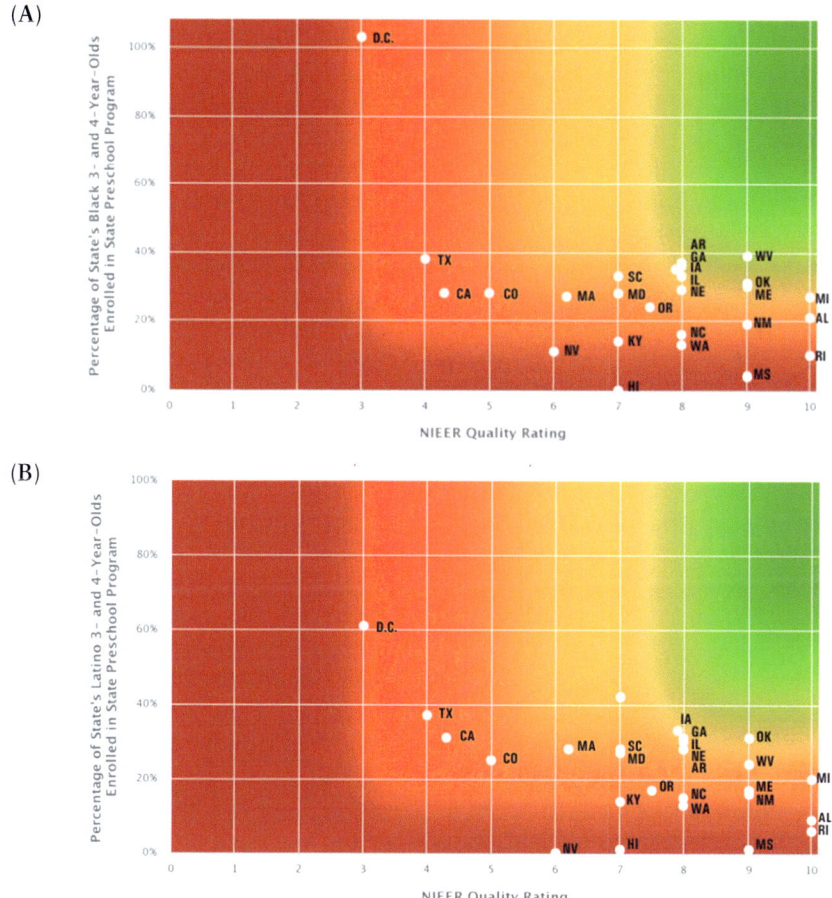

FIGURE 2-6 Percentage of states' populations of 3- and 4-year-olds enrolled in state preschool programs by number of National Institute for Early Education Research (NIEER) quality benchmarks. (A) Black 3-and 4-year-olds; (B) Latino 3- and 4-year-olds.
NOTE: Access in some states—including Alabama, Georgia, Hawaii, Maine, Michigan, Mississippi, North Carolina, Oklahoma, and Rhode Island—looks particularly low because their state-funded preschool programs serve only 4-year-olds and not 3-year-olds.
SOURCE: Gillispie, 2019.

at 185% of the federal poverty threshold) were enrolled in high-quality preschool, compared with 29% of their peers in families above this income level. Similar patterns are seen between children in rural and urban/semi-urban areas—15% versus 30%, respectively. No differences were seen on average in the quality of preschool classroom experiences for dual language learners and children speaking English only (Nores & Barnett, 2014).

Evidence does suggest that quality tends to be lower in classrooms that serve a high percentage of children from low-income families or minoritized populations (Friedman-Krauss et al., 2014; Bassok & Galdo, 2016; Valentino, 2018; Aguiar & Aguiar, 2020). However, specific high-quality programs have shown differing patterns. For example, no average differences across groups were seen in the Seattle Preschool Program (Nores et al., 2017), while in Georgia's universal preschool program, lower quality was experienced by children from low-income families and communities of color (Bassock & Galdo, 2016).

Program quality is often categorized according to two interrelated dimensions: structural quality, which includes such factors as teacher:child ratios, class sizes, and teacher credentials; and process quality, which includes such factors as teacher–child closeness and teacher–child interactions. It is important to consider that structural and process quality are interrelated and are both driven by broader systemic drivers of opportunity, such as funding and policies (as discussed in Chapter 1). Structural quality is influenced by program and community resources and influences process quality, such as the quantity and richness of the interactions teachers have with each child (Chaudry & Sandstrom, 2020).

Importantly, certain dimensions of quality, both structural and process, that have an outsized influence on the experiences of children of color, and those from historically marginalized communities are often omitted from quality frameworks. Discipline policies, for example, which can be considered structural in nature, and biased perceptions of challenging behavior, which affect process quality, both affect the experiences of children in learning settings, and disproportionately Black children (OCRDC, 2014; Gilliam et al., 2016). Access to bilingual staff (structural) and teachers' expectations, cultural responsivity, and relationships with families who speak a language other than English (process) all shape children's experiences, and disproportionately those of immigrant children, Latino and Asian American children, and dual language learners (Suárez-Orozco et al., 2010; Adair, 2015; National Academies, 2017; Limlingan et al., 2020).

As a matter of federal policy, Head Start incorporates many of the indicators typically included in the field's understanding of quality, including low adult:child ratios (fewer children per adult) and group sizes, research-based curriculum, and access to qualified teachers and aides who undergo continuous professional development through coaches and mental health specialists. The program's standards also address many quality indicators that have in the past been omitted from the field's quality frameworks but are critical to the experiences of children from historically marginalized communities. These indicators include requiring exposure to and development of the home language alongside English for dual language learners; prohibitions on expulsions (which disproportionately and unfairly affect Black children); and holistic inclusion of children with disabilities, with close coordination with special educators, early interventionists, and other service providers. These standards are accompanied by a funded system of quality improvement, supported by federal, regional, and local technical assistance. No state child care or pre-K system standards include all of the quality indicators in the Head Start Program Performance Standards. However, the implementation of these standards in Head Start programs varies across the United States, indicating substantial room for improvement (Joshi, Geronimo, & Acevedo-Garcia, 2016).

The committee's overview of differential experiences as they relate to opportunity and outcome gaps takes into account these critical and often overlooked dimensions of quality alongside differential access to the more commonly considered dimensions.

THE IMPORTANCE OF STRUCTURAL QUALITY STANDARDS

Although there is no single national agreed-upon definition of quality in the ECE system or in the early grades, decades of research have identified several common indicators of quality that are associated with children's positive experiences and outcomes (Ramey & Ramey, 1998; Zigler, Gilliam, & Jones, 2006; Minervino, 2014; Barnett & Friedman-Krauss, 2016; Reynolds et al., 2017; Weiland et al., 2018; Meloy, Gardner, & Darling-Hammond, 2019; Reynolds, 2019). They include, among others, learning experience with small classes and low teacher:child ratios; a highly skilled and supported workforce; research-based curriculum and meaningful assessment; and developmentally appropriate, play-based pedagogy. With respect to curricula, there is some evidence for the benefits of skill-specific curricula in targeted developmental domains (Joo et al., 2020).

Dosage and duration also appear to play an important role. Most recently, Wasik and Snell (2019) found that full-day, high-quality programs appear to yield stronger results compared with partial-day programs, particularly for children from low-income households. In addition, evidence is starting to emerge that 2 years rather than 1 year of ECE may lead to longer-term outcomes (Arteaga et al., 2014; Ou, Arteaga, & Reynolds, 2019; Jung & Barnett, 2021).

Research has found that failure to produce the desired outcomes in ECE settings can most commonly be attributed to deviation from critical program standards that results from implementation failure, design failure, and/or inadequate funding. Another likely contributor is lack of attention to dimensions of quality that disproportionately shape the experiences of children from historically marginalized communities. A comparison of Head Start, state pre-K, and other center-based programs by Bassok et al. (2016b) found that higher quality and better child cognitive outcomes are associated with programs following more "stringent regulations" (p. 15). Through its State of Preschool yearbooks, NIEER has tracked state spending, program components, and access for publicly funded preschool programs, as reported by state program administrators (Friedman-Krauss et al., 2022). With respect to characteristics of program design, this source tracks general aspects of structural quality, such as, among others, class size, teacher:child ratios, teacher qualifications, the existence of comprehensive standards, and professional development components, as well as integrated child screenings; the aspects tracked are not exhaustive but serve as minimum features of quality pre-K as supported by research (Barnett & Boocock, 1998; Frede, 1998; NRC, 2001; Clements & Sarama, 2008; Kauerz & Coffman, 2013; Tout et al., 2013; Yoshikawa et al., 2013; Minervino, 2014; Weiland, 2016; Manning et al., 2017; Burchinal, 2018). Significant variation is seen in the number of benchmarks present across the 62 state preschool programs rated, although there have been some improvements over the last decade. Local preschool initiatives differ from state preschool programs in standards and program components, with differences seen in curriculum requirements, teacher:child ratios, class sizes, and teacher qualifications across programs (Barnett & Kasmin, 2018; Patterson & Weisenfeld, 2021; CityHealth, 2022). These differences are in addition to differences in funding per child, with funding most commonly being based on resource decisions at the state and city levels instead of on the cost of providing quality programming (Friedman-Krauss et al., 2021; Patterson & Weisenfeld, 2021).

Inequities in children's experiences of structural quality are wide-ranging and are undergirded by historical and continuing inequities in funding and resource allocation for learning systems that serve young children. The subsections that follow review the literature on several key dimensions of structural quality, with a focus on how gaps in these dimensions are associated with gaps in opportunity and outcomes.

Physical Infrastructure

Research has identified several infrastructure- and facility-related challenges in ECE settings, as in K–12, that could have wide-ranging effects on children's health, safety, development, and learning outcomes. A report published by HHS's Office of the Inspector General examining nine states and one territory found that 96% of child care programs receiving public funding through CCDBG had facilities with one or more potentially hazardous conditions, including water damage and broken gates (Department of Health and Human Services [HHS], 2019). Previous studies at the state and local levels have found similarly concerning issues, ranging from high carbon monoxide levels to rodent infestations, mold, and lead paint (Pardee, 2011; Bipartisan Policy Center; 2019).

Access to clean drinking water is a crucial component of a safe learning environment. Research has found that children in low-income households and children of color are the most vulnerable to lead exposure (National Academies, 2019a) resulting from underresourced communities and infrastructural failures. According to a survey conducted by the Government Accountability Office (GAO), 43% of Head Start programs had not tested lead levels in drinking water in the year prior to the survey, with another 31% reporting that they did not know whether this testing had been done (GAO, 2020). With respect to child care programs, GAO found that the federal Office of Child Care largely left the issue up to state licensing and other regulations, which vary significantly in their requirements and processes for remedying problems and holding programs accountable.

Research has shown that these physical infrastructural issues are associated with teacher and child outcomes, including teacher self-efficacy and child attendance and academic outcomes, as well as health outcomes (Barrett, Carolan, & Johns, 2013; Lafortune & Schonholzer, 2018; Barrett et al., 2019). One study of ECE environments found that physical features of the environment, including light, temperature, and air quality, among others, accounted for 16% of academic performance (Barrett et al., 2013). See Chapter 3 for further discussion of environmental toxins and their association with the opportunity gap.

Ratios and Class Sizes

A robust literature examines the effects of adult:child ratios, group sizes, and class sizes on child outcomes in the early years and the early grades. Small class sizes and lower teacher:child ratios characterize existing effective programs, as well as seminal early childhood programs with long-term demonstrated benefits, such as the Perry Preschool program (10–13 children per class) and Abecedarian program (12 children per class [for 4-year-olds]; e.g., Barnett & Masse, 2007; Barnett et al., 2013; Weiland & Yoshikawa, 2013; Wechsler et al., 2016; Bowne et al., 2017; Reynolds et al., 2017). In general, studies examining the effects of ratio and class size indicate that fewer children and more adults positively impact program quality, children's experiences, and specific child outcomes (NRC, 2001; Barnett et al., 2003; Bowne et al., 2017). A recent randomized controlled trial found that children in preschools with smaller class size (i.e., 15 children) compared with regular class size (i.e., 20 children) engaged in more interactions with their teachers and had gained more early literacy skills at the end of the year. No differences were noted in vocabulary or math (Francis & Barnett, 2019). For young children, low ratios and small class sizes are not only important to developmental or academic gains, but also necessary to ensure appropriate supervision, emotional responsivity, and healthy and safe environments. Studies have found that lower ratios and smaller class sizes are associated with higher-quality programming, more stimulating and warm teacher–child interactions, more individualized attention and learning opportunities, and less time spent on classroom and behavior management (Barnett et al., 2003). Lower ratios and smaller class sizes have also been linked to child outcomes, including greater receptive language, verbal initiative, general knowledge, and cooperative behavior and fewer conflictual relationships with peers (Ruopp & Smith, 1979). More recent research has found that smaller class sizes in preschool are associated with significant gains in literacy and in the number of adult–child interactions, but has documented no effects on math or global quality scores (Francis & Barnett, 2019). One experimental study found that elementary school students in small classes (13–17 students) outperformed their peers in large classes (22–26 students) on all tests, across every subject, in every grade (Mosteller, 1995).

Still, effect sizes for the relationship of ratio and class size to child outcomes vary. Several contextual factors likely influence these inconsistencies in effect size reported in the literature, including the degree to which ratio or class size is reduced (e.g., 30 vs. 25 vs. 15 students), teacher quality, and other structural dimensions of programs (e.g., Burchinal, Zaslow, & Tarullo, 2016; Perlman et al., 2017; Howes et al., 2018). Some research suggests a threshold effect, whereby effects are notable only when reductions in class ratio or size are substantial (Burchinal et al., 2000; NICHD Early Child Care Research Network, 2002; Bowne et al., 2017).

Few studies have examined ratio and class size with attention to how their effects may differ for specific subgroups of children, including those in low-income households and those of color, and in turn, how these differences may contribute to opportunity gaps among these groups. One study found that Hispanic children were more likely to attend ECE programs with larger class sizes (Valentino, 2018), a finding replicated in the early elementary grades (Reardon et al., 2019). Two large-scale studies in the early elementary grades—one in Tennessee and one in Indiana—found that smaller class sizes were more strongly associated with outcomes for Black children and children from low-income communities than for other groups (Mueller, Chase, & Walden, 1988; Word et al., 1990; Achilles, Finn, & Gerber, 2000). Another study using data from the National Institute of Child

Health and Human Development's Study of Early Child Care and Youth Development found that smaller class sizes were associated with growth in early math skills for Black but not White children (Burchinal et al., 2011).

Language of Instruction

There have been relatively fewer studies of the effects of dual language programming in the earlier years. Nonetheless, the robust evidence for the benefits of bilingualism, including early cognitive benefits, higher self-esteem, the impact of early language exposure on later development, and job-related opportunities (National Academies, 2017), supports exposing children to high-quality input in their home language, including and especially in the earliest years. Studies examining dual language models in ECE programs generally have found that children exposed to versus those not exposed to these models make significantly more gains in home language development, either in tandem with greater growth in English development or at the very least, at no cost to English development (National Academies, 2017; Oliva-Olson, 2019). In fact, comprehensive reviews of the research evidence suggest that the development of multiple languages evolved in interrelated fashion. A National Academies report points out that "certain aspects of dual language learning, processing, and usage are significantly and positively correlated and that the development of strong [home language] skills supports the development of English [second language] skills. This interrelationship has been shown to be most evident in domains related to the acquisition of literacy skills and in languages that are typologically similar" (National Academies, 2017, p. 245). These associations are strongest in the development of literacy skills.

Researchers have also highlighted the importance of examining non-academic skills and the influences of the broader context in which learning occurs (Chang et al., 2007; Meek et al., 2020). Such studies have found positive outcomes associated with using children's home language in ECE settings, including improved teacher–child relationships and peer social skills (Chang et al., 2007). One study found an association between Spanish use in the classroom and a variety of executive functioning skills, such as increased frustration tolerance, task orientation, and assertiveness. In contrast, more use of English was associated with teacher-rated conduct and learning problems (Chang et al., 2007).

Bilingual instruction and staff may also facilitate teacher–family relationships and parent involvement—critical components of high-quality early experiences. A related benefit of promoting bilingualism is that it may help support children's positive racial socialization by enabling them to maintain cultural connections and relationships with extended family members (Muller et al., 2020), and scholars have noted that dual language approaches could offer one pathway to more culturally responsive schools (Lindholm-Leary & Hernández, 2011; DeMatthews & Izquierdo, 2018). It is important to note, however, that bilingual and dual language models themselves are not necessarily culturally responsive. Research has found a lack of cultural affirmation and promotion of positive racial identity in some bilingual programs (Chávez-Moreno, 2021), and scholars have suggested that adding these dimensions as explicit goals of dual language and bilingual education models could help address this gap (Palmer et al., 2019).

Most recently, an analysis of English learners in Chicago preschool programs found that those who received bilingual education services compared with their peers who refused those services had stronger academic outcomes, as measured by grades, test scores, and English proficiency, and better attendance. On the other hand, the relatively small percentage of children who had access to dual language immersion classrooms failed to demonstrate advantages in line with those recorded previously in the literature, and scored below their peers on various academic outcomes. The authors suggest caution in interpreting these results, however, as they did not measure any outcomes in children's home language(s) or in social-emotional variables, and the data in English that were collected did not go beyond third grade, notably earlier than the point at which other longitudinal studies, and the literature more broadly, indicate demonstrable positive impacts (i.e., in fifth and eighth grade; Steele et al., 2017). Indeed, some research has found that the strongest effects of high-quality dual language models appear in the later grades (i.e., upper elementary and middle school), after initial delays (Genesee & Lindholm-Leary, 2013).

Despite the evidence summarized above, the vast majority of ECE and early education programs offer instruction exclusively in English. This practice may disadvantage some dual language learners who are not proficient in English, such that they cannot access or take full advantage, at least initially, of the curriculum and of social and learning opportunities, given that it takes several years to acquire oral language proficiency and additional years to acquire academic English proficiency (Collier, 1995; Hakuta, Butler, & Witt, 2000; Menken & Kleyn, 2010). Thus although they may have physical access to educational settings, their ability to engage fully with the content being taught and with their teachers may be hampered. The limited supply of high-quality bilingual or dual language ECE programs and early elementary schools and the limited enrollment of dual language learners in such programs represents an opportunity gap that affects English learners, Latino and Asian students, and immigrant children disproportionately (Castro & Meek, 2022).

Closing opportunity gaps in this area will require specific policies to support the large and growing population of dual language learners in ECE systems today. These policies range from access to high-quality bilingual learning opportunities, to appropriate assessment, to culturally affirming family engagement policies. Required as well is a more linguistically diverse, qualified workforce to provide services in children's home language(s), foster dual language learning, and form partnerships with families that speak a language other than English. Today, policies in ECE designed specifically to support dual language learners are insufficient or altogether lacking. A 2018 report from NIEER documents the complete absence of policies on dual language learners in 18 states (Friedman-Kraus et al., 2019). Those policies that did exist addressed some dimensions of programming for these children but not all. For example, only 24 states collected information on a child's language background, 14 states required written plans for how programs would serve dual language learners, 17 states required assessing children in their home language, and only 6 states required staff training in or qualifications for working with these children (Nores, Krauss, & Frede, 2018).

Harsh and Exclusionary Discipline Policies

It is well documented that exclusionary discipline, including suspension and expulsion, starts early and is disproportionately applied to Black children, boys, and children with disabilities (GAO, 2018). The first study examining preschool expulsion, conducted nearly two decades ago, found that preschoolers were expelled about three times more often than their peers in K–12 settings, and that Black children were twice as likely and boys were four times as likely to be subject to this form of discipline relative to their peers (Gilliam & Shahar, 2006). Nearly a decade after this study was published, the Department of Education's (DOED's) Office for Civil Rights published the first set of federal data on preschool suspension and expulsion through the Civil Rights Data Collection (CRDC). The findings were strikingly similar. Black children made up 19% of the preschool population but 47% of all preschoolers that were suspended, while their White peers made up 41% of enrollment but only 28% of those suspended (OCRDC, 2016). An analysis comparing preschool suspension rates over time found that although the rate of preschool suspension had fallen sharply, by about half, between the last two data collection periods, these racial disparities remained (Fabes et al., 2020).

In addition to exclusionary discipline practices, corporal punishment, defined as inflicting physical pain for purposes of discipline or behavior correction, is a problematic practice in some contexts. Corporal punishment in public schools is legal in 19 states; in private schools, it is legal in 48 states. The CRDC indicates that 851 preschoolers in public pre-K programs were subject to corporal punishment in 1,490 total incidents during the 2017–2018 school year alone (OCRDC, 2018).

Discipline policies and practices contribute to opportunity gaps through a variety of mechanisms. They affect the critical teacher–child and family–teacher relationships that are foundational to early learning experiences (Powell, 2020). Research on the quality of emotional support in ECE settings has found that Black children are more likely to attend programs characterized as lower in emotional support, and that emotional support is negatively associated with "problem behavior" (Iruka et al., 2019). It is important to note that positive discipline cultures can reduce disciplinary injustices in preschool settings (Gansen, 2021). Evidence suggests that children aged 3–5 in early childhood learning environments may be especially at risk for punitive and non–developmentally appropriate discipline and have expulsion rates higher than those in the K–12 system (Gilliam, 2005). In particular, in 2017–2018, Black preschool boys made up 9.6% of preschool enrollment but received both suspensions (34.2%) and expulsions (30.4%) at rates more than three times higher than their share of enrollment. By comparison, White boys, who represent 23.8% of preschool enrollment, received 32.1% of suspensions and 33% of expulsions (OCRDC, 2021). Students facing this kind of discipline in these early years have been shown to be more likely to experience discipline in later school grades, drop out of high school, feel disengaged from school, and be incarcerated later in life (Lamont et al., 2013). In addition, Article 28 of the United Nations Convention on the Rights of the Child states that children have a right to access education on the basis of promoting equal opportunity (UNICEF, 1989). Although this convention has not been ratified in the United States, suspension and expulsion can prevent young children from accessing this right, potentially creating disparities in opportunity.

Policies to address disciplinary practices have had mixed results, for a variety of reasons. With the first federal publication of pre-K suspension and expulsion data in 2014 came greater awareness of how exclusionary discipline was affecting the youngest students, especially Black preschoolers. Shortly thereafter, the Obama administration published guidance on preventing and avoiding exclusionary discipline in ECE programs (HHS & DOED, 2014) and in K–12 settings (Department of Justice and DOED, 2014). In that same year, Congress addressed expulsion in the reauthorized child care law, requiring states to report their policies on child care expulsion and making expulsion prevention and social-emotional development an explicit allowable use of funds to improve the quality of child care. In 2016, HHS updated both the Head Start and child care regulations to include explicit language addressing exclusionary discipline. A wave of state and local policies followed, consisting primarily of new state legislative efforts to limit exclusionary discipline in public pre-K and early education, and modest executive efforts by governors and state agencies to prevent exclusionary discipline in child care by providing professional development, engaging families, and requiring data collection (Loomis et al., 2022).

Despite the large number of new policies, however, the quality of those policies varied by scope of coverage (who was protected—e.g., age, system), content (for what infractions children could or could not be excluded), and accountability (whether there would be consequences for excluding children; Meek et al., 2020; Loomis et al., 2022). Moreover, the latest publication of the CRDC indicates steep declines in preschool suspensions and expulsions, but disparities in exclusionary discipline between Black children and their peers have remained largely unchanged. Exclusionary discipline undermines efforts to expand access to quality ECE and does so in a way that disproportionately disadvantages Black children. Addressing exclusion from education via suspension and expulsion is a critical step toward bridging opportunity gaps across the educational continuum, an issue discussed further in the next chapter.

THE EARLY CARE AND EDUCATION WORKFORCE

A critical component of both ECE and early elementary school experiences is the teaching workforce. Two prior National Academies consensus studies have focused on the workforce of practitioners who contribute to the care and education of children from birth through age 8: *Transforming the Workforce for Children Birth through Age 8* (IOM & NRC, 2015) and *Transforming the Financing of Early Care and Education* (2018). This section examines the factors related to the ECE workforce with the potential to either drive or mitigate disparities in opportunity.

While policies related to workforce competencies, degree requirements, compensation, and systemic supports and coaching are structural in nature, the workforce is undoubtedly the most critical factor in process quality, as discussed below. Research shows that if ECE programs are to reduce opportunity gaps and systemic barriers to services and resources associated with racial, linguistic, cultural, economic, and immigrant background, they must be staffed by well-prepared, well-supported, and competent professionals. Programs staffed by such individuals tend to have more positive impacts on children's learning and development relative to those that lack educators who are intentionally trained for and supported in this work (IOM & NRC, 2015). The effectiveness of ECE educators is driven by a number of interrelated factors (IOM & NRC, 2015):

- Professional preparation and ongoing job-embedded supports that increase educators' understanding and competencies related to (1) the critical array of subject matter and domains of development from an early childhood perspective (language and literacy,

mathematical and scientific thinking, social-emotional development, physical health); (2) children's learning and development trajectory for each content area and domain of development; and (3) the professional approaches and strategies that help children, including those who have learning disabilities or are learning multiple languages, advance in developmentally appropriate ways along these trajectories.
- Policies, systems, and working conditions that allow educators to practice effectively, including professional compensation and benefits and supportive working environments (e.g., paid time for breaks and lesson planning, effective program leaders, adequate materials and supplies). The lack of these supports leads to high turnover rates and places stress on ECE educators' health and well-being, limiting the positive impacts they can have on young children's learning and development.

Critical dimensions of workforce readiness and competence that include providing culturally responsive and affirming learning experiences and being attuned to and actively addressing biases in practice, both of which are discussed further below. Both are necessary for providing quality services to the diverse population of young children in the United States.

Unfortunately, ECE educators lack access to the above professional supports. Whether they have access to any, some, or extensive supports is driven largely by the funding streams, policies, and regulatory systems (i.e., state pre-K, Head Start, child care) that support and govern their work. The results of this uneven approach to supporting ECE educators affect children inequitably. For example Ulrich, Hamm, and Schochet (2017) found that:

- families with higher incomes are able to enroll their children in ECE programs that provide better professional supports for their staff;
- children from families with low incomes who are enrolled in state pre-K or Head Start compared with those in other ECE programs tend to have ECE educators with more professional preparation and ongoing supports and better compensation and working conditions; and
- infants and toddlers compared with preschool-aged children from families with low incomes are less likely to be served by well-trained and well-supported professionals.

Since the ECE workforce is central to the quality of ECE programs, addressing the inequities related to these educators could also help reduce inequities in children's ECE experiences and in turn, the opportunity gaps experienced in the earliest years of life. The following discussion elaborates on disparities related to the ECE workforce in four areas: education and professional preparation, compensation, access to professional development and supportive working conditions, and professional beliefs and practices.

Education and Professional Preparation

Some research indicates that ECE educators' educational attainment and professional preparation are associated with the teacher–child relationship (Chaudry & Sandstrom, 2020). A meta-analysis found that teachers' education levels were associated with more positive teacher–child relationships and child outcomes, as reported by teachers (Howes, Jolena, & Ritchie, 2003; Kelley & Camilli, 2007). It must be noted, however, that long-standing systemic barriers make it more difficult for people of color and people from low-income communities to enroll in and graduate from higher education systems.

As discussed earlier, the major publicly funded ECE programs—Head Start, state-funded pre-K, and child care—were established for different purposes, and accordingly are governed by varying policies related to funding levels, eligibility criteria, and quality definitions and standards. One of the most important areas in which ECE programs differ is policies related to the professional workforce—how they are prepared, paid, and supported. The vast differences among program types (Head Start, pre-K, child care) and settings (centers, homes) can have major implications for these programs' capacity to address opportunity gaps experienced by children in the early years. Strengthening the coordination of policies among the major ECE public funding streams that are focused on compensation and workforce quality can lead to increased workforce recruitment, retention, and stabilization across program types, as well as better outcomes for children. When such policies are uncoordinated, they create instability and inequities in ECE. For example, when policies regarding educator qualifications or compensation differ purely because of how a program is funded, where it is located, or the age group it serves, the result is a two-tiered workforce, with those in better-resourced programs receiving better pay, benefits, and supports. Other programs—and the children they serve—are left with teachers who are less likely to have resources to improve their practice and more likely to struggle with low wages (National Academies, 2018).

Effective, evidence-based ongoing professional development, job-embedded coaching, professional learning communities, and apprenticeship models can provide ECE educators with continuous education, support, and skill development in accessible and equitable ways. Policies that support such intentional approaches can lead to strengthening the workforce without overburdening the ECE workforce to advance their educational attainment (IOM & NRC, 2015).

Examples of differential ECE workforce educational requirements and attainment across programs include the following:

- **State pre-K and Head Start teachers are required to attain higher levels of education and credentials relative to other ECE teachers.**
  In 24 states, pre-K teachers are required to have a bachelor's degree in ECE (McLean et al., 2021). Head Start regulations require that at least half of programs' lead teachers have the same level of professional preparation, although the current workforce well surpasses that mark, with almost 75% of all Head Start teachers having a BA in ECE (Barnett & Friedman-Krauss, 2016). In contrast, no state's child care licensing regulations require this level of professional preparation for lead teachers. The highest level of education required of teachers in licensed child care is an associate's degree for center-based teachers (two states) and a child development associate (CDA) or similar credential (but less than an associate's degree) for home-based providers (six states; McLean et al., 2021).
- **Center-based teachers who work with preschool-aged children have more professional preparation relative to infant–toddler teachers.**
  According to a nationally representative survey from 2012, 45% of center-based teachers of preschoolers had a BA or higher, compared with 19% of infant–toddler teachers. At the same time, 28% of infant–toddler teachers had attained at most a high school diploma, compared with 13% of preschool teachers in centers (NSECEP, 2015).
- **Home-based teachers who are "listed" (recognized and regulated by the state) have lower education levels compared with center-based teachers, but more of them have attained more education and professional preparation in recent years.**
  In 2012, about 30% of home-based teachers had an associate's degree or BA; in 2019, 36% had attained this level of education. In the meantime, the proportion of home-based teachers with a high school diploma or less had decreased from 33% to 25%. Home-based teachers were also more likely to have a CDA in 2019 than in 2012 (52% vs. 42%; Datta et al., 2021).

Increasing the education levels and professional preparation of all ECE educators can help address the uneven quality of ECE programs (as measured by traditional constructs) experienced by young children, especially infants and toddlers and those who participate in home-based programs. But the quality and relevance of the professional preparation experience are critical. A National Academies report from 2015 details what is entailed in effective professional training experiences in higher education and job-embedded contexts (IOM & NRC, 2015). Preparation and continuous professional development in providing culturally and linguistically responsive and affirming care and in understanding and addressing harmful biases are critical. It is also important that the attainment of higher degrees and credentials come with commensurate increases in compensation and benefits. Otherwise, ECE educators may opt to leave their ECE jobs for better-paying opportunities in public schools, in state-funded pre-K or Head Start programs, or outside of the field altogether.

Finally, it is important to note that increasing the education levels and professional preparation of the ECE workforce could lead to *greater* inequity absent an intentional strategy for preserving or increasing the racial and linguistic diversity of the workforce, and an intentional preparation and development strategy that specifically addresses providing culturally and linguistically affirming learning and combating harmful biases. While the ECE workforce is less highly educated than the public education workforce, they are much more representative of the children and communities they serve relative to public school teachers (Austin et al., 2019). Some research, especially in K–12 education, has shown added benefit from children's learning when they are taught by educators who share their racial and cultural backgrounds (Miller, Votruba-Drzal, & Coley, 2013). As discussed earlier, there are also well-established benefits to supporting children's home language and offering bilingual learning opportunities for dual language learners, making a linguistically diverse workforce, reflective of the children they teach, especially important for this population. As discussed in greater detail below, the racial diversity of ECE educators may affect children's early learning experiences, especially those of children of color. Thus, any efforts to increase ECE teachers' education and credentials need also to invest in the recruitment and support of racially and linguistically diverse staff, especially those with fewer financial resources, those with no to minimal experience in higher education, those with children of their own, and those who must remain employed while pursuing higher degrees. ECE systems at the local and state levels have employed a range of strategies to support incumbent educators' efforts in education and professional advancement, including scholarships and wage supplements for achieving higher credentials and degrees; apprenticeships that combine job-embedded learning, higher education supports, and wage increases; cohort programs that allow for robust peer-to-peer support; academic supports, including tutoring and counseling; classes offered online, on weekends, or in community settings; coursework tailored for early childhood educators with limited English proficiency; and the provision of college credit for prior experience or learning (Whitebook et al., 2012; Lieberman et al., 2020).

Compensation

In 2012, the median hourly wage of center-based ECE teachers was $10.60 (NSECEP, 2013), or just above $22,000 per year. According to census data, between 2014 and 2016, the families of 53% of child care workers were enrolled in one of four public assistance programs: Medicaid and the Children's Health Insurance Program, the Supplemental Nutrition Assistance Program, Temporary Assistance for Needy Families, or the earned income tax credit (Whitebook et al., 2018). Similar to educational requirements and access to professional supports, compensation across ECE programs and age groups is inequitable even when educators have college degrees.

- ECE educators in Head Start, publicly funded pre-K, and school-based pre-K are better paid than those in other settings (e.g., licensed child care), although still well below the average of what K–12 teachers earn.
  ECE educators with a BA earn more than $20/hour in school-based pre-K programs, about $16/hour in Head Start and publicly funded pre-K, and less than $14/hour in other settings (NSECEP, 2013).
- ECE educators who work with preschool-aged children are better paid than infant–toddler teachers.
  The median hourly wage for center-based infant–toddler teachers was $9.30 in 2012, compared with $11.90 for preschool teachers in ECE centers (NSECEP, 2013). The Center for Study of Child Care Employment estimates that this disparity amounts to up to $8,375 per year (McLean et al., 2021).

These disparities in compensation are at least in part a function of the fact that Head Start and pre-K teachers are often required to have higher levels of education compared with other ECE teachers. In general, ECE teachers with more education, regardless of program types or age groups served, earn more (NSECEP, 2013; Austin et al., 2019; McLean et al., 2021; see Table 2-2).

Even so, depending on program type, ECE teachers with a BA earn $29,000 to $43,000 per year, compared with about $53,000 for kindergarten teachers and $56,000 for elementary school teachers (National Academies, 2018).

Within-field racial pay disparities exist as well. Black ECE educators—in both preschool and infant–toddler child care settings—are paid less than their peers in similar settings ($0.77 and $1.71 less per hour, respectively). Black teachers are also more likely to teach infants and toddlers than preschoolers, garnering lower wages as discussed above (McLean et al., 2021).

TABLE 2-2 Median Hourly Wages (in dollars) of Center-Based Teachers and Caregivers by Age of Children Served and Sponsorship and Funding of Center-Based Program or Employment

	BA or Higher Staff serving 0–3 only	BA or Higher Staff serving 3–5 only	AA Staff serving 0–3 only	AA Staff serving 3–5 only
School-sponsored	a	20.60	a	13.00[b]
Head Start–funded	10.00[b]	15.90	11.40[b]	12.20
Public pre-K–funded	11.90	16.20	9.00	9.80
All other early care and education	11.40	13.90	9.90	11.00
Total teachers and caregivers, all center types	11.30	15.50	10.00	11.30

NOTE: The Head Start–funded category excludes school-sponsored programs; the public pre-K–funded category excludes school-sponsored and Head Start–funded programs.
[a]Value suppressed because of small sample size.
[b]Interpret data with caution because of small sample size.
SOURCE: NSECEP, 2013.

Access to Professional Development and Supportive Working Conditions

Professional development opportunities, such as in-service training, coaching, and communities of practice, can improve practice, teacher–child relationships, and child outcomes if they also incorporate design and implementation principles that research has associated with effectiveness. However, lack of investments, inconsistent policies, and inequities within the ECE system result in wide variation in the quality of and access to professional development across the field (IOM & NRC, 2015). Other research suggests that teacher training in child development and in-service coaching are predictive of more positive teacher–child relationships (Tout, Zaslow, & Berry, 2005). Although research shows that access to professional development and training benefits quality, access to these supports varies across child care type and by state.

- **Home-based educators participate in professional development at rates similar to those of center-based educators, but are much less likely to receive financial support to do so.**
  Almost half of center-based ECE teachers who reported participating in professional development workshops, college courses, or

coaching said they received financial support to do so, compared with only 15% of home-based educators (NSECEP, 2015).
- **National and state ECE policies generally provide little assurance that educators have the supports that lead to effective professional practice and continuous improvement.**
For example, of the 62 state-funded pre-K programs in the country, only 14 meet the basic standard of providing at least 15 hours of professional development per year, creating individualized professional development plans, and offering coaching (Friedman-Krauss et al., 2021). Compared with their peers in the K–12 public education system, state pre-K teachers are much less likely to have paid time for professional development, lesson planning, and other professional responsibilities, even when they work in the same public schools. Only about half the states offer the same kind of job-embedded coaching to state pre-K teachers that they offer to K–12 teachers (Friedman-Krauss et al., 2019).

ECE educators in child care programs that are not part of pre-K systems fare even worse. These supports are typically not required, and are incentivized and supported only through states' quality rating and improvement systems (QRIS). Even then, QRIS in most states do not include the supports mentioned above as standards of program quality to meet or aspire to. For example, only 15 states' QRIS support or incentivize paid time for professional development for center-based child care programs, and only one state's QRIS does the same for home-based programs. Sixteen states' QRIS include paid planning time as a quality standard for centers, while only eight states do so for home-based programs (McLean et al., 2021). In addition, QRIS have low participation rates in many states across the country, so support through this system alone leaves out many providers and the children they serve (Souto-Mannin & Rabadi-Raol, 2018; Reinke, Peters, & Castner, 2019). This is the case even more so for family care providers and other home-based providers (Schilder et al., 2015; Hallam et al., 2017), as well as providers in predominantly Black communities (Jenkins, Duer, & Connors, 2021). Scholars suggest that this may be due to various requirements that, because of structural inequities, may either be more burdensome for historically marginalized groups to meet or require participation in systems, such as state licensing, in which some communities have less trust. As discussed elsewhere in this chapter, the indicators commonly included in QRIS often lack an emphasis on cultural or linguistic responsiveness, factors that may be particularly important for parents of color and their children (Meek et al., 2022). Finally, one study found that tiered QRIS, which ascribe varying levels of reimbursement based on quality ratings, perpetuate inequities by providing fewer resources to those rated lower in quality. The same study found that Black and Latino providers were most likely to be rated lower in quality, indicating that they receive fewer resources (Babbs Hollett & Frankenberg, 2022).

Beyond access to professional supports, working conditions can have a significant impact on teachers' wellness and the services they provide to young children. Such factors as high teacher:student ratios and group sizes, little to no time for breaks or planning, lack of organizational and leadership support, and poor-quality physical space, paired with low compensation and benefits (including paid sick and vacation time) all can affect teachers' stress and behavior and children's experiences. Research has found, for example, that teacher stress can negatively impact the teacher–child relationship as a result of teacher–child conflict and teachers' hostility and anger toward the children they serve (Goelman & Guo, 1998; Pianta & Hamre, 2009; Hamre et al., 2012; Gastaldi et al., 2014; Chen, Phillips, & Izci, 2018; Chaudry & Sandstrom, 2020). Teacher stress is also associated with a greater likelihood of harshly disciplining children (Gilliam & Shahar, 2006). It is important, then, to consider the policies and funding decisions that affect these working conditions, and how well-resourced programs can ensure that their workforce has healthy working conditions, smaller class sizes and lower ratios, access to mental health specialists and other supports to address social and emotional development, substitute teachers, adequate breaks throughout the day, and paid sick leave.

Professional Beliefs and Practices

Likely related to the above differences between home-based and center-based settings, educators in these two types of settings tend to report different beliefs and practices. In a national survey, for example, 71% of center-based teachers said the main reason they worked in ECE was that it was a career or personal calling, while another 21% said it was to help children. Among listed home-based providers, the proportions with the same responses were 48% and 9%, respectively. The same survey found that 74% of center-based teachers reported using a curriculum, compared with 55% of home-based providers. Almost 90% of center-based providers reported helping families find at least one ancillary service (e.g., developmental assessment, counseling, social services), compared with 44% of home-based providers (NSECEP, 2015).

PROCESS AND INTERACTIONAL QUALITY

All of the previously described structural dimensions of quality, alongside the competencies and credentials, compensation, and conditions of the teaching workforce, determine children's experiences in ECE programs and in some instances, whether children have access to learning opportunities at all. Importantly, these dimensions set the conditions for process quality, including the teacher–child relationship and teacher–child interactions, which researchers agree are critical foundations for learning, secure exploration, and developmental and academic outcomes (IOM & NRC, 2015). This section briefly summarizes the voluminous research literature on different components of ECE process and interactional quality and highlights whether and how the experiences of children of color, low-income children, and dual language learners have been addressed.

Pedagogy, Instruction, and Access to Enrichment

A large body of research examines various pedagogical approaches in ECE settings, concluding that play, structured and unstructured, is important to children's development. Researchers have found that play in preschool is associated with receptive and expressive language skills in young children and with math and reading skills in elementary school (Lewis et al., 2000; Hanline, Milton, & Phelps, 2008; Zosh et al., 2018). Research also has found a negative association between the amount of time dedicated to free play and externalizing behavior (Veiga, Neto, & Rieffe, 2016). A recent study of more than 2,200 children found that unstructured play in the early years was associated with improved self-regulation two years later (Colliver et al., 2022), with previous research having identified the importance of self-regulation to a host of short- and long-term academic and well-being outcomes (Moffitt et al., 2011; Robson, Allen, & Howard, 2020). A meta-analysis found positive effects of guided play compared with direct instruction on early math skills, shape knowledge, task switching, and spatial vocabulary. No differences were noted in other outcomes, notably literacy, prosocial behavior, and social competence (Skene et al., 2022). Overall, the research in this area suggests that a combination of guided play, free play, and developmentally appropriate direct instruction is needed to promote the full range of children's development and learning.

Despite the support for play-based pedagogy and learning opportunities, research indicates that teachers report a lack of competence and confidence in engaging in play-based learning (Bubikova-Moan, Næss Hjetland, & Wollscheid, 2019; Beaven et al., 2020). Research also indicates that Black, Latino, dual language learner, and low-income children are more likely to be in ECE programs that engage in more individual and didactic instruction as opposed to child-directed or play-based models (Chien et al., 2010; Valentino, 2015), which, according to research, may be associated with outcomes related to attention, memory, and motivation.

It is critical to consider that play, across several forms, is differentially perceived for and afforded to children from different backgrounds, especially Black children. Scholars suggest that Black children's play can be curtailed based on negative stereotypes and perceptions of Black people. Specifically, this research indicates that play for Black children is limited by perceptions of boys and girls as being older than they are (i.e., adultification) and boys as being more guilty of a crime (i.e., criminalization), that there are fewer physical spaces in which to play in low-income communities of color, and that the schools most likely to be attended by low-income children of color in the early years are less likely to engage in play-based learning approaches—all of which leads to exclusion from or gaps in opportunities to play and learn through play (Goff et al., 2014; Epstein, Blake, & González, 2017; Bryan, 2019; Pinckney, Bryan, & Outley, 2021).

As an example of differential perceptions of children's play, one study observed children's pretend play as related to child adjustment, as assessed by researchers and reported by teachers. The researchers found no differences in children's observed pretend play profiles or adjustment. But they did find that the association between child pretend play profiles and teacher-rated adjustment was moderated by race, such that teachers rated Black children with imaginative and expressive play profiles more negatively (e.g., more teacher–child conflict, less prepared for school, less peer acceptance), but rated White children with the same pretend play profiles positively (Yates & Marcelo, 2014). These negative perceptions create differential opportunities for play for Black children that can translate into harsher discipline and less emotional support in the classroom (Curenton et al., 2019).

Instructional quality is another important dimension of quality. A robust research base finds that high-quality instruction centered on responsive adult–child interactions, including open-ended questions, expansions, and recasts, implemented across an array of daily activities (e.g., book reading, meal time, pretend play), has a positive impact on child development, particularly in the areas of language and literacy (Stefanou et al., 2004; Reeve, 2009; Pianta, Hamre, & Allen, 2012; IOM & NRC, 2015; Pianta, Downer, & Hamre, 2016).[5] A focus on sequential, direct instruction in code-based characteristics of print has been identified as particularly important to literacy development (Spear-Swerling, 2019). Early writing experiences and instruction are also important, but research has found that preschoolers spend very little time on writing activities, and most of it is focused on fine motor skills and letter formation as opposed to the meaning of written language (Molfese et al., 2011; Pelatti et al., 2014). Other instructional characteristics, such as exposure to varied vocabulary and effective, hands-on math instruction, are also associated with improved outcomes for young

---

[5]For an in-depth discussion of the child development and early learning and educational practices that foster language and literacy skills, see Chapters 4 and 6 of *Transforming the Workforce for Children Birth through Age 8: A Unifying Foundation* (IOM & NRC, 2015).

children (Klein et al., 2011; Wasik & Iannone-Campbell, 2012; Whorall & Cabell, 2016; Starkey et al., 2022).

Embedded instruction, an approach that intentionally embeds sequenced and targeted learning opportunities across activities, is another key instructional concept with a robust evidence base. This approach has been used and evaluated most widely with children with disabilities. A core component of the model is robust planning, implementation, and evaluation of practices (Snyder et al., 2013, 2015). Research has found that this approach is associated with a range of positive developmental outcomes, including communication, preacademic, adaptive, literacy, and social outcomes (Division for Early Childhood & National Association for the Education of Young Children, 2009; Snyder et al., 2015).

Instructional quality is most commonly measured using global classroom quality instruments, such as the Classroom Assessment Scoring System (CLASS), which considers three domains related to supporting learning and development—emotional support, classroom organization, and instructional support. Emotional support includes such dimensions as positive climate, teacher sensitivity, and regard for student perspectives. Classroom organization includes productivity, behavior management, and negative climate. Lastly, the CLASS domain specific to instructional support comprises instructional learning formats, content understanding, analysis and inquiry, quality of feedback, instructional dialogue, and student engagement. This domain assesses the promotion of children's thinking through effective teaching (La Paro, Pianta, & Stuhlman, 2004; World Bank, 2017). Research has found that this domain of quality often scores the lowest for many ECE providers. Recent research on ECE programs considered to be high quality, including programs in Boston and Tulsa, showed higher scores in instructional support in particular (Mashburn et al., 2008; Phillips, Gormley, & Lowenstein, 2009; Moiduddin et al., 2012; Weiland & Yoshikawa, 2013; Yoshikawa et al., 2013; Yoshikawa, Weiland, & Brooks-Gunn, 2016), suggesting that this may be an important indicator for increasing quality broadly and achieving greater child growth and better outcomes. Indeed, scholars posit that pairing focused and targeted curricula with coaching and professional development can help increase instructional quality in ECE settings (Yoshikawa, Weiland, & Brooks-Gunn, 2016).

Little research has examined the differences in instructional quality among various groups of children in the early years and the effects on academic outcomes. Some research has found that Black and Latino children are more likely to experience lower-quality care in general, and specifically in the CLASS domains of emotional and instructional support (Valentino, 2018; Aguiar & Aguiar, 2020). Higher scores on the CLASS have small to moderate positive effects on children's educational outcomes, regardless of race/ethnicity (Soliday Hong et al., 2019), and some positive effects for

Black and Hispanic students (Burchinal et al., 2011; Downer et al., 2012), although there is also evidence of null effects (López, 2011; Stephens et al., 2023). More research is needed to examine the experiences of children of color with instruction in the early years, and the extent to which educators consider culture, language, and bias in their approaches to teaching and learning. Since the CLASS does not consider sociocultural factors associated with children's race/ethnicity or language, new scales have been developed that incorporate more direct measures of these factors. They include the Classroom Assessment of Supports for Emergent Bilingual Acquisition (Figueras-Daniel & Li, 2021) and Assessing Classroom Sociocultural Equity Scales (Curenton et al., 2020).

Strong Family Engagement

The divestment that contributes to the opportunity gap for young people is a symptom of a system that does not always reflect the lived experiences and realities of families, which results in policies and practices that exacerbate inequities. As just one example, families that qualify for child care assistance at the determined state level are often required to stay beneath a certain income threshold to remain eligible for benefits, a requirement that can constrain their employment opportunities. Thus, for instance, some families have made the decision to decline a raise at their place of work so as to remain eligible for child care subsidies (Child Care Assistance Program [CCAP] funding) because the amount of their raise was not enough to cover the increased cost of child care resulting from the loss of benefits (Roll & East, 2014; Anderson et al., 2022). Had CCAP-eligible families been engaged in the design of these policies, they could have informed the development of a more equitable system that would not disincentivize the very type of upward mobility and empowerment that such programs strive to enable.

ECE and early education providers have long recognized the power of the family unit in promoting positive child outcomes and student success (Hayakawaa et al., 2013; Reynolds et al., 2017, 2022). Family engagement, as defined within the field, entails shared responsibility among caregivers, schools, and other community organizations in supporting the learning and development of children (National Family, School, and Community Engagement Working Group, 2009). Research has demonstrated strong correlations between family engagement and myriad positive outcomes for young children, including improved literacy and math skills and social-emotional learning that contribute to overall school readiness (Van Voorhis et al., 2013).

Although the definition of family engagement provides guidance for best practices (e.g., use of the term "shared responsibility" indicates the need for meaningful relationships among the adults in a child's life), family engagement has not received adequate attention and support among policy makers and practitioners interested in promoting quality in care and education for young children or closing opportunity gaps. Indeed, family engagement has often manifested as a set of standardized, transactional practices among caregivers, schools, and community organizations that present barriers to entry for lower-income families. For example, a 2017 Education Week Research Center analysis of federal survey data found that families with an annual income of more than $75,000 versus those making less than $30,000 were twice as likely to report having volunteered at a child's school and reported attending nearly twice as many school meetings (Sparks & Harwin, 2017). These fixed, transactional practices do not foster authentic, equitable engagement that honors families as the most critical stakeholders in children's lives.

An alternative approach—"families as partners"—with corresponding strategies is needed to engage meaningfully with families living in poverty and other divested groups. Quality family engagement requires a true partnership among caregivers, providers, and policy makers, ensuring that family voice and expertise inform providers' practices and policies in much the same way that evidence-based practices can inform and enhance the care families provide at home (Grindal et al., 2016; Joo et al., 2020).

Although an emphasis on parent engagement also characterizes other programs discussed previously in this chapter (e.g., the Chicago Child–Parent Center program), the Head Start model has long been an exemplar of family engagement through efforts to promote parent leadership and advocacy and positive influences that parents can have on child development, including parenting behaviors, economic security, and psychological well-being (Yoshikawa et al., 2013). From its inception, the program was centered around family partnerships and community engagement, and in the years since, the program has developed a Parent, Family, and Community Engagement Framework that serves as a model for the broader ECE field. The program requires and funds family advocacy and leadership efforts, has established infrastructure with which to incorporate parental and familial input into programmatic functioning through parent councils and boards, supports the diverse array of needs families may have individually, and supports parents as their children's first and most important teachers.

When considering family engagement, providers can ask themselves three simple questions: Are we doing *to* families? Are we doing *for* families? Or are we doing *with* families? A "families as partners" approach derives from working *with* families, following this general set of principles (Caspe, Lopez, & Hanebutt, 2019):

- Honor the family unit as the most critical stakeholder in the work of serving children. Take every concern a family raises seriously. Take every idea a family suggests into consideration.
- Do not assume the needs, strengths, or aspirations of families. Instead, develop an understanding of the resources needed and desired by each group of families, and make intentional investments in those resources.
- Affirm the identities of families. Learn about each family's unique background.

When these principles are put into practice, family engagement exists as a dynamic, ever-evolving set of strategies for best supporting families in their unique contexts (Wintrop et al., 2021).

The following are examples of practices aligned with these principles that can be embedded into schools and community-based programs:

- Establishing clear expectations for communications with families. Informal connections with families should occur daily. Children's data should be reviewed quarterly. Response to outreach from a family should occur promptly and within the same standard for response time that an organization sets for any stakeholder. Each point of connection with families should allow for at least 75% of the time to be spent in meaningful dialogue, as opposed to "sit and get" meetings where families serve as passive participants.
- Creating multiple modalities for communicating with families and engaging them in the decision-making processes of the school or program. In family policy meetings, spend time as a group learning how resources are utilized within the organization, and provide time for families to advise on how those resources should be spent.
- When families articulate what resources are needed or how resources should be allocated, investing in high-leverage, targeted activities and materials that meet those needs. As an example, if a provider hears that families need more books in their home libraries, the organization can invest in culturally relevant, identity-affirming, and positive books for families to take home through literature "pop-ups." This experience can then be systematized so that literature pop-ups happen consistently, with the associated book resources being made abundantly available.

These principles and practices are only guideposts. Most important, providers need to continually put the concept of "families as partners" into practice alongside families that are currently receiving services. Building systems and structures that allow for ongoing, relationship-based engagement can break the cycle of transactional relationships and strengthen transformational partnerships.

THE IMPACT OF COVID-19 ON CHILDREN'S OPPORTUNITY GAPS

The COVID-19 pandemic has profoundly impacted families and schooling, including ECE in the United States. It must be noted that families of color, specifically Black, Latino, and Indigenous communities, were the hardest hit by the pandemic across health, employment and income, and education. A September 2020 audit by HHS's Office of the Inspector General found that 63% of child care centers and 27% of family child care providers had closed as a result of the pandemic (HHS, 2020). Among state-funded preschool programs that closed at the onset of the pandemic, 28 programs in 21 states required that remote learning be provided to all children, and four required this for some preschool children based only on program location (Friedman-Krauss et al., 2021). In contrast, 31 programs did not require any virtual instruction.

Not surprisingly, the percentage of 3- and 4-year-olds enrolled in preschool is estimated to have fallen from 54% in 2019 to 40% in 2020 (McElrath, 2021). Children in the lowest-income families had the lowest in-person preschool participation in the 2020–2021 school year, at just 14% compared with 42% of all other children. Thus a significant concern arising from the pandemic is the reversal or stagnation of any progress made in access to and equity in preschool, as is documented in the areas of access and funding in the most recent report on state preschool programs. That report shows that the pandemic erased a decade of progress in preschool enrollment in state-funded preschool programs, preschool special education, and Head Start (Friedman-Krauss et al., 2021).

As families shifted to adapt to all the changes in structure and family life resulting from the pandemic, prioritizing children's learning became difficult. The disruption of ECE services forced families (particularly mothers) to take on additional child care responsibilities (NASEM, 2022). A comprehensive review of national, state, and local studies across the United States found that the pandemic exacerbated gaps in ECE participation (Ford, Kwon, and Tsotsoros, 2021; Weiland et al., 2021), with the decrease in enrollment being greater for low-income children (Weisenfeld, 2021) and for Hispanic and Black children (Cascio, 2021). A national survey found that even by spring 2021, participation rates remained quite low for Hispanic children (Jung & Barnett, 2021), and to date, child enrollment has not returned to the levels that existed before the onset of the pandemic (National Association for the Education of Young Children, 2021).

CONCLUSIONS

A robust research base finds definitively that access to high-quality ECE is associated with long-term positive outcomes spanning education, employment, and health, among other domains of life. The research is also clear, however, that the ECE system and early education have fallen short in realizing their promise. Indeed, the literature consistently finds that children from historically marginalized communities, including children of color, immigrant children, dual language learners, children with disabilities, and children from low-income households, among others, face significant inequities in opportunities for learning and education in formal settings—starting from the introduction of those opportunities (or lack thereof) in child care or preschool, and extending throughout these children's educational trajectories.

Decades of evidence point to the potential of ECE to reduce the opportunity gaps in the earliest years of children's lives and contribute to significant social returns. Yet despite this evidence, the nation has underinvested in expanding families' access to high-quality ECE, with children of color, children from low-income families, children who speak languages other than English at home, and children with disabilities facing the greatest barriers to accessing high-quality, inclusive ECE experiences. None of the major publicly funded ECE programs have sufficient funding to serve all eligible children, and families with lower incomes are less likely to enroll their children in publicly funded child care, pre-K, or Head Start. Many of the policy decisions about funding levels, quality standards, and eligibility for public assistance stem from U.S. society's historical view of ECE as a personal responsibility, a view that persists to this day. The younger the child, the lower is the level of public investment (as demonstrated, for example, by the shortage of infant–toddler care and low compensation for infant–toddler providers).

The underinvestment in ECE and in its workforce reflects a deeply racialized history. The work of child care has historically been performed disproportionately by Black, Latina, and Asian women for free or for minimal pay, as evidenced by a variety of metrics, such as the significant differences in pay between child care providers and other professionals with BAs. Today, still, ECE educators receive near-poverty-level salaries and minimal employment benefits, which affects their own health and wellness and the quality of services they can provide.

Most ECE investments in the United States are targeted to low-income children and families, but they have been far from sufficient to serve even all eligible children or ensure high-quality experiences for all children served. Access is further hampered by state and federal policies and systems that create administrative barriers to access, and communities of color and immigrant families are disproportionately impacted by these administrative burdens. Moreover, those children who have access to publicly funded ECE programs have widely varying experiences within these systems. Children of color and children in low-income households are most likely to have lower-quality experiences compared with their wealthier, White counterparts as a result of underinvestment (historically and currently) in communities, programs, and specific segments of the ECE system and workforce; misguided policies; and lack of attention to culture, language, and bias and their effects on teacher–child relationships and instruction. In addition, certain populations are less likely to access publicly funded ECE programs.

Quality frameworks may sometimes be narrowly focused on standards that neglect issues and lived experiences that, uniquely or disproportionately, tend to affect children from historically marginalized communities, including Black, Latino, Asian, and Native American children; children with disabilities; children who speak a language other than English at home; immigrant children; and children from low-income communities. These neglected issues include structural biases, such as using English exclusively as the language of instruction, which disproportionately impacts children who speak a language other than English at home; harsh, exclusionary, and developmentally inappropriate discipline policies that disproportionately affect Black children, Indigenous children, and children with disabilities; and a lack of inclusion and appropriate accommodations, high-quality services, and supports for children with disabilities in general education and early learning programs. Global classroom quality measures that are aimed at addressing process quality and are often part of broader quality frameworks also fail to consider issues particularly important to the experiences of these populations, such as biases related to expectations, language, empathy, and challenging behavior that affect teacher–child relationships and teacher–child interactions. Yet even by these measures, differences across programs and geographic locations are stark and paint a bleak picture of opportunities for young children.

The lack of a coherent approach to ECE in the United States—with a predominant emphasis on work support over child development goals—results in inconsistent and scarce access to programs of varying quality. Today's ECE system is a patchwork of chronically underfunded programs, defined by quality frameworks that are designed for different goals and fail to capture the experiences and needs of children from historically marginalized communities. Geographic differences in the proportion of children served by ECE highlight the effect of vastly differing state and local policies. Gaps in access are most pronounced for children from low-income families and those living in rural communities. Although more than 80% of parents report that they would utilize a universal pre-K system, current analyses show that about 5 million more preschool seats would be needed to provide a universal system. The result is opportunity gaps experienced by children who do not have access to ECE, those who have access only to lower-quality programs, and those who face bias and differential treatment within learning systems.

REFERENCES

Acevedo-Garcia, D., Joshi, P.K., Ruskin, E., Walters, A.N., Sofer, N., & Guevara, C.A. (2021). Including children in immigrant families in policy approaches to reduce child poverty. *Child Poverty and Health 2021*: Addressing Equity and Economic Justice, 21(8 Suppl), S117–25. https://doi.org/10.1016/j.acap.2021.06.016

Achilles, C., Finn, J., & Gerber, S.B. (2000). *Small classes do reduce the test-score achievement gap*. Paper presented at the Annual Meeting of the Council of Great City Schools. ERIC Clearing House. Available: https://catalogue.nla.gov.au/Record/5682676

Ackert, E., Ressler, R., Ansari, A., & Crosnoe, R. (2018). Maternal employment, community contexts, and the child-care arrangements of diverse groups. *Journal of Marriage and Family*, 80(5), 1210–24. https://doi.org/10.1111/jomf.12501

Adair, J.K. (2015). *The impact of discrimination on the early schooling experiences of children from immigrant families*. Migration Policy Institute. Available: https://www.migrationpolicy.org/research/impact-discrimination-early-schooling-experiences-children-immigrant-families

Adams, G., & Pratt, E. (2021). *Assessing child care subsidies through an equity lens: A review of policies and practices in the Child Care and Development Fund*. Urban Institute. Available: https://www.urban.org/research/publication/assessing-child-care-subsidies-through-equity-lens-review-policies-and-practices-child-care-and-development-fund

Administration for Children and Families. (2022). *Fundamentals of CCDF administration*. Child Care Technical Assistance Network, Department of Health and Human Services. Available: https://childcareta.acf.hhs.gov/ccdf-fundamentals

Aguiar, A.L., & Aguiar, C. (2020). Classroom composition and quality in early childhood education: A systematic review. *Children and Youth Services Review*, 115, 105086. https://doi.org/10.1016/j.childyouth.2020.105086

Aikens, N., Klein, A.K., Tarullo, L.B., & West, J. (2013). *Getting ready for kindergarten: Children's progress during Head Start—FACES 2009 Child Outcomes Report*. (OPRE Report No. 2013-21a). Office of Planning, Research and Evaluation, Administration for Children and Families, Department of Health and Human Services. Available: https://www.acf.hhs.gov/opre/report/getting-ready-kindergarten-childrens-progress-during-head-start-faces-2009-child

Alford, M.T. (2009). *Long-term benefits of Head Start: Evidence from the Panel Study of Income Dynamics*. (Thesis No. 2972). Mississippi State University. Available: https://scholarsjunction.msstate.edu/td/2972

Allen, R., Shapland, D.L., Neitzel, J., & Iruka, I.U. (2021). Creating anti-racist early childhood spaces. *YC Young Children*, 76(2), 49–54. Available: https://fpg.unc.edu/publications/viewpoint-creating-anti-racist-early-childhood-spaces

Alvira-Hammond, M., & Gennetian, L.A. (2015). *How Hispanic parents perceive their need and eligibility for public assistance*. Bethesda, MD: National Research Center on Hispanic Children & Families.

Anderson, T., Coffey, A., Daly, H., Hahn, H., Maag, E., & Werner, K. (2022). *Balancing at the edge of the cliff: Experiences and calculations of benefit cliffs, plateaus, and trade-offs*. Urban Institute. Available: https://www.urban.org/research/publication/balancing-edge-cliff

Arteaga, I., Humpage, S., Reynolds, A., & Temple, J. (2014). One year of preschool or two: Is it important for adult outcomes? *Economics of Education Review*, 40, 221–37. https://doi.org/10.1016/j.econedurev.2013.07.009

Artiles, A.J. (2019). Fourteenth annual Brown lecture in education research: Reenvisioning equity research: Disability identification disparities as a case in point. *Educational Researcher*, 48, 325–35. https://doi.org/10.3102/0013189X19871949

Artiles, A.J., Dorn, S., & Bal, A. (2016). Objects of protection, enduring nodes of difference: Disability intersections with "other" differences, 1916 to 2016. *Review of Research in Education*, 40(1), 777–820. https://doi.org/10.3102/0091732x16680606

Austin, L.J., Edwards, B., Chávez, R., & Whitebook, M. (2019). *Racial wage gaps in early education employment*. Center for the Study of Child Care Employment. University of California at Berkeley. Available: https://cscce.berkeley.edu/publications/brief/racial-wage-gaps-in-early-education-employment/

Babbs Hollett, K., & Frankenberg, E. (2022). A critical analysis of racial disparities in ECE subsidy funding. *Education Policy Analysis Archives*, 30(14). https://doi.org/10.14507/epaa.30.7003

Bai, Y., Ladd, H.F., Muschkin, C.G., & Dodge, K.A. (2020). Long-term effects of early childhood programs through eighth grade: Do the effects fade out or grow? *Children and Youth Services Review*, 112, 104890. https://doi.org/10.1016/j.childyouth.2020.104890

Bailey, D., Duncan, G.J., Odgers, C.L., & Yu, W. (2017). Persistence and fadeout in the impacts of child and adolescent interventions. *Journal of research on educational effectiveness*, 10(1), 7–39.

Bailey, D.B., Jr., Hebbeler, K., Scarborough, A., Spiker, D., & Mallik, S. (2004). First experiences with early intervention: A national perspective. *Pediatrics*, 113(4), 887–96. https://doi.org/10.1542/peds.113.4.887

Bailey, M.J., Sun, S., & Timpe, B. (2021). Prep school for poor kids: The long-run impacts of head start on human capital and economic self-sufficiency. *American Economic Review*, 111(12), 3963–4001. https://doi.org/10.1257/aer.20181801

Baldiga, M., Joshi, P., Hardy, E., & Acevedo-Garcia, D. (2018). Child care affordability for working parents. [Research brief]. Brandeis University Heller School for Social Policy and Management and diversitydatakids.org. Available: https://www.diversitydatakids.org/research-library/research-brief/child-care-affordability-working-parents

Barnes, C.Y. (2021). "It takes a while to get used to": The costs of redeeming public benefits. *Journal of Public Administration Research and Theory*, 31(2), 295–310. https://doi.org/10.1093/jopart/muaa042

Barnett, S., Carolan, M., & Johns, D. (2013). *Equity and excellence: African-American children's access to quality preschool*. Rutgers University Center on Enhancing Early Learning Outcomes and National Institute for Early Education Research. Available: https://nieer.org/wp-content/uploads/2019/09/CEELO-NIEERequityExcellence-2013.pdf

Barnett, W.S. (2011). Effectiveness of early educational intervention. *Science*, 333(6045), 975–8. https://doi.org/10.1126/science.1204534

Barnett, W.S., & Boocock, S.S. (1998). *Early care and education for children in poverty: Promises, programs, and long-term results*. Albany, NY: State University of New York Press.

Barnett, W.S., & Friedman-Kraus, A. (2016). *States of Head Start*. National Institute for Early Education Research. Rutgers University. Available: https://nieer.org/wp-content/uploads/2016/12/HS_Full_Reduced.pdf

Barnett, W., & Kasmin, R. (2018). Fully funding pre-K through K–12 funding formulas. *State Education Standard*, 18(1), 22–8. Available: https://www.researchgate.net/publication/328293262_Fully_Funding_Pre-K_through_K-12_Funding_Formulas

Barnett, W.S., & Masse, L.N. (2007). Comparative benefit–cost analysis of the Abecedarian program and its policy implications. *Economics of Education Review*, 26(1), 113–25. https://doi.org/10.1016/j.econedurev.2005.10.007

Barnett, W.S., Hustedt, J.T., Robin, K.B., & Schulman, K. (2003). *The state of preschool: 2003 state preschool yearbook*. Rutgers, NJ: National Institute for Early Education Research.

Barr, A., & Gibbs, C.R. (2022). Breaking the cycle? Intergenerational effects of an antipoverty program in early childhood. *Journal of Political Economy*, 11(130). https://doi.org/10.1086/720764

Barrett, P., Zhang, Y., Moffat, J., & Kobbacy, K. (2013). A holistic, multi-level analysis identifying the impact of classroom design on pupils' learning. *Building and Environment*, 59, 678–89. https://doi.org/10.1016/j.buildenv.2012.09.016

Barrett, P., Treves, A., Shmis, T., & Ambasz, D. (2019). The impact of school infrastructure on learning: A synthesis of the evidence. *International Development in Focus*. World Bank. https://doi.org/10.1596/978-1-4648-1378-8

Bartik, T.J., Gormley, W., & Adelstein, S. (2012). Earnings benefits of Tulsa's pre-K program for different income groups. *Economics of Education Review*, 31(6), 1143–61. https://doi.org/10.1016/j.econedurev.2012.07.016

Bassok, D., & Galdo, E. (2016). Inequality in preschool quality? Community-level disparities in access to high-quality learning environments. *Early Education and Development*, 27(1), 128–44. https://doi.org/10.1080/10409289.2015.1057463

Bassok, D., Finch, J.E., Lee, R., Reardon, S.F., & Waldfogel, J. (2016a). Socioeconomic gaps in early childhood experiences: 1998 to 2010. *AERA Open*, 2(3). https://doi.org/10.1177/2332858416653924

Bassok, D., Fitzpatrick, M., Greenberg, E., & Loeb, S. (2016b). Within- and between-sector quality differences in early childhood education and care. *Child Development*, 87(5), 1627–45. https://doi.org/10.1111/cdev.12551

Beaven, E., Cady, A., Fyfe, B., & Woods, T.A. (2020). *Ideal pathways: How ideal learning approaches prepare and support early childhood educators*. Trust for Learning. Available: https://trustforlearning.org/resource/ideal-pathways/

Belfield, C., & Schwartz, H. (2007). *The cost of high-quality preschool in New Jersey*. Education Law Center. Available: https://www.researchgate.net/publication/254659996_The_Cost_of_High-Quality_Preschool_in_New_Jersey

Bipartisan Policy Center. (2019). *Early childhood initiative. Early Head Start–child care partnerships: Spotlighting early successes across America*. Bipartisan Policy Center. Available: https://bipartisanpolicy.org/report/early-head-start-child-care-partnerships-spotlighting-early-successes-across-america/

Bitler, M., Hoynes, H.W., & Domina, T. (2014). *Experimental evidence on the distributional effects of Head Start*. (Working Paper No. 20434). National Bureau of Economic Research. Available: https://www.nber.org/system/files/working_papers/w20434/w20434.pdf

Bowne, J.B., Magnuson, K.A., Schindler, H.S., Duncan, G.J., & Yoshikawa, H. (2017). A meta-analysis of class sizes and ratios in early childhood education programs: Are thresholds of quality associated with greater impacts on cognitive, achievement, and socioemotional outcomes? *Educational Evaluation and Policy Analysis*, 39(3), 407–428. https://doi.org/10.3102/0162373716689489

Bruno, E.P., & Iruka, I.U. (2022). Reexamining the Carolina Abecedarian project using an antiracist perspective: Implications for early care and education research. *Early Childhood Research Quarterly*, 58, 165–76. Available: https://doi.org/10.1016/j.ecresq.2021.09.001

Bryan, N. (2019). "Playing with or like the girls": Advancing the performance of "multiple masculinities in Black boys' childhood play" in U.S. early childhood classrooms. *Gender and Education*, 31(3), 309–26. https://doi.org/10.1080/09540253.2018.1447091

Bubikova-Moan, J., Næss Hjetland, H., & Wollscheid, S. (2019). ECE teachers' views on play-based learning: A systematic review. *European Early Childhood Education Research Journal*, 27(6), 776–800. https://doi.org/10.1080/1350293X.2019.1678717

Bucher, E., Meek, S., Smith, L., Sanchez Fuentes, L., Cardona, M., & Palomino, C. (2022). *Spotlight on EHS-CCP grantees during the pandemic: Building supply, enhancing quality, and advancing equity: The early Head Start-child care partnership series*. Children's Equity Project, Bipartisan Policy Center. Available: https://childandfamilysuccess.asu.edu/cep/early-head-start-child-care-partnership-series

Burchinal, J., Zaslow, M., & Tarullo, L. (2016). Quality thresholds, features, and doses in early care and education: Secondary data analyses of child outcomes. *Monographs of the Society for Research in Child Development*, 81(2016), 1–128. https://doi.org/10.1111/mono.12236

Burchinal, M. (2018). Measuring early care and education quality. *Child Development Perspectives*, 12(1), 3–9. https://doi.org/10.1111/cdep.12260

Burchinal, M., Roberts, J., Rhodus, R., Zeisel, S., Neebe, E., & Bryant, D. (2000). Relating quality of center-based child care to early cognitive and language development longitudinally. *Child Development*, 71(2), 339–57. https://doi.org/10.1111/1467-8624.00149

Burchinal, M., McCartney, K., Steinberg, L., Crosnoe, R., Friedman, S.L., McLoyd, V., & Pianta, R. (2011). Examining the black-white achievement gap among low-income children using the NICHD Study of Early Child Care and Youth Development. *Child Development*, 82(5), 1404–20. https://doi.org/10.1111/j.1467-8624.2011.01620.x

Camilli, G., Vargas, S., Ryan, S., & Barnett, W.S. (2010). Meta-analysis of the effects of early education interventions on cognitive and social development. *Teachers College Record*, 112(3), 579–620. https://doi.org/10.1177/016146811011200303

Campbell, F.A., Ramey, C.T., Pungello, E., Sparling, J., & Miller-Johnson, S. (2002). Early childhood education: Young adult outcomes from the Abecedarian Project. *Applied Developmental Science*, 6(1), 42–57. https://doi.org/10.1207/S1532480XADS0601_05

Campbell, F.A., Pungello, E.P., Burchinal, M., Kainz, K., Pan, Y., Wasik, B.A., Barbarin, O.A., Sparling, J., & Ramey, C.T. (2012). Adult outcomes as a function of an early childhood educational program: An Abecedarian Project follow-up. *Developmental Psychology*, 48(4), 1033–43. https://doi.org/10.1037/a0026644

Cannon, J.S., Kilburn, M.R., Karoly, L.A., Mattox, T., Muchow, A.N., & Buenaventura, M. (2017). *Investing early: Taking stock of outcomes and economic returns from early childhood programs.* Santa Monica, CA: RAND Corporation.

Cardona, M., Meek, S., Smith, L., Sanchez Fuentes, Y., & Bucher, E. (2022). *Policy recommendations to growth EHS-CCP in states: Building supply, enhancing quality, and advancing equity: The early Head Start-child care partnership series.* The Children's Equity Project, Arizona State University. Available: https://childandfamilysuccess.asu.edu/cep/early-head-start-child-care-partnership-series

Carr, R.C., Peisner-Feinberg, E.S., Kaplan, R., & Mokrova, I.L. (2021). Effects of North Carolina's pre-kindergarten program at the end of kindergarten: Contributions of school-wide quality. *Journal of Applied Developmental Psychology*, 76, 101317.

Cascio, E.U. (2017). *Does universal preschool hit the target? Program access and preschool impacts.* National Bureau of Economic Research. Available: https://www.nber.org/papers/w23215

Cascio, E.U. (2021). *COVID-19, early care and education, and child development.* Cambridge, MA: National Bureau of Economic Research.

Cascio, E.U., & Schanzenbach, D. (2013). *The impacts of expanding access to high-quality preschool education.* (Working Paper No. 19735). National Bureau of Economic Research. Available: https://www.nber.org/papers/w19735

Caspe, M., Lopez, M.E., & Hanebutt, R. (2019). *A tool for transformative family engagement: A commentary on the family engagement playbook.* Global Family Research Project. Available: https://globalfrp.org/Articles/Family-Engagement-Playbook

Castro, D.C., & Meek, S. (2022). Beyond Castañeda and the "language barrier" ideology: Young children and their right to bilingualism. *Language Policy*, 21, 407–25. https://doi.org/10.1007/s10993-021-09608-x

Chang, F., Crawford, G., Early, D., Bryant, D., Howes, C., Burchinal, M., Barbarin, O., Clifford, R., & Pianta, R. (2007). Spanish-speaking children's social and language development in pre-kindergarten classrooms. *Early Education and Development*, 18(2), 243–69. https://doi.org/10.1080/10409280701282959

Chaudry, A., & Sandstrom, H. (2020). Child care and early education for infants and toddlers. *Future of Children*, 30(2), 165–90. Available: https://futureofchildren.princeton.edu/sites/g/files/toruqf2411/files/foc_vol_30_no_2_compiled.pdf

Chaudry, A., Pedroza, J.M., Sandstrom, H., Danziger, A., Grosz, M., Scott, M., & Ting, S. (2011). *Child care choices of low-income working families*. Urban Institute. Available: https://www.urban.org/research/publication/child-care-choices-low-income-working-families

Chávez-Moreno, L.C. (2021). Dual language as White property: Examining a secondary bilingual-education program and Latinx equity. *American Educational Research Journal*, 58(6), 1107–41. https://doi.org/10.3102/00028312211052508

Chen, S., Phillips, B., & Izci, B. (2018). Teacher–child relational conflict in Head Start: Exploring the roles of child behaviour, teacher stress, and bias, and classroom environment. *Early Child Development and Care*, 190(8), 1–13. https://doi.org/10.1080/03004430.2018.1524378

Chien, N. (2022). *Factsheet: Estimates of child care eligibility and receipt for fiscal year 2019*. Office of the Assistant Secretary for Planning and Evaluation, Department of Health and Human Services. Available: https://aspe.hhs.gov/reports/child-care-eligibility-fy2019

Chien, N.C., Howes, C., Burchinal, M., Pianta, R.C., Ritchie, S., Bryant, D.M., Clifford, R.M., Early, D.M., & Barbarin, O.A. (2010). Children's classroom engagement and school readiness gains in prekindergarten. *Child Development*, 81(5), 1534–49. https://doi.org/10.1111/j.1467-8624.2010.01490.x

CityHealth. (2022). *High-quality, accessible pre-kindergarten*. CityHealth. Available: https://www.cityhealth.org/our-policy-package/high-quality-accessible-pre-k/

Clements, D.H., & Sarama, J. (2008). Experimental evaluation of the effects of a research-based preschool mathematics curriculum. *American Educational Research Journal*, 45(2), 443–94. https://doi.org/10.3102/0002831207312908

Coley, R.L., Votruba-Drzal, E., Collins, M.A., & Miller, P. (2014). Selection into early education and care settings: Differences by developmental period. *Early Childhood Research Quarterly*, 29(3), 319–32. https://doi.org/10.1016/j.ecresq.2014.03.006

Collier, V.P. (1995). *Acquiring a second language for school*. Reading Rockets. Available: https://www.readingrockets.org/article/acquiring-second-language-school

Collins, F.S., Adams, A.B., Aklin, C., Archer, T.K., Bernard, M.A., Boone, E., Burklow, J., Evans, M.K., Jackson, S., Johnson, A.C., Lorsch, J., Lowden, M.R., Nápoles, A.M., Ordóñez, A.E., Rivers, R., Rucker, V., Schwetz, T., Segre, J.A., Tabak, L.A., Hooper, M.W., Wolinetz, C., & NIH UNITE. (2021). Affirming NIH's commitment to addressing structural racism in the biomedical research enterprise. *Cell*, 184(12), 3075–9. https://doi.org/10.1016/j.cell.2021.05.014

Colliver, Y., Harrison, L.J., Brown, J.E., & Humburg, P. (2022). Free play predicts self-regulation years later: Longitudinal evidence from a large Australian sample of toddlers and preschoolers. *Early Childhood Research Quarterly*, 59, 148–61. https://doi.org/10.1016/j.ecresq.2021.11.011

Corcoran, L., & Steinley, K. (2019). Early childhood program participation, results from the National Household Education Surveys Program of 2016. (NCES 2017-101.REV). National Center for Education Statistics, Institute of Education Sciences, Department of Education. Available: https://nces.ed.gov/pubsearch/pubsinfo.asp?pubid=2017101REV

Crosby, D., Mendez, J., & Barnes, A. (2019). *Child care affordability is out of reach for many low-income Hispanic households*. National Research Center on Hispanic Children & Families. Available: https://www.hispanicresearchcenter.org/research-resources/child-care-affordability-is-out-of-reach-for-many-low-income-hispanic-households/

Crosnoe, R., Purtell, K.M., Davis-Kean, P., Ansari, A., & Benner, A.D. (2016). The selection of children from low-income families into preschool. *Developmental Psychology*, 52(4), 599. https://doi.org/10.1037/dev0000101

Cruz, R.A., & Firestone, A.R. (2022). Understanding the empty backpack: The role of timing in disproportionate special education identification. *Sociology of Race and Ethnicity*, 8(1), 95–113. https://doi.org/10.1177/23326492211034890

Cui, J., & Natzke, L. (2021). *Early Childhood Program Participation: 2019* (NCES 2020-075REV). National Center for Education Statistics, Institute of Education Sciences, Department of Education. Available: http://nces.ed.gov/pubsearch/pubsinfo.asp?pubid=2020075REV

Curenton, S.M., Iruka, I.U., Humphries, M.L., Jensen, B., Durden, T.R., Rochester, S.E., Whittaker, J.V., & Kinzie, M.B. (2020). Validity for the Assessing Classroom Sociocultural Equity Scale (ACSES) in early childhood classrooms. *Early Education and Development*, 31(2), 284–303. https://doi.org/10.1080/10409289.2019.1611331

Datta, A.R., & Borton, J. (2020). *How much of children's early care and education participation in 2012 was publicly funded?* Washington, DC: Office of Planning, Research and Evaluation.

Datta, A.R., Milesi, C., Srivastava, S., & Zapata-Gietl, C. (2021). *NSECE chartbook- Home-based early care and education providers in 2012 and 2019: Counts and Characteristics.* (OPRE Report 2021–85). Washington DC: Office of Planning, Research and Evaluation, Administration for Children and Families, Department of Health and Human Services.

DeMatthews, D.E., & Izquierdo, E. (2018). Supporting Mexican American immigrant students on the border: A case study of culturally responsive leadership in a dual language elementary school. *Urban Education*, 55(3), 362–93. https://doi.org/10.1177/004208591875671

DeParle, J. (2021, February 14). A year of hardship, helped and hindered by Washington. *The New York Times.* https://www.nytimes.com/2021/02/14/us/politics/coronavirus-poverty.html

Department of Health and Human Services [HHS]. (2019). *States' payment rates under the child care and development fund program could limit access to child care providers.* (Report in Brief OEI-03-15-00170). Office of Inspector General, Department of Health and Human Services. Available: https://oig.hhs.gov/oei/reports/oei-03-15-00170.pdf

———. (2020). *National snapshot of state agency approaches to child care during the COVID-19 pandemic.* (Report in Brief, No. A-07-20-06092). Office of Inspector General, Department of Health and Human Services. Available: https://oig.hhs.gov/oas/reports/region7/72006092.asp

Department of Health and Human Services (HHS) & Department of Education (DOED). (2014). *Policy statement on expulsion and suspension policies in early childhood settings.* Available: https://www2.ed.gov/policy/gen/guid/school-discipline/policy-statement-ece-expulsions-suspensions.pdf

Department of Justice & Department of Education (DOED). (2014). *Departments of Justice and Education issue school discipline guidance to promote safe, inclusive schools.* Available: https://www.justice.gov/opa/pr/departments-justice-and-education-issue-school-discipline-guidance-promote-safe-inclusive

Derman-Sparks, L., & Moore, E.K. (2016). Our proud heritage: Two teachers look back—The Ypsilanti Perry Preschool, part I. *Young Children*, 71(4). https://www.naeyc.org/resources/pubs/yc/sep2016/ypsilanti-perry-part-1

Division for Early Childhood & National Association for the Education of Young Children. (2009). *Early childhood inclusion: A joint position statement of the Division for Early Childhood (DEC) and the National Association for the Education of Young Children (NAEYC).* Chapel Hill, NC: The University of North Carolina, Frank Porter Graham Child Development Institute.

Downer, J.T., Lopez, M.L., Grimm, K.J., Hamagami, A., Pianta, R., & Howes, C. (2012). Observations of teacher–child interactions in classrooms serving Latinos and dual language learners: Applicability of the Classroom Assessment Scoring System in diverse settings. *Early Childhood Research Quarterly*, 27(1), 21–32. https://doi.org/10.1016/j.ecresq.2011.07.005

Duncan, G.J., & Magnuson, K. (2013). Investing in preschool programs. *Journal of Economic Perspectives*, 27(2), 109–32. https://doi.org/10.1257/jep.27.2.109

Durkin, K., Lipsey, M.W., Farran, D.C., & Wiesen, S.E. (2022). Effects of a statewide prekindergarten program on children's achievement and behavior through sixth grade. *Developmental Psychology*, 58(3), 470–84. https://doi.org/10.1037/dev0001301

Epstein, R., Blake, J.J., & González, T. (2017). *Girlhood interrupted: The erasure of Black girls' childhood*. Georgetown Law Center on Poverty and Inequality. Available: https://www.law.georgetown.edu/povertyinequality-center/wp-content/uploads/sites/14/2017/08/girlhood-interrupted.pdf

Evans, D.L., Feit, M.D., & Trent, T. (2016). African American parents and attitudes about child disability and early intervention services. *Journal of Social Service Research*, 42(1), 96–112. https://doi.org/10.1080/01488376.2015.1081118

Fabes, R.A., Quick, M., Musgrave, A., Meek, S., & Catherine, E. (2020). Exclusionary discipline in U.S. public pre-K programs: An initial look at the 2017-2018 CRDC data. *The Preschool Exclusionary Discipline Project: Research Briefs (Issue 1)*. Arizona State University. Available: https://storymaps.arcgis.com/stories/db517f89380c40b59276d651badc97a3

Farran, D.C., Hofer, K., Lipsey, M., & Bilbrey, C. (2014). *Variations in the quality of TN-VPK classrooms*. Presented March 8, 2014, at the Society for Research on Educational Effectiveness. Available: https://my.vanderbilt.edu/tnprekevaluation/files/2014/03/Farran-SREE-Spring-2014-Presentation.pdf

Feinberg, E., Silverstein, M., Donahue, S., & Bliss, R. (2011). The impact of race on participation in Part C early intervention services. *Journal of Developmental and Behavioral Pediatrics*, 32(4), 284–91. https://doi.org/10.1097/DBP.0b013e3182142fbd

Figueras-Daniel, A., & Li, Z. (2021). Evidence of support for dual language learners in a study of bilingual staffing patterns using the Classroom Assessment of Supports for Emergent Bilingual Acquisition (CASEBA). *Early Childhood Research Quarterly*, 54(1), 271–85. https://doi.org/10.1016/j.ecresq.2020.09.011

Ford, T.G., Kwon, K.A., & Tsotsoros, J.D. (2021). Early childhood distance learning in the U.S. During the COVID pandemic: Challenges and opportunities. *Children and Youth Services Review*, 131, 106297. https://doi.org/10.1016/j.childyouth.2021.106297

Forry, N.D., Tout, K., Rothenberg, L., Sandstrom, H., & Vesely, C.K. (2013). *Child care decision-making literature review*. (OPRE Brief 2013-45). Washington, DC: Office of Planning, Research and Evaluation, Administration for Children and Families, Department of Health and Human Services.

Francis, J., & Barnett, W.S. (2019). Relating preschool class size to classroom quality and student achievement. *Early Childhood Research Quarterly*, 49, 49–58. https://doi.org/10.1016/j.ecresq.2019.05.002

Frede, E.C. (1998). Preschool program quality in programs for children in poverty. *Early care and education for children in poverty: Promises, programs, and long-term results*, 77–98. Albany, NY: State University of New York Press.

Friedman-Krauss, A.H., Raver, C.C., Morris, P.A., & Jones, S.M. (2014). The role of classroom-level child behavior problems in predicting preschool teacher stress and classroom emotional climate. *Early Education and Development*, 25(4), 530–52. https://doi.org/10.1080/10409289.2013.817030

Friedman-Krauss, A.H., Barnett, W.S., Garver, K.A., Hodges, K.S., Weisenfeld, G., & DiCrecchio, N. (2019). *The state of preschool 2018: State preschool yearbook*. National Institute for Early Education Research. Available: https://nieer.org/wp-content/uploads/2019/04/YB2018_Full-ReportR2.pdf

Friedman-Krauss, A.H., Barnett, W.S., Garver, K.A., Hodges, K.S., Weisenfeld, G., & Gardiner, B.A. (2021). *The state of preschool 2020: State preschool yearbook*. New Brunswick, NJ: National Institute for Early Education Research.

Friedman-Krauss, A.H., Barnett, W.S., Garver, K.A., Hodges, K.S., Weisenfeld, G., and Gardiner, B.A., & Merriman Jost, T. (2022). *The state of preschool 2021: State preschool yearbook.* National Institute for Early Education Research, Rutgers Graduate School of Education. Available: https://nieer.org/wp-content/uploads/2022/09/YB2021_Full_Report.pdf

Gansen, H.M. (2021). Disciplining difference(s): Reproducing inequalities through disciplinary interactions in preschool. *Social Problems*, 68(3), 740–60. https://doi.org/10.1093/socpro/spaa011

Gastaldi, F.G.M., Pasta, T., Longobardi, C., Prino, L.E., & Quaglia, R. (2014). Measuring the influence of stress and burnout in teacher-child relationship. *European Journal of Education and Psychology*, 7(1). https://doi.org/10.1989/ejep.v7i1.149

Gelatt, J., Adams, G., & Huerta, S. (2014). *Supporting immigrant families' access to prekindergarten.* Urban Institute. Available: https://www.urban.org/research/publication/supporting-immigrant-families-access-prekindergarten

Genesee, F., & Lindholm-Leary, K. (2013). Two case studies of content-based language education. *Journal of Immersion and Content-Based Language Education*, 1(1), 3–33. https://doi.org/10.1075/jicb.1.1.02gen

Giapponi Schneider, K., Warfield, M.E., Joshi, P., Ha, Y., & Hodgkin, D. (2017). Insights into the black box of child care supply: Predictors of provider participation in the Massachusetts child care subsidy system. *Children and Youth Services Review*, 79, 148–59.

Giapponi Schneider, K., Joshi, P., & Ha, Y. (2021). An examination of child care provider participation in state subsidy contract systems. *Children and Youth Services Review*, 127, 106099.

Gilliam, W. (2005). *Prekindergarteners left behind: Expulsion rates in state prekindergarten systems.* Foundation for Child Development. Available: https://www.zerotothree.org/resource/prekindergarteners-left-behind-expulsion-rates-in-state-prekindergarten-programs

Gilliam, W.S., & Shahar, G. (2006). Preschool and child care expulsion and suspension: Rates and predictors in one state. *Infants & Young Children*, 19(3), 228–45. https://doi.org/10.1097/00001163-200607000-00007

Gilliam, W.S., Maupin, A.N., Reyes, C.R., Accavitti, M., & Shic, F. (2016). *Do early educators' implicit biases regarding sex and race relate to behavior expectations and recommendations of preschool expulsions and suspensions?* Yale Child Study Center. Available: https://marylandfamiliesengage.org/wp-content/uploads/2019/07/Preschool-Implicit-Bias-Policy-Brief.pdf

Gillispie, C. (2019). *Young learners, missed opportunities: Ensuring that Black and Latino children have access to high-quality state-funded preschool.* Education Trust. Available: https://edtrust.org/resource/young-learners-missed-opportunities/

———. (2021). *Our youngest learners. Increasing equity in early intervention.* The Education Trust. Available: https://edtrust.org/increasing-equity-in-early-intervention/

Goelman, H., & Guo, H. (1998). What we know and what we don't know about burnout among early childhood care providers. *Child & Youth Care Forum*, 27, 175–99. https://doi.org/10.1007/BF02589564

Goff, P.A., Jackson, M.C., Di Leone, B.A.L., Culotta, C.M., & Di Tomasso, N.A. (2014). The essence of innocence: Consequences of dehumanizing Black children. *Journal of Personality and Social Psychology*, 106, 526–45. https://doi.org/10.1037/a0035663

Gormley, W. (2017). Universal vs. targeted pre-kindergarten: Reflections for policymakers. In *The current state of scientific knowledge on pre-kindergarten effects*, 51–6. Foundation for Child Development. Available: https://www.fcd-us.org/current-state-scientific-knowledge-pre-kindergarten-effects/

Gormley, W.T., Gayer, T., Phillips, D., & Dawson, B. (2005). The effects of universal pre-K on cognitive development. *Developmental Psychology*, 41(6), 872–84. https://doi.org/10.1037/0012-1649.41.6.872

Gormley, W.T., Amadon, S., Magnuson, K., Claessens, A., & Hummel-Price, D. (2023). Universal pre-K and college enrollment: Is there a link? *AERA Open*, 9. https://doi.org/10.1177/23328584221147893

Government Accountability Office (GAO). (2018). *K-12 education: Discipline disparities for Black students, boys, and students with disability*. (GAO-18-258). Available: https://www.gao.gov/products/gao-18-258

———. (2020). *Child care facilities: Federal agencies need to enhance monitoring and collaboration to help assure drinking water is safe from lead*. (GAO-20-597). Available: https://www.gao.gov/products/gao-20-597

Gray-Lobe, G., Pathak, P.A., & Walters, C.R. (2021). *The long-term effects of universal preschool in Boston*. National Bureau of Economic Research. Available: https://www.nber.org/system/files/working_papers/w28756/w28756.pdf

Greenberg, J.P. (2011). The impact of maternal education on children's enrollment in early childhood education and care. *Children and Youth Services Review*, 33(7), 1049–57.

Grindal, T., Bowne, J.B., Yoshikawa, H., Schindler, H.S., Duncan, G.J., Magnuson, K., & Shonkoff, J.P. (2016). The added impact of parenting education in early childhood education programs: A meta-analysis. *Children and Youth Services Review*, 70, 238–49. https://doi.org/10.1016/j.childyouth.2016.09.018

Ha, Y., Joshi, P., Schneider, K.G., & Hardy, E. (2020). Can administrative changes improve child-care subsidy stability? *Social Service Review*, 94(2). https://doi.org/10.1086/709444

Hakuta, K., Butler, Y.G., & Witt, D. (2000). *How long does it take English learners to attain proficiency?* (Policy Report 2000-1). The University of California Linguistic Minority Research Institute, Stanford University. Available: https://eric.ed.gov/?id=ED443275

Hallam, R., Hooper, A., Bargreen, K., Buell, M., & Han, M. (2017). A two-state study of family child care engagement in Quality Rating and Improvement Systems: A mixed-methods analysis. *Early Education and Development*, 28(6), 669–83. https://doi.org/10.1080/10409289.2017.1303306

Hamre, B., Pianta, R., Field, M., Crouch, J., Downer, J., Howes, C., & LaParo, K. (2012). A course on effective teacher-child interactions: Effects on teacher beliefs, knowledge, and observed practice. *American Educational Research Journal*, 49(1), 88–123. https://doi.org/10.3102/0002831211434596

Han, J., & Neuharth-Pritchett, S. (2021). Predicting students' mathematics achievement through elementary and middle school: The contribution of state-funded prekindergarten program participation. *Child & Youth Care Forum*, 50, 1–24. https://doi.org/10.1007/s10566-020-09595-w

Hanline, M.F., Milton, S., & Phelps, P.C. (2008). A longitudinal study exploring the relationship of representational levels of three aspects of preschool sociodramatic play and early academic skills. *Journal of Research in Childhood Education*, 23(1), 19–28. https://doi.org/10.1080/02568540809594643

Hardy, E., & Huber, R. (2020). *Unequal neighborhood availability of Head Start: Exploring patterns in the data*. Brandeis University, diversitydatakids.org. Available: https://www.diversitydatakids.org/research-library/data-visualization/unequal-neighborhood-availability-head-start-exploring-patterns

Hardy, E., Joshi, P., Ha, Y., & Schneider, K.G. (2018). *Subsidized child care in Massachusetts: Exploring geography, access, and equity*. Institute for Child, Youth, and Family Policy, Brandeis University, Child Care Research Partnership, diversitydatakids.org. Available: https://search.issuelab.org/resource/subsidized-child-care-in-massachusetts-exploring-geography-access-and-equity.html

Hayakawa, M., Englund, M., Warner-Richter, M., & Reynolds, A. (2013). The longitudinal process of early parent involvement and school achievement: A path analysis. *NHSA Dialog: The Research to Practice Journal for the Early Childhood Field*, 16(1), 103–26.

Head Start Early Childhood Learning and Knowledge Center. (2022). *Head Start policy and regulations.* Available: https://eclkc.ohs.acf.hhs.gov/policy/45-cfr-chap-xiii/part-1302-program-operations

Henly, J.R., Kim, J., Sandstrom, H., Pilarz, A.R., & Claessens, A. (2017). What explains short spells on child-care subsidies? *Social Service Review,* 91(3), 488–533. https://doi.org/10.1086/693751

Hill, Z., Gennetian, L.A., & Mendez, J. (2019). A descriptive profile of state Child Care and Development Fund policies in states with high populations of low-income Hispanic children. *Early Childhood Research Quarterly,* 47, 111–23. https://doi.org/10.1016/j.ecresq.2018.10.003

Hillemeier, M.M., Morgan, P.L., Farkas, G., & Maczuga, S.A. (2013). Quality disparities in child care for at-risk children: Comparing Head Start and non-Head Start settings. *Maternal and Child Health Journal,* 17(1), 180–8. https://doi.org/10.1007/s10995-012-0961-7

Hirai, A.H., Kogan, M.D., Kandasamy, V., Reuland, C., & Bethell, C. (2018). Prevalence and variation of developmental screening and surveillance in early childhood. *JAMA Pediatrics,* 172(9), 857–66. https://doi.org/10.1001/jamapediatrics.2018.1524

Howes, C., Jolena, J., & Ritchie, S. (2003). Pathways to effective teaching. *Early Childhood Research Quarterly,* 18, 104–20. https://doi.org/10.1016/S0885-2006(03)00008-5

Howes, C., Burchinal, M., Pianta, R., Bryant, D., Clifford, R., & Barbarin, O. (2018). Ready to learn? Children's pre-academic achievement in pre-kindergarten programs. *Early Childhood Research Quarterly,* 23, 27–50. https://doi.org/10.1016/j.ecresq.2007.05.002

Institute of Medicine (IOM), & National Research Council (NRC). (2000). *From neurons to neighborhoods: The science of early childhood development.* The National Academies Press. https://doi.org/10.17226/9824

———. (2015). *Transforming the workforce for children birth through age 8: A unifying foundation.* The National Academies Press. https://doi.org/10.17226/19401

Iruka, I., Sheridan, S., Knoche, L., & Witte, A. (2019). *Examining child-teacher relationships and classroom quality across racial groups.* Paper presented at the 2019 Biennial SRCD Conference, March 22, 2019. Early Learning Network. Available: https://earlylearningnetwork.unl.edu/wp-content/uploads/2019/04/190410-Iruka-Frontiers-Compressed.pdf

Jenkins, J.M., & Nguyen, T. (2022). Keeping kids in care: Reducing administrative burden in state child care development fund policy. *Journal of Public Administration Research and Theory,* 31(1), 23–40. https://doi.org/10.1093/jopart/muab020

Jenkins, J.M., Duer, J.K., & Connors, M. (2021). Who participates in quality rating and improvement systems? *Early Childhood Research Quarterly,* 54, 219–27. https://doi.org/10.1016/j.ecresq.2020.09.005

Johnson, A.D., Han, W.J., Ruhm, C.J., & Waldfogel, J. (2014). Child care subsidies and the school readiness of children of immigrants. *Child Development,* 85(6), 2140–50. https://doi.org/10.1111/cdev.12285

Johnson, R.C., & Jackson, K.C. (2019). Reducing inequality through dynamic complementarity: Evidence from Head Start and public school spending. *American Economic Journal: Economic Policy,* 11(4), 310–49. https://doi.org/10.1257/pol.20180510

Johnson-Staub, C. (2017). *Equity starts early: Addressing racial inequities in child care and early education policy.* Center for Law and Social Policy. Available: https://www.clasp.org/publications/fact-sheet/equity-starts-early-addressing-racial-inequities-child-care-and-early/

Joo, Y.S., Magnuson, K., Duncan, G.J., Schindler, H.S., Yoshikawa, H., & Ziol-Guest, K.M. (2020). What works in early childhood education programs?: A meta-analysis of preschool enhancement programs. *Early Education and Development,* 31(1), 1–26. https://doi.org/10.1080/10409289.2019.1624146

Joshi, P., Geronimo, K., & Acevedo-Garcia, D. (2016). Head Start since the war on poverty: Taking on new challenges to address persistent school readiness gaps. *Journal of Applied Research on Children: Informing Policy for Children at Risk*, 7(1), 11. Available: https://files.eric.ed.gov/fulltext/EJ1188506.pdf

Joshi, P., Walters, A.N., Noelke, C., & Acevedo-Garcia, D. (2022). Families' job characteristics and economic self-sufficiency: Differences by income, race-ethnicity, and nativity. *RSF: The Russell Sage Foundation Journal of the Social Sciences*, 8(5), 67–95. https://doi.org/10.7758/RSF.2022.8.5.04

Jung, K., & Barnett, W.S. (2021). *Impacts of the pandemic on young children and their parents: Initial findings from NIEER's May-June 2021 preschool learning activities survey*. National Institute for Early Education Research, Rutgers University. Available: https://nieer.org/research-report/impacts-of-the-pandemic-on-young-children-and-their-parents-initial-findings-from-nieers-may-june-2021-preschool-learning-activities-survey

Karoly, L.A., Cannon, J.S., Gomez, C.J., & Whitaker, A.A. (2021). *Understanding the cost to deliver high-quality publicly funded pre-kindergarten programs*. RAND Corporation. Available: https://www.rand.org/pubs/research_reports/RRA252-1.html

Kauerz, K., & Coffman, J. (2013). *Framework for planning, implementing, and evaluating preK-3rd grade approaches*. Foundation for Child Development. Available: https://www.fcd-us.org/framework-for-planning-implementing-and-evaluating-prek-3rd-grade-approaches/

Kay, N.A., & Pennucci, A. (2014). *Early childhood education for low-income students: A review of the evidence and benefit-cost analysis*. Washington State Institute for Public Policy. Available: https://www.wsipp.wa.gov/ReportFile/1547/Wsipp_Early-Childhood-Education-for-Low-Income-Students-A-Review-of-the-Evidence-and-Benefit-Cost-Analysis_Full-Report.pdf

Keating, K.H., Cole, S., Bialik, P., Hains, D., & Schaffner, M. (2022). *State of babies yearbook 2022*. Zero to Three: National Center for Infants, Toddlers, and Families. Available: https://zerotothree.wpenginepowered.com/wp-content/uploads/2022/04/State-of-Babies-2022-Yearbook.pdf

Kelley, P., & Camilli, G. (2007). *The impact of teacher education on outcomes in center-based early childhood education programs: A meta-analysis*. National Institute for Early Education Research, Rutgers University. Available: https://nieer.org/research-report/the-impact-of-teacher-education-on-outcomes-in-center-based-early-childhood-education-programs-a-meta-analysis

Kilander, A., Garver, K., & Barnett, W.S. (2022). *Unworthy wages: State funded preschool teacher salaries and benefits*. The National Institutes for Early Education Research, Rutgers University. Available: https://nieer.org/research-report/unworthy-wages-state-funded-preschool-teacher-salaries-and-benefits

Klein, A., Starkey, P., Deflorio, L., & Brown, E.T. (2011). *Scaling up an effective pre-K mathematics intervention: Mediators and child outcomes*. Society for Research on Educational Effectiveness. Available: https://files.eric.ed.gov/fulltext/ED518141.pdf

Lafortune, J., & Schonholzer, D. (2018). *Do school facilities matter? Measuring the effects of capital expenditures on student and neighborhood outcomes*. Los Angeles, CA: Public Policy Institute of California.

Lamont, J.H., Devore, C.D., Allison, M., Ancona, R., Barnett, S.E., Gunther, R., Holmes, B., Minier, M., Okamoto, J.K., Wheeler, L.S.M., & Young, T. (2013). Out-of-school suspension and expulsion. *Pediatrics*, 131(3), e1000–7. https://doi.org/10.1542/peds.2012-3932

La Paro, K.M., Pianta, R.C., & Stuhlman, M. (2004). The classroom assessment scoring system: Findings from the prekindergarten year. *The Elementary School Journal*, 104(5), 409–26. https://doi.org/10.1086/499760

Latham, S., Corcoran, S.P., Sattin-Bajaj, C., & Jennings, J.L. (2021). Racial disparities in pre-K quality: Evidence from New York City's universal pre-K program. *Educational Researcher*, 50(9), 607–17. https://doi.org/10.3102/0013189X211028214

Lewis, V., Boucher, J., Lupton, L., & Watson, S. (2000). Relationships between symbolic play, functional play, verbal and non-verbal ability in young children. *International Journal of Language & Communication Disorders*, 35(1), 117–27. https://doi.org/10.1080/136828200247287

Lieberman, A., Bornfreud, L., Franchino, E., McCann, C., & Palmer, I. (2020). *Supporting early educator degree attainment: Takeaways from New America's working group.* New America. Available: https://www.newamerica.org/education-policy/reports/supporting-early-educator-degree-attainment/#authors

Limlingan, M.C., McWayne, C.M., Sanders, E.A., & López, M.L. (2020). Classroom language contexts as predictors of Latinx preschool dual language learners' school readiness. *American Educational Research Journal*, 57(1), 339–70. https://doi.org/10.3102/0002831219855694

Lindholm-Leary, K., & Hernández, A. (2011). Achievement and language proficiency of Latino students in dual language programmes: Native English speakers, fluent English/previous ELLS, and current ELLS. *Journal of Multilingual and Multicultural Development*, 32, 531–45. https://doi.org/10.1080/01434632.2011.611596

Lipsey, M.W., Farran, D.C., & Durkin, K. (2018). Effects of the Tennessee Prekindergarten Program on children's achievement and behavior through third grade. *Early Childhood Research Quarterly*, 45, 155–76. https://doi.org/10.1016/j.ecresq.2018.03.005

Loomis, A., Davis, A., Cruden, G., Padilla, C., & Drazen, Y. (2022). Early childhood suspension and expulsion: A content analysis of state legislation. *Early Childhood Education Journal*, 50(2), 327–44. https://doi.org/10.1007/s10643-021-01159-4

López, F. (2011). The nongeneralizability of classroom dynamics as predictors of achievement for Hispanic students in upper elementary grades. *Hispanic Journal of Behavioral Sciences*, 33(3), 350–76. https://doi.org/10.1177/0739986311415222

Ludwig, J., & Miller, D.L. (2007). Does Head Start improve children's life chances? Evidence from a regression discontinuity design. *The Quarterly Journal of Economics*, 122(1), 159–208. https://doi.org/10.1162/qjec.122.1.159

Lumeng, J.C., Kaciroti, N., Sturza, J., Krusky, A.M., Miller, A.L., Peterson, K.E., Lipton, R., & Reischl, T.M. (2015). Changes in body mass index associated with Head Start participation. *Pediatrics*, 135(2), e449–56. https://doi.org/10.1542/peds.2014-1725

Macy, M., Marks, K., & Towle, A. (2014). Missed, misused, or mismanaged: Improving early detection systems to optimize child outcomes. *Topics in Early Childhood Special Education*, 34(2), 94–105. https://doi.org/10.1177/0271121414525997

Malik, R., Hamm, K., Schochet, L., Novoa, C., Workman, S., & Jessen-Howard, S. (2018). *America's child care deserts in 2018.* Center for American Progress. Available: https://www.americanprogress.org/article/americas-child-care-deserts-2018/

Manning, M., Garvis, S., Fleming, C., & Wong, G. (2017). The relationship between teacher qualification and the quality of the early childhood education and care environment. *Campbell Systematic Reviews*, 13, 1–82. https://doi.org/10.4073/csr.2017.1

Markowitz, J.B., Carlson, E., Frey, W.D., Riley, J., Shimshak, A., Heinzen, H., Strohl, J., Klein, S.R., & Hyunshik, L. (2006). *Preschoolers with disabilities: Characteristics, services, and results. Wave 1 overview report from the Pre-elementary Education Longitudinal Study (PEELS).* (NCSER 2006-3003). Washington, DC: National Center for Special Education Research.

Mashburn, A.J., Pianta, R.C., Hamre, B.K., Downer, J.T., Barbarin, O.A., Bryant, D., Burchinal, M., Early, D.M., & Howes, C. (2008). Measures of classroom quality in prekindergarten and children's development of academic, language, and social skills. *Child Development*, 79(3), 732–49. https://doi.org/10.1111/j.1467-8624.2008.01154.x

Mattingly, M.J., & Wimer, C. (2017). *Child care expenses push many families into poverty: National Fact Sheet #36.* University of New Hampshire Carsey School of Public Policy. Available: https://scholars.unh.edu/cgi/viewcontent.cgi?article=1303&context=carsey

McCormick, M.P., Weissman, A.K., Weiland, C., Hsueh, J., Sachs, J., & Snow, C. (2020). Time well spent: Home learning activities and gains in children's academic skills in the prekindergarten year. *Developmental Psychology*, 56(4), 710–26. https://doi.org/10.1037/dev0000891

McCoy, D.C., Yoshikawa, H., Ziol-Guest, K.M., Duncan, G.J., Schindler, H.S., Magnuson, K., Yang, R., Koepp, A., & Shonkoff, J.P. (2017). Impacts of early childhood education on medium- and long-term educational outcomes. *Educational Researcher*, 46(8), 474–87. https://doi.org/10.3102/0013189x17737739

McElrath, K. (2021). *Heightened focus on early childhood education programs as preschool enrollment increased before COVID-19*. U.S. Census Bureau. Available: https://www.census.gov/library/stories/2021/11/pre-pandemic-early-childhood-enrollment-expanded-as-more-enrolled-public-preschool.html

McLean, C., Austin, L.J., Whitebook, M., & Olson, K.L. (2021). *Early childhood workforce index 2020*. Center for the Study of Child Care Employment. Available: https://cscce.berkeley.edu/workforce-index-2020/wp-content/uploads/sites/3/2021/02/Early-Childhood-Workforce-Index-2020.pdf

Meek, S., Smith, L., Allen, R., Catherine, E., Edyburn, K., Williams, C., Fabes, R., McIntosh, K., Garcia, E., Takanishi, R., Gordon, L., Jimenez-Castellanos, O., Hemmeter, M.L., Gilliam, W., & Pontier, R. (2020). *Start with equity. From the early years to the early grades. Data, research, and an actionable child equity policy agenda*. Washington, DC: Bipartisan Policy Center, Children's Equity Project.

Meek, S., Williams, C., Bostic, B., Iruka, I.U., Blevins, D., Catherine, E., & Alexander, B. (2021). *Building a universal preschool system around Head Start. Guiding an equitable pandemic recovery*. Children's Equity Project, The Century Foundation. Available: https://childandfamilysuccess.asu.edu/sites/default/files/2021-08/headstart-report-080221%20%281%29.pdf

Meek, S., Iruka, I. U., Soto-Boykin, X., Blevins, D., Alexander, B., Cardona, M., & Castro, D. (2022). *Equity is quality and quality is equity: Operationalizing equity in quality rating and improvement systems*. The Children's Equity Project, Center for Child and Family Success, Arizona State University. Available: https://childandfamilysuccess.asu.edu/cep/Equity-is-Quality-and-Quality-is-Equity

Meloy, B., Gardner, M., & Darling-Hammond, L. (2019). *Untangling the evidence on preschool effectiveness: Insights for policymakers*. Learning Policy Institute. Available: https://learningpolicyinstitute.org/product/untangling-evidence-preschool-effectiveness-report

Mendez, J.C., Crosby, D., & Siskind, D. (2018). *Access to early care and education for low-income Hispanic children and families: A research synthesis*. Washington, DC: National Research Center on Hispanic Children and Families.

Menken, K., & Kleyn, T. (2010). The long-term impact of subtractive schooling in the educational experiences of secondary English language learners, *International Journal of Bilingual Education and Bilingualism*, 13(4), 399–417. https://doi.org/10.1080/13670050903370143

Merriam-Webster. (2022). Racialization. In *Merriam-Webster*. Available: https://www.merriam-webster.com/dictionary/racialization

Miller, P., Votruba-Drzal, E., & Coley, R.L. (2013). Predictors of early care and education type among preschool-aged children in immigrant families: The role of region of origin and characteristics of the immigrant experience. *Children and Youth Services Review*, 35(9), 1342–55. https://doi.org/10.1016/j.childyouth.2013.04.024

Minervino, J. (2014). *Lessons from research and the classroom: Implementing high-quality pre-K that makes a difference for young children*. Seattle, WA: Bill and Melinda Gates Foundation.

Moffitt, T.E., Arseneault, L., Belsky, D.W., Dickson, N.P., Hancox, R.J., Harrington, H., Houts, R.M., Poulton, R., Roberts, B.W., Ross, S., Sears, M.R., Thomson, W.M., & Caspi, A. (2011). A gradient of childhood self-control predicts health, wealth, and public safety. *Proceedings of the National Academy of Sciences of the United States of America*, 108, 2693–8. https://doi.org/10.1073/pnas.1010076108

Moiduddin, E.M., Aikens, N., Tarullo, L.B., West, J., & Xue, Y. (2012). *Child outcomes and classroom quality in FACES 2009.* (OPRE Report 2012–37a). Office of Planning, Research and Evaluation, Administration for Children and Families, Department of Health and Human Services. Available: https://files.eric.ed.gov/fulltext/ED539265.pdf

Molfese, V.J., Beswick, J.L., Jacobi-Vessels, J.L., Armstrong, N.E., Culver, B.L., White, J.M., Ferguson, M.C., Rudasill, K.M., & Molfese, D.L. (2011). Evidence of alphabetic knowledge in writing: Connections to letter and word identification skills in preschool and kindergarten. *Reading and Writing*, 24, 133–50. https://doi.org/10.1007/s11145-010-9265-8

Morgan, P.L., Farkas, G., Hillemeier, M.M., Mattison, R., Maczuga, S., Li, H., & Cook, M. (2015). Minorities are disproportionately underrepresented in special education: Longitudinal evidence across five disability conditions. *Educational Researcher*, 44(5), 278–92. https://doi.org/10.3102/0013189x15591157

Morgan, P.L., Farkas, G., Hillemeier, M.M., & Maczuga, S. (2017). Replicated evidence of racial and ethnic disparities in disability identification in U.S. Schools. *Educational Researcher*, 46(6), 305–22. https://doi.org/10.3102/0013189x17726282

Mosteller, F. (1995). The Tennessee study of class size in the early school grades. *The Future of Children*, 5(2), 113–27. https://doi.org/10.2307/1602360

Mueller, D.J., Chase, C.I., & Walden, J.D. (1988). The effects of reduced class size in primary classes. *Educational Leadership*, 45(5), 48–50.

Muller, A.E., Hafstad, E.V., Himmels, J., Smedslund, G., Flottorp, S., Stensland, S.Ø., Stroobants, S., Van de Velde, S., & Vist, G.E. (2020). The mental health impact of the COVID-19 pandemic on healthcare workers, and interventions to help them: A rapid systematic review. *Psychiatry Research*, 293, 113441. https://doi.org/10.1016/j.psychres.2020.113441

Muschkin, C.G., Ladd, H.F., & Dodge, K.A. (2015). Impact of North Carolina's early childhood initiatives on special education placements in third grade. *Educational Evaluation and Policy Analysis*, 37, 478–500. https://doi.org/10.3102/0162373714559096

National Academies of Sciences, Engineering, and Medicine (National Academies). (2017). *Communities in action: Pathways to health equity.* Washington, DC: The National Academies Press.

———. (2018). *Transforming the financing of early care and education.* Washington, DC: The National Academies Press.

———. (2019a). *A roadmap to reducing child poverty.* Washington, DC: The National Academies Press.

———. (2019b). *Shaping summertime experiences: Opportunities to promote healthy development and well-being for children and youth.* Washington, DC: The National Academies Press.

———. (2019c). *Vibrant and healthy kids: Aligning science, practice, and policy to advance health equity.* Washington, DC: The National Academies Press.

———. (2019d). *Monitoring educational equity.* The National Academies Press. https://doi.org/10.17226/25389

———. (2022). *Addressing the impact of COVID-19 on the early care and education sector.* Washington, DC: The National Academies Press.

National Association for the Education of Young Children. (2021). *State survey data: Child care at a time of progress and peril.* National Association for the Education of Young Children. Available: https://www.naeyc.org/sites/default/files/wysiwyg/user-74/statedata_july2021_gf_092321.pdf

National Center for Education Statistics (NCES). (2017). *Early Childhood Program Participation Survey of the National Household Education Surveys Program*. (ECPP-NHES: 2012 and 2016). Washington, DC: Department of Education.

———. (2018). *Early Childhood Program Participation Survey of the National Household Education Surveys Program* (ECPP-NHES:1995, 2001, 2005, 2012, and 2016). Washington, DC: Department of Education.

———. (2019). *Early Childhood Program Participation Survey of the National Household Education Surveys Program: Table 202.30a. % age distribution of children who were under 6 years old and not yet in kindergarten, primary reason for difficulty finding child care, and selected child and family characteristics*. Washington, DC: Department of Education.

———. (2021). *Early Childhood Program Participation Survey of the National Household Education Surveys Program* (ECPP-NHES: 2019) Table 202.30. Washington, DC: National Center for Education Statistics.

National Family, School, and Community Engagement Working Group. (2009). *Recommendations for federal policy*. Harvard Family Research Project, Harvard University. Available: https://archive.globalfrp.org/family-involvement/publications-resources/national-family-school-and-community-engagement-working-group-recommendations-for-federal-policy

National Research Council (NRC). (2001). *Eager to learn: Educating our preschoolers*. Washington, DC: The National Academies Press.

———. (2002). *Minority students in special and gifted education*. Washington, DC: The National Academies Press.

National Survey of Early Care and Education Project Team (NSECEP). (2013). *Number and characteristics of early care and education (ECE) teachers and caregivers: Initial findings from the National Survey of Early Care and Education (NSECE)*. (OPRE Report No. 2013-38). Washington, DC: Office of Planning, Research and Evaluation, Administration for Children and Families, Department of Health and Human Services.

———. (2015). *Measuring predictors of quality in early care and education settings in the National Survey of Early Care and Education*. (Methodological Report No. 2015-93). Office of Planning, Research and Evaluation, Department of Health and Human Services. Available: https://www.acf.hhs.gov/sites/default/files/documents/opre/measuring_predictors_of_quality_mpoq_in_the_nsece_final_092315_b508.pdf

National Women's Law Center. (2016). *Annual report 2015-2016*. National Women's Law Center. Available: https://nwlc.org/about/annual-reports-financials/

NICHD Early Child Care Research Network. (2002). Child-care structure—process—outcome: Direct and indirect effects of child-care quality on young children's development. *Psychological Science*, 13(3), 199–206. Available: http://www.jstor.org/stable/40063707

Nores, M., & Barnett, S. (2014). *Access to high quality early care and education: Readiness and opportunity gaps in America*. Center on Enhancing Early Learning Outcomes. Available: https://nieer.org/wp-content/uploads/2014/05/ceelo_policy_report_access_quality_ece.pdf

Nores, M., Barnett, W.S., Joseph, G., Stull, S., Kwanghee, J., & Soderberg, J.S. (2017). *Year 2 report: Seattle pre-K program evaluation*. National Institute for Early Education Research, Cultivate Learning. Available: http://www.seattle.gov/Documents/Departments/Mayor/SPPEvaluation.pdf

Nores, M., Krauss, A.F., & Frede, E. (2018). *Opportunities & policies for young dual language learners: Preschool policy facts*. National Institute for Early Education Research. Available: https://nieer.org/policy-issue/opportunities-policies-for-young-dual-language-learners

Odom, S.L., Buysse, V., & Soukakou, E. (2011). Inclusion for young children with disabilities: A quarter century of research perspectives. *Journal of Early Intervention*, 33(4), 344–56. https://doi.org/10.1177/1053815111430094

Office for Civil Rights Data Collection (OCRDC). (2014). *Civil rights data collection: Data snapshot—School discipline—Issue brief March 2014*. Department of Justice. Available: https://www.ojp.gov/ncjrs/virtual-library/abstracts/civil-rights-data-collection-data-snapshot-school-discipline-issue

———. (2016). *2013-2014 civil rights data collection: A first look.* Department of Education Office for Civil Rights. Available: https://ocrdata.ed.gov/assets/downloads/2013-14-firstlook.pdf

———. (2018). *Number and percentage of public school preschool students subjected to corporal punishment, by race/ethnicity, disability status, and English proficiency, by state: School year 2017-2018.* Department of Education. Available: http://ocrdata.ed.gov

———. (2021). *An overview of exclusionary discipline practices in public schools for the 2017-2018 school year.* Department of Education. Available: https://ocrdata.ed.gov/assets/downloads/crdc-exclusionary-school-discipline.pdf

Office of Child Care. (2022). *OCC fact sheet.* Administration for Children and Families, Department of Health and Human Services. Available: https://www.acf.hhs.gov/occ/fact-sheet

Office of Special Education Programs (OSEP). (2021). *43rd Annual report to Congress on the implementation of the Individuals with Disabilities Education Act.* Department of Education. Available: https://sites.ed.gov/idea/2021-individuals-with-disabilities-education-act-annual-report-to-congress/

Oliva-Olson, C. (2019). *Dos métodos: Two classroom language models in Head Start: Strengthening the diversity and quality of the early care and education workforce paper series.* Urban Institute. Available: https://files.eric.ed.gov/fulltext/ED601890.pdf

Ou, S.R., Arteaga, I., & Reynolds, A. (2019). Dosage effects in the child-parent center preK-to-3rd grade program: A re-analysis in the Chicago Longitudinal Study. *Children and Youth Services Review*, 101, 285–98. https://doi.org/10.1016/j.childyouth.2019.04.005

Pacheco-Applegate, A., Carreon, E.D., Ellis, E., Thomas, W.C., Henly, J. R., Spielberger, J., & Ybarra, M. (2020). *Finding child care in two Chicago communities: The voices of Latina mothers.* The University of Chicago.

Palmer, D.K., Cervantes-Soon, C., Dorner, L., & Heiman, D. (2019). Bilingualism, biliteracy, biculturalism, and critical consciousness for all: Proposing a fourth fundamental goal for two-way dual language education. *Theory into Practice*, 58(2), 121–33. https://doi.org/10.1080/00405841.2019.1569376

Pardee, M. (2011). *Building an infrastructure for quality: An inventory of early childhood education and out-of-school time facilities in Massachusetts.* Children's Investment Fund. Available: https://cedac.org/Uploads/Files/CIFBldgInfrastructureReport.pdf

Parker, F.L., Piotrkowski, C.S., & Peay, L. (1987). Head Start as a social support for mothers: The psychological benefits of involvement. *American Journal of Orthopsychiatry*, 57(2), 220–33. https://doi.org/10.1111/j.1939-0025.1987.tb03532.x

Patterson, C., & Weisenfeld, G.G. (2021). *How can cities find funding and improve the quality of their pre-K programs?* CityHealth. Available: https://www.cityhealth.org/resource/how-can-cities-find-funding-and-improve-the-quality-of-their-pre-k-programs/

Pearman, F.A., Springer, M.P., Lipsey, M., Lachowicz, M., Swain, W., & Farran, D. (2020). Teachers, schools, and pre-K effect persistence: An examination of the sustaining environment hypothesis. *Journal of Research on Educational Effectiveness*, 13(4), 547–73. https://doi.org/10.1080/19345747.2020.1749740

Pelatti, C.Y., Piasta, S.B., Justice, L.M., & O'Connell, A. (2014). Language- and literacy-learning opportunities in early childhood classrooms: Children's typical experiences and within-classroom variability. *Early Childhood Research Quarterly*, 29(4), 445–56. https://doi.org/10.1016/j.ecresq.2014.05.004

Perlman, M., Fletcher, B., Falenchuk, O., Brunsek, A., McMullen, E., & Shah, P.S. (2017). Child-staff ratios in early childhood education and care settings and child outcomes: A systematic review and meta-analysis. *PLoS One*, 12(1), e0170256. https://doi.org/10.1371/journal.pone.017025

Peterson, C.A., Wall, S., Raikes, H.A., Kisker, E.E., Swanson, M.E., Jerald, J., Atwater, J.B., & Wei, Q. (2004). Early Head Start: Identifying and serving children with disabilities. *Topics in Early Childhood Special Education*, 24(2), 76–88. https://doi.org/10.1177/02711214040240020301

Phillips, D., Johnson, A., Weiland, C., & Hutchison, J. (2017). *Public preschool in a more diverse America: Implications for next-generation evaluation research.* (Working Paper No. 2–17). University of Michigan. Available: https://eric.ed.gov/?id=ED594039

Phillips, D.A., Gormley, W.T., & Lowenstein, A.E. (2009). Inside the pre-kindergarten door: Classroom climate and instructional time allocation in Tulsa's pre-K programs. *Early Childhood Research Quarterly*, 24(3), 213–28. https://doi.org/10.1016/j.ecresq.2009.05.002

Phillips, D.A., Johnson, A.D., & Iruka, I.U. (2022). Early care and education settings as contexts for socialization: New directions for quality assessment. *Child Development Perspectives*, 16(3), 127–33. https://doi.org/10.1111/cdep.12460

Pianta, R., & Hamre, B. (2009). Conceptualization, measurement and improvement of classroom processes: Standardized observation can leverage capacity. *Educational Researcher*, 38, 109–19. https://doi.org/10.3102/0013189X09332374

Pianta, R.C., Barnett, W.S., Burchinal, M., & Thornburg, K.R. (2009). The effects of preschool education: What we know, how public policy is or is not aligned with the evidence base, and what we need to know. *Psychological Science in the Public Interest*, 10(2), 49–88. https://doi.org/10.1177/1529100610381908

Pianta, R.C., Hamre, B.K., & Allen, J.P. (2012). Teacher-student relationships and engagement: Conceptualizing, measuring, and improving the capacity of classroom interactions. *Handbook of research on student engagement*, 365–86. Springer. Available: https://bottemabeutel.com/wp-content/uploads/2014/01/Pianta-teacher-student-relationships.pdf

Pianta, R.C., Downer, J., & Hamre, B.K. (2016). Quality in early education classrooms: Definitions, gaps, and systems. *The Future of Children*, 26(2), 119–37. https://doi.org/10.1353/foc.2016.0015

Pilarz, A.R., & Hill, H.C. (2014). Unstable and multiple child care arrangements and young children's behavior. *Early Childhood Research Quarterly*, 29(4), 471–83. https://doi.org/10.1016/j.ecresq.2014.05.007

Pinckney, H.P., Bryan, N., & Outley, C. (2021). Black playcrit: Examining the disruption of play for black male youth. *American Journal of Play*, 13(2–3), 210–29. Available: https://eric.ed.gov/?id=EJ1333521

powell, j.a., Menendian, S., & Ake, W. (2019). *Targeted universalism: Policy & practice.* Othering & Belonging Institute, University of California, Berkley. Available: https://belonging.berkeley.edu/targeted-universalism

Powell, T.M. (2020). *The scars of suspension: Testimonies as narratives of school-induced collective trauma.* Los Angeles, CA: University of California, Los Angeles. Available: https://escholarship.org/uc/item/05p4b41r

Puma, M., Bell, S., Cook, R., Heid, C., Shapiro, G., Broene, P., Jenkins, F., Fletcher, P., Quinn, L., Friedman, J., Ciarico, J., Rohacek, M., Adams, G., & Spier, E. (2010). *Head Start impact study final report.* Administration for Children and Families, Department of Health and Human Services. Available: https://www.acf.hhs.gov/opre/report/head-start-impact-study-final-report-executive-summary

Puma, M., Bell, S., Cook, R., Heid, C., Broene, P., Jenkins, F., Mashburn, A., & Downer, J. (2012). *Third grade follow-up to the Head Start impact study: Final report.* (OPRE Report 2012-45). Office of Planning, Research and Evaluation, Administration for Children and Families, Department of Health and Human Services. Available: https://www.acf.hhs.gov/opre/report/third-grade-follow-head-start-impact-study-final-report

Ramey, C.T. (2018). The Abecedarian approach to social, educational, and health disparities. *Clinical Child and Family Psychology Review*, 21(4), 527–44. https://doi.org/10.1007/s10567-018-0260-y

Ramey, C.T., & Ramey, S.L. (1998). Early intervention and early experience. *American Psychologist,* 53(2), 109–20. https://doi.org/10.1037//0003-066x.53.2.109

———. (2019). Reframing policy and practice deliberations: Twelve hallmarks of strategies to attain and sustain early childhood gains. *Sustaining early childhood learning gains: Program, school, and family influences,* 314–49. Cambridge University Press. https://doi.org/10.1017/9781108349352.016

Reardon, S.F., Weathers, E.S., Fahle, E.M., Jang, H., & Kalogrides, D. (2019). *Is separate still unequal? New evidence on school segregation and racial academic achievement gaps.* (CEPA Working Paper No. 19-06). Center for Education Policy Analysis. Available: https://cepa.stanford.edu/content/separate-still-unequal-new-evidence-school-segregation-and-racial-academic-achievement-gaps

Rebell, M.A., Wolff, J.R., Kolben, N., & Holcomb, B. (2017). *Establishing universal access to prekindergarten as a constitutional right.* Center for Educational Equity. Available: https://files.eric.ed.gov/fulltext/ED586278.pdf

Reeve, J. (2009). Why teachers adopt a controlling motivating style toward students and how they can become more autonomy supportive. *Educational Psychologist,* 44(3), 159–75. https://doi.org/10.1080/00461520903028990

Reinke, S., Peters, L., & Castner, D. (2019). Critically engaging discourses on quality improvement: Political and pedagogical futures in early childhood education. *Policy Futures in Education,* 17(2), 189–204. https://doi.org/10.1177/1478210318788001

Reynolds, A., & Temple, J. (Eds.). (2019). *Sustaining early childhood learning gains: Program, school, and family influences.* Cambridge University Press. https://doi.org/10.1017/9781108349352

Reynolds, A.J. (2019). The child–parent center preschool-to-third-grade program: A school reform model to increase and sustain learning gains at scale. *Sustaining early childhood learning gains: Program, school, and family influences,* 182–209. Cambridge University Press.

Reynolds, A.J., Temple, J.A., Ou, S.R., Arteaga, I.A., & White, B.A. (2011). School-based early childhood education and age-28 well-being: Effects by timing, dosage, and subgroups. *Science,* 333(6040), 360–4. https://doi.org/10.1126/science.1203618

Reynolds, A.J., Hayakawa, M., Ou, S.R., Mondi, C.F., Englund, M.M., Candee, A.J., & Smerillo, N.E. (2017). Scaling and sustaining effective early childhood programs through school-family-university collaboration. *Child Development,* 88(5), 1453–1465. https://doi.org/10.1111/cdev.12901

Reynolds A.J., Ou, S.R., & Temple, J.A. (2018). A multicomponent, peschool to third grade preventive intervention and educational attainment at 35 years of age. *JAMA Pediatrics,* 172(3), 247. https://doi.org/10.1001/jamapediatrics.2017.4673

Reynolds, A.J., Lee, S., Eales, L., Varshney, N., & Smerillo, N. (2022). Parental involvement and engagement in early education contribute to children's success and well-being. *Family-school partnerships during the early school years,* 91–111. Springer International Publishing. https://doi.org/10.1007/978-3-030-74617-9_6

Robinson, C.C., & Rosenberg, S.A. (2004). Child welfare referrals to Part C. *Journal of Early Intervention,* 26(4), 284–91. https://doi.org/10.1177/105381510402600404

Robson, D.A., Allen, M.S., & Howard, S.J. (2020). Self-regulation in childhood as a predictor of future outcomes: A meta-analytic review. *Psychological Bulletin,* 146(4), 324–54. https://doi.org/10.1037/bul0000227

Roll, S., & East, J. (2014). Financially vulnerable families and the child care cliff effect. *Journal of Poverty,* 18(2), 169–87. https://doi.org/10.1080/10875549.2014.896307

Rosenberg, S.A., Zhang, D., & Robinson, C.C. (2008). Prevalence of developmental delays and participation in early intervention services for young children. *Pediatrics,* 121(6), e1503–9. https://doi.org/10.1542/peds.2007-1680

Ruopp, R., & Smith, A.N. (1979). *Children at the center: Final report of the National Day Care Study: Executive summary*. Abt Associates. Available: https://eric.ed.gov/?id=ED168706

Sabol, T.J., & Chase-Lansdale, P.L. (2015). The influence of low-income children's participation in Head Start on their parents' education and employment. *Journal of Policy Analysis and Management*, 34(1), 136–61. https://doi.org/10.1002/pam.21799

Savage, S.A., & Robeson, W. (2022). Child care tradeoffs among Massachusetts mothers. *Community Development Issue Briefs*, 22(3). Federal Reserve Bank of Boston. Available: https://www.bostonfed.org/publications/community-development-issue-briefs/2022/child-care-tradeoffs-among-massachusetts-mothers

Schanzenbach, D.W., & Bauer, L.S. (2016). *The long-term impact of the Head Start program: Economic analysis*. Brookings Institute, The Hamilton Project. Available: https://www.brookings.edu/research/the-long-term-impact-of-the-head-start-program/

Schilder, D., Iruka, I., Dichter, H., & Mathias, D. (2015). *Quality rating and improvement systems: Stakeholder theories of change and models of practice*. Build Initiative. Available: https://buildinitiative.org/resource-library/quality-rating-and-improvement-systems-stakeholder-theories-of-change-and-models-of-practice-study-report-expert-panel-reflections-and-recommendations/

Schindler, H.S., Kholoptseva, J., Oh, S.S., Yoshikawa, H., Duncan, G.J., Magnuson, K.A., & Shonkoff, J.P. (2015). Maximizing the potential of early childhood education to prevent externalizing behavior problems: A meta-analysis. *Journal of School Psychology*, 53(3), 243–63. https://doi.org/10.1016/j.jsp.2015.04.001

Schmit, S., & Walker, C. (2016). *Disparate access: Head Start and CCDBG data by race and ethnicity*. Center for Law and Social Policy. Available: https://www.clasp.org/publications/report/brief/disparate-access-head-start-and-ccdbg-data-race-and-ethnicity/

Schulman, K. (2021). *On the precipice: State childcare assistance policies 2020*. National Women's Law Center. Available: https://nwlc.org/resource/on-the-precipice-state-child-care-assistance-policies-2020/

Schweinhart, L.J., Montie, J., Xiang, Z., Barnett, W.S., Belfield, C.R., & Nores, M. (2005). *Lifetime effects: The High/Scope Perry preschool study through age 40*, 194–215. Ypsilanti, MI: High/Scope Press, High/Scope Educational Research Foundation.

Shuey, E.A., & Leventhal, T. (2018). Neighborhood context and center-based child care use: Does immigrant status matter? *Early Childhood Research Quarterly*, 44, 124–35. https://doi.org/10.1016/j.ecresq.2018.03.009

Simpson, G.A., Colpe, L., & Greenspan, S. (2003). Measuring functional developmental delay in infants and young children: Prevalence rates from the NHIS-D. *Paediatric Perinatal Epidemiology*, 17(1), 68–80. https://doi.org/10.1046/j.1365-3016.2003.00459.x

Skene, K., O'Farrelly, C.M., Byrne, E.M., Kirby, N., Stevens, E.C., & Ramchandani, P.G. (2022). Can guidance during play enhance children's learning and development in educational contexts? A systematic review and meta-analysis. *Child Development*, 93, 1162–80. https://doi.org/10.1111/cdev.13730

Skiba, R.J., Artiles, A.J., Kozleski, E.B., Losen, D.J., & Harry, E.G. (2016). Risks and consequences of oversimplifying educational inequities: A response to Morgan et al. (2015). *Educational Researcher*, 45(3), 221–5. https://doi.org/10.3102/0013189x16644606

Snyder, P. (2021). *Early intervention and early learning in special education*. Presentation to the Committee on Exploring the Opportunity Gap for Young Children from Birth to Age Eight on November 8, 2021. Available: https://www.nationalacademies.org/event/08-11-2021/docs/D6CA4EB5743FF182E2A892F4BFD23F15501A9F51FAEB

Snyder, P., Hemmeter, M.L., Sandall, S., McLean, M., & McLaughlin, T. (2013). Embedded instruction practices in the context of response to intervention. *Handbook of response-to-intervention in early childhood*, 283–300. Baltimore, MA: Paul H. Brookes Publishing Co.

Snyder, P., Rakap, S., Hemmeter, M.L., McLaughlin, T., Sandall, S., & McLean, M. (2015). Naturalistic instructional approaches in early learning: A systematic review of the empirical literature. *Journal of Early Intervention*, Online First, 1–29. https://doi.org/10.1177/1053815115595461

Soliday Hong, S.L., Sabol, T.J., Burchinal, M.R., Tarullo, L., Zaslow, M., & Peisner-Feinberg, E.S. (2019). ECE quality indicators and child outcomes: Analyses of six large child care studies. *Early Childhood Research Quarterly*, 49, 202–17. https://doi.org/10.1016/j.ecresq.2019.06.009

Souto-Manning, M., & Rabadi-Raol, A. (2018). (Re)Centering quality in early childhood education: Toward intersectional justice for minoritized children. *Review of Research in Education*, 42(1), 203–25. https://doi.org/10.3102/0091732X18759550

Sparks, S.D., & Harwin, A. (2017). How parents widen—or shrink—academic gaps. *Families & Community*. EducationWeek. Available: https://www.edweek.org/leadership/how-parents-widen-or-shrink-academic-gaps/2017/04?cmp=eml-contshr-shr

Spear-Swerling, L. (2019). Structured literacy and typical literacy practices: Understanding differences to create instructional opportunities. *Teaching Exceptional Children*, 51(3), 201–11. Available: https://www.readingrockets.org/content/pdfs/structured-literacy.pdf

Starkey, P., Klein, A., Clarke, B., Baker, S., & Thomas, J. (2022). Effects of early mathematics intervention for low-SES pre-kindergarten and kindergarten students: A replication study. *Educational Research and Evaluation*, 27(1–2), 61–82. https://doi.org/10.1080/138036 11.2021.2022316

Steed, E.A., Phan, N., Leech, N., & Charlifue-Smith, R. (2021). Remote delivery of services for young children with disabilities during the early stages of the COVID-19 pandemic in the United States. *Journal of Early Intervention*, 44(2), 110–129. https://doi.org/10.1177/10538151211037673

Steele, J.L., Slater, R., Zamarro, G., Miller, T., Li, J.J., Burkhauser, S., & Bacon, M. (2017). *Dual-language immersion programs raise student achievement in English*. RAND Corporation. https://doi.org/10.7249/RB9903

Stefanou, C.R., Perencevich, K.C., DiCintio, M., & Turner, J.C. (2004). Supporting autonomy in the classroom: Ways teachers encourage student decision making and ownership. *Educational Psychologist*, 39(2), 97–110. https://doi.org/10.1207/s15326985ep3902_2

Stephens, C.M., Crosby, D.A., Yaya-Bryson, D., & Reid, A. (2023). Supporting Spanish-English DLLs in Head Start: Peer language match, instructional language match, and emotional support as predictors of approaches to learning and social skills. *Early Childhood Research Quarterly*, 63(2), 121–32. https://doi.org/10.1016/j.ecresq.2022.11.005

Suárez-Orozco, C., Gaytán, F.X., Bang, H.J., Pakes, J., O'Connor, E., & Rhodes, J. (2010). Academic trajectories of newcomer immigrant youth. *Developmental Psychology*, 46(3), 602.

Tout, K., Zaslow, M., & Berry, D. (2005). Quality and qualifications: Links between professional development and quality in early care and education settings. *Critical issues in early childhood professional development*, 77–110. Baltimore, MA: Paul H. Brookes Publishing Co.

Tout, K., Halle, T., Daily, S., Albertson-Junkans, L., & Moodie, S. (2013). *The research base for a birth through age eight state policy framework*. Bethesda, MD: Child Trends.

Turnbull, H.R., Turnbull, A.P., & Cooper, D.H. (2018). The Supreme Court, *Endrew*, and the appropriate education of students with disabilities. *Exceptional Children*, 84(2), 124–140. https://doi.org/10.1177/0014402917734150

Ullrich, R., Hamm, K., & Schochet, L. (2017). *6 policies to support the early childhood workforce*. Center for American Progress. Available: https://www.americanprogress.org/article/6-policies-to-support-the-early-childhood-workforce/

Ullrich, R., Schmit, S., & Cosse, R. (2019). *Inequitable access to child care subsidies*. Center for Law and Social Policy. Available: https://www.clasp.org/publications/report/brief/inequitable-access-child-care-subsidies/

UNICEF. (1989). *Convention on the Rights of the Child*. Available: https://www.unicef.org/child-rights-convention/convention-text#

Valentino, R. (2018). Will public pre-K really close achievement gaps? Gaps in prekindergarten quality between students and across states. *American Educational Research Journal*, 55(1), 79–116. https://doi.org/10.3102/0002831217732000

Valentino, R.A. (2015). *High quality and effective instruction for young children: Variation by socioeconomic status, race, and language status*. [Dissertation]. Stanford University. Available: https://www.proquest.com/dissertations-theses/high-quality-effective-instruction-young-children/docview/2500419722/se-2

Van Voorhis, F.L., Maier, M.F., Epstein, J.L., & Lloyd, C.M. (2013). *The impact of family involvement on the education of children ages 3 to 8: A focus on literacy and math achievement outcomes and social-emotional skills*. MDRC. Available: https://eric.ed.gov/?id=ED545474

Varshney, N., Temple, J.A., & Reynolds, A.J. (2022). Early education and adult health: age 37 impacts and economic benefits of the Child-Parent Center preschool program. *Journal of Benefit-Cost Analysis*, 13(1), 57–90.

Veiga, G., Neto, C., & Rieffe, C. (2016). Preschoolers' free play—Connections with emotional and social functioning. *International Journal of Emotional Education*, 8, 48–62. Available: https://eric.ed.gov/?id=EJ1098789

Villareal, M.U., & Lee, H.B. (2022). *The impact of a high-quality pre-kindergarten program on educational achievement in third and fourth grades: Evidence from pre-K 4 SA in San Antonio*. The University of Texas at Austin. Available: https://texaserc.utexas.edu/wp-content/uploads/2022/06/77-UTA082-Brief-Public-PreK-6.13.22-REV.pdf

Vogtman, J. (2017). *Undervalued: A brief history of women's care work and child care policy in the United States*. National Women's Law Center. Available: https://nwlc.org/resource/undervalued-a-brief-history-of-womens-care-work-and-child-care-policy-in-the-united-states/

Wasik, B.A., & Iannone-Campbell, C. (2012). Developing vocabulary through purposeful, strategic conversations. *The Reading Teacher*, 66(4), 321–32. https://doi.org/10.1002/TRTR.01095

Wasik, B.A., & Snell, E.K. (2019). Synthesis of preschool dosage: How quantity, quality, and content impact child outcomes. *Sustaining early childhood learning gains: Program, school, and family influences*, 31–51. New York, NY: Cambridge University Press.

Wechsler, M., Kirp, D., Tinubu Ali, T., Gardner, M., Maier, A., Melnick, H., & Shields, P.M. (2016). *The road to high-quality early learning: Lessons from the states*. Learning Policy Institute. Available: https://learningpolicyinstitute.org/product/road-high-quality-early-learning-lessons-states

Weiland, C. (2016). Launching preschool 2.0: A road map to high-quality public programs at scale. *Behavioral Science & Policy*, 2, 37–46. https://doi.org/10.1353/bsp.2016.0005

Weiland, C., & Yoshikawa, H. (2013). Impacts of a prekindergarten program on children's mathematics, language, literacy, executive function, and emotional skills. *Child Development*, 84(6), 2112–30. https://doi.org/10.1111/cdev.12099

Weiland, C., McCormick, M., Mattera, S., Maier, M., & Morris, P. (2018). Preschool curricula and professional development features for getting to high-quality implementation at scale: A comparative review across five trials. *AERA Open*, 4(1), 2332858418757735. https://doi.org/10.1177/2332858418757735

Weiland, C., Greenberg, E., Bassok, D., Markowitz, A.J., Guerrero-Rosada, P., Luetmer, G., Abenavoli, R., Gomez, C.J., Johnson, A.D., Harden, B.J., Maier, M.F., McCormick, M.P., Morris, P.A., Nores, M., Phillips, D.A., & Snow, C. (2021). *Historic crisis, historic opportunity: Using evidence to mitigate the effects of the COVID-19 crisis on young children and early care and education programs.* Urban Institute. Available: https://www.urban.org/policy-centers/center-education-data-and-policy/projects/historic-crisis-historic-opportunity-using-evidence-mitigate-effects-covid-19-crisis-young-children-and-early-care-and-education-programs

Weisenfeld, G.G. (2021). *Impacts of COVID-19 on preschool enrollment and spending: Policy brief.* Institute for Early Education Research, Rutgers University. Available: https://nieer.org/policy-issue/impacts-of-covid-19-on-preschool-enrollment-and-spending

Whitebook, K.F., Almaraz, M., Sakai, L., & Austin, L.J.E. (2012). *Learning together: A study of six B.A. completion cohort programs in early care and education: Year 4.* Berkeley, CA: Center for the Study of Child Care Employment, University of California, Berkeley.

Whitebook, M., McLean, C., Austin, L.J.E., & Edwards, B. (2018). *Early childhood workforce index 2018.* Berkeley: Center for the Study of Child Care Employment, University of California, Berkeley. Available: http://cscce.berkeley.edu/topic/early-childhood-workforce-index/2018/

Whorrall, J., & Cabell, S.Q. (2016). Supporting children's oral language development in the preschool classroom. *Early Childhood Education Journal*, 44(4), 335–41. https://doi.org/10.1007/s10643-015-0719-0

Wiener, J., & Tardif, C.Y. (2004). Social and emotional functioning of children with learning disabilities: Does special education placement make a difference? *Learning Disabilities Research & Practice*, 19(1), 20–32. https://doi.org/10.1111/j.1540-5826.2004.00086.x

Wintrop, R., Barton, A., Ershadi M., & Ziegler L. (2021) *Collaborating to transform and improve education Systems: A playbook for family-school engagement.* Brookings Institute. Available: https://www.brookings.edu/essay/collaborating-to-transform-and-improve-education-systems-a-playbook-for-family-school-engagement/

Word, E., Johnston, J., Pate Bain, H., Fulton, B.D., Boyd Zaharias, J., Achilles, C., Lintz, M.N., Folger, J., & Breda, C. (1990). *Student/teacher achievement ratio (STAR) Tennessee's K-3 class size study: Final summary report 1985-1990.* State Department of Education. Available: https://eric.ed.gov/?id=ED320692

World Bank. (2017). *The Classroom Assessment Scoring System (CLASS).* Available: https://www.worldbank.org/en/programs/sief-trust-fund/brief/the-classroom-assessment-scoring-system-class

Yates, T.M., & Marcelo, A.K. (2014). Through race-colored glasses: Preschoolers' pretend play and teachers' ratings of preschooler adjustment. *Early Childhood Research Quarterly*, 29(1), 1–11. https://doi.org/10.1016/j.ecresq.2013.09.003

Yoshikawa, H., Weiland, C., Brooks-Gunn, J., Burchinal, M., Espinosa, L.M., Gormley, J.W.T., Ludwig, J., Magnuson, K.A., Phillips, D.A., & Zaslow, M. (2013). *Investing in our future: The evidence base on preschool education.* Society for Research in Child Development. Available: https://www.fcd-us.org/the-evidence-base-on-preschool/

Yoshikawa, H., Weiland, C., & Brooks-Gunn, J. (2016). When does preschool matter? *Future of Children*, 26, 21–36. https://files.eric.ed.gov/fulltext/EJ1118535.pdf

Zablotsky, B., Black, L.I., Maenner, M.J., Schieve, L.A., Danielson, M.L., Bitsko, R.H., Blumberg, S.J., Kogan, M.D., & Boyle, C.A. (2019). Prevalence and trends of developmental disabilities among children in the United States: 2009–2017. *Pediatrics*, 144(4), e20190811. https://doi.org/10.1542/peds.2019-0811

Zigler, E., Gilliam, W., & Jones, S.M. (2006). *A vision for universal preschool education.* Cambridge, MA: Cambridge University Press. Available: https://doi.org/10.1017/CBO9781139167284

Zill, N., Resnick, G., Kim, K., McKey, R.H., Clark, C., Pai-Samant, S., Connell, D.C., Vaden-Kiernan, M., O'Brien, R.W., & D'Elio, M.A. (2001). *Head Start FACES: Longitudinal findings on program performance: Third progress report.* Department of Health and Human Services. Available: https://www.acf.hhs.gov/sites/default/files/documents/opre/perform_3rd_rpt.pdf

Zosh, J.M., Hirsh-Pasek, K., Hopkins, E.J., Jensen, H., Liu, C., Neale, D., Solis, S.L., & Whitebread, D. (2018). Accessing the inaccessible: Redefining play as a spectrum. *Frontiers of Psychology,* 9(1124). https://doi.org/10.3389/fpsyg.2018.01124

3

Opportunity Gaps in the Education Experienced by Children in Grades K–3

In this chapter, we continue our discussion of opportunity gaps in education and our analysis of outcomes for students in the context of historical structural drivers that create disparities for young children in the early grades (see Chapter 1 for a broader discussion of historical structural drivers). This chapter reviews the evidence related to these drivers and their effects on student outcomes in grades K–3. We also discuss barriers to access to high-quality education and other supports that can benefit young children and their families, and the differential experiences that children and families may experience in accessing these supports.

Similar to the discussion in Chapter 2, the focus of this chapter is on examining evidence related to gaps in access experienced by children and their families, disparities in quality experiences during the early grades, and the ways in which past and present structural drivers can perpetuate this inequity. We also highlight promising policies, practices, and programs with the potential to close the opportunity gap for children in grades K–3. The review of evidence presented in this chapter informed the committee's recommendations, presented in Chapter 8, for increasing access to equitable and high-quality learning, as well as creating more inclusive quality frameworks.

High-quality early care and education (ECE) followed by quality, well-funded, early elementary education is associated with a host of positive outcomes for children in the early grades, including and especially those who have historically been marginalized (Johnson & Jackson, 2018). Unfortunately, systemic factors in the early elementary grades can sustain and amplify many of the same disparities in opportunities and outcomes that begin earlier in children's educational trajectories. Indeed, recent literature focused on long-term developmental outcomes for young children, in particular those growing up in contexts characterized by lack of access to resources and supportive health and educational services, reexamines classic studies, such as those of the Abecedarian and HighScope Perry Preschool Project and the Head Start Impact Study, finding some evidence of "fade-out" in the elementary school years (Puma et al., 2010; Durkin et al., 2022). By contrast, two other recent meta-analyses looking at the medium- and long-term effects of ECE found that it is beneficial in promoting child well-being and lowering longer-term education costs (McCoy et al., 2017), and that high-quality, well-implemented preschool programs can increase early learning gains that have lasting effects through later years of schooling (Meloy, Gardner, & Darling-Hammond, 2019). Another recent study found evidence of an association between attending high-quality ECE and continued positive outcomes in early academic skills through grade 3 (Horm et al., 2022). Horm and colleagues (2022) note the need for more research to study the mechanisms that help sustain early gains or can cause fade-out in the early grades.

The funding structure for K–12 education relies heavily on local funding, and in many cases, federal and state funding does not adequately compensate for funding gaps at the local level. Research shows that these funding gaps, in combination with policies that have disproportionate negative effects on children from racialized[1] and marginalized backgrounds and interpersonal biases among adults who work with children, result in unequal experiences for young children from racialized backgrounds, those in low-income communities, those who speak a language other than English, and those with disabilities. Further, the misalignment between the ECE and early elementary systems in their definitions and expectations of quality disrupts continuity in gains experienced by young children and further perpetuates opportunity gaps.

The National Academies study *Transforming the Workforce for Children from Birth through Age 8* stresses the importance of continuity across the birth to 8 spectrum—both in the systems in which the education workforce works and in positive, high-quality experiences and environments (Institute of Medicine and National Research Council [IOM & NRC], 2015). The report focuses on two dimensions of continuity: (1) vertical continuity of high-quality experiences across diverse education settings and (2) alignment of learning expectations, curricula, instructional strategies, assessments, and learning environments. The report emphasizes that these

---

[1]Racialization is defined as the act of giving a racial character to someone or something or the process of categorizing, marginalizing, or regarding according to race (Merriam-Webster, 2022).

dimensions of continuity should be based on evidence on child development and be informed by evidence-based best practices. The report also notes that continuity also includes coordinated services and policies that can affect children in this age range and communication among providers, including educators, health care providers and services, mental health professionals, social services, and other community support agencies. They conclude that coordination and collaboration cannot be achieved without removing systemic barriers and improving supports to achieve better communication and interaction among providers and across settings (IOM & NRC, 2015).

CURRENT POLICY, FUNDING, AND SYSTEMS FOR EARLY ELEMENTARY EDUCATION

In the United States, state governments are obligated to provide public education to all school-aged children. Nonetheless, opportunity gaps exist within this system. Funding disparities in K–12 education affect access to well-resourced and quality programs (Lloyd & Harwin, 2021). As with ECE, these disparities impact a disproportionate number of students of color, although there is considerable variability in this regard across and within states (Raikes & Darling-Hammond, 2019). To illustrate, neighboring suburban counties outspend Chicago by more than $10,000 per student (Raikes & Darling-Hammond, 2019).

A key factor shaping funding inequities is the prevailing school funding model that relies on local property taxes. Thus, children who live in low-income neighborhoods are more likely to attend underresourced schools (Raikes & Darling-Hammond, 2019). Funding disparities in school construction and modernization are also shaped by property wealth. Districts with high property wealth—which serve predominantly White learners—spend significantly more on school construction and modernization compared with low-income districts (Brunner, Schwegman, & Vincent, 2022). Furthermore, district size and racial makeup mediate funding patterns. For instance, small school districts serving mainly White students receive $23 billion more than districts serving minority majority districts (EdBuild, 2019). The Education Trust reports that districts educating mainly White students receive $1,800 more per student per year compared with districts serving primarily students of color (Latino, African American, Native American; Morgan & Amerikaner, 2018).

Federal funding for special populations, such as children in low-income communities, English learners, and children with disabilities, is generally insufficient to bridge state and local gaps, largely because these federal funding streams are underfunded. Research indicates that funding gaps exist nationally between White and Black, White and Latino, and higher-income and lower-income students (Shores, Lee, & Williams,

2021). Black students receive about $400 less than White students, while lower-income students receive about $430 less than higher-income students. The largest gap is between White and Latino students, with Latino students receiving about $1,200 less than their White peers. Shores, Lee, and Williams (2021) examined these gaps in per pupil spending at the national, state, and district levels. They found the largest gaps nationally, explained by differences in education spending across states and the distribution of students of color and lower-income students in states that invest less in education. For example, at the state level, Shores, Lee, and Williams found higher per pupil expenditures for Black, Hispanic, and lower-income students than for White and higher-income students. At the district level, more funding is generally allocated to Black, Hispanic, and lower-income students, with the gap between Hispanic and White students being largest. At the national level, however, resource distribution was found to be more regressive, with Black, Hispanic, and lower-income students receiving lower per pupil spending and lower capital expenditures (Shores, Lee, & Williams, 2021).

Probing further the disparities across states, Baker (2017) reports a national perspective on school funding inequalities. His main findings include the following:

- School funding levels continue to be characterized by wide disparities among states, ranging from a high of $18,165 per pupil in New York to a low of $5,838 in Idaho when adjusted for regional differences.
- Many of the lowest-funding states, such as Arizona, Idaho, Nevada, North Carolina, and Texas, allocate a very low percentage of their states' economic capacity to funding for public education.
- Twenty-one states are regressive, providing less funding to school districts with higher concentrations of low-income students.
- Only a handful of states—Delaware, Minnesota, New Jersey, and Massachusetts—have generally high funding levels and also provide significantly more funding to districts where student poverty is highest.
- Low rankings on school funding fairness correlate with poor state performance on key resource indicators, including less access to ECE, noncompetitive wages for teachers, and higher teacher:student ratios.

In light of such funding differences, a research question consistently raised in the literature is whether school spending matters. The available evidence offers an affirmative answer to this question. Increased school funding is associated with better academic performance, higher graduation rates, and improved income in adult life (Jackson, 2018), with the most pronounced effects seen in children from low-income households (Jackson, Johnson, & Persico, 2016). Lafortune, Rothstein, and Schanzenbach (2018) studied the impacts of school finance reforms on student achievement and found that the impacts of increased funding for low-income school districts were immediate, strong, and sustainable. Of significance, Lafortune, Rothstein, and Schanzenbach (2018) found that a one-time $1,000 increment in per student annual spending had a relative achievement impact over a 10-year period of "between 0.12 and 0.24 standard deviations" in low-income districts (p. 6). These researchers also found that funding reforms were effective in reducing inequities across districts, although "other policy tools aimed at closing *within*-district achievement gaps will be needed to address overall equity concerns" (Lafortune, Rothstein, & Schanzenbach, 2018, p. 4 [emphasis in original]), including achievement gaps between students of color and White learners and between high- and low-income groups.

Jackson (2018) conducted a comprehensive review of the research on school spending and student outcomes. The review distinguished between older studies categorized largely as descriptive and recent research aiming to draw causal inferences. A consistent finding across the two kinds of studies was a positive association between increased school spending and learner outcomes. This was "true across studies that use different datasets, examine different time periods, rely on different sources of variation, and employ different statistical techniques" (Jackson, 2018, p. 13). Nevertheless, Jackson cautions about potential contextual effects not yet well understood. For instance, some research on capital construction and Title I spending does not consistently support the link between school funding and learner outcomes. Critically, however, infrastructure and facility investments may have important effects on children beyond academics—for example, in health and safety.

Jackson, Johnson, and Persico (2016) studied the effects of school reform efforts and found that "a 10% increase in per pupil spending each year for all twelve years of public school leads to 0.27 more completed years of education, 7.25% higher wages, and a 3.67 percentage-point reduction in the annual incidence of adult poverty; effects are much more pronounced for children from low-income families" (p. 1). The authors estimate that the effect of a permanent increase in per pupil spending throughout all school years of about 22.7% (about $2,800 in per pupil spending) for low-income learners would eliminate the achievement gap between high- and low-income students. Three states stand out for instituting school spending reforms that have produced noteworthy improvements in student outcomes and achievement gaps (Baker, 2017). Massachusetts, New Jersey, and Minnesota instituted reforms that included increasing funding for school districts serving a sizable number of marginalized learners; expanding enrollment in quality preschool and investing in school readiness programs and Head Start; and strengthening professional capacity and development through measures that included salary increases, higher professional standards, and sustained professional development (Baker, 2017).

School spending also matters for students with disabilities. Cruz and colleagues (2020) report a positive association between greater spending on special education programs and growth in the number of students with disabilities meeting or exceeding standards for English language arts. However, this pattern was not observed in high-poverty schools, which generally had fewer certified teachers compared with low-poverty schools, suggesting that funding and qualified teachers are both critical. It is important to note that the association between increases in spending on special education programs and growth in the number of students meeting or exceeding English language arts standards also benefited learners *without* disabilities in both high- and low-poverty schools (Cruz et al., 2020). Taken together, these findings indicate that school spending reforms are linked to improved academic outcomes for students with and without disabilities (with some important contextual caveats).

Access to and Funding for Out-of-School Time

Access barriers extend into what is traditionally labeled as "after school" and commonly referred to in the youth development sector as out-of-school-time (OST) programming. The trajectory of OST programming is similar to that of ECE programming—born out of labor market shifts and societal needs, OST programs are often underresourced despite the clear evidence of their positive impact on child development gains (Mahoney, Parente, & Zigler, 2009). ECE and OST programs also share a common history of disinvestment and inequity—specifically across communities of color and low-income communities—which manifests in barriers to access, funding, and quality. Families can receive assistance in paying for and accessing school-age care through only two funding streams: the Child Care and Development Block Grant (CCDBG) and the 21st Century Community Learning Centers initiative. CCDBG is the main federal funding source for helping families afford child care, including OST care and care for school-aged children. Although school-age child care is a large part of the child care subsidy system, it is often forgotten in policy and systems conversations. In fact 44% of CCDBG participants are school-aged children between the ages of 5 and 13 (Afterschool Alliance, n.d.). The 21st Century Community Learning Centers program, created in 1994 by Congress, provides grant funding for the creation of community learning centers with the goal of increasing access to academic enrichment opportunities after school and during the summer months for children—in particular, those from lower-performing schools or schools where there is high poverty (Department of Education, 2023).

In 2020, an all-time high of 87% of parents supported public funding for after-school programs (Fortner, Hardy, & Schmit, 2021). According to the Afterschool Alliance, the most prominent barriers families faced in accessing these programs were availability, cost, and the safety of children commuting to and from a program. After-school programs are in limited supply: for every child enrolled in such programs, three are waiting to enroll, suggesting that 24.6 million children might participate in after-school care if it were available. The access issue is even more marked for Black and Latino children in families with low incomes. A survey from the Afterschool Alliance found that, if given the opportunity, 58% of Black children and 55% of Latino children, compared with 46% of White children, would enroll in school-age after-school programs. In rural communities, more than 4.5 million children who are not in OST programming would be if a program were available to them—a 43% increase since 2014; 52% of respondents in rural communities were families with lower incomes. Note that these data were not disaggregated intersectionally by race and income (Afterschool Alliance, 2021, 2022).

As for the workforce, OST providers are paid lower wages and receive fewer benefits compared with other school-age care providers because their positions are often part-time and generally require fewer credentials. The estimated cost to reach all eligible school-age children through CCDBG ranges from $48.4 billion to $79.6 billion, taking into account such variables as increased market-rate payments to states that would go toward higher wages (Fortner, Hardy, & Schmit, 2021).

Regardless of the tremendous need, overall access to OST programming has increased over the last few decades alongside specific program offerings within OST, such as health and wellness programs; science, technology, engineering, and math programs; arts-based programs; and social-emotional learning programs. Yet despite the increase in program offerings overall, the disparity in OST participation between students from wealthy and low-income households has increased (Gardner, Roth, & Brooks-Gunn, 2009). Across demographics, geography, and income, access barriers are consistently increasing as families report challenges related to cost, children having safe transport from school to the program location, lack of available program offerings in the community, and inconvenient program locations. Black (59%) and Latino (56%) families living in rural, predominantly low-income communities report not having a safe way for their children to get from school to the after-school program as a primary barrier to enrollment (Afterschool Alliance, 2022).

Again, consistent with ECE programs, OST after-school programs have seen a surge in demand as the field has shown undeniable evidence of opportunities for positive impacts on children (Lehrer-Small, 2021). However, limited funding, lack of access to and availability of OST programs, and an underpaid workforce continue to demonstrate the pervasiveness of the opportunity gaps children experience as they move along the developmental continuum.

Special Education

Later in childhood, compared with the early years, the percentage of children who qualify for and receive special education almost doubles. In 2019, among children aged 6–21, 6,374,498, or 9.7% of the resident population in that age range, were served in 49 states, the District of Columbia, and Bureau of Indian Education schools. The most common disability categories among children in this age group served under the Individuals with Disabilities Education Act (IDEA) were specific learning disability (37.1%), other health impairment (16.8%), speech or language impairment (16.3%), autism (11.0%), "other disabilities combined" (7%), intellectual disability (6.5%), and emotional disturbance (5.4%). In almost every category, children of color, including Black, Latino, American Indian/Alaska Native, and Hawaiian and other Pacific Islander, were overrepresented in the special education system, generally in the categories of intellectual disabilities, learning disabilities, and emotional/behavioral disorder (NRC, 2002; National Academies, 2019), whereas White and Asian American children were underrepresented in these categories. As elaborated in Table 3-1, representation patterns vary by disability category and racial/ethnic/language group. Cruz and Firestone (2022) conducted a study in a large urban school district in California to trace the timing of special education identification. Their findings indicate that African American and Hispanic/Latino students tended to be identified in later grades (after K–6) and in disability categories associated with greater levels of segregation.

Segregated Learning

In the K–12 system, data on segregated learning among students with disabilities are collected according to the percentage of time children spend in the general education classroom—less than 40%, 40–80%, or more than 80%. According to data from the Department of Education (2021b) for the 2019 school year, while most school-aged students served by IDEA (64.8%) spent 80% or more of their time inside a general education classroom, this figure varied by state, disability type, and racial/ethnic group. Alabama had the highest percentage of children with disabilities who spent 80% or more of the school day alongside their peers without disabilities inside the regular

TABLE 3-1 Risk Ratios for Students with Disabilities Aged 5–21 (served by Individuals with Disabilities Education Act [IDEA] Part B) by Racial/Ethnic Group and Disability Category, Fall 2019

Disability	American Indian or Alaska Native	Asian American	Black or African American	Hispanic/Latino	Native Hawaiian or Other Pacific Islander	White	Two or More Races
All disabilities	1.6	0.5	1.4	1.1	1.5	0.9	1.1
Autism	0.9	1.2	1.1	1.0	1.3	0.9	1.2
Deaf-blindness[a]	1.5	1.0	0.8	0.9	2.6	1.1	1.0
Developmental delay[b]	3.8	0.5	1.5	0.8	2.0	0.9	1.5
Emotional disturbance	1.6	0.2	1.8	0.7	1.1	1.0	1.5
Hearing impairment	1.5	1.2	0.9	1.4	2.6	0.7	0.9
Intellectual disability	1.5	0.5	2.2	1.1	1.8	0.6	0.8
Multiple disabilities	1.9	0.7	1.3	0.8	2.2	1.1	1.0
Orthopedic impairment	1.1	1.0	0.9	1.2	1.8	0.9	0.9
Other health impairment	1.2	0.3	1.4	0.8	1.1	1.1	1.2
Specific learning disability	1.8	0.3	1.4	1.4	1.7	0.7	1.0
Speech or language impairment	1.4	0.7	0.9	1.1	1.1	1.0	1.1

(continued)

TABLE 3-1 Continued

Disability	American Indian or Alaska Native	Asian	Black or African American	Hispanic/Latino	Native Hawaiian or Other Pacific Islander	White	Two or More Races
Traumatic brain injury	1.6	0.5	1.1	0.8	1.2	1.2	1.0
Visual impairment	1.7	0.9	1.1	0.9	1.7	1.0	1.0

[a] Interpret these data with caution. There were 19 American Indian or Alaska Native students, 79 Asian students, 177 Black or African American students, 371 Hispanic/Latino students, 8 Native Hawaiian or Other Pacific Islander students, 817 White students, and 64 students associated with two or more races reported in the deaf-blindness category.

[b] A state's use of the developmental delay category is optional for children and students aged 3–9 and is not applicable to students older than 9.

NOTES: Risk ratio compares the proportion of a particular racial/ethnic group served under IDEA Part B with the proportion served among the other racial/ethnic groups combined. For example, if racial/ethnic group X has a risk ratio of 2 for receipt of special education services, then that group's likelihood of receiving special education services is twice as great as that for all of the other racial/ethnic groups combined. Risk ratio was calculated by dividing the risk index for the racial/ethnic group by the risk index for all the other racial/ethnic groups combined. For the Part B child count and educational environments data collection, fall 2019, states had the option of reporting 5-year-olds by kindergarten status. The table includes only 5-year-olds in kindergarten from those states that chose to report 5-year-old kindergartners in school-age educational environments. It does not include 5-year-olds from those states that chose to report 5-year-old kindergartners in early childhood education environments. All of the results presented in the table should be interpreted with this in mind. Data from U.S. Department of Education, EDFacts Data Warehouse (EDW), Office of Management and Budget (OMB) #1850-0925: IDEA Part B Child Count and Educational Environments Collection, 2019. These data are for 48 states, the District of Columbia, and Bureau of Indian Education schools. Data were not available for Wisconsin and Iowa. Data from U.S. Department of Commerce, U.S. Census Bureau. Intercensal Estimates of the Resident Population by Single Year of Age, Sex, Race, and Hispanic Origin for States and the United States: April 1, 2010 to July 1, 2019, 2019. Data were accessed fall 2020. For actual IDEA data used, go to https://www2.ed.gov/programs/osepidea/618-data/state-level-data-files/index.html

SOURCE: Adapted from Department of Education, 2021b.

classroom, while New Jersey had the lowest percentage. With respect to disability type, children with intellectual disabilities or multiple disabilities were the least likely and children with speech impairments or learning disabilities were the most likely to spend time in general education settings.

There were also differences by race. White children were the most likely to spend most of the day in general education settings compared with children of all other races and ethnicities (Figure 3-1). This evidence indicates gaps in access to inclusive learning opportunities between White children and their peers from other racial/ethnic groups (Fierros & Conroy, 2002; Skiba et al., 2006). Similar patterns have been documented in neighborhood and charter schools (Waitoller & Maggin, 2020).

The disproportionate representation of students of color in special education in general and in segregated settings in particular reflects the complex links between race and disability. These disparities are most noticeable in disability categories—such as learning disabilities, emotional disturbance, and mild intellectual disability—considered most subjective because of the greater role played by professional judgment in diagnostic decisions. Grindal et al. (2019) used individual-level data from three states to analyze racial disparities in special education. They documented greater racial disparities in these more "subjective" disability categories relative to disabilities typically diagnosed in the health care system (e.g., deafness, visual impairment). These authors also found that African American and Latino students were placed in more segregated settings compared with their White counterparts, irrespective of income level. Another study using individual-level data from a large school district and relying on a longitudinal design covering a decade (Cooc, 2022) found that all students with disabilities experienced decreasing levels of inclusion in general education as they became older. Nonetheless, African American learners were the most affected (after controlling for disability type), while Asian American/Pacific Islander students were more included compared with their White and Latino peers. It is important to note that a key challenge in understanding the complex, often ambiguous, and even contradictory findings from studies on racial disparities in special education and disability segregation is the absence of clear theoretical frameworks underlying this knowledge base (Artiles, 2011; Ahram, Voulgarides, & Cruz, 2021).

Indeed, there is a long-standing concern regarding the disproportionate under- and overidentification of learners of color in disability categories. Two National Academies reports addressing this concern were released 20 years apart (NRC, 1982, 2002), and scholarly debates on the issue continue to unfold (Morgan et al., 2015; Skiba et al., 2016). Both patterns can be problematic and can perpetuate opportunity gaps. Underidentification is a problem if children who need services are not diagnosed so that they receive supports. In contrast, overidentification is problematic if a diagnosis

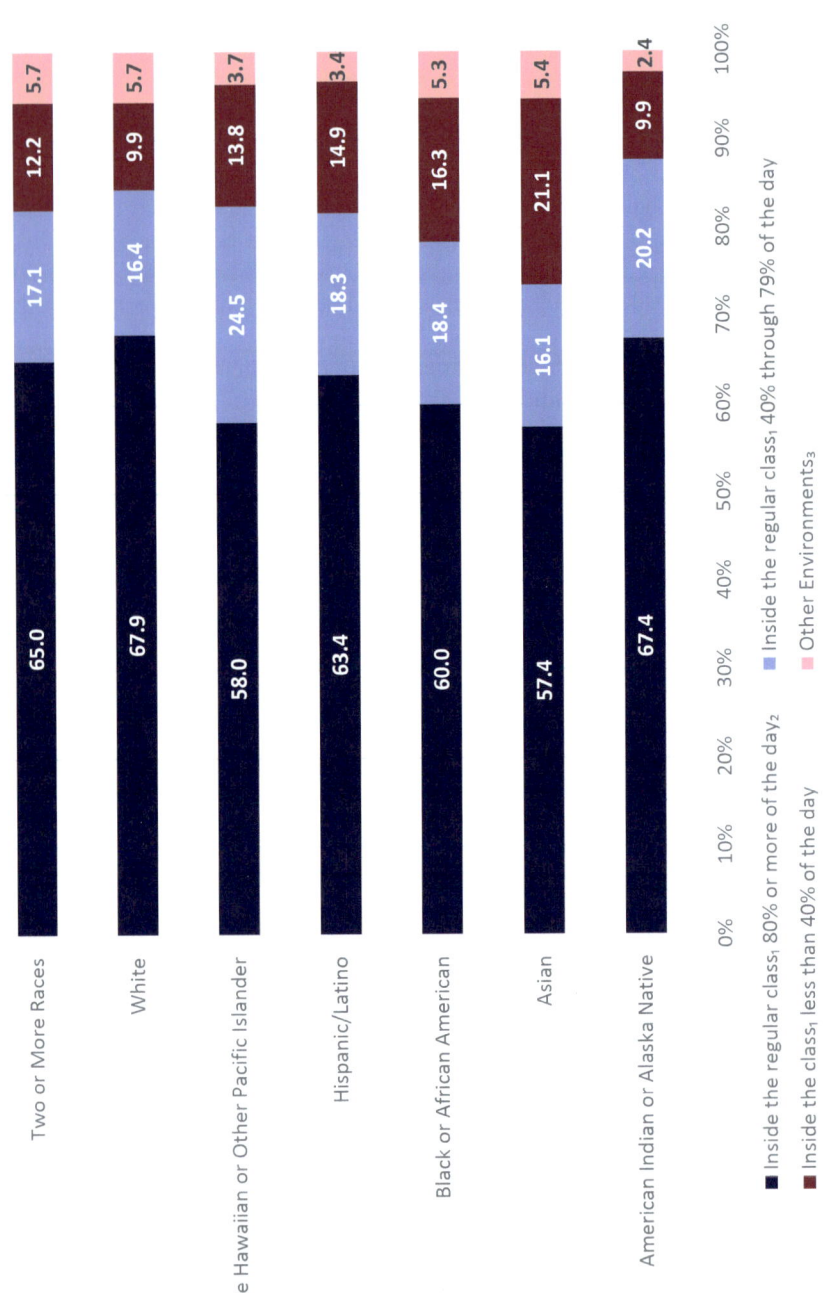

FIGURE 3-1 Percentage of students aged 5–21 served under the Individuals with Disabilities Education Act (IDEA) Part B within racial/ethnic groups, by educational environment, fall 2019.

[1]Percentage of day spent inside the regular class is defined as the number of hours spent each day inside the regular classroom, divided by the total number of hours in the school day (including lunch, recess, and study periods), multiplied by 100.

[2]Students who received special education and related services outside the regular classroom for less than 21% of the school day were placed in the *inside the regular class 80% or more of the day* educational environment category.

[3]"Other environments" consists of separate school, residential facility, homebound/hospital, correctional facilities, and parentally placed in private schools.

NOTES: Percentage was calculated by dividing the number of students aged 5 (school age) through 21 served under IDEA Part B in the racial/ethnic group and educational environment by the total number of students aged 5 (school age) through 21 served under IDEA Part B in the racial/ethnic group and all educational environments, then multiplying the result by 100. The sum of bar percentages may not total 100 because of rounding. For the Part B child count and educational environments data collection, fall 2019, states had the option of reporting 5-year-olds by kindergarten status. The figure includes only 5-year-olds in kindergarten from those states that chose to report 5-year-old kindergartners in school-age educational environments. It does not include 5-year-olds from those states that chose to report 5-year-old kindergartners in early childhood educational environments. All of the results presented in the figure should be interpreted with this in mind. Data from U.S. Department of Education, ED*Facts* Data Warehouse (EDW), Office of Management and Budget (OMB) #1850-0925: IDEA Part B Child Count and Educational Environments Collection, 2019. These data are for 48 states, the District of Columbia, Bureau of Indian Education schools, Puerto Rico, the four outlying areas, and the three freely associated states. Data for Wisconsin and Iowa were not available. Data were accessed fall 2020. For actual IDEA data used, go to https://www2.ed.gov/programs/osepidea/618-data/state-level-data-files/index.html

SOURCE: Adapted from Department of Education, 2021b.

is the result of opportunity gaps, false positives, biases, or the conflation of cultural or linguistic differences with disability.

Disproportionality in identification of learners for special education is a complex phenomenon that takes different forms depending on the level of the system in question (national, state, regional, city, or district); the disability category under consideration; the age and grade level of children and youth; the racial and linguistic backgrounds of students; and the role of contextual and ideological factors, including racism and discrimination (NRC, 1982, 2002; Artiles & Trent, 1994; Skiba et al., 2008; Artiles, 2011; Sullivan & Artiles, 2011; Harry & Klingner, 2014; Cruz & Rodl, 2018; Frederick & Shifrer, 2018; Fish, 2019). Methodological and theoretical considerations shape (often conflicting) findings about disproportionality (Waitoller, Artiles, & Cheney, 2010; Cruz & Rodl, 2018). A complex debate has persisted around the role of race and social class. Some researchers argue that the overrepresentation of learners of color in special education is due to their high levels of poverty, whereas others suggest that race plays a critical role (Skiba et al., 2008; Artiles, 2019). Research findings on this issue have been mixed, and again, methodological factors could explain some of these ambiguous patterns. In a recent review of this literature, Cruz and Rodl (2018, p. 10) conclude that:

> *the ways in which each study conceptualized SES [socioeconomic status] varied, and, thus, results varied. When studies used aggregated measures for SES, they tended to report overrepresentation of students from racially and ethnically diverse backgrounds in more affluent areas. When considering SES by disaggregated free and reduced lunch measures, results were mixed. When using more specific continuous or composite indicators, much of the variability in special education identification could be attributed to SES.*

Other studies with an explicit focus on contextual and cultural historical influences (e.g., history of race relations and racial segregation in the school and community, staff beliefs about race, and deficit views of communities of color) have documented the key role of race in overrepresentation at the district and school levels (Eitle & Eitle, 2002; Skiba et al., 2008; Kramarczuk Voulgarides et al., 2021; Tefera, Siegel-Hawley, & Sjogren, 2022).

The evidence suggests that children of color and those living in rural areas tend to be diagnosed with disabilities later than their White peers of similar age (Barnard-Brak et al., 2021), a problem that creates opportunity gaps in light of the importance of intervening early to provide services for these children (National Academies, 2017). At the same time, there is evidence that some groups of children (e.g., African Americans, Native Americans, English learners) tend to be overidentified in certain categories at the national or sometimes at the regional or state level (Skiba et al., 2008). The issue is most stark in the kinds of more "subjectively" diagnosed disability categories noted earlier, such as intellectual disability, learning disabilities, and emotional disturbance—categories that not only require greater professional (subjective) interpretation in the identification process but also tend to be characterized by overrepresentation of Black and Native American children and placement of learners in segregated settings relative to children in other disability categories. For instance, Cruz and Firestone (2022) found that African American and Latino students were identified in later grades relative to White students in the categories of emotional/behavioral disorders and intellectual disabilities, which tend to be served in more segregated settings compared with other disability categories. Table 3-2 presents the odds ratios for special education identification by grade.

Identification Rates and Placement

Cruz and Firestone (2022) also found that parent education level was positively associated with low-stigma diagnoses (e.g., speech and language impairments, autism). They frame this finding as an instance of opportunity hoarding exercised by privileged parents, given that different disability categories are associated with more or less stigma and services that require more or fewer resources. They explain that "for most disability categories, higher parent education levels were associated with decreased odds of placement; however, for the autism category, as parent education level increased, odds ratios also increased" (Cruz & Firestone, 2022, p. 108; see also Ong-Dean, 2009; Shifrer, 2013).

Disentangling disability from typical language learning for children who speak a language other than English at home has also resulted in under- or overdiagnosis among this group, depending on the context and level of analysis (Castro & Artiles, 2021). English learners tend to be underidentified at the national level in low-incidence categories such as severe autism, moderate/severe intellectual disabilities, and severe emotional/behavioral disorders (National Academies, 2017). Differences in identification rates are shaped by gaps in access related to a host of structural and technical factors, such as variability in referral rates that may be mediated by professionals' misunderstanding of the intersections between speaking multiple languages and disabilities (including myths about second language development), linguistic and cultural barriers in accessing services and service provision, parents' understanding and navigation of health and education service systems, and access to insurance, among other factors (National Academies, 2017). To illustrate, professionals can incorrectly associate English learners' behaviors associated with acquiring a second language with learning disorders, but may hesitate to refer these learners to special education because

TABLE 3-2 Odds Ratios for Special Education Identification by Grade Level and Student Group

Special Education	Pre-K	K	1	2	3	4	5	6	7	8	9	10	11	12
African American	0.50[c]	1.48	1.24	1.03	1.25	0.98	0.98	1.31[b]	1.51[b]	1.48[b]	1.64[a]	1.27	1.17	1.26
Latino	0.66[a]	1.20	1.25[b]	1.09	1.02	0.96	0.97	1.33[a]	1.48[a]	1.50[a]	1.68[a]	1.50[a]	1.52[a]	1.33[a]
AAPI	0.77[b]	0.86	0.81	0.64[a]	0.54[a]	0.49[a]	0.48[a]	0.38[a]	0.39[a]	0.34[a]	0.37[a]	0.32[a]	0.36	0.32[a]
AI/AN	0.78	0.63	0.76	1.04	1.19	1.06	1.06	1.09	0.83	1.30	1.68	1.13	1.81	2.54[a]
Adjusted	Pre-K	K	1	2	3	4	5	6	7	8	9	10	11	12
African American	0.63[b]	1.30	1.12	0.95	1.16	0.94	0.83	1.13	1.32[b]	1.28[b]	1.4[b]	1.10	1.04	1.17
Latino	0.87	0.86	0.97	0.89	0.91	0.75[c]	0.65[a]	0.74[b]	0.82[b]	0.86	1.02	1.01	1.02	0.92
AAPI	1.03	0.69[b]	0.70[a]	0.58[a]	0.49[a]	0.44[a]	0.39[a]	0.32[a]	0.32[a]	0.29[a]	0.33[a]	0.28[a]	0.32[a]	0.28[a]
AI/AN	1.16	0.51	0.67	0.87	1.42	1.03	1.25	0.94	0.62	1.19	1.62	1.15	1.89[b]	2.68[a]
Male	2.80[a]	2.74[a]	3.05[a]	2.96[a]	2.47[a]	2.32[a]	2.22[a]	2.26[a]	2.18[a]	2.33[a]	2.2[a]	2.3[a]	2.14[a]	1.92[s]
FRPL	0.81[b]	1.25	1.34[c]	1.2[b]	1.24[b]	1.17	1.16	1.2[b]	1.17[b]	1.13	1.16[b]	1.11	1.11	1.06
EML	0.33[a]	1.9[a]	1.51[a]	1.36[a]	1.27[c]	1.97[a]	2.33[a]	3.56[a]	4.07[a]	3.98[a]	3.19[a]	2.75[a]	3.15[a]	3.36[a]
Parent Education	1.05	1	1.01	0.97	1.03	1.03	0.98	0.97	0.97	0.96	0.94[c]	0.94[c]	0.94[c]	0.94[c]

[a] $p < .001$.
[b] $p < .05$.
[c] $p < .01$.

NOTES: Highlighted regions indicate the largest two simultaneous cells for each group. Odds ratio = 1.0 indicates parity of probability of being placed in special education. AAPI = Asian American/Pacific Islander; AI/AN = American Indian/Alaska Native; EML = emerging multilingual learner; FRPL = free and reduced-price lunch.
SOURCE: Adapted from Cruz & Firestone, 2022.

of this ambiguity (Klingner et al., 2005; Artiles, Klingner, & Tate, 2006). Table 3-3 outlines similarities in behaviors associated with second language acquisition and learning disability that can potentially lead to incorrect referrals to special education for English learners.

Researchers have documented underidentification of English learners in grades K–12 in urban school districts in California compared with English-proficient and White students (Artiles et al., 2005). When the data

TABLE 3-3 Behaviors Associated with Learning Disabilities and Second Language Acquisition

Behavior Associated with Learning Disability	Behavior Associated with Second Language (L2) Acquisition
Difficulty with auditory discrimination and/or phonological awareness	Students may not be accustomed to hearing sounds in the L2 that are not found in their first language (L1). Unfamiliar sounds in the L2 may also be difficult for the student to produce.
Difficulty with sight words, words with multiple meanings, figurative language, or idioms	Students may be confused by common words, figurative language, or idioms in the L2; however, students may understand the underlying concepts in their L1.
Difficulty understanding which letters make which sounds	Students may be confused by letter sounds in the L2 when different from those in their L1 or when this literacy skill has not been developed in the L1.
Difficulty with story narration and retelling	Students may have difficulty with story narration and retelling when they lack sufficient development of oral proficiency in addition to instruction in reading and writing.
Difficulty with reading fluency	Students may have difficulty reading fluently and conveying expression in the L2. Students may understand more than they are able to convey.
May seem disengaged during instruction	Students may appear disengaged during instruction in the L2 when explanations are provided without visual cues or other scaffolding techniques in place to make instruction more comprehensible.
May seem frustrated or unmotivated	Students may appear frustrated or unmotivated. This can occur if assignments are not at the appropriate level for them or when they do not understand why the assignment is meaningful or relevant.

SOURCE: Adapted from National Academies, 2017.

were disaggregated by grade, however, overrepresentation patterns were noticeable; specifically, this was the case in middle and high school, with particularly large gaps in 12th grade, when English learners were more than three times as likely to be placed in special education compared with their English-proficient counterparts. These districts categorized English learners in two subgroups—those with limited proficiency in English only and those with limited proficiency in both the primary language and English. The latter group represents a theoretically controversial category since it implies that these students are not proficient in any language; the group is described as semilingual or theorized as being languageless in the literature (Rosa, 2016). Of note, this latter group had a substantially higher probability of being identified in the learning disability, language impairment, and intellectual disability categories relative to the other three groups (English learners with limited English proficiency, English-proficient learners, and White learners; Artiles et al., 2005).

IDEA includes provisions on monitoring disproportionality. States have been required to report on disproportionate patterns since 1997, and since 2004 have been expected to create and implement policies and procedures to prevent or remedy inappropriate overidentification or disproportionate representation of learners of color. States cited for disproportionality can use up to 15% of IDEA funds to revise their procedures and eliminate this problem in general education. Unfortunately, because of the lack of clear federal guidance, "a sizable number of states have been able to meet the IDEA mandate by increasing their risk ratio and N criterion without addressing the problem of disproportionality" (Cavendish, Artiles, & Harry, 2014, p. 36; see also Albrecht et al., 2012).

Policies and Practices That Can Create Opportunity Gaps

A number of policy and practice issues create disparities in opportunity for children with disabilities, disproportionately affecting those of color and those in low-income households. Among others, these issues include less or later access to services, a lack of cultural and linguistically responsive services, and greater segregation in learning settings. These issues are in turn undergirded, in large part, by chronic underfunding of IDEA services. As mentioned in Chapter 3, the federal government has never fully funded its share of IDEA, leaving an outsized burden on state and local governments and families. This underfunding has influenced how many children are served by the program and has resulted in long waits for each step of the process, including screening, evaluation, eligibility determination, and service receipt; dosages of services that are often far less than what children need; variations in the quality of services children receive; and lack of coordination with other systems, such as child care.

Absenteeism

Children's learning opportunities may be truncated by everyday experiences that may impact their attendance, whether in ECE programs or in grades K–3. Chronic absenteeism is commonly defined as missing 10% or more of days in the school year (Chang, Bauer, & Byrnes, 2018) or more than 15 days (Department of Education, 2019). Research has shown the negative effects of absenteeism on school performance, achievement, and behavior in the early years and the pattern of absenteeism that continues into the elementary and later grades, as well as higher odds of retention, drop-out, and lifelong behaviors (Rhodes, Thomas, & Liles, 2018). In addition, chronic absenteeism has negative spillover effects on peers (Gottfried, 2009). National-level estimates of chronic absenteeism, most typically reported in the K–12 system, put it at about 10–16% (Chang & Romero, 2008; Department of Education, 2019). But these estimates mask significant geographic variation, with rates of preschool chronic absenteeism being higher in large cities (Gottfried, 2009)—for example, 50% in Newark (Chen & Rice, 2017), 36–45% in Chicago, 20–27% in Baltimore, and 35–37% in the District of Columbia (Connolly & Olson, 2012; Katz, Adams, & Johnson, 2015; Dubay & Holla, 2016; Ehrlich, Gwynne, & Allensworth, 2018). Note also that systematic reporting on attendance and chronic absenteeism has increased as a result of requirements under the Every Student Succeeds Act of 2015 (Katz, Adams, & Johnson, 2015).

Critical to understanding children's early learning opportunities is understanding the roots of absenteeism to the extent that they have been researched and the barriers that may impede high levels of participation. These include considerations related to transportation, hours of operation and program schedule, suspension, chronic illness or disability, housing instability, and community violence or insecurity, as well as misconceptions about the importance of attendance in the early years, among others (Dahlin & Squires, 2016; Chang, Bauer, & Byrnes, 2018; Humm Patnode, Gibbons, & Edmunds, 2018; Ramey & Ramey, 2019).

As a result of these barriers, differences in the incidence of absenteeism emerge across groups. A study conducted by the National Center for Children in Poverty (Romero & Lee, 2007) showed that children from families with income levels below 300% of the federal poverty threshold were four times more likely to have chronic absenteeism relative to children from families with incomes above that level. Findings have been similar for children in households receiving Temporary Assistance for Needy Families (Dubay & Holla, 2015). That study also found a higher incidence of chronic absenteeism in children from minoritized backgrounds and from households led by a single mother, with a high number of children, or with parents with lower educational attainment. Some research has found an association between feelings of discrimination and school absence, pointing to the potential role of racism and school climate in this problem (Bittencourt et al., 2009; Benner & Graham, 2011; Yang & Ham, 2017). Research has shown that maternal depression, substance abuse, homelessness, and mental illnesses of parents may also influence attendance (Gottfried, 2009; Dubay & Holla, 2015; Katz, Adams, & Johnson, 2015). Neighborhood and school factors, including neighborhood safety and the contribution of any tensions with the police and/or with social groups to a lack of safety for specific subgroups (Childs & Lofton, 2021) contribute to higher absenteeism as well (Fuhs, Nesbitt, & Jackson, 2018; Ansari & Pianta, 2019; Singer et al., 2021). Therefore, school infrastructure to support violence prevention, conflict resolution, and related measures is considered important to reducing chronic absenteeism (Kearney & Childs, 2021).

More generally, chronic absenteeism is a multifaceted issue strongly connected to community and poverty conditions, needing further study as well as multifaceted approaches (Childs & Lofton, 2021). Attending ECE programs has been shown to reduce later absenteeism (Gottfried, 2015; Ansari & Purtell, 2018), while initiatives to strengthen parent engagement (Smythe-Leistico & Page, 2018), to have nurses follow up with the families of chronically absent children (Kerr et al., 2011), and to serve breakfast after the start of the school day (Kirksey & Gottfried, 2021) have been found to be associated with increased attendance. A meta-analytical summary of behavioral, family, and academic interventions found small effects, with the authors suggesting that practices to improve attendance may be understudied (Eklund et al., 2022).

DIFFERENTIAL EXPERIENCES IN EARLY ELEMENTARY LEARNING SETTINGS

As in ECE systems, the quality and funding levels of the early elementary system profoundly impact children's experiences and outcomes. Although the term "quality" is used more commonly in discussing ECE, the concepts of structural quality[2] and process quality[3] (as discussed in Chapter 2) continue to be relevant in the early elementary grades, and deficits in both structural and process quality create gaps in opportunity for early elementary learners. Both structural and process quality and the interplay between them are influenced by systemic drivers, such as funding and policies. In communities with fewer resources, for example, larger

---

[2]Structural quality includes such factors as teacher:student ratios, class size, and teacher competencies and credentials.

[3]Process quality includes such factors as teacher–child interactions and closeness of relationships between students and teachers.

class sizes, an element of structural quality, may result in fewer interactions between teachers and children—an element of process quality (Chaudry & Sandstrom, 2020).

As with the ECE system, there is no single or widely agreed-upon framework for quality in elementary school. Nonetheless, several common features have been studied over the years (Lowenstein et al., 2015; Ansari & Pianta, 2019). These include a combination of structural factors (poverty, racial and socioeconomic segregation); school-, district-, or state-level factors (e.g., funding, discipline policies, access to the curricula, ratios/class sizes, use of ability grouping in classrooms, organizational culture, community/family engagement); teacher-level factors (e.g., teacher turnover, teacher absences, distribution of well-qualified educators, educator bias); and child-level factors (e.g., academic outcomes, behavioral infractions; Rimm-Kaufman et al., 2005; Paro et al., 2009; Buttaro & Catsambis, 2019; Darling-Hammond, 2019; Papachristou et al., 2021). Research has examined a variety of teacher factors, for example, including licensure, stress and burnout, compensation, and efficacy, as well as domain-specific (e.g., literacy, math) instructional approaches.

While there is evidence for some factors and some locations (e.g., Montgomery County, Maryland), more work is needed on identifying equitable, holistic frameworks for high-quality elementary experiences that align with and promote continuity with high-quality ECE experiences (Brooks-Gunn, Markman-Pithers, & Rouse, 2016). Research has shown that quality transitions and alignment between ECE and elementary school are important for sustaining learning gains from the early years (Phillips, Austin, & Whitebook, 2016; Johnson & Jackson, 2018; Meloy, Gardner, & Darling-Hammond, 2019; Reynolds & Temple, 2019; Schweinhart, 2019). If quality is high in an ECE program but not in the early grades, it stands to reason that sustainment of ECE achievement gains will likely be low. Evidence also shows that exposure to high-quality processes across the early elementary years results in higher cognitive scores for learners (Vernon-Feagans et al., 2019).

Physical Infrastructure

The health and safety features of the physical buildings and spaces where children learn are perhaps the most foundational dimension of quality, yet research has uncovered profound inequities in this regard. Two Government Accountability Office reports on school infrastructure, separated by more than 20 years, document inequities by race and income (Government Accountability Office, 1996, 2020). Schools with higher proportions of children of color were more likely to cite concerns related to poor physical infrastructure; a recent finding was that low-poverty districts expended about $1 billion more on elementary school construction relative to high-poverty districts. The U.S. Commission on Civil Rights identified additional differences in facility quality by race, stating that schools with higher proportions of students of color were more likely to report poorer facility conditions and more temporary buildings (U.S. Commission on Civil Rights, 2018).

Ratios and Class Sizes

Low teacher:student ratios and smaller class sizes are associated with both developmental and academic gains; they are an important factor in ensuring that students are learning in a healthy and safe environment in which teachers are more likely to meet individual needs, including social-emotional needs. The literature shows that in classrooms with lower teacher:student ratios and smaller class sizes, less time is spent on behavior management, and students have less conflict in their interactions with peers. In addition, these classrooms are associated with higher-quality programming; positive student outcomes, such as greater receptive language and verbal initiative; richer teacher–child interactions; and higher rates of individualized attention (Ruopp, 1979; Barnett, Schulman, & Shore, 2004; Achilles, 2012). One study found that the quality of kindergarten classrooms was related to teacher:student ratios, as well as length of the school day (Paro et al., 2009). An experimental study found that elementary school students in small classes (13–17 students) outperformed their peers in large classes (22–26 students) on all tests, across every subject, in every grade (Finn, Pannozzo, & Achilles, 2003). And studies examining the relationship between elementary school class size and child outcomes in Wisconsin and California also yielded positive findings on academic outcomes, particularly for children from minoritized backgrounds (Molnar et al., 2000; Stecher & Bohrnstedt, 2000). It is important to note, however, that the effects of class size may be affected by other school factors such as high-quality classroom practices, administrative support, school infrastructure, and available space (Graue et al., 2007; Graue, Raucher, & Sherfinski, 2009).

More research is needed to examine the effects of teacher:student ratios and class size on children from various subgroups (e.g., children of color, English learners, children from low-income households) to better understand how these factors may affect opportunity gaps and perpetuate disparate outcomes. It is important to note that many factors come into play in examining ratios and class sizes, including the differences in ratios and class sizes being examined (e.g., 30 vs. 28 vs. 15 students); the availability of teachers and physical space to make it possible to decrease ratios and class sizes; and, critically, teacher quality.

Language of Instruction

Another important dimension of quality is the language of instruction. More than 11 million children, or about a third of all children under the age of 9, have a parent who speaks a language other than English at home (Migration Policy Institute, 2021). With appropriate supports, these children have the potential to become bilingual and biliterate. Bilingualism and biliteracy have been linked to a host of positive cognitive outcomes in the short term (Bialystok, 2017), academic and social outcomes in the medium term (e.g., National Academies, 2017; Steele et al., 2017), and economic and health outcomes in the long term (Callahan & Gándara, 2014; National Academies, 2017). In addition, research has found that a strong first language foundation facilitates language acquisition in subsequent languages. Indeed, children's academic skills and language proficiency in their second language is predicted by skills in their first language (Genesee et al., 2006; Sparks et al., 2008, 2009a, 2009b; August, Shanahan, & Escamilla, 2009). The strengths of bilingualism identified by research stand in stark contrast to the widely held perception that coming from a home where a language other than English is spoken is a deficit that must be remedied, as opposed to a strength to be fostered (Castro & Meek, 2022).

Studies have found that dual language immersion and similar bilingual learning approaches are associated with positive gains for children across a variety of academic and social-emotional domains (Genesee & Lindholm-Leary, 2013; National Academies, 2017). One review of data from 7.5 million student records in 36 school districts in 16 states found that high-quality, long-term bilingual programs closed the achievement gap between English learners and their peers after 5 to 6 years, while English-only and short-term transitional bilingual programs closed only about half of the gap (Collier & Thomas, 2017). Research from one large school district with a robust dual language program found that children—both English learners and those who spoke English at home—randomly assigned to dual language programs outperformed their peers in reading in fifth and eighth grades (Steele et al., 2017); no differences were noted in math and science. This study also found that English learners in dual language programs achieved English proficiency more rapidly relative to their peers in programs in which only English was used for instruction.

Harsh and Exclusionary Discipline Policies

Another structural dimension of quality that influences opportunity gaps is discipline policies and practices. In the 1990s and early 2000s, a zero tolerance approach to discipline took hold across the country, initially as a response to school safety concerns. These policies included mandatory suspensions or expulsions for students for specific infractions. Initially, those infractions included bringing weapons to school or making safety threats, but not long after, they expanded to include infractions unrelated to safety, including dress code violations, truancy, and developmentally appropriate tantrums in younger students. These policies were undergirded by the view that both minor and major disciplinary infractions should be punished harshly (Skiba & Knesting, 2001). Black children were disproportionately impacted by these policies in the form of higher rates of expulsion and suspension, resulting in an array of negative outcomes despite no credible evidence of worse behavior on the part of these children (Meek et al., 2020). Although such practices accelerated during this era, racial disparities in disciplinary practices have existed since schools began integrating after the *Brown vs. Board of Education* decision (Mills, 2016). In fact, data from the early 1970s indicate that the rate of suspension was at least twice as high for Black as for White children across the country (Kaeser, 1979).

Two decades later, these trends remain consistent. An analysis of Civil Rights Data Collection data (2015–2016 school year) for children in pre-K through elementary school found that Black children were disproportionately suspended and expelled in every state in the nation (Meek at al., 2020). The most recent wave of these data, from the 2017–2018 school year, revealed stubbornly consistent racial disparities in this regard between Black children and their peers. In addition, American Indian and Alaska Native children were 1.5 times as likely as their White peers to be suspended, while children with disabilities served under IDEA were 2.5 times as likely as their peers without disabilities to be expelled (Ryberg et al., 2021).

Federal data from the 2017–2018 school year revealed modest declines in exclusionary discipline in the elementary grades, especially compared with the more significant declines in rates for children in pre-K. In sum, exclusionary discipline in the elementary grades declined by 2% between the two most recent data collection periods; however, school-related arrests, expulsions with educational services, and referrals to law enforcement increased by 5%, 7%, and 12%, respectively (Department of Education, 2021a). Black children and boys in all racial/ethnic groups were consistently disciplined disproportionately across all discipline categories. Black girls in particular experienced substantial disproportionality in exclusionary discipline (Losen, 2017). One analysis found that Black girls were suspended at a rate four times greater than that of White girls. Black girls were disciplined disproportionately across every discipline category, including suspension, expulsion, referrals, school transfers due to behavior, and restraint (Epstein et al., 2020). Children with disabilities were disproportionately suspended and expelled compared with their peers without disabilities; these disparities were especially stark for Black children with disabilities, who experienced rates more than four times their share of enrollment. Although discipline

TABLE 3-4 Racial Disparities for Students with Disabilities (SWD) in Days of Lost Instruction per 100 Students Enrolled Due to Disciplinary Removal: Top 10 States (including the District of Columbia)

State	Black SWD Days Lost per 100	White SWD Days Lost per 100	Black–White Racial Gap in Days Lost
Connecticut	128.7	38.9	89.9
District Of Columbia	132.4	18.5	113.9
Missouri	190.1	74.6	115.5
Nebraska	201.2	45.7	155.5
Nevada	182.8	54.5	128.3
North Carolina	158.3	64.1	94.3
Ohio	151.5	47.7	103.8
Tennessee	163.6	59.1	104.5
Texas	181.6	84.0	97.6
Wisconsin	126.4	30.1	96.3
National Average	119	43	76

Source: Data from U.S. Department of Education, EDFacts Data Warehouse (EDW): "IDEA Part B Discipline," 2014-15. Data extracted as of June 6, 2016 from file specifications 005, 006, 007, 088, 143, and 144.
NOTE: To enable comparisons despite enrollment differences for population subgroups, days lost were divided by enrollment and multiplied by 100 to yield days lost per 100 students enrolled.
SOURCE: Losen, 2017.

rates have been inconsistent among Latino students, two recent studies using various methodological approaches identified higher rates of exclusionary discipline for these children compared with their White peers but lower rates compared with their Black peers (Morris & Perry, 2016; Owens & McLanahan, 2020; Gage et al., 2021).

Overall, it has been reported that statewide racial disparities in discipline mask deeper disparities across school districts and schools (Losen, 2017). Although IDEA requires monitoring and intervention on racial disparities in discipline for children with disabilities, only 20 states identified at least one school district with this problem; of the 10 states with the greatest racial disparities in discipline for this population, only four—Wisconsin, Connecticut, Texas, and North Carolina—reported a district with disproportionality patterns (Losen, 2017). See Table 3-4.

Suspensions and expulsions and disparities in these practices are fueled by a number of factors (Meek & Gilliam, 2016), including discipline policies (Skiba & Peterson, 2000), racial bias (Skiba et al., 2002, 2011; Okonofua & Eberhardt, 2015; Gilliam et al., 2016; Carter et al., 2017), lack of teacher preparation and support and poor working conditions (Gilliam & Shahar, 2006), unaddressed childhood trauma resulting from adverse experiences (Zeng et al., 2019), and school climate (McIntosh et al., 2021), among others. A recent study examining the Black–White discipline gap found that nearly half of this gap could be attributed to differential treatment and/or differential support offered to students, the largest single driver of the disparity (Owens & McLanahan, 2020). These authors also found that some of the gap could be attributed to the sorting of children into schools by race and ethnicity (21%), while differences in children's behavior accounted for the smallest amount of variance (Owens & McLanahan, 2020).

Virtually all studies examining differences in child behavior by race have relied on teacher or administrator ratings. Given the breadth of research on the influences of bias on perceptions of Black people, including young children, it is important to apply a critical lens to findings that rely on subjective perceptions of behavior. Indeed, research has found that racial disparities between Black and White students are driven largely by behaviors (e.g., disrespect, defiance) whose perception is subjective in nature, rather than those (e.g., vandalism, smoking) whose perception is objective in nature (Skiba et al., 2014). In addition, Losen (2017) found that school districts with high rates of suspension tended to apply disciplinary sanctions to students of color for minor infractions and nonviolent or nonthreatening behaviors, such as tardiness, loitering in the hall, dress code violations, truancy, profanity, carrying a cell phone, and smoking cigarettes. Research has provided evidence of racial bias in the perceptions of children's behavior and the discipline decisions made by adults in learning systems (see Marcelo & Yates, 2014; Okonofua & Eberhardt, 2015; Gilliam et al., 2016; Meek et al., 2020). A broader evidence base points to negative biases against Black individuals outside the classroom, including misperceiving Black boys as older than they are and less childlike than White boys, and more often mischaracterizing them as angry (Goff et al., 2014; Halberstadt et al., 2020). Likewise, Black girls are rated as more mature and needing less support, comforting, nurturing, and protection than White girls (Epstein et al., 2020). These biases also include empathy bias, whereby people as young as 7 years of age rate Black children as feeling less pain than White children (Goff et al., 2014). They include as well biases unveiled through automatic association tests in which respondents across racial groups more often associate Black versus White individuals with anger and aggression (Duncan, 1976; Hugenberg & Bodenhausen, 2003; Miller, Maner, & Becker, 2010). Collectively, these dimensions of bias influence how adults perceive behavior, whose behavior is scrutinized, and what decisions are made with respect to those perceptions, all of which can lead to disproportionality in exclusionary discipline.

These biases likely mediate responses to student behaviors, resulting in responses that have a negative impact on various outcomes. For instance, although harsher disciplinary sanctions for minor infractions may lead to a reduction in such behaviors, there is evidence that tough discipline models are associated with reduced high school graduation rates and increases in juvenile justice complaints (Sorensen et al., 2022). Principals with a tough discipline stance create conditions associated with lower academic achievement, wider Black–White achievement gaps, and reductions in student attendance (Sorensen et al., 2022). Indeed, research has shown a robust association between the Black–White discipline and achievement gaps after controlling for numerous factors (Pearman et al., 2019). Teacher behavior management approaches also have differential impacts on young children's perceived identities (e.g., "good," "troublemaker") and social relations (Gansen, 2021). Moreover, issues germane to race relations in broader societal contexts are linked to racial disparities in school discipline. For instance, Chin (2021) found that as schools decreased levels of racial segregation, racial disparities in discipline and special education identification increased. Similarly, racial disparities in school discipline were found to be associated with county-level indicators of racial bias (Riddle & Sinclair, 2019). And Perera (2021) documents how school districts with significant equity challenges (e.g., higher levels of racial segregation, substantial racial achievement gaps, larger proportion of racialized students) had a greater probability of receiving civil rights complaints.

Suspension and expulsion result in about 11 million days of missed school in one school year alone, breaking down disproportionately along gender and racial lines. Relative to other groups, Black children and boys in all racial/ethnic groups in one study missed more than twice as many days because of suspensions. Black boys missed the greatest number of days, and Black girls missed about twice as many days as their White female counterparts (Fabes et al., 2021). Losen (2017) reports that, at the national level, Black versus White children lost 76 more days of instruction. Another study found that exclusionary discipline accounted for one-fifth of academic disparities between Black and White children (Morris & Perry, 2016).

Unsurprisingly, suspension and expulsion are positively associated with grade retention, lower achievement, and dropping out of high school, and negatively associated with taking advanced math courses and attending college (Wald & Losen, 2003; Gregory, Skiba, & Noguera, 2010; Fabelo et al., 2011; Morris & Perry, 2016; Losen, 2017; Wolf & Kupchik, 2017; Mittleman, 2018; Pearman et al., 2019; Jabbari & Johnson, 2020)—all of which are outcomes in themselves, but also serve to further perpetuate opportunity gaps going forward. Research has found as well that exclusionary discipline does not reduce challenging behavior; rather, it is associated with increased "delinquent behavior," and these increases are not moderated by race, indicating that these practices have similarly negative influences across groups (Gerlinger et al., 2021).

Since 2014, following the first federal publication of pre-K suspension and expulsion data, policies at the federal level have guided efforts to reduce exclusionary discipline in K–12 settings (Department of Justice & Department of Education, 2014). State and local legislative efforts to limit exclusionary discipline in the early grades, as well as executive branch efforts of state governors and agencies, have followed. These efforts include improving data collection, fostering family engagement, and providing professional development. Despite the number of new policies, however, these policies vary in both quality and content. During the Trump administration, the Obama-era K–12 federal discipline guidance was rolled back, but the effects on state and local policy are currently unclear. Under the Biden administration, federal officials are undertaking a review of the original policy and its subsequent repeal.

Data indicate that efforts aimed at simply reducing rates of exclusionary discipline have proven insufficient in addressing persistent disparities, pointing to the need to develop effective policies targeted specifically at closing the gaps among groups. Addressing this need has proven difficult, however, as researchers have examined statewide efforts to this end and found them to be ineffective at bridging the gaps (Linick, Garcia, & Grandpre, 2021; see also Cruz, Kulkarni, & Firestone, 2021, for a review of efforts to reduce disproportionality in exclusionary discipline; see Losen et al., 2015, for successful interventions to reduce discipline disparities).

Corporal punishment, defined as paddling, spanking, or other forms of physical punishment imposed on a child, is another form of harsh discipline that is used as a disciplinary practice in both pre-K and K–12 settings. The United Nations Convention on the Rights of the Child, which the United States has signed but not ratified, states that no child should be subjected to "physical or mental violence, injury or abuse, neglect or negligent treatment, maltreatment or exploitation" at school or by a parent or legal guardian (United Nations, 1989); however, there is no federal law prohibiting corporal punishment, and it remains legal in public school settings in 19 states across the nation and in private school settings in all but 2 states. According to federal data, roughly 70,000 children across age groups, including more than 800 preschool-aged children, were subjected to corporal punishment during a given year (Department of Education, 2021c). As with exclusionary discipline, Black children, boys, and children with disabilities are disproportionately subjected to corporal punishment. Although only 11% of the nation's school districts practiced corporal punishment in 2013–2014, 10 Southern states accounted for 75% of corporal punishment, with Mississippi, Texas, Alaska, and Alabama accounting for more than 70% (Johnson, 2019)—38% of those suspended at least once and 37% of those corporally punished.

Restraint and seclusion are two additional practices used for disciplinary purposes, despite the fact that they were not intended for that purpose but to address emergencies in case of imminent harm to the child or others. The latest federal data show that 74,000 children in public K–12 settings were physically restrained over the course of a year, and 27,500 were subjected to seclusion—the practice of locking children in a room alone without the ability to get out. As with other forms of harsh discipline, restraint and seclusion are applied disproportionately to Black children and children with disabilities in particular. In K–12 settings, Black children make up 15% of total enrollment but 29% of those restrained and 23% of those secluded; children with disabilities represent 13% of total K–12 enrollment but 78% of those restrained and 77% of those secluded. As with exclusionary discipline and corporal punishment, there is no federal law prohibiting these practices, while a patchwork of state laws limit or place parameters around their use (Meek et al., 2020).

Research suggests that each of these discipline policies and practices is associated with adverse outcomes—academic, social, and psychological—as well as engagement with the criminal justice system later in life. Children who are excluded through suspension and expulsion are stigmatized and isolated (Rosenbaum, 2020) in addition to missing days of school and learning opportunities (Losen & Whitaker, 2018; Fabes et al., 2021). Related to these issues are findings indicating that children who are suspended or expelled have lower school engagement, are more likely to repeat a grade, and are less likely to graduate from high school (Browne, Losen, & Wald, 2001; Karega Rausch & Skiba, 2004; Arcia, 2006; Gregory, Skiba, & Noguera, 2010; Skiba, Arredondo, & Williams, 2014).

THE EDUCATION WORKFORCE IN GRADES K–3

The education workforce in grades K–3 has a profound effect on young children's experiences and outcomes. Three aspects of the workforce—the provision of supportive, enriching, and warm teacher–child relationships and interactions; teacher expectations and perceptions of behavior; and pedagogy, instruction, and access to enrichment—are discussed here.

Supportive, Enriching, and Warm Teacher–Child Relationships and Interactions

Children learn optimally in the context of warm and secure relationships with adults. Indeed, decades of research have revealed that adult–child attachment is predictive of a range of outcomes in children, including advanced cognitive and language development, academic achievement, and a range of social and emotional skills (Ewing & Taylor, 2009; Iruka, Burchinal, & Cai, 2010; IOM & NRC, 2015; Lee & Bierman, 2015; McCormick & O'Connor, 2015; Varghese, Vernon-Feagans, & Bratsch-Hines, 2019). Children typically form these attachments with their parents or primary caregivers, but can also form them with other adults in their lives, including ECE educators and teachers. Researchers have pointed to a number of processes that mediate the association between warm and secure attachments and child outcomes, including early confidence and competence at exploration, effective instruction and guidance, social competence with adults and peers, self-regulatory competence, and stress management (IOM & NRC, 2015).

Studies indicate that teacher–child relationships are associated with children's engagement and ability to optimize their learning experiences in the classroom. When children feel safe and secure in their relationships, they are more confident and better able to explore and engage actively in learning across all domains (Ladd & Burgess, 1999). These relationships form the foundation for the daily interactions that occur inside classroom or home learning environments, both positive and negative, and are associated with an array of factors that influence children's learning experiences. Positive critical teacher–child relationships, and all of their associated processes, are related to third-grade achievement and to children's perceptions of school, including feeling more positive about school and more excited about learning (Birch & Ladd, 1997; NICHD Early Child Care Research Network, 2002; Pianta & Stuhlman, 2004; O'Connor & McCartney, 2007). In turn, negative or conflictual teacher–child relationships have been found to predict challenges with peers (Palermo et al., 2007), as well as internalizing and externalizing behaviors (Roorda et al., 2011; Zatto & Hoglund, 2019). Importantly, research indicates that close and warm teacher–child relationships can play a protective role against discrimination faced by children of color (Redding, 2019). Some research has found that such teacher–child relationships may have a particularly large impact on the outcomes of children from lower-income households (Driscoll & Pianta, 2010).

Research has found that the quality of teacher–child relationships is associated with a number of child demographic characteristics, including gender, race/ethnicity, disability, and socioeconomic status, as well as teacher demographic characteristics. It is important to understand these findings in the context of the systems, policies, and funding decisions that undergird them. That is, it is not the child or teacher demographics per se that are driving these differences, but systemic factors associated with these demographic variables. These systemic factors include differential access to resources and funding, segregation patterns, and other factors previously discussed that influence bias at all levels, from organizational policies to interpersonal interactions (Downey & Pribesh, 2004; Frawley, 2005; Campbell, 2015). Together, these factors drive gaps in the quality of teacher–child relationships and daily interactions, which can contribute to opportunity gaps.

Girls compared with boys are typically rated as having more positive relationships with teachers (Hamre & Pianta, 2001; Palermo et al., 2007; Ewing & Taylor, 2009; Collins et al., 2017). Studies also indicate that girls versus boys may have more to gain from these positive relationships and face more significant consequences when their relationships with teachers are poor (Baker, 2006; Ewing & Taylor, 2009; Ly et al., 2012). One study found that girls having more conflictual relationships with their teachers showed lower levels of math achievement and math growth relative to boys with comparable relationships (McCormick & O'Connor, 2015).

In general, research has found that teachers report having less close and more conflictual relationships with Black and Latino children relative to White children (Hughes, 2005; Garner & Mahatmya, 2015; Goldberg & Iruka, 2022). Research also has found that teachers tend to have more negative perceptions of Black and Latino children (Tenenbaum & Ruck, 2007; Zimmermann, 2018). One study found that those children perceived by kindergarten teachers as visibly being from a racial/ethnic minority group in Canada were 50% less likely to report positive relationships with their teachers in fourth grade (Fitzpatrick et al., 2015). These findings accord with research showing that children's race/ethnicity is associated with various dimensions of adult–child interactions in learning settings (Dobbs & Arnold, 2009); for example, children of color generally receive less praise and positive attention compared with their White peers (see Tenenbaum & Ruck, 2007).

It is critical to interpret these findings in light of data indicating that Black and Latino children are much less likely than their White peers to have teachers who match their race/ethnicity and language background. Research findings with respect to teacher–child racial/ethnic match have been mixed, with some showing positive effects of the match on the learning experiences and academic outcomes of young children of color and others showing minimal measurable effects (Ho, Gol-Guven, & Bagnato, 2012; Garner, Shadur, & Toney, 2021). The issue of teacher–child racial/ethnic match may have particular importance for children with disabilities. One study found that for those children identified as most at risk for emotional or behavioral disorders, racial/ethnic match with their teacher appeared to matter more. That is, greater mismatch predicted teachers' perceived conflict with children, mediated by teachers' classroom management and self-efficacy (Kunemund et al., 2020). Another study found that the teacher–child relationship served as a protective factor for children with developmental delays or disabilities and provided significant advantages for their development compared with their peers with similar delays or disabilities who had less close relationships with their teachers (Baker, 2006). Overall, it is important to consider a number of complex variables, including the structural factors discussed above, language, culture, class, and the interrelationships among all those factors in examining the effects of teacher–child match and interpreting the mixed research findings on this issue to date.

Teacher Expectations and Perceptions of Behavior

Dimensions of the teacher–child relationship that may be less explicit or tangible in nature, such as teacher expectations and perceptions of behavior, can play a significant role in shaping children's experiences in learning systems. Research has identified a positive association between teacher–child relationships and teacher expectations (Trang & Hansen, 2021), and a large and robust research base indicates that teacher expectations are associated with an array of child outcomes, in some cases over and above children's previous performance (McKown & Weinstein, 2008; Harlin, Sirota, & Bailey, 2009; Hinnant et al., 2009; Sorhagen, 2013).

Research also shows, however, that teacher expectations are not always reflective of children's abilities. Black children are rated more negatively by White teachers than by Black teachers across an array of domains, including language, literacy, and behavior (Downer et al., 2016). White compared with Black teachers also have been found to have lower expectations for Black children (Saft & Pianta, 2001; Downey & Pribesh, 2004; Tenenbaum & Ruck, 2007; Murray, Murray, & Waas, 2008; Bates & Glick, 2013). Studies have shown as well that White compared with Black teachers are more likely to recommend exclusionary discipline and special education placement for Black children (Achilles, McLaughlin, & Croninger, 2007; Skiba et al., 2011; Wiley et al., 2013; Sullivan et al., 2014). Other research has found that teachers are more likely to think their classes are too difficult for Black and Latino students than for White students, even after controlling for test scores and homework completion (Cherng, 2017). One study examined teachers' expectations of Latino students' long-term trajectories, and found that most teachers predicted that these students would not go to college but instead would work in the service sector, with many attributing those outcomes to family-related rather than structural factors (Dabach et al., 2018). Research also has revealed differential expectations based on English learner status. One nationally representative study found that teachers had lower expectations for English learners than for learners with English as their first language, expectations that began in kindergarten and grew over time. Importantly, these differential expectations were not observed in bilingual or dual language schools (Umansky & Dumont, 2021). These findings may suggest that teachers' perceptions of children's behavior and abilities and the decisions they make on the basis of those perceptions are influenced by racial, language, and gender-based bias.

The findings of several studies support the role of child race in teachers' assumptions, perceptions, and discipline decisions. One study showed ECE professionals a video of four young children playing in a classroom setting—one Black girl, one Black boy, one White girl, and one White boy. The researchers used eye-tracking technology to examine where on the screen the ECE teachers were looking when asked to predict a challenging behavior. Results indicated that they spent significantly more time looking at the Black boy when anticipating challenging behavior, even though no challenging behavior was ever exhibited in the video (Gilliam et al., 2016). Boonstra (2021) used ethnographic methods to document how racialized and ableist school and classroom discourses constructed pathological identities for Black students and how those identities were in turn associated with surveillance practices that mediated behavioral escalations and physical restraint. This heightened level of scrutiny helps explain racial disparities in exclusionary discipline.

Other research has found similar patterns. One study gave K–12 teachers the behavior reports of two fictitious children and asked a series of questions about the teachers' perceptions of the children and their discipline recommendations. The behavior reports were identical, but researchers manipulated the race of the fictitious children by using stereotypical White (i.e., Greg and Jake) and Black (i.e., Darnell and DeShawn) names. Okonofua, Paunesku, and Walton (2016) found that after the second infraction, teachers were more likely to label Black relative to White children as "troublemakers," which may imply attribution of the behaviors in the report to factors internal to the children and the belief that there was a higher likelihood that the behaviors would continue. Teachers were also more likely to recommend exclusionary discipline for Black children compared with their White peers after the second infraction (Okonofua & Eberhardt, 2015).

These education-specific studies build on a broader base of literature focused on implicit racial bias and its effects on behavior. Studies examining implicit racial bias have found that both White and Black subjects more readily describe White faces with positive words and Black faces with negative words (Nosek, Greenwald, & Banaji, 2005), and that Black men are rated as more angry and aggressive (Duncan, 1976; Hugenberg & Bodenhausen, 2003; Miller, Maner, & Becker, 2010). Research has even found that raising the subject of crime causes participants to think of Black men (Eberhardt et al., 2004). As discussed previously, children are often the subjects of these biases and perceptions.

Empathy has also been found to be an important dimension of teacher–child relationships and has been linked to the quality of those relationships as well as to discipline decisions. Research on empathy interventions demonstrates effects on reducing implicit racial bias of White teachers toward Black individuals (Whitford & Emerson, 2019), increasing empathetic mindsets about challenging behavior, and decreasing suspensions (Okonofua, Paunesku, & Walton, 2016).

Each of these biases and dynamics contributes to classroom climate overall and to teacher–child interactions and relationships. Overall, this body of work indicates that Black children, and in many cases Latino, Indigenous, immigrant, and dual language learner children, are subject to bias across an array of domains, including perceptions of behavior, expectations, and empathy. This bias contributes not only to the quality of teacher–child relationships and interactions but also more generally to reduced opportunities in learning settings that can shape children's learning experiences.

Pedagogy, Instruction, and Access to Enrichment

Schools serving predominantly low-income students of color tend to rely on narrow pedagogies and reductive instructional approaches that stress training in basic skills and reflect low expectations (Darling-Hammond & Baratz-Snowden, 2007). Certain school accountability frameworks, for instance, have negatively impacted educational opportunities for learners of color, as was evident most recently in the No Child Left Behind era. The emphasis on the use of test scores to track educational achievement across subgroups of students shaped the curricula and instruction students experienced. Researchers found, for example, that schools serving marginalized communities devoted an inordinate amount of time to teaching to the test and practicing test-taking skills; cheating practices were also documented (Nichols & Berliner, 2007). Students who were on the cusp of attaining proficiency scores received greater attention and resources relative to their lower-scoring peers, and teacher–student relationships were affected by the daily shuffling experienced by these students in rotating across remedial programs and interventions (Valli & Buese, 2007). Teacher morale declined as outcomes were reduced to test scores, and professional knowledge and judgment were devalued. Because school funding was linked to adequate yearly progress, schools and districts serving predominantly low-income populations of color were more susceptible to funding cuts, which in turn led to the imposition of a "failing school" label and increased the likelihood of teacher attrition (Darling-Hammond & Baratz-Snowden, 2007; Artiles, 2011). These developments substantially altered educational opportunities, including the quality of education and the nature of the curricula and pedagogy available to students of color. There is also evidence that test-based accountability led to lower-quality teachers being assigned to early grades, where students do not yet take standardized tests (Fuller & Ladd, 2013; Henry, McNeill, & Harbatkin, 2022).

As discussed in Chapter 2, a strong theoretical and empirical foundation supports learning through play, play-based pedagogy, and play-based instruction (Hirsh-Pasek et al., 2009; Zosh et al., 2017, 2018; Parker & Stjerne Thomsen, 2019). Research indicates, however, that play is differentially allowed for children of color and those in low-income schools, and also is differentially perceived by adults depending on the demographics of the children engaging in play. Play has been described as a spectrum and defined according to various types, such as sociodramatic or free play, as well as its core features, including joy, active engagement, and meaningfulness (Burghardt, 2011; Zosh et al., 2017, 2018). Play-based learning can unfold through a variety of teacher- or child-led approaches (cooperative learning, project-based learning, inquiry-based learning; Parker & Stjerne Thomsen, 2019). Guided play, a concept that blends teacher- and child-directed learning, allows children to have autonomy and choice in play while ensuring that an adult provides opportunities for direct learning during play by, for example, asking open-ended or inquiry-based questions or exposing children to new concepts or vocabulary (Fisher et al., 2011; Skene et al., 2022). Research has found that this approach to learning engages children in activities that are meaningful to them, and thus intrinsically motivating. According to both research and several theoretical frameworks, learning that is meaningful to children is associated with increased attention, memory, and motivation (Piaget, 1972; Ryan & Deci, 2000; Dang et al., 2012; Hirsh-Pasek et al., 2015; Zosh et al., 2017; Bodrova & Leong, 2019).

There is growing evidence that "community schools" produce positive student and school outcomes, particularly for marginalized learners (Maier et al., 2017). Community schools offer an "integrated focus on academics, health and social services, youth and community development, and community engagement" (Coalition for Community Schools, 2020, p. 1). The design of these schools is flexible and ambitious, offering extended-day and year-round schedules for children and adults. For obvious reasons, community schools offer invaluable resources and opportunities to students and families that face major structural barriers associated with racial and economic inequities. The design of these schools generally rests on four programmatic pillars: integrated student support, expanded learning time and opportunities, family and community engagement, and collaborative leadership and practice. Maier and colleagues (2017) reviewed more than 140 studies as well as various evaluations on the features of community schools. They identified areas that merit additional research, although their overall conclusion is that community schools "offer a promising foundation for progress" (Maier et al., 2017, p. 113).

High-quality and culturally responsive pedagogy and instruction are important factors in children's learning experiences. Access to enrichment programs, such as gifted and talented education, can also have positive effects on children's experiences and trajectories. Yet some research points to inequities in this area as well. For example, there is a long-standing debate about the underidentification of students of color in gifted and talented programs (Ford, 2021), characterized by deficit discourses focused on the ability levels and potential of these students and normative views of gifts and talent (Tenenbaum & Ruck, 2007; Ford, Grantham, & Whiting, 2008; Ford, 2021). Data indicate that Black and Latino students combined make up 41% of school enrollment but only 21% of students enrolled in gifted and talented programs (Patrick, Socol, & Morgan, 2020). A systematic review of referrals to these programs found that across all studies, teachers underreferred Black children (Ford, Grantham, and Whiting, 2008). Other research has found that even when researchers control for children's academic profiles, test scores, and socioeconomic backgrounds, Black children are still underreferred (Grissom & Redding, 2016), pointing to the role of bias in perceptions and expectations of children.

Research and theoretical development have also focused on culturally grounded pedagogy and learning. Several interrelated literatures use the notion of "culture"—in its dynamic and historical meanings—as the cornerstone of learning environments and interventions, encompassing culturally relevant, culturally responsive, and culturally sustaining approaches (Ladson-Billings, 1994; Gay, 2010; Paris, 2012).

Culturally relevant pedagogy, first introduced by Ladson-Billings (1995), centers on the experiences of children, including Black children and other children of color, who historically have been left out of education models. It focuses on changing mindsets and dispositions and ensuring high expectations and long-term academic success while promoting positive cultural and racial identity and enabling critical analysis of social inequalities within and outside of the classroom.

Culturally responsive teaching (Gay, 2010) builds on this theory but places greater emphasis on practice and competencies. It describes the ways teachers can realize culturally grounded learning by building on children's strengths and embracing families' cultural assets, knowledge, and prior experiences to make learning more relevant and engaging. The approach applies a social justice lens and focuses on achieving systemic and interpersonal change to promote success for learners of color. Most recently, scholars have introduced culturally sustaining pedagogy (Paris, 2012). This approach shifts the emphasis from drawing on children's culture for learning to sustaining and strengthening their connections to their culture and language through learning.

The above models for culturally grounded learning share a strengths-based perspective on children and families, with the goal of academic success, development of positive racial and cultural identity, and active engagement with inequality in the broader community. Research has found that many of these dimensions are associated with increased student engagement, persistence, attendance, and academic success (Hammond, 2015; Aronson & Laughter, 2016; Muñiz, 2020). Yet despite these positive outcomes, recent reviews of the literature on culturally relevant education show decreasing attention to this work (Aronson & Laughter, 2016), particularly for Native American students (Castagno & Brayboy, 2008).

THE IMPACT OF COVID-19

The closure of schools during the COVID-19 pandemic had a pronounced impact on families (Weiland et al., 2021). Parents reported high stress levels due to the shift to working from home and managing remote learning, and essential workers who needed to work in person struggled with providing care for their children. Research has shown that parents felt nervous, anxious, or apprehensive about the pandemic (Gonzalez et al., 2020). In addition, parents/guardians described the ways in which the pandemic caused major changes in their families' activities and routines (Gonzalez et al., 2020) and were more concerned about their children's social and emotional development and well-being than they had been prior to the pandemic (Jung & Barnett, 2021). The effects of interruptions in schooling were exacerbated by the disproportionate incidence of COVID-19 among some racial and minoritized groups: illness, hospitalization, and death due to COVID-19 have been higher among Hispanic or Latino, Black, American Indian or Alaska Native, and Native Hawaiian and other Pacific Islander populations (Centers for Disease Control and Prevention, 2020). As a result, children of color have been disproportionately affected by sickness and death among parents and other family members.

The shift to remote schooling during the pandemic introduced changes that were not conducive to social and academic learning (Weiland et al., 2021), and had a significant impact on children's learning opportunities and academic outcomes (EmpowerK12, 2020). Research has shown that many teachers were unable to teach/interact with children effectively online at the onset of the pandemic (Bassok et al., 2021). Reductions in instructional time and quality of instruction have also been documented (Rickles et al., 2020; Weiland et al., 2021). In line with those findings, parents nationally reported high levels of conduct problems, peer problems, and prosocial behavior problems among their children (Jung and Barnett, 2021), and children experienced slower learning growth or unrealized learning opportunities (Dorn et al., 2020; Huff, 2020; Renaissance Learning, 2020; Amplify, 2021; Engzell, Frey, & Verhagen, 2021; Lewis et al., 2021; McGinty et al., 2021; Ohio Department of Education, 2021; Storey & Zhang, 2021; Texas Education Agency, 2021; National Center for Education Statistics [NCES], 2022). A special administration of the National Assessment of Educational

Progress in 2022 found disproportionately large declines in test scores in reading and math overall and inequitable outcomes among different groups of children as a result of the pandemic (NCES, 2022).

The Centers for Disease Control and Prevention surveyed parents of children aged 5–12 between October and November 2020 and found that, compared with parents of children attending school in person, parents of children receiving remote instruction were more likely to report higher levels of emotional distress, conflict between working and providing child care, and difficulty sleeping (Verlenden et al., 2021). Families adapted to the new circumstances with significant changes in their labor market participation (National Academies, 2023).

In addition to these effects, the COVID-19 pandemic has affected school enrollment, which may in turn lead to disparities in school funding. Progressive school funding allocations have been shown to have both short- and long-term effects on student outcomes, especially for students from families with low incomes. In fall 2020, many large school districts reported substantial declines in enrollment—especially in kindergarten, where enrollment decreased by an average of 16%. Schools also saw decreases in attendance during the switch to virtual learning in spring 2020. These declines can negatively affect school funding that is based on enrollment numbers, as well as funding for schools that use attendance measures to allocate funding, and are more likely to affect high-poverty compared with better-resourced districts (Blagg, Gutierrex, & Lee, 2021).

CONCLUSIONS

Although the early elementary system is universally accessible to children and families, gaps in access to quality remain pervasive. As with ECE, differences in quality and funding create disparities in children's experiences and outcomes. This unequal access to both structural and process quality can be influenced by such factors as geography, district size, school infrastructure, funding inequities, teacher and administrator bias, disciplinary policies, and other manifestations of marginalization based on disability status, race, gender, and socioeconomic status. These social and systemic drivers also affect the ways in which structural and process quality interact, leading to a broad spectrum of variation in access to resources and quality educational experiences for young children.

In some cases, federal funding for programs to address the needs of certain populations is insufficient to bridge gaps in state and local funding, resulting in underfunded programs. For students living in states that already have relatively low student spending, this funding gap results in more students at risk—especially students from families with lower incomes and students of color. In 2015, in states with higher levels of poverty, underfunding of Title I, which is meant to ensure that all children receive a quality and equitable education regardless of income, was just over one-eighth the amount required to fully fund the Basic Grants portion. As a result, students from states with higher levels of poverty have received less funding per low-income child relative to states with lower levels of poverty. In the case of IDEA, underfunding has left a large burden for state and local governments and families, affecting the quality, timing, and dosage of services children receive and the quality of coordination with other services.

Children from marginalized populations experience a variety of biases in the early grades related to their race/ethnicity, language status, and disability status that can manifest in differential teacher expectations, perceptions of behavior, and perception of age/maturity. These biases influence experiences in the classroom, relationships with teachers, exposure to harsh and exclusionary disciplinary practices, and other experiences in school that can lead to opportunity gaps and influence both short- and long-term outcomes. These biases can also lead to the misperception that some children do not need environments that help support their learning and development. For children with disabilities, biases can contribute to both under- and overidentification of disabilities, which can prevent children from receiving services to which they are entitled legally or result in children being diagnosed with conditions they do not have. In both cases, the result can be gaps in access to inclusive learning opportunities that adequately support student needs.

Well-funded, high-quality experiences in the early grades that follow well-funded and aligned ECE experiences can improve students' academic performance and in the longer term can lead to more positive outcomes, such as higher graduation rates and reduced adult poverty. It is important to ensure that these early elementary experiences are aligned with the latest science and are specifically designed to close opportunity gaps and ensure that all students succeed, particularly those who have been historically marginalized. These experiences include high-quality instruction and asset-driven pedagogies, assessments, and curricula; social-emotional and mental health supports and policies to explicitly reduce exclusionary and harsh discipline and eliminate disparities in such practices; full inclusion of children with disabilities in general education settings, with high-quality and individualized services and supports; bilingual learning opportunities for children who are English learners and dual language learners; structurally sound, safe, healthy, and engaging learning environments; a well-qualified, fairly compensated, and supported teacher workforce; data-driven, continuous quality improvement efforts targeted at identifying and addressing opportunity and outcome gaps; authentic and meaningful family engagement and partnerships; community partnerships and engagement to promote child and holistic family wellness; and strong partnerships with ECE systems that promote seamless transitions from ECE to the early grades.

REFERENCES

Achilles, C.M. (2012). Class-size policy: The STAR experiment and related class-size studies. *Policy Brief Volume*, 1(2). National Council of Professors of Educational Administration. Available: https://files.eric.ed.gov/fulltext/ED540485.pdf

Achilles, G.M., McLaughlin, M.J., & Croninger, R.G. (2007). Sociocultural correlates of disciplinary exclusion among students with emotional, behavioral, and learning disabilities in the SEELS national dataset. *Journal of Emotional and Behavioral Disorders*, 15(1), 33–45. https://doi.org/10.1177/10634266070150010401

Afterschool Alliance. (n.d.). *Issue: School-age child care: Afterschool programs are a critical resource for working families.* Available: http://afterschoolalliance.org/Issue-School-Age-Child-Care.cfm

Afterschool Alliance & America After 3PM Health & Wellness. (2022). *Promoting healthy futures: Afterschool provides the supports parents want for children's well-being.* Available: https://afterschoolalliance.org/documents/AA3PM/AA3PM-Healthy-Futures-Report-2022.pdf

Ahram, R., Voulgarides, C.K., & Cruz, R.A. (2021). Understanding disability: High-quality evidence in research on special education disproportionality. *Review of Research in Education*, 45, 311–45. https://doi.org/10.3102/0091732X20985069

Albrecht, S., Skiba, R., Losen, D., Chung, C.G., & Middelberg, L. (2012). Federal policy on disproportionality in special education: Is it moving us forward? *Journal of Disability Policy Studies*, 23, 14–25. https://doi.org/10.1177/1044207311407917

Amplify. (2021). *COVID-19 means more students not learning to read.* Amplify Education. Available: https://go.info.amplify.com/download-whitepaper-fy21_general_moydata_national_readingresearch

Ansari, A., & Pianta, R.C. (2019). School absenteeism in the first decade of education and outcomes in adolescence. *Journal of School Psychology*, 76, 48–61. https://doi.org/10.1016/j.jsp.2019.07.010

Ansari, A., & Purtell, K.M. (2018). School absenteeism through the transition to kindergarten. *Journal of Education for Students Placed at Risk*, 23(1–2), 24–38. https://doi.org/10.1080/10824669.2018.1438202

Arcia, E. (2006). Achievement and enrollment status of suspended students: Outcomes in a large, multicultural school district. *Education and Urban Society*, 38(3), 359–69. https://doi.org/10.1177/0013124506286947

Aronson, B., & Laughter, J.C. (2016). The theory and practice of culturally relevant education. *Review of Educational Research*, 86, 163–206. https://doi.org/10.3102/0034654315582066

Artiles, A.J. (2011). Toward an interdisciplinary understanding of educational equity and difference: The case of the racialization of ability. *Educational Researcher*, 40(9), 431–45. https://doi.org/10.3102/0013189X11429391

———. (2019). Fourteenth annual brown lecture in education research: Reenvisioning equity research: Disability identification disparities as a case in point. *Educational Researcher*, 48(6), 325–35. https://doi.org/10.3102/0013189X19871949

Artiles, A.J., & Trent, S.C. (1994). Overrepresentation of minority students in special education: A continuing debate. *The Journal of Special Education*, 27(4), 410–37. https://doi.org/10.1177/002246699402700404

Artiles, A.J., Rueda, R., Salazar, J., & Higareda, I. (2005). Within-group diversity in minority disproportionate representation: English language learners in urban school districts. *Exceptional Children*, 71, 283–300. https://doi.org/10.1177/001440290507100305

Artiles, A.J., Klingner, J.K., & Tate, W.F. (2006). Representation of minority students in special education: Complicating traditional explanations: Editors' introduction. *Educational Researcher*, 35(6), 3–5. https://doi.org/10.3102/0013189X035006003

August, D., Shanahan, T., & Escamilla, K. (2009). English language learners: Developing literacy in second-language learners—Report of the national literacy panel on language-minority children and youth. *Journal of Literacy Research*, 41(4), 432–52. https://doi.org/10.1080/10862960903340165

Baker, B.D. (2017). *How money matters for schools.* Learning Policy Institute. Available: https://learningpolicyinstitute.org/product/how-money-matters-report

Baker, J.A. (2006). Contributions of teacher-child relationships to positive school adjustment during elementary school. *Journal of School Psychology*, 44(3), 211–29. https://doi.org/10.1016/j.jsp.2006.02.002

Barnard-Brak, L., Morales-Alemán, M.M., Tomeny, K., & McWilliam, R.A. (2021). Rural and racial/ethnic differences in children receiving early intervention services. *Family and Community Health*, 44(1), 52–8. https://doi.org/10.1097/FCH.0000000000000285

Barnett, W.S., Schulman, K., & Shore, R. (2004). Class size: What's the best fit? *Preschool Policy Matters*, 9. National Institute for Early Education Research. Available: https://nieer.org/wp-content/uploads/2016/08/9.pdf

Bassok, D., Weisner, K., Markowitz, A.J., & Hall, T. (2021). Teaching young children during COVID-19: Lessons from early educators in Virginia. *Virginia PDG B-5 Evaluation: SEE Partnerships Report and The Study of Early Education Through Partnerships*. EdPolicyWorks at the University of Virginia. Available: https://www.see-partnerships.com/reports--policy-briefs.html

Bates, L.A., & Glick, J.E. (2013). Does it matter if teachers and schools match the student? Racial and ethnic disparities in problem behaviors. *Social Science Research*, 42(5), 1180–90. https://doi.org/10.1016/j.ssresearch.2013.04.005

Benner, A.D., & Graham, S. (2011). Latino adolescents' experiences of discrimination across the first 2 years of high school: Correlates and influences on educational outcomes. *Child Development*, 82(2), 508–19. http://www.jstor.org/stable/29782849

Bialystok, E. (2017). The bilingual adaptation: How minds accommodate experience. *Psychological Bulletin*, 143(3), 233–62. https://doi.org/10.1037/bul0000099

Birch, S.H., & Ladd, G.W. (1997). The teacher-child relationship and children's early school adjustment. *Journal of School Psychology*, 35(1), 61–79. https://doi.org/10.1016/S0022-4405(96)00029-5

Bittencourt, A., Aerts, D., Alves, G., Palazzo, L., Monteiro, L., Vieira, P., & Freddo, S. (2009). Feelings of discrimination among students: Prevalence and associated factors. *Revista de Saúde Pública*, 43, 236–45. https://doi.org/10.1590/s0034-89102009005000008

Blagg, K., Gutierrez, E., & Lee, V. (2021). *How COVID-19-induced changes to K-12 enrollment and poverty might affect school funding.* Washington, DC: Urban Institute.

Bodrova, E., & Leong, D.J. (2019). Tools of the mind: The Vygotskian-Based early childhood program. *Journal of Cognitive Education and Psychology*, 17(3), 223–37. https://doi.org/10.1891/1945-8959.17.3.223

Boonstra, K. (2021). Constructing "behavior problems": Race, disability, and everyday discipline practices in the figured world of kindergarten. *Anthropology & Education Quarterly*, 52(4), 373–90. https://doi.org/10.1111/aeq.12374

Brooks-Gunn, J., Markman-Pithers, L., & Rouse, C.E. (2016). Starting early: Introducing the issue. *The Future of Children*, 26(2), 3–19. http://www.jstor.org/stable/43940578

Browne, J.A., Losen, D.J., & Wald, J. (2001). Zero tolerance: Unfair, with little recourse. *New Directions for Youth Development*, 92, 73–99. https://doi.org/10.1002/yd.23320019206

Brunner, E.J., Schwegman, D., & Vincent, J.M. (2022). How much does public school facility funding depend on property wealth? *Education Finance and Policy*, 18(1), 25–51. https://doi.org/10.1162/edfp_a_00346

Burghardt, G.M. (2011). Defining and recognizing play. *The Oxford handbook of the development of play*, 9–18. Oxford, England: Oxford University Press.

Buttaro, A. Jr., & Catsambis, S. (2019). Ability grouping in the early grades: Long-term consequences for educational equity in the United States. *Teachers College Record*, 121(2), 1–50.

Callahan, R., & Gándara, P. (2014). The bilingual advantage: Language, literacy and the US labor market. *Multilingual Matters*. Bristol, UK: Channel View Publications.

Campbell, T. (2015). Stereotyped at seven? Biases in teacher judgement of pupils' ability and attainment. *Journal of Social Policy*, 44(3), 517–47.

Carter, P.L., Skiba, R., Arredondo, M.I., & Pollock, M. (2017). You can't fix what you don't look at: Acknowledging race in addressing racial discipline disparities. *Urban Education*, 52(2), 207–35. https://doi.org/10.1177/0042085916660350

Castagno, A.E., & Brayboy, B.M.J. (2008). Culturally responsive schooling for Indigenous youth: A review of the literature. *Review of Education Research*, 78(4), 941–93. https://doi.org/10.3102/0034654308323036

Castro, D., & Artiles, A.F. (2021). Language, learning, and disability in the education of young bilingual children. *Multilingual Matters*. Channel View Publications. https://doi.org/10.1080/09500782.2022.2136487

Castro, D.C., & Meek, S. (2022). Beyond Castañeda and the "language barrier" ideology: Young children and their right to bilingualism. *Language Policy*, 21, 407–25. https://doi.org/10.1007/s10993-021-09608-x

Cavendish, W., Artiles, A., & Harry, B. (2014). Tracking inequality 60 years after Brown: Does policy legitimize the racialization of disability? *Multiple Voices for Ethnically Diverse Exceptional Learners*, 14, 30–40. https://doi.org/10.5555/2158-396X.14.2.30

Centers for Disease Control and Prevention. (2020). *Introduction to COVID-19 racial and ethnic health disparities*. Available: https://www.cdc.gov/coronavirus/2019-ncov/community/health-equity/racial-ethnic-disparities/index.html#print

Chang, H., & Romero, M. (2008). *Present, engaged, and accounted for: The critical importance of addressing chronic absence in the early grades*. National Center for Children in Poverty, Mailman School of Public Health, Columbia University. Available: https://www.nccp.org/wp-content/uploads/2008/09/text_837.pdf

Chang, H.N., Bauer, L., & Byrnes, V. (2018). *Data matters: Using chronic absence to accelerate action for student success*. Attendance Works and Everyone Graduates Center. Available: https://www.attendanceworks.org/wp-content/uploads/2019/01/Data-Matters_EXEC-Summary_121418-4.pdf

Chaudry, A., & Sandstrom. (2020). Child care and early education for infants and toddlers. *Future of Children*, 30(2), 165–90. Available: https://files.eric.ed.gov/fulltext/EJ1293558.pdf

Chen, P., & Rice, C. (2017). *Showing up matters: Newark chronic absenteeism in the early years*. Advocates for Children of New Jersey. Available: https://files.eric.ed.gov/fulltext/ED563781.pdf

Cherng, H.-Y.S. (2017). If they think I can: Teacher bias and youth of color expectations and achievement. *Social Science Research*, 66, 170–86. https://doi.org/10.1016/j.ssresearch.2017.04.001

Childs, J., & Lofton, R. (2021). Masking attendance: How education policy distracts from the wicked problem(s) of chronic absenteeism. *Educational Policy,* 35(2), 213–34. https://doi.org/10.1177/0895904820986771

Chin, M.J. (2021). JUE insight: Desegregated but still separated? The impact of school integration on student suspensions and special education classification. *Journal of Urban Economics*, 103389. https://doi.org/10.1016/j.jue.2021.103389

Coalition for Community Schools. (2020). *The coalition for community schools.* Institute for Educational Leadership. Available: https://www.communityschools.org/about/#:~:text=A%20Community%20School%20is%20a,that%20strengthens%20families%20and%20community

Collier, V., & Thomas, W. (2017). Validating the power of bilingual schooling: Thirty-two years of large-scale, longitudinal research. *Annual Review of Applied Linguistics*, 37, 1–15. https://doi.org/10.1017/S0267190517000034

Collins, B.A., O'Connor, E., Supplee, L., & Shaw, D.S. (2017). Behavior problems in elementary school among low-income boys: The role of teacher–child relationships. *The Journal of Educational Research*, 110(1), 72–84. https://doi.org/10.1080/00220671.2015.1039113

Commission on Civil Rights. (2018). *Public education funding inequity in an era of increasing concentration of poverty and resegregation.* Available: https://www.usccr.gov/files/pubs/2018/2018-01-10-Education-Inequity.pdf

Connolly, F., & Olson, L.S. (2012). *Early elementary performance and attendance in Baltimore City Schools' pre-kindergarten and kindergarten.* Baltimore Education Research Consortium. Available: https://eric.ed.gov/?id=ED535768

Cooc, N. (2022). Disparities in general education inclusion for students of color with disabilities: Understanding when and why. *Journal of School Psychology*, 90, 43–59. https://doi.org/10.1016/j.jsp.2021.10.002

Cruz, R.A., & Firestone, A.R. (2022). Understanding the empty backpack: The role of timing in disproportionate special education identification. *Sociology of Race and Ethnicity,* 8(1), 95–113. https://doi.org/10.1177/23326492211034890

Cruz, R.A., & Rodl, J. (2018). An integrative synthesis of literature on disproportionality in special education. *The Journal of Special Education,* 52(1), 002246691875870. https://doi.org/10.1177/0022466918758707

Cruz, R.A., Lee, J.H., Aylward, A.G., & Voulgarides, C.K. (2020). The effect of school funding on opportunity gaps for students with disabilities: Policy and context in a diverse urban district. *Journal of Disability Policy Studies*, 33(1), 3–14. https://doi.org/10.1177/1044207320970545

Cruz, R.A., Kulkarni, S.S., & Firestone, A.R. (2021). A QuantCrit analysis of context, discipline, special education, and disproportionality. *AERA Open*, 7(1), 1–16. https://journals.sagepub.com/doi/10.1177/23328584211041354#con3

Dabach, D.B., Suárez-Orozco, C., Hernandez, S.J., & Brooks, M.D. (2018). Future perfect?: Teachers' expectations and explanations of their Latino immigrant students' postsecondary futures. *Journal of Latinos and Education,* 17(1), 38–52. https://doi.org/10.1080/15348431.2017.1281809

Dahlin, M.S., & Squires, J.H. (2016). *Pre-K attendance: Why it's important and how to support it.* New Brunswick, NJ: Center on Enhancing Early Learning Outcomes. Available: http://ceelo.org/wp-content/uploads/2016/02/ceelo_fastfact_state_ece_attendance_2016_02_01_final_for_web.pdf

Dang, L.C., Donde, A., Madison, C., O'Neil, J.P., & Jagust, W.J. (2012). Striatal dopamine influences the default mode network to affect shifting between object features. *Journal of Cognitive Neuroscience*, 24, 1960–70. https://doi.org/10.1162/jocn_a_00252

Darling-Hammond, L. (2019). *Investing for student success: Lessons from state school finance reforms.* Learning Policy Institute. Available: https://learningpolicyinstitute.org/product/investing-student-success-school-finance-reforms-report

Darling-Hammond, L., & Baratz-Snowden, J. (Eds). (2007). A good teacher in every classroom: Preparing the highly qualified teachers our children deserve. *Educational Horizons*, 85(2), 111–32. Available: https://files.eric.ed.gov/fulltext/EJ750647.pdf

Department of Education. (2019). *Chronic absenteeism in the nation's schools: A hidden educational crisis.* Available: https://www2.ed.gov/datastory/chronicabsenteeism.html

———. (2021a). *2017-2018 State and national estimations.* Office for Civil Rights. Available: https://ocrdata.ed.gov/estimations/2017-2018

———. (2021b). *43rd annual report to Congress on the implementation of the Individuals with Disabilities Education Act, 2021.* Alexandria, VA: Education Publications Center.

———. (2021c). *2017-18 Civil rights data collection, released October 2020, updated May 2021.* Office for Civil Rights. Available: https://ocrdata.ed.gov. https://ocrdata.ed.gov/assets/downloads/Corporal_Punishment_Part4_Updated.pdf

———. (2023). *Nita M. Lowey 21st Century Community Learning Centers.* Office of Elementary and Secondary Education. Office for Civil Rights. Available: https://oese.ed.gov/offices/office-of-formula-grantsschool-support-and-accountability/21st-century-community-learning-centers/

Department of Justice & Department of Education. (2014). *Joint "dear colleague" letter.* Office for Civil Rights. Available: https://www2.ed.gov/about/offices/list/ocr/letters/colleague-201401-title-vi.html

Dobbs, J., & Arnold, D.H. (2009). Relationship between preschool teachers' reports of children's behavior and their behavior toward those children. *School Psychology Quarterly*, 24(2), 95–105. https://doi.org/10.1037/a0016157

Dorn, E., Hancock, B., Sarakatsannis, J., & Viruleg, E. (2020). *COVID-19 and learning loss: Disparities grow and students need help.* McKinsey & Company. Available: https://www.mckinsey.com/industries/public-and-social-sector/our-insights/covid-19-and-learning-loss-disparities-grow-and-students-need-help

Downer, J., Goble, P., Myers, S., & Pianta, R. (2016). Teacher-child racial/ethnic match within pre-kindergarten classrooms and children's early school adjustment. *Early Childhood Research Quarterly*, 37. https://doi.org/10.1016/j.ecresq.2016.02.007

Downey, D., & Pribesh, S. (2004). When race matters: Teachers' evaluations of students' classroom behavior. *Sociology of Education*, 77. https://doi.org/10.1177/003804070407700401

Driscoll, K.C., & Pianta, R.C. (2010). Banking time in Head Start: Early efficacy of an intervention designed to promote supportive teacher-child relationships. *Early Education and Development*, 21(1), 38–64. https://doi.org/10.1080/10409280802657449

Dubay, L., & Holla, N. (2015). *Absenteeism in DC public schools early education program: An update for school year 2013-14.* Washington, DC: Urban Institute.

———. (2016). *Does attendance in early education predict attendance in elementary school? An analysis of DCPS's early education program.* Urban Institute. Available: https://greaterdc.urban.org/publication/does-attendance-early-education-predict-attendance-elementary-school-analysis-dcpss

Duncan, B.L. (1976). Differential social perception and attribution of intergroup violence: Testing the lower limits of stereotyping of Blacks. *Journal of Personality and Social Psychology*, 34(4), 590–8. https://doi.org/10.1037/0022-3514.34.4.590

Durkin, K., Lipsey, M.W., Farran, D.C., & Wiesen, S.E. (2022). Effects of a statewide prekindergarten program on children's achievement and behavior through sixth grade. *Developmental Psychology*, 58(3), 470–84. https://doi.org/10.1037/dev0001301

Eberhardt, J.L., Goff, P.A., Purdie, V.J., & Davies, P.G. (2004). Seeing Black: Race, crime, and visual processing. *Journal of Personality and Social Psychology*, 87(6), 876–93. https://doi.org/10.1037/0022-3514.87.6.876

EdBuild. (2019). *23 billion*. Available: https://edbuild.org/content/23-billion

Ehrlich, S.B., Gwynne, J.A., & Allensworth, E.M. (2018). Pre-kindergarten attendance matters: Early chronic absence patterns and relationships to learning outcomes. *Early Childhood Research Quarterly*, 44, 136–51. https://doi.org/10.1016/j.ecresq.2018.02.012

Eitle, T.M., & Eitle, D.J. (2002). Race, cultural capital, and the educational effects of participation in sports. *Sociology of Education*, 75(2), 123–46. https://doi.org/10.2307/3090288

Eklund, K., Burns, M.K., Oyen, K., DeMarchena, S., & McCollom, E.M. (2022). Addressing chronic absenteeism in schools: A meta-analysis of evidence-based interventions. *School Psychology Review*, 51(1), 95–111. https://doi.org/10.1080/2372966X.2020.1789436

EmpowerK12. (2020). *How COVID-19 regular school closures could impact DC student proficiency in 2020-21*. Available: https://www.empowerk12.org/research-source/covid-school-closures

Engzell, P., Frey, A., & Verhagen, M.D. (2021). Learning loss due to school closures during the COVID-19 pandemic. *Proceedings of the National Academy of Sciences of the United States of America*, 118(17), e2022376118. https://doi.org/10.1073/pnas.2022376118

Epstein, R., Godfrey, E., Gonzalez, T., & Javdani, S. (2020). *Data snapshot: 2017-2018 national data on school discipline by race and gender*. Georgetown Law Center on Poverty and Inequality. Available: https://genderjusticeandopportunity.georgetown.edu/wp-content/uploads/2020/12/National-Data-on-School-Discipline-by-Race-and-Gender.pdf

Ewing, A.R., & Taylor, A.R. (2009). The role of child gender and ethnicity in teacher–child relationship quality and children's behavioral adjustment in preschool. *Early Childhood Research Quarterly*, 24(1), 92–105. https://doi.org/10.1016/j.ecresq.2008.09.002

Fabelo, T., Thompson, M.D., Plotkin, M., Carmichael, D., Marchbanks, M.P., & Booth, E.A. (2011). *Breaking schools' rules: A statewide study of how school discipline relates to students' success and juvenile justice involvement*. (NCJ No. 244572). Office of Justice Programs, U.S. Department of Justice. https://www.ojp.gov/ncjrs/virtual-library/abstracts/breaking-schools-rules-statewide-study-how-school-discipline-0

Fabes, R.A., Catherine, E., Quick, M., Blevins, D., & Musgrave, A. (2021). The price of punishment: Days missed due to suspension in U.S. K-12 public schools. *Psychology in the Schools*, 58, 1980–94. https://doi.org/10.1002/pits.22565

Fierros E.G., & Conroy, J.W. (2002). Double jeopardy: An exploration of restrictiveness and race in special education. *Racial inequity in special education*, 39–70. Harvard Education Publishing Group.

Finn, J., Pannozzo, G., & Achilles, C. (2003). The "why's" of class size: Student behavior in small classes. *Review of Educational Research*, 73, 321–68. https://doi.org/10.3102/00346543073003321

Fish, R.E. (2019). Teacher race and racial disparities in special education. *Remedial and Special Education*, 40(4), 213–24. https://doi.org/10.1177/0741932518810434

Fisher, K., Hirsh-Pasek, K., Golinkoff, R.M., Singer, D.G., & Berk, L. (2011). Playing around in school: Implications for learning and educational policy. *The Oxford handbook of the development of play*, 341–60. Oxford University Press. https://doi.org/10.1093/oxfordhb/9780195393002.001.0001

Fitzpatrick, C., Côté-Lussier, C., Pagani, L.S., & Blair, C. (2015). I don't think you like me very much: Child minority status and disadvantage predict relationship quality with teachers. *Youth & Society*, 47(5), 727–43. https://doi.org/10.1177/0044118X13508962

Ford, D. (2021). *Recruiting & retaining culturally different students in gifted education*. Routledge. https://doi.org/10.4324/9781003237655

Ford, D.Y., Grantham, T.C., & Whiting, G.W. (2008). Culturally and linguistically diverse students in gifted education: Recruitment and retention issues. *Exceptional Children,* 74(3), 289–306. https://doi.org/10.1177/001440290807400302

Fortner, A., Hardy, A., & Schmit, S. (2021). *School-age child care: Overlooked and under-resourced.* The Center for Law and Social Policy. Available: https://www.clasp.org/publications/fact-sheet/school-age-child-care-overlooked-and-under-resourced

Frawley, T. (2005). Gender bias in the classroom: Current controversies and implications for teachers. *Childhood Education,* 81(4), 221.

Frederick, A., & Shifrer, D. (2018). Race and disability: From analogy to intersectionality. *Sociology of Race and Ethnicity,* 5(2), 200–14. https://doi.org/10.1177/2332649218783480

Fuhs, M.W., Nesbitt, K.T., & Jackson, H. (2018). Chronic absenteeism and preschool children's executive functioning skills development. *Journal of Education for Students Placed at Risk,* 23(1–2), 39–52. https://doi.org/10.1080/10824669.2018.1438201

Fuller, S.C., & Ladd, H.F. (2013). School-based accountability and the distribution of teacher quality across grades in elementary school. *Education Finance and Policy,* 8(4), 528–59. Available: https://files.eric.ed.gov/fulltext/ED532767.pdf

Gage, N.A., Katsiyannis, A., Carrero, K.M., Miller, R., & Pico, D. (2021). Exploring disproportionate discipline for Latinx students with and without disabilities: A national analysis. *Behavioral Disorders,* 47(1), 3–13. https://doi.org/10.1177/0198742920961356

Gansen, H.M. (2021). Disciplining difference(s): Reproducing inequalities through disciplinary interactions in preschool. *Social Problems,* 68(3), 740–60. https://doi.org/10.1093/socpro/spaa011

Gardner, M., Roth, J.L., & Brooks-Gunn, J. (2009). Can after-school programs help level the academic playing field for disadvantaged youth? *Equity matters. Research Review No. 4.* Campaign for Educational Equity. Teachers College, Columbia University. Available: https://bgcutah.org/wp-content/uploads/2014/10/Gardner-Roth-and-Brooks-Gunn-Disadvantaged-Youth.pdf

Garner, P.W., & Mahatmya, D. (2015). Affective social competence and teacher–child relationship quality: Race/ethnicity and family income level as moderators. *Social Development,* 24, 678–97. https://doi.org/10.1111/sode.12114

Garner, P.W., Shadur, J.M., & Toney, T. (2021). The effects of teacher–child racial congruence, child race, and emotion situation knowledge on teacher–child relationships and school readiness. *Psychology in Schools,* 58, 1995–2016. https://doi.org/10.1002/pits.22567

Gay, G. (2010). *Culturally responsive teaching: Theory, research, and practice.* New York, NY: Teachers College, Columbia University.

Genesee, F., & Lindholm-Leary, K. (2013). Two case studies of content-based language education. *Journal of Immersion and Content-Based Language Education,* 1(1), 3–33. https://doi.org/10.1075/jicb.1.1.02gen

Genesee, F., Lindholm-Leary, K., Saunders, W.M., & Christian, D. (Eds.). (2006). *Educating English language learners: A synthesis of research evidence.* Cambridge University Press. https://doi.org/10.1017/CBO9780511499913

Gerlinger, J., Viano, S., Gardella, J.H., Fisher, B.W., Chris Curran, F., & Higgins, E.M. (2021). Exclusionary school discipline and delinquent outcomes: A meta-analysis. *Journal of Youth and Adolescence,* 50(8), 1493–509. https://doi.org/10.1007/s10964-021-01459-3

Gilliam, W.S., & Shahar, G. (2006). Preschool and child care expulsion and suspension: Rates and predictors in one state. *Infants & Young Children,* 19(3), 228–45. https://doi.org/10.1097/00001163-200607000-00007

Gilliam, W.S., Maupin, A.N., Reyes, C.R., Accavitti, M.R., & Shic, F. (2016). *Do early educators' implicit biases regarding sex and race relate to behavior expectations and recommendations of preschool expulsions and suspensions?* New Haven, CT: Yale University, Child Study Center. Available: https://medicine.yale.edu/childstudy/zigler/publications/Preschool%20Implicit%20Bias%20Policy%20Brief_final_9_26_276766_5379_v1.pdf

Goff, P.A., Jackson, M.C., Di Leone, B.A.L., Culotta, C.M., & DiTomasso, N.A. (2014). The essence of innocence: Consequences of dehumanizing black children. *Journal of Personality and Social Psychology,* 106(4), 526. https://doi.org/10.1037/a0035663

Goldberg, M., & Iruka, I. (2022). The role of teacher–child relationship quality in black and Latino boys' positive development. *Early Childhood Education Journal.* https://doi.org/0.1007/s10643-021-01300-3

Gonzalez, T., de la Rubia, M.A., Hincz, K.P., Comas-Lopez, M., Subirats, L., Fort, S., & Sacha, G.M. (2020). Influence of COVID-19 confinement on students' performance in higher education. *PLoS One,* 15(10), e0239490. https://doi.org/10.1371/journal.pone.0239490

Gottfried, M.A. (2009). Excused versus unexcused: How student absences in elementary school affect academic achievement. *Educational Evaluation and Policy Analysis,* 31(4), 392–415.

———. (2015). Can center-based childcare reduce the odds of early chronic absenteeism? *Early Childhood Research Quarterly,* 32, 160–173. https://doi.org/10.1016/j.ecresq.2015.04.002

Government Accountability Office. (1996). *School facilities. America's schools report differing conditions.* (HEHS-96-103). Available: https://www.gao.gov/products/hehs-96-103

———. (2020). *K-12 education: School districts frequently identified multiple building systems needing updates or replacement.* (GAO-20-494). Available: https://www.gao.gov/products/gao-20-494

Graue, E., Hatch, K., Rao, K., & Oen, D. (2007). The wisdom of class-size reduction. *American Educational Research Journal,* 44(3), 670–700. https://doi.org/10.3102/00028312073067

Graue, E., Rauscher, E., & Sherfinski, M. (2009). The synergy of class size reduction and classroom quality. *The Elementary School Journal,* 110(2), 178–201. https://doi.org/10.1086/648334

Gregory, A., Skiba, R., & Noguera, P. (2010). The achievement gap and the discipline gap: Two sides of the same coin? *Educational Researcher,* 39, 59–68. https://doi.org/10.3102/0013189X09357621

Grindal, T., Schifter, L.A., Schwartz, G., & Hehir, T. (2019). Racial differences in special education identification and placement: Evidence across three states. *Harvard Education Review,* 89(4), 525–53. https://doi.org/10.17763/1943-5045-89.4.525

Grissom, J., & Redding, C. (2016). Discretion and disproportionality: Explaining the underrepresentation of high-achieving students of color in gifted programs. *AERA Open,* 2(1). https://doi.org/10.1177/2332858415622175

Halberstadt, A., Cooke, A., Garner, P., Hughes, S., Oertwig, D., & Neupert, S. (2020). Racialized emotion recognition accuracy and anger bias of children's faces. *Emotion,* 22(3), 403–17. https://doi.org/10.1037/emo0000756

Hammond, Z. (2015). *Culturally responsive teaching and the brain: Promoting authentic engagement and rigor among culturally and linguistically diverse students.* Thousand Oaks, CA: Corwin/Sage.

Hamre, B.K., & Pianta, R.C. (2001). Early teacher–child relationships and the trajectory of children's school outcomes through eighth grade. *Child Development,* 72(2), 625–38. https://doi.org/10.1111/1467-8624.00301

Harlin, R., Sirota, E., & Bailey, L. (2009). Review of research: The impact of teachers' expectations on diverse learners' academic outcomes. *Childhood Education,* 85(4), 253–6. https://doi.org/10.1080/00094056.2009.10523092

Harry, B., & Klingner, J.K. (2014). *Why are so many minority students in special education? Understanding race & disability in schools.* (2nd ed.). New York: Teachers College Press.

Henry, G.T., McNeill, S.M., & Harbatkin, E. (2022). Accountability-driven school reform: Are there unintended effects on younger children in untested grades? *Early Childhood Research Quarterly,* 61, 190–208. https://doi.org/10.1016/j.ecresq.2022.07.005

Hinnant, J.B., O'Brien, M., & Ghazarian, S.R. (2009). The longitudinal relations of teacher expectations to achievement in the early school years. *Journal of Educational Psychology*, 101(3), 662–70. https://doi.org/10.1037/a0014306

Hirsh-Pasek, K., Golinkoff, R., Berk, L.E., & Singer, D. (2009). *A mandate for playful learning in preschool: Presenting the evidence*. Oxford University Press. https://doi.org/10.1093/acprof:oso/9780195382716.001.0001

Hirsh-Pasek, K., Adamson, L.B., Bakeman, R., Owen, M.T., Golinkoff, R.M., Pace, A., Yust, P. K., & Suma, K. (2015). The contribution of early communication quality to low-income children's language success. *Psychological Science*, 26(7), 1071–83. https://doi.org/10.1177/0956797615581493

Ho, H., Gol-Guven, M., & Bagnato, S.J. (2012). Classroom observations of teacher–child relationships among racially symmetrical and racially asymmetrical teacher–child dyads. *European Early Childhood Education Research Journal*, 20(3), 329–49. https://doi.org/10.1080/1350293X.2012.704759

Horm, D.M., Jeon, S., Clavijo, M.V., & Acton, M. (2022). Kindergarten through grade 3 outcomes associated with participation in high-quality early care and education: A RCT follow-up study. *Education Sciences*, 12(12), 908. https://doi.org/10.3390/educsci12120908

Huff, K. (2020). *Quantifying COVID learning loss: At-home testing raises questions*. Curriculum Associates. Available: https://www.curriculumassociates.com/research-and-efficacy/learning-loss-covid-impact-fall-2020

Hugenberg, K., & Bodenhausen, G.V. (2003). Facing prejudice: Implicit prejudice and the perception of facial threat. *Psychological Science*, 14(6), 640–43. https://doi.org/10.1046/j.0956-7976.2003.psci_1478.x

Hughes, J.E. (2005). The role of teacher knowledge and learning experiences in forming technology-integrated pedagogy. *The Journal of Technology and Teacher Education*, 13, 277–302.

Humm Patnode, A., Gibbons, K., & Edmunds, R.R. (2018). *Attendance and chronic absenteeism: Literature review*. University of Minnesota, College of Education and Human Development, Center for Applied Research and Educational Improvement. Available: http://www.floridarti.usf.edu/resources/format/pdf/Chronic%20Absenteeism%20Lit%20Review%202018.pdf

Institute of Medicine (IOM) & National Research Council (NRC). (2015). *Transforming the workforce for children birth through age 8: A unifying foundation*. Washington, DC: The National Academies Press.

Iruka, I., Burchinal, M., & Cai, K. (2010). Long-term effect of early relationships for African American children's academic and social development: An examination from kindergarten to fifth grade. *Journal of Black Psychology*, 36, 144–71. https://doi.org/10.1177/0095798409353760

Jabbari, J., & Johnson, O. Jr. (2020). The collateral damage of in-school suspensions: A counterfactual analysis of high-suspension schools, math achievement and college attendance. *Urban Education*, 58(5), 801–37. https://doi.org/10.1177/0042085920902256

Jackson, C.K. (2018). *Does school spending matter? The new literature on an old question*. (Working Paper No. 25368). National Bureau of Economic Research. Available: http://www.nber.org/papers/w25368

Jackson, C.K., Johnson, R.C., & Persico, C. (2016). The effects of school spending on educational and economic outcomes: Evidence from school finance reforms. *The Quarterly Journal of Economics*, 131(1), 157–218. https://doi.org/10.3386/w20847

Johnson, D. (2019). *The striking outlier. The persistent, painful and problematic practice of corporal punishment in schools*. Southern Poverty Law Center and The Center for Civil Rights Remedies. Available: https://www.splcenter.org/20190611/striking-outlier-persistent-painful-and-problematic-practice-corporal-punishment-schools

Johnson, R.C., & Jackson, C.K. (2018). *Reducing inequality through dynamic complementarity: Evidence Head Start and public school spending.* (Working Paper No. 23489). National Bureau of Economic Research. https://www.nber.org/papers/w23489

Jung, K., & Barnett, W.S. (2021). *Impacts of the pandemic on young children and their parents: Initial findings from NIEER's May-June 2021 preschool learning activities survey.* New Brunswick, NJ: National Institute for Early Education Research, Rutgers University.

Kaeser, S.C. (1979). Suspensions in school discipline. *Education and Urban Society*, 11(4), 465–84.

Karega Rausch, M., & Skiba, R. (2004). Unplanned outcomes: Suspensions and expulsions in Indiana. *Education Policy Briefs*, 2(2). Indiana Youth Services Association and the Center for Evaluation and Education Policy. Available: https://eric.ed.gov/?id=ED488917

Katz, M., Adams, G., & Johnson, M.C. (2015). *Insights into absenteeism in DCPS early childhood program: Contributing factors and promising strategies.* Urban Institute. Available: https://www.urban.org/research/publication/insights-absenteeism-dcps-early-childhood-program

Kearney, C.A., & Childs, J. (2021). A multi-tiered systems of support blueprint for re-opening schools following Covid-19 shutdown. *Children and Youth Services Review*, 122, 105919. https://doi.org/10.1016/j.childyouth.2020.105919

Kerr, J., Price, M., Kotch, J., Willis, S., Fisher, M., & Silva, S. (2011). Does contact by a family nurse practitioner decrease early school absence? *The Journal of School Nursing*, 28(1), 38–46. https://doi.org/10.1177/1059840511422818

Kirksey, J.J., & Gottfried, M.A. (2021). The effect of serving "breakfast after-the-bell" meals on school absenteeism: Comparing results from regression discontinuity designs. *Educational Evaluation and Policy Analysis*, 43(2), 305–28. https://doi.org/10.3102/0162373721991572

Klingner, J., Artiles, A.J., Kozleski, E., Harry, B., Zion, S., Tate, W., Zamora Durán, G., & Riley, D. (2005). Addressing the disproportionate representation of culturally and linguistically diverse students in special education through culturally responsive educational systems. *Education Policy Analysis Archives*, 13(38). https://doi.org/10.14507/epaa.v13n38.2005

Kramarczuk Voulgarides, C., Aylward, A., Tefera, A., Artiles, A.J., Alvarado, S.L., & Noguera, P. (2021). Unpacking the logic of compliance in special education: Contextual influences on discipline racial disparities in suburban schools. *Sociology of Education*, 94, 208–26. https://doi.org/10.1177/00380407211013322

Kunemund, R., McCullough, S, Williams, C., Miller, C., Sutherland, K., Conroy, M., & Granger, K. (2020). The mediating role of teacher self-efficacy in the relation between teacher-child race mismatch and conflict. *Psychology in the Schools*, 57(11), 1757–70. https://doi.org/10.1002/pits.22419

Ladd, G.W., & Burgess, K.B. (1999). Charting the relationship trajectories of aggressive, withdrawn, and aggressive/withdrawn children during early grade school. *Child Development*, 70(4), 910–29. https://doi.org/10.1111/1467-8624.00066

Ladson-Billings, G. (1994). *The dreamkeepers: Successful teachers of African American children.* Hoboken, NJ: Jossey-Bass.

———. (1995). Toward a theory of culturally relevant pedagogy. *American Educational Research Journal*, 32, 465–91. https://doi.org/10.3102/00028312032003465

Lafortune, J., Rothstein, J., & Schanzenbach, D.W. (2018). School finance reform and the distribution of student achievement. *American Economic Journal: Applied Economics*, 10(2), 1–26. https://doi.org/10.1257/app.20160567

Lee, P., & Bierman, K.L. (2015). Classroom and teacher support in kindergarten: Associations with the behavioral and academic adjustment of low-income students. *Merrill-Palmer Quarterly*, 61(3), 383–411. https://doi.org/10.13110/merrpalmquar1982.61.3.0383

Lehrer-Small, A. (2021, September 22). *"We left those students behind": 1.9 million low-income youth boxed out of afterschool programs, despite surging parent interest in stem offerings*. The74. Available: https://www.the74million.org/we-left-those-students-behind-1-9-million-low-income-youth-boxed-out-of-afterschool-programs-despite-surging-parent-interest-in-stem-offerings

Lewis, K., Kuhfeld, M., Ruzek, E., & McEachin, A. (2021). Learning during COVID-19: Reading and math achievement in the 2020-21 school year. *Center for School and Student Progress*. [Brief]. NWEA Research. Available: https://content.acsa.org/wp-content/uploads/2021/11/Learning-During-COVID-19-Reading-and-Math-NWEA-Brief.pdf

Linick, M.A., Garcia, A.N, & Grandpre, H.D. (2021). *The effect of discipline reform plans on exclusionary discipline outcomes in Minnesota*. Regional Educational Laboratory Program, Institute of Education Sciences. Available: https://ies.ed.gov/ncee/rel/Products/Publication/40022

Lloyd, S., & Harwin, A. (2021). *Nation earns a "C" on school finance, reflecting inconsistency in K-12 funding and equity*. EducationWeek. Available: https://www.edweek.org/policy-politics/nation-earns-a-c-on-school-finance-reflecting-inconsistency-in-k-12-funding-and-equity/2021/06#:~:text=First%2C%20the%20big%20picture%3A%20The,0.3%20points%20over%20last%20year

Losen, D. (2017). *The school-to-prison pipeline: The intersections of students of color with disabilities*. December 8. United States Commission on Civil Rights. Available: https://www.childtrends.org/publications/school-prison-pipeline-intersections-students-color-disabilities

Losen, D.J., & Whitaker, A. (2018). *11 million days lost: Race, discipline, and safety at U.S. public schools (Part 1)*. Center for Civil Rights Remedies, American Civil Liberties Union. Available: https://www.aclu.org/report/11-million-days-lost-race-discipline-and-safety-us-public-schools-part-1

Losen, D.J., Hodson, C.L., Keith, M.A. II, Morrison, K., & Belway, S. (2015). *Are we closing the school discipline gap?* The Civil Rights Project/Proyecto Derechos Civiles. Available: https://escholarship.org/uc/item/2t36g571

Lowenstein, A.E., Wolf, S., Gershoff, E.T., Sexton, H.R., Raver, C.C., & Aber, J.L. (2015). The stability of elementary school contexts from kindergarten to third grade. *Journal of School Psychology*, 53(4), 323–35. https://doi.org/10.1016/j.jsp.2015.05.002

Ly, J., Zhou, Q., Chu, K., & Chen, S.H. (2012). Teacher–child relationship quality and academic achievement of Chinese American children in immigrant families. *Journal of School Psychology*, 50(4), 535–53. https://doi.org/10.1016/j.jsp.2012.03.003

Mahoney, J.L., Parente, M.E., & Zigler, E.F. (2009). Afterschool programs in America: Origins, growth, popularity, and politics. *Journal of Youth Development*, 4(3). https://doi.org/10.5195/jyd.2009.250

Maier, A., Daniel, J., Oakes, J., & Lam, L. (2017). *Community schools as an effective school improvement strategy: A review of the evidence*. Learning Policy Institute. Available: https://learningpolicyinstitute.org/product/community-schools-effective-school-improvement-report

Marcelo, A.K., & Yates, T.M. (2014). Prospective relations among preschoolers' play, coping, and adjustment as moderated by stressful events. *Journal of Applied Developmental Psychology*, 35(3), 223–33. https://doi.org/10.1016/j.appdev.2014.01.001

McCormick, M.P., & O'Connor, E.E. (2015). Teacher–child relationship quality and academic achievement in elementary school: Does gender matter? *Journal of Educational Psychology*, 107(2), 502–16. https://doi.org/10.1037/a0037457

McCoy, D.C., Yoshikawa, H., Ziol-Guest, K.M., Duncan, G.J., Schindler, H.S., Magnuson, K., Yang, R., Koepp, A., & Shonkoff, J.P. (2017). Impacts of early childhood education on medium- and long-term educational outcomes. *Educational Researcher*, 46(8), 474–87. https://doi.org/10.3102/0013189x17737739

McGinty, A., Gray, A., Partee, A., Herring, W., & Soland J. (2021). *Examining early literacy skills in the wake of COVID-19 spring 2020 school disruptions.* University of Virginia. Available: https://pals.virginia.edu/public/pdfs/login/PALS_Fall_2020_Data_Report_5_18_final.pdf

McIntosh, K., Girvan, E.J., McDaniel, S.C., Santiago-Rosario, M.R., St. Joseph, S., Fairbanks Falcon, S., Izzard, S., & Bastable, E. (2021). Effects of an equity-focused PBIS approach to school improvement on exclusionary discipline and school climate, *Preventing School Failure: Alternative Education for Children and Youth*, 65(4), 354–61. https://doi.org/10.1080/1045988X.2021.1937027

McKown, C., & Weinstein, R.S. (2008). Teacher expectations, classroom context, and the achievement gap. *Journal of School Psychology*, 46(3), 235–61. https://doi.org/10.1016/j.jsp.2007.05.001

Meek, S., Smith, L., Allen, R., Catherine, E., Edyburn, K., Williams, C., Fabes, R., McIntosh, K., Garcia, E., Takanishi, R., Gordon, L., Jimenez-Castellanos, O., Hemmeter, M.L., Gilliam, W., & Pontier, R. (2020). *Start with equity: From the early years to the early grades. Data, research, and an actionable child equity policy agenda.* Washington, DC: Children's Equity Project, Bipartisan Policy Center.

Meek, S.E., & Gilliam, W.S. (2016). *Expulsion and suspension in early education as matters of social justice and health equity.* National Academy of Medicine. Available: https://nam.edu/expulsion-and-suspension-in-early-education-as-matters-of-social-justice-and-health-equity

Meloy, B., Gardner, M., & Darling-Hammond, L. (2019). *Untangling the evidence on preschool effectiveness: Insights for policymakers.* Learning Policy Institute. Available https://learningpolicyinstitute.org/product/untangling-evidence-preschool-effectiveness-report

Merriam-Webster. (2022). Racialization. In *Merriam-Webster*. Available: https://www.merriam-webster.com/dictionary/racialization

Migration Policy Institute. (2021). *Young dual language learners in the United States and by state.* Available: https://www.migrationpolicy.org/programs/data-hub/charts/us-state-profiles-young-dlls

Miller, S.L., Maner, J.K., & Becker, D.V. (2010). Self-protective biases in group categorization: Threat cues shape the psychological boundary between "us" and "them." *Journal of Personality and Social Psychology*, 99(1), 62–77. https://doi.org/10.1037/a0018086

Mills, J.M. (2016). From the principal's office to prison: How America's school discipline system defies *Brown. University of San Francisco Law Review*, 50(31), 529.

Mittleman, J. (2018). A downward spiral? Childhood suspension and the path to juvenile arrest. *Sociology of Education*, 91(3), 183–204. https://www.jstor.org/stable/48588580

Molnar, A.S., Zahorik, P., Palmer, J., Halbach, A., & Ehrle, K. (2000). Wisconsin's student achievement guarantee in education (SAGE) class-size reduction program: Achievement effects, teaching and classroom implications. *The CEIC Review*, 9(2). Available: http://www.classsizematters.org/wp-content/uploads/2012/11/Wang-Small-class-size.pdf

Morgan, I., & Amerikaner, A. (2018). *Funding gaps 2018. Too many students do not get their fair share of education funding.* The Education Trust. Available: https://edtrust.org/resource/funding-gaps-2018

Morgan, P.L., Farkas, G., Hillemeier, M.M., Mattison, R., Maczuga, S., Li, H., & Cook, M. (2015). Minorities are disproportionately underrepresented in special education: Longitudinal evidence across five disability conditions. *Educational Researcher*, 44(5), 278–92. https://doi.org/10.3102/0013189X15591157

Morris, E.W., & Perry, B.L. (2016). The punishment gap: School suspension and racial disparities in achievement. *Social Problems,* 63(1), 68–86. https://doi.org/10.1093/socpro/spv026

Muñiz, J. (2020). *Culturally responsive teaching: A reflection guide.* New America. Available: https://www.newamerica.org/education-policy/policy-papers/culturally-responsive-teaching-competencies

Murray, C., Murray, K.M., & Waas, G.A. (2008). Child and teacher reports of teacher-student relationships: Concordance of perspectives and associations with school adjustment in urban kindergarten classrooms. *Journal of Applied Developmental Psychology,* 29(1), 49–61. https://doi.org/10.1016/j.appdev.2007.10.006

National Academies of Sciences, Engineering, and Medicine (National Academies). (2017). *Promoting the educational success of children and youth learning English: Promising futures.* The National Academies Press. https://doi.org/10.17226/24677

———. (2019). *Vibrant and healthy kids: Aligning science, practice, and policy to advance health equity.* The National Academies Press. https://doi.org/10.17226/25466

———. (2023). *Addressing the long-term effects of the COVID-19 pandemic on children and families.* The National Academies Press. https://doi.org/10.17226/26809

National Center for Education Statistics (NCES). (2022). *Reading and mathematics scores decline during COVID-19 pandemic.* Department of Education. Available: https://www.nationsreportcard.gov/highlights/ltt/2022/

National Research Council (NRC). (1982). *Placing children in special education: A strategy for equity.* Washington, DC: The National Academies Press.

———. (2002). *Minority students in special and gifted education.* The National Academies Press. https://doi.org/10.17226/10128

NICHD Early Child Care Research Network. (2002). Early child care and children's development prior to school entry: Results from the NICHD Study of Early Child Care. *American Educational Research Journal,* 39(1), 133–64. http://www.jstor.org/stable/3202474

Nichols, S.L., & Berliner, D.C. (2007). *Collateral damage: How high-stakes testing corrupts America's schools.* Cambridge, MA: Harvard Education Press.

Nosek, B.A., Greenwald, A.G., & Banaji, M.R. (2005). Understanding and using the Implicit Association Test: II. Method variables and construct validity. *Personality and Social Psychology Bulletin,* 31(2), 166–80. https://doi.org/10.1177/0146167204271418

O'Connor, E., & McCartney, K. (2007). Examining teacher-child relationships and achievement as part of an ecological model of development. *American Educational Research Journal,* 44, 340–69. https://doi.org/10.3102/0002831207302172

Ohio Department of Education. (2021). *Data insights: How the pandemic is affecting the 2020-2021 school year.* Available: https://education.ohio.gov/Topics/Reset-and-Restart/Data-Insights-on-the-2020-2021-School-Year

Okonofua, J.A., & Eberhardt, J.L. (2015). Two strikes: Race and the disciplining of young students. *Psychological Science,* 26(5), 617–24. https://doi.org/10.1177/0956797615570365

Okonofua, J.A., Paunesku, D., & Walton, G.M. (2016). Brief intervention to encourage empathic discipline cuts suspension rates in half among adolescents. *Proceedings of the National Academy of Sciences of the United States of America,* 113(19), 5221–6. https://doi.org/10.1073/pnas.1523698113

Ong-Dean, C. (2009). *Distinguishing disability: Parents, privilege, and special education.* University of Chicago Press. https://doi.org/10.7208/chicago/9780226630021.001.0001

Owens, J., & McLanahan, S.S. (2020). Unpacking the drivers of racial disparities in school suspension and expulsion. *Social Forces,* 98(4), 1548–77. https://doi.org/10.1093/sf/soz095

Palermo, F., Hanish, L., Martin, C., Fabes, R., & Reiser, M. (2007). Preschoolers' academic readiness: What role does the teacher-child relationship play? *Early Childhood Research Quarterly,* 22. https://doi.org/10.1016/j.ecresq.2007.04.002

Papachristou, E., Flouri, E., Joshi, H., Midouhas, E., & Lewis, G. (2022). Ability-grouping and problem behavior trajectories in childhood and adolescence: Results from a UK population-based sample. *Child Development,* 93(2), 341–58. https://doi.org/10.1111/cdev.13674

Paris, D. (2012). Culturally sustaining pedagogy: A needed change in stance, terminology, and practice. *Educational Researcher,* 41(3), 93–7. https://doi.org/10.3102/0013189X12441244

Parker, R., & Stjerne Thomsen, B. (2019). *Learning through play at school: A study of playful integrated pedagogies that foster children's holistic skills development in the primary school classroom.* The LEGO Foundation. Available: https://research.acer.edu.au/learning_processes/22

Paro, K.M.L., Hamre, B.K., Locasale-Crouch, J., Pianta, R.C., Bryant, D., Early, D., Clifford, R., Barbarin, O., Howes, C., & Burchinal, M. (2009). Quality in kindergarten classrooms: Observational evidence for the need to increase children's learning opportunities in early education classrooms. *Early Education and Development*, 20(4), 657–92. https://doi.org/10.1080/10409280802541965

Patrick, K., Socol, A., & Morgan, I. (2020). *Inequities in advanced coursework: What's driving them and what leaders can do.* Education Trust. Available: https://edtrust.org/wp-content/uploads/2014/09/Inequities-in-Advanced-Coursework-Whats-Driving-Them-and-What-Leaders-Can-Do-January-2019.pdf

Pearman, F.A., Curran, F.C., Fisher, B., & Gardella, J. (2019). Are achievement gaps related to discipline gaps? Evidence from national data. *AERA Open*, 5(4), 2332858419875440. https://doi.org/10.1177/2332858419875440

Perera, R.M. (2021). *A promise unfulfilled? How modern federal civil rights enforcement is used to address racial discrimination in school discipline.* (Ed Working Paper No. 21-413). Annenberg Insitute at Brown University. Available: https://www.edworkingpapers.com/ai21-413

Phillips, D.A., Austin, L.J., & Whitebook, M. (2016). The early care and education workforce. *The Future of Children*, 26, 139–158. https://doi.org/10.1353/foc.2016.0016

Piaget, J. (1972). Intellectual evolution from adolescence to adulthood. *Human Development*, 15(1), 1–12. https://www.jstor.org/stable/26763966

Pianta, R.C., & Stuhlman, M.W. (2004). Teacher-child relationships and children's success in the first years of school. *School Psychology Review*, 33(3), 444–58. https://doi.org/10.1080/02796015.2004.12086261

Puma, M., Bell, S., Cook, R., Heid, C., Shapiro, G., Broene, P., Jenkins, F., Fletcher, P., Quinn, L., Friedman, J., & Ciarico, J. (2010). *Head Start impact study: Final report.* Administration for Children and Families (HHS), Office of Planning, Research & Evaluation. Available: https://eric.ed.gov/?id=ED507845

Raikes, J., & Darling-Hammond, L. (2019). *Why our education funding systems are derailing the American dream.* Learning Policy Institute. Available: https://learningpolicyinstitute.org/blog/why-our-education-funding-systems-are-derailing-american-dream

Ramey, C.T., & Ramey, S.L. (2019). Reframing policy and practice deliberations: Twelve hallmarks of strategies to attain and sustain early childhood gains. *Sustaining early childhood learning gains: Program, school, and family influences*, 314–49. Cambridge University Press. Available: https://www.cambridge.org/core/books/abs/sustaining-early-childhood-learning-gains/reframing-policy-and-practice-deliberations/37B2B7A346D7ED31A99DE2FBEBFD1ACF

Redding, C. (2019). A teacher like me: A review of the effect of student-teacher racial/ethnic matching on teacher perceptions of students and student academic and behavioral outcomes. *Review of Educational Research*, 89(4), 499–535. https://doi.org/10.3102/0034654319853545

Renaissance Learning. (2022). *How kids are performing: A snapshot of K-12 academic performance and growth, 2021-2022 school year.* Renaissance Learning, Inc. Available: https://www.renaissance.com/how-kids-are-performing/

Reynolds, A., & Temple, J. (Eds.). (2019). *Sustaining early childhood learning gains: Program, school, and family influences.* Cambridge University Press. https://doi.org/10.1017/9781108349352

Rhodes, J., Thomas, J.M., & Liles, A.R. (2018). Predictors of grade retention among children in an elementary school truancy intervention. *Journal of At-Risk Issues*, 21(1), 1–10. Available: https://eric.ed.gov/?id=EJ1187205

Rickles, J., Garet, M., Neiman, S., & Hodgman, S. (2020). *Approaches to remote instruction: How district responses to the pandemic differed across contexts*. [Research Brief]. American Institute for Research. Available: https://www.air.org/sites/default/files/COVID-Survey-Approaches-to-Remote-Instruction-FINAL-Oct-2020.pdf

Riddle, T., & Sinclair, S. (2019). Racial disparities in school-based disciplinary actions are associated with county-level rates of racial bias. *Proceedings of the National Academy of Sciences of the United States of America*, 116(17), 8255–60. https://doi.org/10.1073/pnas.1808307116

Rimm-Kaufman, S.E., La Paro, K.M., Downer, J.T., & Pianta, R.C. (2005). The contribution of classroom setting and quality of instruction to children's behavior in kindergarten classrooms. *The Elementary School Journal*, 105(4), 377–94. https://doi.org/10.1086/429948

Romero, M., & Lee, Y.S. (2007). *A national portrait of chronic absenteeism in the early grades*. National Center for Children in Poverty, Columbia University. https://doi.org/10.7916/D89C7650

Roorda, D.L., Koomen, H.M.Y., Spilt, J.L., & Oort, F.J. (2011). The influence of affective teacher–student relationships on students' school engagement and achievement: A meta-analytic approach. *Review of Educational Research*, 81(4), 493–529. https://doi.org/10.3102/0034654311421793

Rosa, J.D. (2016). Standardization, racialization, languagelessness: Raciolinguistic ideologies across communicative contexts. *Journal of Linguistic Anthropology*, 26, 162–83. https://doi.org/10.1111/jola.12116

Rosenbaum, J.E. (2020). Educational and criminal justice outcomes 12 years after school suspension. *Youth & Society*, 52(4), 515–47. https://doi.org/10.1177/0044118X17752208

Ruopp R. (1979). *Children at the center: Summary findings and their implications*. Abt Books.

Ryan, R.M., & Deci, E.L. (2000). Intrinsic and extrinsic motivations: Classic definitions and new directions. *Contemporary Educational Psychology*, 25(1), 54–67. https://doi.org/10.1006/ceps.1999.1020

Ryberg, R., Her, S., Temkin, D., & Harper, K. (2021). *Despite reductions since 2011-12, Black students and students with disabilities remain more likely to experience suspension*. Child Trends. Available: https://www.childtrends.org/publications/despite-reductions-black-students-and-students-with-disabilities-remain-more-likely-to-experience-suspension

Saft, E.W., & Pianta, R.C. (2001). Teachers' perceptions of their relationships with students: Effects of child age, gender, and ethnicity of teachers and children. *School Psychology Quarterly*, 16(2), 125–41. https://doi.org/10.1521/scpq.16.2.125.18698

Schweinhart, L.J. (2019). Lessons on sustaining early gains from the life-course study of perry preschool. *Sustaining early childhood learning gains: Program, school, and family influences*, 254–67. Cambridge, England: Cambridge University Press.

Shifrer, D. (2013). Stigma of a label: Educational expectations for high school students labeled with learning disabilities. *Journal of Health and Social Behavior*, 54(4), 462–80. https://doi.org/10.1177/0022146513503346

Shores, K., Lee, H., & Williams, N. (2021). *Increasing Title I funds should target largest sources of school spending inequalities—across states*. Brookings Institution. Available: https://www.brookings.edu/blog/brown-center-chalkboard/2021/08/06/increasing-title-i-funds-should-target-largest-sources-of-school-spending-inequalities-across-states/

Singer, J., Pogodzinski, B., Lenhoff, S.W., & Cook, W. (2021). Advancing an ecological approach to chronic absenteeism: Evidence from Detroit. *Teachers College Record*, 123(4), 1–36. https://doi.org/10.1177/016146812112300406

Skene, K., O'Farrelly, C., Byrne, E., Kirby, N., Stevens, E., & Ramchandani, P. (2022). Can guidance during play enhance children's learning and development in educational contexts? A systematic review and meta-analysis. *Child Development*, 93(4), 1162–80. https://doi.org/10.1111/cdev.13730

Skiba, R., & Knesting, K. (2001). Zero tolerance, zero evidence: An analysis of school disciplinary practice. *New Directions for Youth Development*, 92, 17–43. https://doi.org/10.1002/yd.23320019204

Skiba, R.J. & Peterson, R.L. (2000). School discipline at a crossroads: From zero tolerance to early response. *Exceptional Children*, 66(3), 335–47. Available: http://www.rpforschools.net/articles/School%20Programs/Skiba%20&%20Peterson%202000%20School%20discipline%20at%20a%20crossroads%20-%20From%20Zero%20Tolerance%20to%20Early%20Response.pdf

Skiba, R.J., Michael, R.S., Nardo, A.C., & Peterson, R. (2002). The color of discipline: Sources of racial and gender disproportionality in school punishment. *The Urban Review*, 34, 317–42. https://doi.org/10.1023/A:1021320817372

Skiba, R.J., Poloni-Staudinger L., Gallini S., Simmons A.B., & Feggins-Azziz, R. (2006). Disparate access: The disproportionality of African American students with disabilities across educational environments. *Exceptional Children*, 72, 411–24. https://doi.org/10.1177/001440290607200402

Skiba, R.J., Simmons, A., Ritter, S., Gibb, A., Rausch, M., Cuadrado, J., & Chung, C.G. (2008). Achieving equity in special education: History, status, and current challenges. *Exceptional Children*, 74, 264–88. https://doi.org/10.1177/001440290807400301

Skiba, R.J., Horner R.H., Chung C.G., Rausch M.K., May S.L., & Tobin T. (2011). Race is not neutral: A national investigation of African American and Latino disproportionality in school discipline. *School Psychology Review*, 40, 85–107. https://doi.org/10.1080/02796015.2011.12087730

Skiba, R.J., Arredondo, M.I., & Williams, N.T. (2014). More than a metaphor: The contribution of exclusionary discipline to a school-to-prison pipeline. *Equity & Excellence in Education*, 47(4), 546–64. https://doi.org/10.1080/10665684.2014.958965

Skiba, R.J., Chung, C.G., Trachok, M., Baker, T.L., Sheya, A., & Hughes, R.L. (2014). Parsing disciplinary disproportionality: Contributions of infraction, student, and school characteristics to out-of-school suspension and expulsion. *American Educational Research Journal*, 51(4), 640–70. https://doi.org/10.3102/0002831214541670

Skiba, R.J., Artiles, A.A., Kozleski, E.B., Losen, D.J., & Harry, E.G. (2016). Risks and consequences of oversimplifying educational inequities: A response to Morgan et al. (2015). *Educational Researcher*, 45(3), 221–25. https://doi.org/10.3102/0013189X16644606

Smythe-Leistico, K., & Page, L. (2018). Connect-text: Leveraging text-message communication to mitigate chronic absenteeism and improve parental engagement in the earliest years of schooling. *Journal of Education for Students Placed at Risk*, 23(1–2), 139–52. https://doi.org/10.1080/10824669.2018.1434658

Sorensen, L.C., Bushway, S.D., & Gifford, S.J. (2022). Getting tough? The effects of discretionary principal discipline on student outcomes. *Education Finance and Policy*, 17(2), 255–284. https://doi.org/10.1162/edfp_a_00341

Sorhagen, N.S. (2013). Early teacher expectations disproportionately affect poor children's high school performance. *Journal of Educational Psychology*, 105(2), 465–77. https://doi.org/10.1037/a0031754

Sparks, R., Patton, J., Ganschow, L., Humbach, N., & Javorsky, J. (2008). Early first-language reading and spelling skills predict later second-language reading and spelling skills. *Journal of Educational Psychology*, 100, 162–174. https://doi.org/10.1037/0022-0663.100.1.162

Sparks, R., Patton, J., Ganschow, L., & Humbach, N. (2009a). Long-term relationships among early first language skills, second language aptitude, second language affect, and later second language proficiency. *Applied Psycholinguistics, 30,* 725–55. https://doi.org/10.1017/S0142716409990099

———. (2009b). Long-term crosslinguistic transfer of skills from L1 to L2. *Language Learning, 59,* 203–43. https://doi.org/10.1111/j.1467-9922.2009.00504.x

Stecher, B., & Bohrnstedt, G. (2000). *Class size reduction in California: Summary of the 1998-99 evaluation findings.* RAND Corporation. Available: https://www.rand.org/pubs/reprints/RP903z1.html

Steele, J., Slater, R., Zamarro, G., Miller, T., Li, J., Burkhauser, S., & Bacon, M. (2017). Effects of dual-language immersion programs on student achievement: Evidence from lottery data. *American Educational Research Journal, 54,* 282S–306S. https://files.eric.ed.gov/fulltext/ED577026.pdf

Storey, N., & Zhang, Q. (2021). *A meta-analysis of COVID learning loss.* School of Education, Johns Hopkins University. https://doi.org/10.35542/osf.io/qekw2

Sullivan, A., & Artiles, A.J. (2011). Theorizing racial inequity in special education: Applying structural inequity theory to disproportionality. *Urban Education, 46,* 1526–52. https://doi.org/10.1177/0042085911416014

Sullivan, A., Johnson, B., Owens, L., & Conway, R. (2014). Punish them or engage them? Teachers' views of unproductive student behaviours in the classroom. *Australian Journal of Teacher Education, 39.* https://doi.org/10.14221/ajte.2014v39n6.6

Tefera, A.A., Siegel-Hawley, G., & Sjogren, A.L. (2022). The (in)visibility of race in school discipline across urban, suburban, and exurban contexts. *Teachers College Record, 124,* 151–79. https://journals.sagepub.com/doi/10.1177/01614681221093282#con2

Tenenbaum, H.R., & Ruck, M.D. (2007). Are teachers' expectations different for racial minority than for European American students? A meta-analysis. *Journal of Educational Psychology,* 99(2), 253–73. https://doi.org/10.1037/0022-0663.99.2.253

Texas Education Agency. (2021). *Overview of 2021 STAAR results.* Texas Education Agency. Avaiable: https://tea.texas.gov/student-assessment/testing/staar/staar-statewide-summary-reports

Trang, K.T., & Hansen, D.M. (2021). The roles of teacher expectations and school composition on teacher–child relationship quality. *Journal of Teacher Education,* 72(2), 152–167. https://doi.org/10.1177/0022487120902404

United Nations. (1989). *Convention on the Rights of the Child.* Available: https://www.unicef.org/child-rights-convention/convention-text

Umansky, I.M., & Dumont, H. (2021). English learner labeling: How English learner classification in kindergarten shapes teacher perceptions of student skills and the moderating role of bilingual instructional settings. *American Educational Research Journal,* 58(5), 993–1031. https://doi.org/10.3102/0002831221997571

Valli, L., & Buese, D. (2007). The changing roles of teachers in an era of high-stakes accountability. *American Educational Research Journal, 44,* 519–58. https://doi.org/10.3102/0002831207306859

Varghese, C., Vernon-Feagans, L., & Bratsch-Hines, M. (2019). Associations between teacher–child relationships, children's literacy achievement, and social competencies for struggling and non-struggling readers in early elementary school. *Early Childhood Research Quarterly, 47,* 124–33. https://doi.org/10.1016/j.ecresq.2018.09.005

Verlenden, J.V., Pampati, S., Rasberry, C.N., Liddon, N., Hertz, M., Kilmer, G., Viox, M., Lee, S., Cramer, N.K., Barrios, L.C., & Ethier, K.A. (2021). Association of children's mode of school instruction with child and parent experiences and well-being during the COVID-19 pandemic—COVID experiences survey, United States, October 8–November 13, 2020. *Morbidity and Mortality Weekly Report,* 70(11), 369–76. http://dx.doi.org/10.15585/mmwr.mm7011a1

Vernon-Feagans, L., Mokrova, I.L., Carr, R.C., Garrett-Peters, P.T., & Burchinal, M.R. (2019). Cumulative years of classroom quality from kindergarten to third grade: Prediction to children's third grade literacy skills. *Early Childhood Research Quarterly*, 47, 531–40. https://doi.org/10.1016/j.ecresq.2018.06.005

Waitoller, F.R., & Maggin, D.M. (2020). Can charter schools address racial inequities evidenced in access to the general education classroom? A longitudinal study in Chicago public schools. *Remedial and Special Education*, 41(3), 127–38. https://doi.org/10.1177/0741932518800392

Waitoller, F.R., Artiles, A.J., & Cheney, D.A. (2010). The miner's canary: A review of overrepresentation research and explanations. *The Journal of Special Education*, 44(1), 29–49. https://doi.org/10.1177/0022466908329226

Wald, J., & Losen, D. (2003). Defining and redirecting a school-to-prison pipeline. *New Directions for Youth Development*, 99, 9–15. https://doi.org/10.1002/yd.51

Weiland, C., Greenberg, E., Bassok, D., Markowitz, A.J., Guerrero-Rosada, P., Luetmer, G., Abenavoli, R., Gomez, C.J., Johnson, A.D., Harden, B.J., Maier, M.F., McCormick, M.P., Morris, P.A., Nores, M., Phillips, D.A., & Snow, C. (2021). *Historic crisis, historic opportunity: Using evidence to mitigate the effects of the COVID-19 crisis on young children and early care and education programs.* Urban Institute. Available: https://www.urban.org/policy-centers/center-education-data-and-policy/projects/historic-crisis-historic-opportunity-using-evidence-mitigate-effects-covid-19-crisis-young-children-and-early-care-and-education-programs

Whitford, D.K., & Emerson, A.M. (2019). Empathy intervention to reduce implicit bias in pre-service teachers. *Psychological Reports*, 122(2), 670–88. https://doi.org/10.1177/0033294118767435

Wiley, A.L., Brigham, F.J., Kauffman, J.M., & Bogan, J.E. (2013). Disproportionate poverty, conservatism, and the disproportionate identification of minority students with emotional and behavioral disorders. *Education and Treatment of Children*, 36(4), 29–50. https://doi.org/10.1353/etc.2013.0033

Wolf, K.C., & Kupchik, A. (2017). School suspensions and adverse experiences in adulthood. *Justice Quarterly*, 34(3), 407–30. https://doi.org/10.1080/07418825.2016.1168475

Yang, K.E., & Ham, S.H. (2017). Truancy as systemic discrimination: Anti-discrimination legislation and its effect on school attendance among immigrant children. *The Social Science Journal* 54, 216–26. https://doi.org/10.1016/j.soscij.2017.02.001

Zatto, B.R.L., & Hoglund, W.L.G. (2019). Children's internalizing problems and teacher–child relationship quality across preschool. *Early Childhood Research Quarterly*, 49, 28–39. https://doi.org/10.1016/j.ecresq.2019.05.007

Zeng, S., Corr, C.P., O'Grady, C., & Guan, Y. (2019). Adverse childhood experiences and preschool suspension expulsion: A population study. *Child Abuse and Neglect*, 97, 104149. https://doi.org/10.1016/j.chiabu.2019.104149

Zimmermann, C.R. (2018). The penalty of being a young black girl: Kindergarten teachers' perceptions of children's problem behaviors and student–teacher conflict by the intersection of race and gender. *Journal of Negro Education*, 87, 154–68. http://www.jstor.org/stable/10.7709/jnegroeducation.87.2.0154

Zosh, J., Hopkins, E., Jensen, H., Liu, C., Neale, D., Hirsh-Pasek, K., Solis, L., & Whitebread, D. (2017). *Learning through play: A review of the evidence.* [White paper]. The LEGO Foundation. Available: https://cms.learningthroughplay.com/media/wmtlmbe0/learning-through-play_web.pdf

Zosh, J.M., Hirsh-Pasek, K., Hopkins, E.J., Jensen, H., Liu, C., Neale, D., Solis, S.L., & Whitebread, D. (2018). Accessing the inaccessible: Redefining play as a spectrum. *Frontiers in Psychology*, 9. https://doi.org/10.3389/fpsyg.2018.01124

4

Opportunity Gaps in the Physical Health and Health Care Experienced by Young Children and Their Parents

This chapter focuses on the drivers of opportunity gaps related to the physical health and health care experienced by young children and their parents. Physical health is a key determinant of children's ability to participate and thrive in educational settings. Yet there are vast disparities in physical health in the United States. From prenatal and infant health to adolescent health, children from low-income, racial/ethnic minority, and rural backgrounds are more likely to experience health problems. While differences in health care access and quality explain some of these disparities, they are strongly rooted in structural racism and discrimination, as well as underinvestment in economically disadvantaged urban and rural areas (Oberg et al., 2016). Among immigrant children, while those in the first generation are often of lower socioeconomic status but healthier than U.S.-born children on average (the so-called immigrant paradox), the average masks heterogeneity, with worse outcomes among particularly vulnerable groups, such as undocumented children or refugees. Moreover, this paradox often fades by the second generation (Perreira & Allen, 2021).

We also wish to make clear that, by addressing physical and mental health in separate chapters, we do not wish to imply a false dichotomy between the two. We fully recognize the emerging science of brain health as integral to physical health and contextual experiences. Indeed, it is our view that the mental health of children and youth is an essential part of their overall health and a necessary cornerstone of lifelong well-being; we regard neither physical nor mental health as being more or less important than the other, and stress that both are needed to ensure optimal health for children.

Yet opportunity gaps exist in both areas, and ensuring that children thrive will require gaining a comprehensive and global understanding of the status of children's physical and mental health (Laraque-Arena & Stein, 2021).

The first section of this chapter takes a detailed look at drivers of opportunity gaps in health and health outcomes. The discussion starts by examining prenatal conditions and care for mothers. In the United States, one-fifth of all lower-income women of childbearing age lack access to health insurance, leaving them physically and financially vulnerable and without access to pre- or interconception care. These conditions are exacerbated in certain states that have not extended state-level benefits. As a result, 15% of women in the United States lack quality prenatal care (Osterman & Martin, 2018). The discussion then turns to access to preventive and curative health care for young children, as well as the role of proper nutrition and access to sufficient food in children's well-being. Informing this discussion is an increase in recent decades in research identifying the effects of increased food availability and improved nutrition (at all stages of life, but especially in infancy) on the well-being of both children and adults.

In addition to health care and nutrition, this section addresses social and structural causes of poor health among children. For example, poverty helps determine the well-being of young children—for example, by contributing to poor housing conditions, which in turn can lead to increased risk of asthma and other adverse health outcomes.

Safe and healthy environments are another important component of the well-being of young children, representing a key structural determinant of health. The discussion of this issue focuses in particular on the benefits of physical safety and freedom from harm and danger and their role in the opportunity gaps experienced by young children. In one study, approximately 37% of U.S. children were found to have experienced physical assault in the past year; 51.4% had experienced physical assault in their lifetime; and 24.5% and 38.3%, respectively, had witnessed violence in the past year or in their lifetime (Finkelhor et al., 2015). Indeed, gun violence is the leading cause of death among U.S. children, recently overtaking injuries from motor vehicle crashes (Goldstick, Cunningham, & Carter, 2022; Lee et al., 2022). With more than 25% of all children witnessing an act of violence in their home, school, or community and more than 5% witnessing a shooting, the importance of understanding and addressing the physical and mental impacts of this exposure to violence is clear (Finkelhor et al., 2009).

The second section of this chapter reviews existing research on potential solutions to some of the drivers of the opportunity gaps in physical health and health care. It describes existing program interventions, including some introduced during the COVID-19 pandemic, that have been shown to improve these conditions for young children and their mothers.[1]

DRIVERS OF OPPORTUNITY GAPS IN HEALTH AND HEALTH OUTCOMES

Theoretical and empirical work in the field of life-course epidemiology has consistently shown that prenatal and early-life conditions, including powerful social and structural factors, can affect children's physical health later in life (Kuh et al., 2003; Ben-Schlomo, Mishra, & Kuh, 2014). Gaps in opportunities related to health begin before birth and can have both short-term and lifelong consequences for well-being. These gaps are influenced by myriad factors, including access to health care and adequate nutrition, poverty, neighborhood safety, and environmental factors, and are exacerbated by racism, segregation, implicit and explicit bias, and stigma (Adler & Stewart, 2010).

Conditions Prior to Birth and Pregnancy

Adverse outcomes in the perinatal period experienced by children and women/birthing people as a result of often preventable pregnancy and birth complications can have lifelong consequences for children's health and well-being. Most babies in the United States are born healthy and on track for normal physical and cognitive development, but those who are not may need substantial resources and care—not just to survive infancy but to meet the challenges beyond (National Institute of Child Health and Human Development, 2012). Premature birth occurs before the 37th week of pregnancy, a time during which the development of the brain and other organs still benefits substantially from the intrauterine environment (March of Dimes, 2021). Premature birth increases the likelihood of low birthweight (less than 2,500 grams), and can predispose children to breathing and feeding difficulties, vision and hearing problems, developmental delays, and learning disabilities, among other health issues, over the life course (National Institute of Child Health and Human Development, 2012).

Thus gaps in opportunities that emerge before a child is born can have lifelong effects on outcomes. Research is clear that a pregnant person's access to health insurance can influence the use and timing of prenatal care; that adequate prenatal care is associated with healthier birth outcomes, such as a longer period of gestation and healthier birthweight (Creanga et

---

[1] The committee uses the terms "woman" and "mother" in this report; however, we recognize that the terms "pregnant woman," "woman," "mother," and "maternal" may not reflect how some pregnant individuals or others seeking reproductive health care may identify.

al., 2014; Ely & Driscoll, 2019); and that healthier birth outcomes can in turn have substantial benefits for the subsequent health and well-being of the developing child.

While the United States does well on some measures of health according to the Organisation for Economic Co-operation and Development (OECD; e.g., rates of death from heart attack and stroke are below OECD levels), it is important to understand the differences in health expenditures between the United States and OECD countries. In general, the richer a country is, the more resources it devotes to health care as citizens' demands for care increase. However, the United States is also the biggest outlier among the G7 countries in health spending relative to outcomes, with some mortality and morbidity measures falling below the OECD average (e.g., life expectancy is 2 years below the OECD average, and 43% of U.S. children between the ages of 5 and 9 are overweight compared with the OECD average of 31.4% (OECD, 2019, 2022). Unfortunately, an alarming number of people of childbearing age, particularly those with lower incomes, lack access to health insurance, receive inadequate prenatal care, give birth to children who are preterm and of low birthweight, and experience higher rates of infant mortality and maternal mortality and morbidity (a topic discussed further below). These adverse conditions that emerge in the perinatal period are typically more prevalent for people of color, particularly Black birthing people and their infants, and result largely from long-standing oppression and discrimination within health systems (Hoyert & Miniño, 2020; Martin et al., 2019). These early opportunity gaps can widen opportunity gaps and outcomes over the life course.

Maternal Access to Health Insurance

Birthing persons' access to health care and health insurance is vital for their own health, particularly during the perinatal period, and for the health of their children. In the United States, however, more than 16.7% of lower-income women of childbearing age lack access to health insurance (Prenatal-to-3 Policy Impact Center, 2020), leaving them physically and financially vulnerable and without access to pre- or interconception care.

The lack of access to health insurance among lower-income people of childbearing age, particularly people of color, has historical roots in the development and rollout of Medicaid—the primary insurer for births to lower-income birthing people. Medicaid was launched in 1965 and was originally provided only to people eligible to receive cash benefits through the Aid to Families with Dependent Children (AFDC) program, or "welfare." In the 1960s, the AFDC program largely excluded families of color, especially in Southern states, because of racist rules that excluded agricultural and domestic workers. Administration of benefit levels and eligibility for Medicare, the medical insurance program responsible largely for supporting the elderly, occurs at the federal level. By contrast, the administration of Medicaid is left to the states. With minimal federal oversight, states have been allowed to determine income eligibility thresholds, services covered, and reimbursement rates, and these program elements have varied considerably nationwide, with Southern states largely restricting access (Nolen, Beckman, & Sandoe, 2020). Once eligibility has been determined, moreover, continuous coverage for the year is not guaranteed, and even temporary increases in family income can result in loss of coverage and disruption of health care access.

In 2014, the Supreme Court ruled that states could determine whether to implement the expansion of Medicaid in the Affordable Care Act, which provides Medicaid insurance to all individuals with incomes up to 138% of the federal poverty level (FPL). This expansion of Medicaid has reduced the rates of uninsured women of childbearing age significantly, increasing access to and utilization of health care (Kaiser Family Foundation, 2022). To date, however, 12 states have failed to adopt Medicaid expansion, and these states have disproportionately high populations of people of color. In these nonexpansion states, no childless adults are eligible for Medicaid, and the income eligibility threshold for parents varies from a low of 17% of the FPL in Texas to 100% of the FPL in Wisconsin, leaving millions of parents and prospective parents without access to health insurance, a resource that promotes healthier birth outcomes and health across the lifespan.

The percentage of women who lack health insurance is much higher in states that have not expanded Medicaid. In Texas, for example, one of the 12 states that have not expanded Medicaid as part of the Affordable Care Act, nearly half (48.9%) of low-income women aged 19–44 lack health insurance—the highest uninsurance rate in the country (Prenatal-to-3 Policy Impact Center, 2020). These women would be eligible for Medicaid if the state expanded the program, but as noted, under the state rules, no childless adults are eligible for Medicaid, and parents must earn less than 17% of the FPL to qualify. By contrast, fewer than 4% of similar women in the District of Columbia lack health insurance. Not only has the District expanded Medicaid, but it provides coverage to parents with incomes up to 221% of the FPL rather than the 138% required by the Medicaid expansion (Prenatal-to-3 Policy Impact Center, 2020).

In addition, in nearly all states, including Texas, Medicaid income eligibility thresholds for pregnant people are higher than they are for parents or childless adults (in Texas, the threshold for pregnant people is 204% of the FPL, and in the District of Columbia it is 324% of the FPL). And in most states, new parents lose access to Medicaid pregnancy coverage 60 days postpartum. Health insurance is therefore lacking for many new parents, particularly those who cannot remain on traditional Medicaid or buy insurance on the Marketplace (which is unavailable to those with incomes below 138% of the FPL). The American Rescue Plan Act of 2021 allowed states to provide continuous health coverage for up to a year for postpartum birthing people, but to date, few states have fully implemented that policy (American Public Health Association, 2021). Thus many mothers are left without access to health care when they themselves are still at high risk for postpartum conditions, such as depression, that may affect their ability to care for their child.

Uninsurance rates also vary considerably by race and ethnicity. In particular, lower-income Hispanic women of childbearing age (38.5%) are twice as likely to be uninsured as Black (19.1%) or White (17%) women. This disparity is due in part to eligibility restrictions related to immigration status for many state and federal safety net policies and less generous employer benefits for Hispanic women in low-wage jobs (Prenatal-to-3 Policy Impact Center, 2020).

Maternal Access to Adequate Prenatal Care

Related to access to health insurance is access to quality prenatal care, which in turn is linked to healthier birth outcomes and better health for the mother. Access to quality maternity care is a critical component of maternal health and positive birth outcomes, especially in light of the high rates of maternal mortality and severe maternal morbidity in the United States. Yet nearly 15% of women in the United States—ranging from a low of 5% of births in Rhode Island to nearly 25% in New Mexico—do not receive adequate prenatal care. The lack of quality prenatal care can be attributed to the lack of access to health care and health insurance coverage, as well as the limited availability of prenatal programs in an area or region of the country.

The percentage of Black women who do not receive adequate prenatal care (20.1%) is twice as high as the percentage for White women (9.9%; March of Dimes, 2022). This discrepancy is one of the drivers of the stark differences in birth outcomes between Black women and women of other races/ethnicities. Compared with their White and Hispanic counterparts, for example, the proportion of Black babies born preterm (Box 4-1) is 50% higher, and Black babies are more than twice as likely to be born at low birthweight.

Maternity care deserts are counties in which access to maternity health care services is limited or absent as a result of either lack of services or barriers to a woman's ability to access those services (March of Dimes, 2022). More than 2.2 million women of childbearing age live in maternity care deserts (1,095 counties), with no hospital or birth center offering obstetric care and no obstetric provider (March of Dimes, 2022). In 2017, almost

> **BOX 4-1**
> **The Effect of Preterm Birth on Opportunity Gaps**
>
> Preterm birth (defined as live birth at less than 37 weeks gestation) is the second-leading cause of infant mortality in the United States overall and the leading cause of infant mortality among African American/Black infants (Ely & Driscoll, 2019; Heron, 2019). Preterm infants are at higher risk for major adverse health outcomes in both childhood and adulthood (Bhutta et al., 2002; Marlow et al., 2005; Saigal & Doyle, 2008; Evensen et al., 2009; Kaijser et al., 2009; Kajantie et al., 2010; Crump et al., 2011; Dong & Yu, 2011; Kerkhof et al., 2012a; Parkinson et al., 2013; Ramírez-Vélez et al., 2017), and racial disparities in birth outcomes therefore represent a significant public health concern in the United States. While preterm birth declined overall during the past century, African American/Black women consistently experience a rate approximately 1.5–1.6 times higher than that of their White counterparts (Costa, 2004; Martin et al., 2019; Hamilton, Martin, & Osterman, 2020). And although most scientists agree that the causes of this Black–White disparity are complex, factors associated with racism have been posited as one underlying mechanism. Research indicates that racism is an important public health problem with a measurable impact on preterm birth, one that needs to be addressed if racial inequities in birth outcomes are to be eliminated (Bower et al., 2018; Braveman et al., 2021).
>
> Lifelong effects suffered by preterm babies can include cerebral palsy, intellectual development disorders, visual and hearing impairments, and poor health and growth. Motor skill impairment is a commonly reported negative outcome in premature infants, cerebral palsy being its most severe form. Motor dysfunction in children interferes with their ability to explore the world, be involved in social activities, and acquire future gross and fine motor skills (Bélanger et al., 2018). In addition, research on adults born preterm has provided substantial evidence of their increased risk for developing long-term sequelae at various organ sites, including cardiovascular, pulmonary, metabolic, renal, visual, obstetric, and psychiatric impairments (see below; Evensen et al., 2009; Mathai et al., 2012; Kerkhof et al., 2012a,b; Bonamy et al., 2013; Bertagnolli et al., 2016; Crump et al., 2019a,b). Young adults born preterm have been shown to have lower muscular fitness than controls, which may predispose them to cardiometabolic and other chronic diseases (Tikanmäki et al., 2016).
>
> In addition to these adverse physical outcomes, babies born preterm are at higher risk for adverse neurocognitive and behavioral outcomes as they progress from prekindergarten through high school. Epidemiologic studies have for many years identified preterm birth as a significant risk factor for psychiatric disorders, and there has recently been increased interest in neurobehavioral outcomes after preterm birth. There have been few studies using diagnostic psychiatric evaluations, but typically these studies have found a three- to fourfold increased risk for such disorders in middle childhood. Preterm birth and low birthweight have also been identified as risk factors for specific psychiatric disorders, including emotional disorders, attention-deficit/hyperactivity disorder, and autism spectrum disorder (Burd et al., 1999; Gale & Martyn, 2004; Patton et al., 2004; Larsson et al., 2005; Linnet et al., 2006; Nomura et al., 2007; Schendel & Bhasin, 2008; Williams et al., 2008; Abel et al., 2010). These outcomes are associated in turn with a host of reduced opportunities later in life, including lower engagement in school, reduced access to college, and higher unemployment. (See Chapter 6 for a more detailed discussion of opportunity gaps in social-emotional health and well-being.)

150,000 babies were born to women living in maternity care deserts, while an additional 4.8 million women of childbearing age lived in counties with limited access to maternity care (March of Dimes, 2022).

Congress recently reintroduced a sweeping package of 12 maternal health–related bills aimed at addressing racism and racial inequities that disproportionately affect pregnant and birthing people in the United States. The "Momnibus" aims to invest in training a cadre of perinatal health providers to improve upon and better address the significant disparities in maternal and infant health outcomes. For example, although midwives are widely recognized around the world as the primary source of maternal health care, they account for only 8% of U.S. birth workers (*Scientific American* Editors, 2019; Batstone, 2021). Midwives are health care professionals who may be part of the birth care team or stand alone in providing prenatal, delivery, and postpartum care. States that have policies to allow direct-entry midwives—credentialed midwives who are not registered nurses—and certified nurse midwives to practice may increase access to care, especially in underresourced areas (March of Dimes, 2022). Midwifery care, coordinated with care from a physician, can help reduce medical interventions that contribute to the risk of maternal mortality and morbidity in initial and subsequent pregnancies, lower costs, and potentially improve the health of mothers and babies (American College of Nurse-Midwives, 2021). The maternal care team may also include doulas, nonclinical professionals who support women emotionally and physically during the perinatal period, including birth and postpartum. Increased access to doula care can help improve birth outcomes and reduce the higher rates of maternal morbidity and mortality among women of color in the United States.

Troubling as well is that the rate of infant mortality among Black babies (10.8 per 100 births) is twice the national average (5.6 per 100 births; Ely & Driscoll, 2019). Black mothers are also more than twice as likely to die in childbirth or experience severe maternal morbidity, regardless of education level or socioeconomic status (Centers for Disease Control and Prevention [CDC], 2022). Adverse birth outcomes reflect the trauma resulting from discrimination and racism that many Black women have experienced across their life course, as well as their disproportionately lower access to financial security (Alhusen et al., 2016).

Where babies are born is also predictive of their birth outcomes; for example, babies born in Mississippi are nearly twice as likely to be born preterm and nearly three times as likely to die in the first year of life compared with those born in New Hampshire. Again, these differences in opportunities and outcomes are largely a result of state policy choices, such as those discussed previously with regard to Medicaid expansion. Those states that have declined to expand Medicaid are often the same states with weak safety net programs and consequently higher poverty rates, resulting in a combination of forces that exacerbate adverse birth outcomes for marginalized families.

The Medical Home and Developmental Screening

For children, the lack of primary and preventive health services can impact not only physical health but also mental health, social-emotional development, and academic outcomes (Polacheck & Gears, 2020). Preventive (or "well-child") care—including standard vaccinations and flu shots, as well as chronic disease screenings—is an important complement to primary care for physical development and long-term well-being (Regalado & Halfon, 2001; Hagan, Shaw, & Duncan, 2017). Yet obstacles due to the lack of access and health care coverage and to institutional biases reduce the quantity and quality of both primary and preventive care for young children. Also of note, recent data from the Centers for Medicare & Medicaid Services show downward trends in health care utilization during the COVID-19 pandemic for the nearly 40 million children enrolled in Medicaid and the Children's Health Insurance Program (Centers for Medicare & Medicaid Services [CMS], 2020a; Polacheck & Gears, 2020), driven by stay-at-home orders in states across the nation.

The Medical Home

The medical home is an approach to providing comprehensive primary care that facilitates partnerships among patients, clinicians, and families. The pediatric health care/medical home is a model of care that promotes holistic care of children and their families whereby each patient/family has an ongoing relationship with a health care professional (National Association of Pediatric Nurse Practitioners, 2009). A medical home combines place, process, and people. It is not a building, house, or hospital, but an approach to providing comprehensive primary care. The pediatric clinician can help the family and patient access and coordinate specialty care, other health care services, educational services, in- and out-of-home care, family support, and other public and private community services that are important to the overall health of the child and family. Providing a medical home means addressing both the medical and nonmedical needs of the child and family (American Academy of Pediatrics, 2015).

The medical home is significantly associated with positive child health outcomes regardless of household income. However, children living below versus those living above the FPL are at greater risk of lacking access to a medical home (Anker et al., 2018). Parental perceptions and experiences of having a medical home differ by socioeconomic status and race/ethnicity (Diao et al., 2017). And as with health care utilization generally, the percentage of children having access to a medical home visit and/or receiving well-child visits decreased during the COVID-19 pandemic. Well-child visits began to decrease in March 2020, reaching their lowest point of the year in April 2020, reflecting a 47.3% decrease compared with 2018–2019. Visit rates rebounded to 2018–2019 levels in June 2020, reaching a peak in September 2020 and remaining at levels nearly equal to those of 2018–2019 during October–December 2020. In January–March 2021, visits dipped below baseline, with the largest decrease in January 2021 (−9.2%; Kujawski et al., 2022).

Developmental Screening

National guidelines for child preventive care visits recommend that children have 10 preventive care visits from birth to 3 years of age (Hagan, Shaw, & Duncan, 2017). Prior to preschool entry at age 3, child preventive care visits may serve as the only opportunity to screen for, identify, and intervene on a range of social, developmental, and health concerns that can have significant impacts on a child's health and well-being. Yet for many children, particularly those living in poverty, this critical opportunity is often missed, in many cases because of uninsurance or underinsurance or challenges in accessing care, such as those related to transportation and parental work schedules (Bethell et al., 2004, 2011; Halfon et al., 2004; Chung et al., 2006; Norlin et al., 2011).

Routine health care—in particular, well-child visits—is essential for child health and development and can be an important component of lifelong health. When children fall behind on immunizations, they run the risk of developing vaccine-preventable diseases (Santoli et al., 2020). Regular developmental screenings under Early and Periodic Screening, Diagnosis and Treatment guidelines offer an opportunity for pediatric providers to screen for and diagnose physical or cognitive delays early so that early intervention services can be provided (CMS, 2020b). Likewise, failure to identify emerging social-emotional concerns and mental health conditions in childhood or adolescence may result in worsening symptoms over time, potentially leading to increased distress for the child, as well as the need for high-cost inpatient or residential care (Golberstein, Wen, & Miller, 2020). School-based health care and nursing care are a dependable source of pediatric health care for children. When many schools were at least partly closed at the beginning of the COVID-19 pandemic, children and adolescents who previously depended on in-person, school-based mental health care—including a disproportionate number from racial/ethnic minority groups and low-income households—no longer had access to those services (Ali et al., 2019; Golberstein, Wen, & Miller, 2020; Polacheck & Gears, 2020).

Poverty and Health Care

According to a recent National Academies report, poverty has a negative effect on a range of child outcomes in a number of domains (National Academies, 2019). Outcomes related to physical health include low birthweight, structural changes in brain development, child maltreatment, adverse childhood experiences, worse physical health, mental health problems, and increased risky behaviors.

Children and families living in poverty are more likely than their better-resourced counterparts to have needs left unaddressed after a preventive care visit, often as a result of greater social, psychosocial, developmental, and health education and guidance needs that outstrip the 15–20 minutes available for a preventive care visit (Olson et al, 2004; Bethell et al., 2011; Halfon et al., 2011; Norlin et al., 2011; Freeman & Coker, 2018). Pediatric health care visits have traditionally focused on regular immunizations, assessment of growth and developmental milestones, and anticipatory guidance for parents on child development and preventive care to reduce risk for injuries and promote social-emotional learning. Emphasis is increasing, however, on the importance of addressing health-related social needs and social determinants of health within health care through screening; coordinated referrals; colocated and integrated services (including integrated mental health care); and efforts to address institutional and interpersonal racism in medical care through revisions to medical education, leadership development pathways, and policies and protocols (Gottlieb, Sandel, & Adler, 2013).

Beginning at birth, racial and ethnic minorities and those of lower socioeconomic status have poorer access to health care (Flores, 2010). Rural areas are also particularly challenged in terms of health care access, in part because of the difficulty of attracting and retaining high-quality medical providers, as well as transportation and financial difficulties that impede access to care (Douthit et al., 2015). Health care for children is often facilitated through relationships between clinical systems and caregivers, and the broader social context impacts families' engagement with the health care system. For example, since health insurance in the United States is linked to employment or place of residence, with no universal coverage, when parents of children in low-income families change jobs or move, the children's care is often fragmented and disjointed.

Currently, medical care is delivered inequitably. Children of color and lower-income families are more likely to receive fragmented services, episodic and limited care, or care that is not culturally or linguistically competent. These children are also less likely to have a medical home. These inequities are greater for children with learning difficulties and developmental disabilities. Exacerbating these inequities are growing rates of childhood overweight and obesity; mental health and behavioral health challenges; and neurodevelopmental conditions, including autism spectrum disorders (Shonkoff et al., 2012).

Racism and Culturally Responsive Care

Racism is a pervasive stressor, which, like other stressors that operate through physiological pathways, may challenge one's ability to adapt and may increase health risks (Cohen, Kessler, & Gordon, 1997; McEwen, 2005). The National Academy of Medicine report *Vibrant and Healthy Kids* provides an extensive review of stress, traumatic stress, adverse childhood experience, and positive buffers. According to that report:

> *A large body of recent research provides insights into the mechanism by which early adversity in the lives of young children and their families can change the timing of sensitive periods of brain and other organ system development and impact the "plasticity" of developmental processes. Decades of research in the neurobiological sciences have found that responses to pre- and postnatal early life stress are rooted in genetic and environmental interactions that can result in altered molecular and cellular development that impacts the assembly of circuits during sensitive periods of development. There are biologic and physiologic systems involved in cognitive and emotional development that are more sensitive to early disturbances (critical periods) that activate stress response networks, such as the frontal cortex, hippocampus, amygdala, and the hypothalamic-pituitaryadrenal axis, provided a basis for both short- and long-term functional consequences of early life stress. (National Academies, 2019, p. 7)*

Because racism involves prejudicial attitudes, discriminatory treatment, systemic barriers, and internalized oppression due to an immutable personal characteristic fundamental to identity, it can be especially threatening to well-being (Landrine & Klonoff, 1996; Myers, Lewis, & Dominguez, 2003; Williams & Mohammed, 2009), and although most research focuses on direct targets, racism can also have unintended victims. As described by Harrell (2000) regarding racism-related stress for people of color, vicarious racism includes indirect exposure to the prejudice and discrimination experienced by friends, family, and strangers, which can be distressing and may also affect health. Because children develop within the context of their families and wider social environments (Bronfenbrenner, 1979) and are in critical phases of development, they may be particularly vulnerable to the adverse consequences of vicarious racism (Dominguez et al., 2008)—specifically the perceived threats to maltreatment of persons in their environment (Cohen, Kessler, & Gordon, 1997; Kelly, Bécares, & Nazroo, 2013; Priest et al., 2013). In addition, evidence suggests that perceived racism—the subjective experience of discrimination or prejudice—may lead to negative biopsychosocial effects, such as psychological and physiological stress, and other negative health outcomes, such as depression and elevated blood pressure (Clark et al., 1999).

Racism is an established social determinant of children's mental and physical health (Pachter & Coll, 2009). Stress that occurs continually or is triggered by multiple sources not only shapes children's later emotional lives as adults but also affects their physical health and longevity. Race-based traumatic stress associated with direct or indirect (vicarious) social forces and interpersonal or group dynamics (Harrell, 2000) has been linked to anxiety, poor immune functioning, poor sleep, and impaired daily activity (Menakem, 2017).

Racism as it relates to health care has been shown to contribute to the overall health disparities seen among communities of color. Structural or institutional racism results in decreased access to health care and fewer resources for education, often leading to lower health literacy and fewer health care providers of color. Despite progress in treating and preventing many diseases overall, health disparities continue to exist across different groups, with Black individuals experiencing higher rates of diabetes, obesity, asthma, and hypertension compared with their White counterparts (National Center for Health Statistics [NCHS], 2018, 2020; CDC, 2020; Matthew, Clark, & McDavid, 2021).

It must be acknowledged that health care providers contribute to health disparities. Clinicians and health professional students may lack understanding of White privilege and how racism is perpetuated through policies, protocols, practices, and systems, as well as interpersonally. Inequities can be exacerbated by medical teams with limited numbers of members who have lived experiences similar to those of patients from marginalized populations, as well as by a lack of diversity in ethnic and cultural backgrounds among those in decision-making roles. In addition, families may be less likely to access the health care system if they have not received culturally and linguistically appropriate care in the past or if they face additional challenges due to language, transportation issues, cost, and communication (National Academies, 2017). The intersection of race and poverty, especially profound in the context of residential racial segregation (Schickedanz & Coker, 2016; Williams et al., 2010), adds to the problem. Some research has revealed bias and prejudice among pediatric clinicians with respect to caring for lower-income families, reflecting a lack of understanding and training regarding the effects of poverty on children, failure to confront their own personal prejudices and biases, and stigma often attendant to working with low-income families. This research also revealed that providers found it difficult to apply typical diagnostic frameworks to children from low-income families (Smith et al., 2011, 2013).

Relational Health

Caregiver and parenting practices are critical to children's physical, cognitive, and social-emotional health. Relational health—or bidirectional relationships between family members and emotional connectedness—begins in infancy in the parent–child bond and is closely associated with attachment and a number of developmental outcomes, including language development and mental health through adulthood (Bethell et al., 2019; Madigan et al., 2019). Father–child and mother–child relational health are viewed as equally important for health (Roby et al., 2021). In both traditional and nontraditional family structures, other family relationships (e.g., with siblings, grandparents, aunts, and uncles) also are critical for child development. Similarly, teachers and other adult mentors in educational settings can play important roles in promoting child health. The negative consequences of the lack of a responsive parent–child or other adult–child relationship are exacerbated in the context of adversity (Hambrick, Brawner, & Perry, 2019).

Since early relational health is so critical for healthy child development, it has become a key area of focus for both preventive and targeted interventions aimed at improving children's outcomes. Parenting and parent–child relationships therefore represent a central consideration in developmental-behavioral pediatrics. Given that parenting occurs within the context of the greater social and built environments, it is important to address how the stressors of poverty and racism impact the resources, both material and emotional, that parents can devote to their children.

Adultification

Childhood is a social construct that intersects with the social construct of race. As discussed in Chapter 3, relative to their White peers, Black children are more likely to be misperceived as older and more developmentally mature than they are. Beginning at age 5, Black girls are more likely to be viewed as more adult-like, with less need for nurturing, comfort, support, or protection, and to receive harsher punishments (Epstein, Blake, & González, 2017). From age 10, Black boys are viewed as less innocent, misperceived as older, and subject to police violence if accused of a crime (Goff et al., 2014). Research has demonstrated that in general, Black children and youth are more likely than their White peers to receive a punitive response to childlike behavior (Dumas & Nelson, 2016).

Adultification is a term used to describe these differential perceptions of children associated with race (Epstein, Blake, & González, 2017). In this form of implicit bias, the social constructs of childhood and race intersect in a way that disadvantages children of color. A second form of adultification that has been observed in low-resource environments is socialization of children such that they take on more adult responsibilities at younger ages (Burton, 2007). During enslavement, Black children were dehumanized and viewed as chattel, valued on the basis of their ability to work, subjected to brutal forms of punishment, separated from caregivers, and disallowed access to play and to experiencing the world as children (King, 2005). This historical legacy of slavery informs patterns seen today.

Children are afforded unique protections based on social perceptions of innocence associated with understanding of their social and psychological development, as well as moral principles and laws intended to safeguard them from harsh penalties and levels of culpability and responsibility applied to adults. Adultification can result in losing the freedom to engage in the world as children and access to rights and protections of childhood under the law. The misperception that Black children are more mature, and therefore more accountable for their behavior, may help account for disparate outcomes by race in education, social welfare, and juvenile justice (Ocen, 2015).

Perceptions of children of color as more developmentally mature and the association of those perceptions with the way they are treated ultimately have implications for their social, emotional, and physical health. In one study, Black children aged 5–14 were found to be 31% less likely than their White peers to receive medication in the preoperative period to minimize anxiety, although this association was not observed for children younger than 5 and older than 14 (Baetzel et al., 2019). Other studies found that Black children were more likely to be physically restrained in the emergency department compared with their White counterparts (Tolliver et al., 2022), and were less likely to receive any form of analgesia for moderate pain and less likely to receive opioids for severe pain (Goyal et al., 2015), a disparity discussed further below. It is plausible that adultification informs one form of implicit bias that is associated with such disparate treatment and with physical health outcomes. Implicit racial bias toward Black children has been demonstrated at levels similar to those directed at Black adults (Johnson et al., 2017) and has been shown to impact pain management in pediatrics (Sabin & Greenwald, 2012), although other studies have yielded mixed evidence regarding the impact of implicit bias on clinical decision making (Dehon et al., 2017; Voepel-Lewis & Nafiu, 2017).

Researchers and clinicians alike have argued that raising awareness about the prevalence of adultification by tracking data and implementing quality improvement practices to identify adultification and racism, including coding of encounters that are concerning for these forms of discrimination, can help raise awareness among providers, improve recognition of adultification, and help drive intentional efforts to reduce this form of implicit bias (Koch & Kozhumam, 2021, 2022). Providers can support parents in understanding the implications of these perceptions for their children, particularly with respect to encounters with police, educators, and health care providers. "The talk" has been popularized as a strategy for caregivers, educators, and clinicians to help children learn protective strategies for police encounters (Maroney & Zuckerman, 2018), although data showing that these strategies are effective are currently not available. "The talk" may also be based in an expectation that Black children can prematurely assume adult roles and responsibilities in the face of institutional racism, a view that may incur a developmental benefit or toll (Burton, 2007).

Antiracism and Dismantling Race-based Medicine

As the discussion in the last chapter has demonstrated, racism, a system of advantage whereby opportunities and values are assigned on the basis of socially constructed categories of "race," has been identified as a root cause of health and health care inequities (Jones, 2001). Racism operates on multiple levels—interpersonal, institutional, structural, and systemic—although it is perpetuated and reinforced at the structural level. Achieving health equity will therefore require addressing institutional, structural, and systemic racism in health care and public health, and race-based medicine is one area in which systemic racism manifests. It is also worth noting that, while pediatricians have often served as lead clinician in the pediatric medical home, a team-based approach to child health has emerged by which primary care is reconfigured to address access issues. This approach involves the incorporation of mental health in primary care and the medical home, along with an increased role for other health professionals, such as nurse practitioners, school nurses, nurse midwives, social workers, psychologists, doulas, and frontline staff.

History of Race in Medicine

The belief that Black and White individuals have fundamental biological differences was propagated by slaveholders to justify slavery and by scientists and physicians to justify unethical and inhumane medical research conducted on Black people (Cartwright, 1851, as cited in Guillory, 1968; Washington, 2006; Owens, 2017). Today, assumptions about athleticism associated with race/ethnicity are based in beliefs about racial genetics. Although biological conceptions of racial differences are not strongly associated with racist attitudes, they are associated with acceptance of racial inequities as endemic (Williams and Eberhardt, 2008).

The 1985 *Report of the Secretary's Task Force on Black and Minority Health*, commonly known as the Heckler Report, documented racial inequities in health. *Unequal Treatment*, a groundbreaking report of the Institute of Medicine (now known as the National Academy of Medicine), documented racial/ethnic disparities in the quality of care, demonstrating that for almost all diseases among hundreds reviewed, Black Americans received less effective care than their White counterparts even when such factors as insurance and socioeconomic status were matched (Institute of Medicine [IOM], 2003). Implicit bias in the form of unconscious racial stereotypes related to personal and cultural experiences and limited interracial or intercultural engagement is common among health care providers, mirroring the general population (Chapman, Kaatz, & Carnes, 2013; Ansell & McDonald, 2015). Implicit bias is thought to influence administrative decisions on insurance plans accepted, neighborhoods for establishing offices, and selection and inclusion of diverse students in medical education and training and among faculty (Ansell & McDonald, 2015).

Mounting evidence confirms that race is not a reliable proxy for genetic differences. Yet despite these advances in research, the use of race as a proxy for biological and genetic differences with clinical significance has remained embedded in medical practice, education, training, and research.

Diagnostic Algorithms

Diagnostic algorithms and practice guidelines that correct for a patient's race or ethnicity continue to be in common use in clinical medicine (Vyas, Eisenstein, & Jones, 2020), taught in medical education, and included in medical board examinations (Amutah et al., 2021). Race-adjusted clinical algorithms guide clinical decisions and operationalize racism in clinical medicine by directing attention and resources to White patients to the detriment of racial and ethnic minorities (Vyas, Eisenstein, & Jones, 2020). Many of these guidelines offer no rationale for the use of race/ethnicity (Vyas, Eisenstein, & Jones, 2020), or when investigated are found to be rooted in race- and class-based biases and assumptions (Braun, 2014).

Diagnostic algorithms that include race/ethnicity lower estimates of success for people of color, and their use to guide care can exacerbate inequities in health care and outcomes. The vaginal birth after cesarean (VBAC) algorithm, for example, predicts risk associated with a vaginal delivery among those who have had a previous cesarean section. The VBAC calculator was informed by a prior research study that identified variables correlated with VBAC success, including insurance type (Landon et al., 2005). It incorporates two race-based correction factors—one for African American women and another for Hispanic women—that subtract from the overall likelihood of successful VBAC, and these women are therefore assigned a lower chance of success (Vyas, Eisenstein, & Jones, 2020). While this algorithm incorporates race/ethnicity as a correction factor, it does not incorporate other factors, such as insurance type, that were correlated with VBAC success in the referenced study. In the United States, women of color have higher rates of cesarean section in comparison with their White counterparts, as well as three to four times higher rates of maternal mortality and morbidity.

Medical Education

Evidence suggests that medical students and trainees hold false beliefs about fundamental biological and genetic differences by race. The content of medical school curricula reinforces this misperception (Tsai et al., 2016), and this misrepresentation can propagate bias (see Table 4-1; Tsai et al., 2016; Nieblas-Bedolla et al., 2020; Amutah et al., 2021). This misrepresentation can take the form of race-based clinical guidelines; data that tend to associate minoritized populations with increased incidence of disease in the absence of context; association of disease with particular racial groups, which can lead to diagnostic bias; and presentation of racial/ethnic differences in disease burden without addressing the broader social context (Amutah et al., 2021). Race/ethnicity also appears routinely in question banks used to prepare for the United States Medical Licensing Examination (Ripp & Braun, 2017).

Action Steps to Reform Medical Education

The portrayal and misuse of race in medical curricula has been explored, and revisions have been suggested (Amutah et al., 2021). Recommendations include (1) standardizing the language used to describe race/ethnicity; and (2) building relevant medical competencies, such as structural competency, which includes recognizing structures that shape clinical interactions and developing structural interventions (Metzl & Hansen, 2014; Stonington et al., 2018). Training in structural competency can help providers understand the structural and social forces, policies, and historical processes that affect health. More equitable and antiracist care practices could be supported if providers had a deeper understanding of structural and institutional racism and interpersonal discrimination and their impacts on health, clinical encounters, and conditions. To date, however, literature conceptualizing structural racism has not been adequately integrated into medical education, and the majority of empirical studies of racism have focused on interpersonal discrimination rather than structural racism (Bailey et al., 2017).

Implicit Bias

Research has established that the majority of U.S. physicians and medical students have the kinds of implicit biases discussed above that privilege

TABLE 4-1 Misrepresentation of Race in Preclinical Curricula

Domain	Description	Representative Examples
Semantics	Using imprecise and nonbiologic labels that inaccurately conflate race and ancestry	Widespread use of "Caucasian," "Black," "African American," and "Asian" as labels to denote biologic differences between patients
		Describing a Nigerian patient as "African American" in a clinical vignette
Prevalence without context	Presenting racial/ethnic differences in disease burden without contextualization	Teaching students that "Black" patients have higher rates of asthma than "White" patients without reference to the effects on asthma prevalence of residential segregation and unequal access to high-quality housing and health care
		Teaching students that "Black" patients have higher rates of hospital readmission without any discussion of the underlying causes of these disparities
Race-based diagnostic bias	Presentation of links between racial groups and particular diseases	Priming students to view sickle cell disease as affecting only Black people rather than as common in populations at risk for malaria
Pathologizing race	The tendency to link minorities with increased disease burden	In a slide showing the incidence of 13 types of brain tumors in Black patients and White patients, using the title "Incidence rates are higher among Blacks than among Whites," even though 10 of the tumors occurred more frequently in White patients
Race-based clinical guidelines	Teaching of guidelines that endorse the use of racial categories in the diagnosis and treatment of diseases	Teaching students to use different first-line antihypertensive drugs in Black patients than in White patients, without any exposure to literature that questions these practices and misleading interpretations of information

SOURCE: Excerpted from Amutah et al., 2021.

White patients (Haider et al., 2011), with significant proportions of medical students and trainees holding false beliefs about biological differences by race (Hoffman et al., 2016). As noted previously, implicit bias, stereotyping, and prejudice among health care professionals influence inequities in diagnosis, treatment, and care by race/ethnicity (Chapman, Katz, & Carnes, 2013; Hall et al., 2015; FitzGerald & Hurst, 2017), including among common pediatric diagnoses (Sabin & Greenwald, 2012). Medical students who hold such false beliefs were found to be more likely to rate pain lower and make less accurate treatment recommendations for Black versus White patients (Hoffman et al., 2016). Research has documented that Black patients, including children, not only are less likely to receive pain medication but also receive lower quantities and experience greater delays in administration even though they self-report similar levels of pain (Goyal et al., 2015; Singhal, Tien, & Hsia, 2016). Yet despite the disparities resulting from the inequities embodied in diagnostic algorithms and manifest in differential treatment, medical education and clinical practice have been slow to evolve to reflect race as a social construct rather than a biological category, and racism as a systemic factor in shaping social experiences that have biological consequences.

Efforts of Medical Associations and Other Organizations to Confront Systemic Racism

In recent years, medical associations, such as the American Medical Association (AMA), have acknowledged the role of racism in perpetuating health inequities and harms in communities that have historically been marginalized (O'Reilly, 2020; Madara, 2021; Tanne, 2021), and have adopted policies aimed at embedding racial justice and advancing equity in their work (Maybank et al., 2022). In 2021, the AMA adopted guidelines designed to confront systemic racism (American Medical Association, 2021).

The American Academy of Pediatrics (AAP) has recently taken steps to dismantle race-based medicine in clinical practice and medical education. To that end, it is examining and eliminating inaccurately applied "race corrections" or "race adjustment factors" that result in differential approaches to disease management and disparate clinical outcomes. The AAP recently retired clinical guidelines that linked race, as a biologic proxy, to urinary infections in children (Wright et al., 2022). Presently, the AAP is addressing the use of race in guidelines for newborn jaundice. In May 2022, it released a policy statement, "Eliminating Race-Based Medicine," that calls for scrutiny and revision of the suite of clinical guidelines, algorithms, educational materials, textbooks, and literature used to guide clinical practice and for medical education (Wright et al., 2022). And some have called on other prominent health organizations, such as the National Institutes of Health, to examine ways of dismantling racism through research infrastructure (Bear et al., 2022).

Nutrition

It is well known that proper nutrition plays a major role in physical development, and young children are the age group most vulnerable to deficits in nutrition given the important developmental changes that occur during the early years of life. The consequences of poor nutrition may plague children into adolescence and adulthood through stunting and poor cognitive development (De Sanctis et al., 2021; Galler et al., 2021; Pizzol et al., 2021). Existing programs and tax credit policies play an important role in improving nutrition for the poorest children, and recent extensions to these programs may help achieve significant progress toward reducing child hunger and poor nutrition.

Recent decades have seen an increase in research aimed at identifying the effect of increased food availability and improved nutrition on child (and adult) well-being. The techniques used for these studies have leveraged the delayed rollout of programs within the United States to identify the effect of certain U.S. federal and state programs on nutrition outcomes (Almond, Hoynes, & Whitmore Schanzenbach, 2011). For example, increasing evidence indicates that the consumption of nutritious foods during the prenatal period affects the general health and well-being of children and may play a role in their cognitive and physical development (Guan et al., 2021).

Although access to adequate and nutritious food affects development across the life course, it is particularly important for the preconception, prenatal, and early childhood periods. Furthermore, the period from conception to 2 years of age (about the first 1,000 days) is especially critical, as the brain undergoes significant developmental changes during this period that may not be possible later in life (Schwarzenberg et al., 2018). In addition to macronutrients (protein, fat, and glucose), certain micronutrients (zinc, copper, iodine, iron, and selenium) and vitamins and cofactors (vitamin B6, vitamin B12, vitamin A, vitamin K, folate, and choline) are particularly important for healthy early brain development (IOM, 1990; Georgieff, Brunette, & Tran, 2015; Cusick & Georgieff, 2016; Schwarzenberg et al., 2018; National Academies, 2019). Adequate nutrition during later stages of childhood may also play a role in child development. Beyond the above developmental effects, children living in extreme poverty may suffer from insufficient amounts of food that can result in stunting, wasting, or other growth inhibition or delays. Stunting reflects long-term deprivation of nutritious foods, while wasting is the result of more acute periods of food deprivation (Food and Agriculture Organization of the United Nations et al., 2021). Stunting may be indicative of permanent cognitive and/or physical disabilities for children that persist into adulthood.

In addition, poor dietary habits early in life may lead to consumption of foods higher in fat and sugar, which in turn may increase the risk of diabetes (Wen et al., 2014). These habits may be formed in households with little access to nutritious foods because those foods cost more to purchase or prepare, or because supermarkets with these foods are not located conveniently in urban or rural settings.

Food Insecurity for Households with Children

Food insecurity is a pervasive problem in the United States, especially for households with children. The U.S. Department of Agriculture defines food insecurity as a lack of consistent access to enough food for an active and healthy life. In 2016, for example, 13 million (1 in 6) U.S. children were food insecure; 85% of counties with high child food insecurity were rural. Table 4-2 provides a sense of the problem of food insecurity in the United States (National Academies, 2019).

Whereas nutritious foods are important sources of energy, fiber, protein, and key minerals and vitamins needed for healthy development, adequate food is more a measure of whether sufficient quantities of food are available for individuals and households over long periods of time in a sustained manner. Households often face a trade-off between (more costly) nutritious food and adequate quantities of food. Here again, disparities persist within the United States. Although evidence has shown the link between maternal and infant nutrition and children's health and developmental outcomes, access to affordable nutritious food is often more likely to be limited for low-income communities and communities of color (National Academies, 2019).

Safe and Healthy Environments

As discussed previously, young children exist within the contexts of their families and neighborhoods, including the places where they live, learn, and play, and these environments need to be safe and healthy if children are to achieve optimal physical health, growth, and development. Health-promoting neighborhoods provide the physical and social conditions and community resources—social, economic, environmental, and

TABLE 4-2 Food Insecurity by Selected Household Characteristics

Type of Household	Percentage of All Households (%)
Households with children	12.5
Households with children under 6	12.9
Households with children headed by a single woman	24.3
Non-Hispanic Black households	19.8
Hispanic households	16.2
Non-Hispanic White households	7.0
Households with income below the federal poverty threshold	32.1

SOURCE: Data from U.S. Department of Agriculture, 2022.

cultural—that enable young children to be healthy (CDC, 2009; National Academies, 2017). The Child Opportunity Index is a tool used to describe and quantify the neighborhood conditions experienced by U.S. children, ranking them from lowest to highest with regard to the opportunity they provide. Child Opportunity Scores rank all 72,000 neighborhoods in the United States from one to 100 according to this metric (Diversity Data Kids, 2019, Box 1-2). Child Opportunity Scores are also available for metro areas for use in assessing their level of opportunity overall and by race and ethnicity. The opportunity gap between very low- and very high-opportunity neighborhoods represents differences along important dimensions of neighborhood environment. Access to green space, for example, varies widely. In very low-opportunity neighborhoods, almost half of children (48%) lack access to parks and playgrounds, while in very high-opportunity neighborhoods, this is the case for fewer than a quarter of children (22%). As discussed previously, access to nature and to safe places to play is critical for children's health and well-being (Acevedo-Garcia et al., 2019).

After reviewing some methodological considerations regarding the association between neighborhood and child health, this section looks at two specific aspects of neighborhoods thought to be linked most directly with young children's physical health: freedom from environmental contaminants and safety and freedom from violence.

Methodological Considerations

It is important to note that the evidence the committee presents on the association between neighborhoods and child health is complex, and the existing literature is fraught with methodological challenges and pitfalls. For example, associations between neighborhood characteristics and child health may vary based on individual-level characteristics, such as a child's race or immigration status, and effect estimates may be sensitive to the selection of covariates included in models (Paczkowski & Galea, 2010; Auchincloss et al., 2013; Meijer, Bloomfield, & Engholm, 2013; Blair et al., 2014). Given the correlation among different neighborhood factors—such as poverty, racial segregation, housing quality, and environmental contaminants—it is also difficult to separate out the effects of any single neighborhood factor. In addition, results vary widely depending on how a specific health outcome or neighborhood characteristic is measured, and many studies capture only limited subsets of neighborhood factors. As a result, it is difficult to identify specific interventions focused on altering specific neighborhood characteristics to target specific high-risk subgroups. Also, given that true randomized controlled trials are often unethical or infeasible in this realm, causal connections between neighborhood conditions and child health are challenging to validate (Oakes, 2004; Oakes et al., 2015; Glass & Bilal, 2016; Jeffries et al., 2019). For example, existing studies may suffer from selection bias by which unhealthy versus healthy families are more likely to live in disadvantaged neighborhoods.

A handful of studies have overcome some of these methodological limitations. For example, the Moving to Opportunity study randomized families to receive a voucher to move to a low-poverty neighborhood. Analyses of the Moving to Opportunity study have found that children who moved to low-poverty neighborhoods when they were younger were more likely to experience positive social outcomes (e.g., college attendance) later in life, while children who moved at older ages experienced worse outcomes (Chetty, Hendren, & Katz, 2016). The Moving to Opportunity study also showed that girls experienced improved mental health (e.g., decreased risk of major depression), while boys experienced worse outcomes (e.g., increased rates of posttraumatic stress disorder) (Kessler et al., 2014). Yet despite the strength of its randomized study design, the Moving to Opportunity study could not tease apart which aspects of the neighborhood environment mattered, or why this differed for children of different ages and genders. Moreover, the number of physical health conditions examined was limited, and the sample was relatively small (4,604 families, with 98% of households headed by women), restricted to only five U.S. cities, and enrolled in the mid-1990s. Therefore, it may be necessary to address this issue with a broader range of quasi-experimental and observational studies, which of course would have to be interpreted cautiously.

In recent years, an increasing number of quasi-experimental studies have leveraged natural experiments in which families are quasi-randomly assigned to neighborhoods of different levels of disadvantage so the effects of neighborhood characteristics on health can be examined. For example, several studies have found negative health effects of neighborhood disadvantage among refugees quasi-randomly assigned to more deprived neighborhoods in Denmark and Sweden (White et al., 2016; Hamad et al., 2020; Raphael et al., 2020), including increased mental health problems among children (Foverskov et al., 2022). Other studies have examined the effects of the built environment on cardiometabolic disease among older adults forcibly displaced and quasi-randomly assigned to neighborhoods in the wake of the 2011 Great East Japan Earthquake and Tsunami (Shiba et al., 2020). Unfortunately, few of these quasi-experimental studies have focused on child health, and the circumstances underlying the natural experiment, including those just cited, are often "unnatural," hinging on quasi-random variation generated by natural disasters or policies that typically are not generalizable (Hamad, 2020). Nevertheless, quasi-experimental studies provide a balance between randomized studies (which are challenging and/or unethical to conduct and yet methodologically rigorous) and observational studies (which are easier to conduct but can suffer from confounding/

endogeneity), and future research could identify natural experiments with which to focus on child health in the context of U.S. settings in particular.

Environmental Contaminants

Child well-being is affected by environmental determinants related to pollutants and contaminants in the water; the air; and other aspects of a young child's home, school, and play areas. Environmental contaminants have repeatedly been found to be associated with poor health throughout the life course, and the prenatal and early childhood periods represent particularly sensitive developmental windows in which individuals may be especially vulnerable to their effects. Young children may be exposed to thousands of potential contaminants, including through the air they breathe, the water they drink and use, the food they eat, and the consumer products with which they come into contact (Giudice, Woodruff, & Conry, 2017). While these substances may be present in the environment naturally, many are released through human-based processes such as manufacturing, fossil fuel use, and waste disposal (Di Renzo et al., 2015). This section looks at two specific subsets of contaminants—allergens and pollutants that cause asthma, and lead that affects neurological development and cognition—as well as evidence on environmental contaminants more generally.

Allergens/pollutants and asthma Asthma is the most common chronic lung disease in U.S. children (Zahran et al., 2018). It is a serious health condition characterized by inflammation of the lungs and chronic respiratory symptoms such as shortness of breath and coughing, especially with physical activity. Not only does asthma impair quality of life and increase health care utilization, but it also contributes to more than 10.5 million missed days of school annually among U.S. children.

Poor housing conditions can lead to increased risk of asthma in several ways. Research has found links between asthma and cockroaches, dust mites, dampness, and mold (IOM, 2000; Wu & Takaro, 2007; Rauh, Landrigan, & Claudio, 2008). Other work has found an association of higher density of housing code violations and worse public housing conditions with increased risk of health care utilization related to exacerbation of asthma (Beck et al., 2014; Kersten et al., 2014).

Lead Exposure to lead, even in small amounts, is associated with lower IQ and test scores, as well as increased incidence of impulsivity and attention-deficit/hyperactivity disorder (Needleman et al., 1979, 1990; Rauh, Landrigan, & Claudio, 2008; Leventhal & Newman, 2010; Muller, Sampson, & Winter, 2018). Such effects are thought to persist through to later in childhood and have been linked with high adolescent body mass index, impulsivity, anxiety, and depression, as well as lower earnings and criminal activity in adulthood (Kim & Williams, 2017; Winter & Sampson, 2017). Exposure to lead among pregnant mothers has been linked with adverse birth outcomes, possibly through transmission to the fetus (Taylor, Golding, & Emond, 2015). Consistent with prior research on disparities, Black children in these studies have more elevated blood lead levels (BLLs) relative to White children (Miranda et al., 2009). In one study, only one in four Black children had a BLL of 3 micrograms per deciliter (µg/dL) or less, compared with almost half of White children. In a study of BLL and third-grade test scores, non-Hispanic Black students had a mean BLL of 7.7 µg/dL—more than twice that of non-Hispanic White students (3.7 µg/dL; Evens et al., 2015; National Center for Healthy Housing, 2013). Box 4-2 provides an example of how policy changes related to lead exposure succeeded in improving academic performance in children and reducing community-level inequality in Massachusetts.

Other environmental contaminants Numerous other environmental contaminants have been linked to adverse health outcomes at birth and in early childhood. Chemicals from heavy metals and pesticides to carbon monoxide and ozone are thought to affect neurological development and

---

BOX 4-2
Policy Lessons: Lead Exposure and Academic Performance

Beginning in the 1970s, the state of Massachusetts established a Childhood Lead Poisoning Prevention Program making it mandatory to screen children under 6 years of age, provide medical and environmental services to families affected by lead exposure, and implement policies to eliminate potential sources of such exposure (Commonwealth of Massachusetts, 2022). To estimate the benefit of this program, Reyes (2011) used blood-lead data from this program and test scores reported by the Massachusetts Department of Elementary and Secondary Education to determine the relationship between a 1 percentage point increase in blood lead levels (i.e., 10 micrograms/deciliter, or the Centers for Disease Control and Prevention's level of concern) and unsatisfactory test scores. Using these data to simulate the impact of lead policies implemented by the state in the 1990s, the researchers were able to demonstrate that the policies had reduced unsatisfactory academic performance by 5% while also narrowing achievement gaps between low- and middle-income households (Reyes, 2011). By allocating less than $5 million of state government funds per year, Massachusetts has been able to collect data demonstrating that public health policy interventions can simultaneously improve academic performance and reduce community-level inequality. These findings have implications for other local and state policy makers who would like to implement novel policies to improve individual academic outcomes by targeting early childhood influences, policies that can have lasting impacts at the individual level (Almond & Currie, 2010).

contribute to endocrine disruption, with wide-ranging negative effects on asthma as well as on child growth and development, obesity, sexual anatomy, and kidney disorders (Cox et al., 1989; Kalter, 2003; Vandenbergh, 2004; Diamanti-Kandarakis et al., 2009; Nakamura et al., 2012; Manikkam et al., 2013; Di Renzo et al., 2015; Gore et al., 2015; Webb et al., 2016; Weidemann, Weaver, & Fadrowski, 2016; Giudice, Woodruff, & Conry, 2017). The effects of hundreds of contaminants remain untested. Therefore, these contaminants may have both immediate impacts on health and wellness and long-term effects on chronic disease, educational attainment and achievement, and mortality.

Opportunity gaps related to environmental contaminants As the evidence reported above demonstrates, children experience differing levels of exposure to environmental contaminants, such as lead and those that place them at risk of asthma. Exposures vary across an income and race gradient rooted in decades of discriminatory policies and programs. Children whose families have lower incomes and live in substandard housing are more likely to live in greater proximity to known sources of such contaminants, as are children from racial/ethnic minority and immigrant (particularly Latino) groups as a result of the chronic effects of structural racism (Oberg, Colianni, & King-Schultz, 2016; American College of Obstetricians and Gynecologists Committee on Obstetric Practice, 2021). Studies from the United States and other high-income countries also suggest that residence in urban versus rural areas affects the types and quantities of pollutants to which people are exposed (Northridge et al., 2003; Hendryx, Fedorko, & Halverson, 2010; Hulin, Caillaud, & Annesi-Maesano, 2010).

An example is particulate matter 2.5 micrometers or less in diameter ($PM_{2.5}$), which places children at higher risk of asthma. People living in poverty and people of color are exposed to significantly higher levels of $PM_{2.5}$ compared with White individuals (Mikati et al., 2018). Another study found that White individuals experience a "pollution advantage" more generally in that they have 17% less exposure to air pollution on average when the amount to which they are exposed is compared with the amount for which they are responsible; conversely, Black and Latino Americans experience 56% and 64% excess exposure, respectively, when the same comparison is made (National Academies, 2019; Tessum et al., 2019). These inequities persist even as exposure to pollution on average is declining as a result of increased regulation and a shift in population density away from polluted areas. The net result is large racial and socioeconomic disparities in the prevalence of asthma in the United States. Prevalence is highest among Black people (11.1% compared with 8.2% in the population overall), and Black individuals are more than three times more likely than White individuals to visit an emergency department for asthma care (Akinbami, Moorman, & Liu, 2011). And while child deaths from asthma are rare, they are roughly 10 times more likely for Black than for White children (Pate et al., 2021).

Similarly, while more than half a million U.S. children aged 1–5 have BLLs above the reference range according to the most recent prevalence estimates (from 1999 to 2010), this risk is not distributed equally across all groups of children (Wheeler & Brown, 2013). Black children are more than twice as likely as their White peers to have a BLL above 5 μg (5.6% vs. 2.4%), and those who live in poverty or have Medicaid coverage are nearly eight times as likely to have elevated BLLs (Wheeler & Brown, 2013). Even after correcting for risk factors and other variables, such as housing, socioeconomic, status, and age, Black versus White children nationwide have BLLs 1.8 to 5.6 times higher within each risk factor subgroup (Yeter, Banks, & Aschner, 2020).

The primary reason for differential exposures to environmental contaminants is proximity to sources of pollutants, such as traffic and roadways, industrial facilities, power plants, and natural gas wells, that repeatedly have been associated with worse health outcomes for children, including adverse birth outcomes and asthma in particular (Ahmad et al., 2001; Hopenhayn et al., 2003; Tsai et al., 2004; Salam, Islam, & Gilliland, 2008; Clark et al., 2010; Pénard-Morand et al., 2010; Currie & Walker, 2011; Padula et al., 2012; Miranda et al., 2013; Ha et al., 2015; Woodward, Finch, & Morgan, 2015; Casey et al., 2016; Harris et al., 2016; Alexander & Currie, 2017; Fleisch et al., 2017). Proximity to sources of pollutants is in turn determined by other, more upstream risk factors, most notably family poverty, neighborhood poverty and disadvantage, and residential segregation driven by structural racism in housing policies, discussed in turn below.

Families that live in poverty are naturally less likely to be able to afford housing that is high quality (e.g., free of lead and asbestos) and located farther from sources of pollutants (Sandel et al., 2004; Rauh, Landrigan, & Claudio, 2008). Living in older housing also means that outdoor pollutants are more likely to enter the home (Houston et al., 2016). Thus lower-income neighborhoods are more likely to have higher levels of ambient air pollution, while at the same time they have fewer air quality monitoring resources (Stuart, Mudhasakul, & Sriwatanapongse, 2009; Houston et al., 2016).

Like family poverty, neighborhood poverty and disadvantage, experienced disproportionately by families of color, is associated with poor-quality housing and a higher risk of lead contamination (Baek et al., 2021). Although lead paint was banned in 1978, exposure remains high among children living in older homes (particularly in the Northeastern and Midwestern United States), where the paint can peel and be ingested, and among those living close to certain types of manufacturing sites (Rauh, Landrigan, & Claudio, 2008; Muller, Sampson, & Winter, 2018).

Residential segregation is a persistent feature of U.S. neighborhoods, driven by historical racist practices and policies such as redlining and discriminatory banking practices (National Academies, 2017). Although these policies are no longer entrenched in the legal system, their effects are persistent and demonstrated by the continued segregation of many U.S. neighborhoods. These patterns have contributed to the higher levels of poverty and disadvantage experienced by segregated Black neighborhoods because of their limited access to health-promoting resources, including those for children (Acevedo-Garcia et al., 2007, 2008), as well as their greater likelihood of being in proximity to potential pollutants and environmental hazards and of having poor-quality housing (National Academies, 2019).

Safe and Violence-free Environments

Children need environments in which to grow, develop, and thrive that are safe with respect to prevention of unintentional injuries, as well as exposure to violence—whether that exposure is primary (i.e., direct victimization by adults or peers) or secondary (i.e., witnessing violence in the home or community). Young children's exposure to violence in their home or neighborhood is likely to create additional obstacles to their long-term well-being.

Maltreatment Statistics reported for federal fiscal year 2019 document 656,000 victims of child abuse and neglect nationally, which equates to a national rate of 8.9 victims per 1,000 children in the population. The Centers for Disease Control and Prevention (CDC) estimates that in 2019, about 1 in 7 children were affected by maltreatment, and 1,840 of these children died as a result (Department of Health and Human Services, Administration for Children and Families, & Administration on Children, Youth and Families, Children's Bureau, 2021). The youngest children are the most vulnerable to maltreatment: nationally, more than one-quarter (28.1%) of victims are aged 0–2 years. Among school-based children, African American students, students who qualify for free/reduced-price lunch (i.e., those from families with low incomes), students living in relatively high-poverty areas, and students attending urban schools all have an elevated likelihood of being investigated by Child Protective Services for suspected child maltreatment (Jacob & Ryan, 2018). Maltreatment in early childhood is associated with significantly worse academic outcomes, even after controlling for school, neighborhood, race, and other key demographics (Jacob & Ryan, 2018). The total lifetime economic cost associated with child maltreatment in terms of worse outcomes, lower educational attainment, lower probability of employment, and high disability rates was estimated to be about $428 billion in 2015.

The Nurse-Family Partnership (NFP) is often cited as an effective intervention for preventing child abuse and neglect. This program provides nurse home visits to pregnant women with no previous live births, most of whom are: (1) low income, (2) unmarried, and (3) teenagers. The nurses visit the women once or twice per month during their pregnancy and the first two years of their children's lives (Arnold Ventures, 2020). Data on the outcomes of the program in Elmira, New York, and Memphis, Tennessee, show that it reduced verified incidences of abuse and reduced hospitalizations for injuries in young children. Treatment families reported statistically significant decreases in child abuse/neglect and domestic violence and improvements in home learning environments compared with control families.

Injuries Injuries are a leading cause of death among children in the United States, and data on these deaths reveal prominent racial disparities (CDC, 2021). According to a CDC report based on data from 2000–2009, American Indian/Alaska Native children had the highest death rate from injuries at 30.4 per 100,000 in 2000 and 23.8 per 100,000 in 2009—nearly double the rates among Black children (16.2 and 12.8, respectively), the population with the next-highest rate in 2009 (Gilchrist, Ballesteros, & Parker, 2012). There is also a more than sixfold gap between the lowest and highest rates across states (from 4.0 per 100,000 in Massachusetts to 25.1 per 100,000 in Mississippi).

The impact of injury and injury severity on academic outcomes can be substantial. Following an injury, a young person's ability to learn and concentrate can be interrupted, future learning can be affected, and injuries resulting in physical disability have been shown to negatively influence cognitive skills (Ewing-Cobbs et al., 2006; Vu, Babikian, & Asarnow, 2011; Fulton et al., 2012; Kingery et al., 2017; Prasad, Swank, & Ewing-Cobbs, 2017; Treble-Barna et al., 2017). Aside from problems with cognitive performance, seriously injured young people may also experience psychological and physical health problems that can adversely affect their academic performance (Foster et al., 2019a,b). Results of one large population-based study (involving more than 150,000 injured children) suggest that while some young people may fully recover after their injury, others may experience ongoing adverse effects on their school-based academic performance. Overall, injured young people demonstrate poorer performance on school assessments, with increasing injury severity having a greater negative impact. In addition, one study found that injured young people had almost twice the risk of not completing high school compared with their uninjured matched peers (Mitchell et al., 2021).

Exposure to violence Exposure to violence is disturbingly prevalent among U.S. children. Data from the National Survey of Children's Exposure to Violence (2013–2014) show that 37.3% of children had experienced physical assault in the past year; 51.4% had experienced physical assault in their lifetime; and 24.5% and 38.3% had witnessed violence in the past year and in their lifetime, respectively (Finkelhor et al., 2015). Black children have the highest exposure to violence in their communities—9.5% among children aged 5–12, compared with 6.9% for White and 5.7% for Hispanic children (Ullmann, Weeks, & Madans, 2021). Boys are at higher risk than girls.

Opportunity gaps related to safety and exposure to violence Several factors may explain the above disparities in young children's exposure to violence; they include individual, family, and place-based risk factors. On an individual level, babies under 1 year old experience higher rates of injuries and maltreatment (CDC, 2014, 2021). Children with disabilities also are at increased risk, having more than three times greater odds of being victims of violence compared with their peers without disabilities (Jones et al., 2012). In these latter cases, it is likely that increased family conflict and parenting challenges contribute to the greater risk.

At the family level, poverty and structural racism lead to higher levels of chronic stress that may contribute to greater family tensions, which in turn have been found to be associated with increased levels of child maltreatment and violence (Jewkes, 2002; Foster, Brooks-Gunn, & Martin, 2007; Stith et al., 2009). Families living in poverty and parents with limited educational attainment may also be less able to acquire health-promoting resources that can protect against injuries, such as the ability to afford or properly install car seats or to perform adequate childproofing in the home. Similarly, as noted earlier, poverty and structural racism may affect the ability to afford high-quality housing, which is more likely to have appropriate safety measures in place (Reading, Haynes, & Shesnassa, 2005).

Place-based characteristics also contribute to potentially unsafe environments. In addition to the issues with housing quality mentioned above, disadvantaged neighborhoods tend to be the recipients of poor urban planning, with roadways and traffic patterns contributing to traffic injuries (Morency et al., 2012). As noted previously, the distribution of health-promoting community characteristics is racially and socially patterned as a result of historical segregation, placing low-income children and children of color at high risk of exposure to such hazards. The geographic disparities across states discussed above also suggest that aspects of the social and physical environments may play a role, including exposure to place-based hazards (e.g., vehicle-miles traveled, exposure to water settings, urban versus rural environment) and differences in public policy (e.g., gun legislation; Ullmann, Weeks, & Madans, 2021). Additional research is needed to clarify what aspects of disadvantaged neighborhoods are most important to address in this regard (Newgard et al., 2011).

Finally, police brutality, especially in segregated Black, Latino, and Indigenous communities, is a significant driver of health problems in these populations. Beyond police-inflicted violence, these community tensions can also worsen mental health problems among residents, as well as affect downstream outcomes relevant to child health, such as prenatal outcomes among Black women (Alang et al., 2017).

Gun violence is now the leading cause of death for all children and teens aged 1–19 (Figure 4-1). According to the CDC, nearly two-thirds of the 4,368 U.S. children up to age 19 who were killed by guns in 2020 were homicide victims (CDC, 2020). In that year, by comparison, motor vehicle crashes, formerly the leading cause of death for children aged 1 and above, killed nearly 4,000 children. While mass shootings garner the attention of the public and policy makers, routine gunfire kills more children each week than died in the Columbine, Sandy Hook, and Parkland massacres combined. Here, too, there are stark racial disparities. Black children and teens are four times more likely than their White peers to die from gun violence.

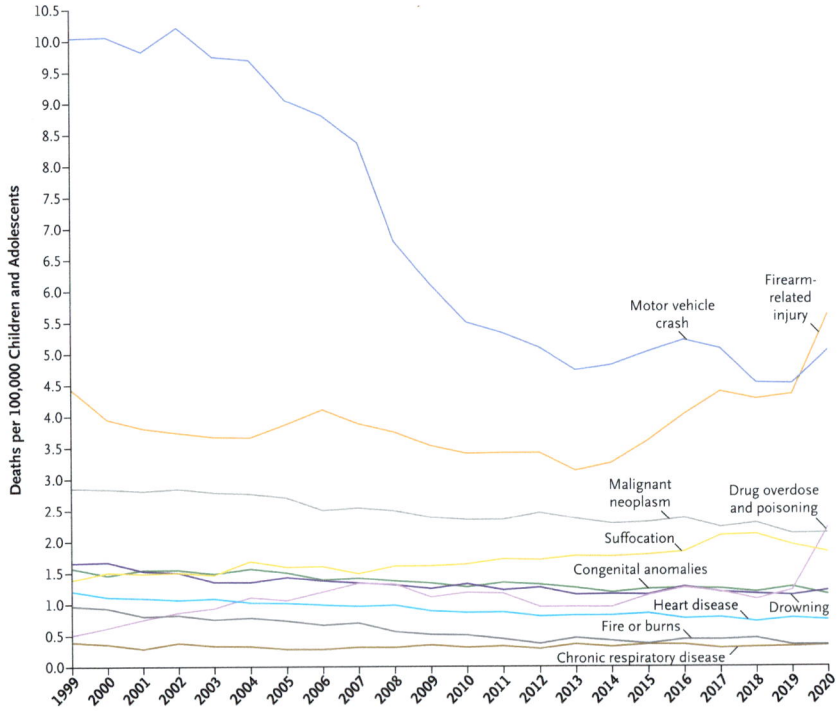

FIGURE 4-1 Leading causes of death among children and adolescents in the United States, 1999–2020.
SOURCE: Goldstick, Cunningham, & Carter, 2022.

U.S. mortality rates among children due to gun violence are the highest across high-income countries and are thought to be due to this country's having the least restrictive gun policies, higher rates of gun ownership, and types of guns available to the public. Differences in state-level gun control policies are also associated with differences in firearm-related morbidity and mortality among children (Rudolph et al., 2015; Raifman et al., 2020).

The consequences of gun violence are pervasive, affecting entire communities in addition to families and children. More than 25% of children witnessed an act of violence in their home, school, or community during 2009, and more than 5% witnessed a shooting. Beyond gun regulation, then, it is essential to address the impact on those who have been injured and traumatized by such violence (Finkelhor et al., 2009; Children's Defense Fund, 2022; Collins and Swoveland, 2022; Goldstick, Cunningham, & Carter, 2022).

While the majority of children who experience injuries or are exposed to violence recover, they often suffer short- and long-term consequences (Schneeberg et al., 2016). Long-term consequences may include impacts on their physical health (e.g., physical disability, asthma, blood pressure), mental health (e.g., posttraumatic stress disorder, sleep disorders), and cognitive health (e.g., cognitive performance, attention disorders). Some of these effects are direct consequences of the injury or violence itself, while others are due to missing school during recovery, and still others are mediated by the impact of stress on dysregulation of biological pathways involving the hypothalamic-pituitary-adrenal axis and autonomous nervous system (Brunton, 2013; Provençal & Binder, 2015; Theall et al., 2017; McGowan and Matthews, 2018; van den Bergh, Dahnke, & Mennes, 2018). Moreover, children exposed to one incident of violence are more likely to be exposed again, including to other forms of violence (Finkelhor, Ormrod, & Turner, 2007; Finkelhor et al., 2009, 2015).

ADDRESSING OPPORTUNITY GAPS IN PHYSICAL HEALTH AND HEALTH CARE

Opportunity gaps in the physical health and health care of young children can be addressed through efforts focused on poverty reduction, access to pediatric and family health care, antiracism and dismantling of race-based medicine, screening for social influences on health, alternative models for delivering health care, and safe and violence-free environments.

Poverty Reduction

As described throughout previous sections of this chapter, poverty is a major contributor to various opportunity gaps for young children—for example, by affecting housing quality, access to health care, and educational settings. Poverty reduction is therefore a major promising focus of efforts to reduce these gaps. According to a prior National Academies report on child poverty (National Academies, 2019), three general sets of forces affect poverty: (1) demographics (e.g., parental age and household size), (2) the economy (e.g., labor markets), and (3) government policy. While the first two forces are challenging to address through interventions, studies of government policy demonstrate promising avenues for programs aimed at reducing child poverty. The above National Academies report reviews in detail the evidence behind such policies and practices, and we briefly summarize them here.

Among those federal governmental programs specifically designed to address poverty are the earned income tax credit, the child tax credit, and the Supplemental Nutrition Assistance Program, which provide cash or in-kind transfers to low-income families, and all of which have been shown to reduce poverty and improve child health outcomes. The temporary expansion of the child tax credit in response to the COVID-19 pandemic had a significant impact on poverty alleviation, reducing child poverty by about 30% and decreasing food insufficiency, with implications for the well-being of many of the nation's most vulnerable children. This expansion has expired, although several states are considering their own child tax credits (Shafer et al., 2022). Indeed, state and local governments have been active in policy making to reduce child poverty, including state supplements to the federal earned income tax credit and programs designed to increase take-up and use of benefits. Nongovernmental organizations have also been active players in pursuing poverty reduction, including by funding research and programs focused on understanding and addressing determinants of low take-up of safety net benefits.

Access to Pediatric and Family Health Care

Research demonstrates that healthy child development begins prior to conception and is dependent upon a strong prenatal foundation. Research has shown, for example, that a family's access to high-quality resources for limiting chronic stress reduces the risk for disrupted development and can alleviate disparities based on race/ethnicity and socioeconomic status (National Academies, 2019). To address psychosocial adversities and social determinants of health within the medical home, providers need culturally competent care models, mental health expertise on the team, and training in screening for and addressing psychosocial adversity (Bair-Merritt et al., 2015). In addition, medical homes need to link intentionally with community-based resources and centralized, colocated community services to optimize transitions in care, promote care coordination, and address health-related social needs (Garg et al., 2012).

Antiracism and Dismantling of Race-based Medicine

Medical providers who receive ongoing training in culturally and linguistically competent care are better able to provide appropriate care to diverse populations (National Academies, 2017). Health care systems can prioritize efforts to address inequities in health and institutional and structural racism by continually reviewing policies, protocols, and strategies, as well as promoting antiracist practices and working to develop trustworthy institutions.

Race-based medicine is a clear driver of opportunity gaps in medical treatment and care. Antiracism is an active practice that involves learning about how racism is constructed, operationalized, and perpetuated and working to dismantle those systems. A number of steps could be taken to dismantle race-based medicine, some of which were discussed earlier in this chapter. They include abandoning the use of race in clinical algorithms and incorporating more complex and nuanced understandings of racism and its impact on health outcomes. In addition, reform of standardized examinations and board exams for medical professionals could eliminate testing on race-based guidelines and racial heuristics. Medical institutions, medical societies, and health care providers could work to advance their recognition of racism in medical research, education, training, and practice, and implement infrastructure for accountability in this regard and motivation to contribute to change. Providers could use clear language to describe racism and racial justice and serve as role models in their own efforts to reduce racial bias.

Screening for Social Influences on Health

The long-term impacts of social adversities on population health are increasingly acknowledged, as is the importance of screening for "health-related social needs" to address social determinants of health (Billioux et al., 2017). Screening for these needs in the pediatric setting holds particular promise for its primary prevention power (Gottlieb, Sandel, & Adler, 2013).

Effective screening is indispensable if pediatric health care providers are to identify and address health-related social needs, thereby helping to prevent and mitigate the health effects of social adversity for families, for children, and for the adults that children will become. These efforts include screening for both risk and protective factors, engaging families and communities in developing screening tools and protocols, establishing person-centered screening priorities for health-related social needs, ensuring that screening is conducted by staff members trained in strengths-based approaches, recognizing that screening is not risk-free for families, and acknowledging family-level risks in a broader historical context (Chung et al., 2016; Andermann, 2018; Flacks & Boynton-Jarrett, 2018; Gears et al., 2021). In addition, providers can ensure that they have the tools to make appropriate referrals to social and other community services if screening results in the identification of such nonmedical needs.

Alternative Models for Delivering Health Care

Group visits for preventive care, in which a group format is used for six to eight families with similarly aged children, have been studied for nearly 50 years (Osborn & Woolley, 1981; Dodds et al., 1993; Rice & Slater, 1997; Taylor, Davis, & Kemper, 1997a,b; Taylor & Kemper, 1998; Jones et al., 2018; Gullett et al., 2019; Fenick et al., 2020). Group visits have also been suggested in systematic and narrative reviews as an effective alternative format for preventive care for young children, particularly for low-income families (Coker et al., 2013; Oldfield, Rosenthal, & Coker, 2020). In group visits, families receive preventive care in a supportive group setting; have more time with providers than they would in an individual visit; and are more likely to have their social, behavioral, and developmental needs addressed (Oldfield, Rosenthal, & Coker, 2020). Yet despite the evidence of effectiveness for group visits, this format for child preventive care has not been widely implemented. There remains a critical need for research comparing models for delivering primary care and examining their impact on racial/ethnic and socioeconomic inequities in preventive care utilization and health outcomes.

Safe and Violence-free Environments

Given the numerous risk factors that place children at higher risk of exposure to unsafe environments, individual and family interventions are unlikely to be sufficient; multilevel societal interventions and policies are needed.

At the family level, counseling and support to alleviate family tension can help reduce the risk of interpersonal violence. In addition, counseling in a health care setting can educate families about restraints for children in vehicles, firearm safety, drowning risks, and other aspects of home safety. Interventions can also address the upstream determinants of family conflict, such as poverty and unemployment, through policies to increase income and promote labor force participation. As noted earlier, for example, the child tax credit and earned income tax credit have been found to improve household resources and reduce child injuries and neglect (Hamad

& Rehkopf, 2016; Klevens et al., 2017; Averett & Wang, 2018; Rostad et al., 2020; Kovski et al., 2022).

At the community level, increasing the supply of high-quality affordable housing can help improve the safety of homes (National Academies, 2019). Additionally, school and health care systems can serve as anchor institutions to help address the root causes of unsafe environments, including housing insecurity, blight, and crime, by supporting neighborhood development (Sharkey, Torrats-Espinosa, & Takyard, 2017; Kelleher, Reece, & Sandel, 2018). Urban planning can improve road safety and prevent traffic and pedestrian deaths among children. Also at the community level, evidence-based programs for young people can be implemented, such as those that include tutoring or mentoring, sports, cognitive-behavioral therapy, and summer jobs, which randomized controlled trials have shown lead to decreased involvement in crime and violence (National Academies, 2019). Finally, to address police brutality that children may witness, better data are needed on the epidemiology of deaths and injuries at the hands of police to inform possible interventions, such as demilitarization or decriminalizing of such behaviors as loitering (Krieger et al., 2015; Alang et al., 2017).

At the policy level, there are multiple ways to address risk factors farther upstream at the population level. To address traffic injuries, for example, policy makers could enact legislation to reduce speed limits, while policies targeting playground injuries could include legislation and enforcement of appropriate standards to reduce risk. Government could also test new Medicaid payment models that would engage providers and other community organizations in addressing housing safety concerns, especially those focused on young children (National Academies, 2019). The World Health Organization's *World Report on Child Injury Prevention* provides additional detail on evidence-based interventions for each of the primary types of injury, including those that are beyond the scope of the present report (Peden et al., 2008).

CONCLUSIONS

Healthy birth, medical care, nutrition, and safe and healthy environments are key determinants in ensuring that children have optimal physical health. In all of these cases, however, notable disparities exist by race/ethnicity, income, rural versus urban residence, and immigration status.

In the prenatal period, adverse outcomes experienced by children and birthing people are often due to preventable pregnancy and birth complications, inadequate access to health insurance, and suboptimal prenatal care. These outcomes can have lifelong consequences for children's health and well-being. Early life, including the in utero and even preconception periods, includes critical points during which exposures can influence the trajectory of physical health. Gaps in opportunities intertwine and build on each other over the life course and across generations. Economic insecurity, for example, drives adverse birth outcomes, which then become determinants of later-life challenges that can impact educational experiences.

Proper nutrition plays a large role in physical development, and young children are the most vulnerable to nutrition deficits given the important developmental changes that occur during the first years of life. Existing programs and tax credit policies play an important role for the poorest children, and recent extensions to these programs may help reduce child hunger and poor nutrition. Children also need safe environments in which to grow, develop, and thrive. They need to have stable and secure housing. Their homes and places of play and schooling need to be free from contaminants (e.g., lead) and allergens (e.g., mold), and from exposure to violence and unsafe conditions.

As noted in other chapters of this report, access to high-quality care and programs that can aid in meeting the above needs can vary significantly from state to state. Programs administered at the state level, such as Medicaid, have differing criteria for eligibility that limit access in ways that affect both parents and children. Lack of access to adequate health care in the early years reduces opportunities to screen for, identify, and intervene on a number of health and developmental concerns. Failure to provide these opportunities early in life can lead to worse outcomes or exacerbate health issues that are cause for concern. Children of color and those from lower-income households are more likely to experience these opportunity gaps. The COVID-19 pandemic and related policies, such as school closures, exacerbated these disparities, because of both the disproportionate burden of disease experienced by low-income communities and people of color and the further limitations placed on access to key material and psychosocial resources among marginalized groups.

Stable access to quality health care is essential for child health and development. For young children, health care involves communication and relationships between clinical systems and caregivers. It is important to understand, however, that the broader social and political context impacts engagement with the health care system for families. Critical to a child's optimal physical health and development are equitable access to a stable medical home, one that provides health promotion and preventive care and is patient and family centered, and a social context that supports child, caregiver, and family well-being. Also essential to the development and well-being of children in their early years is having healthy and well-cared-for parents. The absence of these conditions lays the foundation for opportunity gaps in physical and cognitive well-being in the early years that can persist into adolescence and adulthood.

REFERENCES

Abel, K.M., Wicks, S., Susser, E.S., Dalman, C., Pedersen, M.G., Mortensen, P.B., & Webb, R.T. (2010). Birth weight, schizophrenia, and adult mental disorder: Is risk confined to the smallest babies? *Archives of General Psychiatry*, 67(9), 923–30. https://doi.org/10.1001/archgenpsychiatry.2010.100

Acevedo-Garcia, D., McArdle, N., Tosypuk, T.L., Lefkowitz, B., & Krimgold, B.K. (2007). *Children left behind: How metropolitan areas are failing America's children.* Harvard School of Public Health and the Center for the Advancement of Health. Available: https://escholarship.org/uc/item/28t4f2p4

Acevedo-Garcia, D., Osypuk, T.L., McArdle, N., & Williams, D.R. (2008). Toward a policy-relevant analysis of geographic and racial/ethnic disparities in child health. *Health Affairs*, 27(2), 321–33. https://doi.org/10.1377/hlthaff.27.2.321

Acevedo-Garcia, D., McArdle, N., Noelke, C., Huber, R., Huntington, N., & Sofer, N. (2019). *The child opportunity gap: Inequities in child opportunity within metros.* Brandeis University. Available: https://www.diversitydatakids.org/research-library/data-visualization/child-opportunity-gap

Adler, N.E., & Stewart, J. (2010). Health disparities across the lifespan: Meaning, methods, and mechanisms. *Annals of the New York Academy of Sciences*, 1186(1), 5–23. https://doi.org/10.1111/j.1749-6632.2009.05337.x

Ahmad, S.A., Sayed, M.H., Barua, S., Khan, M.H., Faruquee, M.H., Jalil, A., Hadi, S.A., & Talukder, H.K. (2001). Arsenic in drinking water and pregnancy outcomes. *Environmental Health Perspectives*, 109(6), 629–31. https://doi.org/10.1289/ehp.0110962

Akinbami, L.J., Moorman, J.E., & Liu, X. (2011). Asthma prevalence, health care use, and mortality: United States, 2005–2009. *National Health Statistics Reports*, 32. Washington, DC: Department of Health and Human Services, Centers for Disease Control and Prevention, National Center for Health Statistics.

Alang, S., McAlpine, D., McCready, E., & Hardeman, R. (2017). Police brutality and black health: Setting the agenda for public health scholars. *American Journal of Public Health*, 107(5), 662–5. https://doi.org/10.2105/AJPH.2017.303691

Alexander, D., & Currie, J. (2017). Is it who you are or where you live? Residential segregation and racial gaps in childhood asthma. *Journal of Health Economics*, 55, 186–200. https://doi.org/10.1016/j.jhealeco.2017.07.003

Alhusen, J.L., Bower, K.M., Epstein, E., & Sharps, P. (2016). Racial discrimination and adverse birth outcomes: An integrative review. *Journal of Midwifery & Women's Health*, 61(6), 707–20. https://doi.org/10.1111/jmwh.12490

Ali, M.M., West, K., Teich, J.L., Lynch, S., Mutter, R., & Dubenitz, J. (2019). Utilization of mental health services in educational setting by adolescents in the United States. *Journal of School Health*, 89(5), 393–401. https://doi.org/10.1111/josh.12753

Almond, D., & Currie, J. (2010). *Human capital development before age five.* (Working Paper No. 15827). National Bureau of Economic Research. Available: https://www.nber.org/papers/w15827

Almond, D., Hoynes, H., & Whitmore Schanzenbach, D. (2011). Inside the war on poverty: The impact of food stamps on birth outcomes. *The Review of Economics and Statistics*, 93(2), 387–403. http://www.jstor.org/stable/23015943

American Academy of Pediatrics. (2015). *A medical home where everybody knows your name: What is a medical home?* HealthyChildren. Available: https://healthychildren.org/English/family-life/health-management/Pages/A-Medical-Home-Where-Everybody-Knows-Your-Name.aspx

American College of Nurse-Midwives. (2021). *Congress reintroduces black maternal health "momnibus" legislative package.* Available: https://www.midwife.org/congress-reintroduces-black-maternal-health-momnibus-legislative-package

American College of Obstetricians and Gynecologists Committee on Obstetric Practice. (2021). Reducing prenatal exposure to toxic environmental agents. Opinion No. 832. *Obstetrics and Gynecology*, 138(1), e40–54. https://doi.org/10.1097/AOG.0000000000004449

American Medical Association. (2021). *AMA adopts guidelines that confront systemic racism in medicine.* (Press Release). Available: https://www.ama-assn.org/press-center/press-releases/ama-adopts-guidelines-confront-systemic-racism-medicine

American Public Health Association. (2021). *Expanding Medicaid coverage for birthing people to one year postpartum.* (Policy No. LB21-02). Available: https://www.apha.org/Policies-and-Advocacy/Public-Health-Policy-Statements/Policy-Database/2022/01/07/Expanding-Medicaid-Coverage-for-Birthing-People-to-One-Year-Postpartum

Amutah, C., Greenidge, K., Mante, A., Munyikwa, M., Surya, S.L., Higginbotham, E., Jones, D.S., Lavizzo-Mourey, R., Roberts, D., Tsai, J., & Aysola, J. (2021). Misrepresenting race—The role of medical schools in propagating physician bias. *New England Journal of Medicine*, 384(9), 872–8. https://doi.org/10.1056/NEJMms2025768

Andermann, A. (2018). Screening for social determinants of health in clinical care: Moving from the margins to the mainstream. *Public Health Reviews*, 39(1), 1–17. https://doi.org/10.1186/s40985-018-0094-7

Anker, B., Tripodis, Y., Long, W.E., & Garg, A. (2018). Income disparities in the association of the medical home with child health. *Clinical Pediatrics*, 57(7), 827–34. https://doi.org/10.1177/0009922817733697

Ansell, D.A., & McDonald, E.K. (2015). Bias, black lives, and academic medicine. *New England Journal of Medicine*, 372(12), 1087–9. https://doi.org/10.1056/NEJMp1500832

Arnold Ventures. (2020). *Social programs that work review: Evidence summary for the nurse family partnership.* Available: https://evidencebasedprograms.org/document/nurse-family-partnership-nfp-evidence-summary

Auchincloss, A.H., Mujahid, M.S., Shen, M., Michos, E.D., Whitt-Glover, M.C., & Diez Roux, A.V. (2013). Neighborhood health-promoting resources and obesity risk (the multi-ethnic study of atherosclerosis). *Obesity*, 21(3), 621–8. https://doi.org/10.1002/oby.20255

Averett, S., & Wang, Y. (2018). Effects of higher EITC payments on children's health, quality of home environment, and noncognitive skills. *Public Finance Review*, 46(4), 519–57. https://doi.org/10.1177/1091142116654965

Baek, M., Outrich, M.B., Barnett, K.S., & Reece, J. (2021). Neighborhood-level lead paint hazard for children under 6: A tool for proactive and equitable intervention. *International Journal of Environmental Research and Public Health*, 18(5), 2471. https://doi.org/10.3390/ijerph18052471

Baetzel, A., Brown, D.J., Koppera, P., Rentz, A., Thompson, A., & Christensen, R. (2019). Adultification of black children in pediatric anesthesia. *Anesthesia and Analgesia*, 129(4), 1118–23. https://doi.org/10.1213/ANE.0000000000004274

Bailey, Z.D., Krieger, N., Agénor, M., Graves, J., Linos, N., & Bassett, M.T. (2017). Structural racism and health inequities in the USA: Evidence and interventions. *Lancet*, 389(10077), 1453–63. https://doi.org/10.1016/S0140-6736(17)30569-X

Bair-Merritt, M.H., Mandal, M., Garg, A., & Cheng, T.L. (2015). Addressing psychosocial adversity within the patient-centered medical home: Expert-created measurable standards. *The Journal of Primary Prevention*, 36(4), 213–25. https://doi.org/10.1007/s10935-015-0390-7

Batstone, K. (2021). *The Momnibus Act: Improving black maternal health outcomes by increasing doula and midwifery accessibility.* National Women's Health Network. Available: https://nwhn.org/the-momnibus-act-improving-black-maternal-health-outcomes-by-increasing-doula-and-midwifery-accessibility/

Bear, K., Braveman, P., Dixon-Roman, E., Iruka, I.U., Laraque-Arena, D., LaVeist, T., Murray, V.M., Rodriguez, L.J., & Taylor, S. (2022). Dismantling systemic racism and advancing health equity throughout research infrastructures. *NAM Perspectives*. National Academy of Medicine. Available: https://nam.edu/dismantling-systemic-racism-and-advancing-health-equity-throughout-research/

Beck, A.F., Huang, B., Chundur, R., & Kahn, R.S. (2014). Housing code violation density associated with emergency department and hospital use by children with asthma. *Health Affairs*, 33(11), 1993–2002. https://doi.org/10.1377/hlthaff.2014.0496

Bélanger, R., Mayer-Crittenden, C., Minor-Corriveau, M., & Robillard, M. (2018). Gross motor outcomes of children born prematurely in northern Ontario and followed by a neonatal follow-up programme. *Physiotherapy Canada*, 70, 1–7. https://doi.org/10.3138/ptc.2017-13

Ben-Shlomo, Y., Mishra, G., & Kuh, D. (2014). Life course epidemiology. *Handbook of Epidemiology*. Springer. Available: https://doi.org/10.1007/978-0-387-09834-0_56

Bertagnolli, M., Luu, T.M., Lewandowski, A.J., Leeson, P., & Nuyt, A.M. (2016). Preterm birth and hypertension: Is there a link? *Current Hypertension Reports*, 18(4), 28. https://doi.org/10.1007/s11906-016-0637-6

Bethell, C., Reuland, C.H., Halfon, N., & Schor, E.L. (2004). Measuring the quality of preventive and developmental services for young children: National estimates and patterns of clinicians' performance. *Pediatrics*, 113(6 Suppl), 1973–83. https://doi.org/10.1542/peds.113.S5.1973

Bethell, C., Reuland, C., Schor, E., Abrahms, M., & Halfon, N. (2011). Rates of parent-centered developmental screening: Disparities and links to services access. *Pediatrics*, 128(1), 146–55. https://doi.org/10.1542/peds.2010-0424

Bethell, C., Jones, J., Gombojav, N., Linkenbach, J., & Sege, R. (2019). Positive childhood experiences and adult mental and relational health in a statewide sample: Associations across adverse childhood experiences levels. *JAMA Pediatrics*, 173(11), e193007, 1–10. https://doi.org/10.1001/jamapediatrics.2019.3007

Bhutta, A.T., Cleves, M.A., Casey, P.H., Cradock, M.M., & Anand, K.J. (2002). Cognitive and behavioral outcomes of school-aged children who were born preterm: A meta-analysis. *Journal of the American Medical Association*, 288(6), 728–37. https://doi.org/10.1001/jama.288.6.728

Billioux, A., Verlander, K., Anthony, S., & Alley, D. (2017). Standardized screening for health-related social needs in clinical settings: The accountable health communities screening tool. Discussion Paper. *NAM Perspectives*. National Academy of Medicine. https://doi.org/10.31478/201705b

Blair, A., Ross, N.A., Gariepy, G., & Schmitz, N. (2014). How do neighborhoods affect depression outcomes? A realist review and a call for the examination of causal pathways. *Social Psychiatry and Psychiatric Epidemiology*, 49(6), 873–87. https://doi.org/10.1002/oby.20255

Bonamy, A.K., Holmström, G., Stephansson, O., Ludvigsson, J.F., & Cnattingius, S. (2013). Preterm birth and later retinal detachment: A population-based cohort study of more than 3 million children and young adults. *Ophthalmology*, 120(11), 2278–85. https://doi.org/10.1016/j.ophtha.2013.03.035

Bower, K.M., Geller, R.J., Perrin, N.A., & Alhusen, J. (2018). Experiences of racism and preterm birth: Findings from a pregnancy risk assessment monitoring system, 2004 through 2012. *Womens Health Issues*, 28(6), 495–501. https://doi.org/10.1016/j.whi.2018.06.002

Braun, L. (2014). *Breathing race into the machine: The surprising career of the spirometer from plantation to genetics*. University of Minnesota Press. https://doi.org/10.5749/minnesota/9780816683574.001.0001

Braveman, P., Dominguez, T.P., Burke, W., Dolan, S.M., Stevenson, D.K., Jackson, F.M., Collins, J.W., Driscoll, D.A., Haley, T., Acker, J., Shaw, G.M., McCabe, E.R.B., Hay, W.W., Thornburg, K., Acevedo-Garcia, D., Cordero, J.F., Wise, P.H., Legaz, G., Rashied-Henry, K., Frost, J., Verbiest, S., & Waddell, L. (2021). Explaining the black-white disparity in preterm birth: A consensus statement from a multi-disciplinary scientific work group convened by the March of Dimes. *Frontiers in Reproductive Health*, 3. https://doi.org/10.3389/frph.2021.684207

Bronfenbrenner, U. (1979). Contexts of child rearing: Problems and prospects. *American Psychologist*, 34(10), 844–50. https://doi.org/10.1037/0003-066X.34.10.844

Brunton, P.J. (2013). Effects of maternal exposure to social stress during pregnancy: Consequences for mother and offspring. *Reproduction*, 146(5), R175–89. https://doi.org/10.1530/REP-13-0258

Burd, L., Severud, R., Kerbeshian, J., & Klug, M.G. (1999). Prenatal and perinatal risk factors for autism. *Journal of Perinatal Medicine*, 27(6), 441–50. https://doi.org/10.1515/JPM.1999.059

Burton, L. (2007). Childhood adultification in economically disadvantaged families: A conceptual model. *Family Relations*, 56(4), 329–45. https://doi.org/10.1111/j.1741-3729.2007.00463.x

Casey, J.A., Savitz, D.A., Rasmussen, S.G., Ogburn, E.L., Pollak, J., Mercer, D.G., & Schwartz, B.S. (2016). Unconventional natural gas development and birth outcomes in Pennsylvania, USA. *Epidemiology*, 27(2), 163–72. https://doi.org/10.1097/EDE.0000000000000387

Centers for Disease Control and Prevention (CDC). (2009). *Healthy places terminology*. Available: https://www.cdc.gov/healthyplaces/terminology.htm

———. (2014). *Child maltreatment: Facts at a glance*. Available: https://www.cdc.gov/violenceprevention/pdf/childmaltreatment-facts-at-a-glance.pdf

———. (2020). *Health of Black or African American non-Hispanic population*. Available: https://www.cdc.gov/nchs/fastats/black-health.htm

———. (2021). *Injuries among children and teens*. Available: https://www.cdc.gov/injury/features/child-injury/index.html

———. (2022). *Working together to reduce black maternal mortality*. Available: https://www.cdc.gov/healthequity/features/maternal-mortality/index.html#print

Centers for Medicare & Medicaid Services (CMS). (2020a). *CMS issues urgent call to action following drastic decline in care for children in Medicaid and Children's Health Insurance Program due to COVID-19 pandemic.* (Press Release). Available: https://www.cms.gov/newsroom/press-releases/cms-issues-urgent-call-action-following-drastic-decline-care-children-medicaid-and-childrens-health

———. (2020b). *Early and periodic screening, diagnostic, and treatment*. Available: https://www.medicaid.gov/medicaid/benefits/early-and-periodic-screening-diagnostic-and-treatment/index.html

Chapman, E.N., Kaatz, A., & Carnes, M. (2013). Physicians and implicit bias: How doctors may unwittingly perpetuate health care disparities. *Journal of General Internal Medicine*, 28(11), 1504–10. https://doi.org/10.1007/s11606-013-2441-1

Chetty, R., Hendren, N., & Katz, L.F. (2016). The effects of exposure to better neighborhoods on children: New evidence from the moving to opportunity experiment. *American Economic Review*, 106(4), 855–902. https://doi.org/10.1257/aer.20150572

Chung, E.K., Siegel, B.S., Garg, A., Conroy, K., Gross, R.S., Long, D.A., Lewis, G., Osman, C.J., Messito, M.J., & Wade, R. Jr. (2016). Screening for social determinants of health among children and families living in poverty: A guide for clinicians. *Current Problems in Pediatric and Adolescent Health Care*, 46(5), 135–53. https://doi.org/10.1016/j.cppeds.2016.02.004

Chung, P.J., Lee, T.C., Morrison, J.L., & Schuster, M.A. (2006). Preventive care for children in the United States: Quality and barriers. *Annual Review of Public Health*, 27, 491–515. https://doi.org/10.1146/annurev.publhealth.27.021405.102155

Children's Defense Fund. (2022). *Gun violence prevention*. Available: https://www.childrens-defense.org/policy/policy-priorities/gun-violence-prevention

Clark, N., Demers, P., Karr, C., Koehoorn, M., Lencar, C., Tamburic, L., & Brauer, M. (2010). Effect of early life exposure to air pollution on development of childhood asthma. *Environmental Health Perspectives*, 118, 284–90. https://doi.org/10.1289/ehp.0900916

Clark, R., Anderson, N.B., Clark, V.R., & Williams, D.R. (1999). Racism as a stressor for African Americans: A biopsychosocial model. *American Psychologist*, 54(10), 805.

Cohen, S., Kessler, R., & Gordon, L.U. (1997). *Measuring stress: A guide for health and social scientists*. Oxford, England: Oxford University Press.

Coker, T.R., Windon, A., Moreno, C., Schuster, M.A., & Chung, P.J. (2013). Well-child care clinical practice redesign for young children: A systematic review of strategies and tools. *Pediatrics*, 131(1 Suppl), S5–25. https://doi.org/10.1542/peds.2012-1427c

Collins, J., & Swoveland, E. (2022). The impact of gun violence on children, families, & communities. *Children's Voices*, 23(1). Child Welfare League of America. Available: https://www.cwla.org/the-impact-of-gun-violence-on-children-families-communities/

Commonwealth of Massachusetts. (2022). *Childhood lead poisoning prevention program (CLPPP)*. Available: https://www.mass.gov/orgs/childhood-lead-poisoning-prevention-program

Costa, D.L. (2004). Race and pregnancy outcomes in the twentieth century: A long-term comparison. *The Journal of Economic History*, 64(4), 1056–86. https://www.jstor.org/stable/3874989

Cox, C., Clarkson, T.W., Marsh, D.O., Amin-Zaki, L., Tikriti, S., & Myers, G.G. (1989). Dose-response analysis of infants prenatally exposed to methyl mercury: An application of a single compartment model to single-strand hair analysis. *Environmental Research*, 49(2), 318–32. https://doi.org/10.1016/S0013-9351(89)80075-1

Creanga, A.A., Bateman, B.T., Kuklina, E.V., & Callaghan, W.M. (2014). Racial and ethnic disparities in severe maternal morbidity: A multistate analysis, 2008–2010. *American Journal of Obstetrics and Gynecology*, 210(5), 435.e431–8. https://doi.org/10.1016/j.ajog.2013.11.039

Crump, C., Winkleby, M.A., Sundquist, K., & Sundquist, J. (2011). Risk of diabetes among young adults born preterm in Sweden. *Diabetes Care*, 34(5), 1109–13. https://doi.org/10.2337/dc10-2108

Crump, C., Howell, E.A., Stroustrup, A., McLaughlin, M.A., Sundquist, J., & Sundquist, K. (2019a). Association of preterm birth with risk of ischemic heart disease in adulthood. *JAMA Pediatrics*, 173(8), 736–43. https://doi.org/10.1001/jamapediatrics.2019.1327

Crump, C., Sundquist, J., Winkleby, M.A., & Sundquist, K. (2019b). Preterm birth and risk of chronic kidney disease from childhood into mid-adulthood: National cohort study. *British Medical Journal*, 365, l1346. https://doi.org/10.1136/bmj.l1346

Currie, J., & Walker, R. (2011). Traffic congestion and infant health: Evidence from E-Zpass. *American Economic Journal: Applied Economics*, 3(1), 65–90. Available: https://www.aeaweb.org/articles?id=10.1257/app.3.1.65

Cusick, S.E., & Georgieff, M.K. (2016). The role of nutrition in brain development: The golden opportunity of the "first 1000 days." *The Journal of Pediatrics*, 175, 16–21. https://doi.org/10.1016/j.jpeds.2016.05.013

De Sanctis, V., Soliman, A., Alaaraj, N., Ahmed, S., Alyafei, F., & Hamed, N. (2021). Early and long-term consequences of nutritional stunting: From childhood to adulthood. *Acta Biomedica: The Official Journal of the Society of Medicine and Natural Sciences of Parma*, 92(1), e2021168. https://doi.org/10.23750/abm.v92i1.11346

Dehon, E., Weiss, N., Jones, J., Faulconer, W., Hinton, E., & Sterling, S. (2017). A systematic review of the impact of physician implicit racial bias on clinical decision making. *Academic Emergency Medicine: Official Journal of the Society for Academic Emergency Medicine*, 24(8), 895–904. https://doi.org/10.1111/acem.13214

Department of Health and Human Services, Administration for Children and Families, & Administration on Children, Youth and Families, Children's Bureau. (2021). *Child Maltreatment 2019*. Available: https://www.acf.hhs.gov/sites/default/files/documents/cb/cm2019.pdf

Di Renzo, G.C., Conry, J.A., Blake, J., DeFrancesco, M.S., DeNicola, N., Martin, J.N. Jr., McCue, K.A., Richmond, D., Shah, A., Sutton, P., Woodruff, T.J., van der Poel, S.Z., & Giudice, L.C. (2015). International Federation of Gynecology and Obstetrics opinion on reproductive health impacts of exposure to toxic environmental chemicals. *International Journal of Gynecology & Obstetrics*, 131(3), 219–25. https://doi.org/10.1016/j.ijgo.2015.09.002

Diamanti-Kandarakis, E., Bourguignon, J.P., Giudice, L.C., Hauser, R., Prins, G.S., Soto, A.M., Zoeller, R.T., & Gore, A.C. (2009). Endocrine-disrupting chemicals: An endocrine society scientific statement. *Endocrine Reviews*, 30(4), 293–342. https://doi.org/10.1210/er.2009-0002

Diao, K., Tripodis, Y., Long, W.E., & Garg, A. (2017). Socioeconomic and racial disparities in parental perception and experience of having a medical home, 2007 to 2011–2012. *Academic Pediatrics*, 17(1), 95–103. https://doi.org/10.1016/j.acap.2016.07.006

Diversity Data Kids. (2019). *What is child opportunity?* Brandeis University, diversitydatakids.org. Available: https://www.diversitydatakids.org/research-library/research-brief/what-child-opportunity

Dodds, M., Nicholson, L., Muse, B. III, & Osborn, L.M. (1993). Group health supervision visits more effective than individual visits in delivering health care information. *Pediatrics*, 91(3), 668–670.

Dominguez, T.P., Dunkel-Schetter, C., Glynn, L.M., Hobel, C., & Sandman, C.A. (2008). Racial differences in birth outcomes: The role of general, pregnancy, and racism stress. *Health Psychology*, 27(2), 194–203. https://doi.org/10.1037/0278-6133.27.2.194

Dong, Y., & Yu, J.L. (2011). An overview of morbidity, mortality and long-term outcome of late preterm birth. *World Journal of Pediatrics*, 7(3), 199–204. https://doi.org/10.1007/s12519-011-0290-8

Douthit, N., Kiv, S., Dwolatzky, T., & Biswas, S. (2015). Exposing some important barriers to health care access in the rural USA. *Public Health*, 129(6), 611–20. https://doi.org/10.1016/j.puhe.2015.04.001

Dumas, M.J., & Nelson, J.D. (2016). (Re)Imagining black boyhood: Toward a critical framework for educational research. *Harvard Educational Review*, 86(1), 27–47. https://doi.org/10.17763/0017-8055.86.1.27

Ely, D.M., & Driscoll, A.K. (2019). Infant mortality in the United States, 2017: Data from the period linked birth/infant death file. *National Vital Statistics Reports*, 68(10), 1–20.

Epstein, R., Blake, J., & González, T. (2017). *Girlhood interrupted: The erasure of black girls' childhood*. Center on Poverty and Inequality, Georgetown Law. Available: https://genderjusticeandopportunity.georgetown.edu/wp-content/uploads/2020/06/girlhood-interrupted.pdf

Evens, A., Hryhorczuk, D., Lanphear, B., Lewis, D., Forst, L., & Rosenberg, D. (2015). The effect of childhood lead exposure on school performance in Chicago Public Schools: A population-based retrospective cohort study. *Environmental Health: A Global Access Science Source*, 14, 21. https://doi.org/10.1186/s12940-015-0008-9

Evensen, K.A., Steinshamn, S., Tjønna, A.E., Stølen, T., Høydal, M.A., Wisløff, U., Brubakk, A.M., & Vik, T. (2009). Effects of preterm birth and fetal growth retardation on cardiovascular risk factors in young adulthood. *Early Human Development*, 85(4), 239–45. https://doi.org/10.1016/j.earlhumdev.2008.10.008

Ewing-Cobbs, L., Prasad, M.R., Kramer, L., Cox, C.S., Jr., Baumgartner, J., Fletcher, S., Mendez, D., Barnes, M., Zhang, X., & Swank, P. (2006). Late intellectual and academic outcomes following traumatic brain injury sustained during early childhood. *Journal of Neurosurgery*, 105(4 Suppl), 287–96. https://doi.org/10.3171/ped.2006.105.4.287

Fenick, A.M., Leventhal, J.M., Gilliam, W., & Rosenthal, M.S. (2020). A randomized controlled trial of group well-child care: Improved attendance and vaccination timeliness. *Clinical Pediatrics*, 59(7), 686–91. https://doi.org/10.1177/0009922820908582

Finkelhor, D., Ormrod, R.K., & Turner, H.A. (2007). Re-victimization patterns in a national longitudinal sample of children and youth. *Child Abuse & Neglect*, 31(5), 479–502. https://doi.org/10.1016/j.chiabu.2006.03.012

Finkelhor, D., Turner, H., Ormrod, R., Hamby, S., & Kracke, K. (2009). Children's exposure to violence: A comprehensive national survey. *National Survey of Children's Exposure to Violence*. Office of Justice Programs, Department of Justice. Available: https://www.ojp.gov/pdffiles1/ojjdp/227744.pdf

Finkelhor, D., Turner, H.A., Shattuck, A., & Hamby, S.L. (2015). Prevalence of childhood exposure to violence, crime, and abuse: Results from the national survey of children's exposure to violence. *JAMA Pediatrics*, 169(8), 746–54. https://doi.org/10.1001/jamapediatrics.2015.0676

FitzGerald, C., & Hurst, S. (2017). Implicit bias in healthcare professionals: A systematic review. *BMC Medical Ethics*, 18(1), 19. https://doi.org/10.1186/s12910-017-0179-8

Flacks, J., & Boynton-Jarrett, J.R. (2018). *A strengths-based approach to screening families for health-related social needs*. Center for the Study of Social Policy. Available: https://cssp.org/resource/strengths-based-approaches-screening-families-final/

Fleisch, A.F., Luttmann-Gibson, H., Perng, W., Rifas-Shiman, S.L., Coull, B.A., Kloog, I., Koutrakis, P., Schwartz, J.D., Zanobetti, A., Mantzoros, C.S., Gillman, M.W., Gold, D.R., & Oken, E. (2017). Prenatal and early life exposure to traffic pollution and cardiometabolic health in childhood. *Pediatric Obesity*, 12(1), 48–57. https://doi.org/10.1111/ijpo.12106

Flores, G. (2010). Technical report—Racial and ethnic disparities in the health and health care of children. *Pediatrics*, 125(4), e979–1020. https://doi.org/10.1542/peds.2010-0188

Food and Agriculture Organization of the United Nations, International Fund for Agricultural Development, United Nations Children's Fund, World Food Programme, & World Health Organization. (2021). *The state of food security and nutrition in the world. Transforming food systems for food security, improved nutrition and affordable healthy diets for all*. https://doi.org/10.4060/cb4474en

Foster, H., Brooks-Gunn, J., & Martin, A. (2007). Poverty/socioeconomic status and exposure to violence in the lives of children and adolescents. *The Cambridge handbook of violent behavior and aggression*, 664–87. Cambridge, UK: Cambridge University Press.

Foster, K., Mitchell, R., Van, C., Young, A., McCloughen, A., & Curtis, K. (2019a). Resilient, recovering, distressed: A longitudinal qualitative study of parent psychosocial trajectories following child critical injury. *Injury*, 50(10), 1605–11. https://doi.org/10.1016/j.injury.2019.05.003

Foster, K., Mitchell, R., Young, A., Van, C., & Curtis, K. (2019b). Parent experiences and psychosocial support needs 6 months following paediatric critical injury: A qualitative study. *Injury*, 50(5), 1082–8. https://doi.org/10.1016/j.injury.2019.01.004

Foverskov, E., White, J., Frøslev, T., Sørenson, H., & Hamad, R. (2022). Risk of psychiatric disorders among refugee children and adolescents living in disadvantaged neighborhoods. *Journal of the American Medical Association: Pediatrics*, 176(11), 1107–14. https://doi.org/10.1001/jamapediatrics.2022.3235

Freeman, B.K., & Coker, T.R. (2018). Six questions for well-child care redesign. *Academic Pediatrics*, 18(6), 609–19. https://doi.org/10.1016/j.acap.2018.05.003

Fulton, J.B., Yeates, K.O., Taylor, H.G., Walz, N.C., & Wade, S.L. (2012). Cognitive predictors of academic achievement in young children 1 year after traumatic brain injury. *Neuropsychology*, 26(3), 314–22. https://doi.org/10.1037/a0027973

Gale, C.R., & Martyn, C.N. (2004). Birth weight and later risk of depression in a national birth cohort. *British Journal of Psychiatry*, 184, 28–33. https://doi.org/10.1192/bjp.184.1.28

Galler, J.R., Bringas-Vega, M.L., Tang, Q., Rabinowitz, A.G., Musa, K.I., Chai, W.J., & Valdés-Sosa, P.A. (2021). Neurodevelopmental effects of childhood malnutrition: A neuroimaging perspective. *NeuroImage*, 231, 117828. https://doi.org/10.1016/j.neuroimage.2021.117828

Garg, A., Sandel, M., Dworkin, P.H., Kahn, R.S., & Zuckerman, B. (2012). From medical home to health neighborhood: Transforming the medical home into a community-based health neighborhood. *The Journal of Pediatrics*, 160(4), 535–6. Available: https://www.bmc.org/sites/default/files/About_Us/MAG/health-neighborhood.pdf

Gears, H., Casau, A., Buck, L., & Yard, R. (2021). *Accelerating child health care transformation: Key opportunities for improving pediatric care*. Center for Health Care Strategies. Available: https://www.nationalcomplex.care/wp-content/uploads/2022/06/Accelerating-Child-Health-Care-Transformation-Key-Opportunities-for-Improving-Pediatric-Care.pdf

Georgieff, M.K., Brunette, K.E., & Tran, P.V. (2015). Early life nutrition and neural plasticity. *Development and Psychopathology*, 27(2), 411–23. https://doi.org/10.1017/S0954579415000061

Gilchrist, J., Ballesteros, M., & Parker, E.M. (2012). Vital signs: Unintentional injury deaths among persons aged 0–19 years—United States, 2000–2009. *Morbidity and Mortality Weekly Report*, 61, 270–6. Available: https://www.cdc.gov/mmwr/preview/mmwrhtml/mm6115a5.htm

Giudice, L., Woodruff, T., & Conry, J. (2017). Reproductive and developmental environmental health. *Obstetrics, Gynaecology & Reproductive Medicine*, 27(3), 99–101. https://doi.org/10.1097/GCO.0b013e3283404e59

Glass, T.A., & Bilal, U. (2016). Are neighborhoods causal? Complications arising from the 'stickiness' of ZNA. *Social Science & Medicine*, 166, 244–53. https://doi.org/10.1016/j.socscimed.2016.01.001

Goff, P.A., Jackson, M.C., Di Leone, B.A.L., Culotta, C.M., & DiTomasso, N.A. (2014). The essence of innocence: Consequences of dehumanizing black children. *Journal of Personality and Social Psychology*, 106(4), 526. https://doi.org/10.1037/a0035663

Golberstein, E., Wen, H., & Miller, B.F. (2020). Coronavirus disease 2019 (COVID-19) and mental health for children and adolescents. *JAMA Pediatrics*, 174(9), 819–20. https://doi.org/10.1001/jamapediatrics.2020.1456

Goldstick, J.E., Cunningham, R.M., & Carter, P.M. (2022). Current causes of death in children and adolescents in the United States. *New England Journal of Medicine*, 386(20), 1955–6. https://www.nejm.org/doi/full/10.1056/NEJMc2201761

Gore, A.C., Chappell, V.A., Fenton, S.E., Flaws, J.A., Nadal, A., Prins, G.S., Toppari, J., & Zoeller, R.T. (2015). Executive summary to EDC-2: The Endocrine Society's second scientific statement on endocrine-disrupting chemicals. *Endocrine Reviews*, 36(6), 593–602. https://doi.org/10.1210/er.2015-1093

Gottlieb, L., Sandel, M., & Adler, N. (2013). Collecting and applying data on social determinants of health in health care settings. *The Journal of the American Medical Association: Internal Medicine*, 173(11), 1017–20. https://doi.org/10.1001/jamainternmed.2013.56

Goyal, M.K., Kuppermann, N., Cleary, S.D., Teach, S.J., & Chamberlain, J.M. (2015). Racial disparities in pain management of children with appendicitis in emergency departments. *The Journal of the American Medical Association: Pediatrics*, 169(11), 996–1002. https://doi.org/10.1001/jamapediatrics.2015.1915

Guan, A., Hamad, R., Batra, A., Bush, N., Tylavsky, F., & LeWinn, K. (2021). The revised WIC food package and child development: A quasi-experimental study. *Pediatrics* 147(2), e20201853. https://doi.org/10.1542/peds.2020-1853

Guillory, J.D. (1968). The pro-slavery arguments of Dr. Samuel A. Cartwright. *Louisiana History: The Journal of the Louisiana Historical Association*, 9(3), 209–27. https://www.jstor.org/stable/4231017

Gullett, H., Salib, M., Rose, J., & Stange, K.C. (2019). An evaluation of CenteringParenting: A group well-child care model in an urban federally qualified community health center. *The Journal of Alternative and Complementary Medicine*, 25(7), 727–32. https://doi.org/10.1089/acm.2019.0090

Ha, S., Hu, H., Roth, J., Kan, H., & Xu, X. (2015). Associations between residential proximity to power plants and adverse birth outcomes. *American Journal of Epidemiology*, 182(3). https://doi.org/10.1093/aje/kwv042

Hagan, J.F., Shaw, J.S., & Duncan, P.M. (2017). *Bright futures: Guidelines for health supervision of infants, children and adolescents*. (4th ed.). American Academy of Pediatrics. Available: https://downloads.aap.org/AAP/PDF/Bright%20Futures/BF4_Introduction.pdf

Haider, A.H., Sexton, J., Sriram, N., Cooper, L.A., Efron, D.T., Swoboda, S., Villegas, C.V., Haut, E.R., Bonds, M., Pronovost, P.J., & Lipsett, P.A. (2011). Association of unconscious race and social class bias with vignette-based clinical assessments by medical students. *The Journal of the American Medical Association*, 306(9), 942–51. https://doi.org/10.1001/jama.2011.1248

Halfon, N., Regalado, M., Sareen, H., Inkelas, M., Reuland, C.H., Glascoe, F.P., & Olson, L.M. (2004). Assessing development in the pediatric office. *Pediatrics*, 113(6 Suppl), 1926–33. https://doi.org/10.1016/j.acap.2010.08.008

Halfon, N., Stevens, G.D., Larson, K., & Olson, L.M. (2011). Duration of a well-child visit: Association with content, family-centeredness, and satisfaction. *Pediatrics*, 128(4), 657–64. https://doi.org/10.1542/peds.2011-0586

Hall, W.J., Chapman, M.V., Lee, K.M., Merino, Y.M., Thomas, T.W., Payne, B.K., Eng, E., Day, S.H., & Coyne-Beasley, T. (2015). Implicit racial/ethnic bias among health care professionals and its influence on health care outcomes: A systematic review. *American Journal of Public Health*, 105(12), e60–76. https://doi.org/10.2105/AJPH.2015.302903

Hamad, R. (2020). Natural and unnatural experiments in epidemiology. *Epidemiology*, 31(6), 768–70. https://doi.org/10.1097/EDE.0000000000001242

Hamad, R., & Rehkopf, D.H. (2016). Poverty and child development: A longitudinal study of the impact of the earned income tax credit. *American Journal of Epidemiology*, 183(9), 775–84. https://doi.org/10.1093/aje/kwv317

Hamad, R., Öztürk, B., Foverskov, E., Pedersen, L., Sørensen, H.T., Bøtker, H.E., & White, J.S. (2020). Association of neighborhood disadvantage with cardiovascular risk factors and events among refugees in Denmark. *The Journal of the American Medical Association: Network Open*, 3(8), e2014196. https://doi.org/10.1001/jamanetworkopen.2020.14196

Hambrick, E.P., Brawner, T.W., & Perry, B.D. (2019). Timing of early-life stress and the development of brain-related capacities. *Frontiers in Behavioral Neuroscience*, 13. https://doi.org/10.3389/fnbeh.2019.00183

Hamilton, B.E., Martin., J.A., & Osterman, M.J.K. (2020). Births: Provisional data for 2019. (Report No. 008). *Vital Statistics Rapid Release*. Available: https://www.cdc.gov/nchs/data/vsrr/vsrr-8-508.pdf

Harrell, S.P. (2000). A multidimensional conceptualization of racism-related stress: Implications for the well-being of people of color. *American Journal of Orthopsychiatry*, 70(1), 42–57. https://doi.org/10.1037/h0087722

Harris, M.H., Gold, D.R., Rifas-Shiman, S.L., Melly, S.J., Zanobetti, A., Coull, B.A., Schwartz, J.D., Gryparis, A., Kloog, I., Koutrakis, P., Bellinger, D.C., Belfort, M.B., Webster, T.F., White, R.F., Sagiv, S.K., & Oken, E. (2016). Prenatal and childhood traffic-related air pollution exposure and childhood executive function and behavior. *Neurotoxicology and Teratology*, 57, 60–70. https://doi.org/10.1016/j.ntt.2016.06.008

Hendryx, M., Fedorko, E., & Halverson, J. (2010). Pollution sources and mortality rates across rural-urban areas in the United States. *The Journal of Rural Health*, 26(4), 383–91. https://doi.org/10.1111/j.1748-0361.2010.00305.x

Heron, M. (2019). Deaths: Leading causes for 2017. *National Vital Statistics Reports*, 68(6), 1–77. Available: https://stacks.cdc.gov/view/cdc/79488

Hoffman, K.M., Trawalter, S., Axt, J.R., & Oliver, M.N. (2016). Racial bias in pain assessment and treatment recommendations, and false beliefs about biological differences between blacks and whites. *Proceedings of the National Academy of Sciences of the United States of America*, 113(16), 4296–301. https://doi.org/10.1073/pnas.1516047113

Hopenhayn, C., Ferreccio, C., Browning, S.R., Huang, B., Peralta, C., Gibb, H., & Hertz-Picciotto, I. (2003). Arsenic exposure from drinking water and birth weight. *Epidemiology*, 14(5), 593–602. https://doi.org/10.1097/01.ede.0000072104.65240.69

Houston, D., Dang, A., Wu, J., Chowdhury, Z., & Edwards, R. (2016). The cost of convenience: Air pollution and noise on freeway and arterial light rail station platforms in Los Angeles. *Transportation Research Part D: Transport and Environment*, 49, 127–37. https://doi.org/10.1016/j.trd.2016.09.011

Hoyert, D.L., & Miniño, A.M. (2020). Maternal mortality in the United States: Changes in coding, publication, and data release, 2018. *National Vital Statistics Reports*, 69(2), 1–18. https://stacks.cdc.gov/view/cdc/84769

Hulin, M., Caillaud, D., & Annesi-Maesano, I. (2010). Indoor air pollution and childhood asthma: Variations between urban and rural areas. *Indoor Air*, 20(6), 502–14. https://doi.org/10.1111/j.1600-0668.2010.00673.x

Institute of Medicine (IOM). (1990). *Nutrition during pregnancy: Part I: Weight gain, Part II: Nutrient supplements*. The National Academies Press. https://doi.org/10.17226/1451

———. (2000). *Clearing the air: Asthma and indoor air exposures*. The National Academies Press. https://doi.org/10.17226/9610.

———. (2003). *Unequal treatment: Confronting racial and ethnic disparities in health care*. The National Academies Press. https://doi.org/10.17226/12875.

Jacob, B., & Ryan, J. (2018). *How life outside of school affects student performance in school*. Brookings Institution. Available: https://www.brookings.edu/research/how-life-outside-of-a-school-affects-student-performance-in-school/

Jeffries, N., Zaslavsky, A.M., Diez Roux, A.V., Creswell, J.W., Palmer, R.C., Gregorich, S.E., Reschovsky, J.D., Graubard, B.I., Choi, K., & Pfeiffer, R.M. (2019). Methodological approaches to understanding causes of health disparities. *American Journal of Public Health*, 109(S1), S28–33. https://doi.org/10.2105/AJPH.2018.304843

Jewkes, R. (2002). Intimate partner violence: Causes and prevention. *The Lancet*, 359(9315), 1423–9. https://doi.org/10.1016/S0140-6736(02)08357-5

Johnson, T.J., Winger, D.G., Hickey, R.W., Switzer, G.E., Miller, E., Nguyen, M.B., Saladino, R.A., & Hausmann, L.R. (2017). Comparison of physician implicit racial bias toward adults versus children. *Academic Pediatrics*, 17(2), 120–6. https://doi.org/10.1016/j.acap.2016.08.010

Jones, C.P. (2001). Invited commentary: "Race", racism, and the practice of epidemiology. *American Journal of Epidemiology*, 154(4), 299–304. https://doi.org/10.1093/aje/154.4.299

Jones, K.A., Do, S., Porras-Javier, L., Contreras, S., Chung, P.J., & Coker, T.R. (2018). Feasibility and acceptability in a community-partnered implementation of CenteringParenting for group well-child care. *Academic Pediatrics*, 18(6), 642–9. https://doi.org/10.1016/j.acap.2018.06.001

Jones, L., Bellis, M.A., Wood, S., Hughes, K., McCoy, E., Eckley, L., Bates, G., Mikton, C., Shakespeare, T., & Officer, A. (2012). Prevalence and risk of violence against children with disabilities: A systematic review and meta-analysis of observational studies. *The Lancet*, 380(9845), 899–907. https://doi.org/10.1016/S0140-6736(12)60692-8

Kaijser, M., Edstedt Bonamy, A.K., Akre, O., Cnattingius, S., Granath, F., Norman, M., & Ekbom, A. (2009). Perinatal risk factors for diabetes in later life. *Diabetes*, 58(3), 523–6. https://doi.org/10.2337/db08-0558

Kaiser Family Foundation. (2022). *Medicaid postpartum coverage extension tracker*. Available: https://www.kff.org/medicaid/issue-brief/medicaid-postpartum-coverage-extension-tracker

Kajantie, E., Osmond, C., Barker, D.J.P., & Eriksson, J.G. (2010). Preterm birth—A risk factor for type 2 diabetes? The Helsinki birth cohort study. *Diabetes Care*, 33(12), 2623–5. https://doi.org/10.2337/dc10-0912

Kalter, H. (2003). Teratology in the 20th century: Environmental causes of congenital malformations in humans and how they were established. *Neurotoxicology and Teratology*, 25(2), 131–282. https://doi.org/10.1016/S0892-0362(03)00010-2

Kelleher, K., Reece, J., & Sandel, M. (2018). The healthy neighborhood, healthy families initiative. *Pediatrics*, 142(3), e20180261. https://doi.org/10.1542/peds.2018-0261

Kelly, Y.J., Bécares, L., & Nazroo, J.Y. (2013). Associations between maternal experiences of racism and early child health and development: Findings from the UK Millennium Cohort Study. *Journal of Epidemiology & Community Health*, 67, 35–41. https://doi.org/10.1136/jech-2011-200814

Kerkhof, G.F., Breukhoven, P.E., Leunissen, R.W., Willemsen, R.H., & Hokken-Koelega, A.C. (2012a). Does preterm birth influence cardiovascular risk in early adulthood? *Journal of Pediatrics*, 161(3), 390–6. https://doi.org/10.1016/j.jpeds.2012.03.048

Kerkhof, G.F., Willemsen, R.H., Leunissen, R.W., Breukhoven, P.E., & Hokken-Koelega, A.C. (2012b). Health profile of young adults born preterm: Negative effects of rapid weight gain in early life. *Journal of Clinical Endocrinology & Metabolism*, 97(12), 4498–506. https://doi.org/10.1210/jc.2012-1716

Kersten, E.E., LeWinn, K.Z., Gottlieb, L., Jutte, D.P., & Adler, N.E. (2014). San Francisco children living in redeveloped public housing used acute services less than children in older public housing. *Health Affairs*, 33(12), 2230–7. https://doi.org/10.1377/hlthaff.2014.1021

Kessler, R.C., Duncan, G.J., Gennetian, L.A., Katz, L.F., Kling, J.R., Sampson, N.A., Sanbonmatsu, L., Zaslavsky, A.M., & Ludwig, J. (2014). Associations of housing mobility interventions for children in high-poverty neighborhoods with subsequent mental disorders during adolescence. *Journal of the American Medical Association*, 311(9), 937–47. https://doi.org/10.1001/jama.2014.607

Kim, M.A., & Williams, K.A. (2017). Lead levels in landfill areas and childhood exposure: An integrative review. *Public Health Nursing*, 34(1), 87–97. https://doi.org/10.1111/phn.12249

King, W. (2005). Afterword: African American children in contemporary society. In *African American Childhoods*. Palgrave Macmillan. https://doi.org/10.1007/978-1-349-73165-7_11

Kingery, K.M., Narad, M.E., Taylor, H.G., Yeates, K.O., Stancin, T., & Wade, S.L. (2017). Do children who sustain traumatic brain injury in early childhood need and receive academic services 7 years after injury? *Journal of Developmental & Behavioral Pediatrics*, 38(9), 728–35. https://doi.org/10.1097/DBP.0000000000000489

Klevens, J., Schmidt, B., Luo, F., Xu, L., Ports, K.A., & Lee, R.D. (2017). Effect of the Earned Income Tax Credit on hospital admissions for pediatric abusive head trauma, 1995–2013. *Public Health Reports*, 132(4), 505–11. https://doi.org/10.1177/0033354917710905

Koch, A., & Kozhumam, A. (2021). Addressing adultification of black pediatric patients in the emergency department: A framework to decrease disparities. *Health Promotion Practice*, 23(4), 555–9. https://doi.org/10.1177/15248399211049207

———. (2022). Adultification of black children negatively impacts their health: Recommendations for health care providers. *Nursing Forum*, 57(5), 963–67. https://doi.org/10.1111/nuf.12736

Kovski, N.L., Hill, H.D., Mooney, S.J., Rivara, F.P., Morgan, E.R., & Rowhani-Rahbar, A. (2022). Association of state-level earned income tax credits with rates of reported child maltreatment, 2004–2017. *Child Maltreatment*, 27(3), 325–33. https://doi.org/10.1177/1077559520987302

Krieger, N., Chen, J., Waterman, P., Kiang, M., & Feldman, J. (2015). Police killings and police deaths are public health data and can be counted. *PLoS Medicine*, 12, e1001915. https://doi.org/10.1371/journal.pmed.1001915

Kuh, D., Ben-Shlomo, Y., Lynch, J., Hallqvist, J., & Power, C. (2003). Life course epidemiology. *Journal of Epidemiology and Community Health*, 57(10), 778–83. https://doi.org/10.1136/jech.57.10.778

Kujawski, S.A., Yao, L., Wang, H.E., Carias, C., & Chen, Y.T. (2022). Impact of the COVID-19 pandemic on pediatric and adolescent vaccinations and well child visits in the United States: A database analysis. *Vaccine*, 40(5), 706–13. https://doi.org/10.1016/j.vaccine.2021.12.064

Landon, M.B., Leindecker, S., Spong, C.Y., Hauth, J.C., Bloom, S.L., Varner, M.W., Moawad, A.H., Caritis, S.N., Harper, M., Wapner, R.J., Sorokin, Y., Miodovnik, M., Carpenter, M.W., Peaceman, A.M., O'Sullivan, M.J., Sibai, B.M., Langer, O., Thorp, J.M., Ramin, S.M., . . . & Gabbe, S.G. (2005). The MFMU Cesarean Registry: Factors affecting the success of trial of labor after previous cesarean delivery. *American Journal of Obstetrics and Gynecology*, 193(3), 1016–23. https://doi.org/10.1016/j.ajog.2005.05.066

Landrine, H., & Klonoff, E.A. (1996). The schedule of racist events: A measure of racial discrimination and a study of its negative physical and mental health consequences. *Journal of Black Psychology*, 22(2), 144–68. https://doi.org/10.1177/00957984960222002

Laraque-Arena, D., & Stein, R.E. (2021). Integrating mental health in the comprehensive care of children and adolescents: Prevention, screening, diagnosis and treatment. *Pediatric Medicine*, 4, 21. https://doi.org/10.21037/pm-21-36

Larsson, H.J., Eaton, W.W., Madsen, K.M., Vestergaard, M., Olesen, A.V., Agerbo, E., Schendel, D., Thorsen, P., & Mortensen, P.B. (2005). Risk factors for autism: Perinatal factors, parental psychiatric history, and socioeconomic status. *American Journal of Epidemiology*, 161(10), 916–25. https://doi.org/10.1093/aje/kwi123

Lee, L.K., Fleegler, E.W., Goyal, M.K., Doh, K.F., Laraque-Arena, D., & Hoffman, B.D. (2022). Firearm-related injuries and deaths in children and youth. *Pediatrics*, 150(6). e2022060071. https://doi.org/10.1542/peds.2022-060071

Leventhal, T., & Newman, S. (2010). Housing and child development. *Children and Youth Services Review*, 32(9), 1165–74. https://doi.org/10.1016/j.childyouth.2010.03.008

Linnet, K.M., Wisborg, K., Agerbo, E., Secher, N.J., Thomsen, P.H., & Henriksen, T.B. (2006). Gestational age, birth weight, and the risk of hyperkinetic disorder. *Archives of Disease in Childhood*, 91(8), 655–60. https://doi.org/10.1136/adc.2005.088872

Madara, J.L. (2021). *Reckoning with medicine's history of racism*. The American Medical Association. Available: https://www.ama-assn.org/about/leadership/reckoning-medicine-s-history-racism

Madigan, S., Prime, H., Graham, S.A., Rodrigues, M., Anderson, N., Khoury, J., & Jenkins, J.M. (2019). Parenting behavior and child language: A meta-analysis. *Pediatrics*, 144(4), e20183556. https://doi.org/10.1542/peds.2018-3556

Manikkam, M., Tracey, R., Guerrero-Bosagna, C., & Skinner, M.K. (2013). Plastics derived endocrine disruptors (BPA, DEHP and DBP) induce epigenetic transgenerational inheritance of obesity, reproductive disease and sperm epimutations. *PLoS One*, 8(1), e55387. https://doi.org/10.1371/journal.pone.0055387

March of Dimes. (2021). *2021 March of Dimes report card*. Available: https://www.marchofdimes.org/2021-march-dimes-report-card

———. (2022). *Momnibus*. Available: https://www.marchofdimes.org/momnibus

Marlow, N., Wolke, D., Bracewell, M.A., & Samara, M. (2005). Neurologic and developmental disability at six years of age after extremely preterm birth. *New England Journal of Medicine*, 352(1), 9–19. https://doi.org/10.1056/NEJMoa041367

Maroney, T., & Zuckerman, B. (2018). "The talk," physician version: Special considerations for African American, male adolescents. *Pediatrics*, 141(2). https://doi.org/10.1542/peds.2017-1462

Martin, J.A., Hamilton, B.E., Osterman, M.J.K., & Driscoll, A.K. (2019). Births: Final data for 2018. *National Vital Statistics Reports*, 68(13), 1–47. Available: https://stacks.cdc.gov/view/cdc/82909

Mathai, S., Cutfield, W.S., Derraik, J.G., Dalziel, S.R., Harding, J.E., Robinson, E., Biggs, J., Jefferies, C., & Hofman, P.L. (2012). Insulin sensitivity and β-cell function in adults born preterm and their children. *Diabetes*, 61(10), 2479–83. https://doi.org/10.2337/db11-1672

Matthew, A.J., Clark, M.A, & McDavid, L.M. (2021). Combating racism: The role of the pediatrician. *Pediatric Research*, 90, 708–10. https://doi.org/10.1038/s41390-020-01345-x

Maybank, A., De Maio, F., Lemos, D., & Derige, D.N. (2022). Embedding racial justice and advancing health equity at the American Medical Association. *The American Journal of Medicine*, 135(7), 803–5. https://doi.org/10.1016/j.amjmed.2022.01.058

McEwen, B.S. (2005). Stressed or stressed out: What is the difference? *Journal of Psychiatry & Neuroscience*, 30(5), 315–8.

McGowan, P.O., & Matthews, S.G. (2018). Prenatal stress, glucocorticoids, and developmental programming of the stress response. *Endocrinology*, 159(1), 69–82. https://doi.org/10.1210/en.2017-00896

Meijer, M., Bloomfield, K., & Engholm, G. (2013). Neighbourhoods matter too: The association between neighbourhood socioeconomic position, population density and breast, prostate and lung cancer incidence in Denmark between 2004 and 2008. *Journal of Epidemiology and Community Health*, 67(1), 6–13. https://doi.org/10.1136/jech-2011-200192

Menakem, R. (2017). *My grandmother's hands: Racialized trauma and the pathway to mending our hearts and bodies.* Las Vegas, NV: Central Recovery Press.

Metzl, J.M., & Hansen, H. (2014). Structural competency: Theorizing a new medical engagement with stigma and inequality. *Social Science & Medicine* (1982), 103, 126–33. https://doi.org/10.1016/j.socscimed.2013.06.032

Mikati, I., Benson, A.F., Luben, T.J., Sacks, J.D., & Richmond-Bryant, J. (2018). Disparities in distribution of particulate matter emission sources by race and poverty status. *American Journal of Public Health*, 108(4), 480–5. https://doi.org/10.2105/AJPH.2017.304297

Miranda, M.L., Kim, D., Reiter, J., Overstreet Galeano, M.A., & Maxson, P. (2009). Environmental contributors to the achievement gap. *Neurotoxicology*, 30(6), 1019–24. https://doi.org/10.1016/j.neuro.2009.07.012

Miranda, M.L., Edwards, S.E., Chang, H.H., & Auten, R.L. (2013). Proximity to roadways and pregnancy outcomes. *Journal of Exposure Science & Environmental Epidemiology*, 23(1), 32–8. https://doi.org/10.1038/jes.2012.78

Mitchell, R.J., Cameron, C.M., McMaugh, A., Lystad, R.P., Badgery-Parker, T., & Ryder, T. (2021). The impact of childhood injury and injury severity on school performance and high school completion in Australia: A matched population-based retrospective cohort study. *BMC Pediatrics*, 21(1), 426. https://doi.org/10.1186/s12887-021-02891-x

Morency, P., Gauvin, L., Plante, C., Fournier, M., & Morency, C. (2012). Neighborhood social inequalities in road traffic injuries: The influence of traffic volume and road design. *American Journal of Public Health*, 102(6), 1112–9. https://doi.org/10.2105/AJPH.2011.300528

Muller, C., Sampson, R.J., & Winter, A.S. (2018). Environmental inequality: The social causes and consequences of lead exposure. *Annual Review of Sociology*, 44(1), 263–82. https://doi.org/10.1146/annurev-soc-073117-041222

Myers, H., Lewis, T., & Dominguez, T. (2003). Stress, coping, and minority health: Biopsychosocial perspective on ethnic health disparities. *Handbook of racial and ethnic minority psychology*, 377–400. Thousand Oaks, CA: SAGE Publications.

Nakamura, K., Itoh, K., Dai, H., Han, L., Wang, X., Kato, S., Sugimoto, T., & Fushiki, S. (2012). Prenatal and lactational exposure to low-doses of bisphenol A alters adult mice behavior. *Brain Development*, 34(1), 57–63. https://doi.org/10.1016/j.braindev.2010.12.011

National Academies of Sciences, Engineering, and Medicine (National Academies). (2017). *Communities in action: Pathways to health equity*. The National Academies Press. https://doi.org/10.17226/24624

———. (2019). *Vibrant and healthy kids: Aligning science, practice, and policy to advance health equity*. The National Academies Press. https://doi.org/10.17226/25466

National Association of Pediatric Nurse Practitioners. (2009). NAPNAP position statement on pediatric health care/medical home: Key issues on delivery, reimbursement, and leadership. *Journal of Pediatric Health Care*, 23(3), A23–4.

National Center for Healthy Housing. (2013). *Issue brief: Childhood lead exposure and educational outcomes*. Available: https://nchh.org/resource-library/Childhood_Lead_Exposure.pdf.

National Center for Health Statistics (NCHS). (2018). *Health, United States 2018*. Department of Health and Human Services. Available: https://www.cdc.gov/nchs/data/hus/hus18.pdf#Highlights(2018)

———. (2020). *NCHS Data on racial and ethnic disparities*. Department of Health and Human Services. Available: https://www.cdc.gov/nchs/data/factsheets/factsheet_disparities.pdf

National Institute of Child Health and Human Development. (2012). *The long-lasting effects of preterm birth*. Department of Health and Human Services. Available: https://www.nichd.nih.gov/newsroom/resources/spotlight/012612-effects-preterm-birth

Needleman, H.L., Gunnoe, C., Leviton, A., Reed, R., Peresie, H., Maher, C., & Barrett, P. (1979). Deficits in psychologic and classroom performance of children with elevated dentine lead levels. *New England Journal of Medicine*, 300(13), 689–95. https://doi.org/10.1056/nejm197903293001301

Needleman, H.L., Schell, A., Bellinger, D., Leviton, A., & Allred, E.N. (1990). The long-term effects of exposure to low doses of lead in childhood: An 11-year follow-up report. *New England Journal of Medicine*, 322(2), 83–8. https://doi.org/10.1056/NEJM199001113220203

Newgard, C.D., Schmicker, R.H., Sopko, G., Andrusiek, D., Bialkowski, W., Minei, J.P., Brasel, K., Bulger, E., Fleischman, R.J., Kerby, J.D., Bigham, B.L., Warden, C.R., & Resuscitation Outcomes Consortium Investigators. (2011). Trauma in the neighborhood: A geospatial analysis and assessment of social determinants of major injury in North America. *American Journal of Public Health*, 101(4), 669–77. https://doi.org/10.2105/AJPH.2010.300063

Nieblas-Bedolla, E., Christophers, B., Nkinsi, N.T., Schumann, P.D., & Stein, E. (2020). Changing how race is portrayed in medical education: Recommendations from medical students. *Academic Medicine: Journal of the Association of American Medical Colleges*, 95(12), 1802–6. https://doi.org/10.1097/ACM.0000000000003496

Nolen, L.T., Beckman, A.L., & Sandoe, E. (2020). How foundational moments in Medicaid's history reinforced rather than eliminated racial health disparities. *Health Affairs Blog*. Lown Institute. Available: https://lowninstitute.org/headlines/how-foundational-moments-in-medicaids-history-reinforced-rather-than-eliminated-racial-health-disparities/

Nomura, Y., Brooks-Gunn, J., Davey, C., Ham, J., & Fifer, W.P. (2007). The role of perinatal problems in risk of co-morbid psychiatric and medical disorders in adulthood. *Psychological Medicine*, 37(9), 1323–34. https://doi.org/10.1017/S0033291707000736

Norlin, C., Crawford, M.A., Bell, C.T., Sheng, X., & Stein, M.T. (2011). Delivery of well-child care: A look inside the door. *Academic Pediatrics*, 11(1), 18–26. https://doi.org/10.1016/j.acap.2010.12.008

Northridge, M.E., Stover, G.N., Rosenthal, J.E., & Sherard, D. (2003). Environmental equity and health: Understanding complexity and moving forward. *American Journal of Public Health*, 93(2), 209–14. https://doi.org/10.2105/ajph.93.2.209

Oakes, J.M. (2004). The (mis)estimation of neighborhood effects: Causal inference for a practicable social epidemiology. *Social Science & Medicine*, 58(10), 1929–52. https://doi.org/10.1016/j.socscimed.2003.08.004

Oakes, J.M., Andrade, K.E., Biyoow, I.M., & Cowan, L.T. (2015). Twenty years of neighborhood effect research: An assessment. *Current Epidemiology Reports*, 2(1), 80–7. https://doi.org/10.1007/s40471-015-0035-7

Oberg, C., Colianni, S., & King-Schultz, L. (2016). Child health disparities in the 21st century. *Current Problems in Pediatric and Adolescent Health Care*, 46(9), 291–312. https://doi.org/10.1016/j.cppeds.2016.07.001

Ocen, P.A. (2015). (E)rasing childhood: Examining the racialized construction of childhood and innocence in the treatment of sexually exploited minors. *UCLA Law Review*, 62(6). Available: https://papers.ssrn.com/sol3/papers.cfm?abstract_id=2692829

Oldfield, B.J., Rosenthal, M.S., & Coker, T.R. (2020). Update on the feasibility, acceptability, and impact of group well-child care. *Academic Pediatrics*, 20(6), 731–2. https://doi.org/10.1016/j.acap.2020.02.029

Olson, L.M., Inkelas, M., Halfon, N., Schuster, M.A., O'Connor, K.G., & Mistry, R. (2004). Overview of the content of health supervision for young children: Reports from parents and pediatricians. *Pediatrics*, 113(6 Suppl), 1907–16. https://doi.org/10.1542/peds.113.S5.1907

Organisation for Economic Co-operation and Development (OECD). (2019). *Health at a glance 2019: United States*. Available: https://www.oecd.org/unitedstates/health-at-a-glance-united-states-EN.pdf

———. (2022). *Understanding differences in health expenditure between the United States and OECD countries*. Available: https://www.oecd.org/health/Health-expenditure-differences-USA-OECD-countries-Brief-July-2022.pdf

O'Reilly, K.B. (2020). *AMA: Racism is a threat to public health*. American Medical Association. Available: https://www.ama-assn.org/delivering-care/health-equity/ama-racism-threat-public-health

Osborn, L.M., & Woolley, F.R. (1981). Use of groups in well child care. *Pediatrics*, 67(5), 701–6.

Osterman, M.J.K., & Martin, J.A. (2018). Timing and adequacy of prenatal care in the United States, 2016. *National Vital Statistics Reports*, 67(3), 1–14. Available: https://www.cdc.gov/nchs/data/nvsr/nvsr67/nvsr67_03.pdf

Owens, D.C. (2017). *Medical bondage: Race, gender, and the origins of American gynecology*. University of Georgia Press. https://doi.org/10.2307/j.ctt1pwt69x

Pachter, L.M., & Coll, C.G. (2009). Racism and child health: A review of the literature and future directions. *Journal of Developmental & Behavioral Pediatrics*, 30(3), 255–63. https://doi.org/10.1097/DBP.0b013e3181a7ed5a

Paczkowski, M.M., & Galea, S. (2010). Sociodemographic characteristics of the neighborhood and depressive symptoms. *Current Opinion in Psychiatry*, 23(4), 337–41. https://doi.org/10.1097/YCO.0b013e32833ad70b

Padula, A.M., Humblet, O., Mortimer, K., Lurmann, F., & Tager, I. (2012). Exposure to air pollution during pregnancy and pulmonary function growth in the faces lite cohort A49. Presented at the American Thoracic Society 2012 International Conference, May 20. https://doi.org/10.1164/ajrccm-conference.2012.185.1_MeetingAbstracts.A1725

Parkinson, J.R., Hyde, M.J., Gale, C., Santhakumaran, S., & Modi, N. (2013). Preterm birth and the metabolic syndrome in adult life: A systematic review and meta-analysis. *Pediatrics*, 131(4), e1240–63. https://doi.org/10.1542/peds.2012-2177

Pate, C.A., Zahran, H.S., Qin, X., Johnson, C., Hummelman, E., & Malilay, J. (2021). Asthma surveillance—United States, 2006–2018. *Morbidity and Mortality Weekly Report Surveillance Summaries*, 70(5), 1–32. http://dx.doi.org/10.15585/mmwr.ss7005a1

Patton, G.C., Coffey, C., Carlin, J.B., Olsson, C.A., & Morley, R. (2004). Prematurity at birth and adolescent depressive disorder. *British Journal of Psychiatry*, 184, 446–7. https://doi.org/10.1192/bjp.184.5.446

Peden, M., Oyegbite, K., Ozanne-Smith, J., Hyder, A.A., Branche, C., Rahman, A., Rivara, F., & Bartolomeos, K. (Eds.). (2008). WHO guidelines approved by the guidelines review committee. *World report on child injury prevention*. Geneva, Switzerland: World Health Organization.

Pénard-Morand, C., Raherison, C., Charpin, D., Kopferschmitt, C., Lavaud, F., Caillaud, D., & Annesi-Maesano, I. (2010). Long-term exposure to close-proximity air pollution and asthma and allergies in urban children. *European Respiratory Journal*, 36(1), 33. https://doi.org/10.1183/09031936.00116109

Perreira, K.M., & Allen, C.D. (2021). The health of Hispanic children from birth to emerging adulthood. *Annals of the American Academy of Political and Social Science*, 696(1), 200–22. https://doi.org/10.1177/00027162211048805

Pizzol, D., Tudor, F., Racalbuto, V., Bertoldo, A., Veronese, N., & Smith, L. (2021). Systematic review and meta-analysis found that malnutrition was associated with poor cognitive development. *Acta Pædiatrica*, 110(10), 2704–10. https://doi.org/10.1111/apa.15964

Polacheck, S., & Gears, H. (2020). *COVID-19 and the decline of well-child care: Implications for children, families, and states*. Center for Health Care Strategies. Available: https://www.chcs.org/resource/covid-19-and-the-decline-of-well-child-care-implications-for-children-families-and-states

Prasad, M.R., Swank, P.R., & Ewing-Cobbs, L. (2017). Long-term school outcomes of children and adolescents with traumatic brain injury. *Journal of Health Trauma Rehabilitation*, 32(1), e24–32. https://doi.org/10.1097/HTR.0000000000000218

Prenatal-to-3 Policy Impact Center. (2020). *Prenatal-to-3 state policy roadmap 2020: Building a strong and equitable prenatal-to-3 system of care*. Lyndon B. Johnson School of Public Affairs, University of Texas at Austin. Available: https://pn3policy.org/wp-content/uploads/2020/09/Prenatal-to-3-State-Policy-Roadmap-2020.pdf

Priest, N., Paradies, Y., Trenerry, B., Truong, M., Karlsen, S., & Kelly, Y. (2013). A systematic review of studies examining the relationship between reported racism and health and wellbeing for children and young people. *Social Science & Medicine*, 95, 115–27. https://doi.org/10.1016/j.socscimed.2012.11.031

Provençal, N., & Binder, E.B. (2015). The effects of early life stress on the epigenome: From the womb to adulthood and even before. *Experimental Neurology*, 268, 10–20. https://doi.org/10.1016/j.expneurol.2014.09.001

Raifman, J., Larson, E., Barry, C., Siegel, M., Ulrich, M., Knopov, A., & Galea, S. (2020). State handgun purchase age minimums in the US and adolescent suicide rates: Regression discontinuity and difference-in-differences analyses. *British Medical Journal*, 370, m2436. https://doi.org/10.1136/bmj.m2436

Ramírez-Vélez, R., Correa-Bautista, J.E., Villa-González, E., Martínez-Torres, J., Hackney, A.C., & García-Hermoso, A. (2017). Effects of preterm birth and fetal growth retardation on life-course cardiovascular risk factors among schoolchildren from Colombia: The Fuprecol study. *Early Human Development*, 106–107, 53–8. https://doi.org/10.1016/j.earlhumdev.2017.02.001

Raphael, E., White, J.S., Li, X., Cederin, K., Glymour, M.M., Sundquist, K., Sundquist, J., & Hamad, R. (2020). Neighborhood deprivation and mental health among immigrants to Sweden. *Epidemiology*, 31(3), e25–7. https://doi.org/10.1097/EDE.0000000000001160

Rauh, V.A., Landrigan, P.J., & Claudio, L. (2008). Housing and health. *Annals of the New York Academy of Sciences*, 1136(1), 276–88. https://doi.org/10.1196/annals.1425.032

Reading, R., Haynes, R., & Shesnassa, E. (2005). Neighborhood influences on child injury risk. *Children, Youth and Environments*, 15(1), 165–85. Available: https://www.jstor.org/stable/10.7721/chilyoutenvi.15.1.0165

Regalado, M., & Halfon, N. (2001). Primary care services promoting optimal child development from birth to age 3 years: Review of the literature. *Archives of Pediatrics and Adolescent Medicine*, 155(12), 1311–22. https://doi.org/10.1001/archpedi.155.12.1311

Reyes, J.W. (2011). *Childhood lead and academic performance in Massachusetts.* (Working Paper No. 11-3). New England Public Policy Center at the Federal Reserve Bank of Boston. Available: http://www.bostonfed.org/economic/neppc/wp/2011/neppcwp113.htm

Rice, R.L., & Slater, C.J. (1997). An analysis of group versus individual child health supervision. *Clinical Pediatrics*, 36(12), 685–9. https://doi.org/10.1177/000992289703601203

Ripp, K., & Braun, L. (2017). Race/ethnicity in medical education: An analysis of a question bank for step 1 of the United States medical licensing examination. *Teaching and Learning in Medicine*, 29(2), 115–22. https://doi.org/10.1080/10401334.2016.1268056

Roby, E., Piccolo, L.R., Gutierrez, J., Kesoglides, N., Raak, C., Mendelsohn, A., & Canfield, A. (2021). Father involvement in infancy predicts behavior and response to chronic stress in middle childhood in a low-income Latinx sample. *Developmental Psychobiology*, 63(5), 1449–65. https://doi.org/10.1002/dev.22081

Rostad, W.L., Klevens, J., Ports, K.A., & Ford, D.C. (2020). Impact of the United States Federal Child Tax Credit on childhood injuries and behavior problems. *Children and Youth Services Review*, 109, 104718. Available: https://stacks.cdc.gov/view/cdc/87308

Rudolph, K.E., Stuart, E., Vernick, J., & Webster, D. (2015). Association between Connecticut's permit-to-purchase handgun law and homicides. *American Journal of Public Health*, 105(8), e49–54. https://doi.org/10.2105/AJPH.2015.302703

Sabin, J.A., & Greenwald, A.G. (2012). The influence of implicit bias on treatment recommendations for 4 common pediatric conditions: Pain, urinary tract infection, attention deficit hyperactivity disorder, and asthma. *American Journal of Public Health*, 102(5), 988–95. https://doi.org/10.2105/AJPH.2011.300621

Saigal, S., & Doyle, L.W. (2008). An overview of mortality and sequelae of preterm birth from infancy to adulthood. *Lancet*, 371(9608), 261–9. https://doi.org/10.1016/S0140-6736(08)60136-1

Salam, M.T., Islam, T., & Gilliland, F.D. (2008). Recent evidence for adverse effects of residential proximity to traffic sources on asthma. *Current Opinion in Pulmonary Medicine*, 14(1), 3–8. https://doi.org/10.1097/MCP.0b013e3282f1987a

Sandel, M., Phelan, K., Wright, R., Hynes, H.P., & Lanphear, B.P. (2004). The effects of housing interventions on child health. *Pediatric Annals*, 33(7), 474–81. https://doi.org/10.3928/0090-4481-20040701-14

Santoli, J.M., Lindley, M.C., DeSilva, M.B., Kharbanda, E.O., Daley, M.F., Galloway, L., Gee, J., Glover, M., Herring, B., Kang, Y., Lucas, P., Noblit, C., Tropper, J., Vogt, T., & Weintraub, E. (2020). Effects of the COVID-19 pandemic on routine pediatric vaccine ordering and administration—United States, 2020. *Morbidity and Mortality Weekly Report*, 69(19), 591–3. https://doi.org/10.15585/mmwr.mm6919e2

Schendel, D., & Bhasin, T.K. (2008). Birth weight and gestational age characteristics of children with autism, including a comparison with other developmental disabilities. *Pediatrics*, 121(6), 1155–64. https://doi.org/10.1542/peds.2007-1049

Schickedanz, A., & Coker, T.R. (2016). Surveillance and screening for social determinants of health-where do we start and where are we headed? *Current Problems in Pediatric and Adolescent Health Care*, 46(5), 154–6. https://doi.org/10.1016/j.cppeds.2016.02.005

Schneeberg, A., Ishikawa, T., Kruse, S., Zallen, E., Mitton, C., Bettinger, J.A., & Brussoni, M. (2016). A longitudinal study on quality of life after injury in children. *Health and Quality of Life Outcomes*, 14(1), 120. https://doi.org/10.1186/s12955-016-0523-6

Schwarzenberg, S.J., Georgieff, M., Committee on Nutrition, Daniels, S., Corkins, M., Golden, N., Kim, J., Lindsey, C.W., & Magge, S. (2018). Advocacy for improving nutrition in the first 1000 days to support childhood development and adult health. *Pediatrics*, 141(2), e20173716. https://doi.org/10.1542/peds.2017-3716

Scientific American Editors. (2019, February 1). The U.S. needs more midwives for better maternity care. Policy. *Scientific American*. Available: https://www.scientificamerican.com/article/the-u-s-needs-more-midwives-for-better-maternity-care

Shafer, P.R., Gutiérrez, K., Ettinger de Cuba, S., Bovell-Ammon, A., & Raifman, J. (2022). Association of the implementation of Child Tax Credit advance payments with food insufficiency in US households. *JAMA Network Open*, 5(1), e2143296. https://doi.org/10.1001/jamanetworkopen.2021.43296

Sharkey, P., Torrats-Espinosa, G., & Takyar, D. (2017). Community and the crime decline: The causal effect of local nonprofits on violent crime. *American Sociological Review*, 82(6), 1214–40. https://doi.org/10.1177/0003122417736289

Shiba, K., Hanazato, M., Aida, J., Kondo, K., Arcaya, M., James, P., & Kawachi, I. (2020). Cardiometabolic profiles and change in neighborhood food and built environment among older adults: A natural experiment. *Epidemiology*, 31(6), 758–67. https://doi.org/10.1097/EDE.0000000000001243

Shonkoff, J.P., Garner, A.S., Committee on Psychosocial Aspects of Child and Family Health, Committee on Early Childhood, Adoption, and Dependent Care, & Section on Developmental and Behavioral Pediatrics. (2012). The lifelong effects of early childhood adversity and toxic stress. *Pediatrics*, 129(1), e232–46. https://doi.org/10.1542/peds.2011-2663

Singhal, A., Tien, Y.Y., & Hsia, R.Y. (2016). Racial-ethnic disparities in opioid prescriptions at emergency department visits for conditions commonly associated with prescription drug abuse. *PLoS One*, 11(8), e0159224. https://doi.org/10.1371/journal.pone.0159224

Smith, L., Mao, S., Perkins, S., & Ampuero, M. (2011). The relationship of clients' social class to early therapeutic impressions. *Counselling Psychology Quarterly*, 24(1), 15–27. https://doi.org/10.1080/09515070.2011.558249

Smith, L., Li, V., Dykema, S., Hamlet, D., & Shellman, A. (2013). "Honoring somebody that society doesn't honor": Therapists working in the context of poverty. *Journal of Clinical Psychology*, 69(2), 138–51. https://doi.org/10.1002/jclp.21953

Stith, S.M., Liu, T., Davies, L.C., Boykin, E.L., Alder, M.C., Harris, J.M., Som, A., McPherson, M., & Dees, J.E.M.E.G. (2009). Risk factors in child maltreatment: A meta-analytic review of the literature. *Aggression and Violent Behavior*, 14(1), 13–29. https://doi.org/10.1016/j.avb.2006.03.006

Stonington, S.D., Holmes, S.M., Hansen, H., Greene, J.A., Wailoo, K.A., Malina, D., Morrissey, S., Farmer, P.E., & Marmot, M.G. (2018). Case studies in social medicine—Attending to structural forces in clinical practice. *New England Journal of Medicine*, 379(20), 1958–61. https://doi.org/10.1056/NEJMms1814262

Stuart, A.L., Mudhasakul, S., & Sriwatanapongse, W. (2009). The social distribution of neighborhood-scale air pollution and monitoring protection. *Journal of the Air & Waste Management Association*, 59(5), 591–602. https://doi.org/10.3155/1047-3289.59.5.591

Tanne, T. (2021). American Medical Association confronts its racist past with plan for a more equal future. *BMJ*, 373(1314). http://dx.doi.org/10.1136/bmj.n1314

Taylor, C.M., Golding, J., & Emond, A.M. (2015). Adverse effects of maternal lead levels on birth outcomes in the ALSPAC study: A prospective birth cohort study. *British Journal of Obstetrics and Gynaecology*, 122(3), 322–8. https://doi.org/10.1111/1471-0528.12756

Taylor, J.A., & Kemper, K.J. (1998). Group well-child care for high-risk families: Maternal outcomes. *Archives of Pediatrics & Adolescent Medicine*, 152(6), 579–84. https://doi.org/10.1001/archpedi.152.6.579

Taylor, J.A., Davis, R.L., & Kemper, K.J. (1997a). Health care utilization and health status in high-risk children randomized to receive group or individual well child care. *Pediatrics*, 100(3), e1. https://doi.org/10.1542/peds.100.3.e1

———. (1997b). A randomized controlled trial of group versus individual well child care for high-risk children: Maternal-child interaction and developmental outcomes. *Pediatrics*, 99(6), e9. https://doi.org/10.1542/peds.99.6.e9

Tessum, C.W., Apte, J.S., Goodkind, A.L., Muller, N.Z., Mullins, K.A., Paolella, D.A., Polasky, S., Springer, N.P., Thakrar, S.K., Marshall, J.D., & Hill, J.D. (2019). Inequity in consumption of goods and services adds to racial-ethnic disparities in air pollution exposure. *Proceedings of the National Academy of Sciences of the United States of America*, 116(13), 6001–6. https://doi.org/10.1073/pnas.1818859116

Theall, K.P., Shirtcliff, E.A., Dismukes, A.R., Wallace, M., & Drury, S.S. (2017). Association between neighborhood violence and biological stress in children. *JAMA Pediatrics*, 171(1), 53–60. https://doi.org/10.1001/jamapediatrics.2016.2321

Tikanmäki, M., Tammelin, T., Sipola-Leppänen, M., Kaseva, N., Matinolli, H.M., Miettola, S., Eriksson, J.G., Järvelin, M.R., Vääräsmäki, M., & Kajantie, E. (2016). Physical fitness in young adults born preterm. *Pediatrics*, 137(1). https://doi.org/10.1542/peds.2015-1289

Tolliver, D.G., Lee, L.K., Patterson, E.E., Monuteaux, M.C., & Kistin, C.J. (2022). Disparities in school referrals for agitation and aggression to the emergency department. *Academic Pediatrics*, 22(4), 598–605. https://doi.org/10.1016/j.acap.2021.11.002

Treble-Barna, A., Schultz, H., Minich, N., Taylor, H.G., Yeates, K.O., Stancin, T., & Wade, S.L. (2017). Long-term classroom functioning and its association with neuropsychological and academic performance following traumatic brain injury during early childhood. *Neuropsychology*, 31(5), 486–98. https://doi.org/10.1037/neu0000325

Tsai, J., Ucik, L., Baldwin, N., Hasslinger, C., & George, P. (2016). Race matters? Examining and rethinking race portrayal in preclinical medical education. *Academic Medicine*, 91(7), 916–20. https://doi.org/10.1097/ACM.0000000000001232

Tsai, S.S., Yu, H.S., Chang, C.C., Chuang, H.Y., & Yang, C.Y. (2004). Increased risk of preterm delivery in women residing near thermal power plants in Taiwan. *Archives of Environmental Health*, 59(9), 478–83. https://doi.org/10.1097/ACM.0000000000001232

Ullmann, H., Weeks, J.D., & Madans, J.H. (2021). Disparities in stressful life events among children aged 5–17 years: United States, 2019. *National Center for Health Statistics Data Brief*, 416. Centers for Disease Control and Prevention. Available: https://www.cdc.gov/nchs/products/databriefs/db416.htm

U.S. Department of Agriculture. (2022). *Household food security in the United States in 2021*. Available: https://www.ers.usda.gov/publications/pub-details/?pubid=104655

van den Bergh, B.R.H., Dahnke, R., & Mennes, M. (2018). Prenatal stress and the developing brain: Risks for neurodevelopmental disorders. *Development and Psychopathology*, 30(3), 743–62. https://doi.org/10.1017/S0954579418000342

Vandenbergh, J.G. (2004). Animal models and studies of in utero endocrine disruptor effects. *Institute for Laboratory Animal Research Journal*, 45(4), 438–42. https://doi.org/10.1093/ilar.45.4.438

Voepel-Lewis, T., & Nafiu, O.O. (2017). Reflecting on racial disparities in pediatric care: Can perianesthesia care nurses make a difference? *Journal of PeriAnesthesia Nursing*, 32(6), 668–70. https://doi.org/10.1016/j.jopan.2017.09.002

Vu, J.A., Babikian, T., & Asarnow, R.F. (2011). Academic and language outcomes in children after traumatic brain injury: A meta-analysis. *Exceptional Children*, 77(3), 263–81. https://doi.org/10.1177/001440291107700301

Vyas, D.A., Eisenstein, L.G., & Jones, D.S. (2020). Hidden in plain sight—Reconsidering the use of race correction in clinical algorithms. *The New England Journal of Medicine*, 383(9), 874–82. https://doi.org/10.1056/NEJMms2004740

Washington, H.A. (2006). *Medical apartheid: The dark history of medical experimentation on black Americans from colonial times to the present*. New York, NY: Doubleday Books.

Webb, E., Hays, J., Dyrszka, L., Rodriguez, B., Cox, C., Huffling, K., & Bushkin-Bedient, S. (2016). Potential hazards of air pollutant emissions from unconventional oil and natural gas operations on the respiratory health of children and infants. *Reviews on Environmental Health*, 31(2), 225–43. https://doi.org/10.1515/reveh-2014-0070

Weidemann, D.K., Weaver, V.M., & Fadrowski, J.J. (2016). Toxic environmental exposures and kidney health in children. *Pediatric Nephrology*, 31(11), 2043–54. https://doi.org/10.1007/s00467-015-3222-3

Wen, X., Kong, K.L., Eiden, R.D., Sharma, N.N., & Xie, C. (2014). Sociodemographic differences and infant dietary patterns. *Pediatrics*, 134(5), e1387–98. https://doi.org/10.1542/peds.2014-1045

Wheeler, W., & Brown, M.J. (2013). Blood lead levels in children aged 1–5 years—United States, 1999–2010. *Morbidity and Mortality Weekly Report*, 62(13), 245–8. Available: https://www.cdc.gov/mmwr/preview/mmwrhtml/mm6213a3.htm

White, J.S., Hamad, R., Li, X., Basu, S., Ohlsson, H., Sundquist, J., & Sundquist, K. (2016). Long-term effects of neighbourhood deprivation on diabetes risk: Quasi-experimental evidence from a refugee dispersal policy in Sweden. *The Lancet Diabetes & Endocrinology*, 4(6), 517–24. https://doi.org/10.1016/S2213-8587(16)30009-2

Williams, D.R., & Mohammed, S.A. (2009). Discrimination and racial disparities in health: Evidence and needed research. *Journal of Behavioral Medicine*, 32(1), 20–47. https://doi.org/10.1007/s10865-008-9185-0

Williams, D.R., Mohammed, S.A., Leavell, J., & Collins, C. (2010). Race, socioeconomic status, and health: Complexities, ongoing challenges, and research opportunities. *Annals of the New York Academy of Sciences*, 1186, 69–101. https://doi.org/10.1111/j.1749-6632.2009.05339.x

Williams, K., Helmer, M., Duncan, G.W., Peat, J.K., & Mellis, C.M. (2008). Perinatal and maternal risk factors for autism spectrum disorders in New South Wales, Australia. *Child: Care, Health and Development*, 34(2), 249–56. https://doi.org/10.1111/j.1365-2214.2007.00796.x

Williams, M.J., & Eberhardt, J.L. (2008). Biological conceptions of race and the motivation to cross racial boundaries. *Journal of Personality and Social Psychology*, 94(6), 1033–47. https://doi.org/10.1037/0022-3514.94.6.1033

Winter, A.S., & Sampson, R.J. (2017). From lead exposure in early childhood to adolescent health: A Chicago birth cohort. *American Journal of Public Health*, 107(9), 1496–501. https://doi.org/10.2105/AJPH.2017.303903

Woodward, N., Finch, C.E., & Morgan, T.E. (2015). Traffic-related air pollution and brain development. *AIMS Environmental Science*, 2(2), 353–73. https://doi.org/10.3934/environsci.2015.2.353

Wright, J.L., Davis, W.S., Joseph, M.M., Ellison, A.M., Heard-Garris, N.J., & Johnson, T.L. (2022). Eliminating race-based medicine. *Pediatrics*, 150(1), e2022057998. https://doi.org/10.1542/peds.2022-057998

Wu, F., & Takaro, T.K. (2007). Childhood asthma and environmental interventions. *Environmental Health Perspectives*, 115(6), 971–5. https://doi.org/10.1289/ehp.8989

Yeter, D., Banks, E.C., & Aschner, M. (2020). Disparity in risk factor severity for early childhood blood lead among predominantly African-American black children: The 1999 to 2010 US NHANES. *International Journal of Environmental Research and Public Health*, 17(5), 1552. https://doi.org/10.3390/ijerph17051552

Zahran, H., Bailey, C., Damon, S., Garbe, P., & Breysse, P. (2018). Vital signs: Asthma in children—United States, 2001–2016. *Morbidity and Mortality Weekly Report*, 67(5), 149–55. Available: https://www.cdc.gov/mmwr/volumes/67/wr/mm6705e1.htm?s_cid=mm6705e1_w

5

Opportunity Gaps in the Social-Emotional Development, Well-being, and Mental Health Experienced by Young Children

Opportunity gaps in social-emotional development, well-being, and mental health result from numerous factors experienced both by children and their parents or other caregivers. The committee begins its discussion of these gaps by showing that the path to mental health and well-being in adolescence and adulthood starts at birth (Institute of Medicine & National Research Council [IOM & NRC], 2000): the dyadic relationship that is established between the parental caregiver and infant is crucial to the growing child's development of self-regulation and social-emotional competence (Sroufe, 2005). In turn, parents' readiness to engage in the tasks of parenting at the birth of an infant is affected by their own mental health (Kamis, 2021), stress (Vismara et al., 2016), material support (Larson et al., 2008), social support (Luecken, Roubinov, & Tanaka, 2013), and ability to draw on community institutional resources (Rostad et al., 2018).

To set the stage for the discussion in this chapter, some definitions are in order. First, in addressing parents' mental health and well-being, we are talking not just about formal psychiatric disorders in the *Diagnostic and Statistical Manual of Mental Disorders, Fifth Edition* (American Psychiatric Association, 2013), such as substance abuse disorder, depressive illness, anxiety disorder, and posttraumatic stress disorder, but also about factors that hinder well-being, such as domestic violence, daily work stress, hassles, worry about minimal material goods, lack of neighborhood safety, racism, and pessimism. A child's healthy development requires more than a parent's lack of mental illness: the parent must be ready to parent, which requires sufficient emotional well-being and energy to be able to devote attention to the child's well-being. Second, when we discuss the mental health of infants and young children, we are referring to the emergent ability to regulate one's own emotions and behavior; a positive sense of self and agency; appropriate social connections to parents and peers; and freedom from significant internalizing and externalizing behavior problems, attention deficits, and developmental delays.

We assert in this chapter that outcome gaps in overall adjustment in childhood, adolescence, and adulthood result from gaps in opportunities that facilitate positive parent and child mental health and well-being during the early years of life. As discussed in prior chapters, opportunity gaps, in turn, have evolved across generations through biased institutional practices. The good news is that by identifying culpable policies and practices, societal leaders can implement changes that the committee believes hold promise for reducing these opportunity gaps and hence, helping to enable healthy developmental outcomes for all children. This chapter also examines how a parent's ability to draw on community resources to support the tasks of parenting is a function of historical institutions, laws, norms, and practices, many of which have been discriminatory (Condon et al., 2022). Finally, the chapter identifies policies and practices that affect family functioning and mental health and well-being in the first several years of life as potential targets for efforts to eliminate opportunity gaps in social-emotional development, well-being, and mental health.

CONTEMPORARY CHILD DEVELOPMENT SCIENCE

For many years, educators, pediatricians, and scientists thought that what happened to a child during the child's early years did not matter much for later development. When universal public education was first contemplated in the United States some 200 years ago, the age at which education would first be offered was established as 7, known then as the "age of reason" (Shapiro & Perry, 1976), or the age at which a child could begin to reason and to absorb instruction. Formal education before that age was assumed to be useless. Only later did early childhood education emerge as a field (Lillard, 2016), through leaders such as Maria Montessori (1966) and Loris Malaguzzi (1998). Likewise, pediatricians used to believe that the focus of early childhood should be on physical health and possibly play. In the 1920s, the American Medical Association publicly opposed governmental support for home visiting to families of infants on the grounds that it would be useless and might even disrupt the mother's breastfeeding and material support of her infant (Madgett, 2017). Child development science, which offered a new perspective on the early childhood years, became a well-formulated field only in the past hundred years with the theories of Jean Piaget (1936), Lev Vygotsky (1962), and John Dewey (1922).

In contrast, and perhaps to compensate for past failures, contemporary child development science has embraced the importance of the first 5 years of life (and even the prenatal period) as a sensitive period for learning that has a tremendous impact on ultimate life outcomes. The report *From Neurons to Neighborhoods: The Science of Early Childhood Development* (IOM & NRC, 2000) highlighted the importance of early ecological experiences for brain development, with profound impact across the lifespan. Rapid developments in brain science through imaging (magnetic resonance imaging [MRI] and functional MRI) studies have shown that early traumatic experiences (De Bellis & Zisk, 2014) and poverty (Brito & Noble, 2014) are associated with smaller brain volume and impaired development in critical regions that affect higher cognitive and social-emotional functioning (Bauer et al., 2009). Careful prospective studies of community samples have demonstrated the power of early life experiences, both positive and adverse, to predict later child outcomes (Béatrice et al., 2012).

Scientific findings on child development over the past several decades have shown what kinds of environmental experiences are essential for optimal cognitive, social-emotional, and behavioral development. It is now known that a primary caregiver needs to interact synchronously and reciprocally with an infant for the infant to develop a secure dyadic attachment (Ainsworth, 1979) that will enable the infant to use the caregiver as a secure base for venturing into other social relationships with competence and confidence.

Known now as well is that both material and emotional supports are essential for an infant to grow, and the lack of these supports leads to failure-to-thrive syndrome (Scholler & Nittur, 2012). Research has shown that young children reared in orphanages and home environments lacking in sufficient emotional and cognitive stimulation are likely to grow into troubled older children and adolescents (Nelson, Fox, & Zeanah, 2014), and that a sense of physical and emotional safety based on a safe and cohesive home and neighborhood is essential for a young child's growing sense of efficacy (Bandura et al., 2001).

Infants and young children are now known to need an optimal level of cognitive and social-emotional stimulation (neither overly excitatory nor void of novelty) to develop the cognitive and social-emotional skills that provide the basis for eventual school readiness and long-term academic functioning and adult well-being (Kessler et al., 2005; Mashburn et al., 2008). In current economic conditions that require almost every able-bodied adult living in a home with young children to work outside the home to make financial ends meet, it is extremely difficult for parents of any background to provide all the emotional support needed by young children. Parents therefore rely increasingly on early care and education (ECE) outside the home to supplement the emotional support and cognitive stimulation they are able to provide within the home. Parents who understand the importance of these community supplements and can access high-quality ECE are able to provide these opportunities to their young children.

It is now known further that opportunities for play and peer interaction without bullying or threat are essential for the young child's development of social skills that lay the foundation for healthy friendships and emotional well-being (Dodge et al., 2015; Rubin, Bukowski, & Bowker, 2015). And finally, it is known that education can disrupt the intergenerational transmission of disadvantage (Andersen et al., 2021).

HOW DISPARITIES IN CHILD OUTCOMES DEVELOP

The same studies that identify the environmental opportunities that enable young children to learn and grow also provide the basis for understanding that if there are disparities in these opportunities across groups based on income, race, ethnicity, or geography, disparities in outcomes for children will result (McLoyd, Hill, & Dodge, 2005). A growing body of literature, described later in this chapter, shows that some groups of families in the United States are not afforded sufficient opportunities to enable the growth and learning essential for their young children to reach their full potential.

Particularly large inequities exist in the structural supports available to families, leading to disparities in parental stress (Nomaguchi & House, 2013), parenting (Brody et al., 2008), maternal and infant health and well-being (Bailey, Feldman, & Bassett, 2021), parent mental health (McNeil et al., 2014), and parental efficacy (Anderson et al., 2015). Disparities experienced by parents in housing, education, job opportunities, health care, and access to community resources are responsible for disparities in their readiness to parent and in the resources available to them to invest in their children in ways essential to a child's development of essential competencies.

As an example, consider the hypothetical parent who observes that her 36-month-old child is exhibiting frequent temper tantrums and unable to calm down despite his mother's best attempts. How does this parent know whether this behavior represents a developmental lag and a problem that could be solved with early professional intervention, or merely a modest developmental challenge that will disappear on its own? How does this parent know where to get professional screening and, if indicated, comprehensive assessment that could lead to early intervention that could put this child on a positive trajectory? How does this parent get access to funds that could subsidize professional assessment and intervention? How does this parent come to understand that seeking help is a sign of parental competence and strength rather than parental incompetence and weakness?

Numerous studies show that group disparities exist in all of the domains referenced above. Families from low-income and minoritized backgrounds, in particular, lack access to scientific information and evidence-based interventions that could help parents provide optimal resources to their young children. The inequities are so pronounced that they have fed into some parents' lack of confidence in science itself and in mainstream professional intervention. The result is that inequities in opportunities continue.

Historical and Current Inequities in Families' Access to Community Resources

Although the United States is one of the wealthiest countries in the world, it has historically had higher rates of child poverty compared with most other developed nations (Haider, 2021). According to the most recent census data (2019), one in seven (14.4%) children in the United States live in poverty; the rate is even higher (15.4%) for younger children, under the age of 6. Children of color are overrepresented in these numbers, representing 71% of this group of children (Children's Defense Fund, 2021).

Children from impoverished communities experience a range of inequities with respect to their child care and school settings, health care, and neighborhoods, and these inequities limit their opportunities for optimal developmental outcomes. These disparities in families' access to community resources (and in their willingness to access those resources) are rooted in four centuries of slavery and racial injustice (Diptee, 2006). A counterargument to the statement that some families are unable to access the community resources they need is that laws and policy reforms over the last half-century have largely reduced the overt racism of the past. While this counterargument can readily be refuted, it must be recognized that parents become able to access community resources and opportunities through relationships and informal networks of peers, and inequities in these culturally based assets will continue to persist even if systemic racism is eliminated. Passive government policy that requires families to lift themselves up by their own bootstraps constitutes passive racism because it enables inequity in access to continue.

Disparities and Opportunity Gaps in Mental Health in Early Childhood

The mental health of young children is critical for their academic outcomes and general health and well-being (Mashburn et al., 2008). Children who experience compromised mental health are at increased risk for later challenges with respect to their physical health, social relationships, psychological well-being, and financial stability (Kessler et al., 2005; Merikangas et al., 2010). Thus, it is critical to promote mental health in early childhood to enhance long-term mental health and other aspects of well-being for children from impoverished and minoritized backgrounds.

According to nationally representative parent report data (Cree et al., 2018), 17.4% of American young children (i.e., aged 2–8 years) have a mental, behavioral, or developmental disorder, and a substantial evidence base documents mental health disparities based on socioeconomic status and race/ethnicity. Research suggests that these disparities often appear in early childhood and increase throughout childhood, adolescence, and adulthood (e.g., Alegría et al., 2015; Robinson et al., 2017). However, it is difficult to disentangle whether disparities in child mental health are due to socioeconomic status or racial/ethnic minority status given the confounding of these two factors in the United States. Further complicating the issue is evidence that children from minoritized and impoverished backgrounds are more likely to be pathologized with regard to their mental health functioning (Hansen, Bourgois, & Drucker, 2014; Downer et al., 2016; Meek & Gilliam, 2020). Examining national data from the parents of children 2–8 years of age, Cree et al. (2018) found that children from families with lower incomes were more likely to receive a diagnosis of a mental, behavioral, or developmental disorder compared with families with midlevel incomes.

Nevertheless, extant data point to a stark difference in the mental health outcomes for children from low-income backgrounds compared with their middle-class counterparts. A systematic review of the research by Reiss (2013), for example, found that children and adolescents from low-income backgrounds were two to three times more likely than their middle-class counterparts to present with mental health problems. Chronic poverty was associated with higher rates of mental health problems, and children who experienced decreases in socioeconomic status had increased levels of mental health problems. Moreover, mental health disparities related to socioeconomic status were more apparent in younger than in older children (Jones Harden & Slopen, 2022).

A robust literature is focused on mental health disparities among children from different racial/ethnic groups (Gonzalez, Alegria, & Prihoda, 2005; Alegría, Vallas, & Pumariega, 2015). For example, African American children are more likely to have externalizing disorders but less likely to have internalizing disorders compared with their White counterparts (Coker et al., 2009). Relative to White children, Asian American children have higher levels of internalizing problems and inadequate interpersonal relationships (Huang et al., 2012). Overall Latin American versus White children have higher rates of mood disorders (Merikangas et al., 2010), although the ratios within this population vary based on country of origin (e.g., low levels among Central American children). Finally, although the data are scant, Native American children and adolescents may have higher rates of substance use, internalizing problems, and externalizing problems relative to all other racial/ethnic groups (Sarche et al., 2011). In general, although much of the data on racial/ethnic disparities comes from studies of older children, Alegría and colleagues (2015) point to early childhood as critical for the emergence of racial/ethnic disparities because of the vulnerability to adversity that characterizes this developmental period.

Notably, when socioeconomic status is controlled for in many studies of racial/ethnic disparities in health, the differences among groups disappear (Hayward et al., 2000; LaVeist et al., 2007; Tackett et al., 2017). These findings suggest that the poverty experienced by many minoritized groups may explain their higher rates of mental health problems. As Yoshikawa and colleagues (2012) suggest, however, race and ethnicity may moderate the effects of poverty on mental health, rendering poverty's impact more pronounced for certain racial/ethnic groups given the risks emanating from discrimination and other factors beyond poverty. Indeed, some studies suggest that race/ethnicity contributes to disparities beyond what can be attributed to minoritized families' socioeconomic status (Alegría et al., 2015; Assari, 2020). Notably, such disparities may be traceable to the overdiagnosing of young children from minoritized backgrounds as having attentional and behavioral disorders, as discussed previously (Williams & Williams-Morris, 2000; Coker et al., 2016; Ballentine, 2019).

The paths toward optimal social-emotional functioning and mental health for young children reflect the factors that promote young children's optimal development writ large. As the preceding section of this chapter suggests, young children's mental health is grounded in individual, familial, and neighborhood processes, including sensitive and responsive caregiving, safe and stable home and neighborhood environments, and opportunities for supports outside the home. However, young children from families with low socioeconomic status and certain racial/ethnic backgrounds are deprived of many of these individual and environmental resources, a disparity that creates a large opportunity gap between them and children from less marginalized groups.

To elucidate the mechanisms that lead to optimal mental health outcomes among children from impoverished backgrounds, Yoshikawa, Aber, and Beardslee, (2012) propose a conceptual framework that identifies three types of mediators between poverty and children's mental, emotional, and behavioral health: (1) individual factors, (2) relational factors, and (3) institutional factors. Similarly, Alegría et al. (2015) offer a conceptual model for racial/ethnic disparities in child mental health that identifies protective and risk factors, including childhood socioeconomic status, childhood adversity and supports, family structure, and neighborhood factors. Although these two models address two different types of disparities, the mechanisms they identify to explain these disparities are similar on many levels.

On the individual level, specific aspects of child and parent functioning are related to child mental health; they include child stress and behavior, as well as family structure, parent stress, and parent mental health (Yoshikawa, Aber, & Beardslee, 2012; Alegría et al., 2015). For example, Robinson et al. (2017) argue that early childhood stressors can affect children's neurologic systems, which in turn can adversely affect subsequent social-emotional functioning. On the relational level, children's experiences of safety, security, stability, and sensitivity from their parents and other caregivers are critical to their optimal mental health. However, the parents of children from impoverished families tend to experience higher levels of stress, which may be associated with more negative parenting practices and ultimately with children's mental health challenges, such as behavior problems (Mazza et al., 2016; Schenck-Fontaine & Panicio, 2019). Further, research has consistently revealed a strong link between poverty and both parental mental illness (e.g., depression), and child emotional and behavioral challenges (Aber, Jones, & Cohen, 2000; Yoshikawa, Aber, & Beardslee, 2012; Ridley et al., 2020). It is important to note here that some factors on the relational level—including family religiosity, social support, and neighborhood stability—may protect children from low socioeconomic status and minoritized groups against negative mental health outcomes (Alegría et al., 2015).

The higher likelihood of stress in the families of children from low-income and minoritized backgrounds may constitute an opportunity gap with regard to the parenting and other caregiving experiences of these children. The lack of mental health, parenting, and other services for these families may result in lower levels of parental functioning due to a lack of support in dealing with stressful experiences, which in turn may increase this opportunity gap for their children (Lyons-Ruth, Wolfe, & Lyubchik, 2000; Yoshikawa, Aber, & Beardslee, 2012). Children may also experience myriad systemic opportunity gaps, such as institutional factors—including experiences in ECE and school, parental job quality and stability, neighborhood resources, and access to health care—that affect children from impoverished and minoritized backgrounds (Yoshikawa, Aber, & Beardslee, 2012; Alegría et al., 2015).

The quality of school experiences, whether in ECE or the primary grades—including structural quality (group or class size) and process quality (e.g., teacher–child interactions)—can significantly affect children's mental health (Weist, 2005; Baker-Henningham, 2014; Jones Harden & Slopen, 2022). Many studies on classroom climate have reported that the absence of responsive, supportive interactions with adult caregivers strongly affects young children's social-emotional functioning (Pianta & Hamre, 2009; Gilliam et al., 2016; Jones Harden & Slopen, 2022). Also linked to negative social-emotional outcomes for young children is the decreased use of effective instructional practices, such as developmentally appropriate didactic and play experiences (Pianta & Hamre, 2009; Jones Harden &

Slopen, 2022). Scholars have suggested that children from low-income and minoritized backgrounds are more likely to experience low-quality ECE and primary school settings compared with their counterparts from middle-income and racial/ethnic majority backgrounds (Iruka, 2022; see Chapters 2 and 3, respectively).

Other research on ECE and school quality has suggested that teacher functioning plays a role in creating mental health disparities. For example, robust evidence shows that ECE teachers perceive African American and Latin American children (especially African American boys) as behaviorally problematic (Gilliam, 2005; Barbarin & Crawford, 2006; Gilliam et al., 2016) when their behaviors are similar to those of other children in the classroom, perceptions that have led to disproportionate rates of suspension and expulsion of African American boys from both preschool programs and the early grades (see Chapters 2 and 3, respectively, for further discussion of this issue).

Extensions of this area of research have documented that the mental health and well-being (e.g., depression, stress) of teachers and child care providers affect their perceptions of children as behaviorally problematic (Gilliam, 2005; Perry et al., 2008, 2010). Many educational programs are supported by school psychologists and other mental health personnel who help teachers develop the capacity to provide social-emotional support in the classroom as well as address the individual mental health needs of vulnerable children (Splett et al., 2013). Head Start programs, which serve low-income children and families, typically have some level of mental health support, such as a consultant who helps teachers create a positive social-emotional climate in their classrooms or addresses the individual needs of children with behavior problems (Yoshikawa & Zigler, 2000; Gonzales-Ball & Bratton, 2019). However, child care centers and homes, as well as schools in poor neighborhoods, often lack the resources to offer such supports (Johnston & Brinamen, 2006; Masia-Warner, Nangle, & Hansen, 2006; Azzi-Lessing, 2010), creating an opportunity gap with respect to the mental health of young children in the early education arena.

Parental job quality and stability are compromised for parents from low-income backgrounds and minoritized racial/ethnic groups. For example, these parents are more likely to have low-paying jobs that offer fewer benefits and are often characterized by greater physical demands, less autonomy, irregular hours, and fewer opportunities for advancement (Morris & Levine-Coley, 2004; Earle et al., 2014). These parents are also more likely to experience job instability and higher levels of job loss. Multiple studies have found these job-related factors to be related to children's mental health outcomes—in particular, challenging behaviors. For example, Strazdins et al. (2010) found that children of parents who had poorer-quality jobs (e.g., limited security, control, flexibility, and paid family leave) were more likely to have emotional and behavioral difficulties, especially if they were from low-income families. In her summary of the literature on parental employment and young child outcomes, Heinrich (2014) suggests that low-income mothers' employment in jobs with nonstandard hours can affect their social-emotional connections with their young children, partly because of the decreased time available to interact with them.

Neighborhood quality has also been linked to children's mental health outcomes. Some research has focused on neighborhood, whether by socioeconomic status or race/ethnicity, and its relationship to child mental health outcomes (Leventhal & Brooks-Gunn, 2003). For example, neighborhood support appears to have an impact on parents, and the lack of this support may hinder their parenting capacity and thus their children's social-emotional functioning (Xue et al., 2005). On the other hand, one study found that parents' lack of ties to their community (i.e., knowing few neighbors) was associated with lower levels of preschool children's internalizing problems if they lived in low-income neighborhoods (Jones Harden & Slopen, 2022). Other studies have examined the role of the neighborhood built environment in children's mental health. In a review of these studies, Alderton and colleagues (2019) found mental health challenges in childhood to be linked to less access to and/or fewer neighborhood green or public open spaces. Finally, research has looked at environmental toxins, finding that early childhood exposure to air pollution and lead paint, among other toxins in their neighborhoods, may lead to higher levels of mental health problems, such as attention-deficit/hyperactivity disorder (ADHD) and autism spectrum disorder (ASD; Morello-Frosch & Shenassa, 2006; Payne-Sturges et al., 2019).

A key opportunity gap lies in access to and engagement in mental health care among low-income and minoritized groups (Bringewatt & Gershorff, 2010). The Institute of Medicine (now the National Academy of Medicine; Institute of Medicine, 2003; McGuire et al., 2006) has defined a health service disparity as differences in treatment and/or access that are not explained by differences in groups' health status or preferences. Using such a definition, many studies have documented disparities in mental health services for low-income and racial/ethnic minority groups in the United States (McGuire et al., 2006; Morello-Frosch & Shenassa, 2006; Alegría et al., 2015; Marrast, Himmelstein, & Woolhandler, 2016). For example, Cree and colleagues (2018) report that young children from low-income families were less likely to see a health care provider and to receive needed care for a mental or behavioral disorder compared with their counterparts from higher-income families. In a review of the relationship between poverty and mental health services, Santiago, Kaltman, and Miranda (2013) suggest that the majority of children from low-income backgrounds who need mental health services do not receive them because of logistical challenges, parents' perceptions about mental health services, and system-level barriers. However, some research points to a strong sense of racial and ethnic identity as a protective factor for minority mental health, as it can combat system-level barriers (i.e., racism, discrimination) and strengthen social network support (Sellers et al., 2006; Edwards & Romero, 2008; Birman & Simon, 2013; Morris et al., 2021).

Although disparities in access to and engagement in mental health intervention and treatment by socioeconomic status are a critical consideration, access to and engagement in mental health promotion and preventive services are equally important (IOM & NRC, 2009). For example, universal programs such as home visiting and social-emotional learning approaches in school and child care settings have been found to improve children's social-emotional outcomes (Zhai, Raver, & Jones 2015; Sama-Miller & Baumgartner, 2017). Although there is a federal home visiting program—the Maternal, Infant, and Early Childhood Home Visiting (MIECHV) Program—that is targeted to low-income families, it does not serve close to the number of potentially eligible families. According to the National Home Visiting Resource Center 2021 Yearbook, there are potentially 16.4 million families with young children who are eligible for home visiting services through MIECHV; in 2020, 71,000 families were served. Similarly, child care centers serving low-income children (apart from Head Start) lack the resources to incorporate specialized social-emotional services (Azzi-Lessing, 2010).

Individuals from minoritized groups are also less likely to have their mental health needs met, as evidenced by the rates and patterns of use of mental health services among these groups (Chow, Jaffee, & Snowden, 2003; Guevara et al., 2005; Marrast, Himmelstein, & Wooldhandler, 2016). Specifically, individuals from minoritized groups are underrepresented in outpatient mental health services but overrepresented in inpatient and emergency treatment (Chow, Jaffee, & Snowden, 2003; Marrast, Himmelstein, & Wooldhandler, 2016), a differential that may be attributable to the lack of treatment during the early phases of mental health challenges. Additionally, research suggests that individuals from minoritized groups are more likely to have their treatment prematurely terminated, are less likely to have appropriate insurance coverage, and are more likely to consider mental health problems in the context of religious and cultural beliefs around healing instead of engaging with professional providers (Chow, Jaffee, & Snowden, 2003; Loewenthal, 2006).

According to Alegría and colleagues (2015), children and youth from minority groups have lower utilization of mental health services compared with their White counterparts despite their greater need for those services. Likewise, Butler and Rogers (2019) underscore that African American and Latino children and youth are less likely to receive specialized mental health care for such issues as substance use and depression. These authors also emphasize that minority children and youth are less likely to receive mental health services in other child-serving sectors, such as schools and the child welfare system.

In addition to disparities in access to mental health treatment, researchers have examined issues relevant to mental health service providers. Substantial research suggests that the lack of linguistically matched and culturally sensitive mental health providers contributes to unequal access to mental health services for minoritized racial/ethnic groups (Chow, Jaffee, & Snowden, 2003; Aratani & Cooper, 2012; Avila & Bramlett, 2013). Because parents must navigate the mental health service sector for their children, parental perceptions that mental health service providers are not sensitive to their needs may decrease their children's engagement in these services. Cook and colleagues (2013) found that community supply of mental health providers was related to the use of mental health services, particularly for Latin American and African American groups.

Racial/ethnic disparities in access to and engagement in mental health services may be partly attributable to the socioeconomic status of minoritized families. For example, Chow, Jaffee, and Snowden (2003) found that neighborhood poverty interacted with race/ethnicity to create disparities in utilization of mental health services among African, Latin, and Asian Americans. Specifically, individuals in high-poverty areas were more likely to use emergency and inpatient services and to have coercive referrals. In a study of the use of specialty mental health services, Alegría and colleagues (2002) found that Latin Americans from low-income backgrounds were less likely to receive specialty mental health services compared with White individuals with similar income status. On the other hand, nonpoor African Americans were less likely than their White counterparts to receive specialty mental health care. In their proposed research agenda for improving minority children's access to mental health care, Alegría and colleagues (2015) suggest that racial/ethnic disparities be examined in conjunction with disparities in socioeconomic status to increase understanding of and capacity to promote access to and utilization of mental health services among children from low-income and minoritized groups.

Positive Socialization and Identity Formation

Children are attuned to race from an early age. Racial identity formation is a complex and relational process that develops through stages (Tatum, 2017). By age 3 months, infants demonstrate a preference for faces from their own racial/ethnic group (Kelly et al., 2005) unless regularly exposed to other ethnic groups (Anzures et al., 2012), a phenomenon not seen in newborns. Preschool children develop a sense of "race constancy"—the idea that race is a permanent part of their identity. Preschoolers also develop implicit preferences and adopt racial stereotypes. By the start of kindergarten, children demonstrate implicit racial attitudes of the dominant society (McKown & Weinstein, 2003) and "in-group" preferences (Dunham, Baron, & Banaji, 2008). Research indicates that racial bias in the perception of others' pain emerges as early as age 7 and is strong and reliable by age 10 (Dore et al., 2014). Adolescents begin to incorporate racial and ethnic identity more formally into their self-concept.

Racial socialization involves actively communicating with children and youth about experiences informed by race and racism, and may buffer racial trauma. Strategies for racial socialization, which includes opportunities to explore cultural pride in combination with preparation for addressing bias, have been shown to be successful (Anderson & Stevenson, 2019). In addition to racism, colorism—prejudicial or preferential treatment associated with skin tone (Walker, 1983)—can impact family processes (Landor et al., 2013), as well as experiences of discrimination and the ways in which parents racially socialize their children. As with racism, social hierarchies associated with skin tone that elevate lighter-skinned above browner-skinned individuals can lead to microaggression and discrimination and serve as a source of traumatic stress (Landor & McNeil Smith, 2019).

REDUCING OPPORTUNITY GAPS IN MENTAL HEALTH IN EARLY CHILDHOOD

Because of the myriad mechanisms that lead to opportunity gaps in mental health among young children, a multifaceted approach to these disparities is warranted. Dodge (2018) advocates for a comprehensive system of care for young children and their families that addresses the individual needs of children and their families at multiple levels of risk. In this framework, programs would incorporate preventive services at the primary level (preventing the onset of mental health disorders), secondary level (intervening for those at risk of a disorder), and tertiary level (mitigating the outcomes of mental health disorder). Similarly, preventive services would include universal (population-wide), selected (targeted toward a high-risk group), and indicated (provided based on a diagnosis) approaches.

Overall, a comprehensive approach is critical to address opportunity gaps in mental health for children from low-income and minoritized backgrounds. Fusar-Poli (2019) argues for the use of such an approach during childhood as a means of improving adult mental health outcomes. Robinson and colleagues (2017) advocate for the integration of relationship-based prevention and intervention services during the early childhood period. They emphasize collaboration across child-serving programs, utilization of data, and a public health approach to integrating systems to support child mental health. A large and growing body of evidence is available to guide social-emotional learning programs for children (e.g., the Incredible Years, Second Step, Fast Track).

Although Butler and Rogers (2019) highlight the lack of attention to mental health disparities in childhood, strategies have been developed at multiple levels for addressing the opportunity gaps that lead to these disparities. Many of these strategies are incorporated in Project LAUNCH (Linking Actions for Unmet Needs in Children's Health), the federal initiative designed to promote the mental health and wellness of young children from birth to age 8 (Goodson et al., 2014). Consistent with Dodge's (2018) comprehensive approach, the Project LAUNCH framework calls for a multipronged approach to improving the mental health and wellness of young children, including screening and assessment, incorporation of behavioral health in primary care, mental health consultation in ECE and schools, enhanced home visiting, and family strengthening. The framework specifies that these strategies should be implemented with attention to workforce development, public awareness, systems integration, and evaluation.

In addition to promoting children's physical, social, emotional, cognitive, and behavioral development, Project LAUNCH focuses on addressing risk and protective factors at the individual and community levels. By targeting impoverished communities, this initiative is designed to improve access to and engagement in mental health and other services among children from low-income families. Additionally, it is designed to reduce racial/ethnic health disparities by implementing strategies to increase access, service use, and outcomes among young children from minoritized families.

Preliminary findings, based on a cross-site implementation study and state-level studies, suggest that Project LAUNCH has had a positive impact on providers, parents, and children (Goodson et al., 2014; Molnar et al., 2018). Specifically, providers reported increased knowledge of children's socioemotional development and of services for children with behavioral problems, as well as increased utilization of mental health consultation. Additionally, parents reported positive perceptions of the helpfulness of programs for their families, their parenting skills, and their children's development. Given these preliminary findings, the framework for Project LAUNCH can be useful in devising an overall strategy for addressing opportunity gaps in young children's mental health. In what follows, we address specific strategies incorporated in the Project LAUNCH framework, including those relevant to screening and assessment, family strengthening, home visiting, early childhood mental health interventions, and integration of services into other child-serving sectors (i.e., ECE, schools, and primary health care). In this discussion, we consider the empirical evidence supporting the effectiveness of these strategies in addressing opportunity gaps in the mental health arena for young children from minoritized groups and families with low socioeconomic status.

Screening and Assessment Strategies for Reducing Opportunity Gaps

Evidence demonstrates an opportunity gap in screening and assessing children for mental health diagnoses. The Department of Health and Human Services (HHS) has proposed "increasing the proportion of children with mental health problems who receive treatment" as one of its Healthy People 2020 objectives (Healthy People 2020, 2020). Given the high rates (Halfon & Newacheck, 1999; Bitsko et al., 2022) and increasing prevalence of childhood behavioral and developmental conditions (Pastor & Reuben, 2008; Kogan et al., 2009; Blumberg et al., 2013; Bitsko et al., 2022), promptly identifying and treating these conditions is important so that children's functional outcomes can be maximized. In addition, since long-term treatment of childhood behavioral and developmental conditions is expensive (Jacobson & Mulick, 2000; Swensen et al., 2003; Pelham, Foster, & Robb, 2007) intervention in early childhood has the potential to yield large cost savings (IOM & NRC, 2000).

Racial, ethnic, and language disparities are seen in the diagnosis and treatment of early childhood behavioral and developmental conditions. For instance, compared with other children, African American and Latino children are less likely to be diagnosed with an ASD, and are more likely to be diagnosed at older ages and with more severe symptoms (Croen et al., 2002; Mandell et al., 2002, 2009; Palmer et al., 2010; Fountain, King, & Bearman, 2011; Pedersen et al., 2012). Likewise, Black and Latino children are less likely to be diagnosed with ADHD and are less likely to be treated with a stimulant medication once diagnosed (Bussing et al., 1998, 2003; Pastor & Reuben, 2005; Stevens, Harman, & Kelleher, 2005). Table 5-1 summarizes recent peer-reviewed studies of diagnostic disparities in ASD and ADHD, two common early childhood developmental conditions. Similar disparities exist in the areas of overall developmental risk (Stevens, 2006), depression and mental health disorders (Chabra, Chávez, & Harris, 1999; Chabra et al., 1999; Zimmerman, 2005), use of psychotropic medications (Leslie et al., 2003), and use of mental health services (Garland et al., 2005). These racial and ethnic disparities deserve increased attention given recent demographic trends: census estimates suggest that the U.S. population younger than age 5 is approximately 50% racial/ethnic minority, and some states are now "majority minority" for children (Frey, 2018; Jensen et al., 2021).

Many of these disorders are identified through the pediatric medical home and at school by either a teacher or school nurse. Developmental surveillance and standardized screening are critical. Standardized developmental screening as recommended by the American Academy of Pediatrics is offered during specific times in a child's series of well-child visits, and if necessary, referral to therapeutic services takes place after those screening

TABLE 5-1 Racial and Ethnic Differences in Diagnosis Rates for Attention-Deficit/Hyperactivity Disorder (ADHD) and Autism Spectrum Disorder (ASD)

Author	Data Source	Major Findings
ADHD		
Rowland et al., 2002	School-based sample of 7,333 children	African American children were less likely than White children to be diagnosed with ADHD and to currently be taking medication to treat ADHD.
Stevens, Harman, & Kelleher, 2005	18,708 children in 1997–2000 Medical Expenditure Panel Survey	Latino and African American children were less likely than White children to be diagnosed with ADHD by parent report. African American children with ADHD were less likely than White children with ADHD to initiate stimulant medication.
Pastor & Reuben, 2005	21,294 children in the 1997–2001 National Health Interview Survey	Latino and African American children, compared with White children, had less frequent parental reports of ADHD.
Miller, Nigg, & Miller, 2009	Systematic review/ meta-analysis	African American children were less likely than White children to have an ADHD diagnosis and when diagnosed, had higher severity scores.
ASD		
Mandell et al., 2002	Medicaid claims for 406 children diagnosed with autism	African American children were diagnosed with autism at older ages relative to White children, and required more time in treatment before receiving an autism diagnosis.

TABLE 5-1 Continued

Author	Data Source	Major Findings
Croen et al., 2002	Birth certificate and health service agency records for >3 million children in California	Children of African American mothers were more likely than children of White mothers to have ASD. Children of Latino mothers and of Mexican immigrants were less likely than White children to have ASD.
Liptak et al., 2008	102,353 children in the 2003 National Survey of Children's Health	Parent-reported prevalence of ASD was lower for Latino than for White children; rates were similar for African American and White children.
Kogan et al., 2009	78,037 children included in the 2007 National Survey of Children's Health	African American children were less likely than White children to have ever had or currently have an ASD.
Mandell et al., 2009	Review of medical and education records for 2,168 children in a multisite network	African American, Latino, and other race children were less likely to have a documented ASD.
Palmer et al., 2010	Data from Texas Educational Agency and Health Resources and Services Administration	School districts with more Latino children had lower rates of ASD.
Fountain, King, & Bearman, 2011	Linked birth and administrative records on 17,185 children with diagnoses of autistic disorder born in California between 1992 and 2001	African American, Latino, and Asian children and those of "other" race were diagnosed with ASD at older ages relative to White children.
Jarquin et al., 2011	Data from Metropolitan Atlanta	Prevalence of ASD was higher for non-Hispanic White than for non-Hispanic Black children.

SOURCE: Zuckerman et al., 2014.

tests. Despite these recommendations, however, recent studies have shown that Spanish-speaking Latino parents and Black parents are less likely to be asked by a provider about their developmental concerns, a difference that persists even when their child is at high risk of a developmental disorder (Zuckerman et al., 2009; Guerrero, Rodriguez, & Flores, 2011). In addition, developmental assessment and therapy may be poorly covered by insurance, making care unaffordable to many minority families (Markus et al., 2005). Even if available, specialty mental health services often are not located where minority children live. Sturm, Ringel, and Andreyeva (2003) found that geographic disparities in mental health care account for many apparent differences in mental health utilization according to race/ethnicity (Sturm, Ringel, & Andreyeva, 2003). Minority families may also have difficulty accessing services because of financial, transportation, or child care issues (Zuckerman et al., 2013).

Parent Beliefs about Child Development, Behavior, and Use of Mental Health Services

Many evaluations of a child's mental or developmental status begin with a parental concern, and racial/ethnic and cultural variation in parental concerns may affect whether and for what reason a child receives a developmental and behavioral evaluation. Several studies have found that parents' differing understandings of the limits of typical child behavior may impact their perception of specific developmental and behavioral problems and result in different rates of utilization of mental health care (Zuckerman et al., 2013, Table 2). For instance, in a large survey of parents of youth with identified mental health problems, Yeh and colleagues (2004) showed that African American, Asian/Pacific Islander, and Latino parents were less likely than non-Hispanic White parents to view emotional/behavioral problems as having a mental health basis (Kinser et al., 2018), a view that is associated with lower rates of use of mental health services (Pachter & Dworkin, 1997; Bornstein & Cote, 2004). Moreover, because of cultural beliefs, historical factors, and long-standing mistreatment of minorities by health care and educational systems, some parents may be less likely to feel that there is value in interacting with those systems to obtain developmental and behavioral treatment for their children. Indeed, parents from minoritized populations may be more likely to distrust the health care system in general (Yeh et al., 2004) and mental health treatment in particular.

Additionally, many families worry about the stigma associated with seeking mental health services, a concern that has been linked with a lower likelihood of attending mental health appointments. This stigma stems from a variety of misperceptions, including parents' belief that mental health treatment is ineffective or unhelpful (Atkins et al., 2006; García,

Méndez Pérez, & Ortiz, 2000; McKay & Bannon, 2005). In a survey of 235 low-income families of school-age children, Richardson (2001) found that African American parents were twice as likely as White parents to expect disapproval from family members and to be embarrassed with respect to seeking mental health care for their children, twice as likely to perceive mental health professionals as untrustworthy and disrespectful, and three times as likely to expect poor care (Bussing et al., 1998).

Other studies have shown that cultural differences have important implications for families seeking and attending care. In particular, Latino and other minority parents do not bring their children for care because they feel that providers fail to understand cultural differences (Kummerer, Lopez-Reyna, & Hughes, 2007), and when surveyed, have expressed the view that providers have negative attitudes toward minorities or treat minority families poorly (Guarnaccia & Parra, 1996). Many of these views are likely rooted in lived experiences in which the mental health system has not performed as well for minority and other underserved families as for their White counterparts (Yeh et al., 2005; Zimmerman, 2005).

Strengthening Families' Work Supports to Reduce Opportunity Gaps

The first few months after childbirth is a period in which mothers need time away from work to recover physically and bond with their infants. Consistent and sensitive parent–child interactions and routines provide the scaffolding for infants' emotional regulation, attachment, and brain function, which in turn lay the foundation for the subsequent development of social, cognitive, and language skills in early childhood (IOM & NRC, 2000). Beyond infant bonding and caregiving, fathers need time to support mothers' recovery (Yogman & Eppel, 2022), which includes being alert for maternal stress and depression (Kotelchuck, 2021). Parents adopting children or becoming foster parents also need time to engage in responsive caregiving and build strong connections, establish routines, and create stable environments (Center on the Developing Child, 2016). Elevated stress from family and financial changes is normal after childbirth or adoption. The concern is whether those changes turn into chronic stress, depression, and financial insecurity that adversely affect parents' mental health and infant development (Shonkoff et al., 2012).

Children's social-emotional development may also be affected by the onset of and care for their own or other family members' serious medical conditions. Whether a newly diagnosed or worsening chronic condition, this health issue may require parents to be away from the workforce temporarily. Adequate time to recover from or provide care for these conditions can help decrease family stress, prevent economic hardship, improve health management, encourage earlier treatment, and facilitate the return to work (Smalligan & Boyens, 2020).

Policies providing for paid family leave offer an opportunity for working parents to take time off from work temporarily to spend time with infants, adopted children, or foster children during a critical bonding period that sets the stage for healthy developmental outcomes across the life course. These policies also support taking leave to provide care for serious medical conditions, including inpatient services for mental health care. Paying wages when parents are temporarily away from their jobs is essential to mitigate financial stress and stabilize income during times of health vulnerability. Conversely, limited access to paid leave creates an opportunity gap for young children by limiting bonding time for parents and infants or adopted children, decreasing the time available to take care of serious health issues, elevating family stress, and exposing children to financial uncertainty, all of which can negatively affect children's social-emotional development.

Although paid family leave policies benefit parents' and young children's mental health, their effects can vary. Positive effects on maternal mental health are consistent across studies. In most studies, paid leave had positive effects on fathers' mental health and reduced fathers' alcohol use, which may indicate less psychological distress (Lee et al., 2020). Evidence is mixed on the differential effects of paid leave on mental health by income and race/ethnicity, likely because of the diversity of study samples (with respect to geographic location and definition of eligible parents) and parents' uneven access and take-up rates. Some studies found that paid leave had greater mental health benefits for parents and children in working families with low incomes (Bullinger, 2019) and lower maternal educational attainment (Kozak et al., 2021). Another study found greater improvements in parents' mental health for White and middle-income parents, with Black children experiencing increased behavioral problems (Irish et al., 2021). Given that White, married, and highly educated mothers have higher take-up rates for maternity leave (Han, Ruhm, & Waldfogel, 2009), the design of programs with respect to length of leave, the extent to which wages are replaced, and whether workplaces and supervisors support leave taking will likely affect whether programs can benefit Black and Hispanic families and those with lower incomes.

Overall, research suggests that paid family leave policies are effective in improving social-emotional well-being for parents and their young children. These policies can be improved by reducing racial/ethnic disparities in take-up of leave through less restrictive eligibility criteria, higher wage replacement rates, targeted outreach, and improved administrative systems.

Home Visiting Strategies to Reduce Opportunity Gaps

Since the launch of the Maternal, Infant, and Early Childhood Home Visiting (MIECHV) Program a large number of families from low-income backgrounds (more than 140,000 in fiscal year 2020) have received home visiting services through the program (Health Resources and Services Administration, 2022). Yet this number represents only a small fraction of eligible families. According to the *National Home Visiting Yearbook* (National Home Visiting Resource Center, 2021), approximately 17.6 million pregnant women and families with young children could potentially benefit from early childhood home visiting programs (National Home Visiting Resource Center, 2021). Of these potential beneficiaries, 23% (more than 4 million pregnant women and families) have incomes below the federal poverty threshold; 14% are Black/African American, and 23% are Hispanic/Latino. Thus, there is a clear need to expand home visiting services to prevent mental health challenges for families and their young children, an expansion that could be accomplished within the parameters of the MIECHV Program.

The key provisions of the MIECHV legislation are that HHS: (1) distribute funding to the states to provide home visiting services to eligible populations, (2) provide technical assistance to the states and programs on effective program implementation, (3) conduct formative and impact evaluations of the home visiting programs, and (4) create and implement a procedure for identifying effective home visiting models that states can select to receive funding. This latter mandate, called Home Visiting Evaluation and Effectiveness (HomVEE; Administration for Children and Families, 2022), calls for periodic reviews of interventions in which home visiting is the primary service delivery strategy to determine whether they improve outcomes in specific legislatively mandated domains, including maternal and child health; positive parenting practices and reductions in child maltreatment; child development and school readiness; family economic self-sufficiency; linkages and referrals to community resources and supports; and reductions in juvenile delinquency, family violence, and crime.

Evaluations of home visiting programs (including those that are and are not reviewed by HomVEE) have produced a rich set of findings. Most notably, the home visiting models being implemented by states and communities have a record of producing benefits for low-income children and families across a variety of domains that are relevant for the positive mental health of participant children (see Sama-Miller & Baumgartner, 2017, for a review).

Research has documented the positive impact of home visiting programs at the primary prevention level on outcomes related to global parenting and maltreatment (see Table 5-2 for examples).

TABLE 5-2 Outcomes of Interest for Home Visiting Programs at the Primary Prevention Level

Program	Outcome(s) of Interest
Early Head Start	Increase in parents' emotional support, decrease in their use of spanking, and reduction in their depression and parenting stress; reduction in children's social, emotional, and behavioral problems (Chazan-Cohen et al., 2007)
Family Check-Up	Reduction in children's social, emotional, and behavioral problems (Dishion et al., 2014; Gill, Dishion, & Shaw, 2014; Sitnick et al., 2015)
Family Connects	Reduction in child maltreatment (Dodge & Goodman, 2019)
Parents as Teachers	Reduction in children's social, emotional, and behavioral problems (Wagner, Spiker, & Linn, 2002; Zigler, Pfannenstiel, & Seitz, 2008)

Programs at the secondary prevention level (e.g., Healthy Families America) have shown reduced maltreatment (DuMont et al., 2011; Lee et al., 2018), more positive parenting practices (e.g., LeCroy & Krysik, 2011), improved home environments, and decreased violence in the home (LeCroy & Lopez, 2020). Compared with primary-level programs, secondary-level programs tend to be more intensive in content and format, briefer in duration, and more experiential (e.g., using active coaching and/or video feedback to promote improved parenting). Evaluations of such programs have highlighted numerous benefits (see Table 5-3 for examples).

Tertiary-level home visiting programs are typically therapeutic and are targeted at children and families that display mental health challenges. Some of these programs are relationship based, with providers using nurturance and reflection to improve parent–child interaction, as well as parent and child functioning. Evaluations of relationship-based programs have documented:

- increases in secure attachment and decreases in disorganized attachment among maltreated children (Child Parent Psychotherapy: Stronach et al., 2013), and reductions in behavior problems and trauma-related symptoms (Lieberman, Ghosh Ippen, & van Horn, 2006); and

TABLE 5-3 Outcomes of Interest for Secondary-Level Home Visiting Programs

Program	Outcome(s) of Interest
Attachment and Bio-behavioral Catchup	Increases in sensitive and responsive parenting and reductions in child behavior problems (Dozier & Bernard, 2019; Jones Harden, Martoccio, & Berlin, 2021; West et al., 2022); increases in emotion regulation, compliance, and attachment security (Jones Harden, Martoccio, & Berlin, 2021)
Cognitively-Enhanced Home Visiting	Less physical punishment (Bugental & Schwartz, 2009)
Family Connections	Improved child safety (Collins et al., 2011)
Healthy Families America	Reductions in maltreatment (DuMont et al., 2011; Lee et al., 2018); more positive parenting practices (e.g., LeCroy & Krysik 2011); improved home environments and decreased violence in the home (LeCroy & Lopez, 2020)
Nurse-Family Partnership	Reduction in child maltreatment (Eckenrode et al., 2016) and in children's social, emotional, and behavioral problems (Olds, 2006; Holland et al., 2014; Miller, 2015)
Play and Learning Strategies	Young children were more likely to be cooperative and socially engaged and less likely to display negative affect (Landry et al., 2008)
Promoting First Relationships	Increased sensitive and responsive parenting (Oxford et al., 2016)
Safe Care	Reduced child abuse recidivism (Chaffin et al., 2012)

- decreases in parental stress, maternal psychopathology, and child externalizing behavior problems (Child First; Lowell et al., 2011).

Other home visiting programs may have a parent management orientation and coach parents to alter negative interaction patterns with their children. Evaluations of such programs have shown reductions in disruptive child behavior, dysfunctional parenting, parental distress and relationship conflict, negative parental attribution for children's misbehavior, and unrealistic parental expectations (Triple P; Prinz et al., 2009; Sanders et al., 2014).

The legislatively mandated impact evaluation associated with MIECHV—the Mother and Infant Home Visiting Program Evaluation (Michalopoulos et al., 2019)—found that four major home visiting programs (Early Head Start, Healthy Families, Nurse-Family Partnership, and Parents as Teachers) improved participant children's ecological contexts compared with those of their nonparticipating counterparts; benefits included improved quality of the home environment, reduced frequency of psychological aggression toward the child, fewer emergency department visits, decreases in mothers' experience with intimate partner violence and increases in mothers' use of domestic violence services, and reductions in parental depression and stress. Consistent with the literature on home visiting, most of these benefits accrued to families. However, one child outcome finding was related to child mental health: that children enrolled in home visiting programs compared with their nonparticipating counterparts had fewer behavioral problems. Notably, all the positive outcomes found in this evaluation were similar across a range of family characteristics, including race/ethnicity.

Although there has been an increase in services for young children at all three prevention levels—primary, secondary, and tertiary—research suggests that opportunity gaps exist at each of these levels for children from racially/ethnically and socioeconomically marginalized backgrounds. Thus, the need is great for scholars, policy makers, and practitioners to devote particular attention to reducing opportunity gaps for young children and families across systems designed to address their mental health needs.

Program Strategies for Reducing Opportunity Gaps in Early Childhood Mental Health

Mental health programs are another set of interventions designed to reduce the opportunity gaps and disparate mental health outcomes experienced by children and families from racially/ethnically and socioeconomically marginalized populations. The goal of infant and early childhood mental health programs is to foster the optimal social-emotional functioning of young children, specifically regarding the development of positive relationships with adults and peers, the expression and regulation of emotions, and the creation of a solid sense of identity and autonomy. These foundational social-emotional processes may prevent the emergence of mental health problems in infancy and early childhood, as well as later in development.

Many scholars and policy makers have decried the lack of a comprehensive mental health system for children and families (Bringewatt & Gershoff, 2010; Cummings, Wen, & Druss, 2013). Extant mental health services are fragmented with respect to the provider agencies and funding sources. Nonetheless, there has been a robust response to the need for mental health interventions for young children. Like home visiting programs, interventions in the infant and early childhood mental health arena can be categorized as primary, secondary, or tertiary, in accordance with the Pyramid Model for promoting social-emotional competence in young children (Hemmeter, Ostrosky, & Fox, 2006; Hemmeter et al., 2016). In this model, primary interventions **promote** children's positive social-emotional functioning through universal supports such as nurturing and responsive relationships and high-quality supportive environments. Secondary interventions are designed to **prevent** the onset of mental health challenges by providing targeted social-emotional services such as explicit instruction and supports for children at risk for mental health difficulties. Finally, tertiary strategies are used to **intervene** with children already displaying symptoms of mental health difficulties, as exemplified by intensive treatment, skill-building, and family-centered interventions. Evidence suggests that children in Pyramid Model classrooms have improved social skills and reduced challenging behavior (Hemmeter, Ostrosky, & Fox, 2006; Hemmeter et al., 2016).

Building on the Pyramid Model and other similar models, the Center of Excellence for Infant and Early Childhood Mental Health Consultation (IECMHC) provides consultation to programs, classroom staff, and families (Duran et al., 2009; Brinamen, Taranta, & Johnston, 2012; Ash, Mackrain, & Johnston, 2013). At the program level, IECMHC consultants collaborate with administrators to develop policies and procedures (e.g., disciplinary policies, communication strategies, professional development opportunities) that promote children's social-emotional competence and a positive climate. IECMHC consultants support teachers in classrooms in the use of positive behavior supports and strategies for managing their classrooms and addressing the needs of specific children. IECMHC consultants may also collaborate with teachers and parents to create supports for children already showing challenging behavior, which may result in fewer child suspensions and expulsions.

A growing evidence base is documenting the effectiveness of IECMHC at the child, teacher, school, and family levels (Brennan et al., 2008; Perry et al., 2010; Hepburn et al., 2013; Substance Abuse and Mental Health Services Administration, 2014; Center of Excellence for Infant & Early Childhood Mental Health Consultation [IECMHC], 2020). Studies have shown that IECMHC consultations lead to improved social-emotional competence and reduced behavior problems among participant children. IECMHC is also associated with improved teacher–child relationships and classroom climate. Participating teachers also have less stress and better skills in teaching social-emotional lessons. One study found that participation in an IECMHC program attenuated the association between teacher depression and child expulsion (Silver & Zinsser, 2020). At the school level, IECMHC has led to lower suspension and expulsion rates, less teacher turnover, and better staff interactions. And parents participating in IECMHC displayed better relationships with their children and missed fewer work days.

One study explicitly examined whether IECMHC programs in a state reduced racial/ethnic disparities in teacher beliefs and discipline policies in preschool (Shivers, Faragó, & Gal-Szabo, 2022). Examining change over the course of a year, the authors documented a strong decrease in conflict scores for teachers and African American children and a trend toward lower risk of expulsions for African American boys over the course of IECMHC consultation. Overall, these findings suggest that disparities in mental health outcomes and the sequelae of these outcomes (e.g., suspension, expulsion) can be reduced by IECMHC programs (Center of Excellence for IECMHC, 2020; Shivers, Faragó, & Gal-Szabo, 2022).

As noted previously, research shows that children from minoritized and socioeconomically disadvantaged communities are more likely to display mental health difficulties and challenging behavior relative to their White and better-resourced peers (Shivers, Faragó, & Gal-Szabo, 2022). Yet they also have far less opportunity to participate in child-serving settings that utilize the models discussed above or in school-based, clinic-based, and community-based mental health supports in general (NRC & IOM, 2009; Alegría, Vallas, & Pumariega, 2010; Atkins et al., 2017). Overall, there is evidence that children and families from minoritized and low-income communities have a lower likelihood of engagement in high-quality mental health services (Hodgkinson et al., 2017; Rodgers et al., 2022).

Specific to early childhood mental health care, scholars have called for increased attention to young children in need of mental health care (Robinson et al., 2017). Although the previously discussed Pyramid and IECMHC models have often been implemented in Head Start and child care programs that serve children from minoritized and low-income communities (Corso, 2003; Fox & Hemmeter, 2009), these models need to be expanded so they can benefit more children, families, teachers, and programs in these communities. Important as well is to adapt these models to meet the specific cultural and community needs of participant children and families, including by hiring providers that reflect the community's racial/ethnic composition (Cappella et al., 2008).

School Nursing to Reduce Opportunity Gaps in School

Strengthening school-based mental health systems and supports could help in addressing the growing mental and social-emotional health challenges seen in young children (Johnson, 2017; Kodzis, 2021). School nurses stand at the intersection of health and education, of supports needed to reduce barriers to learning and promote healthy children, families, and communities. They have a broad scope of practice and offer services ranging from screening tests to care for life-threatening allergy and asthma events. School nurses ensure that all children have access to appropriate educational opportunities regardless of their state of health. To this end, it is essential for their referral options to include comprehensive school mental health systems as well as primary care providers, mental health specialists, telemedicine, and school-based health centers (Centers for Disease Control and Prevention, 2018; National Center for School Mental Health, 2019). School nurses and school-based health clinics have a foundational role, not only providing direct services for students with health problems but also promoting the health and well-being of the communities in which they live and serve. Indeed, according to the National Academies (2019), programs that engage children and families, especially those of lower socioeconomic status, and the community can best achieve positive health outcomes.

School nurses are responsible for the health and wellness of 56 million students. Their role includes detecting illnesses early, managing chronic conditions, providing mental health services, and monitoring outbreak-related illnesses (i.e., flu, RSV, COVID-19). As noted above, the need for mental health services has grown tremendously among young people, especially during the COVID-19 pandemic. Prior to the pandemic, about one-third of student health visits to school nurses were related to mental health. As previously noted, students from minoritized populations face more barriers to accessing mental health treatment relative to other groups, and structural racism can exacerbate these conditions. It is possible that school nurses can help overcome many of these barriers and play a vital role in increasing access to health care, advancing health equity, and keeping children in school. It is important to note in this connection that funding for school nurses has increased recently, including via the Coronavirus Aid, Relief, and Economic Security Act in 2020 and the Build Back Better Act in 2021.

Behavioral and mental wellness is essential for students to be healthy, safe, and ready to learn. As noted, the COVID-19 pandemic took a tremendous toll on children's mental health, in line with the general need for enhanced monitoring of children's mental health during public health crises (Leeb et al., 2020; see Box 5-1). The loneliness and social isolation imposed by disease mitigation measures has been shown to predict mental health problems for up to 9 years postevent (Loades et al., 2020). School nurses are frequently the first to identify and address students' mental and behavioral health concerns and connect them and their families with systems of support. In collaboration with the interdisciplinary education team, they can provide critical links to prevention, early identification, intervention, and referral for behavioral/mental health concerns (Immerfall & Ramirez, 2019). Appropriate funding mechanisms and alignment of incentives is necessary to support these services in school-based settings. Since 2014, all

> **BOX 5-1**
> **How the COVID-19 Pandemic Exacerbated the Opportunity Gap**
>
> It is well known that large economic and health shocks to a society bring particularly high stress to families, and the COVID-19 pandemic is no exception. Gassman-Pines, Ananat, and Fitz-Henley (2020) were in the field surveying parents who work in the services industry when the pandemic struck. They quickly added a new survey to their protocol. Between March 23 and April 26, 2020, 86% of families with a young child reported a COVID-19–related hardship, such as work layoff, loss of income, illness, school and child care closure, and unplanned caregiver burden. These hardships, in turn, predicted parents' daily reports of their increased negative mood and sleep disruption and their children's anxiety and uncooperative behavior. Other surveys during the same period found similar adverse effects on parents' anxiety, substance use problems, sleep problems, and disruptions in interpersonal relationships (Pollard, Tucker, & Green, 2020; Dodge et al., 2021). Well-established findings from other societal shocks suggest that these stressors are likely to accumulate and will have long-term adverse impacts on children's development (Evans & Whipple, 2013).
>
> As with many adversities, families of color and low-income families have suffered the most during the COVID-19 pandemic. Communities of color faced high rates of infection (Haynes et al., 2020), were particularly vulnerable to job loss (Kurmann, Lalé, & Ta, 2020), and experienced high rates of stress (Ananat & Gassman-Pines, 2020). This unequal impact has likely increased the opportunity gap for young children, exacerbating disparities in their long-run outcomes. These research findings suggest the need for policy remedies to address the plight of families with young children, particularly families of color and low-income families, during such events.

states have been able to bill Medicaid for school nurse services, but only a handful have taken advantage of this funding source, in part because of the complicated billing process (National Academies, 2021). Expanding Medicaid coverage for school nursing services offers an opportunity for children to have greater access to health care and preventive health services.

CONCLUSIONS

Families with children aged 0–5 have no universal system of community care to support their children's social-emotional learning, mental health, and well-being, and access to quality care in this domain can vary significantly across communities. For families with fewer resources, accessing care can be particularly challenging. The lack of a universal system means that families are on their own to identify their young children's needs and find resources to address those needs and support their children's healthy development. As a consequence, well-resourced and advantaged families are more able to access those resources, while the gaps in opportunities to support young children's social-emotional development grow. This gap in the earliest years of life stands in contrast with the universal education as well as support for specialized needs in learning, nutrition, health, and social-emotional well-being provided by the K–12 system.

Access not only to mental health intervention but also to mental health promotion and prevention services is critical to parents, caregivers, and children. In many care settings, however, a lack of culturally informed and linguistically matched care can exacerbate inequalities for marginalized groups. Well-implemented universal programs such as home visiting and social-emotional learning approaches in ECE and school settings can improve social-emotional outcomes. In addition, policies that support the mental health and well-being of parents can improve outcomes for children. Access to paid family leave, in particular, gives parents opportunities to bond with their young children and enhances their ability to address serious health issues while decreasing family stress and financial uncertainty, all of which is particularly important in the early years, a critical period that can affect healthy development across the life course.

Many of the systems in the United States that are responsible for children lack coordination and interoperability. Many families—especially those experiencing poverty, job insecurity, or health issues—interact with multiple service sectors, such as health care, mental health care, child care, education, job training, substance abuse programs, and housing agencies that work independently of one another. They do not work together to coordinate services for children and families; rather, each agency has its own eligibility requirements, service providers, and practices, creating a burden on families and providing inefficient, duplicative, and siloed services.

Active policies and support for accessing proven programs is necessary to help all children thrive socially and emotionally and to eliminate centuries-old inequities in opportunities that are responsible for disparities in outcomes in this realm. Although there are many promising practices that can help close this opportunity gap, unequal access to services and resources that promote positive social-emotional development and well-being remains a barrier to promoting equitable outcomes for young children.

REFERENCES

Aber, J.L., Jones, S., & Cohen, J. (2000). The impact of poverty on the mental health and development of very young children. *Handbook of infant mental health*. (2nd ed.) New York, NY: The Guilford Press.

Administration of Children and Families. (2022). *What is home visiting evidence of effectiveness?* Department of Health and Human Services. Available: https://homvee.acf.hhs.gov/

Ainsworth, M.S. (1979). Infant–mother attachment. *American Psychologist*, 34(10), 932–7. https://doi.org/10.1037/0003-066X.34.10.932

Alderton, A., Villanueva, K., O'Connor, M., Boulangé, C., & Badland, H. (2019). Reducing inequities in early childhood mental health: How might the neighborhood built environment help close the gap? A systematic search and critical review. *International Journal of Environmental Research and Public Health*, 16(9), 1516. https://doi.org/10.3390/ijerph16091516

Alegría, M., Canino, G., Ríos, R., Vera, M., Calderón, J., Rusch, D., & Ortega, A.N. (2002). Inequalities in use of specialty mental health services among Latinos, African Americans, and non-Latino whites. *Psychiatric Services*, 53(12), 1547–55. https://doi.org/10.1176/appi.ps.53.12.1547

Alegría, M., Vallas, M., & Pumariega, A.J. (2010). Racial and ethnic disparities in pediatric mental health. *Child and Adolescent Psychiatric Clinics of North America*, 19(4), 759–74. https://doi.org/10.1016/j.chc.2010.07.001

Alegría, M., Green, J.G., McLaughlin, K.A., & Loder, S. (2015). *Disparities in child and adolescent mental health and mental health services*. William T. Grant Foundation. Available: http://cfs.cbcs.usf.edu/projects-research/_docs/Disparities_in_child_and_adolescent_health.pdf

American Psychiatric Association. (2013). *Diagnostic and statistical manual of mental disorders*. (5th ed.). American Psychiatric Association Publishing. https://doi.org/10.1176/appi.books.9780890425596

Ananat, E., & Gassman-Pines, A. (2020). Snapshot of the COVID crisis impact on working families. *Econofact*. Edward R. Murrow Center for a Digital World at The Fletcher School at Tufts University. Available: https://econofact.org/snapshot-of-the-covid-crisis-impact-on-working-families

Andersen, S.H., Richmond-Rakerd, L.S., Moffitt, T.E., & Caspi, A. (2021). Nationwide evidence that education disrupts the intergenerational transmission of disadvantage. *Proceedings of the National Academy of Sciences of the United States of America*, 118(31), e2103896118. https://doi.org/10.1073/pnas.2103896118

Anderson, R.E., & Stevenson, H.C. (2019). Recasting racial stress and trauma: Theorizing the healing potential of racial socialization in families. *American Psychologist*, 74(1), 63. https://doi.org/10.1037/amp0000392

Anderson, R.E., Hussain, S.B., Wilson, M.N., Shaw, D.S., Dishion, T.J., & Williams, J.L. (2015). Pathways to pain: Racial discrimination and relations between parental functioning and child psychosocial well-being. *Journal of Black Psychology*, 41(6), 491–512. https://doi.org/10.1177/0095798414548511

Anzures, G., Wheeler, A., Quinn, P.C., Pascalis, O., Slater, A.M., Heron-Delaney, M., Tanaka, J.W., & Lee, K. (2012). Brief daily exposures to Asian females reverses perceptual narrowing for Asian faces in Caucasian infants. *Journal of Experimental Child Psychology*, 112(4), 484–95. https://doi.org/10.1016/j.jecp.2012.04.005

Aratani, Y., & Cooper, J.L. (2012). Racial and ethnic disparities in the continuation of community-based children's mental health services. *Journal of Behavioral Health Services & Research*, 39(2), 116–29. https://doi.org/10.1007/s11414-011-9261-z

Ash, J., Mackrain, M., & Johnston, K. (2013). Early childhood mental health consultation: Applying central tenets across diverse practice settings. *Journal of Zero to Three*, 33(5), 28–33. Available: https://www.zerotothree.org/wp-content/uploads/2022/06/Early-Childhood-Mental-Health-Consultation-13-May-Digital-Journal-Issue.pdf

Assari, S. (2020). Socioeconomic status inequalities partially mediate racial and ethnic differences in children's amygdala volume. *Studies in Social Science Research*, 1(2), 62–79. https://doi.org/10.22158/sssr.v1n2p62

Atkins, M.S., Frazier, S.L., Birman, D., Adil, J.A., Jackson, M., Graczyk, P.A., Talbott, E., Farmer, A.D., Bell, C.C., & McKay, M.M. (2006). School-based mental health services for children living in high poverty urban communities. *Administration and Policy in Mental Health*, 33(2), 146–59. https://doi.org/10.1007/s10488-006-0031-9

Atkins, M.S., Cappella, E., Shernoff, E.S., Mehta, T.G., & Gustafson, E.L. (2017). School and children's mental health: Realigning resources to reduce disparities and advance public health. *Annual Review of Clinical Psychology* 13, 123–47. https://doi.org/10.1146/annurev-clinpsy-032816-045234

Avila, R.M., & Bramlett, M.D. (2013). Language and immigrant status effects on disparities in Hispanic children's health status and access to health care. *Maternal and Child Health Journal*, 17(3), 415–23. https://doi.org/10.1007/s10995-012-0988-9

Azzi-Lessing, L. (2010). Meeting the mental health needs of poor and vulnerable children in early care and education programs. *Early Childhood Research & Practice*, 12(1). Available: https://eric.ed.gov/?id=EJ889716

Bailey, Z.D., Feldman, J.M., & Bassett, M.T. (2021). How structural racism works—racist policies as a root cause of U.S. racial health inequities. *New England Journal of Medicine*, 384(8), 768–73. https://doi.org/10.1056/NEJMms2025396

Baker-Henningham, H. (2014). The role of early childhood education programmes in the promotion of child and adolescent mental health in low- and middle-income countries. *International Journal of Epidemiology*, 43(2), 407–33. https://doi.org/10.1093/ije/dyt226

Ballentine, K.L. (2019). Understanding racial differences in diagnosing ODD versus ADHD using critical race theory. *Families in Society*, 100(3), 282–92. https://doi.org/10.1177/1044389419842765

Bandura, A., Barbaranelli, C., Caprara, G.V., & Pastorelli, C. (2001). Self-efficacy beliefs as shapers of children's aspirations and career trajectories. *Child Development*, 72(1), 187–206. https://doi.org/10.1111/1467-8624.00273

Barbarin, O., & Crawford, G.M. (2006). Acknowledging and reducing stigmatization of African American boys. *Young Children*, 61(6), 79–86.

Bauer, P.M., Hanson, J.L., Pierson, R.K., Davidson, R.J., & Pollak, S.D. (2009). Cerebellar volume and cognitive functioning in children who experienced early deprivation. *Biological Psychiatry*, 66(12), 1100–6. https://doi.org/10.1016/j.biopsych.2009.06.014

Béatrice, N., Lise, G., Victoria, Z.M., & Louise, S. (2012). Longitudinal patterns of poverty and health in early childhood: Exploring the influence of concurrent, previous, and cumulative poverty on child health outcomes. *BMC Pediatrics*, 12(1). https://doi.org/10.1186/1471-2431-12-141

Birman, D., & Simon, C.D. (2013). Acculturation research: Challenges, complexities, and possibilities. *APA handbook of multicultural psychology*. American Psychological Association. Available: https://www.researchgate.net/publication/255991744_Acculturation_research_Challenges_complexities_and_possibilities

Bitsko, R.H., Claussen, A.H., Lichstein, J., Black, L.I., Jones, S.E., Danielson, M.L., Hoenig, J. M., Davis Jack, S.P., Brody, D.J., Gyawali, S., Maenner, M.J., Warner, M., Holland, K. M., Perou, R., Crosby, A.E., Blumberg, S.J., Avenevoli, S., Kaminski, J.W., ... & Meyer, L.N. (2022). Mental health surveillance among children—United States, 2013–2019. *Morbidity and Mortality Weekly Reports: Supplements*, 71(2), 1–42. https://doi.org/10.15585/mmwr.su7102a1

Blumberg, S., Bramlett, M., Kogan, M., Schieve, L., Jones, J., & Lu, M. (2013). Changes in parent-reported prevalence of autism spectrum disorder in school-aged US children: 2007 to 2011–12. *National Health Statistics Report*, (65), 1–11.

Bornstein, M.H., & Cote, L.R. (2004). "Who is sitting across from me?" Immigrant mothers' knowledge of parenting and children's development. *Pediatrics*, 114(5), e557–64. Available: https://www.researchgate.net/publication/254303944_The_Evidence_Base_for_Mental_Health_Consultation_in_Early_Childhood_Settings_Research_Synthesis_Addressing_Staff_and_Program_Outcomes

Brennan, E.M., Bradley, J.R., Allen, M.D., & Perry, D.F. (2008). The evidence base for mental health consultation in early childhood settings: Research synthesis addressing staff and program outcomes. *Early Education and Development*, 19(6), 982–1022. https://doi.org/10.1080/10409280801975834

Brinamen, C.F., Taranta, A.N., & Johnston, K. (2012). Expanding early childhood mental health consultation to new venues: Serving infants and young children in domestic violence and homeless shelters. *Infant Mental Health Journal*, 33(3), 283–93. https://doi.org/10.1002/imhj.21338

Bringewatt, E.H., & Gershoff, E.T. (2010). Falling through the cracks: Gaps and barriers in the mental health system for America's disadvantaged children. *Children and Youth Services Review*, 32(10), 1291–9.

Brito, N.H., & Noble, K.G. (2014). Socioeconomic status and structural brain development. *Frontiers in Neuroscience*, 8. https://doi.org/10.3389/fnins.2014.00276

Brody, G.H., Chen, Y.F., Kogan, S.M., Murry, V.M., Logan, P., & Luo, Z. (2008). Linking perceived discrimination to longitudinal changes in African American mothers' parenting practices. *Journal of Marriage and Family*, 70(2), 319–31. https://doi.org/10.1111/j.1741-3737.2008.00484.x

Bugental, D.B., & Schwartz, A. (2009). A cognitive approach to child mistreatment prevention among medically at-risk infants. *Developmental Psychology*, 45(1), 284–8. https://doi.org/10.1037/a0014031

Bullinger, L.R. (2019). The effect of paid family leave on infant and parental health in the United States. *Journal of Health Economics*, 66, 101–16. https://doi.org/10.1016/j.jhealeco.2019.05.006

Bussing, R., Schoenberg, N.E., Rogers, K.M., Zima, B.T., & Angus, S. (1998). Explanatory models of ADHD: Do they differ by ethnicity, child gender, or treatment status? *Journal of Emotional and Behavioral Disorders*, 6(4), 233–42. https://doi.org/10.1177/106342669800600405

Bussing, R., Zima, B.T., Gary, F.A., & Garvan, C.W. (2003). Barriers to detection, help-seeking, and service use for children with ADHD symptoms. *The Journal of Behavioral Health Services & Research*, 30(2), 176–89. https://doi.org/10.1007/BF02289806

Butler, A.M., & Rodgers, C.R.R. (2019). Developing a policy brief on child mental health disparities to promote strategies for advancing equity among racial/ethnic minority youth. *Ethnicity & Disease*, 29(2 Suppl), 421–6. https://doi.org/10.18865/ed.29.S2.421

Cappella, E., Frazier, S.L., Atkins, M.S., Schoenwald, S.K., & Glisson, C. (2008). Enhancing schools' capacity to support children in poverty: An ecological model of school-based mental health services. *Administration and Policy in Mental Health*, 35(5), 395–409. https://doi.org/10.1007/s10488-008-0182-y

Center on the Developing Child. (2016). *Applying the science of child development in child welfare systems*. Harvard University Center on the Developing Child. Available: www.developingchild.harvard.edu

Center of Excellence for Infant & Early Childhood Mental Health Consultation. (2021). *Annotated bibliography: The evidence base for infant and early childhood mental health consultation (IECMHC)*. Georgetown University Center for Child and Human Development. Available: http://www.iecmhc.org/documents/CoE-Annotated-Bibliography.pdf

Centers for Disease Control and Prevention. (2018). *Mental health services for children*. [Policy brief]. Available: https://www.cdc.gov/ruralhealth/child-health/policybrief.html

Chabra, A., Chávez, G.F., & Harris, E.S. (1999). Mental illness in elementary-school-aged children. *Western Journal of Medicine*, 170(1), 28.

Chabra, A., Chávez, G.F., Harris, E.S., & Shah, R. (1999). Hospitalization for mental illness in adolescents: Risk groups and impact on the health care system. *Journal of Adolescent Health*, 24(5), 349–56. https://doi.org/10.1016/s1054-139x(98)00116-5

Chaffin, M., Hecht, D., Bard, D., Silovsky, J.F., & Beasley, W.H. (2012). A statewide trial of the SafeCare home-based services model with parents in Child Protective Services. *Pediatrics*, 129(3), 509–15. https://doi.org/10.1542/peds.2011-1840

Chazan-Cohen, R., Stark, D.R., Mann, T.L., & Fitzgerald, H.E. (2007). Early Head Start and infant mental health. *Infant Mental Health Journal*, 28(2), 99–105. https://doi.org/10.1002/imhj.20124

Children's Defense Fund. (2021). *The state of America's children 2021*. Available: https://www.childrensdefense.org/state-of-americas-children/

Chow, J.C.-C., Jaffee, K., & Snowden, L. (2003). Racial/ethnic disparities in the use of mental health services in poverty areas. *American Journal of Public Health*, 93(5), 792–7. https://doi.org/10.2105/ajph.93.5.792

Coker, T.R., Elliott, M.N., Kanouse, D.E., Grunbaum, J.A., Schwebel, D.C., Gilliland, M.J., Tortolero, S.R., Peskin, M.F., & Schuster, M.A. (2009). Perceived racial/ethnic discrimination among fifth-grade students and its association with mental health. *American Journal of Public Health*, 99(5), 878–84. https://doi.org/10.2105/AJPH.2008.144329

Coker, T.R., Elliott, M.N., Toomey, S.L., Schwebel, D.C., Cuccaro, P.M., Emery, S.T., Davies, S.L., Visser, S.N., & Schuster, M.A. (2016). Racial and ethnic disparities in ADHD diagnosis and treatment. *Pediatrics*, 138(3), e20160407. https://doi.org/10.1542/peds.2016-0407

Collins, K.S., Strieder, F.H., DePanfilis, D., Tabor, M., Clarkson, P.A., Linde, L., & Greenberg, P. (2011). Trauma adapted family connections: Reducing developmental and complex trauma symptomatology to prevent child abuse and neglect. *Child Welfare*, 90(6), 29–48. https://www.jstor.org/stable/48625368

Condon, E.M., De Mendoza, V.B., Ibrahim, B.B., Crusto, C.A., & Taylor, J.Y. (2022). Racial discrimination, mental health, and parenting among African American mothers of preschool-aged children. *Journal of the American Academy of Child and Adolescent Psychiatry*, 61(3), 402–12. https://doi.org/10.1016/j.jaac.2021.05.023

Cook, B.L., Doksum, T., Chen, C.-N., Carle, A., & Alegría, M. (2013). The role of provider supply and organization in reducing racial/ethnic disparities in mental health care in the U.S. *Social Science & Medicine*, 84, 102–9. https://doi.org/10.1016/j.socscimed.2013.02.006

Corso, R. (2003). The Center on the Social and Emotional Foundations for Early Learning. *Young Children*, 58(4), 46–7.

Cree, R.A., Bitsko, R.H., Robinson, L.R., Holbrook, J.R., Danielson, M.L., Smith, C., Kaminski, J.W., Kenney, M.K., & Peacock, G. (2018). Health care, family, and community factors associated with mental, behavioral, and developmental disorders and poverty among children aged 2–8 years - United States, 2016. *Morbidity and Mortality Weekly Report*, 67(50), 1377–83. https://doi.org/10.15585/mmwr.mm6750a1

Croen, L.A., Grether, J.K., Hoogstrate, J., & Selvin, S. (2002). The changing prevalence of autism in California. *Journal of Autism and Developmental Disorders*, 32(3), 207–15. https://doi.org/10.1023/a:1015453830880

Cummings, J.R., Wen, H., & Druss, B.G. (2013). Improving access to mental health services for youth in the United States. *Journal of the American Medical Association*, 309(6), 553–4. https://doi.org/10.1001/jama.2013.437

De Bellis, M.D., & Zisk, A. (2014). The biological effects of childhood trauma. *Child and Adolescent Psychiatric Clinics of North America*, 23(2), 185–222. https://doi.org/10.1016/j.chc.2014.01.002

Dewey, J. (1922). *Human nature and conduct: An introduction to social psychology*. New York: Henry Holt and Company.

Diptee, A.A. (2006). African children in the British slave trade during the late eighteenth century. *Slavery and Abolition*, 27(2), 183–96. https://doi.org/10.1080/01440390600765458

Dishion, T.J., Brennan, L.M., Shaw, D.S., McEachern, A.D., Wilson, M.N., & Jo, B. (2014). Prevention of problem behavior through annual family check-ups in early childhood: Intervention effects from home to early elementary school. *Journal of Abnormal Child Psychology*, 42(3), 343–54. https://doi.org/10.1007/s10802-013-9768-2

Dodge, K.A. (2018). Toward population impact from early childhood psychological interventions. *The American Psychologist*, 73(9), 1117–29. https://doi.org/10.1037/amp0000393

Dodge, K.A., & Goodman, W.B. (2019). Universal reach at birth: Family connects. *The Future of Children*, 29(1), 41–60. https://doi.org/10.1353/foc.2019.0003

Dodge, K.A., Malone, P.S., Lansford, J.E., Sorbring, E., Skinner, A.T., Tapanya, S., Tirado, L.M., Zelli, A., Alampay, L.P., Al-Hassan, S.M., Bacchini, D., Bombi, A.S., Bornstein, M.H., Chang, L., Deater-Deckard, K., Di Giunta, L., Oburu, P., & Pastorelli, C. (2015). Hostile attributional bias and aggressive behavior in global context. *Proceedings of the National Academy of Sciences of the United States of America*, 112(30), 9310–5. https://doi.org/10.1073/pnas.1418572112

Dodge, K.A., Skinner, A.T., Godwin, J., Bai, Y., Lansford, J.E., Copeland, W.E., Goodman, W.B., McMahon, R.J., Goulter, N., & Bornstein, M.H. (2021). Impact of the COVID-19 pandemic on substance use among adults without children, parents, and adolescents. *Addictive Behaviors Reports*, 14. https://doi.org/10.1016/j.abrep.2021.100388

Dore, R.A., Hoffman, K.M., Lillard, A.S., & Trawalter, S. (2014). Children's racial bias in perceptions of others' pain. *British Journal of Developmental Psychology*, 32(2), 218–31. https://doi.org/10.1111/bjdp.12038

Downer, J.T., Goble, P., Myers, S.S., & Pianta, R.C. (2016). Teacher-child racial/ethnic match within pre-kindergarten classrooms and children's early school adjustment. *Early Childhood Research Quarterly*, 37, 26–38. https://doi.org/10.1016/j.ecresq.2016.02.007

Dozier, M., & Bernard, K. (2019). *Coaching parents of vulnerable infants: The attachment and biobehavioral catch-up approach*. New York, NY: The Guilford Press.

DuMont, K., Kirkland, K., Mitchell-Herzfeld, S., Ehrhard-Dietzel, S., Rodriguez, M.L., Lee, E., Lane, C., & Greene, R. (2011). *A randomized trial of Healthy Families New York (HFNY): Does home visiting prevent child maltreatment?* National Institute of Justice. Available: https://www.ojp.gov/pdffiles1/nij/grants/232945.pdf

Dunham, Y., Baron, A.S., & Banaji, M.R. (2008). The development of implicit intergroup cognition. *Trends in Cognitive Sciences*, 12(7), 248–53. https://doi.org/10.1016/j.tics.2008.04.006

Duran, F., Hepburn, K., Irvine, M., Kaufmann, R., Anthony, B., Horen, N., & Perry, D. (2009). *What works? A study of effective early childhood mental health consultation programs*. Georgetown University Center for Child and Human Development. Available: https://www.aecf.org/resources/what-works-a-study-of-effective-early-childhood-mental-health-consultation

Earle, A., Joshi, P., Geronimo, K., & Acevedo-Garcia, D. (2014). Job characteristics among working parents: Differences by race, ethnicity, and nativity. *Monthly Labor Review*. Available: https://www.bls.gov/opub/mlr/2014/article/job-characteristics-among-working-parents.htm

Eckenrode, J., Campa, M., Morris, P., Henderson, C., Bolger, K., Kitzman, H., & Olds, D. (2016). The prevention of child maltreatment through the nurse family partnership program. *Child Maltreatment*, 22(2), 92–9. https://doi.org/10.1177/1077559516685185

Edwards, L.M., & Romero, A.J. (2008). Coping with discrimination among Mexican descent adolescents. *Hispanic Journal of Behavioral Sciences*. 30(1), 24–39. https://doi.org/10.1177/0739986307311431

Evans, G.W., Li, D., & Whipple, S.S. (2013). Cumulative risk and child development. *Psychological Bulletin*, 139(6), 1342–96. https://doi.org/10.1037/a0031808

Fountain, C., King, M.D., & Bearman, P.S. (2011). Age of diagnosis for Autism: Individual and community factors across 10 birth cohorts. *Journal of Epidemiology & Community Health*, 65(6), 503–10. https://doi.org/10.1136/jech.2009.104588

Fox, L., & Hemmeter, M.L. (2009). A programwide model for supporting social emotional development and addressing challenging behavior in early childhood settings. *Handbook of positive behavior support*, 177–202. Springer Publishing Company. https://doi.org/10.1007/978-0-387-09632-2_8

Frey, W.H. (2018). *Diversity explosion: How new racial demographics are remaking America*. Washington, DC: Brookings Institution Press.

Fusar-Poli, P. (2019). Integrated mental health services for the developmental period (0 to 25 years): A critical review of the evidence. *Frontiers in Psychiatry*, 10, 355. https://doi.org/10.3389/fpsyt.2019.00355

García, S.B., Méndez Pérez, A., & Ortiz, A.A. (2000). Mexican American mothers' beliefs about disabilities: Implications for early childhood intervention. *Remedial and Special Education*, 21(2), 90–120. https://doi.org/10.1177/074193250002100204

Garland, A.F., Lau, A.S., Yeh, M., McCabe, K.M., Hough, R.L., & Landsverk, J.A. (2005). Racial and ethnic differences in utilization of mental health services among high-risk youths. *American Journal of Psychiatry*, 162(7), 1336–43. https://doi.org/10.1176/appi.ajp.162.7.1336

Gassman-Pines, A., Ananat, E.O., & Fitz-Henley, J. (2020). COVID-19 and parent-child psychological well-being. *Pediatrics*, 146(4). https://doi.org/10.1542/peds.2020-007294

Gill, A.M., Dishion, T.J., & Shaw, D.S. (2014). The family check-up: A tailored approach to intervention with high-risk families. *Wellbeing in children and families*, 385–405. Hoboken, NJ: Wiley-Blackwell.

Gilliam, W. (2005). *Prekindergarteners left behind: Expulsion rates in state prekindergarten systems*. Foundation for Child Development. Available: https://www.fcd-us.org/prekindergartners-left-behind-expulsion-rates-in-state-prekindergarten-programs/

Gilliam, W.S., Maupin, A.N., Reyes, C.R., Accavitti, M., & Shic, F. (2016). *Do early educators' implicit biases regarding sex and race relate to behavior expectations and recommendations of preschool expulsions and suspensions?* New Haven, CT: Yale University, Child Study Center.

Gonzalez, J.M., Alegria, M., & Prihoda, T.J. (2005). How do attitudes toward mental health treatment vary by age, gender, and ethnicity/race in young adults? *Journal of Community Psychology*, 33(5), 611–29. https://doi.org/10.1002/jcop.20071

Gonzales-Ball, T.L., & Bratton, S.C. (2019). Child–teacher relationship training as a Head Start early mental health intervention for children exhibiting disruptive behavior. *International Journal of Play Therapy*, 28(1), 44. https://doi.org/10.1037/pla0000081

Goodson, B., Grindal, T., Darrow, C., Gwaltney, M., Walker, D., Wyant, B., & Price, C. (2014). *Outcomes of project launch: Cross-site evaluation findings, Volume II*. (OPRE Report No. 2014–88). Washington, DC: Office of Planning, Research and Evaluation, Administration for Children and Families, Department of Health and Human Services.

Guarnaccia, P.J., & Parra, P. (1996). Ethnicity, social status, and families' experiences of caring for a mentally ill family member. *Community Mental Health Journal*, 32(3), 243–60. https://doi.org/10.1007/BF02249426

Guerrero, A.D., Rodriguez, M.A., & Flores, G. (2011). Disparities in provider elicitation of parents' developmental concerns for US children. *Pediatrics*, 128(5), 901–9. https://doi.org/10.1542/peds.2011-0030

Guevara, J.P., Feudtner, C., Romer, D., Power, T., Eiraldi, R., Nihtianova, S., Rosales, A., Ohene-Frempong, J., & Schwarz, D.F. (2005). Fragmented care for inner-city minority children with attention-deficit/hyperactivity disorder. *Pediatrics*, 116(4), e512–7. https://doi.org/10.1542/peds.2005-0243

Haider, A. (2021). *The basic facts about children in poverty*. Center for American Progress. Available: https://www.americanprogress.org/article/basic-facts-children-poverty/

Halfon, N., & Newacheck, P.W. (1999). Prevalence and impact of parent-reported disabling mental health conditions among US children. *Journal of the American Academy of Child & Adolescent Psychiatry*, 38(5), 600–9. https://doi.org/10.1097/00004583-199905000-00023

Han, W.J., Ruhm, C., & Waldfogel, J. (2009). Parental leave policies and parents' employment and leave-taking. *Journal of Policy Analysis and Management*, 28(1), 29–54. https://doi.org/10.1002/pam.20398

Hansen, H., Bourgois, P., & Drucker, E. (2014). Pathologizing poverty: New forms of diagnosis, disability, and structural stigma under welfare reform. *Social Science & Medicine*, 103, 76–83. https://doi.org/10.1016/j.socscimed.2013.06.033

Haynes, N., Cooper, L.A., & Albert, M.A., on Behalf of the Association of Black Cardiologists. (2020). At the heart of the matter: Unmasking and addressing the toll of COVID-19 on diverse populations. *Circulation*, 142(2), 105–7. https://doi.org/10.1161/CIRCULATIONAHA.120.048126

Hayward, M.D., Miles, T.P., Crimmins, E.M., & Yang, Y. (2000). The significance of socioeconomic status in explaining the racial gap in chronic health conditions. *American Sociological Review*, 910–30. https://www.jstor.org/stable/2657519

Health Resources and Services Administration. (2022). *Maternal, Infant, and Early Childhood Home Visiting (MIECHV) Program*. Available: https://mchb.hrsa.gov/programs-impact/programs/home-visiting/maternal-infant-early-childhood-home-visiting-miechv-program

Healthy People 2020. (2020). *Healthy People 2020*. Washington, DC: Department of Health and Human Services, Office of Disease Prevention and Health Promotion.

Heinrich, C.J. (2014). Parents' employment and children's wellbeing. *Future of Children*, 24(1), 121–46. http://www.jstor.org/stable/23723386.

Hemmeter, M., Ostrosky, M., & Fox, L. (2006). Social and emotional foundations for early learning: A conceptual model for intervention. *School Psychology Review*, 35(4), 583–601. https://doi.org/10.1080/02796015.2006.12087963

Hemmeter, M.L., Snyder, P.A., Fox, L., & Algina, J. (2016). Evaluating the implementation of the pyramid model for promoting social-emotional competence in early childhood classrooms. *Topics in Early Childhood Special Education*, 36(3), 133–46. https://doi.org/10.1177/0271121416653386

Hepburn, K.S., Perry, D. F., Shivers Marie, M.E., & Gilliam, W.S. (2013). Early childhood mental health consultation as an evidence-based practice. *Journal of Zero to Three*, 33(5), 10–9. Available: https://www.zerotothree.org/wp-content/uploads/2022/06/Early-Childhood-Mental-Health-Consultation-13-May-Digital-Journal-Issue.pdf

Hodgkinson, S., Godoy, L., Beers, L.S., & Lewin, A. (2017). Improving mental health access for low-income children and families in the primary care setting. *Pediatrics*, 139(1), e20151175. https://doi.org/10.1542/peds.2015-1175

Holland, M.L., Xia, Y., Kitzman, H.J., Dozier, A.M., & Olds, D.L. (2014). Patterns of visit attendance in the nurse-family partnership program. *American Journal of Public Health*, 104(10), e58–65. https://doi.org/10.2105/AJPH.2014.302115

Huang, K.Y., Calzada, E., Cheng, S., & Brotman, L.M. (2012). Physical and mental health disparities among young children of Asian immigrants. *The Journal of Pediatrics*, 160(2), 331–6. https://doi.org/10.1016/j.jpeds.2011.08.005

Immerfall, S.J., & Ramirez, M.R. (2019). Link for Schools: A system to prevent trauma and its adverse impacts. *National Association of School Nurses School Nurse*, 34(1), 21–4. https://doi.org/10.1177/1942602X18785010

Institute of Medicine. (2003). *Unequal treatment: Confronting racial and ethnic disparities in health care*. Washington, DC: National Academy Press.

Institute of Medicine (IOM) & National Research Council (NRC). (2000). *From neurons to neighborhoods: The science of early childhood development*. Washington, DC: The National Academy Press.

———. (2009). *Preventing mental, emotional, and behavioral disorders among young people: Progress and possibilities*. Washington, DC: The National Academies Press.

Irish, A.M., White, J.S., Modrek, S., & Hamad, R. (2021). Paid family leave and mental health in the U.S.: A quasi-experimental study of state policies. *American Journal of Preventive Medicine*, 61(2), 182–91. https://doi.org/10.1016/j.amepre.2021.03.018

Iruka, I.U. (2022). Delivering on the promise of early childhood education for black children: An equity strategy. *New Directions for Child and Adolescent Development*, 2022 (183–184), 27–45. https://doi.org/10.1002/cad.20483

Jacobson, J.W., & Mulick, J.A. (2000). System and cost research issues in treatments for people with autistic disorders. *Journal of Autism and Developmental Disorders*, 30(6), 585–93. https://doi.org/10.1023/a:1005691411255

Jarquin, V.G., Wiggins, L.D., Schieve, L.A., & Van Naarden-Braun, K. (2011). Racial disparities in community identification of autism spectrum disorders over time; metropolitan Atlanta, Georgia, 2000–2006. *Journal of Developmental & Behavioral Pediatrics*, 32(3), 179–87. https://doi.org/10.1097/DBP.0b013e31820b4260

Jensen, E., Jones, N., Rabe, M., Pratt, B., Medina, L., Orozco, K., & Spell, L. (2021). The chance that two people chosen at random are of different race or ethnicity group has increased since 2010. United States Census Bureau. Available: https://www.census.gov/library/stories/2021/08/2020-united-states-population-more-racially-ethnically-diverse-than-2010.html

Johnson, K. (2017). Healthy and ready to learn: School nurses improve equity and access. *Online Journal of Issues in Nursing*, 22(3), 1. https://doi.org/10.3912/OJIN.Vol22No03Man01

Johnston, K., & Brinamen, C. (2006). Mental health consultation in child care: Transforming relationships among directors, staff, and families. *Journal of Zero to Three*. National Center for Infants, Toddlers and Families. Available: https://www.zerotothree.org/wp-content/uploads/2022/06/Early-Childhood-Mental-Health-Consultation-13-May-Digital-Journal-Issue.pdf

Jones Harden, B., & Slopen, N. (2022). Inequitable experiences and outcomes in young children: Addressing racial and social-economic disparities in physical and mental health. *Annual Review of Developmental Psychology*, 4, 133–59. https://doi.org/10.1146/annurev-devpsych-121020-031515

Jones Harden, B., Martoccio, T.L., & Berlin, L.J. (2021). Maternal psychological risk moderates the impacts of attachment-based intervention on mother-toddler mutuality and toddler behavior problems: A randomized controlled trial. *Prevention Science: The Official Journal of the Society for Prevention Research*. https://doi.org/10.1007/s11121-021-01281-0

Kamis, C. (2021). The long-term impact of parental mental health on children's distress trajectories in adulthood. *Society and Mental Health*, 11(1), 54–68. https://doi.org/10.1177/2156869320912520

Kelly, D.J., Quinn, P.C., Slater, A.M., Lee, K., Gibson, A., Smith, M., Ge, L., & Pascalis, O. (2005). Three-month-olds, but not newborns, prefer own-race faces. *Developmental Science*, 8(6), F31–6. https://doi.org/10.1111/j.1467-7687.2005.0434a.x

Kessler, R.C., Berglund, P., Demler, O., Jin, R., Merikangas, K.R., & Walters, E.E. (2005). Lifetime prevalence and age-of-onset distributions of DSM-IV disorders in the National Comorbidity Survey Replication. *Archives of General Psychiatry*, 62(6), 593–602. https://doi.org/10.1001/archpsyc.62.6.593

Kinser, K., Parlakian, R., Sanchez, G.R., Manzano, S., & Barreto, M. (2018). *Millennial connections: Findings from ZERO TO THREE's 2018 parent survey*. (Executive summary). Zero to Three. Available: https://www.zerotothree.org/our-work/national-parent-survey-millennial-connections/

Kodzis, K. (2021). *Considerations for school nurses: Health equity implications during COVID-19 pandemic*. Silver Spring, MD: National Association of School Nurses.

Kogan, M.D., Blumberg, S.J., Schieve, L.A., Boyle, C.A., Perrin, J.M., Ghandour, R.M., Singh, G.K., Strickland, B.B., Trevathan, E., & van Dyck, P.C. (2009). Prevalence of parent-reported diagnosis of autism spectrum disorder among children in the US, 2007. *Pediatrics*, 124(5), 1395–403. https://doi.org/10.1542/peds.2009-1522

Kotelchuck, M. (2021). The impact of fatherhood on men's health and development. *Engaged fatherhood for men, families and gender equality: Healthcare, social policy, and work perspectives*, 63–91. New York, NY: Springer International Publishing.

Kozak, K., Greaves, A., Waldfogel, J., Angal, J., Elliott, A.J., Fifier, W.P., & Brito, N.H. (2021). Paid maternal leave is associated with better language and socioemotional outcomes during toddlerhood. *Infancy*, 26(4), 536–50. https://doi.org/10.1111/infa.12399

Kummerer, S.E., Lopez-Reyna, N.A., & Hughes, M.T. (2007). Mexican immigrant mothers' perceptions of their children's communication disabilities, emergent literacy development, and speech-language therapy program. *American Journal of Speech Language Pathology*, 16(3), 271–82. https://doi.org/10.1044/1058-0360(2007/031)

Kurmann, A., Lalé, E., & Ta, L. (2020). *The impact of COVID-19 on small business employment and hours: Real-time estimates with homebase data*. Drexel University. Available: https://www.lebow.drexel.edu/sites/default/files/1588687497-hbdraft0504.pdf

Landor, A.M., & McNeil Smith, S. (2019). Skin-tone trauma: Historical and contemporary influences on the health and interpersonal outcomes of african Americans. *Perspectives on Psychological Science*, 14(5), 797–815. https://doi.org/10.1177/1745691619851781

Landor, A.M., Simons, L.G., Simons, R.L., Brody, G.H., Bryant, C.M., Gibbons, F.X., Granberg, E.M., & Melby, J.N. (2013). Exploring the impact of skin tone on family dynamics and race-related outcomes. *Journal of Family Psychology*, 27(5), 817–26. https://doi.org/10.1037/a0033883

Landry, S.H., Smith, K.E., Swank, P.R., & Guttentag, C. (2008). A responsive parenting intervention: The optimal timing across early childhood for impacting maternal behaviors and child outcomes. *Developmental Psychology*, 44(5), 1335–53. https://doi.org/10.1037/a0013030

Larson, K., Russ, S.A., Crall, J.J., & Halfon, N. (2008). Influence of multiple social risks on children's health. *Pediatrics*, 121(2), 337–44. https://doi.org/10.1542/peds.2007-0447

LaVeist, T.A., Thorpe, R.J. Jr., Mance, G.A., & Jackson, J. (2007). Overcoming confounding of race with socio-economic status and segregation to explore race disparities in smoking. *Addiction*, 102(2 Suppl), 65–70. https://doi.org/10.1111/j.1360-0443.2007.01956.x

LeCroy, C.W., & Krysik, J. (2011). Randomized trial of the healthy families Arizona home visiting program. *Children and Youth Services Review*, 33(10), 1761–6. https://doi.org/10.1016/j.childyouth.2011.04.036

LeCroy, C.W., & Lopez D. (2020). A randomized controlled trial of healthy families: 6-month and 1-year follow-up. *Prevention Science*, 21(1), 25–35. https://doi.org/10.1007/s11121-018-0931-4

Lee, B.C., Modrek, S., White, J.S., Batra, A., Collin, D.F., & Hamad, R. (2020). The effect of California's paid family leave policy on parent health: A quasi-experimental study. *Social Science & Medicine*, 251, 112915. https://doi.org/10.1016/j.socscimed.2020.112915

Lee, E., Kirkland, K., Miranda-Julian, C., & Greene, R. (2018). Reducing maltreatment recurrence through home visitation: A promising intervention for child welfare involved families. *Child Abuse & Neglect*, 86, 55–66. https://doi.org/10.1016/j.chiabu.2018.09.004

Leeb, R.T., Bitsko, R.H., Radhakrishnan, L., Martinez, P., Njai, R., & Holland, K.M. (2020). Mental health-related emergency department visits among children aged <18 Years during the COVID-19 Pandemic - United States, January 1–October 17, 2020. *Morbidity and Mortality Weekly Report*, 69(45), 1675–80. https://doi.org/10.15585/mmwr.mm6945a3

Leslie, L.K., Weckerly, J., Landsverk, J., Hough, R.L., Hurlburt, M.S., & Wood, P.A. (2003). Racial/ethnic differences in the use of psychotropic medication in high-risk children and adolescents. *Journal of the American Academy of Child & Adolescent Psychiatry*, 42(12), 1433–42. https://doi.org/10.1097/00004583-200312000-00010

Leventhal, T., & Brooks-Gunn, J. (2003). Children and youth in neighborhood contexts. *Current Directions in Psychological Science*, 12(1), 27–31. https://doi.org/10.1111/1467-8721.01216

Lieberman, A.F., Ghosh Ippen, C., & Van Horn, P. (2006). Child-parent psychotherapy: 6-month follow-up of a randomized controlled trial. *Journal of the American Academy of Child and Adolescent Psychiatry*, 45(8), 913–8. https://doi.org/10.1097/01.chi.0000222784.03735.92

Lillard, A.S. (2016). *Montessori: The science behind the genius.* New York: Oxford University Press.

Liptak, G.S., Benzoni, L.B., Mruzek, D.W., Nolan, K.W., Thingvoll, M.A., Wade, C.M., & Fryer, G.E. (2008). Disparities in diagnosis and access to health services for children with autism: Data from the national survey of children's health. *Journal of Developmental and Behavioral Pediatrics*, 29(3), 152–60. https://doi.org/10.1097/DBP.0b013e318165c7a0

Loades, M.E., Chatburn, E., Higson-Sweeney, N., Reynolds, S., Shafran, R., Brigden, A., Linney, C., McManus, M.N., Borwick, C., & Crawley, E. (2020). Rapid systematic review: The impact of social isolation and loneliness on the mental health of children and adolescents in the context of COVID-19. *Journal of the American Academy of Child and Adolescent Psychiatry*, 59(11), 1218–39. https://doi.org/10.1016/j.jaac.2020.05.009

Loewenthal, K. (2006). *Religion, culture and mental health.* Cambridge, UK: Cambridge University Press.

Lowell, D.I., Carter, A S., Godoy, L., Paulicin, B., & Briggs-Gowan, M.J. (2011). A randomized controlled trial of Child FIRST: A comprehensive home-based intervention translating research into early childhood practice. *Child Development,* 82(1), 193–208. https://doi.org/10.1111/j.1467-8624.2010.01550.x

Luecken, L.J., Roubinov, D.S., & Tanaka, R. (2013). Childhood family environment, social competence, and health across the lifespan. *Journal of Social and Personal Relationships*, 30(2), 171–8. https://doi.org/10.1177/0265407512454272

Lyons-Ruth, K., Wolfe, R., & Lyubchik, A. (2000). Depression and the parenting of young children: Making the case for early preventive mental health services. *Harvard Review of Psychiatry*, 8(3), 148–53. https://doi.org/10.1093/hrp/8.3.148

Madgett, K. (2017). *Sheppard-Towner Maternity and Infancy Protection Act (1921).* Embryo Project Encyclopedia. Available: https://embryo.asu.edu/pages/sheppard-towner-maternity-and-infancy-protection-act-1921

Malaguzzi, L. (1998). *The hundred languages of children.* London, England: Ablex Publishing Corporation.

Mandell, D.S., Listerud, J., Levy, S.E., & Pinto-Martin, J.A. (2002). Race differences in the age at diagnosis among Medicaid-eligible children with autism. *Journal of the American Academy of Child & Adolescent Psychiatry*, 41(12), 1447–53. https://doi.org/10.1097/00004583-200212000-00016

Mandell, D.S., Wiggins, L.D., Carpenter, L.A., Daniels, J., DiGuiseppi, C., Durkin, M.S., Giarelli, E., Morrier, M.J., Nicholas, J.S., Pinto-Martin, J.A., Shattuck, P.T., Thomas, K.C., Yeargin-Allsopp, M., & Kirby, R.S. (2009). Racial/ethnic disparities in the identification of children with autism spectrum disorders. *American Journal of Public Health*, 99(3), 493–8. https://doi.org/10.2105/AJPH.2007.131243

Markus, A.R., Rosenbaum, S.J., Stewart, A.M., & Cox, M.A. (2005). *How medical claims simplification can impede delivery of child developmental services.* [Executive summary]. The Commonwealth Fund. Available: https://www.commonwealthfund.org/publications/fund-reports/2005/aug/how-medical-claims-simplification-can-impede-delivery-child

Marrast, L., Himmelstein, D.U., & Woolhandler, S. (2016). Racial and ethnic disparities in mental health care for children and young adults: A national study. *International Journal of Health Services*, 46(4), 810–24. https://doi.org/10.1177/0020731416662736

Mashburn, A.J., Pianta, R.C., Barbarin, O.A., Bryant, D., Hamre, B.K., Downer, J.T., Burchinal, M., Early, D.M., & Howes, C. (2008). Measures of classroom quality in prekindergarten and children's development of academic, language, and social skills. *Child Development*, 79(3), 732–49. http://www.jstor.org/stable/27563514

Masia-Warner, C., Nangle, D.W., & Hansen, D.J. (2006). Bringing evidence-based child mental health services to the schools: General issues and specific populations. *Education and Treatment of Children*, 29(2), 165–72. http://www.jstor.org/stable/42899880

Mazza, J.R., Pingault, J.B., Booij, L., Boivin, M., Tremblay, R., Lambert, J., Zunzunegui, M.V., & Côté, S. (2016). Poverty and behavior problems during early childhood: The mediating role of maternal depression symptoms and parenting. *International Journal of Behavioral Development*, 41(6), 670–80. https://doi.org/10.1177/0165025416657615

McGuire, T.G., Alegria, M., Cook, B.L., Wells, K.B., & Zaslavsky, A.M. (2006). Implementing the institute of medicine definition of disparities: An application to mental health care. *Health Services Research*, 41(5), 1979–2005. https://doi.org/10.1111/j.1475-6773.2006.00583.x

McKay, M.M., & Bannon, W.M. Jr. (2004). Engaging families in child mental health services. *Child and Adolescent Psychiatric Clinics of North America*, 13(4), 905–21. https://doi.org/10.1016/j.chc.2004.04.001

McKown, C., & Weinstein, R.S. (2003). The development and consequences of stereotype consciousness in middle childhood. *Child Development*, 74(2), 498–515. https://doi.org/10.1111/1467-8624.7402012

McLoyd, V.C., Hill, N.E., & Dodge, K.A. (Eds.). (2005). *African American family life: Ecological and cultural diversity*. New York, NY: The Guilford Press.

McNeil, S., Harris-McKoy, D., Brantley, C., Fincham, F., & Beach, S.R. (2014). Middle class African American mothers' depressive symptoms mediate perceived discrimination and reported child externalizing behaviors. *Journal of Child and Family Studies*, 23(2), 381–8. https://doi.org/10.1007/s10826-013-9788-0

Meek, S.E., & W.S. Gilliam. (2016). Expulsion and suspension in early education as matters of social justice and health equity. [Discussion Paper]. *NAM Perspectives*, 6(10). https://doi.org/10.31478/201610e

Merikangas, K.R., He, J.P., Burstein, M., Swanson, S.A., Avenevoli, S., Cui, L., Benjet, C., Georgiades, K., & Swendsen, J. (2010). Lifetime prevalence of mental disorders in U.S. adolescents: Results from the National Comorbidity Survey Replication—Adolescent Supplement (NCS-A). *Journal of the American Academy of Child and Adolescent Psychiatry*, 49(10), 980–9. https://doi.org/10.1016/j.jaac.2010.05.017

Michalopoulos, C., Faucetta, K., Hill, C.J., Portilla, X.A., Burrell, L., Lee, H., Duggan, A., & Knox, V. (2019). *Impacts on family outcomes of evidence-based early childhood home visiting: Results from the mother and infant home visiting program evaluation*. (OPRE Report No. 2019-07). MDRC. Available: https://www.acf.hhs.gov/sites/default/files/documents/opre/mihope_impact_report_final20_508_0.pdf

Miller, T.R. (2015). Projected outcomes of nurse-family partnership home visitation during 1996–2013, USA. *Prevention Science*, 16(6), 765–77. https://doi.org/10.1007/s11121-015-0572-9

Miller, T.W., Nigg, J.T., & Miller, R.L. (2009). Attention deficit hyperactivity disorder in African American children: What can be concluded from the past ten years? *Clinical Psychology Review*, 29(1), 77–86. https://doi.org/10.1016/j.cpr.2008.10.001

Molnar, B.E., Lees, K.E., Roper, K., Byars, N., Méndez-Peñate, L., Moulin, C., McMullen, W., Wolfe, J., & Allen, D. (2018). Enhancing early childhood mental health primary care services: Evaluation of MA Project LAUNCH. *Maternal and Child Health Journal*, 22(10), 1502–10. https://doi.org/10.1007/s10995-018-2548-4

Montessori, M.M. (1966). *The human tendencies and Montessori education.* Amsterdam, the Netherlands: Association Montessori Internationale.

Morello-Frosch, R., & Shenassa, E.D. (2006). The environmental "riskscape" and social inequality: Implications for explaining maternal and child health disparities. *Environmental Health Perspectives*, 114(8), 1150–3. https://doi.org/10.1289/ehp.8930

Morris, J.E., & Levine Coley, R. (2004). Maternal, family, and work correlates of role strain in low-income mothers. *Journal of Family Psychology,* 18(3), 424–32. https://doi.org/10.1037/0893-3200.18.3.424

Morris, S.L., Hospital, M.M., Wagner, E.F., Lowe, J., Thompson, M.G., Clarke, R., & Riggs, C. (2021). SACRED connections: A university-tribal clinical research partnership for school-based screening and brief intervention for substance use problems among Native American Youth. *Journal of Ethnic & Cultural Diversity in Social Work*, 30(1), 149–62. https://doi.org/10.1080/15313204.2020.1770654

National Academies of Sciences, Engineering, and Medicine (National Academies). (2019). *Vibrant and healthy kids: Aligning science, practice, and policy to advance health equity.* Washington, DC: The National Academies Press.

———. (2021). *The future of nursing 2020–2030: Charting a path to achieve health equity.* The National Academies Press. https://doi.org/10.17226/25982.

National Center for School Mental Health. (2019). *Advancing comprehensive school mental health systems: Guidance from the field.* Available: https://www.schoolmentalhealth.org/media/SOM/Microsites/NCSMH/Documents/Bainum/Advancing-CSMHS_September-2019.pdf

National Home Visiting Resource Center. (2021). *2021 Home visiting yearbook.* James Bell Associates and the Urban Institute. Available: https://nhvrc.org/yearbook/2021-yearbook/

National Research Council (NRC) & Institute of Medicine (IOM). (2009). *Preventing mental, emotional, and behavioral disorders among young people: Progress and possibilities.* The National Academies Press. https://doi.org/10.17226/12480

Nelson, C.A., Fox, N.A., & Zeanah, C.H. (2014). *Romania's abandoned children: Deprivation, brain development, and the struggle for recovery.* Boston, MA: Harvard University Press.

Nomaguchi, K., & House, A.N. (2013). Racial-ethnic disparities in maternal parenting stress: The role of structural disadvantages and parenting values. *Journal of Health and Social Behavior*, 54(3), 386–404. https://doi.org/10.1177/0022146513498511

Olds, D.L. (2006). The nurse–family partnership: An evidence-based preventive intervention. *Infant Mental Health Journal,* 27(1), 5–25. https://doi.org/10.1002/imhj.20077

Oxford, M.L., Spieker, S.J., Lohr, M.J., & Fleming, C.B. (2016). Promoting First Relationships® randomized trial of a 10-week home visiting program with families referred to Child Protective Services. *Child Maltreatment*, 21, 267–77. https://doi.org/10.1177/1077559516668274

Pachter, L.M., & Dworkin, P.H. (1997). Maternal expectations about normal child development in 4 cultural groups. *Archives of Pediatrics & Adolescent Medicine*, 151(11), 1144–50. https://doi.org/10.1001/archpedi.1997.02170480074011

Palmer, R.F., Walker, T., Mandell, D., Bayles, B., & Miller, C.S. (2010). Explaining low rates of autism among Hispanic schoolchildren in Texas. *American Journal of Public Health*, 100(2), 270–2. https://doi.org/10.2105/AJPH.2008.150565

Pastor, P.N., & Reuben, C.A. (2005). Racial and ethnic differences in ADHD and LD in young school-age children: Parental reports in the national health interview survey. *Public Health Reports*, 120(4), 383–392. https://doi.org/10.1177/003335490512000405

___. (2008). Diagnosed attention deficit hyperactivity disorder and learning disability: United States, 2004–2006: Data from the National Health Interview Survey. *Vital and Health Statistics. Series 10, Data from the National Health Survey*, (237), 1–14.

Payne-Sturges, D.C., Marty, M.A., Perera, F., Miller, M.D., Swanson, M., Ellickson, K., Cory-Slechta, D.A., Ritz, B., Balmes, J., Anderko, L., Talbott, E.O., Gould, R., & Hertz-Picciotto, I. (2019). Healthy air, healthy brains: Advancing air pollution policy to protect children's health. *American Journal of Public Health*, 109(4), 550–4. https://doi.org/10.2105/AJPH.2018.304902

Pedersen, A., Pettygrove, S., Meaney, F.J., Mancilla, K., Gotschall, K., Kessler, D.B., Grebe, T.A., & Cunniff, C. (2012). Prevalence of autism spectrum disorders in Hispanic and non-Hispanic white children. *Pediatrics*, 129(3), e629–35. https://doi.org/10.1542/peds.2011-1145

Pelham, W.E., Foster, E.M., & Robb, J.A. (2007). The economic impact of attention-deficit/hyperactivity disorder in children and adolescents. *Journal of Pediatric Psychology*, 32(6), 711–27. https://doi.org/10.1016/j.ambp.2006.08.002

Perry, D.F., Dunne, M.C., McFadden, L., & Campbell, D. (2008). Reducing the risk for preschool expulsion: Mental health consultation for young children with challenging behaviors. *Journal of Child and Family Studies*, 17(1), 44–54. https://doi.org/10.1007/s10826-007-9140-7

Perry, D.F., Allen, M., Brennan, E.M., & Bradley, J. (2010). The evidence base for mental health consultation in early childhood settings: A research synthesis addressing children's behavioral outcomes. *Early Education and Development*, 21(6), 795–824. https://doi.org/10.1080/10409280903475444

Piaget, J. (1936). *Origins of intelligence in the child*. London, UK: Routledge & Kegan Paul.

Pianta, R.C., & Hamre, B.K. (2009). Conceptualization, measurement, and improvement of classroom processes: Standardized observation can leverage capacity. *Educational Researcher*, 38(2), 109–19. https://doi.org/10.3102/0013189X09332374

Pollard, M.S., Tucker, J.S., & Green, H.D. Jr. (2020). Changes in adult alcohol use and consequences during the COVID-19 pandemic in the U.S. *JAMA Network Open*, 3(9), e2022942. https://doi.org/10.1001/jamanetworkopen.2020.22942

Prinz, R.J., Sanders, M.R., Shapiro, C.J., Whitaker, D.J., & Lutzker, J.R. (2009). Population-based prevention of child maltreatment: The U.S. Triple P System Population Trial. *Prevention Science: The Official Journal of the Society for Prevention Research*, 10(1), 1–12. https://doi.org/10.1007/s11121-009-0123-3

Reiss, F. (2013). Socioeconomic inequalities and mental health problems in children and adolescents: A systematic review. *Social Science & Medicine*, 90, 24–31. https://doi.org/10.1016/j.socscimed.2013.04.026

Richardson, L.A. (2001). Seeking and obtaining mental health services: What do parents expect? *Archives of Psychiatric Nursing*, 15(5), 223–31. https://doi.org/10.1053/apnu.2001.27019

Ridley, M., Rao, G., Schilbach, F., & Patel, V. (2020). Poverty, depression, and anxiety: Causal evidence and mechanisms. *Science*, 370(6522). https://doi.org/10.1126/science.aay0214

Robinson, L., Bitsko, R., Thompson, R., Dworkin, P., McCabe, M., Peacock, G., & Thorpe, P. (2017). CDC grand rounds: Addressing health disparities in early childhood. *Morbidity and Mortality Weekly Report*, 66, 769–72. http://dx.doi.org/10.15585/mmwr.mm6629a1

Rodgers, C.R.R., Flores, M.W., Bassey, O., Augenblick, J.M., & Cook, B.L. (2022). Racial/ethnic disparity trends in children's mental health care access and expenditures from 2010–2017: Disparities remain despite sweeping policy reform. *Journal of the American Academy of Child and Adolescent Psychiatry*, 61(7), 915–25. https://doi.org/10.1016/j.jaac.2021.09.420

Rostad, W.L., Moreland, A.D., Valle, L.A., & Chaffin, M.J. (2018). Barriers to participation in parenting programs: The relationship between parenting stress, perceived barriers, and program completion. *Journal of Child and Family Studies, 27,* 1264–74. https://doi.org/10.1007/s10826-017-0963-6

Rowland, A.S., Umbach, D.M., Stallone, L., Naftel, A.J., Bohlig, E.M., & Sandler, D.P. (2002). Prevalence of medication treatment for attention deficit-hyperactivity disorder among elementary school children in Johnston county, North Carolina. *American Journal of Public Health,* 92(2), 231–4. https://doi.org/10.2105/ajph.92.2.231

Rubin, K.II., Bukowski, W., & Bowker, J. (2015). Children in peer groups. *Handbook of child psychology and developmental science: Ecological settings and processes,* 175–222. New York, NY: John Wiley & Sons, Inc.

Sama-Miller, E., & Baumgartner, S. (2017). *Features of programs designed to help families achieve economic security and promote child well-being.* (No. 2017–49). Washington, D.C.: Office of Planning, Research and Evaluation, Administration for Children and Families, Department of Health and Human Services.

Sanders, M.R., Kirby, J.N., Tellegen, C.L., & Day, J.J. (2014). The Triple P-Positive Parenting Program: A systematic review and meta-analysis of a multi-level system of parenting support. *Clinical Psychology Review,* 34(4), 337–57. https://doi.org/10.1016/j.cpr.2014.04.003

Santiago, C.D., Kaltman, S., & Miranda, J. (2013). Poverty and mental health: How do low-income adults and children fare in psychotherapy? *Journal of Clinical Psychology,* 69(2), 115–26. https://doi.org/10.1002/jclp.21951

Sarche, M.C., Spicer, P., Farrell, P., and Fitzgerald, H.E. (2011). *American Indian and Alaska native children and mental health: Development, context, prevention, and treatment.* Santa Barbara, CA: Praeger/ABC-CLIO.

Schenck-Fontaine, A., & Panico, L. (2019). Many kinds of poverty: Three dimensions of economic hardship, their combinations, and children's behavior problems. *Demography,* 56(6), 2279–305. https://doi.org/10.1007/s13524-019-00833-y

Scholler, I., & Nittur, S. (2012). Understanding failure to thrive. *Paediatrics and Child Health,* 22(10), 438–42. https://doi.org/10.1016/j.paed.2012.02.007

Sellers, R.M., Copeland-Linder, N., Martin, P.P., & Lewis, R.L.H. (2006). Racial identity matters: The relationship between racial discrimination and psychological functioning in African American adolescents. *Journal of Research on Adolescence,* 16(2), 187–216.

Shapiro, T., & Perry, R. (1976). Latency revisited. *The Psychoanalytic Study of the Child,* 31(1), 79–105. https://doi.org/10.1080/00797308.1976.11822310

Shivers, E.M., Faragó, F., & Gal-Szabo, D.E. (2022). The role of infant and early childhood mental health consultation in reducing racial and gender relational and discipline disparities between black and white preschoolers. *Psychology in the Schools,* 59, 1965–83. https://doi.org/10.1002/pits.22573

Shonkoff, J.P., Garner, A.S., Committee on Psychosocial Aspects of Child and Family Health, Committee on Early Childhood, Adoption, and Dependent Care, & Section on Developmental and Behavioral Pediatrics (2012). The lifelong effects of early childhood adversity and toxic stress. *Pediatrics,* 129(1), e232–46. https://doi.org/10.1542/peds.2011-2663

Silver, H.C., & Zinsser, K.M. (2020). The interplay among early childhood teachers' social and emotional well-being, mental health consultation, and preschool expulsion. *Early Education and Development,* 31(7), 1133–50. https://doi.org/10.1080/10409289.2020.1785267

Sitnick, S.L., Shaw, D.S., Gill, A., Dishion, T., Winter, C., Waller, R., Gardner, F. & Wilson, M. (2015). Parenting and the family check-up: Changes in observed parent-child interaction following early childhood intervention. *Journal of Clinical Child & Adolescent Psychology,* 44(6), 970–84.

Smalligan, J., & Boyens, C. (2020). *Paid medical leave.* Washington Center for Equitable Growth. Available: https://equitablegrowth.org/research-paper/paid-medical-leave-research/?longform=true

Splett, J.W., Fowler, J., Weist, M.D., McDaniel, H., & Dvorsky, M. (2013). The critical role of school psychology in the school mental health movement. *Psychology in the Schools*, 50(3), 245–58. https://doi.org/10.1002/pits.21677

Sroufe, L.A. (2005). Attachment and development: A prospective, longitudinal study from birth to adulthood. *Attachment & Human Development*, 7(4), 349–67. https://doi.org/10.1080/14616730500365928

Stevens, G.D. (2006). Gradients in the health status and developmental risks of young children: The combined influences of multiple social risk factors. *Maternal and Child Health Journal*, 10(2), 187–99. https://doi.org/10.1007/s10995-005-0062-y

Stevens, J., Harman, J.S., & Kelleher, K.J. (2005). Race/ethnicity and insurance status as factors associated with ADHD treatment patterns. *Journal of Child & Adolescent Psychopharmacology*, 15(1), 88–96. https://doi.org/10.1089/cap.2005.15.88

Strazdins, L., Shipley, M., Clements, M., Obrien, L.V., & Broom, D.H. (2010). Job quality and inequality: Parents' jobs and children's emotional and behavioural difficulties. *Social Science & Medicine*, 70(12), 2052–60. https://doi.org/10.1016/j.socscimed.2010.02.041

Stronach, E.P., Toth, S.L., Rogosch, F., & Cicchetti, D. (2013). Preventive interventions and sustained attachment security in maltreated children. *Development and Psychopathology*, 25(4 Pt 1), 919–30. https://doi.org/10.1017/S0954579413000278

Sturm, R., Ringel, J.S., & Andreyeva, T. (2003). Geographic disparities in children's mental health care. *Pediatrics*, 112(4), e308. https://doi.org/10.1542/peds.112.4.e308

Substance Abuse and Mental Health Services Administration. (2014). *Expert convening on infant and early childhood mental health consultation*. Available: https://www.samhsa.gov/sites/default/files/programs_campaigns/IECMHC/iecmhc-expert-convening-summary.pdf

Swensen, A.R., Birnbaum, H.G., Secnik, K., Marynchenko, M., Greenberg, P., & Claxton, A. (2003). Attention-deficit/hyperactivity disorder: Increased costs for patients and their families. *Journal of the American Academy of Child & Adolescent Psychiatry*, 42(12), 1415–23. https://doi.org/10.1097/00004583-200312000-00008

Tackett, J.L., Herzhoff, K., Smack, A.J., Reardon, K.W., & Adam, E.K. (2017). Does socioeconomic status mediate racial differences in the cortisol response in middle childhood? *Health Psychology*, 36(7), 662. https://doi.org/10.1037/hea0000480

Tatum, B.D. (2017). *Why are all the black kids sitting together in the cafeteria? And other conversations about race*. London, England: Hachette UK.

Vismara, L., Rollè, L., Agostini, F., Sechi, C., Fenaroli, V., Molgora, S., Neri, E., Prino, L.E., Odorisio, F., Trovato, A., Polizzi, C., Brustia, P., Lucarelli, L., Monti, F., Saita, E., & Tambelli, R. (2016). Perinatal parenting stress, anxiety, and depression outcomes in first-time mothers and fathers: A 3- to 6-months postpartum follow-up study. *Frontiers in Psychology*, 7, 938. https://doi.org/10.3389/fpsyg.2016.00938

Vygotsky, L.S. (1962). *Thought and language*. Cambridge, MA: MIT Press.

Wagner, M., Spiker, D., & Linn, M.I. (2002). The effectiveness of the Parents as Teachers Program with low-income parents and children. *Topics in Early Childhood Special Education*, 22(2), 67–81. https://doi.org/10.1177/02711214020220020101

Walker, A. (1983). *In search of our mothers' gardens: Womanist prose*. Boston, MA: Houghton Mifflin Harcourt.

Weist, M.D. (2005). Fulfilling the promise of school-based mental health: Moving toward a public mental health promotion approach. *Journal of Abnormal Child Psychology*, 33(6), 735–41. https://doi.org/10.1007/s10802-005-7651-5

West, A.L., Berlin, L.J., Goodman, A., Endy, K., Manzon, C., & Harden, B.J. (2022). Home-based early Head Start plus attachment and biobehavioral catch-up: A qualitative study of implementation outcomes. *Journal of Child and Family Studies*, 31, 1057–68. https://doi.org/10.1007/s10826-021-02189-7

Williams, D.R., & Williams-Morris, R. (2000). Racism and mental health: The African American experience. *Ethnicity & Health*, 5(3–4), 243–68. https://doi.org/10.1080/713667453

Xue, Y., Leventhal, T., Brooks-Gunn, J., & Earls, F.J. (2005). Neighborhood residence and mental health problems of 5- to 11-year-olds. *JAMA Archive of General Psychiatry*, 62(5), 554–63. https://doi.org/10.1001/archpsyc.62.5.554

Yeh, M., Hough, R.L., McCabe, K., Lau, A., & Garland, A. (2004). Parental beliefs about the causes of child problems: Exploring racial/ethnic patterns. *Journal of American Academy of Child and Adolescent Psychiatry*, 43(5), 605–12. https://doi.org/10.1097/00004583-200405000-00014

Yeh, M., McCabe, K., Hough, R.L., Lau, A., Fakhry, F., & Garland, A. (2005). Why bother with beliefs? Examining relationships between race/ethnicity, parental beliefs about causes of child problems, and mental health service use. *Journal of Consulting and Clinical Psychology*, 73(5), 800–7. https://doi.org/10.1037/0022-006X.73.5.800

Yogman, M.W., & Eppel, A.M. (2022). The role of fathers in child and family health. *Engaged fatherhood for men, families and gender equality*, 15–30. New York, NY: Springer International Publishing.

Yoshikawa, H., & Zigler, E. (2000). Mental health in Head Start: New directions for the twenty-first century. *Early Education and Development*, 11(3), 247–64. https://doi.org/10.1207/s15566935eed1103_2

Yoshikawa, H., Aber, J.L., & Beardslee, W.R. (2012). The effects of poverty on the mental, emotional, and behavioral health of children and youth: Implications for prevention. *American Psychology*, 67(4), 272–84. https://doi.org/10.1037/a0028015

Zhai, F., Raver, C.C., & Jones, S.M. (2015). Social and emotional learning services and child outcomes in third grade: Evidence from a cohort of Head Start participants. *Children and Youth Services Review*, 56, 42–51. https://doi.org/10.1016/j.childyouth.2015.06.016

Zigler, E., Pfannenstiel, J.C., & Seitz, V. (2008). The Parents as Teachers program and school success: A replication and extension. *The Journal of Primary Prevention*, 29(2), 103–20. https://doi.org/10.1007/s10935-008-0132-1

Zimmerman, F.J. (2005). Social and economic determinants of disparities in professional help-seeking for child mental health problems: Evidence from a national sample. *Health Services Research*, 40(5 Pt 1), 1514–33. https://doi.org/10.1111/j.1475-6773.2005.00411.x

Zuckerman, K.E., Boudreau, A.A., Lipstein, E.A., Kuhlthau, K.A., & Perrin, J.M. (2009). Household language, parent developmental concerns, and child risk for developmental disorder. *Academic Pediatrics*, 9(2), 97–105. https://doi.org/10.1016/j.acap.2008.12.006

Zuckerman, K.E., Perrin, J.M., Hobrecker, K., & Donelan, K. (2013). Barriers to specialty care and specialty referral completion in the community health center setting. *The Journal of Pediatrics*, 162(2), 409–14. https://doi.org/10.1016/j.jpeds.2012.07.022

Zuckerman, K.E., Mattox, K.M., Sinche, B.K., Blaschke, G.S., & Bethell, C. (2014). Racial, ethnic, and language disparities in early childhood developmental/behavioral evaluations: A narrative review. *Clinical Pediatrics*, 53(7), 619–31. https://doi.org/10.1177/0009922813501378

6

The Economic Costs of the Opportunity Gap[1]

This chapter presents the committee's estimation of the economic costs posed by the opportunity gap, using traditional approaches from cost-benefit analysis. These numbers, appropriately discounted, mark the upper bound of, or the maximum of, the benefit side of a calculation of the value of "investing in strategies, interventions, and policies to address opportunity gap concerns for children from birth to age 8," which was part of the committee's statement of task (Box 1-1 in Chapter 1). If interventions could entirely close this gap, that would represent the benefit side of the calculation, and the price of carrying out those interventions would represent the cost side (along with any unintended consequences).

After presenting these estimates, the chapter draws on existing high-quality causal research to draw inferences about a range of the share of this benefit that could be achieved by policy intervention, which likely is below 1 but surely is well above 0. The committee faced several challenges in finding this evidence. First, not all of this work is based on randomized controlled trials (RCTs), which are often viewed as the gold standard for research evidence. Thus, we had to rely on quasi-experimental studies and other approaches, and not all differences in outcomes can be examined in this fashion. Second, data are not always available with which to document differences in outcomes in order to consider the results of either RCT interventions or quasi-experimental designs, so the upper bound described above would be underestimated if the largest effects were for difficult-to-measure

---

[1] This chapter is adapted from a paper commissioned by the committee for this study (Bitler & Oh, 2022).

outcomes. Third, while the public costs of interventions are often easy to measure and are incurred right away, many of the benefits of these investments take many years to materialize. For example, if an intervention has intergenerational benefits, as has been documented for the Medicaid expansions of the late 1980s and early 1990s (e.g., East et al., 2023), it could take multiple decades for these benefits to materialize. Finally, some of the evidence stems from settings in the past (e.g., policy changes during the war on poverty leading to long-run improvements) or in different contexts (e.g., evidence about the effects of parental leave from Europe), and the literature on how well estimates from one setting apply to another is underdeveloped. Thus, there is a tension between high-quality evidence that provides comprehensive evaluations of total net benefits and interventions that fit today's context and setting.

In the remaining sections of this chapter we briefly discuss approaches that have been used traditionally to evaluate these trade-offs (cost-benefit analysis, cost-effectiveness analysis), and then touch on the marginal value of public funds (e.g., Hendren & Sprung-Keyser, 2020), provide representative calculations from the literature for three interventions, and present the conclusions that can be drawn from these findings.

THE OPPORTUNITY GAP: COST ESTIMATES

This section provides rough estimates of the economic costs of the opportunity gap that are due to mortality and morbidity as a percentage of gross domestic product (GDP). We derive these estimates by determining a possible upper bound for the cost of disparities in education; health; and social-emotional development, well-being, and mental health.

Obviously, it is difficult to find an ethical way of determining the value to society of lives lost, but given this task, we require some way to value these differences quantitatively across groups. For purposes of regulatory impact evaluation, for example, the Department of Health and Human Services (HHS; 2016) summarizes the value of a statistical life (VSL) and value of a statistical life year appropriate for considering the benefits of reducing risks of mortality and morbidity through interventions.[2] The calculation is derived from the thought experiment of measuring a person's willingness to pay to reduce the risk of dying from a particular cause or condition, and VSL is then presumed to be constant for small differences in risk. The midpoint in the review cited in these guidelines in 2014 dollars is $9.3 million,

---

[2] As stated in the HHS guidelines, "Values for mortality risk reduction reflect the rate of tradeoff between money and small changes in mortality risk, referred to as the marginal rate of substitution between wealth and risk" (Hammitt, 2000, p. 13). The guidelines describe many caveats and issues associated with using VSL (and quality-adjusted life year).

with a range of $4.4–14.2 million. It is important to note that this is not a value to always be applied to a certain mortality reduction. When the mortality reduction and/or any costs occur in a different time period than the present, the costs must be discounted to the present.

Morbidity reductions (improvements in health) are more difficult to value, but if alternatives are not available, the HHS guidance suggests using estimates of the monetary value of a quality-adjusted life year (QALY). QALY is a measure that incorporates "duration and severity of illness" to make it possible to "compare health status across individuals or population groups," and represents the value of one more year in perfect health (Department of Health and Human Services, 2016, p. 18). The total QALYs of experiencing a particular condition for a specific length of time are calculated by determining how much time a person spends in that condition and multiplying that time by the health-related quality of life associated with the condition—a number ranging from 0 (death) to 1 (full health), measured from populations experiencing the condition. Thus the QALY gain of an intervention is the sum of the change in QALY across a statistical person's lifespan after versus before the intervention of interest, and then for regulatory purposes, the future is discounted as in other cost-benefit or cost-effectiveness calculations. Table 3.2 of the guidelines (HHS, 2016) reports a monetized value per QALY in 2014 dollars, which ranges from $490,000 to $820,000 for average VSL.

Chapters 1 through 5 of this report summarize existing work on the existence and sources of differences across groups—racial/ethnic, immigrant/nonimmigrant, place of birth/residence, and family advantage (human capital, income, wealth). The simple statistics document significant differences in health outcomes by many of these characteristics. For example, a National Center for Health Statistics Data Brief from 2011 summarizes infant mortality rates by race and Hispanic origin of the mother, using 2007 data (MacDorman & Matthews, 2011). Babies born to non-Hispanic Black mothers had an infant mortality rate (mortality in the first year of life) of 13.31/1,000 live births. By comparison, the rate for babies born to American Indian or Alaska Native mothers was 9.22/1,000 live births; for those born to Puerto Rican mothers was 7.71/1,000 live births; for those born to non-Hispanic White mothers was 5.63/1,000 live births; and for those born to Mexican, Cuban, Asian or Pacific Islander, or Central and South American mothers was even lower (MacDorman & Matthews, 2011). Were we simply to use the middle level of VSL, moving the infant mortality rates for non-Hispanic Black and American Indian or Alaska Native mothers to the average would result in a savings of $67 billion in 2014 dollars. We note further that these different groups have different levels of low birthweight and preterm birth, which represent additional risks, so eliminating these additional infant health differences would result in additional savings that would be much more difficult to value.

Next, we considered differences in mortality for children aged 1–8. Data on mortality rates in 2018 for children aged 1–8 from the Centers for Disease Control and Prevention's WONDER database were used to assess the savings from moving mortality for groups with higher levels to the mean. With these 2018 data, the mortality rate for this age group was 17.7 per 100,000. Non-Hispanic Black children had a mortality rate nearly twice as high, 31.6 per 100,000. American Indian and Alaska Native children also had an elevated rate, at 18.3 per 100,000, and Native Hawaiian or other Pacific Islander children had higher mortality than the average, at 20.39 per 100,000. Non-Hispanic White children, those of more than one race, Asian children, and Hispanic White and Black children had lower rates than the average. Eliminating this disparity would lead to a savings of $5.8 billion in 2014 dollars. The mortality savings alone would yield $72.8 billion in savings, or 0.4% of GDP in 2014, based on these rough estimates.

Earlier chapters of this report also review at length other disparities among young children in learning, physical health, safety and security, social-emotional development, and other outcomes. Eliminating these disparities would undoubtedly add further savings. Monetizing these outcomes is even more complicated, however, and requires many more assumptions, especially as assessing morbidity requires using a specific discount factor, such as that suggested by the Office Management and Budget. There is also interest in measuring the effects of these gaps on children's development and future earnings. Assessing the benefits of avoiding outcomes such as low birthweight due to follow-on effects on outcomes across the life course, such as earnings and children's development, is complicated, and raises issues about double counting. If averting low birthweight, low gestational age, and other health differences at birth affects later adult earnings, one should count either the properly measured present discounted value of the lower birthweight or lower gestational age and other health differences or the positive carry-on effects of these improved outcomes, but not both.

SHARE OF OPPORTUNITY GAPS AND THEIR COSTS THAT CAN BE AFFECTED BY POLICY

The previous section presented some examples of calculations of the net savings to society from closing opportunity gaps, detailed some of the mortality differences across groups that would be eliminated, and described challenges with making even rough estimates for valuing benefits of these changes. This section addressed what is known from causal research about the share of opportunity gaps that policy could plausibly be expected to affect. We are certain the number is much higher than 0, but also suspect it is not 1. Currie (2005) discusses the extent to which disparities in health contribute to racial gaps in school readiness, exploring a host of health conditions as well as maternal health and behaviors and suggests these factors may account for as much as a quarter of the racial gap in school readiness. If this is the case, policy interventions around birth and health after birth could at most address one-fourth of this gap. Currie points out that incomplete take-up—the fact that many individuals eligible for programs do not participate in them—is also an important issue. This idea is worth considering when suggesting interventions, in that universal rather than targeted programs may be more effective. However, well-targeted programs with low barriers to take-up appear promising.

It is of course challenging to understand the right share of the savings from eliminating disparities that can be attributed to particular interventions, and the share likely varies across programs, populations, and settings. But any program that will eliminate disparities must either leave advantaged children unaffected or have greater impacts on the disadvantaged groups.

APPROACHES TO EVALUATING THE NET BENEFITS OF INVESTMENT IN MITIGATING THE OPPORTUNITY GAP

Even though a specific policy intervention might prove to be highly effective in mitigating the opportunity gap, it may not be feasible if it incurs tremendous costs relative to benefits. On the other hand, if a long-term benefit generated by a policy is substantial and even greater than its costs, investing in that policy could have the dual advantage of closing the opportunity gap while not overtaxing a government budget. To evaluate the effectiveness of various public programs quantitatively, social scientists use welfare analysis. In this section, we summarize three methods commonly used to measure the welfare impact of a public policy: cost-benefit analysis, cost-effectiveness analysis, and the marginal value of public funds (MVPF) framework. Although results of these welfare analyses should be interpreted carefully and cautiously because they depend on strong assumptions, the analyses are valuable as they provide a guideline for policy makers.

Cost-benefit analysis is a traditional method used in public policy. It is also commonly adopted when governments attempt to assess whether proposed regulations or policies are "worth it." From this perspective, interventions for which the present discounted value of the costs is outweighed by the present discounted value of the benefits are considered worthwhile. Suppose the total benefit of a policy is estimated to be greater than its cost, so that its cost-benefit ratio is larger than 1. In that case, the policy is deemed to generate a positive net social benefit. To encompass benefits and costs generated over the lifetime of a program, researchers usually calculate the present discounted value of the expected benefits and costs associated with the program. Importantly, costs are not accounting costs, but incorporate the opportunity cost of the resources used (their next-best alternative use). Costs and benefits are discounted, as a dollar today is worth an amount 1 + r next year, where r is the rate of return if the dollar were not used on this program. Should the government need to borrow, the relevant interest rate is the net of inflation rate, and a large literature focuses on the right rate and how to calculate it in the short versus the long run. Additionally, it is important to note that this simple approach does not take account of the fact that different persons may experience the costs and the benefits differently, and many of the estimates, including those around the value of saving lives, face challenges with representing uncertainty.

Cost-benefit analysis is very intuitive and easy to understand. However, reporting of the costs and benefits is not comprehensive, making it difficult to compare the gain or loss in social welfare across different welfare policies because different strands of literature usually adopt different measures. For instance, studies on early childhood education programs such as Head Start report costs and benefits using the internal rate of return or the ratio of benefit to cost of a program (Heckman et al., 2010; Carneiro & Ginja, 2014). On the other hand, studies on taxes often focus on the marginal deadweight burden or marginal efficiency cost of funds (Saez, Slemrod, & Giertz, 2012).

Cost-effectiveness analysis (often referred to as cost-utility analysis) is another method commonly used for welfare analysis. When the benefits are considered difficult to monetize or, alternatively, it is agreed that the benefits are useful, cost-effectiveness analysis is a good alternative to cost-benefit analysis. With this method, the lowest-cost way of achieving a common goal is preferred. For instance, two options for reducing infant deaths by 50% can be considered: expanding Medicaid coverage to disadvantaged pregnant women or expanding Medicaid coverage to families with newborn babies. If the former could achieve the goal at less cost than the latter, the cost-effectiveness analysis would consider the first policy more effective. Since cost-effectiveness analysis is particularly useful when it is difficult to measure the benefits of a policy quantitatively, it is commonly adopted in health economics literature, where it is difficult or sometimes perceived as impossible to measure the value of the life or health of a human being quantitatively. For example, estimates of the effects of Medicaid expansion sometimes address cost-effectiveness by converting impacts into costs per life saved (Currie & Gruber, 1996) or a more simple estimate of the number of deaths that could have been avoided (Miller, Johnson, & Wherry, 2021).

Finally, the MVPF framework aims to improve the comparability of net benefits across programs. Hendren and Sprung-Keyser (2020) suggest use of this framework as a unified method for welfare analysis of different government policies (see Finkelstein & Hendren, 2020, for more detail). A mathematical definition of MVPF is the ratio of the benefit of a specific policy to its net cost, accounting for any policy externalities (such as spillovers from a given intervention beyond the direct intended effects). The "net" cost in the denominator is calculated by adding up any negative externalities or subtracting positive externalities induced by the policy. For example, if increasing the benefit provided by a cash transfer program makes a recipient work less and thus decreases the labor supply, which in turn reduces tax revenue, then the net cost of the program to the government will be greater than the direct cost of program implementation. By contrast, if individuals work more and thereby increase the labor supply to be eligible for additional benefits from the earned income tax credit, that policy externality will decrease the net cost of that program.[3]

Intuitively, the larger the MVPF, the greater the net benefits generated by a policy. The maximum possible value of an MVPF is infinity, which implies that a long-term benefit from a policy is significant enough to cover the policy's initial and long-term costs. In this case, the policy helps the government save money over time. If the MVPF of a welfare program is larger than 1, the program generates larger benefits than its cost; if the MVPF is smaller than 1—for instance, 0.5—the program generates $0.50 worth of benefits for every $1.00 spent. If a program has large or even infinite MVPF, there is no reason not to adopt it. However, a low MVPF does not necessarily mean that a program is worthless; the program's worth depends on values the society pursues.

EVIDENCE FOR WHETHER IMPLEMENTATION MAKES SENSE: REPRESENTATIVE EXAMPLES OF EFFECTIVE POLICIES IN THREE ARENAS

Many high-quality causal studies have found that the safety net programs providing resources during early life have both short- and long-term positive effects on children's later-life outcomes, including labor market outcomes, health, and educational achievement. This section summarizes findings about the effectiveness of such programs in closing the opportunity gap. In addition, we provide findings from previous research about whether a certain welfare program generates a larger benefit than its cost based on MVPF estimates. We focus on three major U.S. welfare programs: the Supplemental Nutrition Assistance Program (SNAP, formerly known

---

[3]Although the mathematical formulas of the MVPF framework and the ratio of benefits to costs—an alternative way to carry out cost-benefit analysis—are quite similar, one big difference between the two lies in how positive externalities of a government policy are incorporated. The MVPF includes any positive externalities in its denominator together with any negative externalities. In contrast, the ratio of benefit to cost sums up all positive externalities in its numerator while placing negative externalities in the denominator.

as Food Stamps), Medicaid, and Head Start. These programs were chosen because there is a large body of work on them in the U.S. context, but we note that it is likely worth considering many other programs as well, such as family or parental leave, that have less complete U.S. evidence but have been shown to be effective.

Reducing the Opportunity Gap Due to Income Differences through Cash and Near-Cash Means-Tested Assistance

Unconditional cash assistance programs are traditional welfare programs in the United States. A typical example is Aid to Families with Dependent Children (AFDC), replaced by Temporary Assistance for Needy Families (TANF), a block grant program, in 1996. The AFDC program transferred a cash benefit to families with dependent children aged 0–18 as long as their income was below a certain threshold. Public spending on and participation rates for AFDC/TANF fell significantly after the 1996 welfare reform since the TANF program was no longer an entitlement, and many states chose to funnel spending on that program to other purposes. Nonetheless, some studies have found long-term positive effects of exposure to cash assistance programs during early childhood before this change occurred. For instance, Aizer and colleagues (2016) showed that people who received cash transfers during childhood from the Mother's Pension program, a predecessor of AFDC operated between 1911 and 1931, experienced significant improvements in health, educational attainment, and income in adulthood. Moreover, the magnitude of those effects was greatest for children from the poorest families and those who were exposed at younger ages. These findings imply that this cash transfer program closed some portion of the opportunity gap in health, education, and adult income for children from the poorest families.

A large body of literature on the effects of the SNAP/Food Stamp program provides valuable information about its effects in closing many aspects of the opportunity gap. SNAP currently provides a voucher that can be used to purchase food by low-income families that have gross incomes below 130% of the federal poverty threshold or otherwise satisfy gross income limits and have net incomes below 100% of the federal poverty threshold. Starting in 1961 under the Kennedy administration as a core mechanism of the war on poverty, this program has supplemented the food budgets of many disadvantaged families. Leveraging the quasi-random variation of the program's rollout, researchers have found that exposure to Food Stamps in utero and in early childhood was particularly effective in improving adult health, educational attainment, and labor market outcomes (Hoynes, Schanzenbach, & Almond, 2016; Bitler & Figinski, 2019; Bailey et al., 2020). This program has been highly effective in improving outcomes in early and later life; however, it is worth noting that its effects have been found to be heterogeneous across different subgroups.

What are the cumulative benefits of exposure to SNAP starting in early childhood? Using their estimates of increased income and longevity and reduced incarceration rates and public assistance spending, Bailey and colleagues (2020) estimated that the MVPF of providing SNAP from in utero up to age 5 is 56, which implies that for each $1 spent on the program, children exposed to the program in early childhood garner benefits worth $56 in the long run.

Reducing the Opportunity Gap Due to Inequitable Access to Health Care and Health Insurance through Medicaid

Since being established in 1965 and gradually adopted by states, Medicaid has provided basic health insurance to low-income individuals. Medicaid coverage was closely tied to AFDC participation until the early 1980s, but eligibility dramatically expanded to a broader population (Hoynes & Schanzenbach, 2018). Today, Medicaid is the most extensive safety net program for low-income families in terms of the amount of federal spending: according to the Congressional Budget Office, Medicaid spending for children totals $89 billion annually (Hoynes & Schanzenbach, 2018) and covers almost half of all births in the United States (Markus et al., 2013).

Focusing on the introduction of Medicaid and its expansions during the 1980s and 1990s, a body of research has found that exposure to the program in utero and/or in early childhood had substantial positive effects on the educational attainment, adult health, and earnings in early adulthood of exposed children (Meyer & Wherry, 2012; Miller & Wherry, 2018; Brown, Kowalski, & Lurie, 2020; Goodman-Bacon, 2021). For instance, Goodman-Bacon (2021) provides specific estimates of the public savings due to the introduction and expansion of Medicaid, respectively, in the long run. He estimates that the introduction of the Medicaid program yielded a total of 10 million additional QALYs, meaning that the program resulted in 10 million more years of life in perfect health compared with a counterfactual world without Medicaid. East and colleagues (2023) show that the program's effects are even multigenerational, as women who experience in utero exposure to Medicaid are more likely to have healthy babies with respect to birthweight and gestational age. This intergenerational transmission of positive health impacts implies even more considerable social benefits from the program. These findings strongly indicate that the Medicaid program may be particularly effective in reducing the opportunity gap by race and income in health, educational attainment, and earnings by improving outcomes in adulthood of exposed children, most of whom are likely to be from vulnerable families.

The enormous private and public benefits of Medicaid are captured by an infinite MVPF, meaning that its fiscal externalities are large enough to fully cover its initial cost (Hendren & Sprung-Keyser, 2020). In addition, according to the estimates of Goodman-Bacon (2021), Medicaid saved more than twice its initial cost for 1976 birth cohorts. Brown, Kowalski, and Lurie (2020) focus on the expansion of the Medicaid program during the 1980s and estimate that $1.00 in spending on Medicaid recoups 0.90 cents by age 28, meaning that 56% of the expenditure for the 1980s expansion would be paid after 60 years.

Reducing the Opportunity Gap Due to Unequal Access to Early Education through the Head Start Program

Launched in 1965 as part of the war on poverty, the Head Start program has offered comprehensive child development services for children from low-income families from birth to age 5 with the aim of promoting the school readiness of disadvantaged children. The program encompasses not only early learning but also health, nutrition, and family well-being. Approximately 900,000 children aged 3–5 participate in the program annually; the program's budget in fiscal year 2022 was about $11 billion (Gibbs et al., 2016; Administration for Children and Families, 2022).

Many studies have found positive causal effects of exposure to Head Start on children's long-run outcomes, although these findings should be interpreted cautiously as many derive from retrospective analyses. Findings include substantial impacts in terms of increases in high school graduation rates, college attendance, earnings, and household income (Currie & Thomas, 1995; Garces, Thomas, & Currie, 2002; Deming, 2009; Thompson, 2018; Johnson and Jackson, 2019; Bailey, Sun, & Timpe, 2021); improvements in health (Ludwig & Miller, 2007; Carneiro & Ginja, 2014); and reduction in crime rates (Deming, 2009; Carneiro & Ginja, 2014; Johnson & Jackson, 2019). Effects are larger for more disadvantaged children and women (De Haan & Leuven, 2020) and for African American children (Bauer & Schanzenbach, 2016).

The above findings imply that the early-life intervention of the Head Start program has been effective in mitigating opportunity gaps in education, earnings, and health across income and racial groups. However, another strand of studies suggests that the effects of the Head Start program have not lasted long. For instance, results from the Head Start Impact Study, a randomized evaluation of Head Start conducted in 2002, indicate that the immediate gain in test scores that followed participation in the program faded out quickly in the following years (HHS and Administration for Children and Families, 2010; Puma et al., 2012). Although such findings do not negate the Head Start program's contribution to closing the opportunity gap in early educational attainment, they do raise concern about the program's cost-effectiveness (Haskins, 2004; Barnett, 2011). It would be useful to follow up with the children included in the Head Start Impact Study to see whether positive effects reemerge in the longer run.

Although there is not yet clear consensus on the size of the net social benefit of the Head Start program, two recent studies suggest that the program pays for itself. Kline and Walters (2016) estimate that the MVPF measured from the Head Start Impact Study data is well above 1 (1.86 according to their preferred estimation). The MVPF of 1.86 implies that expansions of the program are likely to improve social welfare by generating $1.86 in benefits for every $1.00 spent. Bailey, Sun, and Timpe (2021) provide a traditional cost-benefit analysis using the staggered rollout of the Head Start program between 1965 and 1980. Focusing on gains in the accumulation of human capital and improvement in economic self-sufficiency, they estimate that the Head Start program generates positive fiscal externalities by reducing public assistance expenditures and increasing tax revenue (from approximately $576 to $2,331 annually per program participant) as a result of the additional wages earned by the exposed children. This estimated gain could be larger if the positive effects of the Head Start program are transmitted intergenerationally (Barr & Gibbs, 2022) or if the program is a good complement to other programs, such as Medicaid (Bailey, Sun, & Timpe, 2021).

CONCLUSIONS

This chapter has examined—at the broadest level—the added benefit accompanying a reduction in infant and child mortality, showing substantial benefit even when conservative estimates of VSL are employed. The overall annual benefit of a reduction in infant mortality could safely be estimated at approximately $67 billion, while a reduction in child mortality (ages 1–8) would result in a savings of approximately $73 billion per year.

Our review of the literature on the evaluation of social welfare programs focused on the three most heavily studied programs: SNAP, Medicaid, and Head Start. Our analysis found that the benefits of these programs exceed the costs, although to varying degrees. For SNAP/Food Stamps, the evidence shows (while results differ across different subgroups in the population) that every $1 spent on the program results in about $56 in benefits across the life course. Medicaid (and its expansions) has been shown to have very high rates of return—often exceeding the initial costs during the program's early years—due to improved health and longevity. Finally, the potential benefits from funding the Head Start program also tend to exceed the initial costs; an initial investment of $1 yields a return of about $1.86, indicating that the program is more than cost-effective.

The analyses presented in this chapter provide a conservative estimate of the potential benefits of targeted interventions aimed at closing the opportunity gap for children aged 0–8. Overall, research evidence provides some quantification of the monetary and fiscal returns to reducing the opportunity gap for these young children. These benefits accrue at the level of the individual, the family, and society. Analysis of additional policies and programs, while sometimes challenging, is a key area for future research related to understanding the economic costs of the opportunity gap.

REFERENCES

Administration for Children and Families. (2022). *FY 2022 Head Start funding increase ACF-PI-HS-22-02*. Department of Health and Human Services. Available: https://eclkc.ohs.acf.hhs.gov/policy/pi/acf-pi-hs-22-02

Aizer, A., Eli, S., Ferrie, J., & Lleras-Muney, A. (2016). The long-run impact of cash transfers to poor families. *American Economic Review*, 106(4), 935–71. https://doi.org/10.1257/aer.20140529

Bailey, M., Hoynes, H., Rossin-Slater, M., & Walker, R. (2020). *Is the social safety net a long-term investment? Large-scale evidence from the food stamps program*. (Working Paper No. 26942). National Bureau of Economic Research. https://doi.org/10.3386/w26942

Bailey, M.J., Sun, S., & Timpe, B. (2021). Prep school for poor kids: The long-run impacts of head start on human capital and economic self-sufficiency. *American Economic Review*, 111(12), 3963–4001. https://doi.org/10.1257/aer.20181801

Barnett, W.S. (2011). Effectiveness of early educational intervention. *Science*, 333(6045), 975–8. https://doi.org/10.1126/science.1204534

Barr, A., & Gibbs, C. (2022). Breaking the cycle? The intergenerational effects of an anti poverty program in early childhood. *Journal of Political Economy*, 130(12). Available: http://people.tamu.edu/~abarr/Head%20Start%20Intergen_1_31_2022.pdf

Bauer, L., & Schanzenbach, D.W. (2016). *The long-term impact of the Head Start program: Economic analysis*. The Brookings Institution, The Hamilton Project. https://www.hamiltonproject.org/papers/the_long_term_impacts_of_head_start?_ga=2.95710620.1446079228.1670529729-979225845.1663104239

Bitler, M., & Oh, S. (2022). [Economic costs of the Opportunity Gap]. Commissioned paper for the Committee on Exploring the Opportunity Gap for Young Children from Birth to Age 8.

Bitler, M.P., & Figinski, T.F. (2019). *Long-run effects of food assistance: Evidence from the Food Stamp program economic self-sufficiency policy research institute*. University of California at Davis. Available: https://arefiles.ucdavis.edu/uploads/pub/2021/02/09/bitler-figinski-fsp-2019-8-29-full-paper.pdf

Brown, D.W., Kowalski, A.E., & Lurie, I.Z. (2020). Long-term impacts of childhood Medicaid expansions on outcomes in adulthood. *The Review of Economic Studies*, 87(2), 792–821. https://doi.org/10.1093/restud/rdz039

Carneiro, P., & Ginja, R. (2014). Long-term impacts of compensatory preschool on health and behavior: Evidence from Head Start. *American Economic Journal: Economic Policy*, 6(4), 135–73. https://doi.org/10.1257/pol.6.4.135

Currie, J. (2005). Health disparities and gaps in school readiness. *Future Child*, 15(1), 117–38. https://doi.org/10.1353/foc.2005.0002

Currie, J., & Gruber, J. (1996). Saving babies: The efficacy and cost of recent changes in the Medicaid eligibility of pregnant women. *Journal of Political Economy*, 104(6), 1263–96. http://www.jstor.org/stable/2138939

Currie, J., & Thomas, D. (1995). Does Head Start make a difference? *American Economic Review*, 85(3), 341–64. http://www.jstor.org/stable/2118178

De Haan, M., & Leuven, E. (2020). Head Start and the distribution of long-term education and labor market outcomes. *Journal of Labor Economics*, 38(3), 727–65. http://dx.doi.org/10.1086/706090

Deming, D. (2009). Early childhood intervention and life-cycle skill development: Evidence from Head Start. *American Economic Journal: Applied Economics*, 1(3), 111–34. https://doi.org/10.1257/app.1.3.111

Department of Health and Human Services (HHS). (2016). *Guidelines for regulatory impact analysis*. Office of the Assistant Secretary for Planning and Evaluation. Available: https://aspe.hhs.gov/reports/guidelines-regulatory-impact-analysis

Department of Health and Human Services (HHS), Administration for Children and Families. (2010). *Head Start impact study: Final report*. Available: https://www.acf.hhs.gov/opre/report/head-start-impact-study-final-report-executive-summary

East, C.N., Miller, S., Page, M., & Wherry, L.R. (2023). Multigenerational impacts of childhood access to the safety net: Early life exposure to Medicaid and the next generation's health. *American Economic Review*, 113(1), 98–135. https://doi.org/10.1257/aer.20210937

Finkelstein, A., & Hendren, N. (2020). Welfare analysis meets causal inference. *The Journal of Economic Perspectives*, 34(4), 146–67. https://www.jstor.org/stable/26940894

Garces, E., Thomas, D., & Currie, J. (2002). Longer-term effects of Head Start. *American Economic Review*, 92(4), 999–1012. Available: http://www.jstor.org/stable/3083291

Gibbs, C., Ludwig, J., Miller, D.L., & Shenhav, N. (2016). *Short-run fade-out in Head Start and implications for long-run effectiveness*. [Policy Brief]. Center for Poverty, University of California at Davis. Available: https://poverty.ucdavis.edu/policy-brief/short-run-fade-out-head-start-and-implications-long-run-effectiveness

Goodman-Bacon, A. (2021). The long-run effects of childhood insurance coverage: Medicaid implementation, adult health, and labor market outcomes. *American Economic Review*, 111(8), 2550–93. https://doi.org/10.1257/aer.20171671

Hammitt, J.K. (2000). Valuing mortality risk: Theory and practice. *Environmental Science & Technology*, 34(8), 1396–400. https://doi.org/10.1021/es990733n

Haskins, R. (2004). *Competing visions*. The Brookings Institution. Available: https://www.brookings.edu/articles/competing-visions/

Heckman, J.J., Moon, S.H., Pinto, R., Savelyev, P.A., & Yavitz, A. (2010). The rate of return to the High/Scope Perry Preschool Program. *Journal of Public Economics*, 94(1–2), 114–28. https://doi.org/10.1016/j.jpubeco.2009.11.001

Hendren, N., & Sprung-Keyser, B. (2020). A unified welfare analysis of government policies. *The Quarterly Journal of Economics*, 135(3), 1209–318. https://doi.org/10.1093/qje/qjaa006

Hoynes, H., & Schanzenbach, D. (2018). Safety net investments in children. *Brookings Papers on Economic Activity*, 2018, 89–150. Available: https://www.brookings.edu/bpea-articles/safety-net-investments-in-children/

Hoynes, H., Schanzenbach, D.W., & Almond, D. (2016). Long-run impacts of childhood access to the safety net. *American Economic Review*, 106(4), 903–34.

Johnson, R.C., & Jackson, C.K. (2019). Reducing inequality through dynamic complementarity: Evidence from Head Start and public school spending. *American Economic Journal: Economic Policy*, 11(4), 310–49. https://doi.org/10.1257/pol.20180510

Kline, P., & Walters, C.R. (2016). Evaluating public programs with close substitutes: The case of Head Start. *The Quarterly Journal of Economics*, 131(4), 1795–848. https://doi.org/10.1093/qje/qjw027

Ludwig, J., & Miller, D.L. (2007). Does Head Start improve children's life chances? Evidence from a regression discontinuity design. *The Quarterly Journal of Economics*, 122(1), 159–208. https://doi.org/10.1162/qjec.122.1.159

MacDorman, M.F., & Matthews, T.J. (2011). *Understanding racial and ethnic disparities in U.S. infant mortality rates.* (NCHS Data Brief No. 74). Hyattsville, MD: National Center for Health Statistics.

Markus, A.R., Andres, E., West, K.D., Garro, N., & Pellegrini, C. (2013). Medicaid covered births, 2008 through 2010, in the context of the implementation of health reform. *Womens Health Issues*, 23(5), e273–80. https://doi.org/10.1016/j.whi.2013.06.006

Meyer, B., & Wherry, L. (2012). *Saving teens: Using a policy discontinuity to estimate the effects of Medicaid eligibility.* (Working Paper No. 18309). National Bureau of Economic Research. Available: https://www.nber.org/papers/w18309

Miller, S., & Wherry, L.R. (2018). The long-term health effects of early life Medicaid coverage. *Journal of Human Resources*, 54(3), 785–824. https://doi.org/10.3368/jhr.54.3.0816.8173R1

Miller, S., Johnson, N., & Wherry, L.R. (2021). Medicaid and mortality: New evidence from linked survey and administrative data. *The Quarterly Journal of Economics*, 136(3), 1783–829. https://doi.org/10.1093/qje/qjab004

Puma, M., Bell, S., Cook, R., Heid, C., Broene, P., Jenkins, F., Mashburn, A.J., & Downer, J.T. (2012). *Third grade follow-up to the Head Start impact study: Final report.* (OPRE Report No. 2012-45). Washington, DC: Office of Planning, Research and Evaluation, Administration for Children and Families, Department of Health and Human Services.

Saez, E., Slemrod, J., & Giertz, S. (2012). The elasticity of taxable income with respect to marginal tax rates: A critical review. *Journal of Economic Literature*, 50, 3–50. https://doi.org/10.1257/jel.50.1.3

Thompson, O. (2018). Head Start's long-run impact: Evidence from the program's introduction. *Journal of Human Resources*, 53. https://doi.org/10.3368/jhr.53.4.0216-7735R1

7

Research, Policy, and Practice: Contexts and Efforts to Address Opportunity Gaps

The committee's overview of opportunity gaps and outcomes in education, physical health, and social-emotional health and well-being in previous chapters has highlighted the numerous ways in which policies, practices, and social contexts in each of these domains interact and often exacerbate opportunity gaps for young children. In this chapter, the committee discusses policies with the potential to improve outcomes for young children and their families. The chapter begins with a discussion of income augmentation programs and policies, and then turns to the effects of poor parental job quality on opportunity gaps for children, as well as policy interventions that address parents' job quality. We then discuss policies, programs, and practices that address opportunity gaps and outcomes in these domains of interest. The chapter concludes with a discussion of human-centered design and policy development and the role of public–private partnerships.

INCOME AUGMENTATION PROGRAMS AND POLICIES

Programs that directly increase individual or family incomes are potential solutions to the opportunity gap for children. Several national and state programs with this focus have been implemented over the past 50 years, starting with those under the Great Society. This section describes three income augmentation programs and policies—minimum wage, the earned income tax credit (EITC), and paid family and medical leave—and the ways in which they may reduce opportunity gaps for young children. A fourth policy, the child tax credit (CTC), is briefly discussed in a later section.

Minimum Wage

Policies that enhance financial resources also impact birth outcomes. One prominent example is federal and state minimum wage increases, which raise the wage floor and boost the incomes of low-wage workers and their families. Higher family incomes can lead, in turn, to better social, economic, and health outcomes for parents and children (Wehby, Dave, & Kaestner, 2020). Greater access to resources such as housing, food, health care, and transportation can lower parental stress, improving a child's caregiving environment and reducing the likelihood that a child will experience abuse, neglect, or other adverse experiences at home (Hill & Romich, 2018). Higher minimum wages also facilitate greater health care access, which can reduce the prevalence of low birthweight and increase use of prenatal care, all of which may positively impact children's later health outcomes (Wehby, Dave, & Kaestner, 2020).

A 2016 study examined data on U.S. birth outcomes from 1980 to 2011 and found that state minimum wages that were higher than the federal floor were significantly linked to reduced prevalence of infant mortality and low birthweight. In particular, each dollar above the federal minimum wage led to a 4% decrease in infant mortality and a 1–2% decrease in the prevalence of low birthweight (Komro et al., 2016). A 2018 study using data from 1995 to 2013 found that a 10% increase in the minimum wage was associated with a 3.2% reduction in infant mortality among mothers with a high school degree or less (Jalali, 2018). A 2020 analysis examined 46 million births between 1989 and 2012 that occurred to women with a high school degree or less and found that a $1 minimum wage increase was linked to a significant 2 gram increase in birthweight and a significant, though small, increase in gestation length (0.01 weeks) and fetal growth (0.03 grams per week; Wehby, Dave, & Kaestner, 2020). Given the standard low birthweight threshold of 2,500 grams, these are very small effects that likely reached statistical significance as a result of the study's large sample size. The $1 wage increase had small, insignificant effects on reducing the number of preterm births in the authors' preferred specification.

A 2020 study assessed the impacts on birth outcomes of increasing "subminimum wages"—the wages that may be paid to tipped workers, which are often set much lower than the floor for nontipped workers. For example, the federal subminimum wage has been set at $2.13 per hour since 1991 (equivalent to about $4.63 in 2022 dollars, when adjusted for inflation), and the federal minimum wage was last increased to $7.25 per hour in 2009 (equivalent to about $12.00 per hour in 2022 dollars). The study found that when the tipped wage was set at the full federal minimum wage level, the birthweight of the smallest 5% of infants increased, and the birthweight of the largest 5% of infants decreased, leading to overall healthier birthweights for gestational age (Andrea et al., 2020). A 2021 study using data from 2001 to 2018 examined the relationship between state preemption laws (which prevent cities, counties, and other local jurisdictions from adopting minimum wages higher than the state level) and infant mortality. The study found that each additional $1 increase in the minimum wage reduced the infant mortality rate by 1.3%, and as a result, state preemption laws that restricted local increases were linked to as many as 605 preventable infant deaths in 2018 (Wolf, Monnat, & Montez, 2021).

A 2019 study found that higher state minimum wages significantly reduced infant mortality among infants born to Black mothers (a 20% reduction among states at or above the 75th percentile of state minimum wage levels), whereas no significant impact was found for infants with White mothers (Rosenquist et al., 2020), suggesting that minimum wage policies may have the largest impact among those with the worst birth outcomes at baseline.

Earned Income Tax Credit

The EITC is a poverty-reducing and work-support policy that involves tax refunds disbursed annually to low-income working families. More than 25 million tax filers receive the benefit annually, and the average refund size is about $2,500 (National Conference of State Legislatures [NCSL], 2022). Beyond the federal EITC, more than half of states now have their own supplemental EITC programs of varying generosity. Through the increased income it provides, the EITC is expected to promote greater use of health care, greater ability to purchase food and other household resources, and reduced stress among low-income women, which may lead to better birth outcomes (Markowitz et al., 2017; Lenhart, 2019). While there have been mixed findings on the impacts of increased use of prenatal care in terms of healthier births, research has demonstrated that state EITCs have positive impacts on birth outcomes, although the effect sizes are generally small (Prenatal-to-3 Policy Impact Center, 2022). A study from 2017 found that higher local and state credits in New York City were associated with a small but statistically significant reduction in rates of low birthweight at the community level (Wicks-Lim & Arno, 2017).

Another study with a large sample of single mothers found that the state EITC was associated with a 0.5 ounce (16 grams) increase in birthweight (Strully, Rehkopf, & Xuan, 2010). Research on the District of Columbia's credit expansions over time found beneficial effects on both birthweight and gestational age—of note, 1.9–4.7 fewer low-birthweight births per 100 live births and 48–104 gram increases in average birthweight (depending on the generosity of the credit, with the 104 gram increase being linked to a 40% EITC). The District of Columbia study also found an increase in gestational age ranging from 0.12 to 0.43 weeks, depending on the generosity of the EITC (10–40%; Wagenaar et al., 2019). This finding has been replicated in a study of Montgomery County, Maryland, which found that the introduction of the EITC reduced the likelihood of low birthweight by 1.9–2.4 percentage points among likely eligible mothers. Moreover, the EITC significantly increased birthweights by 27.3 grams in states with generous, refundable credits (generosity being defined as 10% or more of the federal credit; Hill & Gurley-Calvez, 2019). While high credits yielded greater benefits in infant outcomes, even states with less generous or nonrefundable credits saw significant benefits in these measures compared with states with no EITC, but the benefits were smaller (Hill & Gurley-Calvez, 2019).

This research has further implications as we consider efforts to improve health equity, especially with respect to Black mother and infant dyads. A subsequent analysis by the same authors using the same data found that the improvements were greater in magnitude (37.2 grams and 0.15 gestation weeks) for Black mothers in states with generous, refundable credits compared with the effects for White and Hispanic mothers. This finding shows that the state credit has the potential to reduce racial disparities in birth outcomes and increase health equity for infants, as Black infants disproportionately experience low birthweight and preterm birth (Komro et al., 2019). The EITC has also been associated with improved child health beyond the perinatal period, including improvements in food security, test scores, and behavioral problems (Dahl & Lochner, 2012; Hamad & Rehkopf, 2016; Batra & Hamad, 2021).

Paid Family and Medical Leave

The United States lacks a national paid family and medical leave policy. Of the 34 Organisation for Economic Co-operation and Development countries, the United States is the only country that does not guarantee paid leave to mothers of infants, and one of only two countries that does not guarantee paid leave to both parents (Joshi et al., 2019; Raub et al., 2018). Yet as discussed in Chapter 5, while paid family leave policies and their effects can vary, their positive effects on maternal mental health are consistent across studies.

U.S. policy in family and medical leave is regulated by the Family and Medical Leave Act (FMLA), an unpaid job-protected leave program that covers about half of working parents (Joshi et al., 2020). Workers in 13 states and the District of Columbia receive paid family and medical leave benefits (or will have these benefits by 2024). These benefits are also available in a growing number of cities and counties (Joshi et al., 2019; A Better Balance, 2021). Some employers provide access to paid family leave, but these benefits cover only 23% of civilian (private- and public-sector) workers and are available primarily to workers in higher-wage occupations (BLS, 2021); they are less available to Black, Hispanic, and immigrant workers (Bartel, Kim, & Nam, 2019) and working parents in lower-wage occupations (Adelstein & Peters, 2019).

California has the first and longest-running paid leave program, established in 2004. Quasi-experimental studies have provided strong evidence that the California program improved mental health and parent–infant interactions among parents participating in the program. These improvements include parents' higher self-rated health, lower psychological distress, better coping with demands of parenthood, increased parental reading to infants, and higher ratings of infant health (Bullinger, 2019; Lee et al., 2020; Irish et al., 2021). Several cross-sectional studies have found that it is not just access to paid leave but also the duration of the leave that matters for mothers' mental health. Longer paid leaves are associated with reduced maternal postpartum depression and major depressive disorder (Chatterji & Markowitz, 2012; Dagher, McGovern, & Dowd, 2014; Kornfeind & Sipsma, 2018; Mandal, 2018), and can buffer potential adverse effects of mothers' depressive symptoms on their relationships with infants (Clark et al., 1997). Both parents in dual-earner families need access to paid family leave since only one working parent's leave-taking was found to have negatively affected the other's mental health. One study found that mothers' longer paid maternity leave decreased fathers' anxiety across the year after childbirth (Perry-Jenkins et al., 2017), while another found that fathers' increased flexibility to take paternity leave in Sweden improved mothers' mental health outcomes (Persson & Rossin-Slater, 2019).

Paid leave can have direct effects on children's developmental outcomes, as well as indirect effects on children through changes in parents' mental health or family income. Recent U.S. studies of infants with working mothers who took paid maternity leave found that their leave was associated with improved outcomes in infancy and toddlerhood, including higher infant brain function compared with infants of mothers taking unpaid leave. Higher physiological stress among mothers taking unpaid leave was identified as one pathway that may be associated with less mature patterns of infants' brain activity (Brito et al., 2021). Taking paid leave also benefits children's development over time. Infants whose mothers took paid leave were found to have better linguistic and social-emotional outcomes in toddlerhood compared with infants whose mothers took unpaid leave (Kozak et al., 2021).

Paid family leave also has been shown to increase breastfeeding, which has been linked with improvements in bonding and later child and maternal health. One of two rigorous quasi-experimental studies of mothers in California (Hamad et al., 2019) found that the ability to spend the first few weeks with a newborn significantly increased the ability to breastfeed and facilitated its continuation. The other of these studies (Huang & Yang, 2015) found that paid leave increased breastfeeding during the first 3, 6, and 9 months postpartum. Other studies in the United States as well as other high-income countries have found that maternity leave lasting at least 8 weeks results in increased probability of establishing breastfeeding (National Academies, 2019b). Paid parental leave may also increase attachment between mothers and children and give parents more time to develop skills and establish social supports that can allow the continuation of breastfeeding after return to work (National Academies, 2016).

Other studies have shown that maternity leave leads to lower infant and child mortality (National Academies, 2019b). Research has also found that paid maternity leave could lead to a reduction in low birthweight and early births, with larger effects for unmarried and Black women (Stearns, 2015).

While there is a robust literature on paid family leave, there have been few studies of medical leave. However, evidence from paid sick leave (which is shorter in duration than medical leave) indicates positive effects on workers' take-up of preventive health care for themselves and their children (Shepherd-Banigan et al., 2017). Paid sick leave can help workers with moderate mental health issues stay employed (Goorin, Frank, & Glied, 2021) and can lessen stress related to missing a paid day of work (Hill, 2013). One study found that access to sick leave was associated with less psychological distress and helped prevent negative spillover effects into other aspects of life and day-to-day activities (Stoddard-Dare et al., 2018).

In addition to the strong evidence showing that paid family and medical leave positively impacts children's health outcomes, these programs also have been found to improve women's employment outcomes (Baum & Ruhm, 2013; Byker, 2016), with no negative effects on employers (Bartel, Kim, & Nam, 2019). Across studies, however, there is evidence of limited access to both unpaid leave under the FMLA and paid leave for all workers. Access is disproportionately lower for low-income, Black, Hispanic, and immigrant workers, resulting in their children's greater exposure to opportunity gaps. Reasons for this lower access include the unaffordability of taking unpaid or partially paid leave, restrictive eligibility criteria, administratively burdensome systems, and lack of knowledge about programs.

Unpaid leave guaranteed by the FMLA is out of reach for many working parents, but especially for low-income and Black and Hispanic working families because of issues of affordability and restrictive eligibility criteria. A nationally representative employee survey found that workers earning hourly wages under $15 and Black and Hispanic workers were less likely to take FMLA leave even when they needed it for a qualifying health reason (Brown et al., 2020). Workers who had experienced an unmet need for leave cited the inability to afford leave as their main reason for not taking it. The result for these workers' own or another family member's health was postponing (44%) or forgoing (39%) medical treatment (Brown et al., 2020).

Beyond affordability, the FMLA's strict eligibility requirements, such as the number of hours and weeks worked and firm size, limit access for women (Heymann et al., 2021) and Hispanic and immigrant workers (Joshi et al., 2020). For example, Hispanic and immigrant workers have lower access because they disproportionately work for small businesses that do not meet the FMLA's eligibility criteria. More Black workers are eligible because they have higher rates of employment in the public sector, which provides automatic eligibility for the FMLA (Joshi et al., 2020).

To address the limitations of the FMLA, a growing number of states and cities have developed their own paid family and medical leave programs that address affordability issues and increase take-up rates. Research has found that paid leave programs increase the use of leave among Black and Hispanic working mothers who previously had low leave take-up rates (Rossin-Slater, Ruhm, & Waldfogel, 2013). One study estimates that if national policy changed from unpaid to paid leave, Black workers would benefit more relative to White workers since by taking unpaid leave, they stand to lose more wages relative to total family income (Joshi et al., 2019). Newer state and local paid leave programs target higher wage replacement for low-wage workers. Such programs can help reduce racial/ethnic disparities, but no research is available on their impact as yet.

Administratively burdensome application and benefit systems can decrease access to family and medical leave (Grant et al., 2019). One qualitative study found that the application process was cumbersome for some low-income parents, and that some qualifying families abandoned the application because of the lack of information and guidance regarding the submission process. There were also delays in employers and health care providers completing their portions of the application (Setty, Skinner, & Wilson-Simmons, 2016). Since each employer designs its own process for employees to take unpaid leave through the FMLA, and similarly, each state agency designs its own administrative system for paid leave, the application processes, required documentation, outreach, and assistance offered will vary. Most leave programs require medical certification and documentation of family relationships, which creates administrative complexity without a straightforward process for use by workers to request and transfer forms from the health care system and vital records to employers.

Both surveys and qualitative studies have found that gaps in knowledge about programs limit access to and use of family and medical leave programs among low-income workers. Surveys conducted in California (statewide) and in greater San Francisco suggest that lower-income mothers had limited program knowledge (Goodman, Elser, & Dow, 2020) and that immigrant and Hispanic workers who had a qualifying event also had lower awareness (Appelbaum & Milkman, 2011).

The evidence base on family and medical leave has some limitations that could be improved with new and better data collection. First, most national surveys do not include comprehensive measures of employment, access to and take-up of employer-provided or publicly available paid leave, and adult and child health outcomes. Similarly, administrative databases that track paid leave applications and usage do not always collect data on race/ethnicity and generally are not linked to health databases, making it difficult to estimate the impact of having access to leave on health or health disparities. The implementation of unpaid leave under the FMLA and paid family and medical leave programs is not tracked systematically, so it is difficult to document FMLA enforcement and the access and outreach issues in paid family and medical leave programs. More information is needed on implementation to inform the design of practices that improve knowledge and take-up of programs.

PARENTS' POOR JOB QUALITY AND OPPORTUNITY GAPS FOR CHILDREN

Parents' job characteristics are a social determinant of their children's health. The quality of parents' jobs is an important but overlooked component of the resources available to children that affect their healthy development (Heinrich, 2014). As highlighted in Figure 7-1, parents' jobs have direct and indirect pathways to children's health and development. Parents' jobs present opportunity gaps for children if they do not provide enough resources, wages, and benefits, or if they entail unpredictable work schedules, or require working at night or on weekends, making it difficult to arrange child care and producing family stress. The role of parents' jobs in creating opportunity gaps is important to consider since most families with children (89%) include at least one working parent (Department of Labor, 2022), and earnings make up more than 75% of household income (Shrider et al., 2021).

While parents' employment provides the main source of family resources to invest in children, there are trade-offs between the resources gained and potentially less parental time with children, as well as the quality of care arrangements to which children are exposed when parents are working (Becker, 1981; Peters, 1995). Moreover, parents' positive or negative experiences at work can spill over to affect their psychological well-being, family interactions, and children's social-emotional development (Repetti & Wang, 2014). While research shows that unemployment has a consistent negative effect on mental health, studies of employment have found both

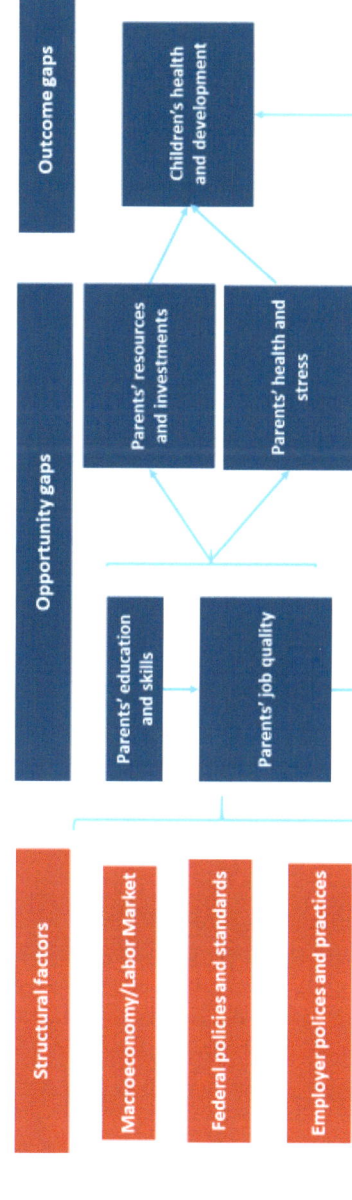

FIGURE 7-1 Hypothesized pathways between parents' job quality and children's health and development.
SOURCE: Adapted from Joshi et al., 2020.

positive and negative effects depending on job quality, including wages, hours, schedules, and stability (Antonisse & Garfield, 2018).

Beyond employment status, the quality of parents' jobs affects children's healthy development. While there is no standard definition of job quality, both economic and noneconomic dimensions affect parents' health, family dynamics, and resources available to invest in children. These dimensions include compensation, such as earnings and benefits (health insurance, pensions, paid leave); working conditions (hours, predictability of schedules, job security, safety); business culture and job design (mission and autonomy); and opportunities for skill development and advancement (Howell & Kalleberg, 2019; Congdon et al., 2020).

Studies show that some characteristics of parents' jobs directly affect financial and health resources available for their children, whereas other characteristics, such as work schedules, hours, tasks, and relationships affect children indirectly through their parents (Menaghan & Parcel, 1995). Heinrich (2014) posits that exposure to lower wages and benefits and unpredictable hours and schedules can increase family stress, which negatively affects both parents' and children's mental health (Heinrich, 2014). Conversely, higher-wage jobs that provide work–family support and the opportunity to engage in creative work have been linked to improved mental health (Burgard & Lin, 2013).

A growing nonexperimental evidence base confirms that parents' job characteristics are associated with outcomes for both parents and children in the predicted directions. Indices of poor-quality job characteristics are associated with children's grade repetition and behavior issues (Kalil & Ziol-Guest, 2005; Strazdins et al., 2010) and mothers' worse postpartum mental health (Cooklin et al., 2011). Several studies establish a negative association between nonstandard schedules (Joshi & Bogen, 2007; Li et al., 2014) or unpredictable schedules (Carrillo et al., 2017; Schneider and Harknett, 2019a,b; Ananat et al., 2022) and parents' well-being and children's behavioral health and quality care arrangements. Evidence suggests that precarious work schedules may also make it more difficult for individuals and families to meet work requirements for safety net programs (Karpman, Hahn, & Gangopadhyaya, 2019). In contrast, higher-quality jobs are associated with children's improved reading and math scores and behavioral outcomes (Lombardi & Coley, 2013) and help improve new parents' mental health in dual-earner couples (Perry-Jenkins et al., 2017). In addition, more consistent work schedules and higher-quality jobs can increase options for many families to access higher-quality schools through school choice programs when their neighborhood school is underperforming, especially when those programs require families to provide transportation and child care (Sandstrom, 2015; Chingos & Blagg, 2017; McShane & Shaw, 2020; Collier, 2021). Although the preponderance of evidence suggests that lower job quality has negative implications for families, a causal relationship cannot be determined because of potential selection bias.

Over the past 40 years, wages have failed to keep up with inflation, and employers have offered fewer benefits, making it difficult for the average working family with children to cover a basic family budget that includes the costs of housing, food, child care, and health insurance (Howell & Kalleberg, 2019). At the same time, wage growth at the upper end of the labor market has significantly increased wage inequality (Howell & Kalleberg, 2019). Other dimensions of poor job quality discussed above have increased as well, including nonstandard work hours (in the evening, at night, or on weekends) and unpredictable scheduling practices, such as last-minute scheduling changes (Henly, Lambert, & Dresser, 2021). Growing wage inequality and declining job quality mean lower access to resources for lower- and middle-income families, in turn widening parental job–related opportunity gaps for children.

A recent study found that one-third of families working full-time year-round do not earn enough to cover a basic family budget, and more than three-quarters of low-income full-time working families do not have enough income to cover basic costs, including child care, transportation, housing, food, and other expenses (Joshi et al., 2022). Figure 7-2 shows the significant proportions of working families (14%) and low-income families (31%) that do not earn enough wages from full-time work to cover basic expenses or have any access to health insurance or pensions through their employers. These jobs are the most concerning in terms of providing adequate resources for families with children.

It is well known that racial inequities in wages and employer-provided benefits are an enduring feature of the U.S. labor market (Kristal, Cohen, & Navot, 2018; Howell & Kalleberg, 2019). Black, Hispanic, and foreign-born working parents disproportionately experience low job quality (Earle et al., 2014). Figure 7-2 shows significant racial/ethnic and nativity differences in the quality of jobs held by full-time year-round working families. Approximately 30% of Hispanic families have full-time jobs that do not provide enough wages to cover basic expenses and do not offer health insurance or pension benefits. While many families need access to income assistance to make up for these shortfalls in job resources, low-income Hispanic (43%) and immigrant (41%) families are in particular need because they disproportionately have earnings that do not cover family expenses or work for employers that do not offer benefits. In addition to lower wages and less access to employer-provided benefits, Black and Hispanic workers are more likely than workers from other racial/ethnic groups to work in jobs that require nonstandard work schedules during the evening, at night, and on weekends (Presser & Ward, 2011); to work part-time hours involuntarily (e.g., they would like to work full-time; Golden & Kim, 2020); and to

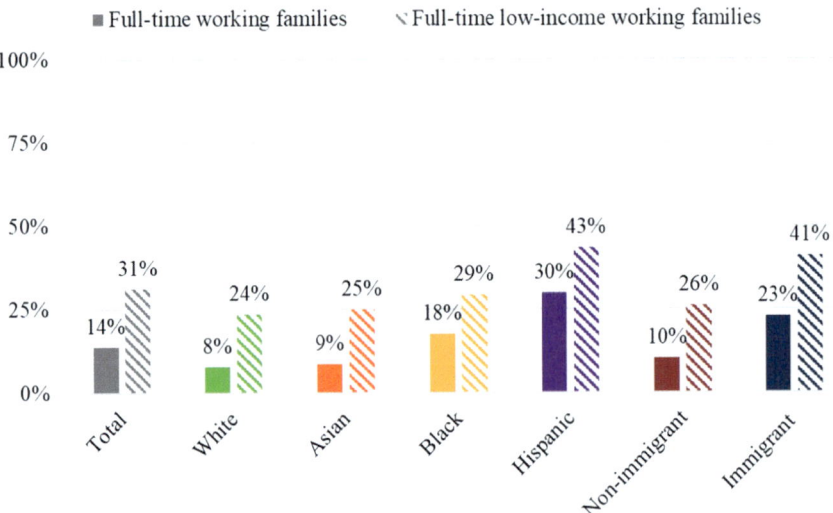

FIGURE 7-2 Share of full-time working families with jobs without adequate family-supporting wages or benefits, by race/ethnicity and foreign-born status.
NOTES: Calculations based on the Current Population Survey Annual Social and Economic Supplement 2015–2019. Adequate family-supporting wages denotes whether total family earnings from full-time work are greater than the costs of basic expenses in a family budget, including food, child care, medical care, transportation, and housing. Working families are coded as having health insurance if at least one working parent or working spouse/partner is the policyholder in an employer-provided plan. Families' access to pensions is measured by whether working parents are offered employer- or union-provided pensions.
SOURCE: Adapted from Joshi et al., 2022.

have last-minute shift changes (Storer, Schneider, & Harknett, 2020). Thus, Black, Hispanic, immigrant, and low-income children have higher exposure to opportunity gaps stemming from their parents' lower-quality jobs.

These racial/ethnic and nativity differences in job quality are driven by structural factors such as occupational segregation, racial/ethnic discrimination in hiring and promotion, policy choices such as exclusion from laws that provide worker protections, and differences in access to educational opportunities and attainment (Derenoncourt & Montialoux, 2020; Shakesprere, Katz, & Loprest, 2021). To the extent that Black, Hispanic, and immigrant families have higher exposure to poor job quality, they experience greater opportunity gaps in resources to invest in children, which in turn contributes to racial/ethnic disparities in children's health (Burgard & Lin, 2013). Studies of the effects of parents' job quality on children do not disaggregate the effects of job quality on families by income, race/ethnicity, or nativity, mainly because of low sample sizes.

POLICY INTERVENTIONS AND PROGRAMS THAT ADDRESS PARENTS' JOB QUALITY

Research has established a clear need for public policies to address the child opportunity gaps created by parents' low job quality. Federal policies set minimum wages; protect family income in the event of job loss; and supplement low earnings to help offset the high costs of everyday expenses such as food, rent, and child care. Income supplements, provided by means-tested programs and tax credits, are targeted primarily to families and children with the greatest need. Limited employer-provided benefits are supplemented through public health insurance. Some social insurance programs, such as unemployment insurance, replace a portion of lost wages when workers lose their jobs. Other programs provide education and training to enable access to higher-quality jobs. Since many of these policies were established long ago, adjustments are needed to better address economic changes that affect families' economic outcomes and social-emotional health. As discussed previously, structural changes in the economy that create opportunity gaps for children include persistently low wage growth, nonstandard work schedules demanded by a 24/7 economy, and employers' unstable scheduling practices. The disparate negative effects of the economic crises associated with the COVID-19 pandemic on Black, Hispanic, and immigrant working families highlighted the need for more comprehensive policy interventions.

The United States, however, lacks a comprehensive approach to addressing structural economic changes. A complex set of policies and programs addresses low earnings, and limited benefits are available through employers, but these measures do not fully address all aspects of poor job quality, do not serve all children, and can be difficult to know about or access. These limitations translate to persistent resource gaps that elevate family stress and are tied to children's social-emotional health. Higher exposure to poor job quality and uneven access to policies that alleviate it for low-income, Black, Hispanic, and immigrant families exacerbate child opportunity gaps that can lead to disparate outcomes.

This section reviews the evidence on the effectiveness of policies for promoting economic security and social-emotional health for all families with children, with attention to whether they effectively reduce gaps in family job quality experienced by low-income Black, Hispanic, and immigrant working families with children. The discussion concludes with promising practices for improving programs to better address family economic security, promote child development, and reduce racial/ethnic and nativity gaps in jobs that provide adequate compensation and schedules amenable to raising children.

Federal Labor Standards and Social Protection Policies

Federal laws enacted in the 1930s establish basic national labor standards, including minimum wages, overtime provisions, restrictions on child labor, unpaid job-protected leave, and unemployment insurance. These laws were enacted at a time when the economy and families looked very different from the way they are today. While labor standards have been updated over time, for example, to provide break times for nursing mothers or to cover previously excluded occupations that employed a high proportion of Black and Hispanic workers (Dixon, 2021), policies are antiquated, particularly for working women, who do the lion's share of caregiving (Ansel & Boushey, 2017). Compared with other countries, the United States has robust child labor laws but lower labor standards to protect families from economic insecurity and limited policies to address caregiving for children (e.g., child care, paid sick leave, and paid family and medical leave; WORLD Policy Analysis Center, 2022).

Burgeoning evidence shows that labor standards establishing minimum wages and unemployment insurance help families with children by reducing downward mobility and family stress and improving social-emotional health. Whereas the federal minimum wage is low ($7.25 per hour) and has not kept pace with inflation, there is evidence that an increase in the minimum wage throughout childhood is associated with improvements in child health, particularly from birth to age 5, and with small to no decreases in employment (Wehby, Dave, & Kaestner, 2020). Although the evidence on the effect of minimum wages on adult health is mixed, a recent review of rigorously designed studies found that raising minimum wages led to a decrease in the prevalence of low birthweight, a decrease in smoking prevalence among adult women, and reduced absences from work due to illness among employed adults (Leigh & Du, 2018). Moreover, improving minimum wage coverage over time by bringing in more sectors that employ Black workers significantly reduced Black–White earnings gaps (Derenoncourt & Montialoux, 2020), and correlational evidence shows reduced poverty for Black children (Spriggs, 2019). This evidence suggests that expansion of minimum wage provisions could improve parents' job quality, increase the resources available to children, and reduce racial/ethnic child opportunity gaps. However, the minimum wage would need to be greatly increased (to more than $10.25 per hour) to have a significant impact on reducing child poverty (National Academies, 2019a).

In addition to minimum wages, social insurance systems such as unemployment insurance protect working families with children from downward economic mobility and prevent declines in families' health due to parents' job loss. Unemployment insurance provides temporary partial replacement of earnings for unemployed workers who lost their jobs through no fault of their own but because of structural factors such as downsizing. Rules and benefit coverage under the joint federal–state program vary by state, but most programs replace up to half of wages up to a maximum of 26 weeks (Congressional Research Service, 2019).

Parents' job loss negatively affects families and children through reduced financial resources, greater income instability, and elevated stress (Kalil, 2013). An extensive literature establishes that involuntary job loss is associated with worse adult physical and mental health (Catalano et al., 2011), including increased risk of men's premature death (Sullivan & von Watcher, 2009) and infants' lower birth weight (Lindo, 2011). Both correlational and causal studies show that unemployment and job loss have negative consequences for children's outcomes as well, particularly in low-income families. Job loss is associated with both short- and long-term education outcomes for children, such as a greater likelihood of grade repetition (Kalil & Ziol-Guest, 2008; Stevens & Schaller, 2011), lower math and reading scores (Ananat et al., 2011), more challenges with classroom behavior (Johnson, Kalil, & Dunifon, 2010; Hill et al., 2011), and greater psychological strain (McLoyd et al., 1994; Coelli, 2011). Some evidence indicates that unemployment has particularly large long-term negative effects on Black children's educational attainment (Kalil & Wightman, 2011).

Unemployment insurance is an essential support for children whose parents lose their jobs. Using a variety of modeling techniques that minimize selection bias, research has established that unemployed workers receiving unemployment insurance benefits have better self-rated health and mental health compared with workers who do not receive these benefits (O'Campo et al., 2015; Cylus & Avendano, 2017). A growing body of rigorous research shows that the generosity of unemployment benefits, especially during recessions, reduces suicide rates (Sullivan & von Wachter, 2009; Cylus, Glymour, & Avendano, 2014), significantly improves adults' self-rated health, and is not associated with increases in health risks such as alcohol consumption (Kuka, 2020). During the early years of the COVID-19 pandemic, expanded unemployment insurance benefits were associated with reduced risk of depression and anxiety (Berkowitz & Basu, 2021). Although there have been few studies of unemployment insurance focused on children, there is some evidence that the generosity of these benefits is positively associated with academic achievement (Kukla-Acevedo & Heflin, 2014; Regmi, 2019). An extensive body of evidence shows that extensions of unemployment insurance during the Great Recession (Rothstein, 2011; Farber, Rothstein, & Valletta, 2015; Chodorow-Reich, Coglianese, & Karabarbounis, 2019) and the COVID-19 pandemic had negligible effects on unemployment rates (Altonji et al., 2020; Bartik et al., 2020; Petrosky-Nadeu & Valletta, 2021) and reduced poverty (Chen & Shrider, 2021). These studies do not focus on racial/ethnic differences in outcomes.

Without access to unemployment insurance to mitigate the economic and health effects of job loss, particularly during recessions, the risk of downward family economic mobility increases, potentially widening child opportunity gaps. One study found that only one-third of children with an unemployed parent lived in families that received unemployment insurance (Issacs, 2013). Yet several studies document challenges with the design of the unemployment insurance program (von Wachter, 2019) and access to benefits (U.S. Bureau of Labor Statistics [BLS], 2019). More than half of unemployed workers do not apply for unemployment insurance benefits; a much higher proportion of these workers indicated that their reason for not applying was thinking they were not eligible rather than having to deal with administrative hassles (Gould-Werth & Schaefer, 2012). These issues disproportionately affect unemployed workers without college degrees and Hispanic workers (Gould-Werth and Schaefer, 2012). Moreover, low-income workers, those arguably in most need of assistance, have a lower proportion of their earnings replaced compared with middle- and higher-income workers (East and Simon, 2020). The unemployment insurance program appears to better serve workers with higher education and income, thus exacerbating opportunity gaps.

Studies have found that Black and Hispanic children are more exposed to unemployment compared with their White peers (Parolin, 2020), since Black and Hispanic versus White workers have higher unemployment rates and longer duration of unemployment, even in tight labor markets (Aaronson, Barnes, & Edelberg, 2021; BLS, 2021). Structural factors such as hiring discrimination (Neumark, 2018), mass incarceration (Pager, 2003), and increased likelihood of being the first fired as the business cycle weakens (Couch & Fairlie, 2010) contribute to the persistent racial unemployment gap. Yet Black and Hispanic versus White workers were less likely to receive unemployment benefits prior to and during the COVID-19 pandemic (Nichols & Simms, 2012; U.S. Government Accountability Office [GAO], 2021). Many states, especially those in the South that have larger shares of Black and Hispanic residents, have made it increasingly difficult to access unemployment benefits and offer lower amounts and fewer weeks of benefits (Kofman & Fresques, 2020). Based on the evidence base, it has been recommended that the effectiveness of the unemployment insurance program could be improved by modernizing eligibility and administrative processes; making benefits more generous, particularly during recessions; and resolving budget shortfalls (Gould-Werth & Schaefer, 2012; Isaacs, 2013; von Wachter, 2019). To improve the effectiveness of unemployment insurance specifically for families, states could institute or expand a dependent allowance targeting increased benefits to support for children during times of economic instability and heighted family stress (von Wachter, 2019). Given the greater barriers to access to unemployment insurance faced by Black, Hispanic, and immigrant workers, these policy improvements have the potential to help close racial/ethnic and income-based opportunity gaps.

Social Protection Policies

Federally funded social protection programs designed to supplement low job wages and limited employer-provided benefits have positive effects on both parents' employment and children's developmental outcomes (Boushey & Mitukiewicz, 2014). These programs provide direct income support in the form of tax credits to working families (e.g., the EITC and CTC), in-kind benefits to pay for food (the Supplemental Nutrition Assistance Program [SNAP]), and subsidies to help pay for child care (the Child Care and Development Fund), as well as programs such as Medicaid, which supplement the lack of health insurance in many low-wage jobs. The CTC is designed to provide income support to children, which also helps families make up for wages that have not kept pace with inflation, while programs such as the EITC and child care subsidies are associated with increases in employment and earnings among low-income workers (Ha, 2009; Ha & Miller, 2015; Hoynes & Patel, 2018) as well as reduced poverty (National Academies, 2019a). Yet despite these benefits, differential access to these programs can cause opportunity gaps. The CTC, for example, is contingent on employment and provides benefits largely to middle-income families, offering minimal or no benefits for the lowest-income families. Research on the recent expansion of the CTC, however, found that the revised program reduced poverty, food insecurity, and material hardship (Parolin et al., 2021) and did not reduce employment (Roll, Hamilton, & Chun, 2021).

Many social policies benefit the health of both adults and children (Osypuk et al., 2014), benefits that persist for children into adulthood (East & Page, 2020). An extensive literature review documented in two other reports of the National Academies established that the EITC generates significant improvements in child health (National Academies, 2019a,b; see also Braga, Balvin, & Gangopadhyaya, 2020). And studies of SNAP show that making eligibility criteria more inclusive for immigrants improves child health for this population over time (East, 2020). There has been less research on the CTC, but early evidence indicates that it has positive effects on reducing injuries and behavior problems when the tax credit is refundable and extended to families with low incomes (Rostad et al., 2020).

One of the above-referenced National Academies studies shows that a significant expansion of the safety net could reduce poverty overall by half and significantly reduce poverty among Black and Hispanic families

(National Academies, 2019a). However, children in immigrant families, who are largely Hispanic, are exposed to particularly large income-based opportunity gaps due to their exclusion from safety net programs; thus children in noncitizen families have much higher poverty rates compared with other children, yet they are excluded from the EITC even when they are U.S. citizens (Acevedo-Garcia et al., 2021a). Children in noncitizen families face not only the standard set of complex rules and administrative systems that all families face, but also additional barriers, such as categorical eligibility based on immigration status, stricter income eligibility, and reduced benefit levels (Heinrich, 2018; Acevedo-Garcia et al., 2021b).

State and Local Paid Family and Medical Leave and Scheduling Laws

As discussed earlier, since there is no federal guarantee of paid family and medical leave or sick leave, and no federal laws address employers' unpredictable scheduling practices, some states and localities have passed laws to fill these gaps. With respect to paid leave, although rigorous research demonstrates that it positively impacts child and maternal health outcomes, women's employment outcomes, and economic returns to employers, there is some evidence of small decreases in employment for one subgroup of younger women (out of multiple groups tested; Das & Polachek, 2015) and for women who used paid leave right after it was implemented in California in 2004 (Bailey et al., 2019). The positive impacts of paid leave detailed in this chapter largely outweigh concerns about lower women's employment. However, more research is needed on the long-term impacts on women's employment to identify any resulting gender discrimination by employers due to women's potential need for maternity leave (Mathur et al., 2017).

With respect to unpredictable scheduling, a growing number of cities and one state have implemented laws designed to improve the predictability and stability of work schedules, mainly in the service sector. These laws bar employers from using irregular and unpredictable scheduling practices, including little or no advance notice of scheduling and inconsistent scheduling from week to week—practices that can increase income instability and make it difficult for parents to plan ahead for child care, take classes, or work second jobs. Oregon is the only state with a law on predictable scheduling. Six cities—San Francisco and Emeryville in California, Chicago, New York City, Philadelphia, and Seattle—have implemented ordinances barring such practices (Harknett & Schneider, 2020), and more than 12 cities have ongoing initiatives to pass such laws (Lambert, 2020). Typically, however, these ordinances apply only to large employers (e.g., in Seattle, establishments with >500 employees; Wolfe, Jones, & Cooper, 2018).

Since mid-2017, Seattle's Secure Schedule Ordinance has required employers to post schedules at least 14 days in advance and pay employees additional compensation (called "predictability pay") for each employer-requested schedule change that occurs after the original schedule posting (Harknett, Schneider, & Irwin, 2021b). Two years after the ordinance was implemented, a rigorous evaluation found an increase in the predictability of scheduling, predictability-related pay, job satisfaction, and employees' overall happiness, and a decrease in employees' material hardship (Harknett, Schneider, & Irwin, 2021a). No significant effect on psychological distress among employees was found.

Evidence is also emerging from Emeryville's 2017 Fair Workweek Ordinance (FWO), which required two weeks' advance scheduling notice and allowed workers to decline unscheduled hours without retaliation. Research using a difference-in-difference design found that the FWO significantly reduced scheduling unpredictability mainly by reducing surprise shifts and last-minute scheduling (Ananat, Gassman-Pines, & Fitz-Henley, 2022). The ordinance had some effects on labor market outcomes, including a decrease in the likelihood of working on any given day and an increase in the length of shifts that may have potential implications for earnings (Ananat, Gassman-Pines, & Fitz-Henley, 2022). The ordinance also had significant and positive effects on workers' sleep quality, but no effects on parenting behaviors (e.g., losing temper) or child's behavior (e.g., uncooperative, worrying).

State-level laws on paid family and medical leave and scheduling address the lack of federal policies focused on improving job quality. While there is strong evidence of the health impacts of paid family and medical leave, scheduling laws are more recent. Emerging research evidence on scheduling laws shows some effects on workers' health but no spillover effects on parenting or child health. Both paid leave and scheduling laws require workers to negotiate time with supervisors, whether time away from or at work. Studies highlight that the nuts and bolts of scheduling laws can be complex; thus both supervisors and employees must know and understand the laws well enough to ensure that they are implemented correctly (Mitchell, Baumle, & Cloud, 2021). Since these laws are relatively new and localities may not be in full compliance, stronger health effects may emerge over time (Lambert, 2020). Moreover, since low wages and supervisor discretion are common in the retail sector, significant impacts of these laws on child health may be seen in that sector only with improvements in labor laws and the social safety net and even more advance scheduling notices (e.g., retail stores in Germany provide 6 months' advance notice; Carré & Tilly, 2017).

Programs Designed to Supplement Low Wages and Limited Benefits and Promote Career Advancement

Funded by federal agencies and private foundations, a number of innovative community-based programs are designed to improve job quality by providing some combination of earnings supplements, access to subsidized benefits, career-specific job training, job placement, and support services. Some programs target low-income families with children, sometimes using a dual-generation approach (serving parents and their children), while other programs target workers without a high school degree. A recent review identified 52 programs targeting family economic security, low-wage employment, and child well-being, but many of these programs were pilots or in the early stages of development and have not been rigorously evaluated (Sama-Miller & Baumgartner, 2017). Since the committee's focus is on identifying opportunity gaps in job quality that affect children's resources and well-being, we summarize two approaches that have been evaluated using experimental or quasi-experimental designs and that showed positive impacts on employment and earnings, as well as health and well-being.[1]

The first approach to improving parents' job quality is based on supplementing low-wage full-time jobs and providing parents with support to help maintain their employment. The New Hope program, one of the earliest comprehensive programs designed to supplement poor job quality, operated in Milwaukee during the welfare reform era from 1994 to 1998. The program offered a combination of wage subsidies, income supplements (child allowance), work supportive benefits (subsidized child care and health insurance), a community service job if needed, and case management. The program's design was premised on the idea that full-time work (defined as 30 hours per week) should not result in family incomes under the federal poverty threshold and that access to support services should not be administratively burdensome. New Hope supplemented wages from full-time jobs with a menu of benefits from which families could choose. More than half of New Hope parents were Black (55%), more than one-quarter were Hispanic (29%), and the majority were mothers (90%) (Huston et al., 2005). The program was evaluated using a randomized controlled design, and the

---

[1] During the 1990s, there were several rigorous evaluations of welfare-to-work programs that included some combination of education, job training, and support services. These studies found mixed impacts on parents' employment and children's outcomes (National Academies, 2019b). Given the significant decline in families' participation in the welfare program (Temporary Assistance to Needy Families), the results of these evaluations are less relevant today since they are focused on the impact of imposing work requirements to receive public benefits rather than on a comprehensive and intentional strategy for improving job quality and children's outcomes. The negative outcomes found by the evaluations of welfare-to-work programs led the National Academies' Committee on Vibrant and Healthy Kids to recommend eliminating those work requirements (National Academies, 2019b).

evaluation identified short-term positive impacts during the program and longer-term impacts three and five years after the program had ended.

The New Hope evaluation found significant impacts on employment, earnings, and poverty reduction during the three years of program operation that lasted beyond program participation for families with low to moderate barriers to work (Miller et al., 2008). The program also reduced adults' depression and improved their physical well-being (Miller et al., 2008). Positive effects were observed on children's academic performance (reading), positive behavior, and enrollment in child care and structured activities, and these effects lasted three years after the program ended (Huston et al., 2005). Five years after the program ended, new findings for children emerged. Children were less likely to repeat a grade, receive poor grades, or be placed in special education (Miller et al., 2008). Generally, the effects were stronger for boys than girls. For example, boys in program group families, particularly Black boys, had positive future work orientation and employment experiences compared with the control group (McLoyd et al., 2011).

Other studies of employment programs that provided earnings supplements found similar positive effects on employment and children's achievement (Duncan et al., 2009). Taken together, the findings for New Hope and programs that subsidized low wages suggest that ensuring earnings for full-time work that are above the federal poverty threshold is effective at helping to improve job quality and children's health in low-income families. For families at the lowest end of the income gradient, studies found that employment-focused programs not providing comprehensive support had negative impacts on parents' mental health and resulted in less use of formal child care (Alderson et al., 2008). An employment-focused approach that does not provide child care and other benefits and supports for parents' emotional and psychological well-being may therefore be insufficient to improve parents' job quality and will not address opportunity gaps, particularly for children living in families with the lowest incomes.

The second approach to improving job quality uses a sectoral strategy that provides training and connects workers to jobs in specific high-demand industries. Sectoral job training programs generally target workers (who may or may not be parents) who are younger (aged 18–24) and do not have education beyond high school, or they target low-income parents while simultaneously providing services to their children (a two-generation approach). These job training programs have been implemented in the health care, information technology, and manufacturing sectors.

There have been several experimental evaluations of sectoral job training programs that include screening, placement, and wraparound services for workers who met preenrollment criteria (ranging from minimum educational attainment to drug screening). Not all of these programs target parents. A recent review of the evidence found that four multisite programs

(WorkAdvance, Project Quest, Year Up, and sites included in the Sectoral Employment Impact Study) have significant impacts on gains in earnings (12–34%) that are sustained long after program participation (Katz et al., 2022). More than 75% of participants have been Black and Hispanic workers, suggesting that these programs can help improve racial/ethnic disparities in job quality.

One of the above sectoral training programs, Project Quest, is particularly relevant to reducing opportunity gaps associated with parents' jobs, since more than 70% of participants had children at program entry. This program's impact on annual earnings was found to be much higher for participants who had at least one child under 18 compared with those who had no children (Roder & Elliot, 2019). Although the program does not track impacts on children, these findings highlight significant increases in resources available to children. Earnings gains far exceed the costs of the program and participants' college attendance (Roder & Elliot, 2021).

In contrast to sectoral training targeted to adults, dual-generation programs target parents and children. CareerAdvance targets education and training services to parents with children enrolled in Head Start programs run by community action organizations in Tulsa, Oklahoma. Using a sectoral training approach targeting jobs in the health care sector, the program offers intensive services to support parents' participation, such as tuition coverage, as well as in-kind services, such as after-school care or transportation, to offset wages lost while attending school. The program also coordinates parents' and children's schedules, and the same support staff work with both parents and children. The program's goals are to improve economic outcomes, family dynamics, and children's educational and health outcomes (Sabol et al., 2021).

While there have been fewer evaluations of dual-generation versus other sectoral programs, a quasi-experimental evaluation of CareerAdvance—a two-generation program that provides postsecondary credentialing and career training for parents of children enrolled in Head Start—found that parents were employed more in health care than in other sectors and had improved psychological well-being after one year of participation. After two years, parents had higher incomes and improved psychological well-being and physical health, and children had higher school attendance and lower chronic absenteeism (Sommer et al., 2020). Since children in both the treatment and comparison groups are enrolled in high-quality Head Start centers, the lack of significant differences in children's educational and behavioral outcomes on average is not unexpected. Positive effects of CareerAdvance were found both among children who were less school ready as well as among children whose parents were more college ready (Sabol et al., 2019).

Employer Policies and Practices

There have been relatively few rigorous studies of employer practices that improve job quality and reduce employee stress, thereby improving parents' mental health and work–family outcomes. The Work, Family, and Health Study and the Stable Scheduling Study are two group randomized controlled trials of interventions designed to improve employer practices. Both interventions were designed to improve health outcomes by reducing work–family conflicts, but they varied in approach and by sector.

Designed to promote employees' control over work schedules and increase supervisors' support for employees' family and personal life, the Work, Family, and Health intervention targeted two different occupations and industries: professionals in the information technology (IT) sector and hourly service workers in nursing homes. Through facilitated discussions and supervisor training, the intervention aimed to redesign work to modify practices that cause stress in families and do not benefit productivity. For IT professionals, the intervention reduced turnover and had several beneficial impacts on social-emotional health, including lower levels of employee burnout, perceived stress, and psychological stress (Moen et al., 2016) and improvements in the functioning of parents' biological stress systems (Almeida et al., 2018). Improved outcomes for working parents and children included more daily shared time for parents and children (Davis et al., 2015), increased positive affect among youth (Lawson et al., 2016), and modifications of adolescents' negative sleep patterns (McHale et al., 2015). This example points to the potential for work quality interventions to address systemic issues in other sectors that impede family and child health. In contrast, for hourly workers in the long-term care sector who are paid lower wages than IT professionals and engage in hands-on work with patients, the intervention lowered cardiometabolic risk, but results across other health outcomes were mixed (Lovejoy et al., 2021). Psychosocial stress did improve, but only among employees who had significant elder care responsibilities (Kossek et al., 2019).

Designed to increase the stability and predictability of work schedules, the Stable Scheduling Study included two group-randomized controlled trials conducted in the retail sector (clothing stores). The first trial focused on changing one work practice—requiring managers to post the full month's schedule at least seven days before the start of the month. The study found that this intervention did significantly increase the number of weeks and days schedules were posted in advance but had no effects on perceived stress, work–family conflict, or turnover (Lambert, Henly, & Kim, 2019). The second trial went further by giving workers two weeks' advance notice of scheduling and eliminating all on-call shift work. At some stores in the intervention group, employees received a mobile application that enabled them to easily swap shifts and a guaranteed minimum number of work hours. The intervention significantly improved productivity and employees' sleep quality and physical health (symptoms of headaches, muscle pain, and stomachaches), but there were no significant differences in perceived stress and work–family conflict (Williams et al., 2018, 2019).

ADDRESSING OPPORTUNITY GAPS AND OUTCOMES IN EDUCATION

It is clear from the literature that expanding access to high-quality early care and education (ECE), followed by well-resourced, high-quality elementary experiences, has the potential to bridge opportunity gaps associated with children's academic and learning outcomes in both the short and long terms (Pearman et al., 2019; Cascio, 2021; Bailey, Sun, & Timpe, 2022). Yet ECE programs remain insufficiently funded, and unable to serve all eligible children and families, to ensure equitable access to quality programs, and to support the competency and well-being of the ECE workforce (National Academies, 2018). The limited public investment in ECE has disproportionately impacted children of color and those from immigrant families, especially those from low-income communities. These shortfalls have been shaped in part by societal attitudes toward safety net spending and aid for people living in poverty, which in turn are entangled with racism, class bias, and a meritocratic ethos (DeParle, 2022). Contrary to such attitudes, however, the research evidence shows that strengthening safety net supports (income supplements) is associated with later average higher earnings, better health, and reduced criminal arrests (National Academies, 2019a).

Full Funding

Although adequate funding of education programs and policies is essential, it has never been realized in the United States in the early years or the early grades. As a result of funding shortfalls, existing programs never reach all eligible children, and for those that they do reach, quality is inadequate and uneven. Research has found that increased investments in Head Start and in K–12 education are positively associated with educational attainment and earnings, and negatively associated with the likelihood of poverty and incarceration (Johnson & Jackson, 2019). Research in the K–12 system similarly has found that school spending and school funding reform, the latter typically stemming from court mandates, are both associated with increased achievement, educational attainment, and even wages in adulthood (Candelaria & Shores, 2015, 2017; Hyman, 2017; Lafortune, Rothstein, & Schanzenbach, 2018). Importantly, Johnson and Jackson (2019) found that the effects of Head Start increase when participation is followed by well-funded K–12 education, and that the effects on children of investments in K–12 education are magnified when children first participate in Head Start, pointing to the importance of the interconnectedness of these systems to children's outcomes and of continuity in funding and quality experiences.

Remedying the many opportunity gaps caused by these inadequacies in funding will require significant new resources across the birth to age 8 continuum, and encompassing ECE, general education, and education for children with disabilities under the Individuals with Disabilities Education Act (IDEA). As discussed in Chapters 2 and 3, an essential component of a fully funded education system is a significant investment in the workforce, across age groups and settings, that guarantees compensation and benefits commensurate with credentials and experience. The current lack of full funding for education for children aged 0–8 points to the lack of a strategic national plan for supporting these young children. Considering the powerful role of adult–child interactions and relationships in children's early learning experiences, it is clear that without this piece of the puzzle, quality in young children's education will be unattainable, and opportunity gaps will remain.

Inclusive, Quality Standards

Most quality frameworks fail to include factors that uniquely affect the learning experiences of children from historically marginalized communities. But while these factors are rarely examined in the broader context of quality, they have an outsized impact on the experiences of children of color, those who are dual language learners, and those with disabilities (Meek et al., 2020). This gap can be filled by expanding quality frameworks to go beyond the traditional markers of quality, such as small class sizes and credentialed teachers. Research suggests that a new system, based in a core set of standards informed and driven by closing opportunity gaps, might include structurally safe and healthy learning spaces; low teacher:student ratios and small class sizes; inclusion of children with disabilities with fully funded and appropriate services and supports; culturally affirming and research-based pedagogy and instruction; bilingual learning (i.e., learning both in English and in the home language) for dual language learners; a supported, competent, and fairly compensated workforce; and attention to bias and racism in adult–child relationships and interactions. This reenvisioning of quality frameworks is relevant from the early years to the early grades and is critical if significant resources are to be dedicated to improving the quality of early education.

A Supported, Fairly Compensated, Competent Workforce

A previous study of the National Academies on transforming the ECE workforce notes that an inclusive model of ECE quality would expand on the conception of what constitutes an effective and competent early childhood educator. The ECE field has spent decades defining what such an educator should know and be able to do (Institute of Medicine [IOM] & National Research Council [NRC], 2015). A more inclusive definition of workforce quality could be applied to all early childhood educators, including home child care workers, regardless of what age group they serve, what funding streams support them, or what setting they work in while allowing for specialized skills needed for different program types (IOM & NRC, 2015). Research shows that early childhood educators need access to professional preparation and ongoing supports to meet this standard, and this is especially so for those with limited financial resources and those from communities of color, who experience systemic barriers to higher education and other career pathways (IOM & NRC, 2015).

Data, Monitoring, and Accountability

Accountability measures, including quality standards and use of enforcement mechanisms—such as federal offices for civil rights—together with technical assistance systems, can be used to close opportunity gaps. Indeed, the opportunity gaps discussed in this report will be closed only if states, districts, and programs identify and monitor existing gaps, adequately fund interventions to close those gaps, and implement accountability standards to track progress.

The federal government has traditionally funded services, although incompletely and imperfectly, for historically marginalized groups, such as through supplemental education funding (e.g., Titles I and III), Head Start, or IDEA. But accountability for failing to bridge opportunity gaps has been weak. Indeed, a lack of accountability for reducing disparities in outcomes across publicly funded programs is common and serves as a significant hindrance to progress (Meek et al., 2020). This lack of accountability manifests in program standards that do not address the unique experiences of children from historically marginalized communities, monitoring systems that do not look for inequities in experiences, and accountability systems that impose no consequences for failing to address and therefore maintaining inequities.

A well-documented example of this lack of accountability is school segregation. After *Brown v. Board of Education* was decided, the government issued desegregation orders, and as a result, integration, albeit flawed and incomplete, increased sharply. Yet several court cases in the past 40 years have reversed oversight and requirements first implemented in the period after the *Brown* decision, and different administrations over time have failed to prioritize civil rights enforcement, including on the issue of segregation. Today, schools are more segregated than they were in 1970 (Orfield & Frankenberg, 2014).

ADDRESSING OPPORTUNITY GAPS AND OUTCOMES IN PHYSICAL HEALTH

Disparities in health outcomes often begin in early childhood as the result of a number of factors previously described in this report. Addressing these factors can not only improve health outcomes for parents and young children in the short term but also promote more positive health outcomes across the lifespan. Variations in access to health care and healthy environments from state to state and within communities create substantial differences in how—and the extent to which—these factors negatively impact different groups of children to create opportunity gaps. This section highlights a number of policies, programs, and approaches that can be implemented to promote positive and equitable health outcomes for children and their families.

Improving Maternal Health and Birth Outcomes

California has successfully reversed trends in maternal mortality. Between 2006 and 2013, during a period of collaboration among the California Department of Public Health, the California Maternal Quality Care Collaborative, and the California Hospital Association, the state's rate of maternal mortality dropped by 50%, even as the national rate continued to rise (Main, 2018). Research shows, however, that this decline did not include an overall reduction in racial disparities in maternal mortality and morbidity. Since that time, the California Maternal Quality Care Collaborative has launched the California Birth Equity Collaborative, and an evaluation of this collaborative is ongoing.

State policies have also begun focusing on ways to reduce adverse birth outcomes. One approach to this end is illustrated by Perinatal Quality Collaboratives (PQCs) and Maternal Mortality Review Committees (MMRCs). These statewide, multidisciplinary networks promote evidence-based clinical practices by bringing key stakeholders together, produce issue briefs and strategic plans, and convene symposia and other events. MMRCs operate at the state level to identify and analyze maternal deaths, disseminate findings, and develop recommendations. PQCs often serve as the "action arm" of MMRCs, translating MMRC findings into clinical reforms (Bellazaire & Skinner, 2019). Together, MMRCs and PQCs are thought to improve birth outcomes through systemwide changes across a state. Involvement of state governments in these efforts includes participation of key leaders in PQCs; states can also use legislation to mandate and fund MMRCs. In addition, federal grants provide funding to establish and support existing MMRCs in states. Currently, most states have active PQCs and MMRCs (Prenatal-to-3 Policy Impact Center, 2020).

Another state-level approach to improving birth outcomes is participation in the Alliance for Innovation on Maternal Health (AIM), which works to bring efforts to improve maternal health at the national, state, and hospital levels into alignment (Mahoney, 2018). For example, AIM provides hospitals with toolkits and bundles of medical information—generally articles, guidelines, and educational documents—regarding evidence-based practices for improving specific patient outcomes. A bundle, for example, might address a particular medical cause of maternal mortality and morbidity (such as preeclampsia or obstetric hemorrhage). In contrast to a PQC, a toolkit or bundle is thought to improve birth outcomes not through systemwide changes but through adjustments to practices in particular hospital settings. To date, research on this approach is limited to observational studies; although research suggests that toolkits and bundles can help reduce maternal morbidity, more rigorous studies would help in drawing firm conclusions about causality.

Improved access to information and best practices in clinical and prenatal care for mothers has been shown to improve health outcomes for infants across U.S. states. The sharing and transmission of data, information, and research is an important foundation for healthy infant and newborn outcomes. Additionally, there is evidence that increased income for parents results in a reduction in adverse health outcomes and birth experiences. Studies looking at raising minimum wages and expanding the EITC have shown that these policies produce significant reductions in infant mortality and increased birthweights.

Medicaid

Numerous policies and programs can improve the health of birthing people during the prenatal period, birth outcomes, and well-being during the perinatal period, which in turn can have lifelong positive impacts on children's health. One such policy is expanding income eligibility for health insurance, which research shows may improve birth outcomes (Prenatal-to-3 Policy Impact Center, 2021). Before Medicaid expansion, low-income women without children had more limited access to family planning services, preventive care before conception, and prenatal care in the earliest stages of pregnancy (Bhatt & Beck-Sagué, 2018). The ability of women and birthing persons to access care during the preconception and interconception periods gives clinicians a window of opportunity to assess and treat health conditions prior to pregnancy, which can lead to safer and healthier pregnancies and births and thus reduce maternal and infant mortality, low birthweights, and preterm births (Bhatt & Beck-Sagué, 2018).

Although the income limit to qualify for Medicaid is higher for pregnant versus nonpregnant people, these differing income eligibility guidelines can cause interruptions in health insurance coverage around childbirth known as perinatal churn. As a result, access to care is often restricted during the postpartum period, which can exacerbate health disparities and negatively impact maternal health. There has been some effort through state Medicaid expansion to decrease the gap in Medicaid eligibility between nonpregnancy and pregnancy, thus reducing the numbers of individuals susceptible to perinatal insurance churn compared with the numbers in nonexpansion states (Daw, Backes Kozhimannil, & Admon, 2019; Searing & Ross, 2019).

Evidence shows that although state Medicaid expansions are not significantly associated with improved birth outcomes in the overall population, the expansions do help reduce racial disparities in preterm birth and infant mortality, as well as both overall rates of and racial disparities in maternal mortality (Prenatal-to-3 Policy Impact Center, 2021). One study found that state Medicaid expansion was significantly associated with a 0.1 percentage point reduction in the incidence of very low birthweight and a 0.4 percentage point reduction in preterm birth rates among non-Hispanic Black infants compared with White infants. A second study found 52.6 fewer infant deaths per 1,000 live births among Hispanic infants in Medicaid expansion versus nonexpansion states. A 2020 quasi-experimental study also found that Medicaid expansion was associated with 6.7 fewer maternal deaths overall per 100,000 live births; when disaggregated by race, the findings showed 16.3 fewer deaths among Black mothers, six fewer deaths among Hispanic mothers, and no significant impacts among White mothers. Thus, while the Medicaid expansion may not have observable impacts at the population level, it may have significant impacts for particularly vulnerable populations.

Nutrition Assistance Programs

Three programs—SNAP, the National School Breakfast and Lunch Programs, and the Special Supplemental Nutrition Program for Women, Infants, and Children (WIC)—provide nutritional assistance and improve outcomes for vulnerable children and families.

Supplemental Nutrition Assistance Program (SNAP)

Hoynes, Schanzenbach, and Almond (2016) found that every $100 in SNAP benefits saved families $70 of their own income that they would otherwise have had to spend on food but could now spend on additional resources for their children. About $30 of this amount went to additional food purchases, thus increasing total spending on food by 30%. The remaining money saved by receiving SNAP benefits was available for other household expenditures.

Receiving SNAP benefits also translated into improvements in child outcomes beyond nutrition. Children from households with SNAP benefits had observed improvements in attendance at school and at medical checkups (National Academies, 2019a). Other research found that receipt of food aid led to a significantly reduced incidence of low birthweight and improvements in infant health (Almond, Hoynes, & Schanzenbach, 2011). More recent research has shown that the loss of SNAP benefits for those who exceed the income threshold results in worse caregiver and child health, and also increases the incidence of food insecurity (Ettinger de Cuba et al., 2019).

An important extension of this analysis has been additional research following up on long-run outcomes for children affected by SNAP/Food Stamp benefits during their childhood. In one study, researchers found that the children had improved health outcomes as adults as well (Hoynes, Schanzenbach, & Almond, 2016), which suggests that improvements in household resources that enable improved nutrition translate into better long-term health for affected children. In fact, a recent National Academies study (National Academies, 2019a) found that SNAP improves birth outcomes as well as many child and health outcomes. And research has shown that the pandemic electronic benefit transfer (EBT) program reduced food insecurity by more than seven percentage points in at-risk households (Bauer et al., 2020).

National School Breakfast and Lunch Programs

While there are a number of nutrition-focused programs in the United States, research on their short- and long-term impacts is not abundant. One study (Gundersen, Kreider, & Pepper, 2012) used data from the National Health and Nutrition Examination Survey to investigate the National School Lunch Program (NSLP) which provides free and reduced-price lunches for children in pre-K and grades K–12—approximately 4.9 billion lunches were provided in fiscal year 2019 (pre-COVID-19; National Academies, 2016; USDA, 2022a). Gunderson and colleagues (2012) estimate that the NSLP reduced food insecurity by at least 3.8%, reduced poor health in children by at least 29%, and reduced rates of obesity in children by at least 17%. Bhattacharya and colleagues (2006) found that the School Breakfast Program (SBP) improved healthy eating habits, increased the quality of calories consumed, reduced vitamin and mineral deficiencies, and improved the quality of diets for both children and their families, all of which could lead to better health and well-being for households with children who utilize the program. And recent research has shown that the pandemic EBT program, which provided food vouchers to cover the cost of meals for students while school was not in session, reduced food insecurity by more than 7 percentage points in at-risk households (Bauer et al., 2020).

For many students, there is well-documented stigma associated with using the NSLP and SBP; however, the program's Community Eligibility Provision (CEP) may be a promising strategy for reducing this stigma (Radsky et al., 2022). Currently, a students' family income is used to determine their eligibility to receive free or reduced-price meals at school. The CEP allows schools to offer free meals to all students, eliminating processes that differentiate between those who do and do not pay full price. Research suggests that universal provision of school meals—through the CEP or other universal meal programs—can increase student achievement (Kitchen et al., 2013; Gordanier et al., 2020; Ruffini, 2020; Schwartz & Rothbart, 2020; Radsky et al., 2022). A 2022 study of the implementation of the CEP in Oregon found that the program improved student nutrition, reduced administrative burden, and had a statistically significant effect on reducing student suspension rates by the third year of implementation. The protective effect on suspension was particularly pronounced for students from low-income families. The use of this program to reduce stigma highlights its potential value not only in providing meals but also in promoting equity in other domains (Radsky et al., 2022).

Special Supplemental Nutrition Program for Women, Infants, and Children

WIC provides healthy food packages, nutrition education, and breastfeeding support for low-income pregnant and postpartum women and children under age 5. In 2019, nearly 11 million people were eligible for the WIC program (USDA, 2022b). A review of the research on WIC (Carlson & Neuberger, 2021) found that women who participate in WIC have healthier babies compared with those who do not participate. The WIC program allows women to access more nutritious foods and improves infant feeding; specifically, WIC participants consume more high-quality, nutrient-dense foods. Mental development among children whose mothers participated in WIC was found to be higher than that among children whose mothers did not participate. Revisions to WIC in 2009 that improved the nutritional content of the food package and added a fruit and vegetable voucher were shown to have improved dietary quality, birth outcomes, and child health (Tester, Leung, & Crawford, 2016; Hamad et al., 2019; Guan et al., 2021; Pulvera, Collin, & Hamad, 2022). During the COVID-19 pandemic, the value of the fruit and vegetable voucher was increased, although as of this writing, these benefits are set to expire.

The National Academies report *Vibrant and Healthy Kids* (National Academies, 2019b, p. 15) includes a recommendation that various levels of governmental agencies strive to remove barriers to participation for both WIC and SNAP. In particular, the report states that these benefits should not be conditioned on parental employment in families with young children or pregnant women—conditions that could reduce eligibility for these programs among the poorest families with the greatest need. At present, WIC take-up is high for infants (nearly 100%) but only 50% for women and 25% as children reach age 4. Moreover, WIC benefits expire when children turn 5, leaving many children without nutrition benefits and with worsening household food insecurity until they start school and qualify for reduced-price lunch (Bitler et al., 2022; USDA, 2022b).

Reduction of Environmental Contaminants

Multilevel approaches are required to address inequities in the distribution of environmental contaminants, including actions at the government, industry, community/clinic, and household levels (Schulz et al., 2016). A recent National Academies report (National Academies, 2019b) summarizes current regulatory approaches to addressing environmental factors and children's health via existing government bodies, including the Centers for Disease Control and Prevention, Environmental Protection Agency (EPA), U.S. Food and Drug Administration, and U.S. Consumer Product Safety Commission. Several states have also asserted regulatory authority over particular environmental toxicants, including bisphenol A, cleaning agents in schools, and flame retardants (NCSL, 2017). The President's Task Force on Environmental Health Risks and Safety Risks to Children has made recommendations in three domains: (1) strengthen environmental protection in ECE settings through expanded workforce training, program monitoring, and regulations; (2) support expanded or innovative models for training prenatal and childhood health care providers on screening, counseling, and interventions to prevent or mitigate toxic environmental exposures; and (3) encourage relevant federal agencies to continue to support and enforce efforts to prevent and mitigate the impact of environmental toxicants during preconception through early childhood (National Academies, 2019b).

In all three of these domains, it is important to incorporate civil rights approaches that promote racial equity in environmental justice. Such approaches can mitigate inequitable burdens, lower or remove barriers to community participation in decision making, and improve access to health and environmental benefits (USDA, 2012; National Academies, 2017). Such might include, for example, describing proposals in terms that are understandable to all, analyzing the benefits and burdens for high-risk subgroups and not just the population at large, and including low-income people and people of color in all steps of the process (National Academies, 2019b). In addition to these policy changes, there are downstream interventions for each of these three domains, as detailed below.

Allergens/Pollutants and Asthma

Interventions focused at the family/household level have the potential to reduce allergen- and pollutant-driven asthma triggers. These interventions are focused on improving indoor air quality and reducing allergens by, for example, providing mattress and pillow covers, high-efficiency particulate air vacuum cleaners and air filters, and cleaning; controlling cockroaches; and eliminating leaks and removing moldy items (Krieger et al., 2010). Such interventions have been found to reduce asthma symptoms and school absenteeism among children in both rural and urban areas, and are often carried out by home visitors or community health workers (Crain et al., 2002; Chew et al., 2003; Morgan et al., 2004; Levy et al., 2006; Crocker et al., 2011). Moreover, these interventions have been found to reduce disparities in asthma-related outcomes based on race/ethnicity and income (Postma, Karr, & Kieckhefer, 2009).

Lead

A report by the Health Impact Project (2017, pp. 3–4) includes the following recommendations for promoting community interventions to reduce lead exposure and disparities in exposure:

- Reduce lead in drinking water in homes built before 1986 and other places children frequent. Removing leaded drinking water service lines from the homes of children born in 2018 would protect more than 350,000 children and yield $2.7 billion in future benefits, or about $1.33 per dollar invested.
- Remove lead paint hazards from low-income housing built before 1960 and other places children spend time. Eradicating lead paint hazards from older homes of children from low-income families

would provide $3.5 billion in future benefits, or approximately $1.39 per dollar invested, and protect more than 311,000 children.
- Increase enforcement of the federal renovation, repair, and painting rule. Ensuring that contractors comply with the EPA rule that requires lead-safe renovation, repair, and painting practices would protect about 211,000 children born in 2018 and provide future benefits of $4.5 billion, or about $3.10 per dollar spent.
- Reduce air lead emissions. Eliminating lead from airplane fuel would protect more than 226,000 children born in 2018 who live near airports, generate $262 million in future benefits, and remove roughly 450 tons of lead from the environment every year.
- Clean up contaminated soil.
- Improve blood lead testing among children at high risk of exposure, and find and remediate the sources of their exposure.
- Ensure access to developmental and neuropsychological assessments and appropriate high-quality programs for children with elevated blood lead levels.

It is important to note that, to support many of these initiatives, Medicaid can cover home investigations of lead exposures; case management for exposed children; and support to states for implementing education, screening, and outreach efforts in areas at high risk of lead exposure, although such programs would have to be applied at the local level (Tong, Artiga, & Rudowitz, 2022). In addition, greater collaboration with tribal nations is needed to improve state screening and registry efforts (President's Task Force on Environmental Health Risks and Safety Risks to Children, 2016).

With more than 13 million preschoolers in child care every day, including six million infants and toddlers, child care settings are also critical sites with the potential for lead exposure (Amoah et al., 2016). These highly heterogeneous settings include individual homes, community centers, and office buildings, and licensing guidelines also vary greatly at the local level. Interventions addressing these settings could involve regulations and policies, as well as requirements for training child care workers in environmental risk assessment, which prior studies have shown to be effective for both lead and other contaminants (Amoah et al., 2016).

Other Environmental Contaminants

Multilevel approaches are also required to address inequities in the distribution of other environmental contaminants. These approaches could include improving manufacturing and industrial processes to minimize pollution, evaluating construction and urban development plans to reduce dependence on automobile transportation, and involving communities in assessment processes to effect broader policy change (Schulz et al., 2016).

The only environmental exposure screening that receives Medicaid support is that for lead because of the magnitude, frequency, and duration of exposure; the significance of health impacts; and the potential for prevention (Honsberger, McCaman, & VanLandeghem, 2018). This could be an avenue of policy change for other environmental toxicants.

In summary, pollutants and environmental contaminants have potentially significant impacts on child health outcomes. These pollutants may also play a role in school achievement and attendance in the case of asthma or other chronic disease, and there are racial/ethnic and socioeconomic disparities in exposure and risk for children from vulnerable communities. Depending on the type of contaminant, potential solutions range from local community development and environmental cleaning efforts to local, state, and federal policies to legislate change.

HUMAN-CENTERED DESIGN AND POLICY DEVELOPMENT

In recent years, the application of human-centered design (HCD) principles and approaches has expanded at all levels of the social services domain. Service providers from different systems can adopt an HCD approach to establishing an effective family engagement framework as a way to improve their services. Policy makers, advocates, and agency staff with roles in designing and implementing policies can use HCD to ensure that their work centers on the needs and experiences of the user or consumer from the beginning so the policies will have the intended impact for children, families, and communities.

First applied to the development of consumer goods and online applications and websites, HCD is based on the premise that working with the stakeholders most directly affected by a particular issue is critical to develop the most effective solutions. The approach entails three phases: inspiration, ideation, and implementation (IDEO.org, 2015). In general, HCD turns on its head the notion that only trained "experts" should lead the design process, whether its intended outcome is a commercial product, a website, or the development or implementation of a policy.

Exploring how an HCD approach can be operationalized in a school, community, or policy context can inform the planning and implementation of authentic family engagement within processes, systems, and day-to-day practices. In the context of policy development and implementation, an HCD approach will incorporate the following principles:

- The approach goes beyond getting feedback from end users, instead collaborating with them as codesigners with equal decision-making power (Pahlka, 2018; Weeby, 2018). "In short, community voice without community leadership is significantly less effective" (Weeby, 2018, p. 10).
- The design process intentionally dismantles barriers to access to publicly funded services and benefits so policies can lead to equitable outcomes across race and ethnicity, linguistic group, socioeconomic status, gender, geography, and other social factors associated with unequal opportunities and outcomes (Pahlka, 2018).
- The design process involves multidisciplinary teams that include not only policy makers but also stakeholders such as design professionals, subject matter experts, policy implementers, and procurement and compliance professionals (Pahlka, 2019).
- Iterative processes and feedback loops are incorporated to improve policy design and implementation, driven by real-time, actionable data from user experience, allowing for "experimentation that can inform policy development with the knowledge of what's actually working towards the original intent" (Pahlka, 2019, p. 6).

Applying an HCD approach to policy requires that policy leaders take additional steps to ensure that equity is at the center of the process. Otherwise, the work will exclude critical voices and result in policies and implementation processes that continue to create barriers for certain communities to access publicly funded services to which they are entitled. First, the definition of "end users" in HCD includes those whose voices are often not at the table and who face the greatest barriers to accessing services and benefits. Participation in HCD processes takes time, and involving users who happen to be able to engage will likely perpetuate the inequities in current systems (Weeby, 2018). Also, HCD processes need to "take into consideration the historical and social contexts within which many social 'problems' exist" (Weeby, 2018, p. 11). As discussed earlier, barriers to accessing publicly funded programs that can reduce opportunity gaps are as much a result of historical disinvestment and disenfranchisement of low-income communities and communities of color as of poorly designed or implemented policies. Neglecting this history will only lead to incomplete solutions, even when the "end users" are at the center of the process (Weeby, 2018).

To date, HCD approaches have been used to good effect in a number of public policy areas. Examples include designing the Centers for Medicare & Medicaid Services' strategy for transferring health care delivery from a procedure-based to a value-based system (Sinai, Leftwich, & McGuire, 2020); creating prototypes of tools that school districts can test and adapt to implement public school funding reform in California (Knudson, 2019); identifying key lessons and developing outreach materials to improve the implementation of paid family leave in New Jersey (Schulte, 2021; Zucker, 2021) and increasing participation in EITC programs in New York (Rodriguez et al., 2021).

Taken together, the experience thus far in applying HCD to the policy arena shows that the approach holds great promise for creating more equitable policies and implementation processes that address many of the causes of the opportunity gaps discussed in this report. A fundamental overhaul of the systems that have contributed to these opportunity gaps for children and their families is needed, and providers and policy makers alike need to bring families to the table as authentic partners in informing policies and systems. Only then will the shared responsibility for the learning and development of children translate to deep and sustainable impact.

PUBLIC–PRIVATE PARTNERSHIPS

Public–private partnerships are an increasingly effective approach for fostering multisectoral collaboration and leveraging the strengths of stakeholders from a wide variety of disciplines and sectors. Opportunity gaps exist across a number of domains. Many of the factors that drive opportunity gaps in education, physical health, and social-emotional development and well-being cut across these domains; a multisectoral approach will be required to reduce, mitigate, and eliminate them. Through public–private partnerships, the public sector, philanthropic organizations, private-sector businesses, and other stakeholders can combine and sustain efforts to address opportunity gaps more efficiently.

A number of states already use public–private partnerships to support programs, interventions, and services aimed at addressing disparities in outcomes in a variety of health, education, and developmental domains. For example, some of these partnerships have focused on increasing school readiness; funding the development of community-level early care, health, and education systems; increasing access to health services; providing parent education and family support to promote health and social-emotional health; and facilitating the alignment of foundation funding in such areas as school attendance, home visiting, and policy advocacy to promote improvements in outcomes for children (U.S. Department of Health and Human Services, 2014; NCSL, 2012).

Part of the committee's task was to identify the potential roles, actions, and supports that would enable the philanthropic community to assist in addressing the opportunity gap. Public–private partnerships are one way in which philanthropic organizations can engage with other stakeholders to this end. Philanthropic organizations are well positioned to engage communities at the national, state, and local levels to help deliver community-driven solutions for promoting equity across a variety of sectors. The 2017 National Academies report *Communities in Action: Pathways to Health Equity* highlighted a number of ways in which the philanthropic community could promote health equity—for example, supporting community organizing, building capacity, supporting enforcement of civil rights laws to target injustice, and prioritizing equity in the social determinants of health by investing in minoritized and low-income communities (National Academies, 2017). While the focus of that report was on health equity, many of these concepts and actions can be applied more broadly to promoting equity in education and social-emotional health and well-being as well.

Philanthropic organizations can take on a number of roles in efforts to reduce the opportunity gap. They can serve as conveners to bring together members of government, community organizations, and individuals to identify community needs; work within to communities to develop and fund grants to address local needs; create opportunities to develop leaders who can help sustain efforts and build capacity; develop, fund, implement, test, and scale promising interventions to promote equity; and fund research that focuses on the needs of groups experiencing the greatest disparities and builds the knowledge base needed to address the numerous opportunity gaps that exist across sectors. It is important to note, however, that philanthropic organizations cannot meet the demand for programs, services, and infrastructure alone. It is through partnership with other stakeholders—community members, employers, government, and other community institutions—that they can play a key role in addressing and responding to the needs of the communities and populations they serve and fostering and sustaining innovative approaches to promoting equity.

CONCLUSIONS

There is strong evidence that the social safety net reduces child poverty. Safety net programs are crucial for providing the resources needed to address the opportunity gaps discussed in this report, improving economic security, and countering structural racism. These programs include the EITC, WIC, SNAP, Medicaid, minimum wages, and paid family leave. Increased investment for support of these programs is associated with improved outcomes across a variety of domains. However, differences in state policies can create geographic disparities in the supports available through these programs, and administrative burden can limit access and exacerbate inequities. The complexity of programs and uncertainties related to eligibility, continued participation, and benefit levels create stress and insecurity within households. In addition, eligibility restrictions significantly limit the ability of safety net programs to reduce opportunity gaps for children in Hispanic and immigrant families that could be mitigated by more inclusive eligibility rules and reduced administrative burden.

Because of the lack of comprehensive surveys, limitations of program administrative data, and the lack of program implementation studies, a number of equity-focused research questions about paid family and medical leave remain unanswered. A growing nonexperimental evidence base shows that parents' poor job quality is associated with greater social-emotional issues for young children by raising parents' stress levels. Black, Hispanic, immigrant, and low-income children have higher exposure to opportunity gaps associated with parents' low-quality jobs. More comprehensive data sets that include measures of parents' jobs and children's outcomes are needed to understand how differential exposure to opportunity gaps in parents' job quality affects differences in children's health and education outcomes by income, race/ethnicity, and immigrant status.

Parental job characteristics are an often overlooked social determinant of health for young children. Recent rigorous studies demonstrate that the implementation of scheduling laws in the lower-wage retail sector leads to improved scheduling practices. Studies have found that scheduling laws have positive impacts on job satisfaction, overall happiness, and sleep quality, but null impacts on social-emotional health for adults or children. However, evidence suggests that inconsistent or unreliable work schedules can make it difficult for some families to meet the work requirements necessary for them to access safety net programs. Earnings subsidies, sectoral job training, and wraparound service approaches help improve parents' job quality and can open doors for Black and Hispanic workers to enter higher-wage sectors; however, none of these approaches addresses structural issues such as racial discrimination in hiring, wages, or advancement. Thus, programs can potentially help reduce racial/ethnic opportunity gaps in parents' job quality and psychological stress that influence children's development, but more research is needed to test rigorously whether these strategies reduce gaps in children's social-emotional outcomes.

Taken together, results from these interventions show that proactively changing employer practices with the goal of reducing stress from work–family conflicts can be effective in improving the social-emotional and physical health of working parents, which in turn positively affects children's health. These studies also show that, to improve social-emotional outcomes, interventions need to be improved and tailored for parents who work in lower-wage occupations and in the service sector. These are challenging to redesign because of narrow profit margins and lean staffing (Kelly & Moen, 2020). Since Black, Hispanic, low-income, and immigrant working parents work disproportionately in the service sector and are underrepresented in professional occupations (Earle et al., 2014), opportunity gaps in job quality by income and race/ethnicity will remain unless employer scheduling practices are improved.

Despite the number of programs and policies in the United States with the potential to close the opportunity gap, the complex system of these programs and policies is not equally accessible to all children and families—especially those who are in greatest need of services. Both state-to-state and intrastate variations in the implementation and funding of various programs and policies (e.g., Medicaid expansion, minimum wages, the EITC) lead to persistent inequities in outcomes for children.

REFERENCES

Aaronson, S., Barnes, M., & Edelberg, W. (2021). *A hot labor market won't eliminate racial and ethnic unemployment gaps.* Brookings Institution. Available: https://www.brookings.edu/blog/up-front/2021/09/02/a-hot-labor-market-wont-eliminate-racial-and-ethnic-unemployment-gaps/

Acevedo-Garcia, D., Joshi, P.K., Ruskin, E., Walters, A.N., & Sofer, N. (2021a). Restoring an inclusionary safety net for children in immigrant families: A review of three social policies. *Health Affairs,* 40(7), 1099–107. https://doi.org/10.1377/hlthaff.2021.00206

Acevedo-Garcia, D., Joshi, P.K., Ruskin, E., Walters, A.N., Sofer, N., & Guevara, C.A. (2021b). Including children in immigrant families in policy approaches to reduce child poverty. *Child Poverty and Health 2021: Addressing Equity and Economic Justice,* 21(8 Suppl), S117–25. https://doi.org/10.1016/j.acap.2021.06.016

Adelstein, S., & Peters, H.E. (2019). *Parents' access to work-family supports.* Urban Institute. Available: https://www.urban.org/research/publication/parents-access-work-family-supports

Alderson, D.P., Gennetian, L.A., Dowsett, C.J., Imes, A., & Huston, A.C. (2008). Effects of employment-based programs on families by prior levels of disadvantage. *Social Service Review,* 82(3), 361–94. https://doi.org/10.1086/592360

Almeida, D.M., Lee, S., Walter, K.N., Lawson, K.M., Kelly, E.L., & Buxton, O.M. (2018). The effects of a workplace intervention on employees' cortisol awakening response. *Community, Work & Family,* 21(2), 151. https://doi.org/10.1080/13668803.2018.1428172

Almond, D., Hoynes, H., & Schanzenbach, D. (2011). Inside the war on poverty: The impact of food stamps on birth outcomes. *Review of Economics and Statistics,* 93. http://www.jstor.org/stable/23015943

Altonji, J., Contractor, Z., Finamor, L., Haygood, R., Lindenlaub, I., Meghir, C., O'Dea, C., Scott, D., Wang, L., & Washington, E. (2020). *Employment effects of unemployment insurance generosity during the pandemic.* Tobin Center for Economic Policy. Available: https://tobin.yale.edu/sites/default/files/files/C-19%20Articles/CARES-UI_identification_vF(1).pdf

Amoah, A.O., Witherspoon, N.O., Pérodin, J., & Paulson, J.A. (2016). Findings from a pilot environmental health intervention at early childhood centers in the District of Columbia. *Journal of Public Health,* 38(3), e209–17.

Ananat, E.O., Gassman-Pines, A., Francis, D., & Gibson-Davis, C. (2011). *Children left behind: The effects of statewide job loss on student achievement.* (Working Paper No. 17104). National Bureau of Economic Research. Available: https://www.researchgate.net/publication/228200308_Children_Left_Behind_The_Effects_of_Statewide_Job_Loss_on_Student_Achievement

Ananat, E.O., Gassman-Pines, A., & Fitz-Henley II, J. (2022). *The effects of the Emeryville fair workweek ordinance on the daily lives of low-wage workers and their families.* (Working Paper No. 29792). National Bureau of Economic Research. http://doi.org/10.3386/w29792

Andrea, S.B., Messer, L.C., Marino, M., Goodman, J.M., & Boone-Heinonen, J. (2020). A nationwide investigation of the impact of the tipped worker subminimum wage on infant size for gestational age. *Preventive Medicine,* 133, 106016. https://doi.org/10.1016/j.ypmed.2020.106016

Ansel, B., & Boushey, H. (2017). *Modernizing U.S. labor standards for 21st-century families.* (Policy Proposal No. 2017-08). Brookings Institution. Available: https://www.brookings.edu/research/modernizing-u-s-labor-standards-for-21st-century-families/

Antonisse, L., & Garfield, R. (2018). *The relationship between work and health: Findings from a literature review.* (Issue Brief). Available: https://www.kff.org/medicaid/issue-brief/the-relationship-between-work-and-health-findings-from-a-literature-review/

Appelbaum, E., & Milkman, R. (2011). *Leaves that pay: Employer and worker experiences with paid family leave in California.* Center for Economic and Policy Research. Available: https://www.cepr.net/documents/publications/paid-family-leave-1-2011.pdf

Bailey, M., Sun, S., & Timpe, B. (2022). *Is universal preschool worth it? Headstart offers encouraging results.* Brookings Institute. Available: https://www.brookings.edu/blog/brown-center-chalkboard/2022/02/09/is-universal-preschool-worth-it/

Bailey, M.J., Byker, T.S., Patel, E., & Ramnath, S. (2019). *The long-term effects of California's 2004 paid family leave act on women's careers: Evidence from U.S. Tax data.* (Working Paper No. 26416). National Bureau of Economic Research. https://doi.org10.3386/w26416

Bartel, A., Kim, S., & Nam, J. (2019). *Racial and ethnic disparities in access to and use of paid family and medical leave: Evidence from four nationally representative datasets. Monthly Labor Review.* Bureau of Labor Statistics. https://doi.org/10.21916/mlr.2019.2

Bartik, A.W., Bertrand, M., Lin, F., Rothstein, J., & Unrath, M. (2020). *Measuring the labor market at the onset of the COVID-19 crisis.* (Working Paper No. 27613). National Bureau of Economic Research. Available: https://www.nber.org/system/files/working_papers/w27613/w27613.pdf

Batra, A., & Hamad, R. (2021). Short-term effects of the earned income tax credit on children's physical and mental health. *Annals of Epidemiology,* 58, 15–21. https://doi.org/10.1016/j.annepidem.2021.02.008

Bauer, L.P., Ruffini, A., Schanzenbach, K., & Whitmore, D. (2020). *The effect of pandemic EBT on measures of food hardship.* Brookings Institute. Available: https://www.brookings.edu/research/the-effect-of-pandemic-ebt-on-measures-of-food-hardship/

Baum, C.L., & Ruhm, C.J. (2013). *The effects of paid family leave in California on labor market outcomes.* (Working Paper No. 19741). National Bureau of Economic Research. https://doi.org/10.3386/w19741

Becker, G. (1981). *A treatise on the family.* Harvard University Press. Available: https://www.nber.org/books-and-chapters/treatise-family

Bellazaire, A.S., & Skinner, E. (2019). *Preventing infant and maternal mortality: State policy options.* National Conference of State Legislatures. Available: https://www.ncsl.org/health/preventing-infant-and-maternal-mortality-state-policy-options

Berkowitz, S.A., & Basu, S. (2021). Unemployment insurance, health-related social needs, health care access, and mental health during the COVID-19 pandemic. *JAMA Internal Medicine,* 181(5), 699–702. https://doi.org/10.1001/jamainternmed.2020.7048

A Better Balance. (2021). *Comparative chart of paid family and medical leave laws in the United States.* Available: https://www.abetterbalance.org/resources/paid-family-leave-laws-chart/

Bhatt, C.B., & Beck-Sagué, C.M. (2018). Medicaid expansion and infant mortality in the United States. *American Journal of Public Health*, 108(4), 565–7. https://doi.org/10.2105/AJPH.2017.304218

Bhattacharya, J., Currie, J., & Haider, S.J. (2006). Breakfast of champions? The school breakfast program and the nutrition of children and families. *Journal of Human Resources*, 41(3), 445–66. Available: http://www.jstor.org/stable/40057265

Bitler, M., Currie, J., Hoynes, H.W., Ruffini, K., Schulkind, L., & Willage, B. (2022). *Mothers as insurance: Family spillovers in WIC*. (Working Paper No. 30112). National Bureau of Economic Research. https://doi.org/10.3386/w30112

Boushey, H., & Mitukiewicz, A. (2014). *Job quality matters: How our future economic competitiveness hinges on the quality of parents' jobs*. Washington Center for Equitable Growth. Available: https://equitablegrowth.org/job-quality-matters-future-economic-competitiveness-hinges-quality-parents-jobs/

Braga, B., Blavin, F., & Gangopadhyaya, A. (2020). The long-term effects of childhood exposure to the earned income tax credit on health outcomes. *Journal of Public Economics*, 190(104249). https://doi.org/10.1016/j.jpubeco.2020.104249

Brito, N.H., Wechan, D., Brandes-Aitken, A., Yoshikawa, H., Greaves, A., & Zhang, M. (2021). Paid maternal leave is associated with infant brain function at 3-months of age. *Child Development*, 93(4), 1030–43. https://doi.org/10.1111/cdev.13765

Brown, S., Herr, J., Roy, R., & Klerman, J.A. (2020). *Employee and worksite perspectives of the family and medical leave act: Results from the 2018 surveys*. Abt Associates. Available: https://www.dol.gov/sites/dolgov/files/OASP/evaluation/pdf/WHD_FMLA2018SurveyResults_FinalReport_Aug2020.pdf

Bullinger, L.R. (2019). The effect of paid family leave on infant and parental health in the United States. *Journal of Health Economics*, 66, 101–16. https://doi.org/10.1016/j.jhealeco.2019.05.006

Bureau of Labor Statistics (BLS). (2019). What would a comprehensive reform of the Unemployment Insurance program look like? Washington, DC: *Monthly Labor Review*. Available: https://www.bls.gov/opub/mlr/2019/book-review/unemployment-insurance-reform.htm

———. (2021). *Labor force characteristics by race and ethnicity, 2020*. BLS Report 1095. Washington, DC: Bureau of Labor and Statistics. Available: https://www.bls.gov/opub/reports/race-and-ethnicity/2020/home.htm

Burgard, S.A., & Lin, K.Y. (2013). Bad jobs, bad health? How work and working conditions contribute to health disparities. *American Behavioral Scientist*, 57(8), 1105–27. https://doi.org/10.1177/0002764213487347

Byker, T.S. (2016). Paid parental leave laws in the United States: Does short-duration leave affect women's labor-force attachment? *American Economic Review*, 106(5), 242–6. https://doi.org/ 10.1257/aer.p20161118

Candelaria, C.A., & Shores, K.A. (2015). *The sensitivity of causal estimates from court-ordered finance reform on spending and graduation rates*. Stanford University. Available: https://cepa.stanford.edu/sites/default/files/shores_candelaria_causal_estimate.pdf

———. (2017). *Court-ordered finance reforms in the adequacy era: Heterogenous causal effects and sensitivity*. Stanford University Center for Education Policy Analysis. Available: https://cepa.stanford.edu/content/court-ordered-finance-reforms-adequacy-era-heterogeneous-causal-effects-and-sensitivity

Carlson, S., & Neuberger, Z. (2021). *WIC works: Addressing the nutrition and health needs of low-income families for more than four decades*. Center on Budget and Policy Priorities. Available: https://www.cbpp.org/research/food-assistance/wic-works-addressing-the-nutrition-and-health-needs-of-low-income-families

Carré, F., & Tilly, C. (2017). *Where bad jobs are better. Retail jobs across countries and companies*. Russell Sage Foundation. Available: https://www.russellsage.org/publications/where-bad-jobs-are-better-0

Carrillo, D., Harknett, K., Logan, A., Luhr, S., & Schneider, D. (2017). Instability of work and care: How work schedules shape child-care arrangements for parents working in the service sector. *Social Service Review*, 91(3), 422–55.

Cascio, E. (2021). *Early childhood education in the United States: What, when, where, who, how, and why*. (Working Paper No. 28722). National Bureau of Economic Research. https://doi.org/10.3386/w28722

Catalano, R., Goldman-Mellor, S., Saxton, K., Margerison-Zilko, C., Subbaraman, M., LeWinn, K., & Anderson, E. (2011). The health effects of economic decline. *Annual Review of Public Health*, 32, 431–50. https://doi.org/10.1177/0002716213500453

Chatterji, P., & Markowitz, S. (2012). Family leave after childbirth and the mental health of new mothers. *Journal of Mental Health Policy and Economics*, 15(2), 61–76.

Chen, F., and Shrider, E. (2021). *Expanded unemployment insurance benefits during pandemic lowered poverty rates across all racial groups*. Washington, DC: U.S. Census Bureau. Available: https://www.census.gov/content/dam/Census/library/publications/2021/demo/p60-273.pdf

Chew, G.L., Perzanowski, M.S., Miller, R.L., Correa, J.C., Hoepner, L.A., Jusino, C.M., Becker, M.G., & Kinney, P.L. (2003). Distribution and determinants of mouse allergen exposure in low-income New York City apartments. *Environmental Health Perspectives*, 111(10), 1348–51. https://doi.org/10.1289/ehp.6124

Chingos, M., & Blagg, K. (2017). *Student transportation and educational access*. Urban Institute. Available: https://www.urban.org/research/publication/student-transportation-and-educational-access

Chodorow-Reich, G., Coglianese, J., & Karabarbounis, L. (2019). The macro effects of unemployment benefit extensions: A measurement error approach. *The Quarterly Journal of Economics*, 134(1), 227–79. https://doi.org/10.1093/qje/qjy018

Clark, R., Hyde, J.S., Essex, M.J., & Klein, M.H. (1997). Length of maternity leave and quality of mother-infant interactions. *Child Development*, 68(2), 364–83.

Coelli, M.B. (2011). Parental job loss and the education enrollment of youth. *Labour Economics*, 18(1), 25–35. https://doi.org/10.1016/j.labeco.2010.04.015

Collier, M. (2021). *Child care access for families with non-standard work hours*. Research-to-Policy Collaboration. Available: https://research2policy.org/child-care-for-families-with-non-standard-work/

Congdon, W.J., Scott, M.M., Katz, B., Loprest, P., Nightingale, D., & Shakesprere, J. (2020). *Understanding good jobs: A review of definitions and evidence*. Urban Institute. https://www.urban.org/research/publication/understanding-good-jobs-review-definitions-and-evidence

Congressional Research Service. (2019). *Unemployment insurance: Programs and benefits*. RL33362. https://crsreports.congress.gov/product/pdf/RL/RL33362

Cooklin, A.R., Canterford, L., Strazdins, L., & Nicholson, J.M. (2011). Employment conditions and maternal postpartum mental health: Results from the longitudinal study of Australian children. *Archives of Women's Mental Health*, 14(3), 217–25. https://doi.org/10.1007/s00737-010-0196-9

Couch, K.A., and Fairlie, R. (2010). Last hired, first fired? Black-white unemployment and the business cycle. *Demography*, 47(1), 227–47. https://doi.org/10.1353/dem.0.0086

Crain, E.F., Walter, M., O'Connor, G.T., Mitchell, H., Gruchalla, R.S., Kattan, M., Malindzak, G.S., Enright, P., Evans, R., 3rd, Morgan, W., & Stout, J.W. (2002). Home and allergic characteristics of children with asthma in seven U.S. urban communities and design of an environmental intervention: The inner-city asthma study. *Environmental Health Perspectives*, 110(9), 939–45. https://doi.org/10.1289/ehp.02110939

Crocker, D.D., Kinyota, S., Dumitru, G.G., Ligon, C.B., Herman, E.J., Ferdinands, J.M., Hopkins, D.P., Lawrence, B.M., Sipe, T.A., & Task Force on Community Preventive Services (2011). Effectiveness of home-based, multi-trigger, multicomponent interventions with an environmental focus for reducing asthma morbidity: A community guide systematic review. *American Journal of Preventive Medicine,* 41(2 Suppl 1), S5–32. https://doi.org/10.1016/j.amepre.2011.05.012

Cylus, J., & Avendano, M. (2017). Receiving unemployment benefits may have positive effects on the health of the unemployed. *Health Affairs,* 36(2), 289–96. https://doi.org/10.1377/hlthaff.2016.1040

Cylus, J., Glymour, M.M., & Avendano, M. (2014). Do generous unemployment benefit programs reduce suicide rates? A state fixed-effect analysis covering 1968–2008. *American Journal of Epidemiology,* 180(1), 45–52. https://doi.org/10.1093/aje/kwu106

Dagher, R.K., McGovern, P.M., & Dowd, B.E. (2014). Maternity leave duration and postpartum mental and physical health: Implications for leave policies. *Journal of Health Politics, Policy and Law,* 39(2), 369–416.

Dahl, G.B., & Lochner, L. (2012). The impact of family income on child achievement: Evidence from the earned income tax credit. *American Economic Review,* 102(5), 1927–56. http://dx.doi.org/10.1257/aer.102.5.1927

Das, T., & Polachek, S.W. (2015). Unanticipated effects of California's paid family leave program. *Contemporary Economic Policy,* 33(4), 619–35. https://doi.org/10.1111/coep.12102

Davis, E.E., Krafft, C., Madill, R., & Halle, T. (2015). *Continuity of subsidy participation and stability of care in the child care subsidy program in Maryland.* (Research Brief No. 2015-41). Child Trends. Available: https://www.childtrends.org/publications/continuity-of-subsidy-participation-and-stability-of-care-in-the-child-care-subsidy-program-in-maryland

Daw, J.R., Backes Kozhimannil, K., & Admon, L.K. (2019). High rates of perinatal insurance churn persist after the ACA. *Forefront Group.* https://doi.org/10.1377/forefront.20190913.387157

DeParle, J. (2022). Expanded safety net drives sharp drop in child poverty. *The New York Times.* Available: https://www.nytimes.com/2022/09/11/us/politics/child-poverty-analysis-safety-net.html

Department of Health and Human Services. (2014). New HHS data shows major strides made in patient safety, leading to improved care and savings. https://innovation.cms.gov/files/reports/patient-safety-results.pdf

Department of Labor. (2022). *Employment characteristics of families - 2021.* USDL-22-0673. Washington, DC. Available: https://www.bls.gov/news.release/pdf/famee.pdf

Derenoncourt, E., & Montialoux, C. (2020). Minimum wages and racial inequality. *The Quarterly Journal of Economics,* 136(1), 169–228. https://doi.org/10.1093/qje/qjaa031

Dixon, R. (2021). *From excluded to essential: Tracing the racist exclusion of farmworkers, domestic works, and tipped workers from the Fair Labor Standards Act. Testimony of Rebecca Dixon.* Hearing before the U.S. House of Representatives Education and Labor Committee, Workforce Protections Subcommittee. Available: https://s27147.pcdn.co/wp-content/uploads/NELP-Testimony-FLSA-May-2021.pdf

Duncan, G.J., Bos, H., Gennetian, L.A., & Hill, H. (2009). New Hope: A thoughtful and effective approach to "make work pay". *Northwestern Journal of Law and Social Policy,* 4(1), 101–15. Available: https://scholarlycommons.law.northwestern.edu/njlsp/vol4/iss1/6/

Earle, A., Joshi, P., Geronimo, K., & Acevedo-Garcia, D. (2014). Job characteristics among working parents: Differences by race, ethnicity, and nativity. *Monthly Labor Review.* Bureau of Labor Statistics. Available: https://www.bls.gov/opub/mlr/2014/article/job-characteristics-among-working-parents.htm

East, C.N. (2020). The effect of food stamps on children's health evidence from immigrants' changing eligibility. *Journal of Human Resources,* 55(2), 387–427. https://doi.org/10.3368/jhr.55.3.0916-8197R2

East, C.N., & Page, M.E. (2020). Introduction: What does it take to achieve equality of opportunity for children? *How do early-life health experiences affect future generations' equality of opportunity?* American Psychological Association. https://doi.org/10.1037/0000187-001

East, C.N., & Simon, D. (2020). *How well insured are job losers? Efficacy of the public safety net.* (Working Paper No. 28218). National Bureau of Economic Research. https://doi.org/10.3386/w28218

Ettinger de Cuba, S., Chilton, M., Bovell-Ammon, A., Knowles, M., Coleman, S.M., Black, M.M., Cook, J.T., Cutts, D.B., Casey, P.H., Heeren, T.C., & Frank, D.A. (2019). Loss of SNAP is associated with food insecurity and poor health in working families with young children. *Health Affairs (Project Hope),* 38(5), 765–773. https://doi.org/10.1377/hlthaff.2018.05265

Farber, H.S., Rothstein, J., & Valletta, R.G. (2015). The effect of extended unemployment insurance benefits: Evidence from the 2012-2013 phase-out. *American Economic Review,* 105(5), 171–6. https://doi.org/10.1257/aer.p20151088

Golden, L., & Kim, J. (2020). *The involuntary part-time work and underemployment problem in the U.S.* Center for Law and Social Policy. Available: https://www.clasp.org/publications/report/brief/involuntary-part-time-work-and-underemployment-problem-us/

Goodman, J.M., Elser, H., & Dow, W.H. (2020). Among low-income women in San Francisco, low awareness of paid parental leave benefits inhibits take-up. *Health Affairs,* 39(7), 1157–65. https://doi.org/10.1377/hlthaff.2020.00157

Goorin, A., Frank, R.G., & Glied, S. (2021). Addressing mental illness requires workplace policy as well as health care policy. *Health Affairs Forefront.* https://doi.org/10.1377/forefront.20210615.243332

Gordanier, J., Ozturk, O., Williams, B., & Zhan, C. (2020). Free lunch for all! The effect of the community eligibility provision on academic outcomes. *Economics of Education Review,* 77, 101999. https://doi.org/10.1016/j.econedurev.2020.101999

Gould-Werth, A., & Schaefer, H.L. (2012). Unemployment insurance participation by education and by race and ethnicity. *Monthly Labor Review,* 135(10), 14. Available: https://www.bls.gov/opub/mlr/2012/article/unemployment-insurance-participation-by-education-and-by-race-and-ethnicity.htm

Government Accountability Office (GAO). (2021). *Management report: Preliminary information on potential racial and ethnic disparities in the receipt of unemployment insurance benefits during the COVID-19 pandemic.* GAO-21-599R. Washington, DC. Available: https://www.gao.gov/products/gao-21-599r

Grant, K., Brumfield, C., Khan, S., Aderonmu, F., & Dutta-Gupta, I. (2019). *The paid family and medical leave opportunity.* Washington, DC: Center on Poverty and Inequality (Georgetown Law).

Guan, A., Hamad, R., Batra, A., Bush, N.R., Tylavsky, F.A., & LeWinn, K.Z. (2021). The revised WIC food package and child development: A quasi-experimental study. *Pediatrics,* 147(2), e20201853. https://doi.org/10.1542/peds.2020-1853

Gundersen, C., Kreider, B., & Pepper, J.V. (2012). The impact of the National School Lunch Program on child health: A nonparametric bounds analysis. *Journal of Econometrics,* 166, 79–91. https://doi.org/10.1016/j.jeconom.2011.06.007

Ha, Y. (2009). Stability of child-care subsidy use and earnings of low-income families. *Social Service Review,* 83(4), 495–523. https://doi.org/10.1086/650352

Ha, Y., & Miller, D.P. (2015). Child care subsidies and employment outcomes of low-income families. *Children & Youth Services Review*, 59, 139–48. https://doi.org/10.1016/j.childyouth.2015.11.003

Hamad, R. & Rehkopf, D.H. (2016). Poverty and child development: A longitudinal study of the impact of the earned income tax credit. *American Journal of Epidemiology*, 183(9), 775–84. https://doi.org/10.1093/aje/kwv317

Hamad, R., Collin, D.F., Baer, R.J., & Jelliffe-Pawlowski, L.L. (2019). Association of revised WIC food package with perinatal and birth outcomes: A quasi-experimental study. *JAMA Pediatrics*, 173(9), 845–52. https://doi.org/10.1001/jamapediatrics.2019.1706

Harknett, K., & Schneider, D. (2020). *Precarious work schedules and population health* (Health Policy Brief). Project HOPE. https://doi.org/10.1377/hpb20200206.806111

Harknett, K., Schneider, D., & Irwin, V. (2021a). *Evaluating the impacts of the Seattle secure scheduling ordinance*. Department of Labor, Labor Research and Evaluation Grants, 19. Harvard Kennedy School. Available: https://www.hks.harvard.edu/publications/evaluating-impacts-seattle-secure-scheduling-ordinance

Harknett, K., Schneider, D., & Irwin, V. (2021b). *Seattle's secure scheduling ordinance: Year 2 worker impact report*. Cambridge, Mass.: The Shift Project.

Health Impact Project. (2017). *10 policies to prevent and respond to child lead exposure*. The Pew Charitable Trust. Available: https://www.pewtrusts.org/en/research-and-analysis/reports/2017/08/10-policies-to-prevent-and-respond-to-childhood-lead-exposure

Heinrich, C.J. (2014). Parents' employment and children's wellbeing. *Future of Children*, 24(1), 121–46. Available: http://www.jstor.org/stable/23723386

———. (2018). Presidential address: "A thousand petty fortresses:" Administrative burden in U.S. immigration policies and its consequences. *Journal of Policy Analysis and Management*, 37(2), 211–39. https://doi.org/10.1002/pam.22046

Henly, J.R., Lambert, S.J., & Dresser, L. (2021). The new realities of working-class jobs: Employer practices, worker protections, and employee voice to improve job quality. *Annals of the American Academy of Political and Social Science*, 695(1), 208–24.

Heymann, J., Sprague, A., Earle, A., McCormack, M., Waisath, W., & Raub, A. (2021). US sick leave in global context: US eligibility rules widen inequalities despite readily available solutions. *Health Affairs*, 40(9), 1501–9. https://doi.org/10.1377/hlthaff.2021.00731

Hill, B., & Gurley-Calvez, T. (2019). Earned income tax credits and infant health: A local EITC investigation. *National Tax Journal*, 72(3), 617–46. https://doi.org/10.17310/ntj.2019.3.06

Hill, H.D. (2013). Paid sick leave and job stability. *Work & Occupations*, 40(2), 143–73. https://doi.org/10.1177/0730888413480893

Hill, H.D., & Romich, J. (2018). How will higher minimum wages affect family life and children's well-being? *Child Development Perspectives*, 12(2), 109–14. https://doi.org/10.1111/cdep.12270

Hill, H.D., Morris, P.A., Castells, N., & Walker, J.T. (2011). Getting a job is only half the battle: Maternal job loss and child classroom behavior in low-income families. *Journal of Policy Analysis and Management*, 30(2), 310–33. https://doi.org/10.1002/pam.20565

Honsberger, K., McCaman, L., & VanLandeghem, K. (2018). State strategies to improve childhood lead screening and treatment services under Medicaid and CHIP. *A Publication of the National Academy for State Health Policy*.

Howell, D.R., & Kalleberg, A.L. (2019). Declining job quality in the United States: Explanations and evidence. *The Russell Sage Foundation Journal of the Social Sciences*, 5(4), 1–53. https://doi.org/10.7758/RSF.2019.5.4.01

Hoynes, H.W., & Patel, A.J. (2018). Effective policy for reducing poverty and inequality? The earned income tax credit and the distribution of income. *Journal of Human Resources*, 53(4), 859–90. https://doi.org/10.3368/jhr.53.4.1115.7494R1

Hoynes, H., Schanzenbach, D.W., & Almond, D. (2016). Long-run impacts of childhood access to the safety net. *American Economic Review*, 106(4), 903–34. https://doi.org/10.1257/aer.20130375

Huang, R., & Yang, M. (2015). Paid maternity leave and breastfeeding practice before and after California's implementation of the nation's first paid family leave program. *Economics and Human biology*, 16, 45–59. https://doi.org/10.1016/j.ehb.2013.12.009

Huston, A.C., Duncan, G.J., MeLoyd, V.C., Crosby, D.A., Ripke, M.N., Weisner, T.S., & Eldred, C.A. (2005). Impacts on children of a policy to promote employment and reduce poverty for low-income parents: New Hope after 5 years. *Developmental Psychology*, 41(6), 902–18. https://doi.org/10.1037/0012-1649.41.6.902

Hyman, J. (2017). Does money matter in the long run? Effects of school spending on educational attainment. *American Economic Journal: Economic Policy*, 9(4), 256–80. https://doi.org/10.1257/pol.20150249

IDEO.org. (2015). *The field guide to human-centered design*. Ideo.org. Available: https://www.designkit.org/resources/1

Institute of Medicine (IOM) & National Research Council (NRC). (2015). *Transforming the workforce for children birth through age 8: A unifying foundation*. Washington, DC: The National Academies Press. https://doi.org/10.17226/19401.

Irish, A.M., White, J.S., Modrek, S., & Hamad, R. (2021). Paid family leave and mental health in the U.S.: A quasi-experimental study of state policies. *American Journal of Preventive Medicine*, 61(2), 182–91. https://doi.org/10.1016/j.amepre.2021.03.018

Isaacs, J. (2013). *Unemployment from a child's perspective*. (Research Report). The Urban Institute. Available: https://www.urban.org/research/publication/unemployment-childs-perspective

Jalali, A.A. (2018). The minimum wage and infant mortality. *Social Science Research Network*. https://doi.org/10.2139/ssrn.3308213

Johnson, R., & Jackson, C. (2019). Reducing inequality through dynamic complementarity: Evidence from head start and public school spending. *American Economic Journal: Economic Policy*, 11, 310–49. https://doi.org/10.1257/pol.20180510

Johnson, R.C., Kalil, A., & Dunifon, R.E. (2010). *Mothers' work and children's lives: Low-income families after welfare reform*. W.E. Upjohn Institute for Employment Research. https://doi.org/10.17848/9781441644886

Joshi, P., & Bogen, K. (2007). Nonstandard schedules and young children's behavioral outcomes among working low-income families. *Journal of Marriage & Family*, 69(1), 139–56. doi.org/10.1111/j.1741-3737.2006.00350.x

Joshi, P., Baldiga, M., Earle, A., Huber, R., Osypuk, T., & Acevedo-Garcia, D. (2019). How much would family and medical leave cost workers in the US? Racial/ethnic variation in economic hardship under unpaid and paid policies. *Community, Work & Family*, 24(5), 517–40. https://doi.org/10.1080/13668803.2019.1704398

Joshi, P., Baldiga, M., Huber, R., & Acevedo-Garcia, D. (2020). *Policy equity assessment: Family and medical leave act*. Institute for Child, Youth & Family Policy (ICYFP), Heller School for Social Policy & Management. Brandeis University. Available: https://www.diversitydatakids.org/research-library/policy-equity-assessment/policy-equity-assessment-family-and-medical-leave-act

Joshi, P., Walters, A.N., Noelke, C., & Acevedo-Garcia, D. (2022). Families' job characteristics and economic self-sufficiency: Differences by income, race/ethnicity, and nativity. *RSF: The Russell Sage Foundation Journal of the Social Sciences*, 8(5), 67–95. https://doi.org/10.7758/RSF.2022.8.5.04

Kalil, A. (2013). Effects of the great recession on child development. *Annals of the American Academy of Political and Social Science*, 650(1), 232–50. https://doi.org/10.1177/0002716213500453

Kalil, A., & Wightman, P. (2011). Parental job loss and children's educational attainment in black and white middle-class families. *Social Science Quarterly*, 92(1), 57–78. https://doi.org/10.1111/j.1540-6237.2011.00757.x

Kalil, A., & Ziol-Guest, K.M. (2005). Single mothers' employment dynamics and adolescent well-being. *Child Development*, 76(1), 196–211. https://doi.org/10.1111/j.1467-8624.2005.00839.x

———. (2008). Parental employment circumstances and children's academic progress. *Social Science Research*, 37(2), 500–15. https://doi.org/10.1016/j.ssresearch.2007.08.007

Karpman, M., Hahn, H., & Gangopadhyaya, A. (2019). *Precarious work schedules could jeopardize access to safety net programs targeted by work requirements.* (Brief). Urban Institute. Available: https://www.urban.org/research/publication/precarious-work-schedules-could-jeopardize-access-safety-net-programs-targeted-work-requirements

Katz, L.F., Roth, J., Hendra, R., & Schaberg, K. (2022). Why do sectoral employment programs work?: Lessons from WorkAdvance. *Journal of Labor Economics*, 40(S1). https://doi.org/10.1086/717932

Kelly, E.L., & Moen, P. (2020). Overload: How good jobs went bad and what we can do about it. *Work and Occupations*, 49(1), 135–8. https://doi.org/10.1177/07308884211031976

Kitchen, S., Tanner, E., Brown, V., Payne, C., Crawford, C., Dearden, L., Greaves, E., & Purdon, S. (2013). *Evaluation of the free school meals pilot: Impact report*. Department for Education. Available: https://assets.publishing.service.gov.uk/government/uploads/system/uploads/attachment_data/file/184047/DFE-RR227.pdf

Knudson, J. (2019). *Improving LCFF implementation through user-centered design: Year 1 of the LCFF test kitchen.* Policy and practice brief. Available: https://files.eric.ed.gov/fulltext/ED596439.pdf

Kofman, A., & Fresques, H. (2020). *Black workers are more likely to be unemployed but less likely to get unemployment benefits.* Pro Publica Inc. Available: https://www.propublica.org/article/black-workers-are-more-likely-to-be-unemployed-but-less-likely-to-get-unemployment-benefits

Komro, K., Livingston, M., Markowitz, S., & Wagenaar, A. (2016). The effect of an increased minimum wage on infant mortality and birth weight. *American Journal of Public Health*, 106(8), 1514–6. https://doi.org/10.2105/AJPH.2016.303268

Komro, K.A., Markowitz, S., Livingston, M.D., & Wagenaar, A.C. (2019). Effects of state-level earned income tax credit laws on birth outcomes by race and ethnicity. *Health Equity*, 3(1), 61–7. https://doi.org/10.1089/heq.2018.0061

Kornfeind, K.R., & Sipsma, H.L. (2018). Exploring the link between maternity leave and postpartum depression. *Women's Health Issues*, 28(4), 321–6. https://doi.org/10.1016/j.whi.2018.03.008

Kossek, E.E., Thompson, R.J., Lawson, K.M., Bodner, T., Perrigino, M.B., Hammer, L.B., Buxton, O.M., Almeida, D.M., Moen, P., Hurtado, D.A., Wipfli, B., Berkman, L.F., & Bray, J.W. (2019). Caring for the elderly at work and home: Can a randomized organizational intervention improve psychological health? *Journal of Occupational Health Psychology*, 24(1), 36–54. https://doi.org/10.1037/ocp0000104

Kozak, K., Greaves, A., Waldfogel, J., Angal, J., Elliott, A.J., Fifier, W.P., & Brito, N.H. (2021). Paid maternal leave is associated with better language and socioemotional outcomes during toddlerhood. *Infancy*, 26(4), 536–50.

Krieger, J., Jacobs, D.E., Ashley, P.J., Baeder, A., Chew, G.L., Dearborn, D., Hynes, H.P., Miller, J.D., Morley, R., Rabito, F., & Zeldin, D.C. (2010). Housing interventions and control of asthma-related indoor biologic agents: A review of the evidence. *Journal of Public Health Management and Practice*, 16(5 Suppl), S11–20. https://doi.org/10.1097/PHH.0b013e3181ddcbd9

Kristal, T., Cohen, Y., & Navot, E. (2018). Benefit inequality among American workers by gender, race, and ethnicity, 1982–2015. *Sociological Science*, 5, 461–88. https://doi.org/10.15195/v5.a20

Kuka, E. (2020). Quantifying the benefits of social insurance: Unemployment insurance and health. *Review of Economics and Statistics*, 102(3), 490–505. https://doi.org/10.1162/rest_a_00865

Kukla-Acevedo, S., & Heflin, C.M. (2014). Unemployment insurance effects on child academic outcomes: Results from the National Longitudinal Survey of Youth. *Children and Youth Services Review*, 47, 246–52. https://doi.org/10.1016/j.childyouth.2014.09.019

Lafortune, J., Rothstein, J., & Schanzenbach, D.W. (2018). School finance reform and the distribution of student achievement. *American Economic Journal: Applied Economics*, 10(2), 1–26. https://www.jstor.org/stable/26528381

Lambert, S. (2020). *Fair work schedules for the U.S. economy and society: What's reasonable, feasible, and effective*. Washington Center for Equitable Growth. Available: https://equitablegrowth.org/fair-work-schedules-for-the-u-s-economy-and-society-whats-reasonable-feasible-and-effective/

Lambert, S.J., Henly, J.R., & Kim, J. (2019). Precarious work schedules as a source of economic insecurity and institutional distrust. *The Russell Sage Foundation Journal of the Social Sciences*, 5(4), 218. https://doi.org/10.7758/RSF.2019.5.4.08

Lawson, K.M., Davis, K.D., McHale, S.M., Almeida, D.M., Kelly, E.L., & King, R.B. (2016). Effects of workplace intervention on affective well-being in employees' children. *Developmental Psychology*, 52(5), 772–7. https://doi.org/10.1037/dev0000098

Lee, B.C., Modrek, S., White, J.S., Batra, A., Collin, D.F., & Hamad, R. (2020). The effect of California's paid family leave policy on parent health: A quasi-experimental study. *Social Science & Medicine*, 251, 112915. https://doi.org/10.1016/j.socscimed.2020.112915

Leigh, J.P., & Du, J. (2018). *Effects of minimum wages on population health*. (Health Policy Brief). Project HOPE. https://doi.org/10.1377/hpb20180622.107025

Lenhart, O. (2019). The effects of income on health: New evidence from the earned income tax credit. *Review of Economics of the Household*, 17(2), 377–410. https://doi.org/10.1007/s11150-018-9429-x

Levy, J.I., Brugge, D., Peters, J.L., Clougherty, J.E., & Saddler, S.S. (2006). A community-based participatory research study of multifaceted in-home environmental interventions for pediatric asthmatics in public housing. *Social Science & Medicine*, 63(8), 2191–203. https://doi.org/10.1016/j.socscimed.2006.05.006

Li, J., Johnson, S.E., Han, W.-J., Andrews, S., Kendall, G., Strazdins, L., & Dockery, A. (2014). Parents' nonstandard work schedules and child well-being: A critical review of the literature. *Journal of Primary Prevention*, 35(1), 53–73. doi.org/10.1007/s10935-013-0318-z

Lindo, J.M. (2011). Parental job loss and infant health. *Journal of Health Economics*, 30(5), 869–79. https://doi.org/10.1016/j.jhealeco.2011.06.008

Lombardi, C.M., & Coley, R.L. (2013). Low-income mothers' employment experiences: Prospective links with young children's development. *Family Relations*, 62(3), 514–28.

Lovejoy, M., Kelly, E.L., Kubzansky, L.D., & Berkman, L.F. (2021). Work redesign for the 21st century: Promising strategies for enhancing worker well-being. *American Journal of Public Health*, 111(10), 1787–95. https://doi.org/10.2105/AJPH.2021.306283

Mahoney, J. (2018). The Alliance for Innovation in Maternal Health Care: A way forward. *Clinical Obstetrics and Gynecology*, 61(2), 400–10. https://doi.org/10.1097/GRF.0000000000000363

Main, E.K. (2018). Reducing maternal mortality and severe maternal morbidity through state-based quality improvement initiatives. *Clinical Obstetrics and Gynecology*, 61(2), 319–31. https://doi.org/10.1097/GRF.0000000000000361

Mandal, B. (2018). The effect of paid leave on maternal mental health. *Maternal and Child Health Journal*, 22(10), 1470–6. https://doi.org/10.1007/s10995-018-2542-x

Markowitz, S., Komro, K.A., Livingston, M.D., Lenhart, O., & Wagenaar, A.C. (2017). Effects of state-level earned income tax credit laws in the U.S. on maternal health behaviors and infant health outcomes. *Social Science & Medicine*, 194, 67–75. https://doi.org/10.1016/j.socscimed.2017.10.016

Mathur, A., Sawhill, I.V., Boushey, H., Gitis, B., Haskins, R., Holtz-Eakin, D., Holzer, H.J., Jacobs, E., McCloskey, A.M., Rachidi, A., Reeves, R.V., Ruhm, C.J., Stevenson, B., & Waldfogel, J. (2017). *Paid family and medical leave: An issue whose time has come*. Brookings Institute. Available: https://www.brookings.edu/research/paid-family-and-medical-leave-an-issue-whose-time-has-come/

McHale, S.M., Lawson, K.M., Davis, K.D., Casper, L., Kelly, E.L., & Buxton, O. (2015). Effects of a workplace intervention on sleep in employees children. *The Journal of Adolescent Health: Official Publication of the Society for Adolescent Medicine*, 56(6), 672–7. https://doi.org/10.1016/j.jadohealth.2015.02.014

McLoyd, V.C., Jayaratne, T.E., Ceballo, R., & Borquez, J. (1994). Unemployment and work interruption among African American single mothers: Effects on parenting and adolescent socioemotional functioning. *Child Development*, 65(2), 562–89. https://doi.org/10.2307/1131402

McLoyd, V.C., Kaplan, R., Purtell, K.M., & Huston, A.C. (2011). Assessing the effects of a work-based antipoverty program for parents on youth's future orientation and employment experiences. *Child Development*, 82(1), 113–32. https://doi.org/10.1111/j.1467-8624.2010.01544.x

McShane, M.Q., & Shaw, M. (2020). *Transporting school choice students: A primer on states' transportation policies related to private, charter, and open enrollment students*. EdChoice. Available: https://eric.ed.gov/?id=ED605559

Meek, S., Smith, L., Allen, R., Catherine, E., Edyburn, K., Williams, C., Fabes, R., McIntosh, K., Garcia, E., Takanishi, R., Gordon, L., Jimenez-Castellanos, O., Hemmeter, M.L., Gilliam, W., & Pontier, R. (2020). *Start with equity. From the early years to the early grades. Data, research, and an actionable child equity policy agenda*. Children's Equity Project, Bipartisan Policy Center. Available: https://childandfamilysuccess.asu.edu/sites/default/files/2020-07/CEP-report-071520-FINAL.pdf

Menaghan, E.G., & Parcel, T.L. (1995). Social sources of change in children's home environments: The effects of parental occupational experiences and family conditions. *Journal of Marriage and the Family*, 57(1), 69–84. https://doi.org/10.2307/353817

Miller, C., Huston, A.C., Duncan, G.J., McLoyd, V.C., & Weisner, T.S. (2008). *New hope for the working poor*. MDRC. Available: https://www.mdrc.org/sites/default/files/full_458.pdf

Mitchell, S.M., Baumle, D., and Cloud, L.K. (2021). *Using law to combat unpredictable scheduling practices for women in U.S. workplaces*. (Policy Brief). Philadelphia, PA: Temple University Beasley School of Law. Available: https://phlr.org/sites/default/files/uploaded_images/UnpredictableScheduling_TUMU-PolicyBrief_Oct2021.pdf

Moen, P., Kelly, E.L., Fan, W., Lee, S.-R., Almeida, D., Kossek, E.E., and Buxton, O.M. (2016). Does a flexibility/support organizational initiative improve high-tech employees' well-being? Evidence from the work, family, and health network. *American Sociological Review*, 81(1), 134–64. https://doi.org/10.1177/0003122415622391

Morgan, W.J., Crain, E.F., Gruchalla, R.S., O'Connor, G.T., Kattan, M., Evans, R. 3rd, Stout, J., Malindzak, G., Smartt, E., Plaut, M., Walter, M., Vaughn, B., & Mitchell, H. (2004). Results of a home-based environmental intervention among urban children with asthma. *New England Journal of Medicine*, 351(11), 1068–80. https://doi.org/10.1056/NEJMoa032097

National Academies of Sciences, Engineering, and Medicine (National Academies). (2016). *Parenting matters: Supporting parents of children ages 0-8*. The National Academies Press. https://doi.org/10.17226/21868

---. (2017). *Communities in action: Pathways to health equity.* The National Academies Press. https://doi.org/10.17226/24624
---. (2018). *Transforming the financing of early care and education.* The National Academies Press. https://doi.org/10.17226/24984
---. (2019a). *A roadmap to reducing child poverty.* The National Academies Press. https://doi.org/10.17226/25246
---. (2019b). *Vibrant and healthy kids: Aligning science, practice, and policy to advance health equity.* The National Academies Press. https://doi.org/10.17226/25466
National Conference of State Legislatures (NCSL). (2012). *Backgrounder: Public-private partnerships.* Available: https://www.ncsl.org/documents/cyf/Ounce_Public_Private_Partnership.pdf.
---. (2017). *NCSL policy update: State statutes on chemical safety.* Available: http://www.ncsl.org/research/environment-and-natural-resources/ncsl-policy-update-state
---. (2022). *Earned income tax credit overview.* Available: https://www.ncsl.org/research/labor-and-employment/earned-income-tax-credits-for-working-families.aspx
Neumark, D. (2018). Experimental research on labor market discrimination. *Journal of Economic Literature,* 56(3), 799–866. https://doi.org/10.1257/jel.20161309
Nichols, A., & Simms, M. (2012). *Racial and ethnic differences in receipt of unemployment insurance benefits during the great recession.* (Policy Brief No. 04). Urban Institute. Available: https://www.urban.org/sites/default/files/publication/25541/412596-Racial-and-Ethnic-Differences-in-Receipt-of-Unemployment-Insurance-Benefits-During-the-Great-Recession.PDF
O'Campo, P., Molnar, A., Ng, E., Renahy, E., Mitchell, C., Shankardass, K., St. John, A., Bambra, C., & Muntaner, C. (2015). Social welfare matters: A realist review of when, how, and why unemployment insurance impacts poverty and health. *Social Science & Medicine,* 132, 88–94. https://doi.org/10.1016/j.socscimed.2015.03.025
Orfield, G., & Frankenberg, E. (2014). Increasingly segregated and unequal schools as courts reverse policy. *Educational Administration Quarterly,* 50(5), 718–34. https://doi.org/10.1177/0013161X14548942
Osypuk, T.L., Joshi, P., Geronimo, K., & Acevedo-Garcia, D. (2014). Do social and economic policies influence health? A review. *Current Epidemiology Reports,* 1(3), 149–64. https://doi.org/10.1007/s40471-014-0013-5
Pager, D. (2003). The mark of a criminal record. *American Journal of Sociology,* 108(5), 937–75. https://doi.org/10.1086/374403
Pahlka, J. (2018). *Delivery-driven government: Principles and practices for government in the digital age.* Medium. Available: https://medium.com/code-for-america/delivery-driven-government-67e698c57c7b
---. (2019). *Delivery-driven policy: Policy designed for the digital age.* Code for America. Available: https://codeforamerica.org/news/delivery-driven-policy/
Parolin, Z. (2020). Unemployment and child health during covid-19 in the USA. *The Lancet Public Health,* 5(10), e521–2. https://doi.org/10.1016/S2468-2667(20)30207-3
Parolin, Z., Collyer, S., Curran, M., & Wimer, C. (2021). *The potential poverty reduction effect of the American Rescue Plan.* Center on Poverty and Social Policy, Columbia University. Available: https://static1.squarespace.com/static/610831a16c95260dbd68934a/t/6116a2c1cb768c23269b1add/1628873410837/Poverty-Reduction-Analysis-American-Families-Plan-CPSP-2021.pdf
Pearman, F.A., Curran, F.C., Fisher, B., & Gardella, J. (2019). Are achievement gaps related to discipline gaps? Evidence from national data. *AERA Open,* 5(4). https://doi.org/10.1177/2332858419875440
Perry-Jenkins, M., Smith, J.Z., Wadsworth, L.P., & Halpern, H.P. (2017). Workplace policies and mental health among working-class, new parents. *Community, Work & Family,* 20(2), 226–49. doi.org/10.1080/13668803.2016.1252721

Persson, P., & Rossin-Slater, M. (2019). *When dad can stay home: Fathers' workplace flexibility and maternal health*. (Working Paper No. 25902). National Bureau of Economic Research. https://doi.org/10.3386/w25902

Peters, H.E. (1995). An economic approach to the study of child well-being: Gary Becker on altruism and household production. *Journal of Family Issues*, 16(5), 587–608. https://doi.org/10.1177/019251395016005005

Petrosky-Nadeau, N., & Valletta, R.G. (2021). *UI generosity and job acceptance: Effects of the 2020 CARES Act*. (Working Paper No. 2021-13). Federal Reserve Bank of San Francisco. Available: https://www.frbsf.org/economic-research/wp-content/uploads/sites/4/wp2021-13.pdf

Postma, J., Karr, C., & Kieckhefer, G. (2009). Community health workers and environmental interventions for children with asthma: A systematic review. *Journal of Asthma*, 46(6), 564–76. https://doi.org/10.1080/02770900902912638

Prenatal-to-3 Policy Impact Center. (2020). *Prenatal-to-3 state policy roadmap 2020: Building a strong and equitable prenatal-to-3 system of care*. Child and Family Research Partnership. Vanderbilt University. https://pn3policy.org/pn-3-state-policy-roadmap/complete-roadmap/

———. (2021). *Expanded income eligibility for health insurance*. Vanderbilt University. Available: https://pn3policy.org/resources/2021-evidence-of-impact-for-expanded-income-eligibility-for-health-insurance/#download-pdf

———. (2022). *Prenatal-to-3 policy clearinghouse evidence review: State earned income tax credit (ER 05C.1022)*. Vanderbilt University. Available: https://pn3policy.org/policy-clearinghouse/ state-earned-income-tax-credit/

President's Task Force on Environmental Health Risks and Safety Risks to Children. (2016). *Key federal programs to reduce childhood lead exposures and eliminate associated health impacts*. Environmental Protection Agency. Available: https://www.epa.gov/lead/federal-action-plan-reduce-childhood-lead-exposure

Presser, H.B., & Ward, B.W. (2011). *Nonstandard work schedules over the life course: A first look*. Bureau of Labor Statistics. Available: https://www.bls.gov/opub/mlr/2011/07/art1full.pdf

Pulvera, R., Collin, D.F. & Hamad, R. (2022). The effect of the 2009 WIC revision on maternal and child health: A quasi-experimental study. *Paediatric and Perinatal Epidemiology*, 36(6), 851–60. https://doi.org/10.1111/ppe.12898

Radsky, V., Domina, T., Clark, L.R., & Bhaskar, R. (2022). *Stigma free lunch: School meals and student discipline*. (Working Paper No. CES-22-23). U.S. Census Bureau. Available: https://www.census.gov/library/working-papers/2022/adrm/CES-WP-22-23.html

Raub, A., Nandi, A., Earle, A., Chorny, N.D.G., Wong, E., Chung, P., Batra, P., Schickendanz, A., Bose, B., Jou, J., Franken, D., & Heymann, J. (2018). *Paid parental leave: A detailed look at approaches across OECD countries*. (Policy Analysis). WORLD Policy Analysis Center. Available: https://www.worldpolicycenter.org/sites/default/files/WORLD%20Report%20-%20Parental%20Leave%20OECD%20Country%20Approaches_0.pdf

Regmi, K. (2019). Examining the externality of unemployment insurance on children's educational achievement. *Economic Inquiry*, 57(1), 172–87. https://doi.org/10.1111/ecin.12733

Repetti, R.L., & Wang, S.-W. (2014). Employment and parenting. *Parenting: Science & Practice*, 14(2), 121–32. http://dx.doi.org/10.1080/15295192.2014.914364

Roder, A., & Elliott, M. (2019). *Nine year gains: Project Quest's continuing impact*. Available: https://economicmobilitycorp.org/nine-year-gains-project-quests-continuing-impact/

———. (2021). *Project Quest's investment continues to pay dividends*. Economic Mobility Corporation. https://economicmobilitycorp.org/wp-content/uploads/2021/09/Mobility_Eleven-Year-Gains.pdf

Rodriguez, A., Kaur, N., Nichols, I., Namdol, T., & Rachakonda, S. (2021). *Improving service delivery in EITC for New Yorkers*. New America. Available: https://www.newamerica.org/new-practice-lab/blog/improving-service-delivery-in-eitc-for-new-yorkers/

Roll, S., Hamilton, L., & Chun, Y. (2021). *Expanded child tax credit payments have not reduced employment: Evidence from Census data*. Social Policy Institute. https://openscholarship.wustl.edu/cgi/viewcontent.cgi?article=1057&context=spi_research

Rosenquist, N.A., Cook, D.M., Ehntholt, A., Omaye, A., Muennig, P., & Pabayo, R. (2020). Differential relationship between state-level minimum wage and infant mortality risk among US infants born to white and black mothers. *Journal of Epidemiology and Community Health*, 74(1), 14. https://doi.org/10.1136/jech-2019-212987

Rossin-Slater, M., Ruhm, C., & Waldfogel, J. (2013). The effects of California's paid family leave program on mothers' leave-taking and subsequent labor market outcomes. *Journal of Policy Analysis and Management*, 32(2), 224–45. https://doi.org/10.1002/pam.21676

Rostad, W.L., Klevens, J., Ports, K.A., & Ford, D.C. (2020). Impact of the United States federal child tax credit on childhood injuries and behavior problems. *Children and Youth Services Review*, 109. https://doi.org/10.1016/j.childyouth.2019.104718

Rothstein, J. (2011). *Unemployment insurance and job search in the great recession*. (Working Paper No. 17534). Cambridge, MA: National Bureau of Economic Research. Available: https://www.brookings.edu/wp-content/uploads/2011/09/2011b_bpea_rothstein.pdf

Ruffini, K. (2020). Universal access to free school meals and student achievement: Evidence from the Community Eligibility Provision. *Journal of Human Resources*, 0518-9509R3. Available: https://edopportunity.org/papers/Ruffini_CEP_achievement_JHR.pdf

Sabol, T.J., Sommer, T.E., Chase-Lansdale, P.L., Morris, A., Brooks-Gunn, J., King, C., & Guminski, S. (2019). *What are the effects of a two-generation human capital program on children's outcomes in Head Start?* (Policy Brief No. 2). Aspen Institute. Available: https://www.ipr.northwestern.edu/documents/nu2gen-docs/cap-fls-year-1-and-2-findings_brief-ii_may-2019.pdf

Sabol, T.J., Sommer, T.E., Chase-Lansdale, P.L., & Brooks-Gunn, J. (2021). Intergenerational economic mobility for low-income parents and their children: A dual developmental science framework. *Annual Review of Psychology*, 72, 265–92. https://doi.org/10.1146/annurev-psych-010419-051001

Sama-Miller, E., & Baumgartner, S. (2017). *Features of programs designed to help families achieve economic security and promote child well-being*. (Report No. 2017-49). Office of Planning, Research and Evaluation, Administration for Children and Families, Department of Health and Human Services. Available: https://www.acf.hhs.gov/opre/report/features-programs-designed-help-families-achieve-economic-security-and-promote-child

Sandstrom, H. (2015). *Why parents' nonstandard work schedules matter for children: Is it the hours or the instability?* Urban Institute. Available: https://www.urban.org/urban-wire/why-parents-nonstandard-work-schedules-matter-children-it-hours-or-instability

Schneider, D., & Harknett, K. (2019a). Consequences of routine work-schedule instability for worker health and well-being. *American Sociological Review*, 84(1), 82–114. https://doi.org/10.1177/0003122418823184

———. (2019b). *Parental exposure to routine work schedule uncertainty and child behavior*. Washington Center for Equitable Growth. Available: https://equitablegrowth.org/working-papers/parental-exposure-to-routine-work-schedule-uncertainty-and-child-behavior/

Schulte, B. (2021). *Want to design policies that really work? Test them on the users who need them first*. New America. Available: https://www.newamerica.org/better-life-lab/blog/want-to-design-policies-that-really-work-test-them-on-the-users-who-need-them-first/

Schulz, A.J., Mentz, G.B., Sampson, N., Ward, M., Anderson, R., de Majo, R., Israel, B.A., Lewis, T.C., & Wilkins, D. (2016). Race and the distribution of social and physical environmental risk: A case example from the Detroit metropolitan area. *Du Bois Review: Social Science Research on Race*, 13(2), 285–304. https://doi.org/10.1017/S1742058X16000163

Schwartz, A.E., & Rothbart, M.W. (2020). Let them eat lunch: The impact of universal free meals on student performance. *Journal of Policy Analysis and Management, 39*(2), 376410. https://doi.org/10.1002/pam.22175

Searing, A.R., & Ross, D.C. (2019). *Medicaid expansion fills gaps in maternal health coverage leading to healthier mothers and babies.* Health Policy Institute, Center for Children and Families, Georgetown University. Available: https://ccf.georgetown.edu/2019/05/09/medicaid-expansion-fills-gaps-in-maternal-health-coverage-leading-to-healthier-mothers-and-babies/

Setty, S., Skinner, C., & Wilson-Simmons, R. (2016). *Protecting workers, nurturing families: Building an inclusive family leave insurance program.* New York, NY: National Center for Children in Poverty, Mailman School of Public Health, Columbia University.

Shakesprere, J., Katz, B., & Loprest, P. (2021). *Racial equity and job quality: Causes behind racial disparities and possibilities to address them.* (Policy Brief). Urban Institute. Available: https://www.urban.org/sites/default/files/publication/104761/racial-equity-and-job-quality.pdf

Shepherd-Banigan, M., Bell, J.F., Basu, A., Booth-LaForce, C., & Harris, J.R. (2017). Mothers' employment attributes and use of preventive child health services. *Medical Care Research and Review, 74*(2), 208–26. https://doi.org/10.1177/1077558716634555

Shrider, E.A., Kollar, M., Chen, F., & Semega, J. (2021). *Income and poverty in the United States: 2020.* (Report No. P60-273). U.S. Government Publishing Office. Available: https://www.census.gov/library/publications/2021/demo/p60-273.html

Sinai, N.L., Leftwich, D., & McGuire, B. (2020). *Human-centered policymaking: What government policymaking can learn from human-centered design and agile software development.* Harvard Kennedy School Belfer Center for Science and International Affairs. https://www.belfercenter.org/sites/default/files/2020-04/HumanPolicyMaking.pdf

Sommer, T.E., Schneider, W., Chor, E., Sabol, T.J., Chase-Lansdale, P.L., Brooks-Gunn, J., Yoshikawa, H., Morris, A., & King, C. (2020). A two-generation education intervention and children's attendance in head start. *Child Development, 91*(6), 1916–33. https://doi.org/10.1111/cdev.13397

Spriggs, W.E. (2019). *Wage policies to address rising economic inequality and why they are needed: Testimony prepared for U.S. House of Representatives Committee on the Budget.* 116th Congress, First Session. Hearing on Solutions to Rising Economic Inequality. Available: https://www.congress.gov/116/meeting/house/109948/witnesses/HHRG-116-BU00-Bio-SpriggsPhDW-20190919.pdf

Stearns, J. (2015). The effects of paid maternity leave: Evidence from temporary disability insurance. *Journal of Health Economics, 43,* 85–102. https://doi.org/10.1016/j.jhealeco.2015.04.005

Stevens, A.H., & Schaller, J. (2011). Short-run effects of parental job loss on children's academic achievement. *Economics of Education Review, 30*(2), 289–99. https://doi.org/10.1016/j.econedurev.2010.10.002

Stoddard-Dare, P., DeRigne, L., Collins, C.C., Quinn, L.M., & Fuller, K. (2018). Paid sick leave and psychological distress: An analysis of U.S. workers. *American Journal of Orthopsychiatry, 88*(1), 1–9. https://doi.org/10.1037/ort0000293

Storer, A., Schneider, D., & Harknett, K. (2020). What explains racial/ethnic inequality in job quality in the service sector? *American Sociological Review, 85*(4), 537–72. https://doi.org/10.1177/0003122420930018

Strazdins, L., Shipley, M., Clements, M., Obrien, L.V., & Broom, D.H. (2010). Job quality and inequality: Parents' jobs and children's emotional and behavioural difficulties. *Social Science and Medicine (1982), 70*(12), 2052–60.

Strully, K.W., Rehkopf, D.H., and Xuan, Z. (2010). Effects of prenatal poverty on infant health: State earned income tax credits and birth weight. *American Sociological Review, 75*(4), 534–62. https://doi.org/10.1177/0003122410374086

Sullivan, D., & von Wachter, T. (2009). Job displacement and mortality: An analysis using administrative data. *The Quarterly Journal of Economics*, 124(3), 1265–306. https://doi.org/10.1162/qjec.2009.124.3.1265

Tester, J.M., Leung, C.W., and Crawford, P.B. (2016). Revised WIC food package and children's diet quality. *Pediatrics*, 137(5), e20153557. https://doi.org/10.1542/peds.2015-3557

Tong, M., Artiga, S., & Rudowitz, R. (2022). Mitigating childhood lead exposure and disparities: Medicaid and other federal initiatives. *Kaiser Family Foundation*. Available: https://www.kff.org/racial-equity-and-health-policy/issue-brief/mitigating-childhood-lead-exposure-and-disparities-medicaid-and-other-federal-initiatives/

U.S. Department of Agriculture (USDA). (2012). Environmental justice strategic plan: 2012-2014. Available: https://www.dm.usda.gov/emd/responserestoration/docs/Final%20USDA%20EJ%20STRAT%20Scan_1.pdf

———. (2022a). *National School Lunch Program*. https://www.ers.usda.gov/topics/food-nutrition-assistance/child-nutrition-programs/national-school-lunch-program/

———. (2022b). *WIC 2019 Eligibility and Coverage Rates*. https://www.fns.usda.gov/wic/2019-eligibility-coverage-rates

von Wachter, T. (2019). Unemployment insurance reform. *Annals of the American Academy of Political and Social Science*, 686(1), 121–46. https://doi.org/10.1177/0002716219885339

Wagenaar, A.C., Livingston, M.D., Markowitz, S., and Komro, K.A. (2019). Effects of changes in earned income tax credit: Time-series analyses of Washington DC. *SSM - Population Health*, 7, 100356. https://doi.org/10.1016/j.ssmph.2019.100356

Weeby, J. (2018). *Creating more effective, efficient, and equitable education policies with human-centered design*. Boston, MA: Bellwether Education Partners. Available: https://files.eric.ed.gov/fulltext/ED585907.pdf

Wehby, G., Dave, D., & Kaestner, R. (2020). Effects of the minimum wage on infant health. *Journal of Policy Analysis and Management*, 39(2), 411–43.

Wicks-Lim, J., and Arno, P.S. (2017). Improving population health by reducing poverty: New York's earned income tax credit. *SSM - Population Health*, 3, 373–81. https://doi.org/10.1016/j.ssmph.2017.03.006

Williams, J.C., Lambert, S.J., Kesavan, S., Fugiel, P.J., Ospina, L.A., Rapoport, E.D., Jarpe, M., Bellisle, D., Pandem, P., McCorkell, L., & Adler-Milstein, S. (2018). *Stable scheduling increases productivity and sales: The stable scheduling study*. San Francisco, CA: Center for WorkLife Law, University of California, Hastings College of the Law. Available: https://worklifelaw.org/projects/stable-scheduling-study/report/

Williams, J.C., Lambert, S.J., Kesavan, S., Korn, R.M., Carreon, E.D., Bellisle, D., Jarpe, M., & McCorkell, L. (2019). *Stable scheduling study: Health outcomes report*. San Francisco, CA: Center for WorkLife Law, University of California, Hastings College of the Law. Available: https://worklifelaw.org/projects/stable-scheduling-study/stable-scheduling-health-outcomes/

Wolf, D.A., Monnat, S.M., & Montez, J.K. (2021). Effects of US state preemption laws on infant mortality. *Preventive Medicine*, 145, 106417. https://doi.org/10.1016/j.ypmed.2021.106417

Wolfe, J., Jones, J., & Cooper, D. (2018). *'Fair workweek' laws help more than 1.8 million workers: Laws promote workplace flexibility and protect against unfair scheduling practices*. Washington, DC: Economic Policy Institute. https://www.epi.org/publication/fair-workweek-laws-help-more-than-1-8-million-workers/

WORLD Policy Analysis Center. (2022). *Labor*. Available: https://www.worldpolicycenter.org/topics/labor/methods

Zucker, G. (2021). *Implementing paid family and medical leave: Lessons for state administrators from research in New Jersey*. New America. Available: https://www.newamerica.org/better-life-lab/reports/implementing-paid-family-and-medical-leave/

8

Key Conclusions and Recommendations

Existing disparities in opportunity have been shaped by historical contexts and continue to persist as a result of current policies and practices that create barriers to access, barriers that prevent many children—especially those from marginalized populations—from reaching their full potential. Throughout this report, the committee has described disparities that exist across multiple domains and family contexts and the ways in which these inequities create an opportunity gap that affects outcomes for young children not only from birth through age 8, but also across the life course. The committee was asked in its statement of task (see Box 1-1 in Chapter 1) to develop recommendations for education policy, practice, and research that could promote success for all students, as well as for steps that could be taken to improve conditions and promote success for children at home, in communities, and in schools. The committee's evidence review informed the key conclusions and recommendations that follow, which highlight ways in which existing mechanisms across sectors could be used to promote greater equity and access to opportunity across all levels of the ecosystems in which children live.

KEY CONCLUSIONS

A number of common themes emerged during the committee's evaluation of the literature related to the domains discussed in this report—education, physical health, and social-emotional health and well-being—and are reflected in the key conclusions that follow. These conclusions lay out what is known about the causes of the opportunity gap experienced by many young children and areas in which changes to policies and social structures could help close this gap. These conclusions also informed the committee's recommendations.

> Conclusion 1: *Differential experiences and access to resources in early childhood result in opportunity gaps, which can lead to long-term gaps in outcomes in education, physical health, and social-emotional development that are harmful to individuals, communities, and society.*

There are a number of drivers of opportunity gaps in health and health outcomes in the early years and even before birth. The historical origins of many of these gaps—policies that intentionally segregated and limited access for various populations—can be seen in current policies and practices, which continue to perpetuate inequitable access to opportunity. Lack of accessible, high-quality health care can prevent parents from seeking care for both themselves and their children. Parents' stress due to illness, unstable work schedules, and poverty can affect their ability to meet their children's needs. Communities with fewer resources or unsafe and unhealthy neighborhood conditions can deprive children and families of opportunities to engage in activities that promote healthy development. In all these cases, both short- and long-term costs are borne not just by individuals but by society at large.

> Conclusion 2: *There is substantial evidence describing effective policies and practices that can increase opportunity across multiple domains. These domains range from health, such as increasing maternal access to prenatal care, access to health care, and insurance coverage to access to antipoverty programs and to early care and education. However, differential access as a matter of policy or practice, as well as inconsistent—and in some cases, uncoordinated—implementation and inadequate funding, has allowed barriers to accessing opportunities to persist, leaving the most vulnerable populations underserved. These barriers must be addressed for these promising policies and practices to be implemented equitably and effectively.*

A positive finding in this report is the number of promising policies and practices with the potential to address opportunity gaps. However, their inconsistent—and in some cases uncoordinated—implementation has allowed these gaps to persist, leaving the most vulnerable populations underserved. For example, maternal access to prenatal care has been linked to better outcomes for both children and mothers, yet nearly 15% of women in the United States do not receive adequate prenatal care. Lack of access to health care and insurance coverage are key drivers of this disparity. Access to adequate nutrition also plays an important role in children's cognitive and physical development, as the consequences of poor nutrition can extend well beyond the early years into adolescence and even adulthood. Yet take-up of safety net nutrition programs is often low, in part because of administrative hurdles. Disparities in access to care and nutrition by race/ethnicity and socioeconomic status lead to disparities in outcomes that in turn can become and perpetuate opportunity gaps (see Conclusion 5). The policies and programs that can address these disparities are not equally accessible to all.

> *Conclusion 3: Restrictive eligibility criteria set at the federal and state levels and differences in state and local implementation of policies lead to vastly different experiences for children and families depending on who they are and where they live. Access to resources and services has been impeded by some state and federal policies, as well as service systems that create administrative barriers to access, barriers that disproportionately affect communities of color, immigrant families, and families with low income. These differences occur across all domains examined by the committee, from school funding and access, to quality schools and teachers, to access to health care and health insurance, to the neighborhood-level resources that shape the ability of parents to support and care for their children and provide the supports needed for healthy development.*

Numerous systemic factors make variations in opportunities available to children and parents highly dependent on federal, state, and local policy choices; at the same time, however, the disparities that can result from these variations can be addressed through policy changes at all levels of government. In such efforts, federal guidance can help shape state and local policy to promote more equitable outcomes. As noted in Chapter 6 of this report, which examines the three most heavily studied social welfare programs—the Supplemental Nutrition Assistance Program (SNAP), Medicaid, and Head Start—the benefits of investing in these supports exceed the costs. Although the extent to which this is the case depends on the program, the committee's analyses provide a conservative estimate of the potential returns on investing in targeted interventions to address the opportunity gap. For example, the committee found that every $1.00 spent on the SNAP program results in about $56.00 in benefits across the life course. Likewise, Medicaid and Medicaid expansion have high rates of return due to improved health and longevity, and a $1.00 investment in Head Start yields a return of about $1.86. These findings point to the potential for investments in targeted interventions that close the opportunity gap to yield benefits at the individual, family, and societal levels.

> *Conclusion 4: Research shows that income from full-time employment does not cover the cost of basic needs for many working families. In addition, many employers do not provide benefits such as paid leave or child care. Limited access to paid family leave creates an opportunity gap for young children by limiting parents' and infants' bonding time, decreasing the time available to take care of serious health issues, elevating family stress, and exposing children to financial uncertainty. Limited access to high-quality child care can create opportunity gaps by limiting parents' employment, earnings, and job stability, ultimately leading to family economic insecurity.*

Multiple studies have found parents' precarious job conditions to be related to children's mental health outcomes, including emotional and behavioral difficulties and decreased opportunities for social-emotional connections with parents. Of concern as well is the lack of employer-provided paid family leave, since access to paid leave has been shown to promote healthy developmental outcomes and to allow parents to see to their own and their children's health. Research suggests that paid family leave is an effective policy that benefits the well-being of young children and parents and reduces financial uncertainty.

> *Conclusion 5: Differential experiences and access to resources are associated with factors such as race/ethnicity, income, social class, gender, national origin, language background, and disability; however, the intersections of these factors with social determinants can result in interdependent systems of disadvantage that multiply negative effects. Thus, opportunity gaps for one age group can persist and compound, becoming the cause of future opportunity gaps.*

This report identifies numerous opportunity gaps that the committee refers to collectively as "the opportunity gap." However, the outcomes of many opportunity gaps for the youngest children can themselves become future opportunity gaps. Differential experiences are associated with such factors as race/ethnicity, social class, gender, national origin, language background and disability, and the intersections of these social determinants can result in interdependent systems of disadvantage that multiply negative effects. An intersectional approach is therefore necessary to fully understand how opportunity gaps are perpetuated and how they can be eliminated.

> *Conclusion 6: Structural racism and discrimination perpetuate opportunity gaps and the achievement gap. Systematic exclusion, structural racism, racial and ethnic discrimination, poverty, unequal allocation of resources and services, labor market inequalities, biases in access to and*

experiences in services, and policies that create administrative burden for families all affect the ways in which families experience opportunity. While many of these structures have their origins in the past, they persist, and their effects—now compounded—continue to affect outcomes and the well-being of children and families.

A number of social and structural factors have created and continue to perpetuate a confluence of disparities in opportunity for young children. The National Institutes of Health defines structural racism and discrimination as "macro-level conditions (e.g., residential segregation and institutional policies) that limit opportunities, resources, power, and well-being of individuals and populations based on race/ethnicity and other statuses, including but not limited to: gender, sexual orientation, gender identity, disability status, social class or socioeconomic status, religion, national origin, immigration status, limited English proficiency, or physical characteristics or health conditions" (National Institutes of Health, 2023). Systematic exclusion, structural racism, unequal allocation of resources and services, labor market inequalities, biases in access to services, and policies that create administrative burden for families all affect the ways in which families experience opportunity, and in turn are associated with a variety of outcomes. Disparities in outcomes across education and wellness are deeply rooted in hundreds of years of policies and practices (e.g., segregation, discriminatory housing policies, employment policies, insufficient social safety nets) that have caused some communities of color to have fewer and/or differential access to resources. While many of these structures have their origins in the past, they persist, and their effects, now compounded, continue to affect the well-being of children and families.

RECOMMENDATIONS

The committee's recommendations draw on evidence-based conclusions presented throughout the report to identify actions that can be taken by policy makers, practitioners, community organizations, philanthropic organizations, and other stakeholders. These recommendations are designed to address opportunity gaps, improve data collection, and identify future research needs.

Recommendation 1: Federal entities and agencies and private philanthropic organizations that collect data and fund research related to child health and development should create and adequately support an effective equity-focused policy- and services-monitoring data infrastructure (collection of both quantitative and qualitative data, data analysis, and program evaluation) to guide federal, state, and local policy decisions aimed at closing the opportunity gap across income, race/ethnicity, disability, gender, language background, and immigrant status. This data infrastructure should also be made available for research and learning.

To further a research agenda addressing the opportunity gap, actions such as the following could be taken by federal entities and private philanthropic organizations:

- All federal data (and data reported to the federal government by states and local communities) could be disaggregated for groups listed in Executive Order 13985, On Advancing Racial Equity and Support for Underserved Communities through the Federal Government.
- Data could be shared across agencies that are responsible for individual safety net and social insurance programs (e.g., the Department of Health and Human Services/Centers for Medicare & Medicaid Services for Medicaid, the Internal Revenue Service for the earned income tax credit/child tax credit, the Department of Labor for unemployment insurance) and linked when possible to create merged data sets. These data could be used by each agency to monitor program access, quality, and outcomes across groups known to experience gaps in opportunity through internal and external research studies.
- The Office of Management and Budget (OMB), with input from the Office of Science and Technology Policy, could direct all federal agencies to conduct audits and examine disparate treatment and administrative burden in state and local service systems responsible for serving families and children.
- OMB could direct each federal agency with significant federal expenditures on young children to create an equity research, evaluation, and technical assistance center.
- OMB could direct federal statistical agencies to assess current data collection on families and young children and make recommendations on improvements aimed at addressing opportunity and outcome gaps that can be evaluated and prioritized for investment.
- The Department of Labor could use its existing data to monitor differential trends in job quality, including wages, employer-provided benefits, schedules, and health and safety standards for all workers and working families with young children. With input from the relevant offices of the Executive Office of the President (e.g. the

Council of Economic Advisers), the data could be used to formulate policy recommendations and set goals for improving job quality.
- The National Institutes of Health, National Science Foundation, and Institute of Education Sciences could prioritize studies that fill gaps in knowledge about policies, programs, and practices that reduce opportunity gaps for subgroups of young children that are underrepresented in the existing evidence base.
- The Internal Revenue Service and the Census Bureau could create a linked data system for use in analyzing all families' access to and take-up of tax credits—the most robust antipoverty programs, including the earned income tax credit and the child tax credit—in support of the development of a systematic outreach approach to reduce the burden associated with and increase take-up.
- The Department of Education could require the "What Works Clearinghouse" to report the evidence for subgroups of children and results from rigorous quasi-experimental studies.
- The Interagency Forum on Child and Family Statistics could evaluate each agency's existing systems for collecting data on young children and whether and how these systems could be linked. This assessment would lead to recommendations for improving these data systems so they could be used to evaluate and monitor developmental outcomes of young children, including disparities among groups in access, take-up, and outcomes across multiple programs.
- The philanthropic community could prioritize investments in further developing state and local data systems that include linked data on children's health and education outcomes, as well as measures of opportunity gaps by race/ethnicity, income, nativity, language, and disability, at a minimum. To monitor child opportunity across communities and target funding to communities with lower resources, a consistent set of state/local measures from these systems could be added to the Child Opportunity Index. Investments are also needed to bolster the evaluation efforts of community-based organizations aimed at identifying, piloting, and expanding evidence-based practices that make families' access to systems more equitable and user friendly and their experiences within systems positive and promotive.

Monitoring and accountability are a key issue for the successful implementation of all of the committee's recommendations. Given the complexities surrounding the opportunity gap for young children, a system of metrics is needed to track disparities in opportunities and resources, such as access to qualified educators, rigorous and inclusive curricula, school funding, school ecologies that support learning, quality health care, and resources that promote healthy social and emotional well-being and development. In addition to tracking of these metrics, systematic cataloging of evidence-based, effective, and equitable policies and program interventions across domains in a centralized database/registry would provide a significant resource to communities, policy makers, researchers, and philanthropic organizations working to reduce disparities in opportunity for children. While there is evidence that policies and programs reduce opportunity gaps on average, information often is lacking as to whether policies are effective in reducing gaps for different subgroups of children.

This recommendation cuts across all chapters of the report, in which a range of evidence and a variety of innovative approaches are highlighted. Chapter 1 outlines the racialized distribution of resources in the United States (e.g., Parolin et al., 2021) that contributes to gaps in opportunity and achievement, as well as the historical and current drivers of inequities in education (e.g., Reardon, 2015), physical health, and social and emotional well-being. This introductory chapter also details the administrative burden associated with benefit programs and their state-by-state shortcomings, and includes a robust discussion of how poverty perpetuates the opportunity gap (National Academies, 2019a). The following five chapters detail gaps in data collection, funding, and administrative coordination that impact early care and education (ECE), early elementary education, child health, and social-emotional development. Chapter 6 then provides an estimation of the economic costs of the opportunity gap, and illustrates how it can be reduced using the examples of SNAP (Hoynes, Schanzenbach, & Almond, 2016; Bitler & Figinski, 2019), Medicaid (Miller & Wherry, 2019; Goodman-Bacon, 2021), and the Head Start program (Ludwig & Miller, 2007; Johnson & Jackson, 2019; Bailey et al., 2021). Chapter 7 summarizes evidence on two approaches for reducing opportunity gaps related to job quality and resulting positive impacts on employment, earnings, and health and well-being (e.g., Miller et al., 2008; Duncan et al., 2009; Katz et al., 2021; Roder & Elliot, 2021; Sabol et al., 2021). In addition, the effect of the earned income tax credit on improved child health and educational outcomes demonstrate the importance of coordinated and sustained efforts to increase uptake of such programs (Dahl & Lochner, 2012; Markowitz et al., 2017; Komro et al., 2019; Lenhart, 2019; Batra & Hamad, 2021).

Recommendation 2: The federal government and states should establish early learning opportunities—accompanied by both legal accountability guaranteeing access and inclusive, intentional quality standards that are aligned with scientific evidence—as a right afforded to all children and families who need and want services.

A robust body of research demonstrates the benefits of ECE and its power as a strategy for reducing opportunity gaps. Ironically, however, policies that impose rigorous eligibility criteria and enrollment processes create access barriers for those who stand to benefit the most from ECE programs. One promising approach for reducing opportunity gaps in ECE would be to reenvision it as a public good, like K–12 education, that all children and families have the choice to claim (Sawhill, 1999; Barnett, Schulman, & Shore, 2004; Ladd, 2017; DeAngelis, Holmes Erickson, & Ritter, 2020; Bailey, Shuqiao, & Timpe, 2022).

Many young children are not getting what they need to grow, learn, and develop optimally. Developmental science long ago established that children are born learning, and neuroscience has demonstrated for decades that the early years are among the most sensitive periods in the life course for brain development. High-quality ECE is indeed a public good with social and economic returns that benefit all, and is recognized as a fundamental right in many countries around the world. Despite this fact, ECE is available only to some and exists as a patchwork system of varying quality. As a result, many families, disproportionately those from marginalized backgrounds, are left in difficult positions, balancing the safety, care, and education of their children and their employment.

Considering the wealth of evidence, the federal government and states should establish early learning opportunities—accompanied by legal accountability guaranteeing access and inclusive, intentional quality standards that are aligned with scientific evidence—as a right afforded to all children and families who need and want these services. To this end, federal and state actors should consider codifying ECE as both a civil and a human right of all young children. This could be achieved at the federal level by ratifying the United Nations Convention on the Rights of the Child, which would build on existing precedent established at the federal level through, for example, the right to preschool services for young children with disabilities under the Individuals with Disabilities Education Act (IDEA).

Chapter 1 of this report describes the historical and structural drivers of gaps in early learning opportunities (e.g., segregation, poverty, and economic opportunity), and provides evidence supporting the assertion that ECE investments have been inadequate to bridge opportunity gaps for historically marginalized groups (Institute of Medicine [IOM] & National Research Council [NRC], 2015; Lombardi et al., 2016; Malik et al., 2018; National Academies, 2018; Ullrich & Schmit, 2019; Keating, Cole, & Schaffner, 2020; Meek et al., 2020; Friedman-Krauss et al., 2022a, 2022b). Chapter 2 explores the short- and long-term benefits of ECE for a child's long-term trajectory (e.g., schooling and labor market outcomes; see Gormley, 2017; Bai et al., 2020; Bailey, Sun, & Timpe, 2021; Gray-Lobe, Pathak, & Walters, 2021; Jung & Barnett, 2021). That chapter also describes the uncoordinated current policies, systems, and funding streams whose shortcomings impede efforts to advance early learning goals for all children. Evidence related to disparities in access, gaps in availability, and administrative barriers demonstrate clear differential experiences in learning settings and the need for coordinated quality standards (National Academies, 2018).

> Recommendation 3: The federal government—in partnership with states—should fully implement a voluntary universal high-quality public early care and education system using a targeted universal approach (i.e., setting universal goals that are pursued using processes and strategies targeted to the needs of different groups). Such programs should be responsive to community needs, reflect the true cost of quality, and have strong monitoring and accountability systems that specifically address gaps in opportunity.

Such a unified system would:

- ensure that children and families from communities listed in Executive Order 13985, Advancing Racial Equity and Support for Underserved Communities through the Federal Government, are prioritized;
- allocate greater resources to historically marginalized communities to compensate for historical and current inequities in resources, experiences, and opportunities;
- allocate greater resources for parts of the ECE system that have traditionally received fewer resources;
- require evidence-based program standards that improve population outcomes and explicitly remedy opportunity gaps;
- build a corps of diverse, competent, well-trained, well-supported, and appropriately compensated early childhood educators and program leaders, across all age groups and program settings; and
- require disaggregated data collection that can be linked with other relevant data sources, as well as continuous quality improvement aimed at bridging opportunity and outcome gaps.

Underinvestment in high-quality ECE disproportionately affects children from low-income families, children of color, children who speak languages other than English at home, and children with disabilities. This underinvestment is the result of a complex array of factors, starting with the racialized[1] origins of ECE work and the perspective that ECE is an individual family's responsibility. This underinvestment in ECE persists today despite the well-documented benefits—individual and societal—of

---

[1] Racialization is defined as the act of giving a racial character to someone or something or the process of categorizing, marginalizing, or regarding according to race (Merriam-Webster, 2022).

high-quality ECE. Underinvestment has hit the ECE workforce particularly hard, resulting in high rates of poverty and economic insecurity among those who care for and teach young children. Efforts to target ECE investments to children from households with low income have not ensured high-quality experiences or been sufficient in scope to serve all eligible children.

Quality frameworks adopted by the field may not, in many instances, include indicators that have a particularly salient effect on opportunity gaps and the experiences of children from historically marginalized communities, such as issues related to bias, language of instruction, and inclusion of children with disabilities. Underfunded and fragmented programs, underpaid workers, inconsistent access to high-quality programming, and inadequate quality frameworks contribute to opportunity gaps. Wide-scale implementation of such a system should take into account the challenges that can occur during scale-up, such as insufficient capacity to implement programs, lack of sustained funding, a mismatch between demand for and supply of programs, lack of demand for programs, or barriers to access for targeted populations. A systematic approach to scaling up should be used to ensure that goals are clear and measurable, that progress is assessed regularly, and that challenges and opportunities are identified as they occur to inform iterative improvements in implementation. Two prior consensus studies of the National Academies—*Transforming the Workforce for Children Birth through Age 8* (IOM & NRC, 2015) and *Transforming the Financing of Early Care and Education* (2018)—offer additional comprehensive recommendations that provide guidance to support improvements in the quality of professional practice for ECE professionals, as well as in the funding of ECE in a way that makes high-quality programs accessible and affordable for families.

Chapter 1 of this report details segregation by socioeconomic status, disability status, and language, which structures the ECE system to benefit wealthier families and widen the educational achievement gap by limiting equitable access to quality educational opportunities for all children (Owens, Reardon, & Jencks, 2016; Gormley, 2017; Gándara, 2020; Meek et al., 2020; Cascio, 2021; Gillispie, 2021). Chapter 2 presents evidence from individual studies on the short- and long-term benefits of both targeted and universal preschool programs, and these studies report positive outcomes for children in low-income households, as well as those from marginalized communities (Bartik, Gormley, & Adelstein, 2012; Cascio & Schanzenbach, 2013; Phillips et al., 2017; Jung and Barnett, 2021). In addition, findings from meta-analyses support the substantial positive effects of high-quality pre-K on child learning and development across a range of domains (Camili et al., 2010; Duncan & Magnuson, 2013; Kay & Pennucci, 2014; Schindler et al., 2015; Joo et al., 2020). Because compulsory public education does not extend to ECE except for children with disabilities (under IDEA), many children and their families have no legal recourse to challenge inequitable access to quality education.

Recommendation 4: The federal government, states, local communities, and districts should adequately and equitably support elementary school education and out-of-school programs. Elementary school education should operate under a common quality framework, with quality benchmarks aligned with those in the early care and education system and based on evidence-based policies and practices.

Such a system would:

- address structural drivers of education opportunity, including segregation in learning settings by language, disability, race, and income; and
- be adequately funded to support the implementation of high-quality benchmarks aligned with those in the ECE system, including
  o high-quality instruction and asset-driven pedagogies, assessments, and curricula;
  o social-emotional and mental health supports and policies to explicitly reduce exclusionary and harsh discipline and eliminate disparities in such practices;
  o full inclusion of children with disabilities in general education settings, with high-quality and individualized services and supports;
  o bilingual learning opportunities for children who are English learners and dual language learners;
  o structurally sound, safe, healthy, and engaging learning environments;
  o a well-qualified, fairly compensated, and supported workforce;
  o data-driven continuous quality improvement efforts targeted at identifying and addressing opportunity and outcome gaps;
  o authentic and meaningful family engagement and partnerships;
  o strong partnerships with ECE systems that promote seamless transitions from ECE to the early grades; and
  o community partnerships and engagement to promote holistic family wellness.

Increasing funding for education, particularly for low-income students, has significant effects (e.g., improving achievement and graduation rates, employment, and wages and reducing poverty rates). Thus, resource allocation would need to prioritize underserved populations, including high-poverty and minoritized communities and children with unique needs, such as English learners and students with disabilities. Increased resources could be used in a targeted way to meet quality benchmarks, close opportunity gaps, and meet the holistic and academic needs of students. ECE and the early grades would also need to be aligned so that what was attained in the early years would be built upon and expanded in the later grades rather than repeated or dropped altogether. Families and communities must be a part of these systems to ensure that children are immersed in the environments and conditions they need to thrive across settings.

Chapter 3 of this report catalogs evidence related to differential experiences in early elementary learning settings, and includes a discussion of the common features of quality elementary school (e.g., structural factors, school- and district-level factors, teacher-level factors, and child-level outcomes; Paro et al., 2009; Lowenstein et al., 2015; Ansari & Pianta, 2019; Buttaro & Catsambis, 2019; Darling-Hammond, 2019). Poor physical infrastructure, large class sizes, singular language of instruction, and harsh and exclusionary discipline practices can further widen these gaps for children from marginalized communities. Evidence supporting the importance of warm, supportive, and enriching teacher–child relationships is presented in the context of the systems, policies, and funding that influence those relationships, as well as the child and teacher demographic characteristics that may mediate them (IOM & NRC, 2015).

> Recommendation 5: The Department of Education should fully integrate Individuals with Disabilities Education Act programming with general early childhood and K–12 education. As part of achieving this goal, the Department of Education, states, and districts should undertake specific reforms explicitly addressing opportunity gaps identified in this report, including
>
> a. uneven access to early intervention and preschool special education;
> b. uneven quality and dosage of early intervention and preschool special education;
> c. inclusion of children with disabilities across age groups, especially preschoolers, who are the most likely to be served in separate settings;
> d. nonbiased, accurate identification, specifically addressing over- and underidentification of specific groups of children, such as children of color, English learners, and others; and
> e. prohibition of harsh forms of discipline, including suspensions, expulsions, all forms of corporal punishment, seclusion, and inappropriate restraint for all students with disabilities, with special attention to students of color, who are disproportionately subject to these practices.

The maximum federal share of funding for IDEA determined by Congress is 40% of the national average per pupil expenditure. Unfortunately, Congress has never met this goal, and today funds only about 18% of what it costs to educate children with disabilities. Indeed, the inadequate funding of these services has resulted in states restricting eligibility criteria, lowering the dosage of services, or stretching wait times for the evaluation and service delivery process to the upper limits of what is allowable by law.

IDEA policy reforms, through reauthorization, regulation, technical assistance, and monitoring and accountability systems, must intentionally address gaps in access, particularly for children of color; accuracy in identification; inclusion in general ECE settings; and the harsh discipline to which children with disabilities are disproportionately subject. Unaddressed, these funding and policy issues will continue to perpetuate opportunity and outcome gaps between children with disabilities and their peers.

Chapter 1 of this report details the current shortcomings of IDEA in meeting the need for sufficient quantity and dosage of high-quality services for children who access special education, as well as issues with accurate identification of and provision of services to children of color who may experience disproportionately high rates of harsh discipline (Meek et al., 2020; National Center for Learning Disabilities, 2020; Smith et al., 2020; Department of Education, 2021; Gillispie, 2021; Hinds, Newby, & Korman, 2022). Chapter 2 presents a detailed comparison of child care, Head Start, and state pre-K programs and their coverage by IDEA (e.g., Table 2-1), and provides a lengthy discussion of the benefit of inclusive special education services for academic and social outcomes for children with disabilities, as well as the barriers that preclude access for many children.

> **Recommendation 6:** The Department of Health and Human Services (HHS) should create, lead, and be accountable for coordinating an interagency group focused on children's mental health and social-emotional well-being that includes the several HHS operating divisions, including the Administration for Children and Families, the Health Resources and Services Administration, the Substance Abuse and Mental Health Services Administration, the Centers for Disease Control and Prevention, and the Centers for Medicare & Medicaid Services, among others, as well as the Department of Education, the Department of Justice, the Department of Housing and Urban Development, and other relevant agencies, for the purpose of designing, implementing, and evaluating a comprehensive system of primary psychosocial care for young children and their families.

Such a comprehensive system of primary psychosocial care for young children and their families would include:

- universal support from the prenatal period through third grade, consisting of regular screening and identification of needs in mental health and social-emotional development for both families and children, followed by facilitated access that community resources to address those needs;
- sufficient community capacity to address young children's needs through a comprehensive array of well-funded evidence-based intervention programs and resources;
- an integrated data system, much like a child's electronic medical record, that charts a child's needs and interventions across the life course, to facilitate cross-agency communication and program and policy evaluation, and serve as a resource for future providers; and
- an evaluation plan and support for research to understand systemic and structural drivers (e.g., racism) that create or worsen physical and mental health challenges among young children from historically marginalized communities.

For families with children, no universal system provides care to support the social and emotional development, mental health, and well-being of their child from birth until age 5 when they enter the K–12 system with continuity of supports and services through the early school-age years. Chapter 5 of this report describes how families are faced with the burden of identifying the needs of their children, as well as accessing the resources to address those needs. During these early years, disparities in opportunity can grow as more advantaged families are able to use their resources to support the social-emotional needs of their children. Families from minoritized groups (both parents and children) are disproportionately exposed to hardships and stress across the life course, including stress related to racism and discrimination; are less likely to have their mental health needs met; and are more likely to have treatment prematurely terminated (e.g., Reiss, 2013; Cree et al., 2018; Jones Harden & Slopen, 2022). In addition, children from minoritized groups are less likely to have access to mental health services in schools and in the child welfare system (IOM, 2003; McGuire et al., 2006). For many families, especially those experiencing poverty, health issues, and precarious jobs, uncoordinated public systems that are charged with providing support for the well-being of children create barriers to access and burden these families in their efforts to access services and supports (Aber, Jones, & Cohen, 2000; Yoshikawa, Aber, & Beardslee, 2012; Alegría et al., 2015; Mazza et al., 2017; Schenck-Fontaine & Panico, 2019; Ridley et al., 2020).

Given the complexity of the system proposed in Recommendation 6, an interagency working group offers the potential to ensure that the design of this system is informed by the work of agencies whose policies have an impact on children's mental health and social-emotional well-being, and that the system's implementation is consistent and coordinated. A centralized system for identifying and cataloging effective, evidence-based intervention programs, policies, and resources that exist within a particular community should be part of the development of this system of primary psychosocial care. That system would support local community efforts to select appropriate evidence-based interventions, which could then be evaluated and used to understand drivers of challenges affecting specific communities.

Recommendation 7: The Department of Labor and the Department of Health and Human Services, in partnership with other relevant federal agencies, should review, update, and enforce existing labor standards and employment policies to address disparities that disproportionately affect working families with young children.

To implement this recommendation, the federal government could:

- build on the current job protections offered under the unpaid Family Medical Leave Act to create a paid social insurance program, administered by the Social Security Administration, to support parents needing time away from work to care for infants and newly adopted children and attend to their own and their family members' serious health issues;
- address documented issues in access to paid family and medical leave for low-income families and families from marginalized communities by implementing progressive wage replacement rates, making coverage more inclusive by eliminating firm-size requirements, and using existing hours and duration criteria for Social Security Disability Insurance or Medicare Hospital Insurance;
- develop recommendations on the definition of good-quality jobs for families with children, an effort that should include setting standards for family-sustaining wages and family-friendly employer practices;
- update existing labor standards and policies, raise the minimum wage floor, make work schedules more predictable, budget more resources for enforcement, and incentivize employers to provide training and career ladders; and
- partner with philanthropic organizations to conduct research on job quality standards and metrics to guide policy and employer-based interventions.

Research shows that many working families do not earn enough from full-time employment to cover basic needs, and that many employers do

KEY CONCLUSIONS AND RECOMMENDATIONS 395

not provide benefits such as paid sick or medical leave, parental leave, or child care. Lack of access to paid leave creates an opportunity gap for young children by limiting bonding time for parents and infants, decreasing the time available to attend to serious health issues, elevating family stress, and exposing children to financial uncertainty. Overall, this body of research suggests that paid family and medical leave is an effective policy that improves the social-emotional well-being of parents and the health of their young children. Moreover, making the program nearly universal would lower per worker costs. The policy could be further improved by reducing racial/ethnic and income disparities in take-up of leave through less restrictive eligibility criteria, higher wage replacement rates, targeted outreach, and improved administrative systems.

Chapter 5 of this report describes the evidence on paid family leave and its positive effects on mental health outcomes for both children and caregivers (e.g., Bullinger, 2019; Irish et al., 2021; Kozak et al., 2021). Chapter 7 further reports on the benefits of lengthy, accessible paid leave for caregivers' mental health outcomes (Chatterji & Markowitz, 2012; Dagher, McGovern, & Dowd, 2014; Kornfeind & Sipsma, 2018; Mandal, 2018), as well as infants' physical health and attachment (National Academies, 2016, 2019b; Hamad, Modrek, & White, 2019). In addition, that chapter presents research on the current limitations of the Family and Medical Leave Act and paid leave for all workers (e.g., Joshi et al., 2019, 2020), as well as the role of parental job quality as a social determinant of a child's health (e.g., Burgard & Lin, 2013; Repetti & Wang, 2014; Antonisse & Garfield, 2018; Congdon et al., 2020).

Recommendation 8: The federal government, in partnership with state and local governments, philanthropy, and relevant public and private organizations, should support policies and interventions targeting social determinants of health that create and perpetuate opportunity gaps at the community level.

To further the development of targeted policies and interventions for addressing the opportunity gap at the community level, the following actions should be taken by federal, state, and local entities and private philanthropic organizations:

- Federal and state governments should expand existing safety net programs that have been shown to address poverty and food insecurity as social determinants of health, including the special Supplemental Nutrition Program for Women, Infants, and Children, SNAP, and the earned income tax credit, as well as the 2021 expanded child tax credit. Eligibility applications for these programs

- could be unified and streamlined to reduce administrative hurdles to take-up.
- As with other programs such as child care subsidies, to reduce disruptions in insurance and health care access, the federal government should ensure continuous coverage with Medicaid for a minimum 12-month period even if families experience temporary changes in income during the year that make them ineligible, and Medicaid should be provided to women for at least 12 months postpartum.
- Federal, state, and local governments should increase the supply of affordable high-quality housing, which would include access to green spaces, playgrounds, and parks.
- Local governments should engage in urban planning improvements to enhance traffic safety and eliminate road hazards (e.g., legislate speed limits), especially in marginalized communities.
- Governments at the federal, state, and local levels and philanthropy should prioritize support for communities with a level of high need and low resources, as measured by the Child Opportunity Index, program administrative data, and historical budget data.
- Early learning, education, and health care systems should act as anchor institutions and be coordinated through shared data systems and integrated service delivery to promote family wellness and community development by offering onsite or providing connections to health, mental health, after-school, nutritional support, and economic wellness services. The federal government should build on and expand existing programming that can facilitate this anchor organization approach, such as full-service community schools, Head Start, and federally qualified health centers.
- Community organizations, philanthropy, and local governments should support evidence-based programs for young people, such as those that include tutoring or mentoring; sports; and early childhood mental health programs, including parent–child interaction and cognitive-behavioral therapeutic approaches.

Children living in poverty and those from other marginalized populations are subject to inequities in experiences with and access to resources related to health care, child care, school quality, safe and healthy home environments and neighborhood contexts, along with access to supportive programs. These inequities in access to resources and programs that strongly influence developmental outcomes lead to persistent opportunity gaps for young children. Creation of a centralized resource cataloguing effective, evidence-based practices across domains that eliminate disparities in opportunity among young children—similar to the What Works

Clearinghouse, for example—could allow communities to share and learn from experiences with promising and effective intervention programs and policies. In addition, state and local governments could examine existing policies that have demonstrated promising outcomes for young children, and leverage resources and partnerships with the private sector to invest in interventions with the potential to close opportunity gaps for young children and support their healthy development.

Chapter 1 provides examples of federal, state, and local influences on the opportunity gap and associated racial/ethnic disparities, as well as effects on marginalized communities, including differences in achievement and inequitable access to mental and physical supports for health and well-being (e.g., Bell, 1965; Vogtman, 2017; Minoff, 2020; Derenoncourt & Montialoux, 2021; Parolin et al., 2021). These examples extend to discriminatory housing policies and urban planning and community development that can contribute to increased injuries and environmental exposure to toxins (Morency et al., 2012; Rothstein, 2017; National Academies, 2019b). Chapter 4 provides a brief history of Medicaid, including the role of states in determining income and eligibility thresholds (Nolen, Beckman, & Sandoe, 2020); Chapter 6 describes the implications of expanding Medicaid coverage for pregnant people and families (e.g., reducing infant deaths by 50%), and Chapter 7 presents evidence on the positive effects of exposure to Medicaid on educational outcomes and adult health (Meyer & Wherry, 2012; Miller & Wherry, 2019; Brown, Kowalski, & Lurie, 2020; Goodman-Bacon, 2021). In addition, Chapter 4 expands on the opportunity for anchor institutions to support neighborhood development, reduce housing insecurity and crime, and increase community safety (Sharkey, Torrats-Espinosa, & Takyar, 2017; Kelleher, Reece, & Sandel, 2018; National Academies, 2019a). This coordinated approach can leverage political will and private and public funding at a variety of levels to support sustained and synergistic interventions with the potential to remediate the opportunity gap.

Recommendation 9: Early learning and K–12 education systems, health care systems, and employers should test and institute policies and protocols for identifying and addressing manifestations of institutional racism to reduce inequities in access to resources and quality services in education, health care, and public health.

To identify and address manifestations of institutional racism that create and perpetuate the opportunity gap, the following specific actions should be taken to reduce inequities in access to resources and quality services in education, health care, and public health:

- Systems leaders and administrators across all levels of government (federal, state, local) should work to address institutional racism and increase culturally and linguistically appropriate health care, public health, early care and education, and early grade education.
- Policy makers should take into account historical inequities in resource distribution and current manifestations of racism and marginalization in developing policy and making budgetary decisions.
- Federal research agencies (e.g., the National Institutes of Health, the National Science Foundation) and philanthropic organizations should support and prioritize historically marginalized communities and groups to improve their access to professional development programs, apprenticeships, and scholarships and diversify the pipeline of health care professionals, public health practitioners, teachers, early educators, and early childhood researchers.
- National professional organizations and accreditors should improve curriculum training and require minimum competencies in antiracist approaches; social determinants of health inequities; and culturally competent, trauma-informed, and resilience-building health care, early care and education, and early grade education.

A consistent finding across issue areas (e.g., early education, health, social-emotional development) is that opportunity is associated with race, and that race intersects with multiple other identities to result in compounded gaps in opportunity and outcomes. Many gaps in opportunity and outcomes are the products of centuries of systemic racism across numerous domains of life, including financial/wealth, health, and education. Any attempt to address unequal opportunity requires understanding and remedying historical inequities and their manifestations today.

Chapter 1 of this report describes the historical precedents of the opportunity gap in educational systems, the role of segregation in widening this gap, and structural and economic policies that further widen these inequities. Chapters 2 and 3 explore the evidence on the intersection of institutional racism with ECE and elementary education, and highlight how program funding, early special education intervention, differential learning settings, and the training of the education workforce are heavily influenced by manifestations of structural racism (e.g., poorly funded programs, under- and overidentification of children of color for special education, harsh disciplinary practices aimed at marginalized children, and poorly paid and trained educators). Chapter 5 connects racialized drivers of opportunity gaps to child and parental health, with evidence demonstrating clear disparities in health care delivery, relational health, and safe and healthy neighborhoods. Chapter 6 extends this discussion to include the impact of institutional racism on opportunity gaps in child mental health, and highlights strategies for reducing these gaps.

FINAL THOUGHTS

Many of the findings and challenges presented in this report are not new; however, the committee's recommendations highlight ways in which changes to the status quo hold the potential to improve the quality of care and education children receive from birth through age 8. Differential access to high-quality experiences, services, programs, and other resources is the result of a diverse array of factors, both historical and current, which have led to disparities in educational outcomes, physical health, mental health, and healthy social-emotional development and well-being that persist and compound. Indeed, these disparities will continue to persist in the absence of investments in increasing equitable access to opportunity. It is important to stress that the question of quality is central to all efforts to close the opportunity gap; the expansion of access to resources and experiences alone is insufficient in the absence of high quality.

Promising approaches highlighted in this report offer the opportunity to reduce disparities in ways that promote healthy development and learning for all children. The committee hopes that implementation of its recommendations, which cut across the systems that serve young children and their families, will guide leaders in federal, state, and local governments; the private sector; and the philanthropic community in developing multifaceted, cross-sectoral approaches that can shape policies, programs, and services to foster the well-being of and improve outcomes for young children, their families, and their communities.

REFERENCES

Aber, J.L., Jones, S., & Cohen, J. (2000). *The impact of poverty on the mental health and development of very young children: Handbook of infant mental health*. (2nd ed.). New York, NY: The Guilford Press.

Alegría, M., Green, J.G., McLaughlin, K.A., & Loder, S. (2015). *Disparities in child and adolescent mental health and mental health services in the U.S.* William T. Grant Foundation. Available: http://cfs.cbcs.usf.edu/projects-research/_docs/Disparities_in_child_and_adolescent_health.pdf

Ansari, A., & Pianta, R.C. (2019). School absenteeism in the first decade of education and outcomes in adolescence. *Journal of School Psychology*, 76, 48–61. https://doi.org/10.1016/j.jsp.2019.07.010

Antonisse, L., & Garfield, R. (2018). *The relationship between work and health: Findings from a literature review*. (Issue Brief). Available: https://www.kff.org/medicaid/issue-brief/the-relationship-between-work-and-health-findings-from-a-literature-review/

Bai, Y., Ladd, H.F., Muschkin, C.G., & Dodge, K.A. (2020). Long-term effects of early childhood programs through eighth grade: Do the effects fade out or grow? *Children and Youth Services Review*, 112, 104890. https://doi.org/10.1016/j.childyouth.2020.104890

Bailey, M.J., Sun, S., & Timpe, B. (2021). Prep school for poor kids: The long-run impacts of Head Start on human capital and economic self-sufficiency. *American Economic Review*, 111(12), 3963–4001. https://doi.org/10.1257/aer.20181801

Bailey, M., Shuqiao, S., & Timpe, B. (2022). Is universal preschool worth it? Head Start offers encouraging long-term results. Available: https://www.brookings.edu/blog/brown-center-chalkboard/2022/02/09/is-universal-preschool-worth-it/

Barnett, W.S., Schulman, K., & Shore, R. (2004). Class size: What's the best fit? *Preschool Policy Matters*, 9. National Institute for Early Education Research. Available: https://nieer.org/wp-content/uploads/2016/08/9.pdf

Bartik, T.J., Gormley, W., & Adelstein, S. (2012). Earnings benefits of Tulsa's pre-K program for different income groups. *Economics of Education Review*, 31(6), 1143–61. https://doi.org/10.1016/j.econedurev.2012.07.016

Batra, A., & Hamad, R. (2021). Short-term effects of the earned income tax credit on children's physical and mental health. *Annals of Epidemiology*, 58, 15–21. https://doi.org/10.1016/j.annepidem.2021.02.008

Bell, W. (1965). *Aid to dependent children*. New York: Columbia University Press.

Bitler, M.P., & Figinski, T. (2019). *Long-run effects of food assistance: Evidence from the Food Stamp program*. (Working Paper No. 20195). Economic Self-Sufficiency Policy Research Institute. Available: https://www.esspri.uci.edu/files/docs/working_papers/ESSPRI%20Working%20Paper%2020195%20Bitler%20Figinski.pdf

Brown, D.W., Kowalski, A.E., & Lurie, I.Z. (2020). Long-term impacts of childhood Medicaid expansions on outcomes in adulthood. *Review of Economic Studies*, 87(2), 792–821. https://doi.org/10.1093/restud/rdz039

Bullinger, L.R. (2019). The effect of paid family leave on infant and parental health in the United States. *Journal of Health Economics*, 66, 101–16. https://doi.org/10.1016/j.jhealeco.2019.05.006

Burgard, S.A., & Lin, K.Y. (2013). Bad jobs, bad health? How work and working conditions contribute to health disparities. *American Behavioral Scientist*, 57(8), 1105–27. https://doi.org/10.1177/0002764213487347

Buttaro, A., Jr., & Catsambis, S. (2019). Ability grouping in the early grades: Long-term consequences for educational equity in the United States. *Teachers College Record*, 121(2), 1–50.

Camilli, G., Vargas, S., Ryan, S., & Barnett, W.S. (2010). Meta-analysis of the effects of early education interventions on cognitive and social development. *Teachers College Record*, 112(3), 579–620. https://doi.org/10.1177/016146811011200303

Cascio, E. (2021). *Early childhood education in the United States: What, when, where, who, how, and why*. (Working Paper No. 28722). National Bureau of Economic Research. https://doi.org/10.3386/w28722

Cascio, E.U., & Schanzenbach, D.W. (2013). *The impacts of expanding access to high-quality preschool education*. (Working Paper No. 19735). National Bureau of Economic Research. https://doi.org/10.338/w19735

Chatterji, P., & Markowitz, S. (2012). Family leave after childbirth and the mental health of new mothers. *Journal of Mental Health Policy and Economics*, 15(2), 61–76.

Congdon, W.J., Scott, M.M., Katz, B., Loprest, P., Nightingale, D., & Shakesprere, J. (2020). *Understanding good jobs: A review of definitions and evidence*. Urban Institute. Available: https://www.urban.org/research/publication/understanding-good-jobs-review-definitions-and-evidence

Cree, R.A., Bitsko, R.H., Robinson, L.R., Holbrook, J.R., Danielson, M.L., Smith, C., Kaminski, J.W., Kenney, M.K. & Peacock, G. (2018). Health care, family, and community factors associated with mental, behavioral, and developmental disorders and poverty among children aged 2–8 years—United States, 2016. *Morbidity and Mortality Weekly Report*, 67(50), 1377.

Dagher, R.K., McGovern, P.M., & Dowd, B.E. (2014). Maternity leave duration and postpartum mental and physical health: Implications for leave policies. *Journal of Health Politics, Policy & Law*, 39(2), 369–416.

Dahl, G.B., & Lochner, L. (2012). The impact of family income on child achievement: Evidence from the earned income tax credit. *American Economic Review*, 102(5), 1927–56. http://dx.doi.org/10.1257/aer.102.5.1927

Darling-Hammond, L. (2019). *Investing for student success: Lessons from state school finance reforms*. Learning Policy Institute. https://learningpolicyinstitute.org/product/investing-student-success-school-finance-reforms-report

DeAngelis, C.A., Holmes Erickson, H., & Ritter, G.W. (2020). What's the state of the evidence on pre-K programmes in the United States? A systematic review. *Educational Review*, 72(4), 495–519.

Department of Education. (2021). *43rd annual report to Congress on the implementation of the Individuals with Disabilities Education Act, 2021*. Available: https://sites.ed.gov/idea/files/43rd-arc-for-idea.pdf

Derenoncourt, E., & Montialoux, C. (2020). Minimum wages and racial inequality. *The Quarterly Journal of Economics*, 136(1), 169–228. https://doi.org/10.1093/qje/qjaa031

Duncan, G.J., & Magnuson, K. (2013). Investing in preschool programs. *Journal of Economic Perspectives*, 27(2), 109–32. https://doi.org/10.1257/jep.27.2.109

Duncan, G.J., Bos, H., Gennetian, L.A., & Hill, H. (2009). New Hope: A thoughtful and effective approach to "make work pay". *Northwestern Journal of Law and Social Policy*, 4(1), 101–15. Available: https://scholarlycommons.law.northwestern.edu/njlsp/vol4/iss1/6/

Friedman-Krauss, A.H., Barnett, W.S. & Duer, J.K. (2022a). *The state(s) of Head Start and Early Head Start: Looking at equity*. New Brunswick, NJ: National Institute for Early Education Research.

Friedman-Krauss, A.H., Barnett, W.S., Garver, K.A., Hodges, K.S., Weisenfeld, G.G., Gardiner, B.A., & Jost, T.M. (2022b). The State of Preschool 2021: State Preschool Yearbook. *National Institute for Early Education Research*.

Gándara, P. (2020). Equity considerations in addressing English learner segregation. *Leadership and Policy in Schools*, 19(1), 141–3. https://doi.org/10.1080/15700763.2019.1711134

Gillispie, C. (2021). *Our youngest learners. Increasing equity in early intervention*. The Education Trust. Available: https://edtrust.org/increasing-equity-in-early-intervention/

Goodman-Bacon, A. (2021). The long-run effects of childhood insurance coverage: Medicaid implementation, adult health, and labor market outcomes. *American Economic Review*, 111(8), 2550–93. https://doi.org/10.1257/aer.20171671

Gormley, W. (2017). Universal vs. targeted pre-kindergarten: Reflections for policymakers. *The current state of scientific knowledge on pre-kindergarten effects*, 51–6. Foundation for Child Development. Available: https://www.fcd-us.org/current-state-scientific-knowledge-pre-kindergarten-effects/

Gray-Lobe, G., Pathak, P.A., & Walters, C.R. (2021). *The long-term effects of universal preschool in Boston*. National Bureau of Economic Research. Available: https://www.nber.org/system/files/working_papers/w28756/w28756.pdf

Hamad, R., Modrek, S., & White, J.S. (2019). Paid family leave effects on breastfeeding: A quasi-experimental study of US policies. *American Journal of Public Health*, 109(1), 164–6. https://doi.org/10.2105/AJPH.2018.304693

Hinds, H., Newby, L., & Korman, H. (2022). *Ignored, punished, and underserved: Understanding and addressing disparities in education experiences and outcomes for Black children with disabilities*. Bellwether. Available: https://bellwether.org/publications/ignored-punished-and-underserved

Hoynes, H., Schanzenbach, D.W., & Almond, D. (2016). Long-run impacts of childhood access to the safety net. *American Economic Review*, 106(4), 903–34. https://doi.org/10.1257/aer.20130375

Institute of Medicine (IOM). (2003). *Unequal treatment: Confronting racial and ethnic disparities in health care*. The National Academies Press. https://doi.org/10.17226/12875.

Institute of Medicine (IOM) & National Research Council (NRC). (2015). *Transforming the workforce for children birth through age 8: A unifying foundation*. The National Academies Press. https://doi.org/10.17226/19401

Irish, A.M., White, J.S., Modrek, S., & Hamad, R. (2021). Paid family leave and mental health in the U.S.: A quasi-experimental study of state policies. *American Journal of Preventive Medicine*, 61(2), 182–91. https://doi.org/10.1016/j.amepre.2021.03.018

Johnson, R.C., & Jackson, C.K. (2019). Reducing inequality through dynamic complementarity: Evidence from Head Start and public school spending. *American Economic Journal: Economic Policy*, 11(4), 310–49. https://doi.org/10.1257/pol.20180510

Jones Harden, B., & Slopen, N. (2022). Inequitable experiences and outcomes in young children. Addressing racial and social-economic disparities in physical and mental health. *Annual Review of Developmental Psychology*, 4, 133–59. https://doi.org/10.1146/annurev-devpsych-121020-031515

Joo, Y.S., Magnuson, K., Duncan, G.J., Schindler, H.S., Yoshikawa, H., & Ziol-Guest, K.M. (2020). What works in early childhood education programs?: A meta–analysis of preschool enhancement programs. *Early Education and Development*, 31(1), 1–26. https://doi.org/10.1080/10409289.2019.1624146

Joshi, P., Baldiga, M., Earle, A., Huber, R., Osypuk, T., & Acevedo-Garcia, D. (2019). How much would family and medical leave cost workers in the US? Racial/ethnic variation in economic hardship under unpaid and paid policies. *Community, Work & Family*, 24(5), 517–40. https://doi.org/10.1080/13668803.2019.1704398

Joshi, P., Baldiga, M., Huber, R., & Acevedo-Garcia, D. (2020). *Policy equity assessment: Family and Medical Leave Act*. Institute for Child, Youth & Family Policy (ICYFP), Heller School for Social Policy & Management. Brandeis University. Available: https://www.diversitydatakids.org/research-library/policy-equity-assessment/policy-equity-assessment-family-and-medical-leave-act

Jung, K., & Barnett, W.S. (2021). *Impacts of the pandemic on young children and their parents: Initial findings from NIEER's May-June 2021 preschool learning activities survey*. National Institute for Early Education Research. Available: https://nieer.org/research-report/impacts-of-the-pandemic-on-young-children-and-their-parents-initial-findings-from-nieers-may-june-2021-preschool-learning-activities-survey

Katz, L.F., Roth, J., Hendra, R., & Schaberg, K. (2021). Why do sectoral employment programs work?: Lessons from WorkAdvance. *Journal of Labor Economics*, 40(S1). https://doi.org/10.1086/717932

Kay, N., & Pennucci, A. (2014). *Full day kindergarten: A review of the evidence and benefit-cost analysis*. Olympia, WA: Washington State Institute for Public Policy.

Keating, K., Cole, P., & Schaffner, M. (2020). *State of babies yearbook 2020*. Zero the Three. Available: https://stateofbabies.org/wp-content/uploads/2020/06/State-of-Babies-2020-Full-Yearbook-061820.pdf

Kelleher, K., Reece, J., & Sandel, M. (2018). The Healthy Neighborhood, Healthy Families initiative. *Pediatrics*, 142(3), e20180261. https://doi.org/10.1542/peds.2018-0261

Komro, K.A., Markowitz, S., Livingston, M.D., & Wagenaar, A.C. (2019). Effects of state-level earned income tax credit laws on birth outcomes by race and ethnicity. *Health Equity*, 3(1), 61–7. https://doi.org/10.1089/heq.2018.0061

Kornfeind, K.R., & Sipsma, H.L. (2018). Exploring the link between maternity leave and postpartum depression. *Women's Health Issues*, 28(4), 321–6. https://doi.org/10.1016/j.whi.2018.03.008

Kozak, K., Greaves, A., Waldfogel, J., Angal, J., Elliott, A.J., Fifer, W.P., & Brito, N.H. (2021). Paid maternal leave is associated with better language and socioemotional outcomes during toddlerhood. *Infancy*, 26(4), 536–50. https://doi.org/10.1111/infa.12399

Ladd, H.F. (2017). *Weighing the benefits and costs of universal versus targeted pre-K programs*. Brookings Institute. Available: https://www.brookings.edu/blog/brown-center-chalkboard/2017/06/27/weighing-the-benefits-and-costs-of-universal-versus-targeted-pre-k-programs/

Lenhart, O. (2019). The effects of income on health: New evidence from the earned income tax credit. *Review of Economics of the Household*, 17(2), 377–410. https://doi.org/10.1007/s11150-018-9429-x

Lombardi, J., Harding, J.F., Connors, M.C., & Friedman-Krauss, A. (2016). Executive summary. *Coming of age: A review of federal early childhood policy 2000-2015*. Build Initiative. Available: https://www.researchgate.net/publication/323400908_Coming_of_Age_A_Review_of_Federal_Early_Childhood_Policy_2000_-_2015

Lowenstein, A.E., Wolf, S., Gershoff, E.T., Sexton, H.R., Raver, C.C., & Aber, J.L. (2015). The stability of elementary school contexts from kindergarten to third grade. *Journal of School Psychology*, 53(4), 323–35. https://doi.org/10.1016/j.jsp.2015.05.002

Ludwig, J., & Miller, D.L. (2007). Does Head Start improve children's life chances? Evidence from a regression discontinuity design. *The Quarterly Journal of Economics*, 122(1), 159–208. https://doi.org/10.1162/qjec.122.1.159

Malik, R., Hamm, K., Schochet, L., Novoa, C., Workman, S., & Jessen-Howard, S. (2018). *America's child care deserts in 2018*. Center for American Progress. Available: https://www.americanprogress.org/article/americas-child-care-deserts-2018

Mandal, B. (2018). The effect of paid leave on maternal mental health. *Maternal and Child Health Journal*, 22(10), 1470–6.

Markowitz, S., Komro, K.A., Livingston, M.D., Lenhart, O., & Wagenaar, A.C. (2017). Effects of state-level earned income tax credit laws in the U.S. on maternal health behaviors and infant health outcomes. *Social Science & Medicine*, 194, 67–75. https://doi.org/10.1016/j.socscimed.2017.10.016

Mazza, J.R., Pingault, J.-B., Booij, L., Boivin, M., Tremblay, R., Lambert, J., Zunzunegui, M.V., & Côté, S. (2017). Poverty and behavior problems during early childhood: The mediating role of maternal depression symptoms and parenting. *International Journal of Behavioral Development*, 41(6), 670–80. https://doi.org/10.1177/0165025416657615

McGuire, T.G., Alegría, M., Cook, B.L., Wells, K.B., & Zaslavsky, A.M. (2006). Implementing the Institute of Medicine definition of disparities: An application to mental health care. *Health Services Research*, 41(5), 1979–2005. https://doi.org/10.1111/j.1475-6773.2006.00583.x

Meek, S., Smith, L., Allen, R., Catherine, E., Edyburn, K., Williams, C., Fabes, R., McIntosh, K., Garcia, E., Takanishi, R., Gordon, L., Jimenez-Castellanos, O., Hemmeter, M.L., Gilliam, W., & Pontier, R. (2020). *Start with equity. From the early years to the early grades. Data, research, and an actionable child equity policy agenda*. Children's Equity Project and Bipartisan Policy Center. Available: https://childandfamilysuccess.asu.edu/cep/start-with-equity

Merriam-Webster. (2022). Racialization. In *Merriam Webster*. https://www.merriam-webster.com/dictionary/racialization

Meyer, B., & Wherry, L. (2012). *Saving teens: Using a policy discontinuity to estimate the effects of Medicaid eligibility*. (Working Paper No. 18309). National Bureau of Economic Research. Available: https://www.nber.org/papers/w18309

Miller, C., Huston, A.C., Duncan, G.J., McLoyd, V.C., & Weisner, T.S. (2008). *New hope for the working poor*. MDRC. Available: https://www.mdrc.org/sites/default/files/full_458.pdf

Miller, S., & Wherry, L.R. (2019). The long-term effects of early life Medicaid coverage. *Journal of Human Resources*, 54(3), 785–824.

Minoff, E. (2020). *The racist roots of work requirements*. Center for the Study of Social Policy. Available: https://cssp.org/resource/racist-roots-of-work-requirements

Morency, P., Gauvin, L., Plante, C., Fournier, M., & Morency, C. (2012). Neighborhood social inequalities in road traffic injuries: The influence of traffic volume and road design. *American Journal of Public Health*, 102(6), 1112–9. https://doi.org/10.2105/AJPH.2011.300528

National Academies of Sciences, Engineering, and Medicine (National Academies). (2016). *Parenting matters: Supporting parents of children ages 0-8*. The National Academies Press. https://doi.org/10.17226/21868

———. (2018). *Transforming the financing of early care and education*. The National Academies Press. https://doi.org/10.17226/24984

———. (2019a). *A roadmap to reducing child poverty*. The National Academies Press. https://doi.org/10.17226/25246

———. (2019b). *Vibrant and healthy kids: Aligning science, practice, and policy to advance health equity*. The National Academies Press. https://doi.org/10.17226/25466

National Center for Learning Disabilities. (2020). *Significant disproportionality in special education. Current trends and actions for impact*. Available: https://www.ncld.org/wp-content/uploads/2020/10/2020-NCLD-Disproportionality_Trends-and-Actions-for-Impact_FINAL-1.pdf

National Institutes of Health. (2023). *Structural racism and discrimination*. National Institute on Minority Health and Health Disparities. Availabile: https://www.nimhd.nih.gov/resources/understanding-health-disparities/srd.html

Nolen, L.T., Beckman, A.L., & Sandoe, E. (2020, September 1). How foundational moments in Medicaid's history reinforced rather than eliminated racial health disparities. *Health Affairs Blog*. https://doi.org/10.1377/hblog20200828.661111

Owens, A., Reardon, S.F., & Jencks, C. (2016). Income segregation between schools and school districts. *American Educational Research Journal*, 53(4), 1159–97. https://doi.org/10.3102/0002831216652722

Paro, K.M.L., Hamre, B.K., Locasale-Crouch, J., Pianta, R.C., Bryant, D., Early, D., Clifford, R., Barbarin, O., Howes, C., & Burchinal, M. (2009). Quality in kindergarten classrooms: Observational evidence for the need to increase children's learning opportunities in early education classrooms. *Early Education and Development*, 20(4), 657–92. https://doi.org/10.1080/10409280802541965

Parolin, Z., Collyer, S., Curran, M., & Wimer, C. (2021). *The potential poverty reduction effect of the American Rescue Plan*. Fact sheet. Center on Poverty and Social Policy at Columbia University. Available: https://www.povertycenter.columbia.edu/publication/2021/poverty-reduction-analysis-american-rescue-plan

Phillips, D., Johnson, A., Weiland, C., & Hutchison, J. (2017). *Public preschool in a more diverse America: Implications for next-generation evaluation research*. (Working Paper No. 2-17). Poverty Solutions, University of Michigan. Available: https://eric.ed.gov/?id=ED594039

Reardon, S.F. (2015). *School segregation and racial academic achievement gaps*. (Working Paper No. 15-12). Stanford Center for Education Policy Analysis. https://cepa.stanford.edu/sites/default/files/wp15-12v201510.pdf

Reiss, F. (2013). Socioeconomic inequalities and mental health problems in children and adolescents: A systematic review. *Social Science & Medicine*, 90(1982), 24–31. https://doi.org/10.1016/j.socscimed.2013.04.026

Repetti, R.L., & Wang, S.-W. (2014). Employment and parenting. *Parenting: Science & Practice*, 14(2), 121–32. http://dx.doi.org/10.1080/15295192.2014.914364

Ridley, M., Rao, G., Schilbach, F., & Patel, V. (2020). Poverty, depression, and anxiety: Causal evidence and mechanisms. *Science*, 370(6522). https://doi.org/10.1126/science.aay0214

Roder, A., & Elliott, M. (2021). *Project Quest's investment continues to pay dividends*. Economic Mobility Corporation. Available: https://economicmobilitycorp.org/wp-content/uploads/2021/09/Mobility_Eleven-Year-Gains.pdf

Rothstein, R. (2017). *The color of law: A forgotten history of how our government segregated America*. New York: Liveright Publishing Corporation.

Sabol, T.J., Sommer, T.E., Chase-Lansdale, P.L., & Brooks-Gunn, J. (2021). Intergenerational economic mobility for low-income parents and their children: A dual developmental science framework. *Annual Review of Psychology*, 72, 265–92. https://doi.org/10.1146/annurev-psych-010419-051001

Sawhill, I.V. (1999). *Kids need an early start: Universal preschool education may be the best investment Americans can make in our children's education—and our nation's future*. Brookings Institute. Available: https://www.brookings.edu/articles/kids-need-an-early-start-universal-preschool-education-may-be-the-best-investment-americans-can-make-in-our-childrens-education-and-our-nations-future/

Schenck-Fontaine, A., & Panico, L. (2019). Many kinds of poverty: Three dimensions of economic hardship, their combinations, and children's behavior problems. *Demography*, 56(6), 2279–305. https://doi.org/10.1007/s13524-019-00833-y

Schindler, H.S., Kholoptseva, J., Oh, S.S., Yoshikawa, H., Duncan, G.J., Magnuson, K.A., & Shonkoff, J.P. (2015). Maximizing the potential of early childhood education to prevent externalizing behavior problems: A meta-analysis. *Journal of School Psychology*, 53(3), 243–63. https://doi.org/10.1016/j.jsp.2015.04.001

Sharkey, P., Torrats-Espinosa, G., & Takyar, D. (2017). Community and the crime decline: The causal effect of local nonprofits on violent crime. *American Sociological Review*, 82(6), 1214–40. https://doi.org/10.1177/0003122417736289

Smith, S., Ferguson, D., Burak, E.W., Granja, M.R., & Ortuzar, C. (2020). *Supporting social-emotional and mental health needs of young children through Part C early intervention: Results of a 50-state survey*. National Center for Children in Poverty, Bank Street Graduate School of Education. Available: www.nccp.org/wp-content/uploads/2020/11/Part-C-Report-Final.pdf

Ullrich, R., & Schmit, S. (2019). *Inequitable access to child care subsidies*. Center for Law and Social Policy. Available: https://www.clasp.org/publications/report/brief/inequitable-access-child-care-subsidies

Vogtman, J. (2017). Undervalued: A brief history of women's care work and child care policy in the United States. *National Women's Law Center*.

Yoshikawa, H., Aber, J.L., & Beardslee, W.R. (2012). The effects of poverty on the mental, emotional, and behavioral health of children and youth: Implications for prevention. *American Psychologist*, 67(4), 272–84. https://doi.org/10.1037/a0028015

Appendix A

A Total Population of Children Ages 0–8 by Race/Ethnicity and Nativity, 2020

TABLE A-1 Total Population of Children Ages 0–8, by Race/Ethnicity and Nativity, 2020

	Total	Hispanic	White	Black	Asian	Multirace	American Indian
Children in immigrant families	8,793,886	4,406,640	1,435,997	807,551	1,563,789	570,192	9,717
Foreign born (first generation)	719,211	261,688	119,142	83,403	224,156	30,532	290
U.S. born (second generation)	8,074,675	4,144,952	1,316,855	724,148	1,339,633	539,660	9,427
Children in nonimmigrant families	25,353,226	4,359,369	15,368,463	3,560,586	211,908	1,643,173	209,727
Total children living with parents	34,147,112	8,766,009	16,804,460	4,368,137	1,775,697	2,213,365	219,444
Children not living with parents	1,256,636	266,075	536,881	308,609	29,938	90,909	24,224
Foreign born (first generation)	33,917	16,379	4,809	4,616	6,418	1,562	133
U.S. born (immigrant status unknown)	1,222,719	249,696	532,072	303,993	23,520	89,347	24,091
Total child population	35,403,748	9,032,084	17,341,341	4,676,746	1,805,635	2,304,274	243,668

NOTES: Immigrant families include at least one foreign-born parent. U.S.-born children include those born abroad with at least one U.S.-born parent. Children in nonimmigrant families are U.S. born and parents are U.S. born. Racial groups include only non-Hispanic members. Hispanic people may be of any race. American Indian includes Alaska Native. Asian includes Pacific Islander. Multirace includes "other race."
SOURCE: Data from diversitydatakids.org calculations of 2020 American Community Survey, 5-year data set, accessed through IPUMS-USA (Steven Ruggles, Sarah Flood, Ronald Goeken, Megan Schouweiler, and Matthew Sobek). IPUMS USA: Version 12.0 (ACS 2020, 5-year data set). Minneapolis, MN: IPUMS, 2022 (https://doi.org/10.18128/D010.V12 [accessed 1/26/23]).

Appendix B

Percentage of Children from Birth through Age 5 and Not Yet in Kindergarten Participating in Various Weekly Nonparental Care Arrangements, by Child and Family Characteristics, 2019

TABLE B-1 Percentage of Children from Birth through Age 5 and Not Yet in Kindergarten Participating in Various Weekly Nonparental Care Arrangements, by Child and Family Characteristics, 2019

Characteristic	Number of children (thousands)	Weekly nonparental care arrangement					
		At least one weekly nonparental care arrangement	Type[a]				No weekly nonparental care arrangement
			Relative care	Nonrelative care	Center-based care[b]		
Total	21,195	59	37	18	62		41
Child's age							
Less than 1 year	4,621	42	58	22	31		58
1–2 years	8,425	55	45	23	46		45
3–5 years	8,149	74	25	13	83		26
Child's sex							
Male	10,992	59	37	17	63		41
Female	10,203	60	37	19	61		40
Child's race/ethnicity							
White, non-Hispanic	10,420	61	33	22	65		39
Black, non-Hispanic	2,706	63	43	9	59		37
Hispanic	5,424	56	45	14	56		44
Asian or Pacific Islander, non-Hispanic	1,181	55	34	10	66		45
Other race, non-Hispanic[c]	1,463	59	32	21	62		41
Family type							
Two parents or guardians	17,105	58	34	19	63		42
One parent or guardian	4,089	65	51	13	58		35

English spoken at home by parents/guardians[d]						
Both/only parent(s)/guardian(s) speak(s) English	18,424	61	38	18	61	39
One of two parents/guardians speaks English	706	41	25	11 !	71	59
No parent/guardian speaks English	2,065	48	30	14	74	52
Highest education level of parents/guardians						
Less than high school	1,884	43	46	13	58	57
High school/GED	4,001	49	49	12	54	51
Vocational/technical or some college	5,061	56	43	16	57	44
Bachelor's degree	5,988	64	33	20	64	36
Graduate or professional degree	4,261	75	28	22	70	25
Labor force status of parents/guardians[e]						
Two-parent/guardian family						
Both full time	6,401	86	36	24	58	14
One full time, one part time	2,860	64	40	18	57	36
One full time, one not in labor force	6,315	31	19	8	83	69
Other	1,371	44	40	12	57	56
Single-parent/guardian family						
Full time	2,136	75	48	16	61	25
Part time	716	78	54	9	51	22
Not in the labor force	936	36	54	7 !	60	64
Looking for work	302	50	59	‡	52	50

(*continued*)

TABLE B-1 Continued

Characteristic	Number of children (thousands)	At least one weekly nonparental care arrangement	Type[a] Relative care	Nonrelative care	Center-based care[b]	No weekly nonparental care arrangement
School enrollment status of parents/guardians						
Both or single parent(s)/guardian(s) enrolled	766	62	50	9!	56	38
Both or single parent(s)/guardian(s) not enrolled	18,175	59	37	18	62	41
One parent/guardian enrolled, one not enrolled (two-parent/guardian households)	2,253	58	37	18	61	42
Region						
Northeast	3,589	66	36	20	64	34
South	7,499	58	35	13	65	42
Midwest	4,744	61	38	22	61	39
West	5,363	55	42	19	57	45
Household income						
$20,000 or less	2,401	51	43	11	61	49
$20,001–$50,000	5,063	46	44	12	59	54
$50,001–$75,000	3,659	55	45	20	50	45
$75,001–$100,000	2,849	58	41	18	59	42
$100,001 or more	5,376	72	32	19	66	28
Poverty status[f]						
At or above poverty threshold	17,316	62	36	19	62	38
Below poverty threshold	3,879	50	44	10	62	50

Assistance to pay for primary care arrangement[g]

Parents received assistance (for one or more arrangements)	1,577	100	26	19	80	†
Parents did not receive assistance	7,013	100	24	25	71	†
No fee for care	4,004	100	64	4	40	†

NOTE: Estimates represent about 12,594,000 children who have at least one weekly nonparental care arrangement. Children may have multiple weekly arrangements across the three types of care; therefore, a single child may be represented in multiple columns of this table. Among all children from birth through age 5 and not yet in kindergarten, 11 percent of children's parents reported having more than one type of regularly scheduled weekly nonparental care arrangement. Detail may not sum to totals because of rounding.

[a] Among children with at least one weekly nonparental care arrangement.

[b] Center-based arrangements include day care centers, Head Start programs, preschools, pre-kindergartens, and other early childhood programs.

[c] "Other, non-Hispanic" includes American Indian/Alaska Native children who are not Hispanic and children who are Two or more races and not Hispanic.

[d] Complete descriptions of the categories for English spoken at home by parents/guardians are as follows: (1) Both parents/guardians or the only parent/guardian learned English first or currently speak(s) English in the home, (2) One of two parents/guardians in a two-parent/guardian household learned English first or currently speaks English in the home, and (3) No parent/guardian learned English first and both parents/guardians or the only parent/guardian currently speak(s) a non-English language in the home.

[e] Full-time employment is defined as working 35 hours or more per week. Part-time employment is defined as working fewer than 35 hours per week.

[f] Determined by the federal government, the poverty threshold is the income necessary to meet the household's needs, given its size and composition. Income is collected in categories in the survey, rather than as an exact amount, and therefore the poverty measures used in this report are approximations of poverty. Detailed information on the poverty status calculation used in this report is available in appendix B.

[g] Assistance could be from a state welfare or family assistance program, a relative, an employer, another social service, or someone else. Parents were asked about assistance only for the primary arrangement within each arrangement type.

† Not applicable.

! Interpret data with caution. The coefficient of variation (CV) for this estimate is between 30 and 50 percent.

‡ Reporting standards not met. Either there are too few cases for a reliable estimate or the coefficient of variation (CV) is 50 percent or greater.

SOURCE: U.S. Department of Education, National Center for Education Statistics, Early Childhood Program Participation Survey of the 2019 National Household Education Surveys Program (ECPP-NHES:2019).

Appendix C

Committee Member and Staff Biosketches

LARUE ALLEN (*Chair*) is Raymond and Rosalee Weiss professor of applied psychology and vice dean for faculty affairs at the Steinhardt School of Culture, Education, and Human Development at New York University. She also directs the Child and Family Policy Center (CFPC), which focuses on bringing social science knowledge to policy makers and practitioners concerned with young children and their families. As part of her work at CFPC, Allen has partnered with the agencies that oversee the publicly funded early care and education system in New York City and State on research initiatives such as authentic assessment in preschool settings, and Family Child Care Workforce Development. Allen was chair of the Committee on the Science of Children Birth to Age 8: Deepening and Broadening the Foundation for Success, which was convened by the Institute of Medicine and authored the 2015 report *Transforming the Workforce for Children Birth through Age 8: A Unifying Foundation*. A follow-up committee, which she also chaired, focused on how to fund early care and education for children from birth to kindergarten entry that is accessible, affordable to families, and of high quality, including a well-qualified and adequately supported workforce consistent with the vision outlined in the prior report. The follow-up committee's report, *Transforming the Financing of Early Care and Education*, was released in 2018. Allen received her doctorate in clinical/community/developmental psychology from Yale University.

RANDALL AKEE is associate professor in the Department of Public Policy and American Indian Studies at the University of California, Los Angeles. Previously, he served as a David M. Rubenstein fellow in economic studies at the Brookings Institution. Akee is an applied microeconomist and has published research on childhood interventions on child health and educational outcomes. He has examined the impact of school quality and access to child outcomes for Indigenous peoples in the United States. Previously, he served on the National Advisory Council on Race, Ethnic, and Other Populations at the U.S. Census Bureau. Akee cowrote a National Academy of Sciences (NAS)–commissioned paper on poverty and American Indian children in 2017. In 2019, he participated in an NAS research conference focusing on the U.S. Census and Differential Privacy. He is a research fellow at the Harvard Project on American Indian Economic Development and a research associate at the National Bureau of Economic Research. Akee completed his doctorate at Harvard University in June 2006.

ALFREDO J. ARTILES is Lee L. Jacks professor of education at Stanford University. He is director of the Stanford Center for Opportunity Policy in Education and director of research at the Center for Comparative Studies in Race & Ethnicity. Artiles' scholarship examines equity paradoxes created by educational policies. He studies how responses to the intersection of disability, race, language, gender, and social class can unwittingly stratify educational opportunities for disparate groups. He has (co)led federally funded national and regional technical assistance centers to reduce educational disparities. Artiles is an elected member of the National Academy of Education, a fellow of the American Educational Research Association and the National Education Policy Center, and a senior research fellow of the Learning Policy Institute. He was a resident fellow of the Center for Advanced Study in the Behavioral Sciences and was elected vice-president of the American Educational Research Association, leading its Social Contexts of Education Division. Artiles served on the National Academy of Sciences' consensus study panels on English Learners and the Future of Education Research at the Institute of Education Sciences, and served on the White House Commission on Educational Excellence for Hispanics.

RENÉE BOYNTON-JARRETT is associate professor at Boston Medical Center and Boston University School of Medicine. A pediatrician and social epidemiologist, she is founding director of the Vital Village Network, which uses a trauma-informed lens to improve community capacity to promote child well-being in Boston and support coalitions nationally through the National Organization for Women Forum. Her scholarship has focused on early-life adversities as life-course social determinants of health, with a specific concentration on psychosocial stress and neuroendocrine and reproductive health outcomes, including obesity, puberty, and fertility. Boynton-Jarrett is nationally recognized for work on the intersection of community violence, intimate partner violence, and child abuse and neglect and neighborhood characteristics that influence these patterns. Through dedicated community partnerships her current work is developing community-based strategies to promote child well-being and prevent childhood adversities.

KENNETH A. DODGE is William McDougall distinguished professor of public policy and professor of psychology and neuroscience at Duke University. He is a leading scholar in the development and prevention of aggressive and violent behaviors. His work provides a framework for understanding how current public policies perpetuate opportunity gaps in the first several years of life but could be reshaped to reduce gaps and support success for all children. Dodge has published more than 500 scientific articles, which have been cited more than 125,000 times. He was elected to the National Academy of Medicine in 2015. He is past-president of the Society for Research in Child Development (2019–2021) and has been awarded the Distinguished Scientific Award from the American Psychological Association. Dodge earned his Ph.D. in psychology (clinical) from Duke University in 1978.

BRENDA P. JONES HARDEN is Ruth Ottman professor of children and family welfare at the Columbia School of Social Work. She directs the Prevention and Early Adversity Research Laboratory, where she and her research team examine the developmental and mental health needs of young children from low-income backgrounds who have experienced early adversity such as maltreatment. A particular focus is preventing maladaptive outcomes in these populations through early childhood programs, including home visitation, parenting interventions, early care and education, and early childhood mental health programs. Jones Harden has numerous publications in the early childhood and early adversity arenas. She has been a Society for Research in Child Development Policy Fellow, in which she worked on early childhood program evaluations and research on children in the child welfare system. She is currently the president of the Board of Zero to Three, a national organization with a mission to ensure that all infants and toddlers have an equitable start in their lives. Jones Harden received a Ph.D. in psychology from Yale University (1996) and a master's in social work from New York University (1980).

PAMELA K. JOSHI is senior scientist and associate director of the Institute for Child, Youth and Family Policy at The Heller School for Social Policy and Management at Brandeis University and policy research director for diversitydatakids.org. Her research investigates how social policies, such as early childhood education, paid family and medical leave, and antipoverty programs, influence children's developmental trajectories and evaluates their effectiveness in reducing racial and ethnic inequities in access to opportunities. Joshi is trained in Cochrane systematic review and policy equity methods and has been funded to undertake comprehensive policy reviews, most recently including the access of children in immigrant families to the social safety net. She serves on several expert panels, including the U.S. Department of Health and Human Services, Administration for Children and Families, Office of Research and Planning Evaluation's Racial and Ethnic Disparities in Human Services project. Joshi and colleagues received the Lawrence R. Klein Award from the U.S. Department of Labor's Bureau of Labor Statistics for their research documenting differential job quality of working parents by race, ethnicity, and nativity. Joshi received her Ph.D. in social welfare policy from Brandeis University and a master of public policy from the University of Michigan.

SHANTEL E. MEEK is professor of practice and founding director of the Children's Equity Project (CEP) in the T. Denny Sanford School of Social and Family Dynamics at Arizona State University. She manages strategic partnerships with CEP partners at 17 universities and nonprofit organizations, policy makers, and national organizations, with a budget of over $1 million, and sets the strategic direction of the CEP. Meek previously served as a consultant in early childhood policy and strategy at the Bipartisan Policy Center in Washington, DC, where she advised senior staff on a range of federal and state equity and early childhood policy issues. Previously, she served in the Obama administration as senior policy advisor for early childhood development at the U.S. Department of Health and Human Services (HHS) and as senior policy advisor for education in the Domestic Policy Council at the White House. During her time in the Obama administration, Meek advised senior officials at HHS and at The White House on a wide array of policy issues, including Head Start, child care, public pre-K expansion, and promoting equity and reducing disparities across the early care and education system. She also worked on drafting official guidance and regulations related to Head Start and the Child Care and Development Block Grant, and worked closely with states and communities on implementation.

BELA MOTÉ is president and CEO of the Carole Robertson Center for Learning in Chicago, Illinois, and is widely recognized as a leader in early childhood education and youth development. She is a seasoned nonprofit executive with successful program, strategy, evaluation, and organizational management experience. Moté has spent her career developing, scaling, and evaluating highly effective programs for children and families that improve systems and funding for underserved families locally, nationally, and internationally. Previously, she served as vice president of evidence-based youth development for the YMCA of the USA. Additionally, Moté has held leadership positions with the YMCA of Metropolitan Chicago; Start Early; Teaching Strategies, Inc.; and the Robert R. McCormick Foundation. She serves on several councils, committees, and commissions at city, state, and national levels. Moté holds an M.Ed. from the Erikson Institute.

MILAGROS NORES is codirector for research and associate research professor at the National Institute for Early Education Research. Her expertise is in early childhood attainment and program evaluation, the economics of education, and international and comparative early care and education. Nores has recently concluded an early childhood study in Colombia and a study on parental–child educational practices for minority children in the United States, and an evaluation of the Seattle preschool program. Currently, she is currently leading evaluations of Philadelphia and West Virginia's preschools programs. Nores consults for various organizations in education projects in Latin America and Asia. Previously, she worked as a postdoctoral research associate at the Taubman Center in Public Policy at Brown University. She has been involved in sponsored research amounting to about $17 million. Nores strongly emphasizes moving beyond descriptive analysis to making inferences about programs and policies, examining the short- and long-term benefits of pre-K, understanding the determinants of preschool access and participation for different types of families, and assessing the impacts of access (or lack thereof) to pre-K on later academic achievement. She has a Ph.D. in education and economics from Columbia University and an Ed.M. in educational administration and social policy from Harvard University.

CYNTHIA OSBORNE is professor of early childhood education and policy at Vanderbilt University's Peabody College of Education and Human Development. She is also founder and executive director of the national Prenatal-to-3 Policy Impact Center, an academic research center that translates research on state policies with demonstrated effectiveness at creating the conditions in which young children and their families can thrive into policy actions states can adopt. Osborne was an appointed member of the National Academies of Sciences, Engineering, and Medicine's Committee on Building an Agenda to Reduce the Number of Children in Poverty by Half in 10 Years and is currently an elected member of the Policy Council for the Association for Public Policy Analysis and Management. Osborne's teaching and research interests are in the areas of social policy, poverty and inequality, family and child well-being, and family demography. She has extensive experience leading long-term evaluations of state and national programs, with the aim of helping organizations understand what works and how to ensure sustainable implementation of effective policies. Osborne holds a

Ph.D. in demography and public affairs from Princeton University, a master in public policy from Harvard University's Kennedy School of Government, and a master of arts in education from Claremont Graduate University.

ALBERT WAT is senior policy director at the Alliance for Early Success, where he supports the organization's strategy and goals for early education, including increasing access to high-quality pre-K, improving the early learning workforce, and enhancing alignment with K–12 policies. Wat has served on two National Academies committees, which created the following reports: *Transforming the Workforce for Children Birth Through Age 8: A Unifying Foundation*; and *Vibrant and Healthy Kids: Aligning Science, Practice, and Policy to Advance Health Equity*. He also serves on the board of the Council for Professional Recognition. In late November 2022, Wat began a nine-month assignment as Senior Policy Advisor at the Administration for Children and Families at the U.S. Department of Health and Human Services to support their initiatives related to the ECE workforce. Wat holds a bachelor's degree in psychology and a master's degree in education from Stanford University, and a master's in education policy from The George Washington University.

2020–2022 James C. Puffer, MD/American Board of Family Medicine Fellow

RITA HAMAD is a social epidemiologist and family physician in the Philip R. Lee Institute for Health Policy Studies and the Department of Family & Community Medicine at the University of California, San Francisco (UCSF). She is director of the Social Policies for Health Equity Research Program at UCSF, and associate director of the UCSF Center for Health Equity. Her research evaluates the health effects of social and economic policies using interdisciplinary quasi-experimental methods, with a specific focus on safety net policies. Hamad has given presentations and provided consultation to policy makers and staff in the California state legislature on the design of economic policies to address health equity. She serves as cochair of the Communications Committee of the Interdisciplinary Association of Population Health Sciences. Hamad received a Ph.D. in epidemiology from Stanford University, an M.D. from UCSF, and an M.P.H. and M.S. from the University of California, Berkeley.

2020–2021 National Academy of Medicine Distinguished Nurse Scholar in Residence and Consultant to the Committee

ASHLEY DARCY-MAHONEY is a neonatal nurse practitioner and researcher who has worked throughout her career to advance nursing research, education, and practice, with a focus on neonatology, infant health, and developmental pediatrics. As director of infant research at The George Washington University's Autism and Neurodevelopmental Institute, Darcy-Mahoney advances the body of research in infant health and developmental outcomes in high-risk infants with a focus on understanding the early brain and development trajectories in this population. She is a fellow of the American Academy of Nurses, is a Robert Wood Johnson Foundation Nurse Faculty Scholar Alumna, and a Josiah Macy Faculty Scholar; she was recently named a Modern Healthcare Rising Star in Nursing. Darcy-Mahoney holds a Ph.D. from the University of Pennsylvania and a B.S.N. from Georgetown University.

Staff

REBEKAH HUTTON (*Study Director*) is senior program officer with the National Academies. She is currently study director of the Committee on Exploring the Opportunity Gap for Young Children from Birth to Age Eight and the Committee on A New Vision for High Quality Pre-K Curriculum. Previously, she was study director of the Committee on Summertime Experiences and Child and Adolescent Education, Health, and Safety. Prior to working at the National Academies, Hutton was an education management and information technology consultant working on projects in the United States, as well as in Haiti, Equatorial Guinea, and Djibouti. She has also worked as a program manager and researcher at the National Center on Performance Incentives at Vanderbilt University and as an English-language lecturer in Tourcoing, France. During her time with the Board on Children, Youth, and Families, Hutton has worked on projects focused on fostering the educational success of children and youth learning English, reducing child poverty, and promoting the mental, emotional, and behavioral health of children and youths. She received her M.Ed. from Vanderbilt University in international education policy and management.

PAMELLA ATAYI serves as program coordinator with the Board on Children, Youth, and Families (BCYF) of the National Academies of Sciences, Engineering, and Medicine. She has been serving with BCYF since 2009. Atayi provides clerical, administrative, and logistical support for the senior board director, board members, and project directors. She also supervises the Board's administrative support staff and serves as liaison between boards and programs of the National Academies, and related external customers, members, and sponsors on clerical and administrative matters. Further, Atayi currently provides logistical and clerical support for the Committee on Exploring the Opportunity Gap for Young Children from Birth to Age Eight. She was awarded the Sandra H. Matthews Cecil Award by the Institute of Medicine (now the Health and Medicine Division) in 2013, and the Division of Behavioral and Social Sciences and Education's Espirit de Corps Award in 2017. She earned her B.A. in English from the University of Maryland University College and a diploma in computer information systems from Strayer University.

MEREDITH YOUNG serves as associate program officer with the Board on Children, Youth, and Families (BCYF) of the National Academies of Sciences, Engineering, and Medicine. She currently supports the Committee on Exploring the Opportunity Gap for Young Children from Birth to Age Eight and the Committee on A New Vision for High Quality Pre-K Curriculum. Before joining BCYF, Young supported the National Academies' Food and Nutrition Board (FNB) as a research associate. During her 5 years at FNB, she contributed to research focused on updating dietary reference intakes, revising federal feeding guidelines, and accelerating progress in childhood obesity prevention and treatment. Young received her M.S. in nutrition science and policy from Tufts University and her B.S. in human nutrition, foods, and exercise with a concentration in dietetics from Virginia Tech.